FREE MOVEMENT OF GOODS IN THE EUROPEAN COMMUNITY

Fourth Edition

AUSTRALIA
Law Book Co.
Sydney

CANADA and **USA**
Carswell
Toronto

HONG KONG
Sweet & Maxwell Asia

NEW ZEALAND
Brookers
Wellington

SINGAPORE and **MALAYSIA**
Sweet & Maxwell Asia
Singapore and Kuala Lumpur

FREE MOVEMENT OF GOODS IN THE EUROPEAN COMMUNITY

UNDER ARTICLES 28 TO 30 OF THE EC TREATY

Fourth Edition

by

PETER OLIVER

MA (Cantab), Licence spéciale (Brussels), Ph.D. (Cantab)
Barrister-at-Law
Legal Advisor, European Commission

assisted by

MALCOLM JARVIS

MA, LL.M. (Cantab), LL.D. (Groningen)
Barrister
20 Essex Street, London

LONDON
SWEET AND MAXWELL
2003

First Edition.........1982
Second Edition......1988
Third Edition........1997
Fourth Edition......2003

Published in 2003 by
Sweet & Maxwell Limited of
100 Avenue Road, London NW3 3PF
Typeset by York House Typographic Ltd, London
Printed in Great Britain by MPG Books, Bodmin

No natural forests were destroyed to make this product;
only farmed timber was used and replanted

A CIP catalogue record for this book is available from the British Library

ISBN 0421 74020 5

ISBN 0-421-74020-5

9 780421 740204

PREFACE

A number of highly significant changes have occurred in the area of law covered by this book since the last edition appeared in 1996.

First and foremost, the Court of Justice has delivered a vast new body of case law on the scope of Article 28, much of which further clarifies the landmark judgment in *Keck* (*e.g. Familiapress, De Agostini, TK-Heimdienst* and *Gourmet International*). Equally important have been the numerous judgments on the justification of restrictions in such areas as environmental protection (*Aher-Waggon, PreussenElektra*) and intellectual property rights (including *Bristol-Myers, Sebago, Silhouette* and *Boehringer*). What is more, the various new rulings on State monopolies of a commercial character, including those decisions relating to the gas and electricity monopolies, have significantly altered the pre-existing principles. Also, the solemn proclamation of the Charter of Fundamental Rights of the European Union, although not binding, constitutes a major step in that area of the law. A number of important developments have taken place in relation to the harmonisation of national provisions such as: major Treaty changes effected by the Treaty of Amsterdam; new case law on the obligation on Member States to notify certain technical standards and norms (see *CIA Security, Lemmens* and *Unilever Italia*); and the renowned *Tobacco Advertising* ruling.

In this edition, we have covered all these developments. We have each contributed in varying degrees to all Chapters, but Peter has been primarily responsible for Chapters 1 to 6, 10, 12 and 13 and Malcolm has been primarily responsible for the remainder, although the intellectual property section of Chapter 8 has been thoroughly re-worked by Christopher Stothers.

Our special thanks go to Christopher for giving us the benefit of his IP expertise, and also for his contribution to Chapter 12. We are also particularly grateful to Herman Speyart for his invaluable advice on intellectual property and to Sven Norberg for his extremely helpful comments on the EEA. Our thanks also go to Karen Banks, John Forman, Hendrik van Lier, Michael Shotter, Denis Martin, Josef Christian Schieferer, Roland Tricot and Philippa Watson.

This edition reflects the law as it stood on September 1, 2002, except where it has been possible to take account of subsequent developments.

Peter Oliver   Malcolm Jarvis
September 2002

v

NOTICE ON THE RENUMBERING
OF THE ARTICLES OF THE TREATY

The proverbial road to hell is paved with good intentions. So it proved when the draftsmen of the Treaty of Amsterdam decided to renumber the articles of the EC Treaty. What was intended as an exercise in simplification has merely created immense confusion and complication—and, what is more, the Treaties are set to be amended again shortly by the Treaty of Nice. The problems are especially acute in the area of law covered by this book: prior to the Treaty of Amsterdam, the prohibition on quantitative restrictions and measures of equivalent effect on imports was enshrined in Article 30, and the main exception clause was to be found in Article 36; today, the prohibition has moved to Article 28, while the old Article 36 has become Article 30!

Manifestly, we cannot set our faces against "progress", so that we have no choice but to apply the new numbering. To assist the reader, it has been decided to give the pre-Amsterdam number of each article in brackets when that article is first mentioned in a chapter (for instance: Article 28 (ex 30)). After that, the reader is on his own—except that a table of equivalences is set out in Annex I.

Peter Oliver   Malcolm Jarvis

CONTENTS

CHAPTER I
Introduction

CHAPTER II
Scope: Subject Matter

CONTENTS

CHAPTER III
Scope: Territory

CHAPTER IV
Scope: Persons Bound

CHAPTER V
Quantitative Restrictions

CHAPTER VI
Measures of Equivalent Effect: General

CONTENTS

CHAPTER VII
Measures of Equivalent Effect: II

CONTENTS

CHAPTER VIII

The Main Exception: Article 30 EC Including the "Mandatory Requirements"

CHAPTER IX
Other Exception Clauses

CHAPTER X
Agriculture

CONTENTS

CHAPTER XI
State Monopolies of a Commercial Character

CHAPTER XII
Community Legislation Relating to the Free Movement of Goods

CONTENTS

CHAPTER XIII
The European Economic Area

ANNEX 1
Treaty of Amsterdam: Table of Equivalences

ANNEX 2
Cases and Materials

ANNEX 3
Table of Cases

ANNEX 4
Selected Bibliography on Articles 28 to 30

TABLE OF CASES

ALPHABETICAL LIST OF CASES BEFORE THE EUROPEAN COURTS*

---

* Cases before the European Court of First Instance can be identified by the "T" prefix in the case number. Cases before the Court of the European Free Trade Association can be identified by the "E" prefix in the case number.

TABLE OF CASES

NUMERICAL LIST OF CASES BEFORE THE EUROPEAN COURT OF JUSTICE*

---

* A list of cases before the European Court of First Instance and a list of cases before the Court of the European Free Trade Association can be found at the end of this table.

TABLE OF CASES

TABLE OF CASES

Cases before the European Court of First Instance

Cases before the Court of the European Free Trade Association

TABLE OF LEGAL PROVISIONS

EUROPEAN UNION TREATIES

REGULATIONS, DIRECTIVES, COUNCIL AND COMMISSION DECISIONS

Decisions

INTERNATIONAL TREATIES

LIST OF ABBREVIATIONS

AöR	Archiv des öffentlichen Rechts
C.D.E	Cahiers de Droit Européen
C.M.L.R.	Common Market Law Reports
C.M.L.Rev.	Common Market Law Review
DÖV	Die Öffentliche Verwaltung
E.C.L.R.	European Competition Law Review
E.C.R.	European Court Reports
E.I.P.R.	European Intellectual Property Review
E.L.Rev.	European Law Review
EuR	Europarecht
EuZW	Europäische Zeitschrift für Wirtschaftsrecht
G.J.	Gaceta Juridica de la CEE
G.R.U.R.Int.	Gewerblicher Rechtsschutz und Urheberrecht – Internationaler Teil
I.C.L.Q.	International and Comparative Law Quarterly
I.I.C.	International Review of Industrial Property and Commercial Law
J.T.D.E.	Journal des Tribunaux - Droit Européen
M.L.R.	Modern Law Review
N.J.W.	Neue Juristische Wochenschrift
O.J.	Official Journal
RabelsZ	Rabelszeitschrift
R.I.W.	Recht der Internationalen Wirtschaft
R.M.C.	Revue du Marché Commun
R.D.U.E	Revue du Droit de l'Union Européenne (ex Revue du Marché Unique Européen)
R.M.U.E.	Revue du Marché Unique Européen
R.P.C.	Reports of Patent Cases
R.T.D.E	Revue Trimestrielle de Droit Européen
S.E.W.	Sociaal en Economische Wetgeving
W.R.P.	Wettbewerb in Recht und Praxis
Y.E.L.	Yearbook of European Law
Z.H.R.	Zeitschrift für das gesamte Handelsrecht und Wirtschaftsrecht

CHAPTER I

Introduction

1.01 At the very heart of the European Community lies the common market, and more particularly the customs union. As testimony to this, the fathers of the original Treaty of Rome chose to set out the provisions relating to the customs union immediately after the eight introductory articles.[1] Likewise, Article 3 which lists the "activities" of the EC, begins with the "elimination, as between Member States, of customs duties and of quantitative restrictions on the import and export of goods, and of all other measures having equivalent effect", followed by "a common commercial policy".

The purpose of this book is to examine only a part of the provisions on the customs union, namely Articles 28 to 30 (formerly Articles 30 to 36)[2], in principle, these provisions prohibit quantitative restrictions and measures of equivalent effect on imports and exports between Member States. Briefly stated, quantitative restrictions are non-tariff quotas or total bans on trade, while the concept of measures of equivalent effect covers a multitude of other trade restrictions not falling under any other Chapter of the Treaty of Rome. It cannot be sufficiently emphasised that this concept is not limited to technical customs matters, but covers such questions as intellectual property, price controls and indications of origin. However, this prohibition on quantitative restrictions and measures of equivalent effect is subject to a number of exceptions, which will also be examined. In addition, this book will briefly consider the powers of the Community to pass legislation to eliminate technical barriers to trade. On the other hand, trade between the EC and third countries falls outside the scope of this work (except trade within the European Economic Area, which is covered by Chapter XIII).

First, Articles 28 to 30 must be put in their context, both in historical terms and in terms of their place in the European Community as a whole. To understand the historical context of these provisions one must glance at two quite separate organisations, the GATT and the OEEC.

1.02 The General Agreement on Tariffs and Trade[3] was concluded by 23

---

[1] The Treaty of Maastricht inserted a new Part II entitled "Citizenship of the Union" immediately before the provisions on the customs union.

[2] The Articles of the Treaty of Rome have been renumbered by the Treaty of Amsterdam (see below).

[3] See generally Dam, *The GATT, Law and International Economic Organisation* (1970); Jackson, *The World Trading System* (1989); McGovern "International Trade Regulation", regularly updated online (*www.globefield.com/itrch.htm*); and Völker, *Barriers to External and Internal Community Trade* (1993).

countries in October 1947 and came into force "provisionally" in January 1948. Its object was and is to guard against protectionism in international trade. It was conceived as part of a much grander plan, the establishment of an International Trade Organisation which never saw the light of day, as it was blocked by the United States. Yet with the aid of a number of changes, the GATT was able to operate on its own without its intended institutional base. By 1994 more than 100 countries from all corners of the globe were party to the GATT. While the GATT provides that tariffs are only to be reduced, it requires the outright abolition of quantitative restrictions: Article XI, entitled "General Elimination of Quantitative Restrictions", provides in paragraph 1 that "no prohibitions or restrictions other than duties, taxes or other charges, whether made effective through quotas, import or export licences or other measures, shall be instituted or maintained" between contracting parties.[4] The subsequent paragraphs and Articles contain a number of exceptions to this rule, the most important of which is the balance of payments exception in Article XII. This permits a contracting party to adopt import restrictions necessary:

"(i) to forestall the imminent threat of, or to stop a serious decline in its monetary reserves, or

(ii) in the case of a contracting party with very low monetary reserves, to achieve a reasonable rate of increase in its reserves".

Without using the term "measures of equivalent effect to quantitative restrictions", the GATT does in fact contain certain rules relating to such measures. These are to be found not only in Article XI already mentioned, but also in Article III.1 which states, *inter alia*, that measures on the sale, transport, distribution or use of products "should not be applied to imported or domestic products so as to afford protection to domestic production"; and Article III.4 which provides:

"The products of the territory of any contracting party imported into the territory of any other contracting party shall be accorded treatment no less favourable than that accorded to like products of national origin in respect of all laws, regulations and requirements affecting their internal sale, offering for sale, purchase, transportation, distribution or use...."

The Uruguay Round of negotiations which commenced in 1986 under the auspices of the GATT resulted in a series of Agreements signed in Marrakesh in April 1994. Those Agreements,[5] which came into force on January 1, 1995,

---

[4] This is the provision of the GATT that was in point in the judgment of the European Court of Justice in the *International Fruit* case (see n.7 below).

[5] [1994] O.J. L336/1; see Jansen, "Die neue Welthandelsorganisation" [1994] EuZW 333; Rasmussen, "L'organisation mondiale du commerce et ses instruments législatifs et juridictionnels" (1994) 4 R.M.U.E. 185; Steenbergen, "De Uruguay Ronde" [1994] S.E.W. 632; as to whether these Agreements are directly applicable despite the case law discussed above, see Mengozzi, "Les droits des citoyens de l'Union européenne et l'applicabilité directe des accords de Marrakech" (1994) 4 R.M.U.E. 165 and Timmermans, "L'Uruguay Round: sa mise en oeuvre par la Com-

provide *inter alia* for the establishment of the World Trade Organisation. Those Agreements created a new GATT ("GATT 1994"), while the old GATT ("GATT 1947") lapsed at the end of 1996; but the language of Articles III, XI and XII remains unchanged. Virtually all countries and territories which were party to GATT 1947—including the European Community and all its Member States— are now party to GATT 1994. Member States of the European Community have long ceased to be bound by GATT as between themselves.[6]

For many years the Court declined to take cognisance of GATT obligations at all on the basis that the GATT was not directly applicable.[7] However, the judgment in *FEDIOL v Commission*[8] heralded a reversal of this position: the Court will now have regard to GATT as regards Community restrictions on trade with third countries, albeit only in cases concerning Community legislation expressly mentioning GATT obligations or which aims to give effect to such obligations.[9] However, a further twist occurred in *Portugal v Council*[10] where, after analysing their "nature and structure", the Court held that the WTO Agreements of 1994 are not "in principle among the rules in the light of which the Court is to review the legality of measures adopted by the Community institutions". Nevertheless, it did add the following proviso:

"It is only where the Community intended to implement a particular obligation assumed in the context of the WTO, or where the Community measure refers expressly to the precise provisions of the WTO agreements, that it is for the Court to

---

munauté" (1994) 4 R.M.U.E. 175; (on this point, note that the final recital to Council Decision 94/800 concluding these agreements states that "by its nature, the Agreement establishing the World Trade Organisation, including the Annexes thereto, is not susceptible to being directly invoked in Community or Member State courts"). See also generally Jackson and Sykes "Implementing the Uruguay Round" (1997).

[6] See in particular Case 10/61 *Commission v Italy* [1962] E.C.R. 1; [1962] C.M.L.R. 187 ("in matters governed by the EEC Treaty, that Treaty takes precedence over agreements concluded between Member States before its entry into force, including agreements made within the framework of GATT"). See generally Emiliou and O'Keeffe (eds.), "The European Union and World Trade Law" (1996); Hilf, Jacobs and Petersmann, "The European Community and GATT" (1986).

[7] See in particular Case 10/61 (see n.6 above); Cases 21–24/72 *International Fruit Company v Produktschap voor Groenten en Fruit* [1972] E.C.R. 1219; [1975] 2 C.M.L.R. 1; Case 9/73 *Schlüter v Hauptzollamt Lörrach* [1973] E.C.R. 1135; Case 38/75 *Nederlandse Spoorwegen v Inspecteur der Invoerrechten* [1975] E.C.R. 1439; [1976] 1 C.M.L.R. 167; Case 112/80 *Dürbeck v Hauptzollamt Frankfurt am Main-Flughafen* [1981] E.C.R. 1095; [1982] 3 C.M.L.R. 314; Case 245/81 *Edeka v Germany* [1982] E.C.R. 2745; Case 266/81 *SIOT v Italian Minister of Finance* [1983] E.C.R. 731; [1984] 2 C.M.L.R. 231; Case 193/85 *Cooperative Co-Frutta v Amministrazione delle Finanze dello Stato* [1987] E.C.R. 2085; Hilf and Petersmann (eds.), *GATT und Europäische Gemeinschaft* (1986); and Petersmann, "Application of GATT by the Court of Justice of the European Communities" [1983] C.M.L.Rev. 397.

[8] Case 188/85 [1988] E.C.R. 4193. See also Case 70/87 *FEDIOL v Commission* [1989] E.C.R 1781; Case 152/88 *Sofrimport v Commission* [1990] E.C.R. I-2477; Case C-69/89 *Nakajima v Council* [1991] E.C.R. I-2069; Case C-163/90 *Administration des Douanes v Legros* [1992] E.C.R. I-4625; and Case C-280/93 *Germany v Council (common market organisation for bananas)* [1994] E.C.R. I-4973, discussed by Hahn and Schuster, "Zum Verstoss von gemeinschaftlichem Sekundärrecht gegen das GATT" [1993] EuR 261. See generally De Burca and Scott, *The EU and the WTO* (2001).

[9] See in particular *Nakajima* (see n.8 above).

[10] Case C-149/96 [1999] E.C.R. I-8395, noted by Hilf and Schorkopf [2000] EuR 74, and by Rosas [2000] C.M.L.Rev. 797. That ruling was confirmed in Cases C-27/00 and C-122/00 *The Queen v Secretary of State for the Environment Ex p. Omega Air* (judgment of March 12, 2002).

review the legality of the Community measure in question in the light of the WTO rules (see, as regards GATT 1947, *Fediol,* paragraphs 19 to 22, and *Nakajima,* paragraph 31)."[11]

1.03 At all events, the Organisation for European Economic Co-operation (OEEC)[12] was set up by a Convention signed shortly after the GATT, in April 1948. It was primarily intended to administer the aid provided under the Marshall Plan for the post-war economic reconstruction of Western Europe. Accordingly, it included all non-communist European States other than Finland, although the Federal Republic of Germany and Spain did not become members until 1949 and 1959 respectively. In addition, the United States and Canada became associate members in 1959, and Yugoslavia took part in certain activities of the Organisation as from 1957. Since the abolition of barriers to trade was seen as being intimately linked to Europe's economic recovery, the Council of the OEEC called on its members as from 1949 to make a series of fixed reductions of their import quotas, subject to certain escape clauses. This culminated in a decision of January 1955 to raise the basic minimum level of liberalisation to 90 per cent of the value of imports, which decision was referred to in the original Articles 31 and 33(6) of the Treaty of Rome; (these provisions have now been repealed by the Treaty of Amsterdam). By the end of 1956 overall liberalisation had covered over 85 per cent of trade, so that much had been done to pave the way for the entry into force of the Treaty of Rome. In 1961, the Organisation was transformed into the Organisation for Economic Co-operation and Development (OECD) including the United States, Canada, Australia, New Zealand and Japan among its members. A number of other developed or relatively developed countries have joined the organisation since then.

1.04 The immediate forerunner of the European Economic Community (EEC) was the European Coal and Steel Community (ECSC), set up by the Treaty of Paris of 1951. That Treaty lapsed in July 2002, as it was concluded for only 50 years (Article 97 ECSC).[13] On January 1, 1958 the ECSC was joined by the EEC itself, established by the Treaty of Rome signed in March of the previous year, and by the European Atomic Energy Community (Euratom) set up by another Treaty of Rome of the same date. These two treaties were concluded for an unlimited period (Article 312 (formerly 240) EC and Article 208 Euratom).

Each of these Communities functions as a separate legal entity according to its own rules, but they are now run by the same institutions—the Commission, the Council of Ministers, the Parliament and the Court of Justice. In reality the EEC (now the EC) is by far the most important of the three Communities. This

---

[11] Para. 49 of the judgment.
[12] See generally Palmer and Lambert, *European Unity—A Survey of the European Organisations* (1968).
[13] See also the Protocol to the Treaty of Nice on the consequences of the expiry of the ECSC Treaty and on the research fund for coal and steel ([2000] O.J. C80/67).

book is therefore confined to the EC.[14] Thus throughout this book the term "Treaty of Rome" will be used to designate the Treaty establishing the EC and not the Euratom Treaty.

1.05 Returning, then, to the Treaty of Rome itself, it is necessary to give a very brief outline of its principal provisions so that Articles 28 to 30 can be seen in the context of the Treaty as a whole. The establishment of a "common market" has always featured first in the list of tasks assigned to the Community by Article 2 of the Treaty. As early as 1982 the Court stated in a celebrated judgment that: "the concept of a common market as defined by the Court in a consistent line of decisions involves the elimination of all obstacles to intra-Community trade in order to merge the national markets into a single market bringing about conditions as close as possible to those of a genuine internal market" (*Gaston Schul v Inspecteur der Invoerrechten*).[15] No-one could seriously deny that this definition is extremely far-reaching, although the words "as close as possible" show that in some respects the common market falls short of a genuine internal market.[16]

More specifically, as stated at the beginning of this Chapter, one of the fundamental aims of the Treaty was and is to set up a customs union between the parties. According to a widely received definition, a customs union, in contrast to a free trade area, does not merely involve liberalisation of trade between the parties; it also entails the establishment of essentially uniform rules for goods coming from third countries.[17] Acceptance of this definition is to be found both in an opinion of the Permanent Court of International Justice of 1931[18] and in Article XXIV of the GATT. The terms of the Treaty of Rome are in line with this definition. Accordingly, in its original form the Treaty contained provisions for the establishment and maintenance of a common customs tariff (Articles 18 to 29); since the majority of these provisions had long been obsolete, the Treaty of Amsterdam repealed them all except Articles 28 and 29, which have now become Articles 26 and 27. By the same token, the Treaty further provides for a common commercial policy with respect to trade with third countries, in Article 133 (formerly Article 113). Likewise, Article 23 (ex Article 9) stipulates that the provisions on the free movement of goods apply

---

[14] But see Ch.2, n.1.

[15] Case 15/81 [1982] E.C.R.1409; [1982] C.M.L.R. 229, para. 33.

[16] For instance, restrictions which are purely internal to a Member State are tolerated (paras 6.96 *et seq.* below); equally, the prohibitions in Arts 28 and 29 are subject to a range of exceptions, of which the most important are contained in Art. 30.

[17] See C-125/94 *Aprile v Amministrazione delle Finanze dello Stato* [1995] E.C.R. I-2919 at para.32 where the Court held: "it must be borne in mind that the Customs Union, which, under Article [23] of the Treaty, is to cover all trade in goods, incorporates a Common Customs Tariff intended to bring about equalization of the charges borne at the external frontiers of the Community by products imported from non-member countries, in order to ensure that trade with such countries is not diverted and that the free movement of products between Member States and the conditions of competition between economic agents are not distorted". See also C-126/94 *Société Cadi Surgelés v Ministre des Finances* [1996] E.C.R. I-5647 at para.14.

[18] On the "customs system between Germany and Austria", Permanent Court of International Justice, the Compendium of Consultative Decrees, Directives and Opinions, Series A-B, no. 41, p.51.

not only to products originating in Member States but also to goods originating in third countries but in free circulation in the Community. This means, in essence, that goods from third countries are assimilated to Community goods for this purpose when they have undergone all the appropriate import formalities and any customs duties payable have been levied.[19]

The Treaty provisions on the free movement of goods fall into two distinct sections—and a bit. Article 25 (formerly Articles 12 to 17) lays down total prohibitions on customs duties and charges of equivalent effect between Member States, which fall outside the scope of this book. As already stated, Articles 28 to 30 cover quantitative restrictions and measures of equivalent effect on imports and exports between Member States. Article 28 prohibits such restrictions and measures when imposed on imports, while Article 29 bans the corresponding restrictions and measures applied to exports. Article 30 constitutes the major exception clause. In addition, Article 31 (formerly 37) relates to trade restrictions linked to or forming part of State monopolies. However, it is far from clear to what extent Article 31 is independent of the other provisions on the free movement of goods, a matter to which Chapter XI of this book is devoted.

The free movement of goods is only one of the "four freedoms" existing between Member States. The others are: the free movement of persons, covering both employed workers on the one hand (Articles 39 to 42 (ex 48 to 51)) and the establishment of self-employed persons and undertakings on the other (Articles 43 to 48 (ex 52 to 58)); the free provision of services (Articles 49 to 55 (ex 59 to 66)) and the free movement of capital (Articles 56 to 60 (ex 73b to 73g)). The similarities between the four freedoms will be discussed further at paragraphs 1.12 and 1.13 below.

Furthermore, Articles 87 to 89 (ex 92 to 94) of the Treaty govern aids granted by Member States. Article 87(1) states in effect that such aids are "incompatible with the common market" in so far as they affect trade between Member States. However, by way of exception, Article 87(2) states that certain rather narrow categories of aid, such as compensation for natural disasters, "shall be considered compatible with the common market". Also, the subsequent provisions lay down the conditions and procedures according to which the Commission or the Council may exempt other aids from the rule in Article 87(1). Next, Article 90 (ex 95) prohibits internal taxation which discriminates against identical or competing imported products in favour of domestic products.

The Treaty also provides for a common agricultural policy (Articles 32 to 38 (ex 38 to 47)) and a common transport policy (Articles 70 to 80 (ex 74 to 84)). In addition, Articles 81 and 82 (ex 85 and 86) prohibit certain types of restrictive agreements and practices and the Commission is empowered to take action against undertakings infringing these prohibitions, if necessary by means of fines.[20] More important for the purposes of this book are Articles 94 and 95 (ex 100 and 100A) which relate to harmonisation and which are considered at

---

[19] See paras 2.15 *et seq.*
[20] See paras 4.26, and 6.33 below.

length in Chapter XII.

A provision of general importance is Article 12 (originally 7, then 6) of the Treaty, which prohibits "within the scope of application of this Treaty ... any discrimination on grounds of nationality". Since it is expressed to be "without prejudice to any special provisions" contained in the Treaty, the Court tended until recently to treat it as being of a residuary nature. However, in recent years it has reversed that approach, so that Article 12 has taken on an increasingly important role as a prohibition in its own right.[21]

These provisions did not all take immediate effect when the Treaty came into force on January 1, 1958. The old Article 8 (now repealed by the Treaty of Amsterdam) provided for a 12-year transitional period consisting of three four-year stages. Some Articles of the Treaty are expressed to take effect during this transitional period; this is the case with Article 29 prohibiting quantitative restrictions and measures of equivalent effect on exports, which took effect at the end of the first stage of the transitional period. Other Articles of the Treaty, such as Article 28 prohibiting the same measures on imports, were not expressed to take effect until the end of the transitional period. However, the Treaty also foresaw the possibility of accelerating certain measures and use was made of this.

1.06 As the reader will be aware, Denmark, Ireland and the United Kingdom did not join the EEC until January 1, 1973. Their Act of Accession set out transitional measures, although certain provisions of the Treaty of Rome took effect at once. Greece acceded to the EEC on January 1, 1981 but also benefited from a similar system of transitional measures.[22] Following the accession of Spain and Portugal on January 1, 1986,[23] Austria, Finland and Sweden became members of the Community on January 1, 1995, but the transitional provisions in their Act of Accession[24] in relation to the free movement of goods are minimal.

1.07 The Single European Act, which was a response to the European Parliament's draft Treaty establishing the European Union[25] and to the Commission's White Paper on Completing the Internal Market,[26] came into force on July 1, 1987. That Treaty effected some major amendments to the Treaty of Rome, including the insertion of a new Article 8A (subsequently Article 7A and now Article 14) into the EEC Treaty, requiring the internal market to be completed by December 31, 1992.

---

[21] See paras 1.13, 4.30 and 6.26 below.
[22] See Treaty of Accession [1979] O.J. L291.
[23] See Treaty of Accession [1985] O.J. L302.
[24] [1994] O.J. C241, as amended by the Decision adopted to take account of the decision of the people of Norway to reject accession ([1995] O.J. L1); see Booss and Forman, "Enlargement: Legal and Procedural Aspects" [1995] C.M.L.Rev. 95.
[25] [1984] O.J. C77/23. See Bieber, Jacqué and Weiler, *An Ever Closer Union* (1985), 110; Capotorti, Hilf, Jacobs and Jacqué, *Le Traité d'union européenne* (1985), *Der Vertrag zur Gründung der Europäischen Union* (1984). See para. 12.12 below.
[26] COM(85)310 final.

The second paragraph of that Article defines the internal market as comprising "an area without internal frontiers in which the free movement of goods, persons, services and capital is ensured in accordance with the provisions of this Treaty". This provision harks back to the Court's renowned definition of the "common market" in *Gaston Schul*,[27] there being no apparent difference between the concepts of "internal market" and "common market".[28] In view of the final limb ("in accordance with the provisions of this Treaty"), it is plain that certain restrictions, which are permitted under various provisions such as Article 30, continue to be tolerated.

At the time of the adoption of the Single European Act, a hotly debated issue was whether the passing of the deadline of December 31, 1992 automatically produced any legal effects, thereby removing barriers to the internal market even if the envisaged legislation was not in place.[29] The Conference of Representatives of the Member States stated in a declaration on the then Article 8A that: "Setting the date of 31 December 1992 does not create an automatic legal effect". The Court has now endorsed this view.[30] At all events, fortunately this deadline was met with respect to goods, with the result that frontier controls on goods (such as customs checks or VAT controls) were abolished. A wealth of Community legislation was adopted to make this historic change possible. In so far as these developments are still relevant today, they are examined below, particularly in Chapter XII.[31]

1.08 The Treaty of European Union (TEU), which was signed at Maastricht,

---

[27] See n.15 above.

[28] Tesauro A.G.'s Opinion in Case C-300/89 *Commission v. Council* ("titanium dioxide") [1991] E.C.R. I-2867 at 2887-9 (see paras 12.41 and 12.66 below); that view was tacitly accepted by the Court. See also Barents "The Internal Market Unlimited: Some Observations on the Legal Basis of Community Legislation" [1993] C.M.L.Rev. 85 at 102; De Ruyt, *L'Acte Unique Européen* (2nd ed., 1989) at 150.

Some authors have claimed that the "internal market" is comprised of the "common market", enriched by the new objectives inserted by the Single European Act, including the abolition of border controls: Ayral "La suppression des contrôles aux frontières intracommunautaires" [1993] R.M.U.E. 13; Bardenhewer and Pipkorn, commentary on former Art.7A in Groeben, Thiesing Ehlermann *Kommentar zum EU-/EG-Vertrag* (5th ed., 1997) at 305-6; Ehlermann, "The Internal Market Following the Single European Act" [1987] C.M.L.Rev. 361 at 369; Waelbroeck, "Le rôle de la Cour de Justice dans la mise en oeuvre de l'Acte unique européen" [1989] C.D.E. 42 at 54. It is a moot point whether this school of thought in fact departs from the view that the terms "internal market" and "common market" are synonymous today: on the latter view, the term "common market" as originally understood in 1958 must have taken on a broader meaning with the Single European Act.

Pescatore "Some Critical Remarks on the 'Single European Act'" [1987] C.M.L.Rev. 9 at 11 took the view that the "internal market" comprises an "arbitrary selection of the Treaty objectives" and is thus narrower than the "common market".

A number of provisions of the Treaty, both in its original and in its current form, speak of the "common market": apart from Art.2, see, *e.g.* Arts 81 and 87.

[29] See Ehlermann, *op. cit.*; Glaesner, "Die Einheitliche Europäische Akte" [1986] EuR 119; Mattera Editorial [1992] R.M.U.E. 5; Pescatore, *op. cit.*; Toth "The Legal Status of the Declarations Annexed to the Single European Act" [1986] C.M.L.Rev. 803; Schermers "The Effect of the Date of 31 December 1992" [1991] C.M.L.Rev. 275.

[30] Case C-378/97 *Wijsenbeek* [1999] E.C.R. I-6207; see also points 11–13 of Jacobs A.G.'s Opinion in Case C-297/92 *INCS v Baglieri* [1993] E.C.R. I-5211, and para. 12.14 below.

[31] See also paras 6.10 and 7.04.

came into force on November 1, 1993.[32] It created a new European Union, to which only the Member States of the Community are party and which "shall be founded on the European Communities" (the ECSC, the EC and Euratom). At the same time, it transformed the European Economic Community into the European Community and renumbered certain provisions of the Treaty of Rome.

One little noticed amendment effected by this Treaty was the merger of the previous Parts II and III. The old Part II had been entitled "Foundations of the Community" and covered the four freedoms together with the two common policies (agriculture and transport). The old Part III ("Policy of the Community") comprised a broad range of matters such as competition, social policy, the environment and the European Investment Bank. The Treaty of Maastricht merged the two Parts into a new Part Three ("Community Policies") embracing virtually all the substantive provisions of the Treaty. This step could conceivably have been regarded as "downgrading" the four freedoms so that they were henceforth to be treated as being of no greater importance to Community integration than, say, the provisions relating to consumer protection or education. Yet the Court has implicitly rejected such an approach. Rather, as explained further at paragraph 1.13 below, the Court has continued to stress the special importance of the four freedoms, including the free movement of goods; indeed, it may even be in the process of raising the status of these freedoms to that of "fundamental right".

1.09 The Treaty of Amsterdam,[33] which came into force on May 1, 1999,[34] affected a series of further changes to the Treaty of Rome. These included the repeal of a number of obsolete provisions such as the old Articles 31 to 35 which had lapsed at the end of 1969. The draftsmen of the new Treaty had the foresight to provide in Article 10(1) that: "The repeal or deletion in this Part of lapsed provisions of the Treaty establishing the European Community … as in force before the entry into force of this Treaty of Amsterdam and the adaptation of certain of their provisions shall not bring about any changes in the legal effects of the provisions of those Treaties, in particular the legal effects arising from the time limits laid down by the said Treaties, nor of Accession Treaties." This provision is designed to preclude novel constructions of the surviving articles of the Treaty of Rome based on the premise that the repealed provisions are to be treated as never having existed.

Far more controversially, the Treaty of Amsterdam effected a total renumbering of all the articles of the Treaty with the unfortunate consequence that

---

[32] The Treaty of Maastricht was inspired in part by the draft Treaty establishing the European Union drawn up by the Parliament in February 1984 ([1984] O.J. C77/23); see Bieber, Jacqué and Weiler, *An Ever Closer Union* (1985), 110; and Capotorti, Hilf, Jacobs and Jacqué, *Le Traité d'union européenne* (1985), 180; and *Der Vertrag zur Gründung der europäischen Union* (1984), 171. For an account of the negotiation of the Treaty of Maastricht itself, see Cloos, Reinesch, Vignes and Weyland, *Le Traité de Maastricht: genèse, analyse, et commentaires* (1993).
[33] [1997] O.J. C340/1.
[34] [1999] O.J. C120/24.

Articles 30, 34 and 36 have become Articles 28, 29 and 30.[35] Various consequential amendments to these three provisions were also introduced,[36] but their substance was not effected.

1.10 Finally, the Treaty of Nice,[37] which was signed on February 26, 2001, will come into force once it has been ratified by all the Member States. At the time of writing, that process of ratification has not yet been completed. That Treaty, which essentially concerns the institutional provisions of the Treaty, will not amend Articles 28 to 30 either.

1.11 None of the amending Treaties or Acts of Accession has altered the substance of the three provisions which lie at the heart of this book, namely Articles 28, 29 and 30. This was recognised by the Court as regards Articles 28 and 30 in its recent judgment in *Echirolles Distribution v Association du Dauphiné.*[38]

Having said that, the abolition of frontier controls between Member States by the Single European Act with effect from December 31, 1992 altered the context in which these provisions applied. Hitherto border controls had been tolerated in so far as they did not exceed the "normal requirements inherent in the crossing of the frontier by any goods, whatever their nature", so that they fell *de facto* beyond the scope of Articles 28 and 29.[39] Henceforth, those provisions became fully applicable to such controls.[40]

1.12 As mentioned in paragraph 1.05 above, the free movement of goods is one of the four economic freedoms enshrined in the Treaty of Rome. Recent years have seen a mushrooming of legal articles discussing the increasing similarities between these freedoms.[41] The prevailing view is that the Court's

---

[35] See the Notice on the renumbering of the articles of the Treaty at the beginning of this book.

[36] The words "without prejudice to the following provisions" in the former Article 30 have been removed. Also, the cross-reference in the opening words of the new Article 30 (ex 36) has inevitably had to be changed.

[37] [2001] O.J. C80/1.

[38] Case C-9/99 [2000] E.C.R. I-8207, para.24 of the judgment.

[39] See paras 7.04, and 12.15 *et seq.* below.

[40] See paras 7.04, and 12.15 *et seq.* below.

[41] See, *e.g.* Barnard, "Fitting the remaining pieces into the goods and persons jigsaw?" [2001] E.L.Rev. 35; Behrens, "Die Konvergenz der wirtschaftlichen Freiheiten im europäischen Gemeinschaftsrecht" [1992] EuR 145; Bernard, "Discrimination and Free Movement in EC Law" [1996] I.C.L.Q. 82 and "La libre circulation des marchandises, des personnes et des services dans le Traité CE sous l'angle de la compétence" [1998] C.D.E. 11; Everling, "Sur la jurisprudence récente de la Cour de justice en matière de libre prestation de services rendus dans d'autres Etats membres" [1984] C.D.E. 3 at 14; Jarass, "Elemente einer Dogmatik der Grundfreiheiten" [1995] EuR 202 and [2000] EuR 705; Marenco, "La notion de restriction aux libertés d'établissement et de prestation des services dans la jurisprudence de la Cour" (1992) Gazette du Palais n°s 124–6, p.4 (also published as "The Notion of Restriction on the Freedom of Establishment and Provision of Services in the Case law of the Court" [1991] Y.E.L. 111); Martin, "'Discriminations', 'entraves' et 'raisons impérieuses' dans le traité CE: trois concepts en quête d'identité" 1ère partie [1998] C.D.E. 261; Mortelmans, "Excepties bij non-tarifaire intracommunautaire belemmeringen: assimilatie in het nieuwe EG-Verdrag?" [1997] S.E.W. 182 at 189 (although he rightly points out that it would be neither possible nor desirable to apply precisely the same rules to all four freedoms); O'Keeffe and Bavasso, "Four Freedoms, One Market and National Competence: In Search of a Dividing Line" Liber Amicorum in Honour of Lord Slynn of Hadley vol. I "Judicial

case law on the principles governing those freedoms is converging, although there are some notable exceptions.[42] Plainly, the analogy between goods and services is particularly close: both are normally the subject of commercial transactions, the chief difference being that goods are tangible, whereas services are not.[43] In consequence, we shall be paying greater attention than in previous editions to judgments relating to the other three freedoms, and the free movement of services in particular. In each case, we shall be inquiring whether there is any obstacle, be it inherent in the nature of the freedoms concerned or enshrined in the Treaty, to transposing those judgments to the free movement of goods.[44]

1.13 The Court has not been sparing in its description of the importance of the free movement of goods, referring to it variously as a "fundamental freedom",[45] "one of the fundamental principles of the Treaty",[46] a "fundamental Community provision"[47] and "one of the foundations of the Community".[48] The other three freedoms have been similarly honoured.[49] Indeed, in one recent case the Court described the free movement of goods as a "fundamental right"[50]—a term which it applied to the free movement of workers as long ago

---

Review in European Union Law" (2000) p.541; Oliver, "Goods and Services: Two Freedoms Compared" in Mélanges en l'honneur de Michel Waelbroeck (1999) vol. 2 p. 1377; Snell, *Goods and Services in EC Law: A Study of the Relationship between the Freedoms* (2002); Timmermans, note on Case C-384/93 *Alpine Investments v Minister van Financiën* [1995] E.C.R. I-1141; [1996] S.E.W. 244; Troberg in Groeben, Thiesing, Ehlermann "Kommentar zum EU/EG-Vertrag" (5th. ed.) 1997 vol. I pp. 1448–9 and 1463; van Gerven, "Articles 30, 48, 52 and 59 after *Keck and Mithouard*" (1996) Columbia Journal of European Law 217; von Wilmowsky, "Ausnahmebereiche gegenüber EG-Grundfreiheiten" [1996] EuR 362.

[42] For examples of such convergence, see Cases C-250/95 *Futura Participations v Administration des Contributions* [1997] E.C.R. I-2471 (a case on establishment where the Court based its reasoning on the case law relating to other freedoms); and C-35/98 *Staatssecretaris van Financiën v Verkooijen* [2000] E.C.R. I-4071 (a case on free movement of capital where the same occurred); and Case C-390/99 *Canal Satélite Digital v Spain* (judgment of January 22, 2002), where the Court even chose not to decide whether the measure in issue constituted a restriction on goods or services. As to the exceptions, see in particular *Alpine Investments* (see n.41 above), where the Court refused to carry over to services the principles which it had laid down with respect to Article 28 in Cases C-267 and 268/91 *Keck and Mithouard* [1993] E.C.R. I-6097.

[43] See *Canal Satélite Digital* (see n.42 above) See also generally Oliver, *op. cit.* at 1378 and Snell, *op. cit.*

[44] See also paras 2.34 *et seq.* below. One notable difference between the Treaty provisions on the free movement of goods on the one hand and those on services and persons on the other is that the latter apply exclusively to Community nationals (see para. 2.24 below).

[45] Cases C-394/97 *Heinonen* [1999] E.C.R. I-3599, para.38; C-390/99 (see n.42 above), paras 28–30.

[46] Cases C-205/89 *Commission v Greece* (pasteurised butter) [1991] E.C.R. I-1361, para.9, C-265/95 *Commission v France* (violent action by farmers) [1997] E.C.R. I-6959, para.27.

[47] Case C-44/89 *Corsica Ferries France v Direction générale des douanes françaises* [1989] E.C.R. I-4441, para.8.

[48] Case C-194/94 *CIA Security v Signalson* [1996] E.C.R. I-2201 para.40, and C-443/98 *Unilever Italia v Central Food* [2000] E.C.R. I-7535, para.40.

[49] *Corsica Ferries* (see n.47 above), para. 8 (all three other freedoms); Cases C-415/93 *UEFA v Bosman* [1995] E.C.R. I-4921, para. 93 (workers); C-281/98 *Angonese* [2000] E.C.R. I-4139, para. 35 (workers).

[50] Case C-228/98 *Dounias v Minister for Economic Affairs* [2000] E.C.R. I-577, para. 64.

as 1983.[51] What significance should be attached to these semantic questions is unclear. Quite probably, it is naïve to construct an entire theory on the basis of one word occurring in an isolated judgment; but where a term is used consistently in a series of judgments, that cannot go unheeded.

At all events, the following well-known pronouncement of Jacobs A.G. in *Konstantinidis*[52] deserves attention: "In my opinion, a Community national who goes to another Member State as a worker or self-employed person under Articles [39, 43, or 49] of the Treaty is entitled not just to pursue his trade or profession and to enjoy the same living and working conditions as nationals of the host State; he is in addition entitled to assume that, wherever he goes to earn his living in the European Community, he will be treated in accordance with a common code of fundamental values, in particular those laid down in the European Convention of Human Rights. In other words, he is entitled to say '*civis europeus sum*' and to invoke that status in order to oppose any violation of his fundamental rights." Whether this radical thinking is shared by the Court and whether it can be transposed to the free movement of goods are moot points, however: the mere use of the term "fundamental right" by the Court cannot necessarily be taken to imply that these two questions should be answered in the affirmative.[53] Indeed, it is notable that Mr Jacobs' view has been described by Gulmann A.G. as "too far-reaching".[54]

Since they relate to the individual's right to live and work in the country of his choice and not be separated from his immediate family, the freedoms relating to the movement of natural persons can more readily be seen as fundamental rights of the kind enshrined in the European Convention than can the free movement of goods. In addition, the Court has frequently linked the free movement of workers to Article 12 (prohibition of discrimination on the grounds of nationality), Article 17 (ex 8, citizenship of the Union)[55] and Article 18 (ex 8A, general right of citizens of the Union to move and reside freely within the territory of the Member States)[56]; plainly, these three provisions are of general application and of major importance. Moreover, Articles 7 and 15 of

---

[51] Case 152/82 *Forcheri v Belgium* [1983] E.C.R. 2323, para. 11; see also Case 222/86 *UNCTEF v Heylens* [1987] E.C.R. 4097, para. 14, and Lenz A.G. in *Bosman* (see n.49 above) at 5007–8. As the Court pointed out in *Forcheri*, the preamble to Regulation (EEC) No.1612/68 of the Council of October 15, 1968 on freedom of movement for workers within the Community ([1968] O.J. L257/1) also describes the free movement of workers as a "fundamental right".

[52] Case C-168/91 [1993] E.C.R. I-1198 at 1211–1212.

[53] As to the literature on this general question, see Poiares Maduro, *We the Court—The European Court of Justice & the European Economic Constitution* (1998) at 166–8, who describes Art. 28 as a "fundamental political right" and a "fundamental economic freedom", but warns: "There is a risk of giving such fundamental economic freedoms a status higher than that awarded to other fundamental rights and values in the Community legal order". See also Kingreen, *Die Struktur der Grundfreiheiten des Europäischen Gemeinschaftsrechts* (1999) at 15, who refers to the four freedoms as significant "subjective public rights" (*subjektiv-öffentliche Rechte*). This view is broadly endorsed by Baquero Cruz, *The Economic Constitutional Law of the European Community: between Competition and Free Movement* (forthcoming), who regards them as "constitutional rights but not fundamental constitutional rights".

[54] In n.12 to his Opinion in Case C-2/92 *The Queen v Ministry of Agriculture Ex p. Bostock* [1994] E.C.R. I-955.

[55] See, *e.g.* Case C-85/96 *Martínez Sala v. Freistaat Bayern* [1998] E.C.R. I-2691.

[56] Case C-135/99 *Elsen v Bundesversicherungsanstalt für Angestellte* [2000] E.C.R. I-10409.

the (non-binding) Charter of fundamental rights of the European Union[57] provide for the respect of the individual's private and family life, and for the freedom to work in any Member State, respectively. Whether the Court sees the free movement of goods in the same light is questionable, but such an eventuality can by no means be ruled out: the citizen's right to purchase the washing-powder of his choice and the corresponding right of another individual to purvey it appear trivial in comparison with human rights such as are bound up with the free movement of workers; but it must not be overlooked that the free movement of goods can be linked to the freedom of expression, as where restrictions are placed on the importation or exportation of books, magazines or video-cassettes.[58] Moreover, the freedom to import and export goods may be seen as an aspect of the freedom to conduct a business, which is enshrined in Article 16 of the Charter.[59] At all events, it will be suggested in Chapter IV that in one significant respect Articles 28 and 29 are probably less far-reaching than Article 39.[60]

1.14 Finally, in Opinion 1/91,[61] on an analysis of the provisions of the Treaty of Rome even as they stood prior to the Treaty of Maastricht, the Court found that the free movement of goods was not an end in itself but was "only a means" for establishing an internal market and economic and monetary union, and making concrete progress towards European unity. What practical consequences, if any, might flow from this ruling remains a matter of speculation.

---

[57] [2000] O.J. C364/1, discussed in para. 8.40 below.

[58] Where information is distributed in intangible form via the internet and television, the provision of services rather than goods is involved (see para. 2.** below). See also Cases 60 and 61/84 *Cinéthèque* [1985] E.C.R. 2605, [1986] 1 C.M.L.R. 365; C-260/89 *ERT v DEP* [1991] E.C.R. I-2925 and C-368/95 *Vereinigte Familiapress v Heinrich Bauer Verlag* [1997] E.C.R. I-3689.

[59] This right was already recognised by the Court: see, *e.g.* Cases C-280/93 *Germany v Council* (bananas) [1994] E.C.R. I-4973, para. 78.

[60] Paras 4.33–4.35 below. As to fundamental rights generally, see also paras 8.38 *et seq.* below

[61] [1991] E.C.R. 6079, paras 17 and 18; see Ch. XIII.

CHAPTER II

Scope: Subject Matter

2.01 This is the first of three Chapters dealing with the scope of the Treaty provisions on the free movement of goods between Member States, and more particularly Articles 28 to 30 (ex 30 to 36). It is the purpose of this Chapter to examine first the concept of goods and then the transactions which benefit from these provisions. Consequently, the initial part of this Chapter is devoted to the definition of the term "goods", while the second part is concerned with the concept of goods "in free circulation" in the Member States. In the third section we shall see that the nationality of the owner of goods is irrelevant for the purposes of the rules on the free movement of goods. Last, we shall consider which transactions are governed by the Treaty provisions on the free movement of goods, and in particular the relationship between these rules and those relating to the other three freedoms enshrined in the Treaty—the free movement of workers, services and capital.

As already mentioned in Chapter I, the ECSC and Euratom Treaties fall outside the scope of this book. Article 305 (ex 232) EC states that the provisions of the EC Treaty shall not "affect" the provisions of the ECSC, nor shall they "derogate" from those of the Euratom Treaty. Therefore Articles 28 to 30 EC do not apply to these Treaties. Consequently, "coal" and "steel" as defined by Annex I to the ECSC Treaty, and "goods subject to the nuclear common market", as defined by Annex IV to the Euratom Treaty, will not be considered here.[1] However, the ECSC Treaty lapsed in July 2002, as it was expressed to be concluded for 50 years only (Article 97); thus the EC Treaty has applied to coal and steel as from that date.[2]

It should also be pointed out that the structure of Title I of Part III of the EC Treaty requires that "goods" have the same meaning for purposes of Article 25 (ex 12 to 17) (customs duties and taxes of equivalent effect) as for Articles 28 to 30 (quantitative restrictions and measures of equivalent effect). This is why some cases on Article 25 will be discussed in this Chapter, although that provision falls outside the scope of this book.

---

[1] Arts 4(a) ECSC and 93 Euratom prohibited quantitative restrictions on imports or exports of the products to which they apply respectively. Measures of equivalent effect are not expressly prohibited in those Treaties, although they are perhaps prohib/prohibited impliedly (see generally Ch.3, n.**). On the ECSC Treaty see generally Cases 9 and 12/60 *Vloeberghs v High Authority* [1961] E.C.R. I97; 36/83 *Mabanaft v Hauptzollamt Emmerich* [1984] E.C.R. 2497; and 45/84R *EISA v EC Commission* [1984] E.C.R. I759.

[2] The only transitional measures are contained in the Protocol on the Financial Consequences of the Expiry of the ECSC Treaty ([2001] O.J. C80/67), which is annexed to the Treaty of Nice. However, that protocol has no bearing on the free movement of goods.

I. THE MEANING OF "GOODS"

2.02 The first point to notice is that, whereas in certain cases such as Article 23(1) (ex 9(1)), the Treaty uses the term "goods", in others such as Articles 23(2) (ex 9(2)) and 24 (ex 10(1)) the expression "products" has been preferred. However, although a similar distinction is to be found in a number of the other versions,[3] this appears to owe more to a desire to ring the changes than to convey any difference of meaning—indeed the German text uses the word "Waren" throughout.[4] Consequently, it is clear that the term "goods" covers "agricultural products" within the meaning of Article 32 (ex 38) of the Treaty, that is products listed in Annex I (formerly Annex II) thereto.[5]

Furthermore, neither Article 28 nor Article 29, which lay down the prohibition on quantitative restrictions respectively on imports and on exports, uses the terms "goods" or "products". Instead they refer respectively to "imports" and "exports". Yet there can be no doubt that by this is meant imports and exports of "goods"—an interpretation which is confirmed by the reference in Article 30 to "restrictions on imports, exports or goods in transit".

2.03 Nowhere in the Treaty is the concept of "goods" defined. However, the Court of Justice has stated in *Commission v Italy* (works of art)[6] that:

> "by goods, within the meaning of [Article 23 of the Treaty], there must be understood products which can be valued in money and which are capable, as such, of forming the subject of commercial transactions."

While this is undoubtedly the *locus classicus* on the matter, Fennelly A.G. was no doubt correct to say in a subsequent case that the Court has never laid down an exhaustive definition and has preferred to "follow a functional approach".[7]

At all events, in *Commission v Italy* the defendant Member State, brought before the Court for failing to lift its duty on exports of articles of an artistic, historic, archaeological or ethnographic nature in accordance with Article 25 claimed that such articles did not constitute "goods". This submission was rejected by the Court, since art treasures fell within its definition of goods. Had the Court reached the opposite conclusion, it would have deprived of all meaning the exception clause in Article 30 covering restrictions justified on the grounds of "the protection of national treasures possessing artistic, historic or archaeological value".[8] As already pointed out, "goods" must have the same meaning under Articles 28 to 30 as under Article 25.

---

[3] The French text uses "marchandises" and "produits", the Italian "merci" and "prodotti" and the Dutch "goederen" and "produkten".
[4] Likewise Danish only uses "varer".
[5] See generally Ch. X.
[6] Case 7/68 [1968] E.C.R. 423; [1969] C.M.L.R. 1.
[7] Case C-97/98 *Jägerskiöld v Gustafsson* [1999] E.C.R. I–7319 at 7328.
[8] Paras 8.115 *et seq.* below.

2.04 Some further light was shed on the meaning of "goods" in the *Sacchi*[9] case. Criminal proceedings had been brought against the operator of a private television station for allegedly infringing the Italian State monopoly over television broadcasting. One question put to the Court was whether the principle of the free movement of goods applied to this activity. In this connection it should be pointed out that the first paragraph of Article 50 (ex 60) states that "services shall be considered 'services' within the meaning of this Treaty where they are normally provided for remuneration, in so far as they are not governed by the provisions relating to the freedom of movement for goods, capital and persons". Thus the rules on the free movement of services and those on the free movement of goods cannot apply to the same aspect of a given measure.

The Court replied in the following terms:

"In the absence of express provision to the contrary in the Treaty, a television signal must, by reason of its nature, be regarded as provision of services.

Although it is not ruled out that services normally provided for remuneration may come under the provisions relating to goods such is however the case as appears from Article [50], only in so far as they are governed by such provisions.

It follows that the transmission of television signals including those in the nature of advertisements, comes, as such, within the rules of the Treaty relating to services.

On the other hand, trade in material sound recordings, films, apparatus and other products used for the diffusion of television signals are subject to the rules relating to freedom of movement for goods".[10]

Confirmation of this ruling is to be found in *Procureur du Roi v Debauve*.[11] A number of individuals and undertakings engaged in the diffusion of cable television had been prosecuted before the Belgian courts for infringing the prohibition on television advertising in Belgium. Asked by the Liège court to rule whether this prohibition contravened the Treaty provisions on the freedom to provide services, the Court began by stating that:

"Before examining those questions the Court recalls that it has already ruled in its judgment of 30 April 1974 (Case 155/73 *Sacchi* [1974] E.C.R. 490), that the broadcasting of television signals including those in the nature of advertisements, comes, as such, within the rules of the Treaty relating to services. There is no reason to treat the transmission of such signals by cable television any differently".[12]

2.05 In *R. v Thompson, Johnson and Woodiwiss*,[13] the Court was called upon to distinguish the concept of goods from those of capital and current payments. At the material time, the provisions on the free movement of capital were to be found in Articles 67 to 73 of the Treaty, but following the Treaty of Maastricht

---

[9] Case 155/73 [1974] E.C.R. 409; [1974] 2 C.M.L.R. 177. See also Case C-260/89 *ERT v DEP* [1991] E.C.R. I–2925.
[10] Paras 6 and 7 of the judgment.
[11] Case 52/79 [1980] E.C.R. 833; [1981] 2 C.M.L.R. 362.
[12] Para.8 of the judgment.
[13] Case 7/78 [1978] E.C.R. 2247; [1979] 1 C.M.L.R. 47.

those provisions were replaced with effect from January 1, 1994 by Articles 73b to 73g (now 56 to 60). Meanwhile, the freedom to effect current payments for liberalised transactions was enshrined at that time in Article 106, but was moved by the Treaty of Maastricht to Article 73b(2) (now 56(2)).[14]

The Treaty has never defined the terms "capital" or "current payments". However, the Council had adopted Directives for the implementation of the then Article 67[15]; although these Directives did not purport to give a definition of "capital" either, they incorporated a list of capital movements.[16]

In *Thompson* the three defendants were charged before the English courts with importing Krugerrands and exporting silver alloy coins between April and June 1975, contrary to various provisions of English law. The coins fell into three categories:

(a) Krugerrands (which were legal tender only in South Africa);

(b) British silver alloy coins which were still legal tender; and

(c) British silver alloy half-crowns minted before 1947 which, although no longer legal tender, could be exchanged at the Bank of England and were protected from destruction other than by the State on the grounds that the State enjoyed a right akin to a property right in them.

In each case the commodity value of the coins far exceeded their face value. When this case came before it on appeal by the defendants, the Court of Appeal referred four questions for a preliminary ruling to ascertain whether the import and export restrictions were compatible with Community law. It sought to do so essentially by asking whether the coins were "capital" within the meaning of the Treaty, and in any case whether these restrictions were justified by Article 30.

The difficulty posed by these questions is underlined by the fact that the first capital Directive[17] included imports and exports of gold and "means of payment of every kind" in the list of capital movements, while the Common Customs Tariff[18] mentioned coins which are not collectors' pieces (heading

---

[14] Given its position in the Treaty and its wording, this provision is ambiguous, since it could be taken as covering only current payments connected with capital movements. However, the Court has held that it relates to current payments for goods and services: Case C-163/94 *Saenz de Lera* [1995] E.C.R. I–4821, para.17.

[15] Directive of May 11, 1960 ([1960] O.J. Spec. Ed. 921) amended by Directive 62/21 of December 18, 1962 ([1963] O.J. Spec. Ed. 62).

[16] After the judgment in *Thompson* (see n.13 above), further amendment was effected by Directives 85/583 ([1985] O.J. L372/39) and 86/566 ([1986] O.J. L332/22). The Directive as thus amended was subsequently replaced by Directive 88/361 ([1988] O.J. L178/5), which in turn lapsed on December 31, 1993 when the new Arts. 73b to 73g (now 56 to 60) came into effect. The Court has nevertheless held that the list of transactions annexed to the latter Directive continues to have "indicative value" as a non-exhaustive definition of "capital": Case C-222/97 *Trummer* [1999] E.C.R. I–1661, paras 20–21, *Jägerskiöld* (see n.7 above), para.34.

[17] Directive of May 11, 1960 (see n.15 above).

[18] The Common Customs Tariff is contained in Annex I to Council Regulation 2658/87 on the tariff and statistical nomenclature and on the Common Customs Tariff ([1987] O.J. L256/1) as replaced from time to time, most recently by Commission Regulation 2031/2001 ([2001] O.J. L279/1).

number 72–01), as well as coins which are collectors' pieces (heading number 99–05) and banknotes (heading number 49–07).

Many of the intervenors before the Court deduced from this that the decision as to which Treaty provisions to apply depended not on the nature of the items, but on the purpose for which they were imported—though as to the exact criterion to be applied there were distinct differences between those intervenors.

However, the Court appears to have concentrated rather on the nature of the articles, since it ruled as follows:

"The aim of [the Treaty provision on current payments] is to ensure that the necessary monetary transfers may be made for the liberalisation of movements of capital and for the free movement of goods, services and persons.

It must be inferred from this that under the system of the Treaty means of payment are not to be regarded as goods falling within the purview of Articles [28 to 31] of the Treaty.

Silver alloy coins which are legal tender in a Member State are, by their very nature, to be regarded as means of payment and it follows that their transfer does not fall within the provisions of Articles [28 to 31] of the Treaty.

Although doubts may be entertained on the question whether Krugerrands are to be regarded as means of legal payment it can nevertheless be noted that on the money markets of those Member States which permit dealings in these coins they are treated as being equivalent to currency.

Their transfer must consequently be designated as a monetary transfer which does not fall within the provisions of the said Articles [28 to 31].

Having regard to the above mentioned considerations it is unnecessary to deal with the question under what circumstances the transfer of these two categories of coins might possibly be designated either as a movement of capital or as a current payment.

Question 1(c) refers to silver alloy coins of a Member State, which have been legal tender in that State and which, although no longer legal tender, are protected as coinage from destruction.

Such coins cannot be regarded as means of payment within the meaning stated above, with the result that they can be designated as goods falling within the system of Articles [28 to 31] of the Treaty."

Thus it held that the coins in categories (a) and (b) were not goods, whereas those in category (c) were goods.[19]

In an area that was already beset with conceptual difficulties, it is perhaps unfortunate that the Court chose to refer to concepts which it did not define. Presumably the notion of "means of payment" is wider than that of legal tender, but how wide is it? Is "means of legal payment" the same as "means of payment"? And what is meant by being "treated as being equivalent to currency"? The only clear proposition that can be distilled from this judgment is that coins which are still legal tender in a Member State are not "goods". One might also deduce from the passage relating to Krugerrands that coins which are legal tender in a third country are not "goods" either.

At all events, in its more recent judgment in *Bordessa*[20] the Court confirmed

---

[19] As to the third category, see para. 8.48 below.
[20] Case C-358/93 [1995] E.C.R. I–361. See also para. 6.32 below.

its earlier ruling in *Thompson* and made it clear that the principles laid down there applied to banknotes and bearer cheques as well as to coins. There is every reason to suppose that these rulings are still good law, despite the above-mentioned changes in the Treaty articles relating to capital and current payments.

2.06 In view of this case law, there seems little room left today for the view that the concept of "capital" in Articles 56 to 60 extends beyond financial assets to include objects of value such as jewellery, furs and pictures.[21] The Capital Directives[22], which have now been replaced, covered such items as gifts and endowments, dowries and inheritances, which might take the form of tangible goods; but it would appear that such assets were only caught by the Directives in so far as they were of a financial nature.[23]

2.07 Quite naturally, in *Commission v Italy* (works of art) the Court defined goods as products having commercial value. Yet refuse, if anything, has a negative value: people are paid to remove it. In the first two editions of this book it was suggested that refuse is nevertheless to be regarded as goods within the meaning of the Treaty. Reference was made to a decision of the United States Supreme Court[24] holding unconstitutional a New Jersey statute prohibiting, subject to limited exceptions, the importation of waste from other States of the Union.

This view was accepted by the Court of Justice in *Commission v Belgium*.[25] The facts of that case bear a striking similarity to those of the New Jersey case, the Region of Wallonia having imposed a total ban on the disposal or storage of waste from other Member States. The defendant Member State contended that waste did not constitute goods, at least when it could not be recycled or reused. The Advocate General rejected this argument in the following terms:

---

[21] The broader interpretation was advanced by Everling in Wohlfart, Everling, Glaesener and Sprung, *Die Europäische Wirtschaftsgemeinschaft, Kommentar zum Vertrag* (Frankfurt and Berlin, 1960), 203; *contra* van Ballegooijen, "Free Movement of Capital in the EEC" (1976) 2 L.I.E.I. 1, 4. See generally Oliver, "Free Movement of Capital between Member States: Art. 67(1) EEC and the Implementing Directives" (1984) E.L.Rev. 401.

[22] See n.15 above.

[23] Member States are entitled under Article 30 to take measures to prevent tax evasion; see para. 8.122 below.

[24] *Philadelphia v New Jersey* 437 U.S. 617, 98 S.Ct.2531 (1987); this judgment has been confirmed by the Supreme Court in *Chemical Waste Management v Hunt US* (1992) USA 1a, 112 SCc 2009, 119 LEd 2d 121; and *Fort Gratiot Sanitary Landfill v Michigan Department of Natural Resources US* (1992) US Mich, 112, SCc 2019, 119 LEd 2d 139. For a comparison between the rules on the free movement of goods under the Treaty of Rome and under the American Constitution, see Bermann, Goebel, Davy and Fox, *Cases and Materials on European Union Law* (2nd ed., 2002) Part III "The Common Market, the Internal Market and the Four Freedoms"; Kommers and Waelbroeck, "Legal Integration and the Free Movement of Goods: The American and European Experience" in Integration through Law, Vol. I, book 3; Roth, *Freier Warenverkehr und staatliche Regelungsgewalt in einem Gemeinsamen Markt* (1976); Slot, *Technical and Administrative Obstacles to Trade in the EEC* (1975); and van Gerven "Constitutional Aspects of the European Court's Case-Law on Articles 30 and 36 EC as Compared with the US Dormant Commerce Clause", Mélanges en Hommage à Michel Waelbroeck (1999) Vol. 2 p. 1629.

[25] Case C-2/90 [1992] E.C.R. I, 4431; see para. 8.160 below.

"In my view, the Treaty provisions on free movement of goods must be taken to apply to all types of waste product, even those which cannot be recycled or reused. While it is clear that such products have no intrinsic commercial value—indeed, they rather have a negative value—they clearly form the subject of commercial transactions in that waste disposal undertakings are paid to dispose of them. Indeed, as the Commission agent pointed out at the hearing, a substantial industry is devoted to the disposal of waste products. Account must also be taken of the purpose of the Community provisions on the free movement of goods, namely the removal of all internal frontiers: the acceptance that certain classes of product do not benefit from these provisions would in practice entail the re-erection of internal frontiers."

In a second Opinion, he added that matter having a negative value could perfectly well be the subject of commercial transactions. Moreover, he pointed out that the distinction between goods which could and those which could not be recycled was unworkable, because the economic feasibility of recycling would depend in each case on a series of variables such as the state of technical knowledge at the time, the cost of the recycling process and the price of competing products. The Court subsequently endorsed his interpretation. It follows that all waste is to be regarded as goods.

2.08 What of electricity? This is not tangible (in the normal sense). Indeed, it is somewhat akin to television signals which were held in *Sacchi* to constitute services, not goods. In *Costa v ENEL*[26] the Court, following the Advocate General, found that an electricity monopoly fell under Article 31 (ex 37). This implied that electricity is to be regarded as goods,[27] although neither the Court nor the Advocate General addressed this particular matter.

In *Almelo v Energiebedrijf IJsselmij*[28] the Court confirmed that electricity constitutes goods for these purposes. It gave three reasons to support this conclusion: that this view was accepted both in Community law and in the laws of the Member States; that electricity was treated as a product in the customs nomenclature; and that it had already ruled to this effect in *Costa v ENEL*. This ruling was confirmed once again in *Commission v Italy* (electricity monopoly).[29] The defendant argued that the previous case law took insufficient account of the technical characteristics of electricity, notably the fact that it is intangible and cannot be stored. The Court's reasoning on this point simply repeats that in *Almelo*.

In *Jägerskiöld v Gustafsson*,[30] Fennelly A.G. acknowledged that it might "appear somewhat surprising that the Court has treated electricity, despite its intangible character, as goods". After repeating the reasoning of the Court in *Almelo*, he added: "To my mind, electricity must be regarded as a specific case, perhaps justifiable by virtue of its function as an energy source and, therefore, in competition with gas and oil."

---

[26] Case 6/64 [1964] E.C.R. 585.
[27] Ch. XI.
[28] Case C-393/92 [1994] E.C.R. I-1477.
[29] Case C-158/94 [1997] E.C.R. I-5789, paras 14–20; see para. 9.12 below
[30] See n.7 above, at pp. 7328–9.

2.09 That intangibles other than electricity fall outside the concept of goods appears to have been established almost definitively in *Jägerskiöld*. The Court had been asked *inter alia* whether fishing rights and fishing permits constituted "goods". Fennelly A.G. remarked that the classic definition of that term in *Commission v Italy* (works of art) "cannot be understood as placing in that category anything of value which is capable of being traded". He then added: "Goods, in the common connotation of the term, possess tangible physical characteristics." Next, he acknowledged that electricity constituted something of an anomaly in this regard, as we have just noticed. In addition, he rejected the claim that intellectual property constituted goods: while "a variety of intellectual property rights may affect trade in goods", "Community law does not classify intellectual property rights themselves as a form of goods". Consequently, he concluded that the grant of fishing rights and permits was not trade in goods, but services. Without referring to the intangible nature of the rights concerned, the Court fully endorsed the Advocate General's approach.

2.10 Finally, we come to the highly anomalous case of the human body. That whole, live human beings fall outside the concept of goods is beyond doubt: if they are nationals of a Member State, they are covered instead by the Treaty provisions on the free movement of persons (Article 39 (ex 48) EC) and those on the citizenship of the Union (Articles 17 to 22 (ex 8 to 8E)). Fortunately, slavery has long since been abolished in the Community.

On the other hand, there appears to be no good reason why human foetuses, blood or body parts should not be regarded as goods. Otherwise, they would escape the Treaty provisions on the four freedoms altogether, since they can obviously not be considered to be persons, services or capital. They would therefore fall into a "black hole" in terms of Community law, which would be wholly undesirable. Manifestly, the most basic considerations of public morality, public policy and public health require that trade in some of these materials should be subject to severe restrictions, if it is allowed at all. However, the exceptions set out in Article 30 are surely adequate to cover such prohibitions or restrictions. The same applies to human corpses, it is submitted.[31]

There is some doubt as to whether these items are covered by the Common Customs Tariff,[32] although Chapter 5 ("Products of animal origin, not elsewhere specified or included") appears to be in point. Indeed, the very first subheading, 0501 00 00, relates to a product of the human body, namely: "human hair, unworked, whether or not washed or scoured; waste of human hair". For good measure, it should be added that sub-heading 6703 00 00 covers "human hair, dressed, thinned, bleached or otherwise worked", while heading 6704 relates to "wigs, false beards, eyebrows and eyelashes ... of human or animal hair". Admittedly, the Commission is on record as stating that "the customs nomenclature covers goods alone, and ... foetuses and foetal material are not

---

[31] As explained at para. 2.32 below, moral considerations should play no part in determining whether an item is to be regarded as "goods" for the purposes of the Treaty.
[32] See n.18 above.

classified therein".[33] In any event, it is submitted that the question as to whether the items concerned are covered by the Common Customs Tariff is not decisive: as we noticed earlier, coins and banknotes that were legal tender were held in *Thompson* and *Bordessa* respectively to fall outside the concept of "goods", even though they featured in the customs nomenclature; conversely, it is suggested that other materials which are not classified in that nomenclature may constitute "goods".

Moreover, it would seem from *Veedfald v Århus*[34] that a human kidney donated for transplant constitutes a "product" for the purposes of Council Directive 85/374 on liability for defective products.[35] In so far as is relevant, Article 2 of that Directive defines "products" as "all moveables".

2.11 The situation may therefore be summarised as follows: "goods" means "products which can be valued in money and which are capable, as such, of forming the subject of commercial transactions"; all tangibles other than "means of payment" (and live human beings) are "goods", including all forms of waste; television signals are not goods, but electricity is. Whether an item is covered by the customs nomenclature would not appear to be decisive.

II. GOODS "ORIGINATING IN MEMBER STATES" AND GOODS FROM THIRD COUNTRIES IN "FREE CIRCULATION" IN THE COMMUNITY

2.12 Article 23(2) (ex 9(2)) of the EC Treaty stipulates that the provisions on the free movement of goods, including Articles 28 to 30, apply to "products originating in Member States and to products coming from third countries which are in free circulation in Member States".[36] Each of these two concepts will be examined in turn.

First, it should be pointed out that Council Regulation 222/77[37] on Community transit and Commission Regulation 223/77,[38] which implemented it, provided in effect that goods were presumed not to fall within either of the two categories set out in Article 23(2); this presumption could only be rebutted by production of the relevant transit documents. In *Trend-Moden Textilhandel v HZA Emmerich*[39] the Court found the provisions in question to be compatible with Articles 23 and 24 (ex 10) of the Treaty. However, this presumption has now

---

[33] Answer to Written Question 442/85 ([1985] O.J. C263/19).
[34] Case C-203/99 [2000] E.C.R. I–3569.
[35] [1985] O.J. L 210/29; that Directive has now been amended by Directive 1999/34 ([1999] O.J. L141/20).
[36] Matters relating to quantitative restrictions and measures of equivalent effect in direct trade between the Community and third countries fall outside the scope of this book (but see Ch. XIII).
[37] [1977] O.J. L38/1.
[38] [1977] O.J. L38/20.
[39] Case C-117/88 [1990] E.C.R. I, 631, criticised by Vaulont, "La suppression des frontières intérieures et la réglementation douanière communautaire" [1994] R.M.U.E. 51. That judgment was confirmed in Case C-237/96 *Amelynck* [1997] E.C.R. I–5103.

been reversed: save in certain specified circumstances, "all goods transported between two points in the customs territory of the Community shall be deemed to be Community goods unless it is established that they do not have Community status".[40]

As to the territorial extent of the Member States for this purpose, the reader is referred to Chapter III of this book.

A. Goods Originating in the Member States

2.13 This concept is nowhere defined in the Treaty. However, assistance is to be derived from Articles 23 to 26 of Council Regulation 2913/92 establishing the Community Customs Code.[41] Article 22 provides that Articles 23 to 26 define the non-preferential origin of goods for the purposes of:

"(a) applying the Customs Tariff of the European Communities...;

  (b) applying measures other than tariff measures established by Community provisions governing specific fields relating to trade in goods;

  (c) the preparation and issue of certificates of origin."

Articles 23 to 26 are in the following terms:

"Article 23

1. Goods originating in a country shall be those wholly obtained or produced in that country.
2. The expression 'goods wholly obtained or produced in one country' means:

  (a) mineral products extracted within that country;
  (b) vegetable products harvested therein;
  (c) live animals born and raised therein;
  (d) products derived from live animals raised therein;
  (e) products of hunting or fishing carried on therein;
  (f) products of sea-fishing and other products taken from the sea outside a country's territorial sea by vessels registered or recorded in the country concerned and flying the flag of that country;
  (g) goods obtained or produced on board factory ships from the products referred to in subparagraph
  (f) originating in that country, provided that such factory ships are registered or recorded in that country and fly its flag;
  (h) products taken from the seabed or subsoil beneath the seabed outside territorial sea provided that that country has exclusive rights to exploit that seabed or subsoil;
  (i) waste and scrap products derived from manufacturing operations and used

---

[40] Art. 313 of Commission Reg. 2454/93 implementing the Community Customs Code ([1993] O.J. L253/1) as last amended by Reg. 993/2001 ([2001] O.J. L141/1); the new rule was first laid down by Council Reg. 2726/90 on Community transit ([1990] O.J. L262/1).
[41] [1992] O.J. L302/1, as last amended by Regulation 2700/2000 ([2000] O.J. L311/17); see Dehousse et Vincent, *Les règles d'origine de la Communauté européénne* (1999); Giffoni, "Droit douanier de la CE et aspects économiques: Législation applicable au 1er janvier 1994" (Commission publication 1993) at 103; Witte, *Zollkodex* (2nd ed., 1998) Ch. 2.

articles, if they were collected therein and are fit only for the recovery of raw materials;

(j) goods which are produced therein exclusively from goods referred to in subparagraphs (a) to (i) or from their derivatives, at any stage of production.

3. For the purposes of paragraph 2 the expression "country" covers that country's territorial sea.

Article 24
Goods whose production involved more than one country shall be deemed to originate in the country where they underwent their last, substantial, economically justified processing or working in an undertaking equipped for that purpose and resulting in the manufacture of a new product or representing an important stage of manufacture.

Article 25
Any processing or working in respect of which it is established, or in respect of which the facts as ascertained justify the presumption, that its sole object was to circumvent the provisions applicable in the Community to goods from specific countries shall under no circumstances be deemed to confer on the goods thus produced the origin of the country where it is carried out within the meaning of Article 24.

Article 26
1. Customs legislation or other Community legislation governing specific fields may provide that a document must be produced as proof of the origin of goods.
2. Notwithstanding the production of this document, the customs authorities may, in the event of serious doubts, require any additional proof to ensure that the indication of origin does comply with the rules laid down by the relevant Community legislation."

The concept of "Community goods" for the purposes of the Code is defined *inter alia by* reference to these Articles. They are supplemented by specific provisions relating to particular products[42]; and by various preferential rules adopted by the Community unilaterally or by treaty,[43] in accordance with Articles 20(3)(d) and (e) and 27 of the Code.

2.14 Nevertheless, it should not be thought that all goods originating in Member States are necessarily in free circulation in the Community. Thus goods produced in the Community under inward processing relief arrangements provided for by Articles 114 to 129 of the Community Customs Code are not in free circulation. Also, once goods having Community origin have been exported from the Community in the normal way pursuant to Articles 161 to 162 of the Code, they cease to be in free circulation in the Community.[44]

---

[42] Arts 35 to 46 of Commission Reg. 2454/93 (see n.40 above).
[43] *e.g.* the Protocol on the concept of "originating products" to the Partnership Agreement with the African, Caribbean and Pacific countries ([2000] O.J. L317/94); see also Arts 66 *et seq.* of Reg. 2454/93 (see n.40 above).
[44] However, Arts 185 to 187 of the Code permit such goods to be returned to the Community in certain circumstances without payment of customs duties.

B. Goods from Third Countries in Free Circulation in the Community

2.15 As regards this second category of goods benefiting from free movement within the Community according to Article 23(2), it is provided in Article 24 (ex 10(1)) of the Treaty that:

> "Products coming from a third country shall be considered to be in free circulation in a Member State if the import formalities have been complied with and any customs duties or charges having equivalent effect which are payable have been levied in that Member State, and if they have not benefited from a total or partial drawback of such duties or charges."

As long ago as 1970, Waelbroeck suggested that these conditions are fulfilled if the customs duties payable have merely been determined, whether or not they have been paid.[45] The Council has manifestly espoused this view, since a number of provisions of the Community Customs Code (*e.g.* Articles 74, 79, 218 and 222 to 232) enable goods to be released for free circulation in the Community provided that the customs authorities have accepted a customs declaration, regardless of whether import duties have actually been paid; indeed, it would appear that the amount of the customs debt need not even have been determined.

Yet no distortion of trade can result, since security must have been lodged (save in exceptional circumstances) and the customs authorities will have in their possession all the information necessary to assess the amount of the duties. Consequently, it is submitted that the Code is in no way at variance with Article 24 of the Treaty, a succinct provision which in any case does not purport to provide in detail for every hypothetical situation.

2.16 The term "drawback" in Article 24 means a repayment or reduction of the import duties payable. Where Community legislation has provided a suspension or reduction of all goods of a particular description and origin, the full amount of the duty is not payable at all. Consequently, in those circumstances no drawback has been granted. Similarly, where for any reason sums paid to the customs authorities exceed the amount lawfully due and the excess is repaid to the importer pursuant to Articles 236 or 237 of the Code, no drawback is granted.

It is unclear whether an individual waiver of duties constitutes a "drawback" within the meaning of Article 24. Such waivers may be granted on equitable grounds by the Commission at the request of the national customs authority in exceptional cases, in accordance with Article 239 of the Code and Articles 905 to 909 of the Commission Regulation 2454/93 implementing the Code.[46] In any event, it is plain from Article 233 of the Code that the grant of such a waiver extinguishes the customs debt.

---

[45] *Le droit de la Communauté économique européenne* (1970) Vol. I, 43.
[46] See n.40 above.

Indeed, it is arguable that the final limb of Article 24 relates only to drawbacks granted by the Member States. The Member States have long since lost the power to grant drawbacks except when they have been specifically empowered to do so by Community legislation. It would follow on this view that the final limb of Article 24 has ceased to have effect.[47] At first sight, this might seem surprising: this article was re-enacted in its present form by the Treaty of Amsterdam, although "lapsed provisions" of the EC Treaty were supposedly "deleted" at Amsterdam (Article 6). Nevertheless, nothing in the language of the later Treaty suggests that *all* such provisions were effectively removed.

2.17   What if there has been fraud or error?[48] Where the goods have never been cleared through customs at all, then presumably they are not in free circulation even if they have been mistakenly treated as being so. On the other hand, where the appropriate customs formalities have been completed but the amount of duties has been incorrectly assessed, it would seem that the goods are in free circulation but the unpaid sums are still due. They may be recovered by the customs authorities in accordance with Articles 78, 220 and 222 of the Code. At all events, as in all customs cases, the utmost importance will be attached to the certificates issued in respect of the goods.

2.18   Article 83 of the Code lists a series of exceptional circumstances in which "goods released for free circulation ... lose their customs status as Community goods". Naturally the same will occur when the goods are definitively exported from the Community.

2.19   Assuming then that goods have been put into free circulation in the Community, what is the consequence of their having that status? The assimilation of goods from third countries put into free circulation in a Member State to goods originating in the Community was categorically underlined by the Court in *Donckerwolcke v Procureur de la République*[49] in the following terms:

> "It appears from Article [23] that, as regards free circulation of goods within the Community, products entitled to 'free circulation' are definitively and wholly assimilated to products originating in Member States.
>   The result of this assimilation is that the provisions of Article [28] concerning the elimination of quantitative restrictions and all measures having equivalent effect are applicable without distinction to products originating in the Community and to those which were put into free circulation in any one of the Member States, irrespective of the actual origin of the products."

A particularly clear illustration of this principle is to be found in *Commission v Ireland*[50] where it was held that the defendant State had infringed Article 28 by

---

[47] This is also implied by Vaulont in his commentary on the former Article 10(1) EC in Groeben, Thiesing and Ehlermann, *Kommentar Zum EU-/EG-Vertrag* (5th ed., 1997) Vol. I at pp. 454–5.

[48] See generally Case 252/87 *HZA Hamburg St. Annen v Kiwall* [1988] E.C.R. 4753.

[49] Case 41/76 [1976] E.C.R. 1921 at 1933; [1977] 2 C.M.L.R. 535 at 550.

[50] Case 288/83 [1985] E.C.R. 1761; [1985] 3 C.M.L.R. 152; see Usher, "The Single Market and Goods imported from Third Countries" [1986] Y.E.L. 159 at 179.

imposing an import licensing system for potatoes originating in Cyprus but in free circulation in the United Kingdom.

2.20 However, this principle does not apply to all matters, as the Court emphasised in the *EMI Records v CBS*[51] cases. There, the facts were as follows: until 1917 one undertaking had held the "Columbia" trade mark for records both in the United States and in Europe. That year saw the first of a series of transactions which resulted in CBS holding the trade mark in the United States and EMI owning it in all the Member States of the Community. EMI brought proceedings against CBS in the United Kingdom, Denmark and Germany, giving rise to three parallel references. The Court held that Article 28 had no bearing on this question, since no movement of goods between Member States was involved. It rejected the defendants' reliance on the principle of the assimilation of third country goods in free circulation in the Member States, in the following terms:

> "Since [Articles 23 and 24] only refer to the effects of compliance with customs formalities and paying customs duties and charges having equivalent effect, they cannot be interpreted as meaning that it would be sufficient for products bearing a mark applied in a third country and imported into the Community to comply with the customs formalities in the first Member State where they were imported in order to enable them to be marketed in the Common Market as a whole in contravention of the rules relating to the protection of the mark."[52]

It is submitted that Warner A.G.'s rather drier response to this particular argument of the defendants is more accurate:

> "The argument of the defendants is, as I understand it, that once records made in America and bearing the mark Columbia have been cleared through customs in a Member State, they are, provided they have not benefited from a drawback, to be assimilated to records originating in a Member State. So they are. But I do not see how this assists the defendants. If they were to manufacture similar records in a Member State, they would not thereby render themselves entitled to market them in infringement of EMI Records Limited's registered marks, either in that Member State or in any other."[53]

2.21 Also, certain Treaty provisions created exceptions to the rule that goods originating in third countries are to be treated as Community goods once the appropriate customs formalities have been completed. Exceptions to this principle will not be recognised lightly, as clear and ambiguous wording is needed to create even short-term derogations of this nature.[54] What is more,

---

[51] Case 51/75 [1976] E.C.R. 811; [1976] 2 C.M.L.R. 235; Case 86/75 [1976] E.C.R. 871; [1976] 2 C.M.L.R. 235; Case 96/75 [1976] E.C.R. 913; [1976] 2 C.M.L.R. 235; see para. 8.216 below.
[52] Paras 16, 19 and 9 of the respective judgments.
[53] at 860.
[54] Thus in Case C-233/97 *KappAhl* [1998] E.C.R. I-8069 the Court did not shrink from adopting what amounted to a wrecking interpretation of Article 99 of the 1994 Act of Accession. That provision granted Finland a 3-year derogation from the Common Customs Tariff for certain products.

with the abolition of border controls on goods passing between the Member States with effect from January 1, 1993 pursuant to Article 14 (ex 7A) EC,[55] the mechanisms for applying such provisions have disappeared and accordingly most of these provisions have been phased out.[56]

The most important of these exceptions was Article 134 (ex 115) of the Treaty which applies where the execution of national commercial policy measures is threatened by "deflection of trade" or where "differences between such measures [of national commercial policy] lead to economic difficulties in one or more of the Member States". In such circumstances the Commission "shall authorise Member States to take the necessary protective measures, the conditions and details of which it shall determine". This provision is briefly considered in Chapter IX of this book, although it is probably obsolete.[57]

2.22   Another exception is contained in the largely forgotten Protocol to the original EEC Treaty on goods originating in and coming from certain countries and enjoying special treatment when imported into a Member State. Article 1 of this Protocol entitled France, Italy and the Benelux respectively to continue to grant privileged customs treatment to goods originating and coming from certain past or present French, Italian and Dutch colonies. Article 2 of the Protocol stipulates:

> "goods imported into a Member State and benefiting from the treatment referred to above shall not be considered to be in free circulation in that State within the meaning of Article 10 [now 24] of this Treaty when re-exported to another Member State."

This Protocol appeared to be obsolete or virtually so. Surprisingly, rather than repeal that Protocol altogether, Article 6 of the Treaty of Amsterdam preserved it, albeit only with respect to Surinamese and Dutch Antillian imports into the Benelux countries.[58] Accordingly, Article 1 of the Protocol now provides that the entry into force of the original EEC Treaty did not require any alteration in "the customs treatment applicable on 1 January 1958 to imports into the Benelux countries of goods originating and coming from Surinam or the Netherlands Antilles". Quite apart from its highly anachronistic nature, this protocol is scarcely a model of transparency, since it fails to specify the content of the customs arrangements to which the products concerned were subject on entering the Benelux on January 1, 1958.

2.23   Last, an exception may still be applicable to Canary bananas by virtue of

---

[55] Paras 6.10 and 7.04 and 12.12 *et seq.* below.

[56] Thus the special regime for imports of New Zealand butter into the United Kingdom, which was based on a specific Protocol to the first Act of Accession, lapsed at the end of 1995: Reg. 3610/93 ([1993] O.J. L328/5), as amended by Reg. 3232/94 ([1994] O.J. L338/12). Article 1(4) of that Protocol provided that the butter and cheese imported into the United Kingdom in accordance with that Protocol "may not become the subject of intra-Community trade". This has been replaced by a GATT concession, currently implemented by Council Regulation 1095/96 ([1996] O.J. L146/1) and Commission Regulation 1374/98 ([1998] O.J. L185/21), as amended.

[57] Paras 9.28 *et seq.*

[58] [1997] O.J. C340/69.

the Protocol on the Canary Islands and Ceuta and Melilla which is annexed to the Act of Accession of Spain and Portugal.[59] As explained below,[60] that Protocol provided that goods originating in or coming from the Canaries were in essence assimilated to goods from third countries; but Council Regulation 1911/91[61] brought those islands within the Community customs territory and thus Articles 28 to 30 apply to trade between them and other Member States. However, Article 10(3) of that Regulation provides: "The provisions of Protocol 2 to the Act of Accession relating to bananas continue to apply". This is a reference to Article 4(2)(a) of the Protocol, which stipulates that bananas originating in the Canaries shall be exempt from customs duties when "released for free circulation" in the rest of Spain (other than Ceuta and Melilla); and which goes on to provide that "bananas imported under the above-mentioned arrangements may not be deemed to be in free circulation in the said part of Spain within the meaning of Article [24] of the [EC] Treaty when they are reconsigned to another Member State".

A common market organisation for bananas has now been established[62] and it seems anomalous that Article 4(2)(a) of the Protocol should still be in force. Moreover, since it would appear that that Canary bananas are subject to this common market organisation,[63] it makes no sense for this exception to continue to apply. Yet it is not stipulated either in Regulation 1911/91 or elsewhere that Article 4(2)(a) would lapse once a common market organisation was in force. This must be regarded as an oversight, which might one day be "corrected" by some imaginative judicial interpretation.

III. THE NATIONALITY OF THE OWNER

2.24 Only the status of goods, and not the nationality of their owner, is the determining factor for the application of the Treaty provisions on the free movement of goods. This has been emphasised by the Court in relation to the prohibition on charges of equivalent effect in Article 25 (formerly 12) EC:

"The Treaty prohibits any pecuniary charge on imports and exports between Member States, irrespective of the nationality of the traders who might be placed at a disadvantage by such measures. Thus, in applying these provisions, there is no justification for a distinction to be made according to whether the measures in question adversely affect certain Member States and their nationals, or all the citizens of the Community, or only the nationals of the Member State which was responsible for the measures in question."[64]

---

[59] [1985] O.J. L302/400.
[60] Para. 3.03.
[61] [1991] O.J. L171/1, as last amended by Council Reg. 2674/99 ([1999] O.J. L326/3).
[62] Council Reg. 404/93 [1993] O.J. L47/1.
[63] See the penultimate recital in the preamble to Reg. 404/93.
[64] Cases 2–3/69 *Sociaalfonds voor Diamantarbeiders v Brachfeld* [1969] E.C.R. 211; [1969] C.M.L.R. 335, paras 24–26 of the judgment.

This statement also holds good for Articles 28 to 30.

In highly exceptional circumstances, it may be otherwise when the owner of the goods is a national of a third state enjoying less than cordial relations with one or more Member States. It might then be possible to have recourse to Articles 297 (ex 224) or 301 (ex 228A) to prohibit imports or exports.[65]

IV. THE TRANSACTIONS COVERED

A. General

2.25   The first two parts of this chapter considered what items benefit from the Treaty provisions governing the free movement of goods between Member States and in particular Articles 28 to 30. This section is concerned with the movements covered, and the relationship between these provisions and those relating to the other three freedoms enshrined in the Treaty, namely: the free movement of persons (Articles 39–48 (ex 48–58)), the free provision of services (Articles 49–55 (ex 59–66)) and the free movement of capital (Articles 56–60 (ex 73b–73g)). The relationship between Articles 28 to 30 and other Treaty provisions relating to goods is considered at paragraphs 6.25 *et seq.* below.

2.26   As the reader will be aware, the classic case involves goods passing from one Member State to another to be sold in the second State.[66]

The same applies where the goods merely transit through the second Member State to be sold in another Member State or even outside the Community. This follows from the fact that transit is simply a particular type of importation and of exportation; it is also expressly stated in Article 30, which begins: "The provisions of Articles 28 to 30 shall not preclude prohibitions or restrictions on imports, exports or goods in transit ...". In *SIOT v Ministry of Finance*[67] the Court deduced from the fact that the Community was a customs union, and from Article 30 in particular, that the freedom of transit within the Community constituted a general principle of Community law. Moreover, in *Monsees v Unabhängiger Verwaltungssenat für Kärnten*,[68] a restriction on the transit of live animals through Austria was held to be contrary to Articles 28 and 29.[69]

2.27   Again, the same applies when goods are imported from one Member State to another where they were produced or where they have already been put on the market. In other words, the provisions on the free movement of goods apply to re-imports. This emerges clearly from *Deutsche Grammophon v Metro*[70]

---

[65] Paras 9.40 *et seq.* below.
[66] As to transactions contrived to speculate in currency or to export capital from a Member State, see paras 6.33, 7.39 and 8.34 below.
[67] Case 266/81 [1983] E.C.R. 731 at 777.
[68] Case C-350/97 [1999] E.C.R. I-2921.
[69] See also Case C-23/99 *Commission v France* (transit of spare parts) [2000] E.C.R. I-7653.
[70] Case 78/70 [1971] E.C.R. 487; [1971] C.M.L.R. 631.

where it was held to be contrary to Article 28 to exercise rights akin to copyright to prevent the reimportation by a parallel importer of records manufactured in Germany; the records had been re-imported with a view to undercutting prices imposed by the manufacturer by means of a retail price maintenance scheme. However, in the specific circumstances of *Leclerc v Au Blé Vert*,[71] which concerned resale price maintenance for books, the Court ruled that Article 28 itself could not be invoked with respect to goods "exported for the sole purpose of re-importation in order to circumvent legislation of the type at issue". It is not easy to reconcile the two cases: the only apparent difference between them is that in *Deutsche Grammophon* the resale price maintenance was imposed by the manufacturer, whereas in *Leclerc* it was imposed by the State.

2.28 The Treaty provisions on the free movement of goods also apply to restrictions on parallel imports. This was spelt out by the Court in *De Peijper*[72] where it held that "rules or practices which result in imports being channelled in such a way that only certain traders can effect these imports, whereas others are prevented from doing so" are measures of equivalent effect under Article 28.[73]

2.29 Also, these Treaty provisions apply to restrictions on imports of raw materials or semi-finished products, even where the finished product is subject to no restrictions. This emerges from the Court's judgment in *Eggers v Freie Hansestadt Bremen*.[74] Conversely, Article 28 also covers restrictions on imports of the finished product when the raw material is subject to no restrictions: *Campus Oil v Minister for Industry and Energy*.[75]

2.30 Equally, the Treaty provisions on the free movement of goods apply where an individual resident in one Member State seeks to import into it goods which he has bought in another Member State. This point was made by Warner A.G. in *R. v Henn and Darby*[76]:

> "There is trade between Member States [for the purposes of Articles 28 to 30] when an individual imports into a Member State for his own use goods that he has bought in another Member State."

This interpretation was confirmed in *Schumacher v HZA Frankfurt*,[77] where the plaintiff resided in Germany and had ordered medicine by post from a pharmacy in Strasbourg for his personal use. Article 28 was held to apply.[78]

---

[71] Case 229/83 [1985] E.C.R. I; [1985] 2 C.M.L.R. 296; see para. 7.85 below. On the abuse of rights, see para. 6.00 below.
[72] Case 104/75 [1976] E.C.R. 613; [1976] 2 C.M.L.R. 271.
[73] See Rothnie, *Parallel Imports* (1993) at 329.
[74] Case 13/78 [1978] E.C.R. 1935; [1979] 1 C.M.L.R. 562.
[75] Case 72/83 [1984] E.C.R. 2727; [1984] 3 C.M.L.R. 544, para.16 of the judgment.
[76] Case 34/79 [1979] E.C.R. 3795 at 3827; [1980] 1 C.M.L.R. 346.
[77] Case 215/87 [1989] E.C.R. 617.
[78] This was confirmed in Case C-62/90 *Commission v Germany* (importation of pharmaceuticals by individuals) [1992] E.C.R. I-2575.

The Court made the point more clearly in *GB-Inno-BM v Confédération du Commerce Luxembourgeois.*[79] The appellants operated a supermarket chain in Belgium, with a branch in Arlon on the border with Luxembourg. They contested a Luxembourg regulation prohibiting them from giving complete information in the Grand Duchy about their special offers, thus making it harder for them to attract custom from across the border. They argued that this legislation was contrary to Article 28. The Court upheld their complaint. For the present purposes the following passage is of particular note:

> "Free movement of goods concerns not only traders but also individuals. It requires, particularly in frontier areas, that consumers resident in one Member State may travel freely to the territory of another Member State to shop under the same conditions as the local population. Consequently a prohibition against distributing such advertising must be examined in the light of Articles [28 to 30] of the Treaty."

2.31 Next, does the Title on the free movement of goods apply to such movements involving no commercial transaction? In *Henn and Darby*, Warner A.G. argued most forcefully that it did. While acknowledging that a number of provisions of this Title such as Articles 23 and 30 used the word "trade", he pointed out that:

> "No-one ... would suggest that, because the word 'trade' is occasionally used in [the pre-Amsterdam Treaty] Articles 12 to 17 [now condensed into Article 25], relating to the elimination of customs duties between Member States, private individuals moving their possessions from one Member State to another may still be subjected to customs duties, or that, because that word is occasionally used in [the pre-Amsterdam Treaty] Articles 18 to 29 [now repealed], relating to the Common Customs Tariff, private individuals who bring their possessions into the Community from outside it are subject, not to the Common Customs Tariff but to the erstwhile tariffs of Member States. By a parity of reasoning, Article [28], which is the leading Article on the elimination of quantitative restrictions between Member States, and which does not itself use the word "trade", cannot be interpreted as limited to transactions by or between traders."[80]

The force of the Advocate General's reasoning—and, in particular, the analogy with the Common Customs Tariff—is considerable. Moreover, in *Commission v Belgium* (waste disposal)[81] Jacobs A.G. also appeared to espouse the view that this Title applied to movements of goods having no economic character. Moreover, the Court appears to have accepted this view in *GB-Inno-BM* when it stated: "Free movement of goods concerns not only traders, but also individuals".

The plain truth is that it can scarcely be argued today that non-economic movements of goods fall outside the Treaty altogether—and this would be the inevitable result of holding that they are not within the provisions on the free movement of goods. For the Court to hold now that such movements are not

---

[79] Case C–362/88 [1990] E.C.R. I-667.
[80] at 3827.
[81] See n.25 above at p. 4456.

caught by the Treaty would be a most surprising and regressive step, particularly since January 1, 1993, the date set by Article 14 for the completion of the internal market. This view was surely confirmed by the Treaty of Maastricht, which transformed the European Economic Community into the European Community, a change manifestly designed to underscore the fact that the Community is no longer solely concerned with economic matters.

2.32   Equally, it seems clear that Articles 28 to 30 apply even where commercial transactions in the goods concerned are prohibited throughout all the Member States. According to a large body of case law, neither prohibited narcotic drugs nor counterfeit currency are subject to customs duties or VAT,[82] supposedly because such trafficking can only give rise to penalties under criminal law and thus fall wholly outside the objectives of the Community provisions concerned.

Manifestly, this is not the place for a detailed discussion of the wisdom of that line of case law. Suffice it then to point out that neither the letter nor the spirit of the provisions in issue provide clear support for the Court's approach. It is not easy to see why those dealing in such egregious products should be granted a financial bonus of this kind. Surely that consideration is not compensated by the desire to prevent the State from profiting from illegal and immoral trade. What is more, the Court has inevitably been led to draw some fine distinctions between transactions which form an inherent part of such trafficking and those more remotely connected with it.[83]

In any event, it is submitted that the arguments against extending such a rule to Articles 28 to 30, so as to bring such banned trade outside the scope of those provisions, are overwhelming. Given that these items clearly qualify as "goods" for the purposes of the Treaty and that consequently no other Treaty provisions are applicable, such a course would be misguided, as it would take them outside the ambit of the Treaty altogether. Besides, the exceptions set out in Article 30 are plainly adequate to cover the prohibition on such trade.

Only once has the Court been called upon to consider this question. The issue arose in *R v Home Secretary ex parte Evans Medical*,[84] which concerned the unusual case of lawful, government controlled trade in opium derivatives carried out in accordance with exceptions to the 1961 New York Convention on Narcotic Drugs. By its first question, the national court asked whether Articles 28 to 30 are "inapplicable to trade in narcotic drugs within the meaning or ambit" of that Convention. The Advocate General opined that these provisions were applicable, but only because the trade in issue was lawful. Fortunately, the Court of Justice chose not to go down that path, replying instead:

---

[82] Cases 50/80 *Horvath v Hauptzollamt Hamburg-Jonas* [1981] E.C.R. 385; Case 221/81 *Wolf v Hauptzollamt Düsseldorf* [1982] E.C.R. 3681; Case 294/82 *Einberger v Hauptzollamt Freiburg* [1984] E.C.R. 1177; Case 269/86 *Mol v Inspecteur der Invoerrechten en Accijnzen* [1988] E.C.R. 3627; Case 289/86 *Happy Family v Inspecteur der Omzetbelasting* [1988] E.C.R. 3655; and C-343/89 *Witzemann v Hauptzollamt München-Mitte* [1990] E.C.R. I-4477, para.20.

[83] Case C-158/98 *Staatssecretaris van Financiën v Coffeeshop "Siberië"* [1999] E.C.R. I-3971.

[84] Case C-324/93 [1995] E.C.R. I-563 at 604.

"According to the Court's case law, goods taken across a frontier for the purposes of commercial transactions are subject to Article [28] of the Treaty, whatever the nature of those transactions (judgment in Case C-2/90 *Commission v Belgium* [1992] E.C.R. I-4431, paragraph 26). Since they have those characteristics, the drugs covered by the Convention and marketed under it are subject to [Article 28]."

The Court therefore concluded that Article 28 applied, regardless of whether the trade was lawful.

2.33 In short, it now seems clear that Articles 28 to 30 cover *all* movements of "goods" between Member States, whatever their nature and purpose. This is subject only to the consideration that, where such movements are merely ancillary to the provision of services, Articles 28 to 30 yield to Articles 49 to 55. As we shall see, the same rule may apply to movements of goods ancillary to movements of persons or capital. These issues will now be considered, beginning with services, the only field in which there is any authority on this point.

B. Ancillary Movements of Goods

(i) Goods and services

2.34 Given that national restrictions often strike at goods and services at the same time, the Court has frequently been called upon to grapple with the complex relationship between Articles 28 to 30 on the one hand and Articles 49 to 58 on the other.[85] That an especially close similarity exists between the two sets of provisions is widely recognised, although goods are tangible while services are not: both freedoms involve economic transactions between Member States which are generally of a commercial nature. Indeed, the distinction between the two is frequently a fine one: it has been pointed out that, when a hard copy of the Financial Times is dispatched from London to Frankfurt, a movement of goods between Member States occurs; whereas, if the same newspaper is sent by fax or other electronic means, then an interstate service has been provided.[86] What is more, the close link between the two freedoms has been highlighted very recently by the *Decker v Caisse de Maladie des Employés Privés*[87] and *Kohll v Union des Caisses de Maladie*,[88] which in essence related to the same issues: both plaintiffs were Luxembourg residents contesting the refusal of the Luxembourg sickness funds to cover expenditure incurred in other Mem-

---

[85] See in particular Müller-Graff, commentary on former Art. 30 in Groeben, Thiesing and Ehlermann, *Kommentar Zum EU-/EG-Vertrag* (5th ed., 1997) vol I especially at p. 733; Troberg, Commentary on former Art. 60 in Groeben, Thiesing, Ehlermann *op. cit.* Vol. I especially at p. 1491; and the materials referred to in n.41 of Ch. I above.

[86] March Hunnings, case note [1980] C.M.L. Rev. 564.

[87] Case C-120/95 [1998] E.C.R. I-1831.

[88] Case C-158/96 [1998] E.C.R. I-1931.

ber States; the only difference was that the plaintiff in *Decker* had purchased spectacles (goods), whereas the other case related to dental care (services).

2.35 In reality, the distinction between goods and services will not always be of great practical importance.[89] Thus it appears from the Court's judgments in *Debauve*[90] and in *Coditel v Ciné Vog*,[91] and more particularly from Warner A.G.'s conclusions in those cases, that the result of applying Article 49 to a given case will often be the same as that of applying Article 28.[92] However, only nationals of Member States can rely on Article 49 *et seq.*, whereas for the application of the Treaty provisions on the free movement of goods the nationality of the owner is irrelevant,[93] but this limitation on the scope of Article 49 can often be circumvented with ease by the creation of a company or firm meeting the conditions of Article 48. A second difference between the two freedoms is that the Court has declined to transpose the ruling in *Keck*[94] to services.[95] Again, where Community legislation is concerned, there may be a difference: there is no equivalent to Article 95(4) (ex 100A(4)) for services in Article 47(2) (ex 57(2)) read with Article 55 (ex 66).

2.36 At all events, the Court's approach is to consider in each case whether the measure predominantly affects goods or services, or perhaps whether the transaction in question primarily relates to goods or to services; (it is not fully clear which of the two tests is to be applied, and in most cases nothing turns on this). At the same time, the Court must bear in mind that Article 50 describes services as a residual category of transaction, since services fall within the purview of Articles 49 to 58 only "insofar as they are not governed by the provisions relating to freedom of movement of goods, capital and persons". However, in recent years that clause has ceased to deter the Court from defining the provisions on services widely, perhaps in consequence of the rising importance of the service sector in Western Europe since 1957 when the Treaty of Rome was signed.[96]

2.37 The manufacture of goods does not constitute the provision of services within the meaning of Article 49. The first case of this kind, *Commission v*

---

[89] Marenco ("The Notion of Restriction on the Freedom of Establishment and Provision of Services in the Case Law of the Court" [1991] Y.E.L. III) goes so far as to say: "the distinction between goods and services is largely formal and has no real economic significance. This distinction is sometimes awkward and normally ought not to entail legal consequences...".
[90] See n.1 above.
[91] Case 62/79 [1980] E.C.R. 881; [1981] 2 C.M.L.R. 362.
[92] Everling, "Sur la jurisprudence récente de la Cour de justice en matière de libre prestation de services rendus dans d'autres Etat membres" [1984] C.D.E. 3. Also, the Court has in effect applied Art. 30 by analogy to services: Case 352/85 *Bond van Adverteerders* [1988] E.C.R. 2085. See also Case C-76/90 *Säger v Dennemeyer* [1991] E.C.R. I-4221, especially Jacobs A.G. at 4234.
[93] Para. 2.24 above.
[94] Case C-267-8/91 [1993] E.C.R. I 6097; see paras 6.54 *et seq.* below.
[95] Case C-384/93 *Alpine Investments v Minister van Financiën* [1995] E.C.R. I-1141.
[96] see generally Everling, "Sur la jurisprudence récente. .." (n.92 above); Troberg, *op. cit.* p. 1447. In Case 186/87 *Cowan v Trésor public* [1989] E.C.R. 195 at 205, Lenz A.G. suggested that the free provision of services should not be treated as a residual freedom at all.

France,[97] related to a tax benefit granted under French law to newspaper publishers in relation to printing expenses on condition that their publications were printed in France. The Commission claimed that this condition infringed Article 28. France argued *inter alia* that Article 28 was not the relevant provision and that instead one must look to the Treaty provisions on services, since printing is a service. The Court dismissed this argument on the grounds that printing "leads directly to the manufacture of a physical article". Also, it referred to the provisions in Article 50 of the Treaty that "services shall be considered to be 'services' within the meaning of this Treaty where they are normally provided for remuneration, in so far as they are not covered by the provisions relating to freedom of movement for goods, capital and persons". In the result this ruling is welcome, since the restriction on imports was the predominant aspect of the measure. Yet a restriction on printers established in other Member States carrying out work in France would surely fall under Article 49.

The Court applied the same test in *Cinéthèque v Fédération Nationale des Cinémas Français*.[98] That case concerned French legislation providing that, once the French authorities had authorised a particular film to be shown in the cinemas, no videocassettes of that film could be sold or hired for private showing within one year. The case concerned two separate films. The copyright owner of each film had granted a licence to produce and issue videocassettes before the expiry of the one-year period. In each case the licensee undertook to exploit his licence, which covered France together with certain other States both inside and outside the Community, to maximum commercial advantage. The copyright owners and the licensees contended that the legislation concerned infringed Articles 28, 29 and 49. The questions posed by the national court referred expressly to all three provisions. The Court held that Article 49 was not in point. When the licensee exploited the licence, he was not providing "services" to the copyright owner; instead he was producing goods. Moreover, the Court referred once again to the rule enshrined in Article 50 that the Treaty provisions on services are subsidiary to those on goods.[99]

As already suggested, it is surely right that, when a Member State imposes a restriction on the manufacture of goods elsewhere in the Community, that measure constitutes an obstacle to imports and thus falls under Article 28. On the other hand, when a Member State imposes restrictions on persons coming from other Member States to manufacture goods on its own territory, then Article 28 is not relevant. Article 49 is then the applicable provision.[100]

2.38 Similarly, *Commission v Ireland*[101] concerned an invitation to tender for the construction of a water main in the Irish town of Dundalk. The Commission

---

[97] Case 18/84 [1985] E.C.R. I339; [1986] 1 C.M.L.R. 605.
[98] Cases 60 and 61/84 [1985] E.C.R. 2605; [1986] 1 C.M.L.R. 365.
[99] The Court did not consider the restriction on the hire of videocassettes. This, it is submitted, fell under Art. 49.
[100] Or Art. 43, as the case may be.
[101] Case 45/87 [1988] E.C.R. 4929.

claimed that a clause in that document requiring the asbestos pressure pipes to conform to Irish standards was contrary to Article 28. Ireland contended that, since the contract at issue related to the performance of work, Article 28 was not in point. The Court dismissed Ireland's defence on the basis that "the fact that a public works contract relates to the provision of services cannot remove a clause in an invitation to tender restricting materials that may be used from the scope of the prohibitions set out in Article [28]". The point here was that the offending clause manifestly related to goods, regardless of the purpose of the invitation to tender as a whole.

2.39 In contrast, it was held in *van Schaik*[102] that a contract to repair a car was to be regarded as the supply of services, not goods: in such a case, the supply of goods involved in the replacement of spare parts is merely ancillary to the provision of services. Restrictions on garages in other Member States carrying out such repairs must therefore be considered under Article 49.

2.40 This question also arose in *Boscher v British Motors Wright.*[103] Boscher were a firm of French auctioneers commissioned by a Hamburg company to auction in France a number of vehicles belonging to the latter company. The prospective sale fell foul of a French law prohibiting auctions unless the owner of the goods had been registered for at least two years in the local trade register. The Court held that this legislation was to be scrutinised under Article 28, not Article 49.

2.41 *Federación de Distribuidores Cinematográficos v Spain*[104] concerned a Spanish decree requiring persons applying for a licence to dub a film from a third country into Spanish to undertake to distribute a Spanish film in return. The plaintiffs maintained that this decree fell foul of Article 28, since it favoured Spanish films against those of other Member States. In contrast, the Commission claimed that Article 49 was the relevant provision, since the measure affected the conditions under which films of whatever origin were shown in Spain. Van Gerven A.G. endorsed the latter view: true, one copy of a film would have to cross the frontier into Spain before the film could be shown there at all, but this was really ancillary to the service consisting of its exploitation. The Court also held that this restriction was to be considered under Article 49, not Article 28.

2.42 The relationship between Articles 28 and 49 came under the Court's scrutiny again in relation to the sale of lottery tickets. In *H.M. Customs and Excise Commissioners v Schindler*[105] the defendants were charged in the English courts with attempting to sell German lottery tickets within the United Kingdom, contrary to English law. The High Court in its reference for a preliminary ruling

---

[102] Case C-55/93 [1994] E.C.R. I-4837.
[103] Case C-239/90 [1991] E.C.R. I-2023.
[104] Case C-17/92 [1993] E.C.R. I-2239.
[105] Case C-275/92 [1994] E.C.R. I-1039.

asked *inter alia* whether lottery tickets constitute goods within the meaning of Article 28 and whether such legislation is to be considered under that provision or under Article 49. The view expressed by the Commission and the nine Member States which intervened was that the transaction in question was to be regarded as the provision of services within the meaning of Article 49, not the sale of goods. Only the defendants disagreed.

Gulmann A.G. endorsed the prevailing view, drawing an analogy between the sale of a lottery ticket and the purchase of an insurance policy or of a bus ticket: in each case the purchased document was simply proof that a service had been provided. The Court also upheld the majority view, in the following terms:

> "The activity pursued by the defendants in the main proceedings appears, admittedly, to be limited to sending advertisements and application forms; and possibly tickets, on behalf of a lottery operator, SKL. However, those activities are only specific steps in the organisation or operation of a lottery and cannot, under the Treaty, be considered independently of the lottery to which they relate. The importation and distribution of objects are not ends in themselves. Their sole purpose is to enable residents of the Member States where those objects are imported and distributed to participate in the lottery.
>
> The point relied on by Gerhart and Jörg Schindler, that on the facts of the main proceedings agents of the SKL send material objects into Great Britain in order to advertise the lottery and sell tickets therein, and that material objects which have been manufactured are goods within the meaning of the Court's case law, is not sufficient to reduce their activity to one of exportation or importation."

The Court distinguished the latter judgment in its subsequent ruling in *Läärä v Finnish State*.[106] That case concerned national legislation which granted to a single public body exclusive rights to exploit the operation of slot machines. The Court recalled that the lotteries at issue in *Schindler* were not activities relating to "goods" whereas slot machines, by contrast, "constitute goods in themselves which may be covered by Article [28] of the Treaty".[107] The Court went on to find that the operation of slot machines constituted a service falling within Article 49, but nevertheless remarked that "the fact that an imported item is intended for the supply of a service does not in itself mean that it falls outside the rules regarding freedom of movement".[108] On this point, the Court expressly endorsed La Pergola A.G.'s statement that: "The present case does not concern a main transaction of which another purely ancillary and incidental transaction forms a part, but rather a commercial transaction involving goods which is instrumental to and linked to a provision of services but *quite distinct in conceptual and economic terms*."[109] Accordingly, the Court proceeded to consider whether legislation of the kind in question was compatible with both Article 28 and Article 49.

---

[106] Case C-124/97 [1999] E.C.R. I-6067.
[107] Para.20 of the judgment.
[108] Para.24 of the judgment.
[109] Para.19 of the Opinion; emphasis in the original.

2.43 *Deutsche Post v GZS and Citicorp Kartenservice*[110] concerned the sending, by electronic means, of credit card statements from Germany to the Netherlands where those statements were then printed off and posted from the Netherlands to customers in Germany. The German post office claimed to be entitled under the Universal Postal Convention to charge internal postage for delivering those statements in Germany, rather than restrict itself to collecting terminal dues from the Dutch postal administration for the delivery of its international mail. Both La Pergola A.G. and the Court dealt with the case on the basis of Articles 49 and 86 (read with Article 82). However, the national court had also referred questions as regards Article 28. La Pergola A.G. dismissed the application of Article 28 in the following terms:

> "... the present case does not come within the scope of the Community rules on the free movement of goods. According to the definition of goods adopted by the Court in relation to the interpretation of Article [28] of the Treaty, the prohibition of national measures which form a barrier to trade between Member States concerns objects which can be valued in money and which can be physically transported across a border with a view to sale or other lawful commercial transactions, whatever the nature of those transactions. Postal items of the kind at issue in this case do not, as such, constitute objects of sale or other transactions. One cannot therefore speak of a commercial transaction in goods, ancillary to, and connected with, the provision of a service but conceptually and economically separable from it, nor of a principal transaction which absorbs another transaction which is purely accessory and incidental to it. The only transaction identifiable in the present case is the provision of international letter-post services..."[111]

The Advocate General thus effectively dismissed the application of Article 28 because the "postal items" in question did not fall within the definition of "goods". For the reasons explained above, the latter view is hard to defend. In contrast, the Court gave the following grounds for rejecting that application of Article 28:

> "As regards the interpretation of Article [28] of the Treaty requested by the national court, suffice it to state that Article [28] does not apply in the main proceedings. International letter-post constitutes a cross-border service provided under the universal postal service, which requires the postal services of the Contracting State to which letter-post items are sent to forward and deliver them."[112]

While it is to be regretted that the Court's reasoning was so terse, its approach is surely sound.

2.44 Restrictions on leasing goods between Member States are to be examined under the Treaty provisions on services, not under Articles 28 to 30, despite the

---

[110] C-147–8/97 [2000] E.C.R. I-825, noted by Bartosch [2001] C.M.L. Rev. 195; and Mortelmans [2000] S.E.W. 342.
[111] Para.22 of the Opinion.
[112] Para.35 of the judgment.

fact that such transactions require goods to pass temporarily from one Member State to another: *Cura Anlagen v Auto Service Leasing.*[113]

2.45 In the present context, a particularly striking recent judgment is that in *Canal Satélite Digital v Spain,*[114] which concerned national legislation subjecting the marketing of certain digital television equipment to the requirement of a prior authorisation. The Court chose to decide the case on the basis of both Article 28 and Article 49 of the Treaty, saying:

> "In the field of telecommunications, however, it is difficult to determine generally whether it is free movement of goods or freedom to provide services which should take priority. As the case in the main proceedings shows, the two aspects are often intimately linked. The supply of telecommunication equipment is sometimes more important than the installation or other services connected therewith. In other circumstances, by contrast, it is the economic activities of providing know-how or other services of the operators concerned which are dominant, whilst delivery of the apparatus, equipment or conditional-access telecommunication systems which they supply or market is only accessory."[115]

2.46 One area in which this question has arisen repeatedly is advertising. On the one hand, the Court has held in *Sacchi*[116] and *Debauve*[117] that prohibitions or restrictions on television advertising fall to be considered under Article 49. This is scarcely surprising, since that activity undoubtedly constitutes a service. On the other hand, the Court held that the following restrictions on advertising or promoting goods from other Member States fall under Article 28: a prohibition on promoting encyclopaedias by free gifts was held to contravene Article 30[118]; a system of restrictions on advertising alcoholic drinks which fell more heavily on imported drinks than equivalent domestic ones[119]; and a ban on the advertising of special offers.[120]

---

[113] Case C-451/99 (judgment of March 21, 2002), para.18. A notable feature of that ruling was that the Court relied in part on the fact that such operations constituted services for the purposes of the Sixth VAT Directive (Council Directive 77/388, [1977] O.J. L145/1, as amended). Jacobs A.G. agreed with the Commission that there should be a uniform definition of "services" in Community law, there being no "discernible reason for differing definitions, which would serve only to confuse the legal position of borderline activities" (Opinion, para.32). There is no suggestion, however, that this is to be treated as an absolute rule.

[114] Case C-390/99 (judgment of January 22, 2002).

[115] Para.32 of the judgment.

[116] See n.9 above.

[117] See n.1 above; also *Bond van Adverteerders v Netherlands* (see n.92 above); Case C-288/89 *Collectieve Antennevoorziening Gouda v Commissariaat voor de Media* [1991] E.C.R. I-4007; and Case C-353/89 *Commission v Netherlands* [1991] E.C.R. I-4069.

[118] Case 286/81 *Oosthoek* [1982] E.C.R. 4575; [1983] 3 C.M.L.R. 428.

[119] Case 152/78 *Commission v France* [1980] E.C.R. 2299; [1981] 2 C.M.L.R. 743; for another restriction on alcohol advertising scrutinised under Art. 28 see Cases C-1 and 176/90 *Aragonesa de Publicidad v Departamento de Sanidad* [1991] E.C.R. I-4151.

[120] *GB-Inno-BM*, n.79 above; also Case C-126/91 *Schutzverband v Yves Rocher* [1993] E.C.R. I- 2361.

It is submitted that there is no contradiction here: in *Sacchi* and *Debauve*, the restriction was more closely connected with services, while in the other cases mentioned it was more closely connected with goods.

2.47 Finally, in the first two editions of this book, it was suggested that movements of goods effected by persons moving between Member States for the purposes of providing or receiving services might conceivably be caught by the provisions of Articles 49 rather than those on the free movement of goods. On this view, where a dentist providing services in another Member State brings his equipment with him, any restrictions on the movement of that equipment would be caught by Article 49, not Articles 28 to 29.

Some support for this view could be derived from Title III, Part B of the Council's General Programme for the abolition of restrictions on the freedom to provide services. This lists among the restrictions to be eliminated by that programme "any prohibition of, or hindrance to, the movement of the item to be supplied in the course of the service or of the materials comprising such item or of the tools, machinery, equipment and other means to be employed in the provision of the service."[121] However, the proviso set out in the opening words of Title III of the general programme states that this was subject to the Treaty provisions on the free movement of goods. What is more, in the light of the case law considered here, there is little room left for the view that imports and exports of goods may fall outside the scope of Articles 28 to 30 merely because they are connected with the provision of services. This is borne out by La Pergola A.G.'s statement in *Läärä* that: "Surgeons purchase scalpels ... for the sole purpose of providing a service, but it could not seriously be argued that intra-Community trade flows of such products fall outside the scope" of the Treaty provisions on the free movement of goods.[122]

(ii) Goods and workers

2.48 Similarly, in the first two editions of this book, the possibility was mooted that a migrant worker settling in another Member State in accordance with Article 39 would have to rely on that provision—and not Articles 23, 28 or 29—to contest restrictions on the transfer of his personal effects to the host State. However, as just mentioned, in view of the development of the case law, there appears to be no room left for this theory today

Nevertheless, it would seem clear that the reasoning in *Schindler*[123] is to be applied by analogy to the confiscation of a passport. Common sense would suggest that that measure would fall to be considered solely under Article 39 read with Article 18 (ex 8a) on the right of citizens of the Union to move freely

---

[121] [1962] O.J. Spec. Ed. 3.
[122] See n.106 above, para.19 of the Opinion.
[123] See n.105 above.

within the territory of the Member States. This is despite the fact that the passport itself undoubtedly constitutes "goods".

(iii) Goods and establishment

2.49 *Pfeiffer Grosshandel v Löwa Warenhandel*[124] concerned Austrian legislation that prohibited the use of trade names as the specific designation of an undertaking, where there was a risk of confusion. In that case, Pfeiffer, which operated a large supermarket in Austria under the trade name "Plus KAUF PARK", sought an order restraining Löwa from establishing in parts of Austria retail outlets under the trade name "Plus". The Court held that such a restraining order would constitute a restriction on the freedom of establishment contrary to Article 43 (ex 52), but that such restriction was capable of "objective justification".[125] Having reached the foregoing conclusion on the basis of Article 43, the Court then turned to Article 28 and held as follows:

> "...although the restraining order which the national court is minded to grant restricts the possibilities open to undertakings established in other Member States of using identical trade names in the Member State concerned, it is not contrary to Article [43] of the Treaty because it is justified by overriding requirements. Consequently, it could conflict with Article [28] of the Treaty concerning the free movement of goods only if, and to the extent that, it restricted the free movement of goods between Member States other than indirectly through the restriction of the freedom of establishment."[126]

In effect, the Court thus held that, where the restriction on the free movement of goods flowed directly or indirectly from the restriction on the freedom of establishment, that restriction would be compatible with Article 28. The Court apparently took the view that further analysis under Article 28 was pre-empted by its finding that the restriction on the freedom of establishment was objectively justified.

In *Mac Quen and Grandvision Belgium*[127] the Court was required to rule on Belgian legislation that reserved the examination of eyesight for purely optical defects to ophthalmologists (who are qualified medical doctors) to the exclusion of opticians (who were not medical doctors). In this case, unlike in *Pfeiffer*, the Court dealt with Article 28 before Article 43. As regards Article 28 the Court held:

> "So far as Article [28] of the Treaty is concerned, even assuming the prohibition under challenge to be restrictive of the free movement of goods, those restrictive effects would be the unavoidable consequence of that prohibition. To the extent that the prohibition might be justified, its effects would have to be accepted for the purposes of Article 28 of the Treaty."[128]

[124] C-255/97 [1999] E.C.R. I-2895.
[125] See paras 19 to 24 of the judgment.
[126] Para.26 of the judgment.
[127] C-108/96 [2001] E.C.R. I-837.
[128] Para.21 of the judgment.

The Court then proceeded to examine the prohibition as a restriction on the freedom of establishment and held that it was capable of being objectively justified. Thus, as in *Pfeiffer*, the Court in effect held that its finding that the restriction on the freedom of establishment was objectively justified had the effect of pre-empting further analysis under Article 28.

It is submitted that the reasoning as regards Article 28 in the *Mac Quen* and *Pfeiffer* cases is open to criticism. There is no good reason, as a matter of principle, why a justified restriction on the freedom of establishment must have the result that any restrictive effects on the free movement to goods would also "have to be accepted". As the Court held in the context of services in *Läärä*,[129] the fact that an imported item is intended for the supply of a service does not of itself mean that it falls outside the free movement of goods provisions. It is submitted that on a proper analysis, the Court should first determine whether or not the restriction on the movement of goods is merely ancillary to the restriction on establishment. If not, the Court ought then to proceed to a separate consideration of those provisions. Having said that, it is in practice likely that a measure which is justified under the provisions on establishment will also be found to be a justified restriction on the free movement of goods.

(iv) *Goods and capital*

2.50   It seems clear that the reasoning in *Schindler* may be applied by analogy to documents proving financial transactions which constitute capital movements for the purposes of Articles 56 to 60. On this basis, the movements of such documents are to be treated as ancillary to the capital movements concerned.

---

[129] See n.106 above.

CHAPTER III

Scope: Territory

Introduction

3.01 Different parts of the Treaty have different territorial application, so that certain territories are subject to some but not all of the provisions of the Treaty.[1] The principal question here, then, is to define the area to which Articles 28 to 30 (ex 30 to 36) of the Treaty apply, both as regards the benefit which they confer and the burden which they impose. A rebuttable presumption exists that the two coincide.

Logically, the area concerned should in principle be co-terminous with that to which Article 25 (ex 12 to 17) applies: that provision is intimately linked to Articles 28 to 30, as it also falls within Part Three, Title I which relates to the Treaty on the free movement of goods. This explains why some of the cases discussed in this Chapter relate to Article 25.

At the end of this Chapter, consideration will also be given briefly to the territorial scope of the harmonising provisions of the Treaty.

3.02 Before considering these questions, mention should be made of Part IV of the Treaty, which is entitled "Association of the Overseas Countries and Territories" and runs from Articles 182 to 188 (ex 131 to 136A). The OCTs are not in the Community at all, as the opening words of Article 182 show clearly: "The Member States agree to associate with the Community the non-European countries and territories which ..." Therefore, in the absence of any reference thereto in Articles 182 to 188, Articles 28 to 30 do not apply to the OCTs. Instead, their trading relationship with the Community is governed by the Decisions adopted from time to time under Article 187.[2]

By virtue of Article 299(3) (ex Article 227(3)) of the Treaty, the regime relating to OCTs in Part IV of the Treaty applies to the territories listed in Annex II thereto. That list includes such non-European territories as the Falk-

---

[1] See generally Groux, "Territorialité et Droit Communautaire" [1987] R.T.D.E. 5.

[2] The current Decision, which is closely modelled on the Fourth Lomé Convention, is Council Decision 91/482 [1991] O.J. L263/1, as amended by Council Decision 97/803 [1997] O.J. L329/50; see also Cases C-100 and 101/89 *Kaefer and Procacci v France* [1990] E.C.R. I-4647; and C-263/88 *Commission v France* [1990] E.C.R. I-4611 noted by Oliver [1991] C.M.L.Rev. 199; C-260/90 *Leplat v French Polynesia* [1992] E.C.R. I-643; C-310/95 *Road Air v Inspecteur der Invoerrechten en Accijnzen* [1997] E.C.R. I-2229, noted by Oliver (1998) C.M.L. Rev. 747; C-390/95P *Antillean Rice Mills v Commission* [1999] E.C.R. I-769; C-181/97 *van der Kooy v Staatssecretaris van Financiën* [1999] E.C.R. I-483; and Case C-17/98 *Emesa Sugar (Free Zone) v Aruba* [2000] E.C.R. I-675.

land Islands, the Netherlands Antilles and the French overseas territories (*e.g.* French Polynesia and the Wallis and Futuna Islands). This list replaces that in Annex IV to the pre-Amsterdam Treaty, which had become obsolete with respect to various territories that had attained independence and had thus ceased *de facto* to be governed by Articles 182 to 188.[3]

The Scope of Articles 28 to 30

3.03 The territorial scope of the Treaty is governed first and foremost by Article 299 of the Treaty.[4] While in most respects that Article differs little from its predecessor (Article 227), it contains a wholly new paragraph 2. That paragraph, which relates to those parts of the Community considered to be outside Europe (the French overseas departments, the Azores, Madeira and the Canary Islands), will be considered separately in paragraph 3.04 below. For the rest, the effects of Article 299 with respect to Articles 28 to 30 can be summarised as follows:

(a) Austria, Belgium, Greece,[5] the Republic of Ireland, Italy, Luxembourg, and Sweden are included in their entirety for all purposes;

(b) The Treaty applies to Denmark, excluding both the Faroe Islands (Article 299(6)(a))[6] and Greenland. While the Faroes are assimilated to a third country, Greenland has enjoyed the status of an OCT since February 1, 1985[7];

(c) As to Finland, by virtue of Article 299(5), the Treaty extends to the Åland islands, subject to certain exceptions laid down in Protocol 2 to the 1994 Act of Accession[8]. However, none of those exceptions relate to Articles 28 to 30, so that those provisions apply to the whole territory of Finland;

(d) All the European territory of France is within the Community. Subject to Article 299(2), the same holds good for the overseas departments, of

---

[3] Case 147/73 *Lensing v Hauptzollamt Berlin-Packhof* [1973] E.C.R. 1543. In addition, Annex IV had been expressly amended by Art. 1 of the Convention of November 13, 1962 ([1964] J.O. 2414), which added the Netherlands Antilles to the list; by Art. 24(2) of the first Act of Accession; and by the Treaty of March 1984 relating to Greenland ([1985] O.J. L29/1).

[4] See generally Stapper, *Europäische Mikrostaaten und autonome Territorien im Rahmen der EG* (1999).

[5] See the Joint Declaration on Mount Athos annexed to the Act of Accession of Greece [1979] O.J. L291/186.

[6] By virtue of Art. 227(5)(a) as originally worded the Danish Government was entitled to make a declaration, at any time up to and including December 31, 1975, to the effect that the Treaty applied to these islands. As no such declaration was ever made, the Faroes are outside the Community. For the sake of clarity, this is now spelt out in Art. 299(6)(a).

[7] The Treaty originally applied to Greenland as from Denmark's accession to the Community. However, by a special Treaty (n.3 above), it was withdrawn from the Community and granted the status of an OCT; see Lefaucheux, "Le nouveau régime de relations entre le Groenland et la Communauté Economique Européenne" [1985] R.M.C. 81 and Weiss, "Greenland's Withdrawal from the European Communities" [1985] E.L.Rev. 173.

[8] This is the result of the declaration made by Finland pursuant to Art. 227(5) EC read with the 1995 Act of Accession ([1995] O.J. L75/18).

which there are now four: Guadeloupe, Guyana, Martinique and Réunion. These are to be distinguished from the French overseas territories and the dependencies of Mayotte and St Pierre-and-Miquelon, which are all OCTs;

(e) The Treaty applies to the whole of the Federal Republic of Germany. As is well known, on October 3, 1990 the former German Democratic Republic ceased to exist and its territory was merged into that of the FRG. This occurred without any amendment being made to the Community Treaties.[9] The Protocol on German Internal Trade, which had been annexed to the Treaty of Rome, thus lapsed automatically on that date;

(f) Only the European part of the Kingdom of the Netherlands falls within the scope of the Treaties.[10] The Netherlands Antilles and Aruba, which also form part of the Kingdom as a matter of Dutch constitutional law, are OCTs[11];

(g) The whole territory of Portugal is within the Community, although the Azores and Madeira are subject to Article 299(2)[12];

(h) By virtue of Articles 24 and 25 of the Act of Accession of Spain and Portugal, the Treaty applies to the whole territory of Spain, subject to certain derogations relating to the Canary Islands and the North African enclaves of Ceuta and Melilla.[13] These derogations, which are set out in Article 25 itself and in the Protocol concerning those territories, are of startling complexity. Suffice it to say here that, according to those provisions, Articles 28 to 30 of the Treaty did not apply to trade between these territories and the rest of the Community. Moreover, subject to limited exceptions, the Common Agricultural Policy (CAP) and the Common Fisheries Policy (CFP) did not apply to these territories.

Those arrangements continue to apply to Ceuta and Melilla. On the other hand, by Regulation 1911/91 on the application of the provisions of Community law to the Canary Islands[14] the Council established a

---

[9] See Commission statement on German unification in EC Bulletin Supplement 4/90 "The European Community and German Unification"; Jacqué, "L'Unification de l'Allemagne et la Communauté européenne" [1990] Revue generale de droit international public 997; Priebe, "Die Beschlüsse des Rates zur Eingliederung der neuen deutschen Bundesländer in die Europäischen Gameinschaften" [1991] EuZW 113; Gudrun Schmidt, "L'unification allemande et la Communauté européenne" [1991] R.M.U. 91; Timmermans, "German unification and Community law" [1990] C.M.L. Rev. 437; and Tomuschat, "A United Germany within the European Community" [1990] C.M.L. Rev. 415.

[10] Protocol on the application of the Treaty establishing the European Economic Community to the non-European parts of the Kingdom of the Netherlands of March 25, 1957.

[11] See Case C-181/97 (see n.2 above).

[12] Like Hong Kong, the former Portuguese colony of Macao was never in the Community, and has now returned to Chinese sovereignty in any event.

[13] See Case C-45/94 *Cámara de Comercio, Ceuta v Municipality of Ceuta* [1995] E.C.R. I-4385.

[14] [1991] O.J. L171/1, as last amended by Reg. 1105/2001 ([2001] O.J. L151/1). This Reg. has been implemented by a series of Council Regs, *e.g.* Regs 1601/92, 1602/92, 1605/92 and 1606/92 [1992] O.J. L173.

wholly new regime for those islands, as it was specifically empowered to do by Article 25(4) of the Act of Accession.

Subject to certain specified provisions, they are now brought within the Community's customs territory and are subject to the CAP and the CFP. It would seem to follow that Articles 28 to 30 now apply to trade between the Canaries and other Member States. However, as explained in paragraph 2.23 above, it may be otherwise in relation to bananas.

Also, the Canaries are now covered by Article 299(2), which is discussed below. However, the mere insertion of that paragraph into the Treaty has not of itself altered the arrangements described here, and in any event no legislation has yet been enacted on the basis of that provision.

(i) In addition to Great Britain and Northern Ireland, the Treaty also applies to various dependencies of the United Kingdom. Article 299(4) states that "the provisions of this Treaty shall apply to the European territories for whose external relations a Member State is responsible". This covers Gibraltar, which is a British colony.[15] Yet it would seem that Articles 28 to 30 do not apply to trade between Gibraltar and the rest of the Community.

Admittedly, no relevant exception clause is to be found in the body of the Treaty of Accession of 1972 or of the appended Act of Accession. The only exception clause there with respect to Gibraltar is Article 28 of that Act of Accession, which reads as follows:

"Acts of the institutions of the Community relating to the products in Annex II to the EEC Treaty and the products subject, on importation into the Community, to specific rules as a result of the implementation of the common agricultural policy, as well as the acts on the harmonisation of legislation of Member States concerning turnover taxes shall not apply to Gibraltar unless the Council, acting unanimously on a proposal from the Commission, provides otherwise."

Plainly, that provision is not in point. Rather, the exception is to be found in Annexes I and II to the Act of Accession, to which Articles 29 and 30 of the Act refer. Annex I, point I.4 amended the Regulation then in force on the Community customs territory without including Gibraltar in that territory; the provisions concerned have now been re-enacted in Article 3 of Council Regulation 2913/92 establishing the Community Customs Code.[16] By the same token, Annex II, point VI, which amended the legislation on trade between the Community and third countries, stated that Gibraltar was "in the same position with regard to the Community's import liberalisation system as it was before accession". In keeping with that stipulation, Gibraltar was listed among the third countries and territories in Council Regulation 288/82[17] on common rules for imports from third countries. Today Gibraltar is still assimilated to a

---

[15] Cases T-195/01 and T-207/01 *Gibraltar v Commission* (judgment of April 30, 2002) para. 12.
[16] [1992] O.J. L302/1, last amended by Reg. 2700/2000 ([2000] O.J. L311/17). Article 3 itself was most recently amended by Annex I, Part XIII of the 1995 Act of Accession and by Reg. 82/97 ([1997] O.J. L17/1).
[17] [1982] O.J. L35/1 as last amended by Reg. 2875/92 ([1992] O.J. L287/1).

third country for these purposes, although the enactment which is the successor to Regulation 288/92 contains no list of third countries and territories.[18]

Moreover, the amendments to Community legislation set out in the Annexes to an Act of Accession have treaty status: *LAISA v Council*.[19] It follows that those amendments cannot be challenged before the courts.

In the light of these considerations, it seems clear that the Treaty provisions on the free movement of goods do not apply to Gibraltar.[20] That view is borne out by the Commission's answer to a written question,[21] in which it stated:

> "On the basis of the 1972 Act of Accession, and in particular the exclusion of Gibraltar from the customs territory, the provisions of the EEC Treaty concerning the free movement of goods within the Community do not apply to Gibraltar and the territory is treated as a 'third country' for the purposes of measures under the common commercial policy directly involving the import or export of goods. These arrangements, which were not covered by the negotiations on Spain's accession, are not affected by Spain's membership..."

Furthermore, Article 299(6)(c) provides that, notwithstanding anything in paragraphs 1 to 5 of that Article, "This Treaty shall apply to the Channel Islands and the Isle of Man only to the extent necessary to ensure the implementation of the arrangements" set out in the Act of Accession. These islands are covered by a special Protocol to the Act of Accession, Article 1(1) of which begins: "The Community rules on customs matters and quantitative restrictions, in particular those of the Act of Accession, shall apply to the Channel Islands and the Isle of Man under the same conditions as they apply to the United Kingdom". Article 1(2) in effect states that the same rules apply to agricultural products. Although only quantitative restrictions and not measures of equivalent effect are expressly mentioned in this provision, it is probable that this wording is sufficient to cover both types of measure.[22] Some confirmation of this view may be derived from the fact that those islands are within the Community customs territory as defined by the legislation referred to above. Equally, in its answer to a written question the Commission declared: "In accordance with Protocol 3 of the Accession Treaty, the Community rules allowing free movement of goods apply in trade between the Isle of Man and other Member States".[23] In view of the

---

[18] Council Reg. No. 3285/94 ([1994] O.J. L349/53).

[19] Cases 31 and 35/86 [1988] E.C.R. 2285, (especially para. 19).

[20] True, the Court of Auditors took the contrary view in its report on the customs territory of the Community ([1993] O.J. C347/1 at 22).

[21] Written question 1823/84 ([1985] O.J. C341/1). See also Written questions 655/85 ([1985] O.J. C341/8) and 1297/88 ([1989] O.J. C262/10).

[22] Ehlermann, in Groeben, Boeckh and Thiesing, *Kommentar zum EWG-Vertrag* (1974) Vol. 276. Jacobs A.G.'s Opinion in Case C-367/89 *Aimé Richardt* [1991] E.C.R. I-4621 at 4640, which is concerned with the analogous problem in relation to Council Reg. 2603/69 establishing common rules for exports ([1969] O.J. L324/25), would appear to bear out this view.

[23] Written question 409/80 ([1980] O.J. C217). On the Channel Islands and the Isle of Man, see generally Simmonds, "The British Islands and the Community" [1968-69] C.M.L. Rev. 153 and [1970] C.M.L. Rev. 454. On Protocol 3 and the Isle of Man, see Case 32/79 *Commission v United Kingdom* [1980] E.C.R. 2043; [1981] 1 C.M.L.R. 219 on fisheries, where, however, the Court avoided the issue; Case C-355/89 *Department of Health and Social Security (Isle of Man) v Barr* [1991] E.C.R. I 3479, noted by Simmonds, [1992] C.M.L. Rev. 799; and Case C-171/96 *Pereira Roque v Governor of Jersey* [1998] E.C.R. I-4607.

subject-matter of the question, the Commission's statement appears to extend to measures of equivalent effect. Furthermore, in answer to other written questions the Commission has declared that under the Protocol the Channel Islands and the Isle of Man are "included in the customs union".[24]

On the other hand, the Treaty does not apply to the Sovereign Base Areas of the United Kingdom in Cyprus: Article 299(6)(b).

All the other overseas dependencies of the United Kingdom appear in the list of OCTs to which the first sub-paragraph of Article 299(3) refers. True, the second sub-paragraph of that provision reads: "This Treaty shall not apply to those overseas countries and territories having special relations with the United Kingdom of Great Britain and Northern Ireland which are not included in the aforementioned list [*i.e.* Annex II to the Treaty]." However, that sub-paragraph, which was introduced by the first Act of Accession, appears to be obsolete today: it was intended to exclude Hong Kong from the scope of the Treaty, including Part IV; but that territory had already returned to the Chinese fold before the Treaty of Amsterdam was even signed; and no other territory would seem to be caught by it.

3.04 The new Article 299(2), which was introduced by the Treaty of Amsterdam and is wholly different from any pre-existing provision in the EC Treaty, reads as follows:

> "The provisions of this Treaty shall apply to the French overseas departments, the Azores, Madeira and the Canary Islands.
> However, taking account of the structural social and economic situation of the French overseas departments, the Azores, Madeira and the Canary Islands, which is compounded by their remoteness, insularity, small size, difficult topography and climate, economic dependence on a few products, the permanence and combination of which severely restrain their development, the Council, acting by a qualified majority on a proposal from the Commission and after consulting the European Parliament, shall adopt specific measures aimed, in particular, at laying down the conditions of application of the present Treaty to those regions, including common policies.
> The Council shall, when adopting the relevant measures referred to in the second subparagraph, take into account areas such as customs and trade policies, fiscal policy, free zones, agriculture and fisheries policies, conditions for supply of raw materials and essential consumer goods, State aids and conditions of access to structural funds and to horizontal Community programmes.
> The Council shall adopt the measures referred to in the second subparagraph taking into account the special characteristics and constraints of the outermost regions without undermining the integrity and the coherence of the Community legal order, including the internal market and common policies."

The new features of this paragraph may be summarised as follows:

–   Whereas the former Article 227(2) related exclusively to the French overseas departments (Guadeloupe, Guyana, Martinique and Réunion), the new provision applies equally to the other parts of the Community

---

[24] Written questions 2116/84 ([1985] O.J. C168/25) and 1408/85 ([1986] O.J. C48/15).

considered to be situated outside Europe, namely the Azores, Madeira and the Canaries;

- The earlier provision stipulated unequivocally that certain parts of the Treaty, including that concerning the free movement of goods, applied to the territories concerned,[25] while empowering the Council to exclude other sections of the Treaty.[26] In contrast, by virtue of the new Article 299(2), all the provisions of the Treaty apply to the territories concerned, although the Council may decide otherwise, provided that the highly ambiguous terms of the final sub-paragraph are observed. In view of that ambiguity, it is a moot point whether the Council is entitled to impose restrictions on the free movement of goods in favour of the territories concerned. Can such a step be taken "without undermining the integrity and the coherence of the Community legal order, including the internal market and common policies"?[27]

Nevertheless, it seems clear that, when construing and applying this provision, regard should be had to the case law relating to the old Article 227(2), and in particular that concerning the import duty on goods entering the French overseas departments known as the *octroi de mer*.[28] In particular, it would be mistake to overlook the fact that the Court has upheld a measure adopted pursuant to that provision which permitted the partial exclusion of Article 90 (ex 95) of the Treaty to those departments—but on the basis that it was only authorised exemptions which were "necessary, proportionate and precisely defined".[29] This is in line with the Court's case law on exception clauses and safeguard clauses.[30]

3.05 As already pointed out, Article 299(4) stipulates that: "The provisions of

---

[25] Thus in Case C-163/90 *Administration des Douanes v Legros* [1992] E.C.R. I-4625 the levy on imports into these departments, known as the *octroi de mer*, was held to be contrary to the prohibition on charges having equivalent effect to customs duties, which is now enshrined in Art. 25 of the Treaty. Moreover, in Case C-363/93 *Lancry v Direction Générale des Douanes* [1994] E.C.R. I-3957 the Court held that Council Decision 89/688 ([1989] O.J. L399/46) which purported to authorise this levy was invalid. The old Art. 227(2) did not, it held, empower the Council to suspend, even temporarily, the application of Art. 25 to the French overseas territories. However, the Court subsequently accepted an amended form of this tax: Case C-212/96 *Chevassus-Marche v Conseil Régional de la Réunion* [1998] E.C.R. I-743, discussed by Boissard "La validité inattendue du nouvel octroi de mer" [1999] R.M.U.E. I-129.

[26] Although Art. 227(2) stipulated that such action could only be taken within two years of the original Treaty entering into force, the Court ruled that there was no bar to it being taken at a later stage: Cases 148/77 *Hansen v HZA Flensburg* [1978] E.C.R. 1787; [1979] 1 C.M.L. Rev. 604; and *Chevassus-Marche* (n.24 above).

[27] See Brial, "La place des régions ultrapériphériques au sein de l'Union européenne" [1998] C.D.E. 639; Omarjee, "Le traité d'Amsterdam et l'avenir de la politique de différenciation en faveur des départements français d'outre-mer" [1998] R.T.D.E. 515. See also generally Council Decision 2002/166 authorising France to extend the application of a reduced rate of excise duty on "traditional" rum produced in its overseas departments [2002] O.J. L55/33.

[28] See n.25 above.

[29] Para. 49 of the judgment in *Chevassus-Marche* (see n.25 above).

[30] See para. 9.01 below.

this Treaty shall apply to the European territories for whose external relations a Member State is responsible". As already mentioned, Gibraltar is caught by this provision. Indeed, it may be the only territory in this position.[31] This appears somewhat anomalous, given that this provision, previously Article 227(4), has remained unaltered since 1958 and might therefore be thought to apply to at least one European dependency of one of the six original Member States.[32]

A joint declaration on future trade arrangements with Andorra appended to the Act of Accession of Spain and Portugal[33] stated that "an arrangement governing trade relations between the Community and Andorra" was to be "finalised within a period of two years of the date of entry into force of the Act of Accession". That undertaking was subsequently implemented, albeit not until the end of 1990.[34] It is clear from these arrangements that Andorra is not caught by Article 299(4): if a Member State were responsible for Andorra's external relations, then it would be in no position to conclude a treaty with the Community.

Monaco does not appear to fall within the scope of this provision. In answer to a written question,[35] the Commission stated that, as Monaco has not signed the Treaty of Rome, it did not form part of the EEC; it went on to add, however, that the provisions on the free movement of goods in the Community apply to goods originating in Monaco since it is within the Community customs territory.[36] This is borne out by the Council Decision concerning the accession of that micro-state to the Convention on the Protection of the Alps.[37]

Since San Marino has concluded an agreement with the Community creating a customs union,[38] it plainly falls outside the scope of Article 299(4). The Vatican is responsible for its own external relations and is therefore not caught by Article 299(4).

3.06 What of the sea and the sea-bed?[39] Article 299(1) provides that the Treaty applies to the Member States, without referring to their respective territories, although the concept of territory does appear in Articles 39 to 43 (ex 48 to 52) on the free movement of workers and the right of establishment respectively. Article 80(2) (ex 84(2)) empowers the Council to extend the common transport policy to sea and air transport. The Court has held[40] that this provision does not prevent the "general rules of the Treaty" such as Article 39 from

---

[31] See generally Sack, "Europas Zwerge: Die Sonderbeziehungen der EG zu den europäischen Zwergstaaten und teilautonomen Gebieten von Mitgliedstaaten" [1997] EuZW. 45.
[32] It would seem that this anomaly is due to the fact that San Marino and Monaco were originally believed to fall within the terms of this provision: Stapper, *op. cit.* at 173.
[33] [1985] O.J. L302/488.
[34] [1990] O.J. L374/13, as amended on the accession of Austria, Finland and Sweden ([1996] O.J. 271/39) and supplemented by a Protocol on veterinary matters ([1997] O.J. L148/16).
[35] Written question 1215/80 ([1980] O.J. C335/10).
[36] See para. 3.08 below.
[37] Decision 98/118 ([1998] O.J. L33/21).
[38] [1992] O.J. L359/13 and [2002] O.J. L84/41.
[39] See generally Groux, *op. cit.* n.1 above, at p. 19.
[40] Case 167/73 *Commission v France* [1974] E.C.R. 359; [1974] 2 C.M.L.R. 216.

applying to sea transport even in the absence of a specific decision by the Council.

Although the Treaty contains no provision dealing specifically with sea fishing, its provisions on agriculture, Articles 32 to 38 (ex 38 to 46), provide an appropriate basis for a common fisheries policy. Legislation on sea fishing has therefore been based on these provisions. Furthermore, Articles 100 to 103 of the first Act of Accession are devoted to this matter. The Court has also had occasion to consider it in a series of cases brought before it. In the present context the first of these cases, *Kramer*,[41] is the most important because one of the questions put to the Court was whether fishing quotas not fixed under Community auspices infringed Article 28 of the Treaty. The Court found that such quotas were compatible with that provision on the grounds that, despite restricting "production" in the short term, they ensured supplies in the long term. In so doing the Court made no allusion to the geographical scope of Article 28, but in the light of that judgment there can be no doubt that that article applies to the resources of the sea: in answer to another question the Court held that the Community has power to "take any measures for the conservation of the biological resources of the sea", even as regards the high seas.

It appears that Articles 28 to 30 apply to products produced or obtained within the territorial seas of the Member States (Article 23(3) of the Community Customs Code). Similarly, it would seem that Articles 28 to 30 apply to fish and other products caught on the high seas by a vessel lawfully flying the flag of a Member State, as is shown by Article 23(2)(f) of that Code. By virtue of that provision "products of sea-fishing and other products taken from the sea outside a country's territorial sea by vessels registered or recorded in the country concerned and flying the flag of that country" are taken to originate in that country.[42]

Moreover, in all probability Articles 28 to 30 also apply to resources extracted from that part of the sea-bed over which Member States exercise sovereign rights. According to Article 23(2)(h) of the Code, products are considered to originate in a country where they have been "taken from the sea-bed or subsoil beneath the seabed outside the territorial sea provided that that country has exclusive rights to exploit that sea-bed or subsoil". In a similar vein, Article 4(3) of Council Regulation 2964/95 introducing registration for crude oil imports and deliveries in the Community[43] provides that oil "extracted from the seabed over which a Member State exercises exclusive rights for the purposes of

---

[41] Cases 3, 4 and 5/76 [1976] E.C.R. 1279; [1976] 2 C.M.L.R. 440; see para. 7.96 below.

[42] See n.15 above. See Case 100/84 *Commission v UK* (joint fishing operations) [1985] E.C.R. 1170; [1985] 2 C.M.L.R. 199, and para. 2.13 above. As regards the application of Community VAT legislation to the high seas, see Cases 168/84 *Berkholz v Finanzamt Hamburg-Mitte-Aldstadt* [1985] E.C.R. 2251; [1985] 3 C.M.L.R. 667; and 283/84 *Trans Tirreno Express v Ufficio Provinciale IVA* [1986] E.C.R. 231; [1986] 2 C.M.L.R 100.

[43] [1995] O.J. L310/5.

exploitation" is not to be considered as having been imported from third countries for the purposes of that Regulation.[44]

3.07 As will be explained below,[45] Articles 28 and 29 apply only to goods passing between Member States; goods moving within a Member State are not caught by these provisions. By the same token, when fish caught by a British ship are landed in the United Kingdom these Articles do not apply, as the ship is assimilated to British territory for these purposes.

3.08 As already mentioned, Article 3 of the Community Customs Code,[46] as amended by Part XIII of Annex I to the latest Act of Accession and Regulation 82/97 of the Parliament and the Council,[47] defines the customs territory of the Community. The following points are worthy of note:

(a) Ceuta and Melilla are outside the Community's customs territory. On this point the Regulation merely incorporates the express stipulation to this effect in Article 1(2) of the Protocol to the Act of Accession relating to these territories. In contrast, the Canaries are now within the customs territory, although they were initially outside. This is in line with Regulation 1911/91 described above;

(b) the Regulation provides that the Channel Islands and the Isle of Man are within the Community's customs territory. However, as already mentioned, it says nothing about Gibraltar, which is therefore outside that territory;

(c) conversely, certain German and Italian territories such as Heligoland and the commune of Livigno are excluded, although they are clearly within the Community;

(d) Monaco is included although it is not in the Community; in contrast, Andorra and San Marino are excluded.

Finally, Article 3(3) provides that the Community's customs territory shall include "the territorial waters, the inland maritime waters and the airspace" of the areas so defined. This would appear to cover the continental shelf below the territorial waters[48]; but, since Article 3 does not refer to the continental shelf, that part of it which lies beyond territorial waters is outside the customs territory.

---

[44] See also the Commission's proposal for a Council Decision on the disposal of disused off-shore installations ([1999] O.J. C158/10); and its answer to Written Question P-3036/96 in which it stated that the Directive of the Parliament and the Council on the posting of workers in the framework of the provision of services ([1997] O.J. L18/1) "applies in particular to situations in which workers are posted to oil rigs or drilling platforms situated, for example, in waters under the jurisdiction of a Member State, such as the continental shelf".

[45] Paras 6.96 *et seq.* below.

[46] See n.15 above.

[47] See n.15 above.

[48] See the Court of Auditors' report (See n.19 above) at 19.

The precise effect of Article 3 on the territorial scope of Articles 28 to 30 is a vexed question. On the one hand, it manifestly seeks to define the customs boundary of the Community for the purposes of the common customs tariff. The Treaty provisions on the free movement of goods clearly cannot extend to goods crossing that boundary. On the other hand, it is questionable whether a mere Regulation can determine the scope of provisions of the Treaty. The better view appears to be that in principle the customs territory of the Community as defined in the Article 3 is identical with the area to which Articles 28 to 30 apply. This presumption may well be ousted in the following cases: those German and Italian territories which are outside the Community customs territory are probably caught by Articles 28 to 30 (since they are part of the Member States and are not excluded by any provision of the Treaty); and Monaco is not likely to be covered by Articles 28 to 30, given that it is a third country.

The Scope of the Provisions on Harmonisation

3.09 The purpose of Community legislation adopted pursuant to Article 95 (ex 100A) of the Treaty for the harmonisation of rules relating to goods is generally to facilitate the free movement of goods.[49] Logic would therefore appear to suggest that the territorial scope of legislation based on that provision and designed to remove obstacles to trade in goods should coincide with that of Articles 25 and 28 to 30. On this view, it would follow, for instance, that such legislation does not apply to Gibraltar, but that it is applicable to the Channel Islands and the Isle of Man.

It seems considerably less likely that the same reasoning can be transposed to legislation relating to goods but based on other provisions of the Treaty—such as Article 175 (ex 130S) on the environment.[50] The reason is simply that those provisions are not so closely linked to the Treaty articles on the free movement of goods.

In any case, having regard to the inherent complexity of these issues and the dearth of authority from the Court, the approach set out here cannot be advocated with any degree of certainty.

---

[49] See paras 12.37 *et seq.* below.
[50] See paras 12.65 *et seq.* below.

CHAPTER IV

Scope: Persons Bound

4.01   The question to be examined in this Chapter is what persons or bodies are bound by Articles 28 to 30 (ex 30 to 36) of the Treaty of Rome. Neither Article 28, nor Article 29 nor Article 30 is expressly directed to the Member States. Precisely the same applies to the new Article 25, which prohibits customs duties and charges of equivalent effect between Member States and which replaced the old Articles 12 to 17 on the entry into force of the Treaty of Amsterdam[1]; since that Article forms part of the Treaty provisions on the free movement of goods, it must also be taken into account. However, many of the provisions repealed by the Treaty of Amsterdam, which related to the transitional period running from January 1958 to December 1969, were indeed expressed to be addressed to the Member States (*e.g.* the old Articles 12, 16, 31, 32, 33, 34(2) and 35). Moreover, according to Article 10(1) of the Treaty of Amsterdam, the "repeal or deletion ... of lapsed provisions of the Treaty establishing the European Community ... as in force before the entry into force of this Treaty of Amsterdam and the adaptation of certain of their provisions shall not bring about any changes in the legal effects of the provisions of those Treaties ..."; this precludes any argument to the effect that the repealed provisions should be deemed never to have existed.

Consequently, there can be no doubt that the Member States are bound by the terms of Articles 28 to 30. However, which entities are to be regarded as forming part of the Member States for these purposes is less clear, and this issue will be the subject of the first section. Next, we shall consider whether the Community institutions are also bound by these provisions before coming to the much more vexed question as to whether private parties (individuals and non-State bodies) are required to observe them.

I. MEMBER STATES

4.02   The first paragraph of the old Article 31 read: "Member States shall refrain from introducing between themselves any new quantitative restrictions or measures having equivalent effect". Similarly the first paragraph of the old Article 32 stipulated that "in their trade with one another Member States shall refrain from making more restrictive the quotas and measures having equivalent effect existing at the date of entry into force of this Treaty". Further clear

---

[1] Para. 1.09 above.

references to the fact that State measures are concerned are to be found in the old Articles 33, 34 and 35. All these provisions have now been repealed by the Treaty of Amsterdam.

4.03 What is meant by the "State" in this context? This concept is to be interpreted widely to cover the public authorities of a Member State in general.[2] This embraces not only central government but also regional and local government[3]: it is irrelevant to the Community whether discrimination against a product from another Member State emanates from the federal, provincial or parish authorities, so long as that discrimination exists. Thus the Commission has sought interim measures against Ireland with respect to a clause inserted in an invitation to tender issued by the town of Dundalk, which was alleged to infringe Article 28. In his Order[4] the President of the Court stated:

"Since that clause was inserted in the specifications by Dundalk Urban District Council, a body subject to the authority of the Minister for the Environment and for whose acts Ireland is responsible, the barrier to intra-Community trade to which it prima facie gives rise is imputable to Ireland."

In its final judgment in the same case[5] the Court simply noted that it was common ground between the parties that Dundalk Urban District Council was a "public body for whose acts the Irish Government is responsible"; and that, moreover, before accepting a tender, the U.D.C. had to obtain the authorisation of the Irish Department of the Environment.

Plainly, though, Articles 28 and 29 cover measures emanating from all local authorities, whatever their precise relationship with central government. Thus in *Aragonesa de Publicidad v Departamento de Sanidad*[6] the Court considered the compatibility with Article 28 of a law enacted by the Autonomous Community of Catalonia. Central government had had no hand in the adoption of the legislation. The Court ruled that Article 28 "may apply to measures adopted by all the authorities of the Member States, be they central authorities, the authorities of a federal State, or other territorial authorities."

4.04 Likewise, Articles 28 to 30 apply to measures not only of the executive, but also of the legislature or of the judiciary. This was made clear by the Court

---

[2] Béraud, "Les mesures d'effet équivalent au sens des articles 30 et suivants du Traité de Rome" [1968] R.T.D.E. 265 at 278; Hecquard-Theron, "La notion d'Etat en droit communautaire" [1990] R.T.D.E. 693.
[3] Graff, *Der Begriff "Maßnahmen gleicher Wirkung wie mengenmässige Einfuhrbeschränkungen" im EWG-Vertrag* (1972) 125 *et seq.*
[4] Case 45/87R *Commission v Ireland* [1987] E.C.R. 1369; [1987] 2 C.M.L.R. 563.
[5] Case 45/87 [1988] E.C.R. 4929.
[6] Case C-1/90 [1991] E.C.R. I 4151; see also Case C-277/91 *Ligur Carni v Unità Sanitare Locale* [1993] E.C.R. I-6621.

in *Dansk Supermarked v Imerco*[7] where it held that Articles 28 and 30:

"...must be interpreted to mean that the judicial authorities of a Member State may not prohibit, on the basis of a copyright or of a trade mark, the marketing on the territory of that State of a product to which one of those rights applies."

In addition, it is generally accepted that an action can be brought under Article 226 (formerly 169) against a Member State with respect to judicial acts.[8] However, this is not to say that a single decision by a national court will necessarily render a Member State liable to a declaration under Article 226, at least where an appeal lies against that decision.

In this connection the following statement by Warner A.G. in *R. v Bouchereau* deserves mention:

"It is obvious ... that a Member State cannot be held to have failed to fulfil an obligation under the Treaty simply because one of its courts has reached a wrong decision. Judicial error, whether due to the misapprehension of facts or to misapprehension of the law, is not a breach of the Treaty. In the judicial sphere, Article [226] could only come into play in the event of a court of a Member State deliberately ignoring or disregarding Community law."[9]

4.05 Moreover, one finds in the Member States a myriad of different types of public undertakings, semi-public bodies and "quangos" (quasi-autonomous national governmental organisations), fulfilling a host of different functions and roles, ranging from the social and cultural to the commercial and industrial. Little clear indication exists as to which acts of such bodies are to be attributed to the State for the present purposes.[10] What is more, an already confused picture is complicated by the existence of Article 31 (ex 37) (which relates specifically to State monopolies of a commercial character and which is the subject of Chapter XI of this book), of Article 86 (ex 90) on public undertakings and other undertakings on which the Member States confer

---

[7] Case 58/80 [1981] E.C.R. 181; [1981] 3 C.M.L.R. 590. See also Case 434/85 *Allen and Hanbury's Ltd. v Generics* [1988] E.C.R. 1245; [1988] 1 C.M.L.R. 701 at para. 25.

[8] In Cases 77/69 *Commission v Belgium* [1970] E.C.R. 237; [1974] 1 C.M.L.R. 203; and 8/70 *Commission v Italy* [1970] E.C.R. 961 the Court held that:

"The obligations arising from the Treaty devolve upon States as such and the liability of a Member State under Art. [226] arises whatever the agency of the State whose action or inaction is the cause of the failure to fulfil its obligations, even in the case of a constitutionally independent institution."

[9] Case 30/77 [1977] E.C.R. 1999 at 2020; [1977] 2 C.M.L.R. 800 at 810; see also generally para. 4.26 below.

[10] Directives can only be relied on against the State: Case C-91/92 *Faccini Dori v Recreb* [1994] E.C.R. I-3325). The Court has on occasion been called upon to rule on what bodies constitute the State for this purpose: *e.g.* Cases 152/84 *Marshall v Southampton Area Health Authority* [1986] E.C.R. 723; 222/84 *Johnston v Chief Constable of the RUC* [1986] E.C.R. 1651; and C-188/89 *Foster v British Gas* [1990] E.C.R. I-3313. In these cases, the Court has held that for these purposes, even when acting merely as an employer, a State enterprise is to be regarded as forming part of the State. The rationale behind this rule is that the State is not entitled to plead its own wrong in failing to implement a directive properly. That consideration does not apply to Arts 28 and 29 which, it is submitted, only relate to acts of imperium emanating from public authorities.

special rights,[11] and of Article 295 (ex 222).[12] None of these provisions is particularly straightforward.

However, where a Member State uses such a body as a medium for the execution of a measure, then that measure plainly emanates from the State, regardless of the precise status of the body concerned. This is what occurred in *Commission v Ireland*.[13] That case concerned the "Buy Irish" campaign, which was launched by the Irish Government but implemented by the Irish Goods Council. Although that organisation took the form of a private company, it had been set up by the Government, members of its management committee were appointed by a Minister and it was predominantly financed by the State. Thus the Court had no difficulty in finding that the campaign had been "introduced" by the Irish Government and "prosecuted with its assistance" and was thus attributable to that Government.[14]

Similarly, when the power to pass binding acts of a legislative or administrative nature is delegated by the State to a public or private body, those acts would seem to be attributable to the State for the purposes of Articles 28 to 30. Thus the Court has held that the acts of the Royal Pharmaceutical Society of Great Britain, a professional body exercising statutory powers, could be caught by Article 28: *R. v Royal Pharmaceutical Society of Great Britain, Ex p. Association of Pharmaceutical Importers*.[15] The Court ruled to the same effect in *Hünermund v Landesapotherkammer Baden-Württemberg*,[16] which concerned a body of a similar nature to the Royal Pharmaceutical Society save that it had no power to discipline its members; the Court held that this difference was immaterial.

One might also have thought that, whenever an act of a private person has been approved by the public authorities as required by law, then that act is attributable to the State. Thus in *Haug-Adrion v Frankfurter Versicherungs-AG*[17] the Commission advanced the view that insurance conditions drawn up by private insurance companies but formally approved by public authorities were attributable to the State. Yet this argument fell on deaf ears. Without deciding the point, the Advocate General inclined to the contrary view, while the Court decided the case on other grounds.

---

[11] See para. 9.04 below.
[12] See para. 9.30 below.
[13] Case 249/81 [1982] E.C.R. 4005; [1983] 2 C.M.L.R. 104; see paras 6.06, 6.29 and 7.19 below.
[14] See also generally Case 290/83 *Commission v France (Crédit Agricole)* [1985] E.C.R. 439, [1986] 2 C.M.L.R. 546 at para. 15.
[15] Cases 266–7/87 [1989] E.C.R. 1295; see also Case 190/73 *Van Haaster* [1974] E.C.R. 1123; [1974] 2 C.M.L.R. 521, where the defendant in the main case was charged before the Dutch courts with infringing a provision of a binding regulation adopted by the Produktschap voor Siergewassen, an organisation of producers of ornamental plants; the Court held this provision to be a measure of equivalent effect to a quantitative restriction. However, the Court did not refer expressly to the question in point here. Also, after its adoption by the Produktschap, the regulation received the approval of the Minister of Agriculture. A similar ruling with respect to a levy imposed by the same body was delivered in Case 51/74 *Van der Hulst's Zonen v Produktshap voor Siergewassen* [1975] E.C.R. 79; [1975] 1 C.M.L.R. 236.
[16] Case C-292/92 [1993] E.C.R. I-6787.
[17] Case 251/83 [1984] E.C.R. 4277; [1985] 3 C.M.L.R. 266, noted by Marenco, "La giurisprudenza communitaria sulle misure di effetto equivalente a una restrizione quantitativa" (1984–1986) Il Foro Padano 1988 IV, p. 166.

4.06 Equally, there is strong authority to the effect that technical standards drawn up by recognised standards institutes may in certain circumstances be attributable to the State. In its answer to Written Question 862/83, the Commission stated:

> "as regards the problem of standards it should be pointed out that they are very often drawn up by private bodies and, as such are not binding. If, however, such standards have been made *de jure* or *de facto* obligatory by the State authorities, their compatibility with the provisions of the Treaty and with the provisions relating to the free movement of goods (in particular Articles [28 to 30]) would have to be reviewed."[18]

That approach is closely reflected in Council Directive 98/34 laying down a procedure for the provision of information in the field of technical standards and regulations.[19] This Directive is expressed to extend to "technical specifications and other requirements, including the relevant administrative provisions, the observance of which is compulsory, *de jure* or *de facto*, in the case of marketing or use in a Member State or a major part thereof ...".[20] Having said that, the examples of *de facto* technical regulations set out in that Directive all involve some positive act of the State, and the Directive gives no indication that the tacit acceptance of a standard by the State would be sufficient.

4.07 The ruling in *Dubois v Garanor*[21] would seem to go still further, in that there the Court appeared to extend the concept of State involvement in a measure to cover the mere tacit delegation of an activity by the State to private parties. Having said that, the particularity of this case lies in the fact that this delegation also entailed a tacit transfer of a financial burden to a private party. The question which arose there was whether a particular charge imposed by a private company pursuant to a contract constituted a charge of equivalent effect to a customs duty on imports contrary to Articles 23 and 25 (ex 9 and 12) of the Treaty. The charge was imposed by the company concerned because the State had *de facto* discharged on that company the burden of carrying out various customs services together with the associated costs; to judge from the Opinion of La Pergola A.G., this process had occurred virtually by default, without any formal State act.

The Court found that a charge of the kind in question did indeed fall foul of these provisions. On the point in issue here, it held: "The nature of the measure requiring economic agents to bear part of the operating costs of customs services is immaterial. Whether the pecuniary charge is borne by the economic agent by virtue of a unilateral measure adopted by the authorities or, as in the present case, as a result of a series of private contracts, it arises in all cases, directly or indirectly, from the failure of the Member State concerned to fulfil

---

[18] [1983] O.J. C315/15.
[19] [1998] O.J. L204/37, amended by Council Directive 98/84 ([1998] O.J. L217/18), see paras 12.77 *et seq.* below.
[20] Art. 1(9).
[21] Case C-16/94 [1995] E.C.R. I-2421.

its financial obligations under Articles [23 and 25] of the Treaty".[22] In short, the abrogation by the State of its responsibility in no way precluded the charge being attributed to the State.

4.08 In addition, if a restriction on trade between Member States is provided for by a State measure, it is of no consequence that an individual or other private party must apply to the authorities to obtain the benefit of that restriction. This is because the measure still flows from the State, as explained at paragraph 4.27 below.

It will be clear from the above that State measures do not necessarily have to be binding to fall foul of Articles 28 to 30. This point is discussed at greater length at paragraph 6.11 below.

4.09 Of a somewhat different order are cases in which, by its failure to act against the obstruction of imports or exports by individuals, the State infringes Article 10 (ex 5) of the Treaty, read with Article 28 or Article 29. At present, the only such case to come before the Court is *Commission v France* (violent action by farmers),[23] in which the Commission's complaint of a breach of Articles 10 and 28 was upheld as regards violent protests against imports of fruit and vegetables. That case will be touched on again briefly later in this Chapter, at paragraph 4.32 below, before being discussed fully at paragraph 6.109.

II. THE COMMUNITY INSTITUTIONS

4.10 Can Community legislation validly prohibit or restrict trade between Member States? Alternatively, can such legislation authorise Member States to take such action? The concept of harmonisation of national rules by the Community (whatever the legal basis) presupposes the power to adopt standards with which products from all the Member States must comply. This will involve the submission of certain goods to particular conditions, such as labelling or packaging requirements, and will sometimes entail the complete prohibition of goods falling within certain categories. While a standard laid down in some but not all Member States may restrict interstate trade, it will cease to do so once it is introduced throughout the Community: all Member States will then apply the same standard so that goods from one Member State can be imported and sold in all the others. In such a case no problem arises as to the compatibility of the Community legislation with the Treaty provisions on the free movement of goods.[24]

---

[22] Para. 20 of the judgment.
[23] Case C-265/95 [1997] E.C.R. I-6959, noted by Jarvis, [1998] C.M.L. Rev. 1371; Meier, [1998] EuZW 87; Muylle, [1998] E.L. Rev. 467; Schwarze [1998] EuR 53.
[24] See paras 6.93 *et seq.* below.

Nevertheless it may happen that the Community institutions decide to subject movements of goods between Member States to certain taxes or procedures, or even to prohibit them altogether.

4.11 The starting point for the consideration of this type of case must be the Court's statement in *Ramel v Receveur des Douanes*[25] that:

> "the extensive powers, in particular of a sectoral or regional nature, granted to the Community institutions in the conduct of the Common Agricultural Policy must, in any event as from the end of the transitional period, be exercised from the perspective of the unity of the market to the exclusion of any measure comprising the abolition between Member States of customs duties and quantitative restrictions or charges or measures having equivalent effect."

The case had arisen out of the "wine war" between France and Italy, which flared up at the end of 1975. Article 31(1) of Council Regulation 816/70[26] laying down additional provisions for the common market organisation in wine prohibited charges of equivalent effect to customs duties in the internal trade of the Community, subject to one exception that is not material here. However, Article 31(2) stated that:

> "by way of derogation from the provisions of paragraph 1, so long as all the administrative mechanisms necessary for the management of the market in wine are not in application ... producer Member States shall be authorised in order to avoid disturbances on their markets to take measures that may limit imports from another Member State."

In 1975 there was an exceptional influx of Italian wine into the French market. With a view to limiting that influx the French Government levied a charge on certain Italian wines. The Commission brought an action under Article 226 against France for failure to comply with its Treaty obligations, but discontinued it when the French measure was repealed.

However, the plaintiffs in the main proceedings had been required to pay the charges at issue on various consignments of wine from Italy and now sought to recover those sums in actions against the French customs authorities. The Tribunal d'Instance of Bourg-en-Bresse, before which these actions were brought, accordingly asked the Court of Justice whether Article 31(2) of the Regulation was compatible with the Treaty and, if so, whether it continued to be applicable.

The Court began by considering Article 32(2) (ex 38(2)) of the Treaty, which reads: "Save as otherwise provided in Articles 33 to 38 [formerly 39 to 46], the rules laid down for the establishment of the common market shall apply to agricultural products." The Court found nothing in Articles 33 to 38—the

---

[25] Cases 80–81/77 [1978] E.C.R. 927.
[26] [1970] O.J. Spec. Ed. (I) 234.

provisions of the Treaty dealing with agriculture—which either expressly or by necessary implication provided for or authorised the introduction of charges of equivalent effect to customs duties in intra-Community trade at the end of the transitional period.[27]

After making the statement already quoted, the Court therefore concluded that: "Article 31(2) of Regulation 816/70 in so far as it authorises producer Member States to prescribe and levy, in intra-Community trade in the products covered by the organisation of the market which that regulation sets up, charges having an effect equivalent to customs duties, is incompatible with [old] Article 13, in particular paragraph (2) thereof, [now Article 25] and with Articles [32 to 38] of the Treaty and is consequently invalid."

4.12 *Ramel* concerned taxes but it is clear from the judgment that the same result will apply to quantitative restrictions and measures of equivalent effect. Indeed, this is also clear from a dictum in *Rivoira*.[28] There the Court was called upon to interpret Regulation 2513/69[29] on the co-ordination and standardisation of the treatment accorded by each Member State to imports of fruit and vegetables from non-member countries, and Regulation 1524/70[30] implementing the Agreement between Spain and the EEC of 1970. It held that the power conferred by those Regulations on Member States to impose quantitative restrictions on Spanish grapes over a certain period was limited to direct imports from third countries, on a proper reading of Article 1 of Regulation 2513/69. It added that:

> "the said Article 1 could not have covered the application by a Member State of restrictions on the importation of products in free circulation within the Community from other Member States, because such an ambit would have constituted a derogation from the fundamental rules of the Treaty on the free movement of goods."[31]

4.13 The same principle applies where tariff or non-tariff quotas on imports from third countries are allocated between Member States, as the Court stated unequivocally in *Commission v Council*[32] (rum quotas). To implement Protocol No. 5 to the Second Lomé Convention the Council adopted a regulation in relation to each annual tariff quota of rum and related products from the ACP States. For 1982/1983 it adopted Regulation 1699/82,[33] Article 4(2) of which provided:

---

[27] A similar approach to the interpretation of Art. 32(2) has been used by the Court in Case 90–91/63 *Commission v Belgium and Luxembourg* [1964] E.C.R. 625; [1965] C.M.L.R. 58; and Case 48/74 *Charmasson v Minister of Economic Affairs* [1974] E.C.R. 1383; [1975] 2 C.M.L.R. 208, discussed at para. 10.02 below.
[28] Case 179/78 [1979] E.C.R. 1147; [1979] 3 C.M.L.R. 456.
[29] [1970] J.O. L318/6.
[30] O.J. Spec. Ed. Second Series I External Relations (1), 269.
[31] See also the A.G. in Case 34/78 *Yoshida v Kamer van Koophandel* [1979] E.C.R. 115 at 147; [1979] 2 C.M.L.R. 747 at 752.
[32] Case 218/82 [1983] E.C.R. 4063; [1984] 2 C.M.L.R. 350.
[33] [1982] O.J. L189/1.

"The United Kingdom shall take the steps necessary to ensure that the quantities imported from the ACP States under the conditions laid down in Articles 1 and 2 are restricted to those meeting its domestic consumption requirements."

The Commission sought the annulment of this provision on the grounds that it required the United Kingdom to restrict exports in contravention of Article 29. In its defence the Council argued, *inter alia,* that the provision did not have this meaning but merely required the United Kingdom to refrain from importing quantities exceeding its domestic needs. To this end, it relied on the French version of Article 4(2), which was more favourable to this interpretation than the English version.

Rozès A.G. found for the Commission. In her view both versions of Article 4(2) constituted export restrictions. She also pointed out that the United Kingdom had in fact adopted legislation making re-exports of ACP rum economically prohibitive. The Court took the opposite view. Confirming *Ramel,* it held:

"If, as the Commission maintains, that provision did contain a prohibition on exportation from the United Kingdom to the other Member States it would indeed be contrary to the Treaty provisions on the free movement of goods; while, therefore, as the Court has confirmed, division of a global tariff quota into national quotas may, in certain circumstances, be compatible with the Treaty, that is subject to the express condition that it does not hinder the free movement of the goods forming part of the quota after they have been admitted to free circulation in the territory of one of the Member States."

In line with its earlier ruling in *Gaston Schul v Inspecteur der Invoerrechten,*[34] it then stated that, when the meaning of a provision of secondary Community law is in doubt, preference must be given to the interpretation rendering that provision compatible with the Treaty. It therefore found for the Council, while upholding the basic principle relied on by the Commission.

A particularly clear illustration of the same principle is to be found in *Migliorini*[35] which also concerned the allocation of a tariff quota between Member States. The Italian authorities had brought criminal proceedings against the defendants for re-exporting to Germany quantities of frozen beef imported into Italy from Czechoslovakia as part of Italy's portion of a Community quota for that product. The Italian authorities regarded the very action of re-exporting the beef as smuggling. In a preliminary ruling, the Court held that the Council Regulation opening the quota and allocating it between Member States did not "authorise the Member States to adopt measures intended to prevent, restrict or affect the re-exportation of goods which have been properly imported under that quota and which are consequently in free circulation in a Member State."

It follows from *Commission v Council* and *Migliorini* that where a Community quota is divided between Member States, that division only affects direct imports

---

[34] Case 15/81 [1982] E.C.R. 1409; [1982] 3 C.M.L.R. 229.
[35] Case 199/84 [1985] E.C.R. 3317.

from the third countries concerned. Once the goods have been put into free circulation in the Community they may move freely between the Member States like any other product.

4.14 Two more recent cases confirm the rule laid down in *Gaston Schul*. In *Delhaize v Promalvin*[36] the Court had occasion to consider a provision in Council Regulation 823/87[37] on quality wines which required Member States to lay down conditions for the use of appellations of origin in relation to such wines produced within their territory. The Court held that such a provision did not authorise the Member States to infringe Article 29.

Similarly, in *Verband Sozialer Wettbewerb v Estée Lauder*[38] the Court was asked whether the use of the word "Clinique" to denote a cosmetic product having no medicinal qualities could be banned by a Member State as being misleading. One of the questions considered was whether such a ban was lawful in view of the fact that Council Directive 76/768[39] on the approximation of laws relating to cosmetic products required Member States to prohibit the use of names "suggesting a characteristic which the products in question do not possess". The Court ruled that such a provision could not be taken to authorise national provisions which infringed Article 28. It went on to find that the restriction would indeed be contrary to Article 28 and therefore was not covered by the Directive.

4.15 It is established, then, that the Community institutions must have regard to the principle of the free movement of goods in framing their legislation. However, certain judgments of the Court indicate that in this matter the Community institutions enjoy a greater measure of freedom than the Member States.

The first of these, *REWE-Zentral v HZA Kehl*,[40] was one of a series of three cases[41] which concerned the validity of Regulation 974/71[42] establishing the system of monetary compensatory amounts (green currencies). Of these only the *REWE* case related to interstate trade and thus raised the question of the compatibility of these levies with Articles 23 and 25 the Treaty prohibiting charges of equivalent effect to customs duties. In answer to a question raised by a national court under Article 234 (ex 177), the Court ruled:

> "Although the compensatory amounts do constitute a partitioning of the market, here they have a corrective influence on the variations in fluctuating exchange rates which, in a system of market organisation for agricultural products based on uniform prices, might cause disturbances in trade in these products.

---

[36] Case C-47/90 [1992] E.C.R. I 3669; see para. 8.245 below.
[37] [1987] O.J. L84/59.
[38] Case C-315/92 [1994] E.C.R. I 317.
[39] [1976] O.J. L262/169.
[40] Case 10/73 [1973] E.C.R. 1175.
[41] The other two cases were Case 5/73 *Balkan-Import-Export v HZA Berlin-Packhof* [1973] E.C.R. 1091; and Case 9/73 *Carl Schlüter v HZA Lörrach* [1973] E.C.R. 1135.
[42] [1971] O.J. L106/1.

Diversion of trade caused solely by the monetary situation can be considered more damaging to the common interest, bearing in mind the aims of the common agricultural policy, than the disadvantages for the measures in dispute.

Consequently these compensatory amounts are conducive to the maintenance of a normal flow of trade under the exceptional circumstances created temporarily by the monetary situation.

They are also intended to prevent the disruption in the Member State concerned of the intervention system set up under Community regulations.

Furthermore, these are not levies introduced by some Member States unilaterally, but Community measures which, bearing in mind the exceptional circumstances of the time, are permissible within the framework of the common agricultural policy. Thus, the Council, by adopting them, did not contravene the provisions referred to by the national court."[43]

4.16 In the second case, *Bauhuis v Netherlands*,[44] the Court was confronted with a rather different type of tax, although it was also confined to agricultural products. In accordance with the provisions of the Dutch law relating to livestock, the plaintiff in the main action was required to pay fees for public health inspection, *inter alia*, on exports of pigs, "bovine animals" and horses. Directive 64/432[45] required the exporting Member State to carry out certain veterinary and public health inspections of pigs and "bovine animals", without stating whether a charge might be levied for such inspections. The object of the Directive was to shift supervision to the exporting Member State so as to avoid the need for multiple inspections at subsequent frontiers, and thereby to facilitate intra-Community trade. The Directive did not apply to horses.

In an action before it in which the plaintiff contested the compatibility of these charges with Community law, the Arrondissementsrechtbank of The Hague asked the Court of Justice to decide whether charges of this kind constituted charges of equivalent effect to customs duties on exports contrary to Article 25 (ex16) of the Treaty.

The Court had already held[46] that, even when an inspection is justified under Article 30 on human or animal health grounds, any sum charged for that inspection constitutes a prohibited charge of equivalent effect to a customs duty, if it is levied according to criteria not comparable with those employed in fixing charges on similar domestic products. Consequently, in *Bauhuis* the Court held that the charges for the inspection of horses were contrary to Article 25, such inspections not being provided for by Community legislation.

Yet the Court adopted a radically different approach to the other charges, since they related to inspections which:

---

[43] The system of MCAS was finally abolished at the end of 1992, specifically with a view to removing border controls contrary to Art. 14 (originally 8A, then 7A) of the Treaty: Council Reg. 3813/92 ([1992] O.J. L387/1). However, this was subject to the transitional measures adopted by the Commission: Reg. 3820/92 ([1992] O.J. L387/22). See also Commission Reg. 1068/93 ([1993] O.J. L108/106).

[44] Case 46/76 [1977] E.C.R. 5.

[45] [1964] O.J. Spec. Ed. 164.

[46] Case 29/72 *Marimex v Italian Finance Administration* [1972] E.C.R. 1309; [1973] C.M.L.R. 486.

"are not[47] laid down unilaterally by each Member State but have been made obligatory and uniform in the case of all the products in question whichever the exporting Member State or the Member State of destination may be.

On the other hand they are not prescribed by each Member State in order to protect some interest of its own but by the Council in the general interest of the Community.

They cannot therefore be regarded as unilateral measures which hinder trade but rather as operations intended to promote the free movement of goods, in particular by rendering ineffective the obstacles to this free movement which might be created by the measures for veterinary and public health inspections adopted pursuant to Article [30]. In these circumstances fees charged for veterinary and public health inspections, which are prescribed by a Community provision, which are uniform and are required to be carried out before despatch within the exporting country do not constitute charges having an effect equivalent to customs duties on exports, provided that they do not exceed the actual cost of the inspection for which they are charged."[48]

4.17 In *REWE-Zentrale v Direktor der Landwirtschaftskammer Rheinland*[49] it was argued for the first time that a Directive fell foul of Article 28. The instrument in question was Council Directive 77/93[50] on protective measures against the introduction into the Member States of harmful organisms of plants or plant products, which is based on Articles 37 and 94 (ex 43 and 100). On a reference for a preliminary ruling the plaintiffs in the main case contended that the Directive was incompatible with Article 28 in so far as it permitted an importing Member State to subject as many as one-third of all consignments of plants and plant products to phytosanitary controls. This was said to be excessive since under the Directive the exporting Member State was required to carry out systematic checks.[51]

The Court stressed once again that the Community institutions were bound to observe the principle of the free movement of goods, which was one of the fundamental principles of the common market. Nevertheless, it found that they enjoyed a measure of discretion in exercising their powers under Articles 37 and 94, which had not been exceeded with respect to the Directive. In reaching this conclusion the Court had regard to the specific problems of phytosanitary protection. It also found that under the Treaty provisions referred to harmonisation may be effected in stages and national obstacles to trade abolished gradually. This necessarily implies that the contested provision may in time cease to be valid. Indeed, Slynn A.G., who took the same view as the Court, said as much.

---

[47] Unfortunately the word "not" appears to be missing in the English text, but the other language versions indicate that it should be there.

[48] For criticisms of this ruling see Barents, "Charges of Equivalent Effect to Customs Duties" [1978] C.M.L. Rev. 415; and Kohler, *Abgaben zollgleicher Wirkung im Recht der Europäischen Gemeinschaften* (1978). In Case 89/76 *Commission v Netherlands* [1977] E.C.R. 1355; [1978] 3 C.M.L.R. 630 the Court reached a similar conclusion with respect to fees charged for the phytosanitary inspection of plant exports provided for not by Community legislation, but by an international convention to which all the Member States were party.

[49] Case 37/83 [1984] E.C.R. 1229; [1985] 2 C.M.L.R. 586. For a more recent case in which a directive was held compatible with Art. 28, see Case C-51/93 *Meyhui v Schott Zwiesel Glaswerke* [1994] E.C.R. I 3879; see para. 8.90 below.

[50] [1977] O.J. L26/20.

[51] See para. 8.113 below.

4.18 In its preliminary ruling in *Denkavit Nederland v Hoofdproduktschap voor Akkerbouwprodukten,*[52] the Court likewise dismissed arguments to the effect that Commission Regulation 1725/79[53] on aid for processed skimmed milk was contrary to Article 29. It followed from Articles 6 and 7 of that Regulation that in the case of exports proof that the conditions for the grant of aid had been met must be furnished by Community T5 documents (or by the Benelux 5 document in the case of Benelux exports). On the other hand, where the finished product was put on the market in the Member State of production, proof was to be furnished according to the method laid down by the Member State, provided that that method ensured adequate guarantees of compliance with the conditions concerned. This disparity resulted in the aid being paid later with respect to exports than with respect to goods put on the national market. Denkavit therefore contended that these provisions were contrary, *inter alia,* to Article 29 and a largely identical provision contained in Article 22(1) of Council Regulation 804/68[54] on the common organisation of the market in milk and milk products. Following the Advocate General, a three-judge Chamber of the Court held the Regulation to be compatible with all the provisions and principles of Community law relied on by Denkavit. In relation to Article 29, it held that the documents of proof required in each case, though not identical, were equivalent. Moreover, the later payment of aid for exports was held to be inevitable: the transmission of documents between the authorities of different Member States was bound to take longer than the forwarding of documents within a single Member State. It is also significant that elsewhere in its judgment, in a passage concerned with the principle of proportionality, the Court pointed to the particular dangers of fraud as regards exports. For instance, the risk of paying aid twice with respect to the same goods might be greater where exports were concerned.

4.19 Again, in *Denkavit Futtermittel v Land Baden-Württemberg*[55] the Court was called upon to rule on the validity of a provision in a Directive which empowered Member States to require certain labelling on the packaging of compound foodstuffs, but did not make it obligatory for Member States to do so. The plaintiffs contended that this provision infringed Article 28 because it enabled Member States to extend such a labelling requirement to imports from other Member States which had opted not to impose this requirement. Subsequently, the Council enacted another Directive making this labelling compulsory throughout the Community. The Court rejected Denkavit's argument, finding that the contested measure was justified *inter alia* on consumer protection grounds; and that "the Community institutions must be recognised as enjoying a discretion in relation to the stages in which harmonisation is to take place, having regard to the particular nature of the field subject to coordination".

---

[52] Case 15/83 [1984] E.C.R. 2171.
[53] [1979] O.J. L199/1.
[54] [1968] O.J. Spec. Ed. (I) 176, subsequently amended.
[55] Case C-39/90 [1991] E.C.R. I-3069, para. 12.111 below.

4.20   In contrast, the recent ruling in *Lancry v Direction Générale des Douanes*[56] shows the Court in a more stringent mood. This case related to a Council Decision based on the old Article 227(2) (now, after substantial revision, Article 299(2)) and Article 308 (ex 235) which purported to authorise France to maintain for three years a levy on imports into the overseas departments, known as the *octroi de mer*. The Court held in no uncertain terms that the Decision was unlawful, as those provisions did not entitle the Council to suspend the application of Articles 23 and 25 "even temporarily". This ruling is no doubt due to the blatantly protectionist nature of the measure, which was manifestly not in the interest of the Community as a whole.[57]

4.21   Finally, a ruling which must undoubtedly rest on its special facts was that in *Kind v Commission and Council.*[58] That case concerned the validity of Article 9(3) of Council Regulation 1837/80 on the common organisation of the markets in "sheepmeat" and "goatmeat"[59] which imposed a clawback on exports of mutton and lamb from the United Kingdom to other Member States. The clawback was equal to the amount of the variable slaughter premium granted by the United Kingdom by virtue of the Regulation, no such premium being granted in the other Member States. The regulations in question were part of the common market organisation for those products, which was not established until October 1980. The plaintiffs brought an action for compensation under Article 288 (ex 215) of the Treaty, arguing, *inter alia*, that the clawback constituted a charge of equivalent effect contrary to Articles 23 and 25.

The Court rejected that argument. It first pointed out that the contested provisions were transitional in nature, being designed to bring about a gradual convergence in the markets in mutton and lamb in the Member States; that convergence was intended to be complete by April 1984, as was stated in the regulations themselves. In a crucial passage the Court then stated:

> "within the framework of a regulation, namely Regulation No. 1837/80, the provisions of which, according to Article [29] thereof, are to be reviewed before 1 April 1984, the charge on exports provided for by Article 9(3) of that regulation is inseparable in principle from the intervention system which is made up of payment of the variable slaughter premium in Community regions where buying-in is not practised by the intervention agencies. Therefore, the charge does not constitute, as the applicant maintains, a charge having an effect equivalent to a customs duty but is in reality intended to offset exactly the effects of the slaughter premium, thereby enabling products from the Member States or regions in which the premium is paid to be exported to other Member States without disturbing their markets. If there were no clawback, offers emanating from a Member State which applies the slaughter premium might be made on markets in other Member States at prices appreciably lower than those obtaining in the latter and might bring, through a fall in prices, the intervention

---

[56] Case C-363/93 [1994] E.C.R. I-3957.
[57] However, the Court subsequently accepted an amended form of this tax: Case C-212/96 *Chevassus-Marche v Conseil Régional de la Réunion* [1998] E.C.R. I-743, discussed by Boissard, "La validité inattendue du nouvel octroi de mer" [1999] R.M.U.E. I-129.
[58] Case 106/81 [1982] E.C.R. 2885, noted by Lenaerts [1983] C.M.L. Rev. 839.
[59] [1980] O.J. L183/1, subsequently replaced.

measures which the Community would thus in fact be called upon to finance for a second time, albeit perhaps in another form."

This ruling seems questionable: the clawback was designed to offset a disparity caused by the fact that the premium was granted in the United Kingdom alone; this disparity, which was sanctioned by Regulation 1837/80, was surely irreconcilable with the fundamental principle that Community law is to be applied uniformly in all the Member States. Moreover, it is hard to see how the supposedly temporary nature of this state of affairs could render the clawback lawful.

At all events, the Court to some extent qualified this ruling in *United Kingdom v Commission*,[60] the sequel to *Kind*. It was held there that the Commission had exceeded its powers under Regulation 1837/80 by imposing a clawback on exports from the United Kingdom of animals and products for which the slaughter premium had not been and could not be granted. In so doing, the Court cited *Ramel* and referred to the provision in Article 43(3)(b) of the Treaty that a common market organisation must ensure "conditions for trade within the Community similar to those existing in a national market". It also noted that, although the disparities in the common market organisation concerned were supposedly transitional in nature, they had still not been removed. It added:

"The incomplete state of such a common organisation of the market, which is due in particular to the fact that a particular support measure is reserved for producers of a specific region and is liable to improve their competitive position, may call for corrective measures to restore equality between producers in all regions so far as their competitive position is concerned. Such measures, in so far as they constitute obstacles to the free movement of goods to which any common organisation of the market must aspire, are necessarily of an exceptional nature and therefore their scope must be strictly limited to their specific objective in the context of bringing about market conditions which come closest to those of an internal market."[61]

4.22 Leaving aside the controversial judgment in *Kind* one may tentatively conclude that Community legislation restricting trade between Member States is lawful if it satisfies the following cumulative conditions:

(a) It must be uniform throughout the Member States. This must, however, be subject to the rule that objectively different situations require different treatment.[62]

---

[60] Case 61/86 [1988] E.C.R. 431; [1988] 2 C.M.L.R. 98; see also Cases 162/86 *R. v Intervention Board for Agricultural Produce, Ex p. Livestock Sales Transport* [1988] E.C.R. 489; [1988] 2 C.M.L.R. 186; C-181/88 *Deschamps v OFIVAL* [1989] E.C.R. I 4381; and C-38/90 *R. v Lomas* [1992] E.C.R. I 1781.

[61] Happily, in 1989 the Council adopted Reg. 3013/89 establishing a new common market organisation for sheepmeat and goat meat ([1989] O.J. L289/1), which phased out the different support regimes for the various zones of the Community, together with the clawback itself, at the end of the 1992 marketing year. The choice of that date for the abolition of this restriction on the free movement of goods is no accident, given that Art. 14 of the Treaty required the internal market to be completed by the end of 1992.

[62] Case 13/63 *Commission v Italy* [1963] E.C.R. 165; [1963] C.M.L.R. 289.

(b) It must be adopted "in the general interest of the Community". It is not clear quite what is meant by this, but in *REWE-Zentral v Bundesmono-polverwaltung für Branntwein*[63] (the *"Cassis de Dijon"* case), discussed at length in Chapter VI of this book, the Court found that national measures constituting obstacles to interstate trade must be accepted in so far as those provisions may be recognised as being necessary in order to satisfy mandatory requirements relating in particular to the effectiveness of fiscal supervision, the protection of public health, the fairness of commercial transactions and the defence of the consumer. The concept of general interest for the purposes of Community legislation must be at least as wide as that obtaining for national measures. At all events, the provisions of Articles 2 and 3 of the Treaty will serve as a general guide to the concept of general interest for these purposes.

(c) It must be "intended to promote the free movement of goods" although in itself it is restrictive of trade between Member States. This requirement may in fact merge with (b) above. In many cases, it is something of a misnomer to describe such measures as restrictive of interstate trade, because they are in fact less restrictive than the measures which would be necessary in their absence. Such is the case, for example, with the public health inspections at issue in *Bauhuis:* in the absence of the export inspections laid down by the directive, the Member States would in practice have been obliged to carry out checks on imports, which would have been justified under Article 30 of the Treaty but which would have constituted a greater restriction on trade.

(d) The restrictive effects of the Community measure must not be greater than is necessary to attain the legitimate end in view. The Court has held in other contexts that, since the principle of the free movement of goods is a fundamental principle of the Treaty, exceptions to it may only be allowed in so far as they are necessary.[64]

4.23 It is probable, though, that the burden of proof is not the same in the case of Community legislation as in the case of national measures. There is a presumption that national measures creating restrictions on interstate trade are not justified,[65] while the converse applies to Community legislation. As has already been pointed out, an apparent obstacle to inter-State trade contained in Community legislation will often turn out not to be an obstacle at all, by comparison with the situation which would have existed in its absence.

4.24 In any case, it can be concluded that the Community institutions are

---

[63] Case 120/78 [1979] E.C.R. 649; [1979] 3 C.M.L.R. 494.
[64] With respect to Art. 30, see para. 8.01 below; see also para. 9.01 below.
[65] See para. 8.11 below.

bound to have regard to the principle of the free movement of goods, when adopting legislation. Having established this, the question arises whether these institutions are bound by the Treaty provisions on the free movement of goods themselves or rather by rules which are analogous to them. No clear indication can be found in the Treaty itself. Although in some instances it states simply that the restrictions in question are prohibited "between Member States" (as in Articles 23, 28 and 29)), in others the obligations in point are expressed to be addressed to the Member States (as in the old Article 31, which stated that "Member States shall refrain from introducing ..."). Little, if any, conclusion can be drawn from the existence of these two forms of words.

In *Ramel*[66] it was held that the Community provision concerned was contrary to the old Article 13 itself, but according to Matthies[67] this was merely because the provision did not itself impose an import duty but merely permitted the Member States to do so. He firmly took the view that the Community legislator is bound by the principle of the free movement of goods, and not by the Treaty articles as such. In his view, the free movement of goods is a fundamental principle of Community law to be observed by the Community institutions in the performance of their tasks, much in the same way as the principles of non-discrimination and of proportionality. This view appears to be supported by *REWE-Zentrale*[68] in which the Court stated:

"although it is true, as the Commission emphasised in its observations, that Articles [28 to 30] of the Treaty apply primarily to unilateral measures adopted by the Member States, the Community institutions themselves must also have due regard to freedom of trade within the Community, which is a fundamental principle of the common market."

4.25 Whatever attitude one adopts to this particular problem, it seems clear that the Court has plotted a middle course: while setting bounds to the freedom enjoyed by the Community institutions in this regard, it has ensured that this freedom is greater than that permitted to the Member States in view of the special tasks which the Community is called upon to perform. In addition, the Community institutions possess special powers under the exception or escape clauses discussed in Chapter IX below.

III. PRIVATE PARTIES

A. Introduction

4.26 There remains the highly vexed question as to whether private parties—individuals and non-State bodies—are bound by the provisions of Articles 28 to

---

[66] See n.25 above.
[67] "Herkunftsangaben und Europäisches Gemeinschaftsrecht" in *Festschrift für Schiedermair* (1976) 395.
[68] See n.49 above.

30.[69] Frequently, restrictions on interstate trade resulting from the action of private parties will fall under Articles 81 and 82 (ex 85 and 86) of the Treaty relating to competition[70]; but these provisions only apply in the case of agreements between undertakings (Article 81) or action taken by one undertaking acting alone where that undertaking has a dominant position (Article 82). Other restrictions on imports and exports due to the actions of private parties fall outside Articles 81 and 82. The following examples are worthy of note:

(a) a farmers' union organises violent protests against imports of agricultural produce from another Member State, which protests have both the purpose and the effect of restricting those imports;

(b) a dockers' union takes industrial action, thereby preventing imports (it is generally considered that trade unions fall outside the scope of the concept of "undertakings" in Articles 81 and 82);

(c) an environmental pressure group such as Greenpeace orchestrates a boycott of goods from another Member State in protest at that State's environmental policy;

(d) an association of traders engages in a "buy national" campaign;

(e) an insurance company without any dominant position refuses to insure imported cars, without being party to any agreement to that effect;

(f) an advertising standards body (made up of private undertakings which have agreed, as a self-regulatory measure, to be bound by a voluntary code of practice) determines that a certain advertising campaign adopted by one of its members must be withdrawn; and

(g) an individual purchaser in one Member State decides to boycott goods from one or more other Member States, whether on political grounds, out of pure xenophobia or for other reasons.

In each case it will be assumed that no Member State has in any way supported

---

[69] See Baquero Cruz, "Free Movement and Private Autonomy" [1999] E.L. Rev. 603; Barents, "New Developments in Measures Having Equivalent Effect" [1981] C.M.L. Rev. 271 at 275; Gormley, *Prohibiting Restrictions on Trade within the EEC* (1985) at 258–262; van Gerven, "The Recent Case Law of the Court of Justice concerning Arts. 30 and 36 of the EEC Treaty" [1977] C.M.L. Rev. 5; Jänsch, *Die unmittelbare Drittwirkung der Grundfreiheiten, Untersuchung der Verpflichtung von Privatpersonen durch Art. 30, 48, 52, 59, 73b EGV* (1997); Kluth, "Die Bindung privater Wirtschaftsteilnehmer an die Grundfreiheiten des EG-Vertrages" [1997] AöR 123; Matthies, *op. cit.* n.67 above; Roth, *Drittwirkung der Grundfreiheiten?* in Feschrift for Ulrich Everling (1995) vol. II p. 1231; Steindorff, *EG-Vertrag und Privatrecht* (1996) pp. 277–301; VerLoren van Themaat, "De artikelen 30–36 van het EEG-Verdrag" (1980) RM Themis 4–5 378.

[70] As to the relationship between Arts 28 to 30 on the one hand and Arts 81 and 82 on the other, see para. 6.34 below. See Mortelmans, "Towards convergence in the application of the rules on free movement and on competition" (2001) 38 C.M.L. Rev. 613.

the action in question; any action encouraged by the State, even in a non-binding form, constitutes a State measure for this purpose.[71]

Three separate questions arise:

(i) Are private parties bound to observe Articles 28 to 30 ?

(ii) If not, can those provisions nevertheless be relied on against private parties in legal proceedings?

(iii) What action can the Commission take with respect to such measures ?

These questions will now be considered in turn.

B. The First Question

4.27 In considering this question, one must have regard to the following lines of case law. The starting-point of this survey should be the Court's ruling in *Dassonville*,[72] where it held that a measure having equivalent effect to a quantitative restriction should be understood as covering "all trading rules enacted by Member States which are capably of hindering, directly or indirectly, actually or potentially, intra-Community trade". The Court's use of the words "enacted by Member States" in this classic definition of measures having equivalent effect provides a powerful suggestion that Article 28 is concerned exclusively with "State" measures.[72a]

4.28 Second, regard should be had to the Court's judgment in *Dansk Super-marked*.[73] The case concerned a dinner service produced in the United Kingdom at the behest of a Danish organisation. It had been agreed between those two parties that "seconds" could be sold in the United Kingdom, but not in Denmark. The validity of that agreement was challenged when some "seconds" nevertheless found their way into Denmark. On this point, the Court stated:

"it is impossible in any circumstances for agreements between individuals to derogate from the mandatory provisions of the Treaty on the free movement of goods. It follows that an agreement involving a prohibition on the importation into a Member State of goods lawfully marketed in another Member State may not be relied upon or taken into consideration in order to classify the marketing of such goods as an improper or unfair commercial practice."[74]

While this ruling is very far-reaching, its significance may be limited: apart from the fact that it was delivered by a Chamber of three judges, it has never been

---

[71] para. 6.11 below. As to "buy national" campaigns orchestrated by the State see Case 249/81 (see n.13 above).

[72] [1974] E.C.R. 837 at para. 5.

[72a] In Case C-159/00 *Sapod Audic v Eco-Emballages* (judgment of June 6, 2002) the Court (Fifth Chamber) relied on that ruling for the proposition that a provision in a contract between individuals does not fall within Art. 28 (para. 74 of the judgment).

[73] See n.7 above.

[74] Para. 17.

confirmed by any subsequent judgments.[75] Moreover, as Capotorti A.G. had remarked,[76] the agreement fell to be considered under Article 81.

4.29 Third, one must have regard to the Court's statement in *Vereniging van Vlaamse Reisbureaus*[77] that "Articles [28 and 29] only cover public measures and not the conduct of undertakings". Arguably, this thinking was already implicit in the earlier judgment in *Van de Haar*[78] in which the Court was called upon to compare Articles 28 and 81. The Court held that, whereas Article 81 "belongs to the rules on competition which are addressed to undertakings and associations of undertakings and which are intended to maintain effective competition in the common market", Article 28 "belongs to the rules which seek to ensure the free movement of goods and, to that end to eliminate measures taken by Member States". Clearly, this judgment runs directly counter to the earlier decision in *Dansk Supermarked*.

At all events, whilst the ruling in *Vereniging van Vlaamse Reisbureaus* is undoubtedly the Court's clearest and most direct pronouncement on the subject, it is by no means the end of the matter. In any case, this statement is unsupported by any reasoning in the judgment; nor did the Advocate General consider this issue.

4.30 Fourth, the Court has delivered a large body of case law[79] stating that the exercise of intellectual property rights to exclude imports from other Member States can in certain circumstances be contrary to Article 28. Certain passages in these judgments suggest that such exercise is to be regarded as the act of the private party concerned. An example is the following passage in *Deutsche Grammophon v Metro*[80]:

> "the essential purpose of the Treaty, which is to unite national markets into a single market ... could not be attained if, under the various legal systems of the Member States, nationals of those States were able to partition the market and bring about arbitrary discrimination or disguised restrictions on trade between Member States."

However, it is widely considered that this case law is not in point: the exercise of industrial property rights by a private person merely constitutes reliance on measures adopted by the Member States; without legislation, patent, trade mark and copyright protection would simply not exist.[81]

---

[75] Baquero Cruz, *op. cit.* n.69 above at 608.
[76] at 201.
[77] Case 311/85 [1987] E.C.R. 3801, para. 30.
[78] Cases 177 and 178/82 [1984] E.C.R. 1797; [1985] 2 C.M.L.R. 566; see also para. 6.34 below.
[79] See paras 8.172 *et seq.* below.
[80] Case 78/70 [1971] E.C.R. 487 at 500; [1971] C.M.L.R. 631 at 657.
[81] See the passage from *Dansk Supermarked* quoted in para. 4.04 above; Warner A.G. in Cases 55 and 57/80 *Musik-Vertrieb Membran v GEMA* [1981] E.C.R. 147 at 174–175; [1981] 2 C.M.L.R. 44 at 56–57; and Baquero Cruz, *op. cit.* at 604; Daniele, "Réflections d'ensemble sur la notion de mesures ayant un effet équivalent à des restrictions quantitatives" [1984] R.M.C. 477 at 479; Matthies, *op. cit.* n.67 above; Muller-Graff, in Groeben, Thiesing and Ehlermann, *Kommentar zum EU-/EG-Vertrag* (5th ed., 1997), Vol. I, p 743. *Contra* Waelbroeck, "Les rapports entre les règles sur la libre

4.31 Fifth, the Court's decision in *Walrave v Union Cycliste Internationale*[82] is of particular importance in this context. That case concerned alleged discrimination on the grounds of nationality within a private sporting organisation. One of the points which arose for decision was whether a private body was bound by Article 39 (ex 48) of the Treaty on the free movement of workers and Article 49 (ex 59) on the free provision of services. Referring also to the general prohibition on discrimination on the grounds of nationality in Article 12 (initially 7, then 6) of the Treaty, the Court ruled as follows:

> "Articles [12, 39 and 49] have in common the prohibition, in their respective spheres of application, of any discrimination on grounds of nationality.
>
> Prohibition of such discrimination does not only apply to the action of public authorities but extends likewise to rules of any other nature aimed at regulating *in a collective manner* gainful employment and the provision of services.
>
> The abolition as between Member States of obstacles to the freedom of movement for persons and to freedom to provide services, which are fundamental objectives of the Community contained in Article 3(c) of the Treaty, would be compromised if the abolition of barriers of national origin could be neutralised by obstacles resulting from the exercise of their legal autonomy by associations or organisations which do not come under public law.
>
> Since, moreover, working conditions in the various Member States are governed sometimes by means of provisions laid down by law or regulation and sometimes by agreements and other acts concluded or adopted by private persons, to limit the prohibitions in question to acts of a public authority would risk creating inequality in their application...
>
> It follows that the provisions of Articles [12, 39 and 49] of the Treaty may be taken into account by the national court in judging the validity or the effects of a provision inserted in the rules of a sporting organisation."[83]

This judgment is particularly interesting in that the structure of the Treaty provisions on services is in one sense analogous to those relating to goods. While Article 49 simply states that "restrictions on freedom to provide services within the Community shall be progressively abolished during the transitional period in respect of nationals of Member States", the former Article 62 (now repealed) was expressed to be addressed to the Member States, as is Article 53 (ex 64).[84] The Court addressed this question in the following terms:

> "Although ... [old Articles 62 and 64] specifically relate, as regards the provision of services, to the abolition of measures by the State, this fact does not defeat the general nature of the terms of Article [49], which makes no distinction between the source of the restrictions to be abolished."[85]

On one view, this case is not so far removed from the *Royal Pharmaceutical*

---

circulation des marchandises et les règles de concurrence applicables aux entreprises de la CEE" in Liber Amicorum Pierre Pescatore (1987) 781. See also para 8.194 below *Terrapin v. Terranora.*
[82] Case 36/74 [1974] E.C.R. 1405; [1975] 1 C.M.L.R. 320.
[83] Paras 16–19 and 25, emphasis added.
[84] See para. 4.01 above.
[85] Para. 19.

Society[86] case, where the State had conferred express powers on the private body in question by statute. Arguably, in *Walrave* the States had tacitly accepted the exercise by the body in question of the power to regulate the sport concerned; this tacit acceptance might be seen as a *de facto* delegation of this power by the States to the sporting body.

Equally, *Walrave* has much in common with *Dubois v Garanor*[87]: in the latter case the Member State had tacitly transferred a financial burden to a private party, whereas in *Walrave* the States had merely tolerated the exercise of power by private parties.

4.32 In any case, the ruling in *Walrave* was subsequently confirmed in a number of cases involving sporting organisations.[88] By their very nature, sporting bodies enjoy *de facto* exclusive powers to regulate the sport for which they are responsible, leaving no room for others to intervene; and State intervention tends to be marginal or non-existent.

4. 33 In its recent judgments in *Ferlini v Centre Hospitalier du Luxembourg*[89] and *Wouters v Nederlandse Orde van Advocaten*,[90] the Court has now extended the same principles beyond the field of sport.

Ferlini concerned an agreement between all the hospitals of a Member State fixing the fees for health care. At the same time, the Court applied those principles for the first time to Article 12 of the Treaty, which prohibits discrimination between nationals of Member States. Referring *inter alia* to *Walrave*, it stated: "According to the caselaw of the Court, the first paragraph of Article [12] of the Treaty also applies in cases where a group or organisation ... exercises a certain power over individuals and is in a position to impose on them conditions which adversely affect the exercise of fundamental freedoms guaranteed under the Treaty".[91] There is no mention here of regulating activities "in a collective manner", although in practice that is precisely what the contested agreement between the hospitals achieved.

Wouters related to measures imposed by the Bar Council of the Netherlands on its Members. Referring once again to *Walrave*, the Court held that compliance with Articles 43 and 49 is required in the case of "rules which are not public in nature but which are designed to regulate, collectively, self-employment and the provision of services".[92] The difference in wording between this

---

[86] See n.15 above.
[87] See n. 21 above.
[88] Cases 13/76 *Donà v Mantero* [1976] E.C.R. 1333; [1976] 2 C.M.L.R. 578; C-415/93 *Union Royale Belge des Sociétés de Football Association v Bosman* [1995] E.C.R. I-4921; C-51/96 and C-191/97 *Deliège v Ligue Belge de Judo* [2000] E.C.R. I-2549; and C-176/96 *Lehtonen v Fédération Royale Belge des Sociétés de Basketball* [2000] E.C.R. I-2681.

   In *Bosman*, the Court applied the principles of *Walrave* to non-discriminatory restrictions falling under Article 39, namely restrictions on transfers of footballers between clubs applying in the same manner within and between Member States.
[89] Case C-411/98 [2000] E.C.R. I-8081.
[90] Case C-309/99 (judgment of February 19, 2002).
[91] Para. 50 of the judgment.
[92] Para. 120.

ruling and that in *Ferlini* is worthy of note, especially the word "collectively".

4.34 The sixth relevant line of case law begins with *Defrenne v Sabena*.[93] That case concerned the interpretation of Article 141 (ex 119) of the Treaty, the first paragraph of which reads:

> "Each Member State shall during the first stage ensure and subsequently maintain the application of the principle that men and women should receive equal pay for equal work."

In reply to a preliminary question, the Court ruled that Article 141 prohibited discrimination in pay between men and women, whether by private or by public organisations. The following passages of the judgment are particularly illustrative in the present context:

> "It is also impossible to put forward arguments based on the fact that Article [141] only refers expressly to 'Member States'.
>
> Indeed, as the Court has already found in other contexts, the fact that certain provisions of the Treaty are formally addressed to the Member States does not prevent rights from being conferred at the same time on any individual who has an interest in the performance of the duties thus laid down…
>
> …in its reference to 'Member States', Article [141] is alluding to those States in the exercise of all those of their functions which may usefully contribute to the implementation of the principle of equal pay…
>
> Therefore, the reference to 'Member States' in Article [141] cannot be interpreted as excluding the intervention of the courts in direct application of the Treaty".[94]

In other words, the judiciary is one of the organs of the Member States and is bound by this provision in the same way as the other organs of the States.

It is probably no coincidence that in the same case the Court described the principal of equal pay as "part of the foundations of the Community".[95] Perhaps it is no accident either that this reasoning was confirmed in another ruling relating to sex equality, namely *Von Colson v Land Nordrhein-Westfalen*.[96] That case concerned Council Directive 76/207 on the implementation of the principle of equal treatment for men and women as regards access to employment and working conditions.[97] In that case the Court held:

> "the Member States' obligation arising from a directive to achieve the result envisaged by the directive and their duty under Article [10] of the Treaty to take all appropriate measures, whether general or particular, to ensure the fulfilment of that obligation, is binding on all the authorities of Member States including, for matters within their jurisdiction, the courts".

---

[93] Case 43/75 [1976] E.C.R. 455; [1976] 2 C.M.L.R. 98.
[94] Paras 30 to 37.
[95] Para. 12.
[96] Case 14/83 [1984] E.C.R. 1891 at 1909; also Case 79/83 *Harz v Deutsche Tradax* [1984] E.C.R. 1921 at 1942.
[97] [1976] O.J. L39/40.

4.35 Seventh, one must have regard to the celebrated ruling in *Commission v France* (violent action by farmers).[98] As already mentioned, the Court held there that, by failing to take action against the violent protests of farmers against imports of fruit and vegetables, the defendant State had fallen foul of Articles 10 and 28 of the Treaty read together. The Court almost pointedly refrained from addressing the question as to whether the farmers' conduct itself breached Article 28. What inference, if any, may be drawn from the Court's reluctance to advert to this issue is unclear. Lenz A.G. expressed the view that this provision did not apply to the acts of private parties,[99] although that statement was not supported by any reasoning.

4.36 Finally, particular importance must be attached to the recent ground-breaking judgment in *Angonese v Cassa di Risparmio di Bolzano,*[100] the importance of which can scarcely be exaggerated. In so far as is relevant, the facts were that the plaintiff in the main case complained of discrimination on the basis of knowledge of the language of the region in which he sought employment (the South Tyrol or Alto Adige). In an action against a private bank which had refused to engage him, he alleged that such discrimination was contrary to Article 39 of the Treaty. Although the defendant bank had purported to apply a collective agreement covering all Italian savings banks, the Court found that the act complained of did not necessarily flow from that agreement. After rehearsing at some length its earlier judgments in *Walrave* and *Defrenne*, the Court ruled that the considerations set out there applied *a fortiori* to Article 39, which "lays down a fundamental freedom and which constitutes a specific application of the general prohibition of discrimination contained in" Article 12. The Court added that, like Article 141, Article 39 is "designed to ensure that there is no discrimination in the labour market". It therefore concluded that "the prohibition of discrimination on grounds of nationality laid down in Article [39] of the Treaty must be regarded as applying to private persons as well". In reaching this conclusion, the Court swept aside the misgivings voiced by Fennelly A.G., who indicated that private parties should only be bound to refrain from direct, but not from indirect discrimination (but one might wonder whether the Advocate General's test would not raise more problems than it solves). This ruling differs fundamentally from that in *Walrave* in that the conduct complained of here was the isolated act of an individual employer. On the other hand, *Angonese* is confined to discrimination, whereas the celebrated ruling in *Bosman* shows that the *Walrave* principles extend to non-discriminatory restrictions.[101] What is more, *Angonese* relates exclusively to the free movement of workers under Article 39.

4.37 Having thus reviewed the relevant strands in the case law, we shall now

---

[98] See n.23 above.
[99] n.5 to his Opinion.
[100] Case C-281/98 [2000] E.C.R. I-4139, noted by Lane and Nic Shuibhne, [2000] C.M.L. Rev. 1237.
[101] n.88 above.

turn to the recent literature, taking as our starting-point Roth's article[102] published in 1995. On an analysis of the case law as it then stood—prior to such crucial judgments as *Bosman* and *Angonese*—he found little evidence that the Treaty provisions on the four freedoms were to be construed as placing any burden directly on private parties. This approach he regarded as sound. In contrast, he saw a close parallel between the more general prohibition in Article 12 on discrimination on the basis of nationality and Article 141, and deduced from this that the principle laid down in *Defrenne* was to be applied to Article 12. Equally, according to him the broader language of Article 12 confirmed this view. At the same time, he approved of the Court's approach to "collective rules" in *Walrave*. He therefore advocated a two-pronged approach: (i) "collective rules" of the *Walrave* type would be caught by the Treaty provisions on the four freedoms; (ii) beyond that, only Article 12 would apply to private action.

While Roth's paper would appear to have influenced the Court in *Ferlini* as to point (ii), the ruling in *Angonese* appears to be at variance with his point (i). The fact is that his approach is beset by a fundamental contradiction: the Court has repeatedly held that Articles 39 and 49 give concrete expression to the more general rule in Article 12[103]; so why should the latter provision impose a burden on private parties and not Articles 39 and 49? Article 12 does not apply at all to discrimination against imports as such[104]; and even the most far-fetched construction of that provision would scarcely permit it to be extended to export restrictions.

Steindorff[105] advocates the application of a proportionality test whereby, in view of their more restrictive nature, the acts of sporting and other associations would be judged more strictly than those of isolated individuals. With the greatest of respect, however, it is by no means clear how such a vague test would operate in practice. This author also appears to overlook the conceptual and practical problems entailed in such a broad approach.

In her detailed analysis of the ruling in *Bosman*, Kluth[106] cautions against overstretching the four freedoms. While conceding that associations may in practice have the power to impose highly restrictive measures on the market, she stresses that those freedoms are primarily designed for the benefit of private parties, and are not in general intended to restrain them. She also warns of the dangers of interfering with the mechanisms of Articles 81 and 82—including the grant of exemptions under Article 81(3)—which are specifically designed for dealing with the acts of private parties.

Baquero Cruz[107] also urges caution, since he would be equally loath to encroach on Articles 81 and 82. He would confine the application of the Treaty provisions on the four freedoms to private action which is akin to State action in

---

[102] n.69 above.
[103] See, *e.g. Walrave*, para. 32, *Angonese*, para. 35.
[104] See para. 6.26 below.
[105] See n.69 above.
[106] See n.69 above.
[107] See n.69 above.

that it operates as a form of "private legislation". This would in effect amount to a version of the *Walrave* test which he believes to be in need of clarification. If a person wishing to exercise an economic activity is *de facto* required to be a member of a particular association, then the measures taken by that association are, he claims, to be regarded as "private legislation"—regardless of whether that association enjoys a monopoly. Yet he would extend the horizontal effect of the free movement provisions beyond the collective rules of such organisations to cover collective acts such as the actions of trade unions.

4.38 How then is the first question to be answered, in the light of these primary and secondary sources? Only a tentative answer can be given in view of the case law which, to say the least, points in a variety of different directions.

At this stage, it appears scarcely conceivable that the Court would apply *Angonese* by analogy to the free movement of goods. Discrimination against migrant workers may entail an affront to the dignity of the individual. Indeed, it may even involve, or be akin to, acts of a racist nature. Save perhaps in highly exceptional cases, no such considerations will arise in relation to restrictions on movements of goods. Where an individual acting alone or as part of an insignificant group chooses to avoid purchasing goods from another Member State, that can scarcely be regarded as an offence to the dignity of the individual manufacturer or trader.

What is more, as we noticed in paragraph 1.13 above, the freedoms relating to the movement of natural persons concern the individual's right to live and work in the country of his choice and not be separated from his immediate family, and are thus closely bound up with rights protected under the European Convention.

Moreover, the economic drawbacks of rendering an "embargo" imposed by an individual acting alone contrary to Community law considerably outweigh the advantages—quite apart from the fact that such a prohibition would be largely unenforceable. As the turbulent years leading up to *Keck*[108] have shown, no useful purpose would be served by construing Article 28 or Article 29 so widely as to render them unworkable.

Another relevant factor is that the Treaty of Amsterdam introduced a new Article 13 into the EC Treaty providing for Council legislation to "combat discrimination based on sex, racial or ethnic origin, religion or belief, disability, age or sexual orientation". On this basis, the Council has enacted Council Directive 2000/43 implementing the principle of equal treatment between persons irrespective of racial or ethnic origin.[109] Subject to exceptions, this instrument prohibits direct or indirect discrimination based on racial or ethnic

---

[108] Cases C-267-8/91 [1993] E.C.R. I 6097; see paras 6.50 *et seq.* below.
[109] [2000] O.J. L180/22. See also generally Council Directive 2000/78 establishing a framework for equal treatment in employment and occupation ([2000] O.J. L303/16), which prohibits, subject to exceptions, direct or indirect discrimination based on religion or belief, disability, age or sexual orientation as regards employment and related matters; and Council Decision 2000/750 establishing a Community action programme to combat discrimination (2001 to 2006) ([2000] O.J. L303/23).

origin as regards employment and related matters, as well as social advantages, education and housing. The Member States are required to implement this Directive by July 19, 2003 at the latest. The language of this Directive leaves no room for doubt that, once it has been duly implemented, private parties will be required to observe it; indeed, Member States are required to provide for "effective, proportionate and dissuasive" sanctions for breaches of national implementing legislation. Since discrimination against migrant workers by private parties will frequently constitute direct or indirect discrimination on racial or ethnic grounds contrary to this Directive, the practical impact of the ruling in *Angonese* may be more limited than might appear at first sight.[110] Accordingly, it is suggested that this is an exception to the general trend of convergence between the four freedoms which we noticed at paragraph 1.12 above.

4.39 On the other hand, nothing would appear to preclude the *Walrave* line of case law being transposed to the free movement of goods, at least in its narrow, pristine form (*i.e.* in so far as it applies to organisations or bodies which regulate an economic activity in a "collective manner"). More questionable is whether the broader test in *Ferlini* should be applied, according to which it suffices to show that "a group or organisation ... exercises a certain power over individuals and is in a position to impose on them conditions which adversely affect the exercise of fundamental freedoms guaranteed under the Treaty". Even the *Walrave* formulation is unduly vague and requires further clarification, as Baquero Cruz has correctly pointed out. Caution perhaps suggests that it should be limited to the clearest cases of "private legislation". Whether it should be extended to the other types of act set out in paragraph 4.26 above is more questionable.

4.40 At all events, one point does seem clear: to the extent that private parties are bound by Articles 28 and 29, they can rely on the exceptions in Article 30 in the same way as the Member States. This emerges from *Bosman*, where the Court extended to individuals the right to rely on exceptions to Article 39, saying: "There is nothing to preclude individuals from relying on justifications on grounds of public policy, public security and public health. Neither the scope nor the content of those grounds of justification is in any way affected by the public or private nature of the rules in question".[111] This approach appears to be entirely logical.[112]

C. The Second Question

4.41 The issue here is whether Articles 28 to 30 may be relied on in court proceedings against a private party, whether or not the acts of such parties are caught by those provisions. In such cases, the private party in question merely

---

[110] This Directive would not, however, apply to the facts of *Angonese* itself, which concerned an Italian national returning to his home State following a period of study in Austria.

[111] Para. 86.

[112] See, *contra*, the note on *Bosman* by Mortelmans, who doubts whether it is right that general interests such as public policy and public security (as opposed to, say, consumer protection) should be left to private organisations: [1996] S.E.W. 1996.

bears the consequences of the fact that the relevant State measure is at variance with these articles. It follows from the Court's rulings on intellectual property considered at paragraph 4.30 above that it has in effect given an affirmative reply to this question.[113]

D The Third Question

4.42 The Treaty provides for no procedure whereby the Commission may take action against private parties for the breach of Articles 28 or 29. The acts of private parties not attributable to the State as such cannot give rise to infringement proceedings under Article 226 of the Treaty, save in the somewhat extreme circumstances set out in the judgment in *Commission v France*. In that event, the Commission must rely on Article 10 of the Treaty as well as Article 28 or 29, as the case may be.

Following that judgment, the Council enacted Regulation 2679/98 on the functioning of the internal market in relation to the free movement of goods among the Member States,[114] which empowers the Commission to call upon a Member State to take immediate action in urgent cases. That instrument applies to obstacles to the free movement of goods involving either the "action" or the "inaction" of Member States. According to Article 1(2), "the term 'inaction' shall cover the case when the competent authorities of a Member State, in the presence of an obstacle caused by actions taken by private individuals, fail to take all necessary and proportionate measures within their powers with a view to removing the obstacle and ensuring the free movement of goods in their territory". Thus this Regulation is clearly applicable to situations such as that in *Commission v France*. However, as explained more fully in paras 12.96 *et seq.* below, the Commission only enjoys limited powers under this provision.

IV. CONCLUSION

4.43 In summary, the Member States in the broadest sense are bound by Articles 28 to 30; they will be held responsible for any act which is *de facto* attributable to them, and this possibly includes measures which they have accepted only tacitly. Equally, the extent to which Community legislation must comply with the same principles is largely settled by the case law. In contrast, a major question mark continues to hang over the extent to which private parties are bound by these provisions.

In principle, the other Chapters of this book concern only those measures which are attributable to the Member States. Measures attributable to the Community institutions or to private parties are only referred to incidentally. Having said that, the principles governing the liability of Member States under Article 10 read with Articles 28 and 29 are considered at paragraph 6.109 below.

---

[113] See also generally Case C-443/98 *Unilever Italia v Central Food* [2000] E.C.R. I-7535; that judgment is discussed at para 12.82 below.
[114] [1998] O.J. L337/8.

CHAPTER V

Quantitative Restrictions

5.01 Quantitative restrictions on imports and exports are prohibited by Articles 28 (ex 30) and 29 (ex 34) respectively of the Treaty of Rome, unless they are justified under Article 30 (ex 36).

This Chapter is divided into three sections covering respectively the timetable for the abolition of these restrictions, the direct applicability of the prohibition, and the definition of the concept of quantitative restrictions. Article 30 is not considered in this Chapter, since it is the subject of Chapter VIII. Other exceptions to the prohibition on quantitative restrictions will be discussed in Chapter IX.

I. THE TIMETABLE

5.02 With respect to imports, the basic prohibition on quantitative restrictions is to be found in Article 28, which provides:

> "Quantitative restrictions on imports and all measures having equivalent effect shall be prohibited between Member States."

This provision underwent certain minor amendments as a result of the Treaty of Amsterdam,[1] but these had no effect on its substance.

5.03 Today Article 28 has long since ceased to be subject to any transitional provisions, but it is nevertheless appropriate to consider briefly the timetable for the abolition of quantitative restrictions. Those interested in a fuller account of these provisions should consult the previous edition of this book.

The transitional provisions concerned (ex Articles 31 to 33 and 35 EC) were removed from the text of the EC Treaty by the Treaty of Amsterdam. The former Articles 31 and 32 EC laid down a "standstill" rule as from the date of entry into force of the Treaty of Rome. The former Article 31 required the Member States to refrain from introducing new quantitative restrictions as between themselves, whereas the first paragraph of the old Article 32 prohibited them from making existing quotas more restrictive. The second paragraph of Article 32 declared that quotas were to be abolished by the end of the transitional period (December 31, 1969) at the latest. Article 33 set out the system for

---

[1] See para. 1.09 above.

their progressive abolition during that period. Article 35 stated that the abolition of quantitative restrictions could be effected more rapidly than was provided for in Article 33.

The Commission took advantage of that possibility by adopting Council Decision 66/532 of July 26, 1966,[2] which required quantitative restrictions to be abolished immediately. However, Article 3 of that decision expressly excludes agricultural products from its scope. All the regulations establishing common market organisations[3] for agricultural products during the transitional period prohibited quantitative restrictions with respect to those products from the date of their entry into force. For agricultural products not yet subject to a common market organisation the prohibition took effect at the end of the transitional period.[4]

5.04 Article 29 EC as amended by the Treaty of Amsterdam reads as follows:

> "Quantitative restrictions on exports, and all measures having equivalent effect, shall be prohibited between Member States."

As with Article 28, the amendments introduced by the Treaty of Amsterdam did not affect the substance of Article 29: the latter Treaty simply removed the second paragraph of the former Article 34, which provided for a transitional period for quantitative restrictions on exports running until the end of the first stage of the transitional period, namely December 31, 1961. The better view is that the prohibition applied to agricultural products as from the same date. Although the Treaty did not expressly require Member States to refrain from introducing new restrictions on exports during the first stage of the transitional period, such an obligation was necessarily implicit.[5]

5.05 The first Act of Accession provided for the abolition of quantitative restrictions on imports and exports between the old and the new Member States as from its entry into force on January 1, 1973: Article 42. However, the prohibition took effect one month later for agricultural products subject to a common market organisation at the date of accession: Articles 60(1) and 151. For other agricultural products quantitative restrictions have been prohibited since January 1, 1978.[6] In addition, Article 43 entitled Member States contained specific provisions on restrictions on exports of waste and scrap metal of iron

---

[2] [1966] J.O. 165. This was preceded by two earlier acceleration decisions: those of May 12, 1960 (J.O. September 12, 1960) and May 15, 1962 (J.O. May 28, 1962).
[3] For the meaning of this term, see para. 10.01 below.
[4] See para. 10.02 below.
[5] This can be deduced in particular from the fact that the former Art. 34(2) required Member States to abolish, by the end of the first stage of the transitional period, export restrictions "which are in existence when this Treaty enters into force": see Waelbroeck, *Le Droit de la Communauté Economique Européenne* (1970), Vol. 1, 113; Wägenbaur in Groeben, Boeckh, Thiesing and Ehlermann, *Kommentar zum EWG-Vertrag* (1983), Vol. 1, 279.
[6] Art. 60(2) Act of Accession, as interpreted by the Court in Cases 118/78 *Meijer v Department of Trade* [1979] E.C.R. 1387; [1979] 2 C.M.L.R. 398; and 231/78; *Commission v United Kingdom (potatoes)* [1979] E.C.R. 1447; [1979] C.M.L.R. 427.

and steel for a two-year period, while Protocols 6 and 7 contained certain transitional measures in favour of Ireland.

5.06 The Act of Accession of Greece[7] likewise provided for the immediate abolition of quantitative restrictions on imports or exports between the Nine and Greece as from the date of accession, namely January 1, 1981: Article 35. This applied also to agricultural products covered by a common organisation of the market: Article 65(1). Transitional provisions for specific products were enshrined in Articles 36 (read with Annex III to the Act), 37 and 65(2).[8]

5.07 Spain and Portugal acceded to the Community on January 1, 1986. By virtue of Article 42 of the Act of Accession[9] quantitative restrictions on imports and exports between the Ten and Spain were to be abolished on the same day. However, that Act of Accession contained a large number of transitional provisions, all of which prevailed over the Single European Act by virtue of Article 28 of the latter instrument.

Transitional exceptions for industrial products were contained in Articles 43, 45, 46, 47 and 49 (read with Protocol 9 to the Act).[10] Agricultural products were subject to the special provisions of Articles 76 *et seq.*[11]

Similarly, Article 202 provided that quantitative restrictions on imports and exports between Portugal and the Ten were to be abolished on January 1, 1986. Transitional exceptions were contained in Articles 203, 206 (read with Protocol 17) 207 (read with Protocol 18) and 209.[12] As regards trade between Portugal and the Ten in agricultural products covered by a common market organisation, Articles 244 *et seq.* mirrored those relating to Spain (Articles 76(1) and 81 to 86).[13] However, for the agricultural products caught by Article 259 a different set of provisions, contained notably in Articles 269 to 279, applied. Trade between Spain and Portugal was governed by Article 54 and 214 (read with Protocol 3), as well as by Articles 88 and 256.

5.08 Austria, Sweden and Finland acceded to the Community on January 1, 1995.[14] Immediately prior to that, all three countries had been party to the EEA Agreement, which is described at length in Chapter XIII. Consequently, as

---

[7] [1979] O.J. L291.

[8] On Art. 65(2), see Case 194/85 *Commission v Greece* (bananas) [1988] E.C.R. 1037.

[9] [1985] O.J. L302, see generally Didier and Grisay, "Adhésion de l'Espagne et du Portugal: régime douanier des échanges de produits industriels" [1987] C.D.E. 255.

[10] Art. 47 contained an important exception relating to patents for pharmaceutical products; see para. 8.205 below.

[11] See also Case 119/86 *Spain v Council and Commission* [1987] E.C.R.

[12] Art. 209 was the counterpart for Portugal to Art. 47.

[13] However, the supplementary trade mechanism has been abolished with respect to a number of products by Council Reg. 743/9 ([1993] O.J. L77/9). Measures matching Council Regs 3817/92 and 3818/92 were also adopted: Council Regs 744/93 ([1993] O.J. L77/11) and 745/93 ([1993] O.J. L77/12).

[14] [1994] O.J. C241/1; this Act was adjusted by the Council Decision of January 1, 1995 to take account of the decision of the people of Norway not to accede ([1995] O.J. L1/1). See Booss and Forman, "Enlargement: Legal and Procedural Aspects" (1995) C.M.L. Rev. 95.

regards industrial products, those States were already part of a free trade area with the Twelve. It follows that no transitional provisions in relation to quantitative restrictions and measures of equivalent effect were necessary with regard to such products.[15] Moreover, Article 137 of the Act of Accession abolished all such restrictions on trade in agricultural products, except where the Act itself provided otherwise. In fact, there were no noteworthy exceptions of this kind. Finally, Article 153 of the Act of Accession provided:

> "In order not to hamper the proper functioning of the internal market, the enforcement of the new Member States' national rules during the transitional period referred to in this Act shall not lead to border controls between Member States."

5.09 As already mentioned, the transitional exceptions to the prohibition on quantitative restrictions in Articles 28 and 29 have all lapsed, so that today those restrictions are subject only to those exceptions discussed in Chapters VIII and IX below.

II. DIRECT EFFECT

5.10 In *Salgoil v Italian Ministry for Foreign Trade*,[16] the Court found that the initial paragraphs of Articles 31 and 32—the contents of which were discussed at the beginning of this Chapter—produced "direct effects on the legal relationships between Member States and those subject to their jurisdiction".[17]

Not until 1977 did the Court decide this point with respect to Article 28 itself, in *Iannelli v Meroni*.[18] It did so in the following terms:

> "The prohibition of quantitative restrictions and measures having equivalent effect laid down in Article [28] of the Treaty is mandatory and explicit and its implementation does not require any subsequent intervention of the Member States or Community institutions.
>
> The prohibition therefore has direct effect and creates individual rights which national courts must protect; this occurred at the end of the transitional period at the latest, that is to say on January 1, 1970 as the provisions of the second paragraph of [the old Article 32] of the Treaty indicate."

Likewise in *Pigs Marketing Board v Redmond*[19] the Court held that Articles 28 and 29 were "directly applicable and that as such they confer on individuals rights which the courts of Member States must protect". It is clear that these pronouncements apply equally to quantitative restrictions and to measures of equivalent effect.

---

[15] See, however, Art. 99 of that Act of Accession and Case C-233/97 *KappAhl* [1998] E.C.R. I-8069 (para. 2.21 above).

[16] Case 13/68 [1968] E.C.R. 453; [1969] C.M.L.R. 181.

[17] In the case of Art. 31 the Court held that such effects were delayed for a period of up to six months, by virtue of the second paragraph of that Article.

[18] Case 74/76 [1977] E.C.R. 557; [1977] 2 C.M.L.R. 688.

[19] Case 83/78 [1978] E.C.R. 2347; [1979] 2 C.M.L.R. 177. See also Case C-179/90 *Merci convenzionali porto di Genova v Siderurgica Gabrielli* [1991] E.C.R. I-5889; and C-277/91 *Ligur Carni v Unità Sanitaria Locale* [1993] E.C.R. I-6621.

III. THE DEFINITION OF QUANTITATIVE RESTRICTIONS

5.11 The Court of Justice has held that "the prohibition on quantitative restrictions covers measures which amount to a total or partial restraint of, according to the circumstances, imports, exports or goods in transit": *Geddo v Ente Nazionale Risi.*[20] In that case it was clear beyond all doubt that the national measure at issue did not fall within that definition.

However, this matter was raised subsequently with a prohibition on importing indecent or obscene articles into the United Kingdom. The case in question was *R. v Henn and Darby*[21] in which the defendants had been convicted before the English courts of contravening this prohibition.

When it was contended before it that this provision was contrary to Article 28, the Court of Appeal[22] rejected this argument, *inter alia* on the grounds that the term "quantitative restrictions" connoted restrictions "concerned with quantity" and not total prohibitions. This ruling caused some surprise, in that one of the principal aims of the Treaty of Rome was to guard against protectionism between the Member States—an aim which would be completely undermined if the Court of Appeal's interpretation were followed. More concretely, the Court of Appeal's judgment was contrary to the ruling of the Court of Justice in the *Geddo* case and failed to take account of the opening words of Article 30:

"The provisions of Articles 28 and 29 shall not preclude *prohibitions*[23] or restrictions on imports, exports or goods in transit justified on grounds of public morality..."

The defendants then appealed to the House of Lords, which made its first reference ever to the Court of Justice on this and other points arising out of the case. It was not contended by any party before the Court of Justice that the Court of Appeal's interpretation had been correct and it was virtually a foregone conclusion that the Court would hold, as indeed it did, that a prohibition on imports of pornographic articles fell under Article 28. Nevertheless it is interesting to note that, although the reference only contemplated the possibility that the prohibition was a measure of equivalent effect, both the Advocate General and the Court specifically found that it was a quantitative restriction pure and simple.

5.12 Thus the concept of quantitative restrictions covers not only "quotas", which term appeared in the old Articles 32 and 33, but also absolute prohibitions on imports or exports, as the case may be. This is so whatever the nature of the imports or exports, be they reimports or goods in transit,[24] or re-exports. Furthermore, a quantitative restriction may be based on legislation or merely be an administrative practice.[25] On the other hand, the Articles in question only

---

[20] Case 2/73 [1973] E.C.R. 865 at 879; [1974] 1 C.M.L.R. 13 at 42.
[21] Case 34/79 [1979] E.C.R. 3795; [1980] 1 C.M.L.R. 246; see paras 8.16 and 8.41 *et seq.* below.
[22] [1978] 1 W.L.R. 1031.
[23] The italics are those of the author.
[24] See paras 2.26 and 2.27 above.
[25] See paras 6.11 *et seq.* below.

cover non-tariff quotas; under these, import or export bans are imposed once the ceiling has been reached. Tariff quotas (under which customs duties are imposed on goods exceeding the ceiling laid down) infringe Article 25 (ex 12 to 16) EC if they are imposed between Member States.

5.13 Nevertheless, the exact dividing line between quantitative restrictions and measures of equivalent effect is not yet fully clear.[26] For instance, the requirement of import or export licences has been held to constitute a measure of equivalent effect.[27] Yet such a requirement amounts to a prohibition on imports or exports without the requisite licence.[28] The same applies with respect to the obligation to produce sanitary or veterinary certificates for imports or exports.[29]

Equally, it is unclear whether an import prohibition designed to protect industrial property rights constitutes a quantitative restriction rather than a measure of equivalent effect.

5.14 In any case, it would seem that the distinction between quantitative restrictions and measures of equivalent effect is only material where exceptionally only the former are expressly prohibited. This has occurred with respect to certain transitional periods.[30] Also, Protocol 3 to the first Act of Accession on the Channel Islands and the Isle of Man begins:

"The Community rules on customs matters and quantitative restrictions, in particular those of the Act of Accession, shall apply to the Channel Islands and the Isle of Man under the same conditions as they apply to the United Kingdom."[31]

Although measures of equivalent effect are not expressly mentioned, it is probable that this Protocol covers such measures[32]—particularly in the light of the Court's above quoted ruling in *Iannelli v Meroni* which suggests that "quotas" in the old Article 32 covered measures of equivalent effect.

Unless otherwise stated, the rules discussed in this book apply in the same way to quantitative restrictions as to measures of equivalent effect.

---

[26] In many other cases concerning measures which might properly be described as quantitative restrictions, the Court has ruled instead that those measures constituted measures of equivalent effect or has simply stated without more that they were contrary to Art. 28; see, *e.g.* Case 40/82 *Commission v United Kingdom (Newcastle disease)* [1982] E.C.R. 2793; [1982] 3 C.M.L.R. 497 and [1984] E.C.R. 283; Case 74/82 *Commission v Ireland* [1984] E.C.R. 317; Case 59/82 *Schutzverband gegen Unwesen in der Wirtschaft v Wienvertriebs* [1983] E.C.R. 1217; [1984] 1 C.M.L.R. 319; and Case 261/85 *Commission v United Kingdom (pasteurised milk)* [1988] 2 C.M.L.R. 11. As to exports, see Case 172/82 *Syndicat National des Fabricants Raffineurs d'Huile de Graissage v Inter-Huiles* [1983] E.C.R. 555; [1983] 3 C.M.L.R. 485. In none of these cases has anything turned on the distinction between quantitative restrictions and measures of equivalent effect.

[27] See para. 7.03 below.

[28] Case 194/85 (see n.8 above) was concerned with an import licensing system under which licences were always or almost always refused. The Court found it unnecessary to decide whether this system constituted a quantitative restriction or a measure of equivalent effect.

[29] See para. 7.05 below.

[30] *e.g.* Decision 66/532 (n.2 above) and Art. 42 of the first Act of Accession.

[31] See para. 3.03 above.

[32] See para. 3.03 above.

CHAPTER VI

Measures of Equivalent Effect: General

6.01 Article 28 (formerly Article 30) provides: "Quantitative restrictions on imports and all measures having equivalent effect shall ... be prohibited between Member States". Article 29 (formerly Article 34) is couched in the same terms, except that it applies to restrictions on exports.

As will be seen, the concept of measures of equivalent effect to quantitative restrictions differs from that of quantitative restrictions themselves in that it is considerably wider and more complex. Indeed the definition of this concept forms the crux of this book. For this reason this Chapter contains more sections than Chapter V. These are: a chronological survey, the meaning of "measures", the definition of measures of equivalent effect on imports, the definition of such measures relating to exports, *de facto* harmonisation, regional measures, "purely national" restrictions, the abuse of Articles 28 and 29, the application of Article 10 in conjunction with Articles 28 and/or 29, and finally the burden of proof. The direct applicability of the prohibition of measures of equivalent effect on imports and exports has already been dealt with in paragraph 5.10 above. The compatibility of specific national measures with Articles 28 and 29 will be considered in Chapter VII.

Finally, in determining whether a particular measure falls under Article 28 (or Article 29), it is imperative to proceed in two stages. The first question to ask is: does this measure restrict imports (or exports) so as to be caught by Article 28 (or Article 29)? If so, then the second question arises, namely: is the measure nevertheless justified in Community law and thus lawful? Justification is considered in Chapter VIII.

I. A CHRONOLOGICAL SURVEY

6.02 The substance of Articles 28 to 30 EC (Articles 30 to 36 prior to the Treaty of Amsterdam) has never been amended, although the latter Treaty renumbered those articles and at the same time removed the transitional provisions which had long since lapsed. However, over the years a number of other Treaty amendments have been introduced, which have altered the context in which these provisions apply. At all events, it is appropriate to begin by considering the original timetable for the abolition of measures of equivalent effect.

A. The Original Timetable

6.03   The reader is referred to paragraphs 5.02 to 5.09 above which cover the timetable for the abolition of quantitative restrictions, since the rules are broadly the same.

As between the original Member States the only difference in the timetable of abolition of quantitative restrictions and measures of equivalent effect is that Decision 66/532[1] only applied to quantitative restrictions. Consequently the prohibition on measures of equivalent effect on imports did not take effect until the end of the transitional period[2] except as regards products already covered by a common market organisation or by a directive based on the old Article 33(7). That paragraph provided:

> "The Commission shall issue directives establishing the procedure and timetable in accordance with which the Member States shall abolish, as between themselves, any measures in existence when this Treaty enters into force which have an effect equivalent to quotas."

This provision did not apply to exports.

6.04   It is clear from the context, and in particular the second paragraph of the old Article 32, that the old Article 33(7) lapsed at the end of the transitional period. That is why both provisions were repealed by the Treaty of Amsterdam. During the transitional period the Commission adopted five directives on the basis of this provision:

— Directive 64/486[3] requiring the Federal Republic of Germany progressively to abolish its import restrictions on potatoes; this Directive was exceptional in that it was addressed to one Member State only, the others being addressed to all the Member States;

— Directive 66/682[4] requiring the Member States to abolish, save for certain listed products, measures by which the importation is made conditional on the exportation or purchase or sale of a domestic product;

— Directive 66/683[5] requiring the Member States to abolish, other than for certain products listed in the annex to the Directive, measures which

---

[1] [1966] J.O. 165.
[2] By some quirk of drafting the Treaty did not actually state that measures of equivalent effect on imports were to be abolished at the end of the transitional period. The second para. of the old Art. 32 stipulated that "quotas shall be abolished by the end of the transitional period at the latest." It appears that the term "quotas" must be stretched beyond its natural meaning to include measures of equivalent effect; this appears to be the approach adopted by the Court in Case 74/76 *Iannelli v Meroni* [1977] E.C.R. 557; [1977] 2 C.M.L.R. 688; see para. 5.10 above. In any case, there cannot be a shadow of doubt that the prohibition on measures of equivalent effect on imports did take effect at the end of the transitional period: see, *e.g.* the *Iannelli* case.
[3] [1964] J.O. 2253.
[4] [1966] J.O. 3745.
[5] [1966] J.O. 3748.

partially or totally prohibit the use of an imported product; or subject the entitlement to a benefit, other than an aid within the meaning of Article 87 (ex 92) of the Treaty, to the total or partial use of a national product;

— Directive 70/32[6] requiring the Member States to abolish legislative provisions and put an end to administrative practices discriminating against the supply of imported goods to public authorities;

— Directive 70/50,[7] which was by far the most important of the five directives; it was not limited to any particular type of measure like the others, but set out a lengthy list of measures which it required the Member States to abolish as being measures of equivalent effect. It also set out the Commission's general thinking as to the scope and meaning of this concept; it will be described in greater detail during the course of this Chapter.

6.05 During the transitional period these directives may well have been directly effective[8] and thus capable of being relied on by individuals before the national courts. However, at the end of the transitional period Article 28 itself acquired direct effect,[9] so that this function of the directives has been superseded. Also, any clauses in the directives exempting particular products or measures lapsed at the end of the transitional period.

In addition, the former Article 33(7) empowered the Commission to issue directives relating only to measures "in existence when this Treaty enters into force."[10] However, it would be anomalous if different criteria were to apply as regards measures adopted after the Treaty came into force. Moreover, in *Commission v Germany*,[11] the Court cited the Court cited Directive 70/50 with approval with respect to a German statute of 1971, albeit without referring to this particular issue.

While the Court has often quoted and followed Directive 70/50, it has also, as we shall see later,[12] implicitly rejected certain aspects of it, in particular its approach to "indistinctly applicable" measures.

6.06 What is the effect of Directive 70/50 since the end of the transitional period? In *Commission v Ireland* ("Buy Irish")[13] the Court declined to rule on the challenge to the directive mounted by the defendant. In Ireland's view the former Article 33(7), on which the directive was based, only empowered the Commission to lay down procedures and timetables for the abolition of mea-

---

[6] [1970] J.O. L13/1, para. 7.18 below.
[7] [1970] J.O. L13/29. See Annex II to this Book.
[8] See generally Case 33/70 *SACE v Italian Ministry of Finance* [1970] E.C.R. 1213; [1971] C.M.L.R. 123.
[9] Para. 5.10 above.
[10] See Graf, *Der Begriff "Maßnahmen gleicher Wirkung wie mengenmässige Einfuhrbeschränkungen" im EWG-Vertrag* (1972) 25.
[11] Case 12/74 [1975] E.C.R. 181 at 193; [1975] 1 C.M.L.R. 340 at 364 *et seq.*; para. 7.54 below.
[12] See paras 6.43 and 7.03 below.
[13] Case 249/81 [1982] E.C.R. 4005; [1983] 2 C.M.L.R. 104.

sures of equivalent effect, without defining that concept. The Commission countered this with the argument that the power to give a non-exhaustive definition of the concept of measures of equivalent effect must have been impliedly conferred on it by Article 33(7). Since that concept was not defined in the Treaty, great uncertainty would have ensued if the Commission had laid down procedures and timetables without defining the concept. Capotorti A.G. endorsed the view put forward by the Irish Government that the directive was *ultra vires.*

Secondly, in *Commission v Italy*[14] the Commission relied on Article 2(3)(b) of Directive 70/50 but the defendant advanced an argument based on the wording of that provision to show that it was not applicable. On this point the Court ruled:

> "With regard to the applicability of the criteria in Directive 70/50, it must be pointed out, as can be seen from the terms of Article 2(3) of that directive, that the measures having equivalent effect listed therein are advanced by way of example. Moreover, Directive 70/50 must be read in the light of Article 28 of the Treaty and it may not be relied upon as a means of defeating the objective set out in that Article, an objective which it itself is also intended to achieve. The Italian Republic's argument based on Directive 70/50 must therefore be rejected."

While in legal theory these directives may have been directly effective since their adoption, as a matter of practice they have been relegated in importance since the end of the transitional period, when Article 28 itself acquired direct effect. With the passage of time, the importance of Directive 70/50 has gradually waned so that today it merely serves as a set of non-binding guidelines to the interpretation of Article 28—in so far as they have not been implicitly set aside by the case law of the Court.

This assessment appears to be fully borne out by the Court's approach to Article 3 of Directive 70/50. In *Torfaen Borough Council v B & Q*[15] it based a crucial step in its reasoning on that provision. However, as explained in detail below, it was not long before that judgment fell out of favour and it was reversed by the decision in *Keck*[16] which proceeds on a quite different basis.

6.07   In any event, it is submitted that, by virtue of Article 14 (ex 7A) EC, part of Article 2(3)(r) lapsed on January 1, 1993. That provision, which was first introduced by the Single European Act, prohibited import controls "other than those inherent in the customs clearance procedure". It is submitted that the words cited here have lapsed. The reasoning behind this is set out below.[17]

---

[14] Case 103/84 (subsidies for the purchase of national vehicles) [1986] E.C.R. 1759; [1987] 2 C.M.L.R. 825.
[15] Case C-145/88 [1989] E.C.R. 3851; see also para. 6.52 below.
[16] Case C-267-8/91 [1993] E.C.R. I-6097.
[17] Paras 6.10, 7.04 and 12.12–12.20.

B. The Acts of Accession

6.08 Under the first Act of Accession, measures of equivalent effect to quantitative restrictions on imports and exports were to be abolished by January 1, 1975 by virtue of Article 42(2) of that Act.[18] The exceptions to that rule are those set out above at paragraph 5.05.

The provisions of the Greek Act of Accession already set out in paragraph 5.06 above also applied to measures of equivalent effect. However, Articles 36 to 38 of that Act set out various transitional periods for certain types of measure of equivalent effect.

As regards the Act of Accession of Spain and Portugal, the reader is referred generally to paragraph 5.07 above. By virtue of Article 42 measures of equivalent effect on imports and exports between Spain and the Ten were to be abolished on the date of accession (January 1, 1986), and the same applied to Portugal by virtue of Article 202. A transitional exception in favour of Spain was contained in Article 44. Transitional exceptions in favour of Portugal were contained in Articles 204 and 205.

Austria, Finland, and Sweden acceded to the Community on January 1, 1995. In so far as relevant, their Act of Accession is considered at paragraph 5.08 above.

6.09 Today all the transitional periods relating to Articles 28 and 29 have lapsed, so that those Articles are subject only to the permanent exception clauses discussed in Chapters VIII and IX.

C. The Single European Act

6.10 The Single European Act, which came into force on July 1, 1987, introduced a new Article 8A into the Treaty of Rome. That provision became Article 7A on November 1, 1993 with the entry into force of the Treaty of Maastricht and, with the renumbering introduced by the Treaty of Amsterdam, it is now Article 14. The first two paragraphs of that Article now read as follows:

> "1. The Community shall adopt measures with the aim of progressively establishing the internal market over a period expiring on 31 December 1992, in accordance with the provisions of this Article and of Articles 15, 26, 47(2), 49, 80, 93 and 95 and without prejudice to the other provisions of this Treaty.
>
> 2. The internal market shall comprise an area without internal frontiers in which the free movement of goods, persons, services and capital is ensured in accordance with the provisions of this Treaty."

This provision is considered at length at paragraphs 12.12 to 12.20 below. Suffice it to say at this juncture that since January 1, 1993 Member States are no longer entitled to carry out controls at their internal borders, save to the extent to which they effect the same controls within their territory. Controls at borders

---

[18] See Cases 15/74 *Centrafarm v Sterling Drug* [1974] E.C.R. 1147; [1974] C.M.L.R. 480; and 16/74 *Centrafarm v Winthrop* [1974] E.C.R. 1183; [1974] C.M.L.R. 480.

between Member States will be caught by Article 28 or Article 29 (depending on whether they relate to imports or to exports). However, they may be justified under Article 30.

Prior to the Single European Act, internal border controls had simply been accepted as a fact of life about which little could be done.[19] They were scarcely questioned. Indeed, Community VAT legislation actually introduced new controls. Article 14 changed all that. With effect from January 1, 1993, it has thus widened the material scope of Article 28 and 29 by making them applicable to border controls between Member States.[20]

II. THE MEANING OF "MEASURES"

A. General

6.11   The Commission has consistently taken the view that even non-binding acts may be caught by Article 28 or 29. This is shown by the preamble to Directive 70/50 where it stated:

> "Whereas for the purpose of Article [28] *et seq.* 'measures' means laws, regulations, administrative provisions, administrative practices, and all instruments issuing from a public authority, including recommendations;
> Whereas for the purposes of this Directive 'administrative practices' means any standard and regularly followed procedure of a public authority; whereas 'recommendations' means any instruments issuing from a public authority which, while not legally binding on the addressees thereof, cause them to pursue a certain conduct …".

In the "*Buy Irish*" case[21] the Court to a considerable extent endorsed the Commission's view that non-binding measures could constitute measures of equivalent effect. The Irish authorities had orchestrated an extensive campaign for the promotion of Irish goods within Ireland. This campaign was aimed at all categories of purchaser, be they individual consumers, industrial or commercial undertakings or State bodies. The Commission considered that taken as a whole these measures infringed Article 28. The Irish Government argued, *inter alia,* that they were not "measures" at all since they were not binding and that they therefore fell outside Article 28 altogether.

The Court rejected this defence. It held that the campaign reflected the Irish Government's "considered intention to substitute domestic products for imported products on the Irish market and thereby to check the flow of imports from other Member States." The campaign amounted:

> "to the establishment of a national practice, introduced by the Irish Government and prosecuted with its assistance, the potential effect of which on imports from other

---

[19] See para. 7.04 below.
[20] *ibid.*
[21] See n. 13 above.

Member States is comparable to that resulting from government measures of a binding nature.

Such practice cannot escape the prohibition laid down by Article [28] of the Treaty solely because it is not based on decisions which are binding upon undertakings. Even measures adopted by the government of a Member State which do not have binding effect may be capable of influencing the conduct of traders and consumers in that State and thus of frustrating the aims of the Community as set out in Article 2 and enlarged upon in Article 3 of the Treaty.

That is the case where, as in this instance, such a restrictive practice represents the implementation of a programme defined by the government which affects the national economy as a whole and which is intended to check the flow of trade between Member States by encouraging the purchase of domestic products, by means of an advertising campaign on a national scale and the organisation of special procedures applicable solely to domestic products and where those activities are attributable as a whole to the government and are pursued in an organised fashion throughout the national territory."

In this passage the Court did not go so far as to state that all non-binding measures emanating from the authorities of a Member State may fall under Article 28. Perhaps the reason for this was a desire to exclude ephemeral acts such as casual remarks by ministers, but they can probably not be described as acts of the Member States in any case. This ruling does not lay down any general criterion for distinguishing between acts constituting "measures" and mere ephemeral acts.

6.12 The same tendency can be discerned in the Court's ruling in *Commission v France* (postal franking machines).[22] That case concerned a British company, which had sought without success to have its franking machines approved by the defendant's authorities, although those machines were in lawful use in a considerable number of other countries throughout the world. The Commission put before the Court a history of lengthy delays and repeated rejections of the company's applications by the defendant's authorities. The Commission did not contend that the relevant French legislation was in any way unlawful, but only its application in practice.

The Court ruled as follows:

"The fact that a law or regulation such as that requiring prior approval for the marketing of postal franking machines conforms in formal terms to Article [28] of the [EC] Treaty is not sufficient to discharge a Member State of its obligations under that provision. Under the cloak of a general provision permitting the approval of machines imported from other Member States, the administration might very well adopt a systematically unfavourable attitude towards imported machines, either by allowing considerable delay in replying to applications for approval or in carrying out the examination procedure, or by refusing approval on the grounds of various alleged technical faults for which no detailed explanations are given or which prove to be inaccurate . . . .

It must however be noted that for an administrative practice to constitute a measure prohibited under Article [28] that practice must show a certain degree of consistency and generality. That generality must be assessed differently according to whether it is a

[22] Case 21/84 [1985] E.C.R. 1356.

market, such as that in postal franking machines, on which only a few undertakings are active. In the latter case, a national administration's treatment of a single undertaking may constitute a measure incompatible with Article [28]."

While it is clearly right to exclude purely ephemeral acts, the criterion laid down here seems excessively narrow: taken at its face value it would appear to leave the door open to abuse by Member States in sectors served by a large number of traders. Why should the lawfulness of an unjustified restriction depend on the number of competitors on the market? Moreover, the test propounded by the Court opens a Pandora's box of conceptual difficulties: "few", "numerous", "traders" and "market"[23] may all have to be defined.

6.13   Other types of non-legislative act may also constitute "measures" for this purpose. Thus, the financing of a scheme or project or the grant of a loan by public authorities may constitute a "measure"—for example the grant of a loan to public officials for the purchase of cars on condition that they buy national cars.[24] Furthermore, a treaty concluded by a Member State can also be a "measure".[25]

6.14   A legislative act on the statute book will be a "measure" even if it is not applied or has not entered into force; this is not least because it will cause confusion and might deter potential importers.[26] Conversely, a legislative measure, which has not yet been formally adopted will constitute a measure if it is applied in practice. What is more, importers may be deterred from importing certain goods if they know that their sale is soon to be prohibited by the Member State in question. Thus, even if it were not applied, a draft legislative measure might contravene Articles 28 to 29, at least if it were used by a Member State to deter potential importers from importing goods which do not conform to the draft measure.

6.15   As has been explained earlier in this book,[27] measures falling under Article 28 or 29 may emanate not only from central government but also from

---

[23] One is reminded of the difficulties encountered in defining the relevant market under Art. 82 (ex 86) EC.

[24] See Case 192/84 (n.26 below) where a State ban on credit for imported farm machinery was held contrary to Art. 28 but see paras 6.25 *et seq.* below.

[25] Case C-3/91 *Exportur v LOR* [1922] E.C.R. I-5529, which concerned an agreement between France and Spain (para. 8 of the judgment). True, the Court referred to the fact the agreement was concluded after January 1, 1958, but it is submitted that no significance is to be attached to this. For the same point in relation to Article 43 EC, see Case C-46/98 *Commission v United Kingdom* (air transport) (judgment of November 5, 2002). However, as regards agreements between a Member State and a third country, see Art. 307 (ex 234) EC (paras 9.45 to 9.53 below).

[26] Para. 17 of the judgment in Case 192/84 *Commission v Greece* (credit for agricultural machinery) [1985] E.C.R. 3967; [1988] 1 C.M.L.R. 420 suggests that any act of a Member State which creates an "ambiguous and uncertain situation" to the detriment of imports may fall under Art. 28; see also the A.G. in Case 173/83 *Commission v France* (waste oils) [1985] E.C.R. 491 at 495; and Cases 167/73 *Commission v France* (merchant navy) [1974] E.C.R. 359; 159/78 *Commission v Italy* (customs agents) [1979] E.C.R. 3247; C-80/92 *Commission v Belgium* (radio communications equipment) [1994] E.C.R. I-1019.

[27] Para. 4.03 above.

regional or local government. They may also emanate from the executive, the legislature or the judiciary.[28]

6.16 A measure is not rendered compatible with Articles 28 and 29 simply because a procedure is provided under national law for obtaining an exemption. Thus in *International Fruit Company v Produktschap voor Groenten en Fruit*[29] the Court held that "a national measure, which requires, *even purely as a formality,* import or export licences or any other similar procedure"[30] was precluded by Articles 28 and 29. Also, in *Van Tiggele*,[31] having held that a particular system of minimum prices was contrary to Article 30, the Court continued:

> "This is the conclusion which must be drawn even though the competent authority is empowered to grant exemptions from the fixed minimum price and though this power is freely applied to imported products, since the requirement that importers and traders must comply with the administrative formalities inherent in such a system may in itself constitute a measure having an effect equivalent to a quantitative restriction."

This has been confirmed on several occasions.[32]

B. No *de minimis* Rule

6.17 As is well known, Article 81 (ex 85) EC relating to competition is subject to a *de minimis* rule.[33] In contrast, ever since its ruling in *Van de Haar*,[34] the Court has always steadfastly refused to apply a *de minimis* rule to restrictions on movements of goods between Member States.[35]

A rare dissenting note on this point is to be detected in Jacobs A.G.'s Opinion in *Leclerc-Siplec v TF1 Publicité*,[36] where he propounded the view that a "substantial restriction" on access to a national market should be shown. As he openly acknowledged, this would amount to a *de minimis* test. However, he did admit that it would be inappropriate to apply such a rule in every case; rather, he proposed that overtly discriminatory measures be covered by a *per se* prohibition, and that the *de minimis* rule would apply only to other restrictions. At all events, the Court implicitly rejected his suggestion.

---

[28] Para. 4.04 above.

[29] Cases 51-54/71 [1971] E.C.R. 1107: see para. 7.03 below.

[30] The italics are those of the author.

[31] Case 82/77 [1978] E.C.R. 25; [1978] 2 C.M.L.R. 528; see, however, para. 8.14 below.

[32] Case 27/80 *Fietje* [1980] E.C.R. 3839; [1981] 3 C.M.L.R. 722; Case C-131/93 *Commission v Germany* (Crayfish) [1994] E.C.R. I-3303; Case C-400/96 *Harpegnies* [1998] E.C.R. I-5121 at para. 33; and Case C-473/98 *Kemikalieinspektionen v Toolex Alpha* [2000] E.C.R. I-5681 at para. 37.

[33] Case 5/69 *Volk v Vervaecke* [1969] E.C.R. 295; Cases C-215 and 216/96 *Bagnasco v Banca Popolare di Novara* [1999] E.C.R. I-135, para. 34; and Commission Notice on *de minimis* agreements ([2001] O.J. C368/13). On the differences between the provisions relating to competition and Arts 28 to 30, see generally paras 4.26 and 6.33.

[34] Cases 177-8/82 [1984] E.C.R. 1797.

[35] See Cases 269/83 *Commission v France* (periodicals) [1985] E.C.R. 837; and Case 103/84, see n.14 above.

[36] Case C-412/93 [1995] E.C.R. I-179 at 195-6; see also the same A.G.'s Opinions in other cases, notably that of July 11, 2002 in Case C-112/00 *Schmidberger v Austria* (pending), paras 65 *et seq.*

The *de minimis* question arose once again in a most acute form in the charming and *clochermerlesque* case of *Bluhme*.[37] The defendant had been charged with infringing a ban on keeping nectar-gathering bees other than the subspecies *Apis mellifera mellifera* on the tiny Danish island of Læsø and certain neighbouring islands. The alleged purpose of this prohibition, which was imposed by the Danish Minister of Agriculture, was to protect this particular strain of bee from extinction on these islands. The Court was called upon to rule *inter alia* on whether, despite its limited geographical scope, such a ban could fall within Article 28.[38]

One of the arguments advanced by Denmark was that the decree fell outside Article 28 as being *de minimis*, since the decree covered only 0.3 per cent of Danish territory. Citing *Van de Haar*, Fennelly A.G. rejected that argument on the grounds that "the slight effect of the Decision, in volume terms, cannot, in itself, prevent the application of Article [28] of the Treaty". The Court ruled to the same effect, although curiously it did not address the *de minimis* point.[39]

6.18   While the Court has never given detailed reasons for rejecting the *de minimis* rule, it is submitted that its approach is fully warranted on a number of grounds.

First, as we noticed in Chapter IV, Articles 28 to 30 are directed predominantly or exclusively at State measures. Any measure emanating from any branch of the State and whatever the level of government—be it the smallest local authority—must be regarded as a matter of inherent importance, and must thus be deemed to have some incidence *per se* on interstate trade. To put it another way, as a consequence of its special position the State bears a higher duty than private bodies.

Second, as the Court pointed out in *Corsica Ferries France v Direction générale des douanes françaises*,[40] " ... the articles of the EEC Treaty concerning the free movement of goods, persons, services and capital are fundamental Community provisions and any restriction, even minor, of that freedom is prohibited".[41] If we are to take the four freedoms seriously as fundamental principles of Community law, then there is surely no room for a *de minimis* rule.

This proposition can be illustrated by reference to universally accepted human rights such as the right not to be imprisoned without due process of law. Surely it would be virtually inconceivable in any jurisdiction where the rule of law prevails for *habeas corpus* to be subject to any kind of *de minimis* rule. Precisely the same reasoning applies—albeit with less force—to the four freedoms enshrined in the Treaty of Rome. To take a relatively clear case, it would be hard

---

[37] C-67/97 [1998] E.C.R. I-8033.
[38] As mentioned at para. 6.95 below, restrictions on imports into part of the territory of a Member State may fall under Article 28.
[39] See also para. 8.23 below.
[40] Case C-49/89 [1989] E.C.R. I-4441, para. 8.
[41] Equally, in Case C-205/89 *Commission v Greece* [1991] E.C.R. I-1361 at 1377, the Court referred to the free movement of goods as "one of the fundamental principles of the common market"; and in Case C-265/95 *Commission v France* (violent protests by farmers) [1997] E.C.R. I-6959 at 6998 that freedom was described as "one of the fundamental principles of the Treaty".

to imagine the Court finding a national measure discriminating against workers from other Member States to be compatible with Article 39 (ex 48) of the Treaty, on the basis that only a small class of persons were affected[42]: for those individuals, the severity of the restriction is in no way lessened by the circumstance that their plight is shared by a relatively insignificant number in terms of the host State taken as a whole. Similarly, for the bee-keeper prevented from keeping the bees of his choice it is little comfort to know that the territory affected by the ban represents only a minute part of the surface area of the Member State concerned; nor will this circumstance be of any avail to him.

Third, the practical problems of applying a *de minimis* rule in relation to the free movement of goods are very considerable. To coin the words of Tesauro A.G., such an exercise would be "very difficult, if not downright impossible".[43] For instance, one might wonder whether the test would be purely statistical or whether other elements are to be taken into account. It would introduce a new element of legal uncertainty and thus make it far harder for national courts to apply Article 28.[44]

Precisely the same considerations apply to Article 29.[45]

III. MEASURES OF EQUIVALENT EFFECT ON IMPORTS

A. General

6.19 Quantitative restrictions always take effect at the borders of the Member State which imposes them. Measures of equivalent effect may do so, but need not. Some classic examples of measures of equivalent effect may be cited from Directive 70/50[46]:

"measures which ...

(f) lower the value of an imported product, in particular by causing a reduction in its intrinsic value, or increase its costs; ...

---

[42] Indeed, in Case C-19/92 *Kraus v Land Baden-Württemberg* [1993] E.C.R. I-1663 at 1677 Van Gerven A.G. said (in n.10 to his Opinion): "The number of Community nationals (compared with the number of Germans) who find themselves in this situation has no bearing, in my view, on the applicability of the principle of abolition of discrimination in Article [39]. The issue is whether the national rules are themselves discriminatory. It is sufficient, in this respect, for the rules to be such as to produce discriminatory effects for nationals, however few or many, of other Member States."

[43] Case C-292/92 *Hünermund v Landesapothekerkammer Baden-Württemberg* [1993] E.C.R. I-6787 at 6810-1.

[44] Assuming that the criterion would be statistical, a threshold would have to be set below which restrictions are to be regarded as insignificant (*e.g.* 5 per cent of the market of the Member State concerned); as with Article 81, this would no doubt be done across the board for all types of restriction. After that, the relevant market would have to be defined in each case, which is no easy matter. See also paras 6.63 and 6.67 *et seq.* below.

[45] However, if, as Jacobs A.G. suggests, the *de minimis* principle were not to apply to discriminatory measures, there would be no scope for any application of that principle to Art. 29 on the Court's current interpretation of that Article. See further section IV below.

[46] n.7 above.

(h)... subject imported products to conditions which are different from those laid down for domestic products and more difficult to satisfy; ...

(j) subject imported products only to conditions, in respect, in particular of shape, size, weight, composition, presentation, identification or putting up, or subject imported products to conditions which are different from those for domestic products and more difficult to satisfy;

(k) hinder the purchase by private individuals of imported products only, or encourage, require or give preference to the purchase of domestic products only;

...".

6.20   That the concept of measures of equivalent effect is indeed a wide one is confirmed by the classic definition of such measures set out in *Procureur du Roi v Dassonville*:

"All trading rules enacted by Member States, which are capable of hindering, directly or indirectly, actually or potentially, intra-Community trade are to be considered as measures having an effect equivalent to quantitative restrictions."[47]

Time and time again this definition has been repeated in the Court's case law, though regrettably with minor variations. For instance, the Court has been known to speak of "a direct or indirect, real or potential hindrance to imports between Member States".[48] Also, the word "trading"—which might with justification be regarded as extremely important—is generally omitted today.[49] However, there are at least three *recent* cases in which the word "trading" does appear.[50] No obvious explanation can be found for these surprising inconsistencies.

6.21   At all events, it is clear from this formula that one must look to the effects of a measure rather than to its aims, in deciding whether it falls under Article 28; yet, there are cases in which the Court has had regard to the object of a measure.[51] Furthermore, it is not necessary to show that a measure actually restricts imports, but only that it potentially does so.

It follows that it is inappropriate to consider statistical evidence as to the volume of imports of products subject to the national measure in question; even if imports have actually increased since the measure was introduced, they might have increased more in the absence of such a measure.[52] These are obviously factors of fundamental importance in the interpretation of Article 28.

---

[47] Case 8/74 [1974] E.C.R. 837 at 852; [1974] 2 C.M.L.R. 436 and 453.

[48] Case 4/75 *Rewe-Zentralfinanz v Landwirtschaftskammer* [1975] E.C.R. 843 at 858.

[49] *e.g.* Cases C-368/95 *Vereinigte Familiapress v Heinrich Bauer Verlag* [1997] E.C.R. I-3689, para. 7; and *Bluhme* (n.37 above), para. 18.

[50] Cases C-189/95 *Franzén* [1997] E.C.R. I-5909, para. 69; C-44/98 *BASF v Präsident des Deutschen Patentamtes* [1999] E.C.R. I-6269, para. 16; and C-254/98 *Schutzverband gegen unlauteren Wettbewerb v TK-Heimdienst Sass* [2000] E.C.R. I-151, para. 22.

[51] See para. 6.64 below. Moreover, the intention of the author of a measure may be evidence that is not justified under Art. 30 (see paras 8.17 and 8.22 below).

[52] Paras 22 and 25 of the "Buy Irish" judgment (n.13 above); Case C-405/98 *Konsumentombudsmannen v Gourmet International Products* (judgment of March 8, 2001), para. 22.

6.22 Just how wide the scope of Article 28 is can be seen from the recent ruling in *Commission v France* (foie gras).[53] In that case, the Commission alleged that France had infringed that provision by laying down standards for goods sold under the trade description *"foie gras"*. The defendant argued that the infringement was purely hypothetical and theoretical, since this product was only produced in very small quantities in other Member States, those States had no specific requirements of their own and products from those States generally complied with the French standards in any event. While La Pergola A.G. accepted this argument, the Court dismissed it in the following terms:

"Article [28] applies ... not only to the actual effects but also to the potential effects of legislation. It cannot be considered inapplicable simply because at the present time there are no actual cases with a connection to another Member State ... ".

6.23 Nevertheless, in a series of cases, of which *Peralta*[54] is perhaps the best known, the Court has held that measures fell outside Article 28 on the grounds that they were indistinctly applicable and that the possibility of their effecting imports was too "uncertain and indirect".

The obvious question posed by this line of case law is this: is the Court merely saying in each case that the measure concerned does not even constitute an indirect or a potential restraint on imports *within* the terms of the *Dassonville* test? Or is this rule of remoteness a separate principle which *qualifies* that test? The answer is unclear, although the ruling in *BASF v Präsident des Deutschen Patentamtes*[55] appears to suggest that the Court adopts the second alternative.

Nevertheless, the first alternative is surely to be preferred: on the latter view, this line of case law would add an additional and, it is submitted, unnecessary principle without giving any guidance as to how the test of "certainty and directness" is to be applied. Also, in some of these cases, the purely fanciful nature of the argument that the contested measure was caught by Article 28 would tend to support the former view. For example, in *Peralta* itself it was contended that the prohibition on Italian vessels discharging caustic soda at sea amounted to an unlawful restriction on imports of that product into Italy!

---

[53] Case C-184/96 [1998] E.C.R. I-6197; see Mattera "L'arrêt 'foie gras' du 22 octobre 1998 : porteur d'une nouvelle impulsion pour le perfectionnement du Marché unique européen" [1998] R.M.U.E. 113.

[54] Case 379/92 [1994] E.C.R. I-3453; see also Cases C-140/94 *DIP v Bassano di Grappa* [1995] E.C.R. I-3257; C-96/94 *Centro Servizi Spediporto v Spedizioni Marittima del Golfo* [1995] E.C.R. I-2883; C-134/94 *Esso Española v Comunidad Autónoma de Canarias* [1995] E.C.R. I-4223; and C-266/96 *Corsica Ferries v Ministero dei Trasporti* [1998] E.C.R. I-3949.

It seems logical to exclude from this category of cases those decided prior to the seminal ruling in *Keck* (see n.16 above) such as: Cases 75/81 *Blesgen v Belgium* [1982] E.C.R. 1211; 69/88 *Krantz v Netherlands* [1990] E.C.R. I-583; and C-23/89 *Quietlynn v Southend Borough Council* [1990] E.C.R. I-3059; and C –93/92 *Motorradcenter v Baskiciogullari* [1993] E.C.R. I-5009. This is because today they would presumably be decided on the basis that the measures concerned were non-discriminatory "selling arrangements" as understood in *Keck*; see generally Müller-Graff, commentary on Art. 30 (old numbering) in Groeben, Thiesing, Ehlermann "Kommentar zum EU-/-EG-Vertrag" (5th ed., 1997) vol. I-at 729-731.

[55] See n.50 above, para. 16 of the judgment.

At all events, to regard this rule of remoteness as a *de minimis* test in disguise[56] would be a misconception: a measure may constitute an actual and direct restriction on a very small proportion of imports. Indeed, that is precisely what occurred in *Bluhme*.[57]

6.24 What is more, Article 28 does not only cover restrictions on imports pure and simple, but also restrictions on:

(a) re-imports[58]; or

(b) goods in transit[59]; or

(c) indirect imports[60]; or

(d) parallel imports[61]; or

(e) imports of raw materials semi-finished products, even where the finished product is subject to no restrictions[62]; or

(f) conversely, imports of the finished product when the raw material is subject to no restrictions.[63]

B. The Relationship with Other Provisions

6.25 In addition, the concept of measures of equivalent effect is not so wide as to cover restrictions on movements of goods falling under other provisions of the Treaty. This was clearly stated by the Court in *Iannelli v Meroni*,[64] in the following terms:

> "However wide the field of application of Article [28] may be, it nevertheless does not include obstacles to trade covered by other provisions of the Treaty.
>
> In fact, since the legal consequences of the application or of a possible infringement of these various provisions have to be determined having regard to their particular purpose in the context of all the objectives of the Treaty, they may be of a different kind and this implies that their respective fields of application must be distinguished, except in those cases which may fall simultaneously within the field of application of two or more provisions of Community law."

Consequently, the following fall outside the scope of Article 28:

— discriminatory measures contrary to Article 12 (ex 6);

— customs duties and charges of equivalent effect within the meaning of Articles 25 (ex 12 to 16);

---

[56] See Schilling, "Rechtsfragen zu Art. 30 EGV" [1994] EuR 50 at 60.
[57] n.37 above.
[58] Para. 2.27 above.
[59] Para. 2.26 above.
[60] As in *Dassonville* (n.47 above) itself.
[61] Para. 2.28 above.
[62] Para. 2.29 above.
[63] *ibid.*
[64] See n.2 above. See also C-228/98 *Dounias v Oikonomikon* [2000] E.C.R. I-577 at para. 39.

— State aids (Articles 87 to 89 (ex 92 to 94)); and

— internal taxation (Articles 90 (ex 95)).

Each of these will be examined in turn, after which the relationship between Article 28 and Articles 81 and 82 will be considered.

On the other hand, the relationship with Article 31 is discussed in Chapter XI, and that with Articles 94 and 95 in Chapter XII. Thus there is no need to consider them at this juncture. Likewise, the relationship between Article 28 and the Treaty provisions relating to the free movement of persons, services and capital has been covered in Chapter II.

6.26 Article 12 of the Treaty prohibits discrimination on the grounds of nationality. At first sight, this provision is far removed from the free movement of goods. However, in recent years the Court has decided a number of cases arising out of trade in goods between Member States. Thus *Mund & Fester v Hatrex*[65] concerned a provision of the German Code of Civil Procedure whereby an order for the seizure of a party's assets could be obtained automatically whenever a judgment would have to be enforced outside the jurisdiction, but was only to be granted in exceptional circumstances if the judgment was to be enforced in Germany. Such a provision was found to contravene Article 12. Following that decision, the Court ruled to the same effect with regard to national laws requiring claimants who resided in and/or were nationals of, other Member States, to furnish security for costs in proceedings brought before domestic courts, when no such requirement was imposed on nationals or residents of the State concerned.[66]

In each of these cases, the Court found that, if the dispute between the parties arose out of a commercial transaction involving imports between Member States or out of any other exercise of one of the four freedoms, then the discriminatory rule of judicial procedure in issue fell "within the scope of application" of the EC Treaty, as required by Article 12. Where Community law guarantees certain freedoms, such as the free movement of goods and the freedom to provide services in the common market, it is the corollary of those freedoms, the Court held, that traders exercising them be able to pursue legal remedies in the courts of the Member State concerned in order to resolve disputes which may arise from their economic activities.[67] Accordingly, Member States are required by Article 12 to guarantee the right of those traders to pursue judicial remedies without being subject to discrimination on the grounds of their nationality.

However, in each case, the link between the contested measure and the importation was considered to be too "indirect" for Article 28 itself to apply:

---

[65] Case C-398/92 [1994] E.C.R. I-467 at 471.
[66] Cases C-43/95 *Data Delecta and Forsberg v MSL Dynamics* [1996] E.C.R. I-4661; C-323/95 *Hayes v Kronenberger* [1997] E.C.R. I-1711; and Case C-122/96 *Saldanha v Hiross* [1997] E.C.R. I-5325. All three cases are noted by Ackerman (1998) C.M.L.Rev. 783.
[67] *Data Delecta*, paras 14 and 15; *Hayes*, paras 16 and 17; *Saldanha*, paras 17 to 24.

the first paragraph of Article 12 was held to be applicable to national procedural rules "without there being any need to connect them with the specific provisions of Articles [28 and 30] ... of the Treaty"[68] in so far as they had "an effect, even though indirect, on trade in goods ... between Member States".[69]

6.27   In *Iannelli* the Court held that customs duties and charges of equivalent effect within the meaning of Article 25 EC do not fall under Article 28. This ruling was confirmed in *Kortmann*[70] in which a parallel importer of pharmaceutical products claimed that costs incurred in registering these products as required under Dutch law, were contrary to Article 28, on the grounds that the registration was superfluous as the "official" importer had already effected such registration. The Court held that such costs fell to be examined under Articles 25 and 90 and not under Article 28.

This is not to say, however, that every measure requiring importers or persons selling imported goods to pay a sum of money falls automatically outside Article 28. We shall see in the next Chapter that the obligation to pay a deposit when importing goods[71] is caught by Article 28, as are certain types of fines.[72] Furthermore, in *Musik-Vertrieb Membran v GEMA*[73] the Court classified copyright royalties as measures of equivalent effect rather than taxes of equivalent effect on the grounds that they were really damages paid for the infringement of copyright. Similarly, in *Orlandi v Minister of Foreign Trade*,[74] Slynn A.G. took the view that an obligation to pay an import deposit which could be forfeited to the State in certain circumstances contravened Article 28, and not Article 25. The Court also considered the measure concerned to violate Article 28, thereby implicitly endorsing the Advocate General's view that it did not constitute a charge of equivalent effect.

6.28   In the *Iannelli* case the Court also considered the relationship between Article 28 and Articles 87 to 89 relating to State aids.[75] Those provisions

---

[68] *Data Delecta*, para. 14 and *Hayes*, para. 16.

[69] *Data Delecta*, para. 15 and *Hayes*, para. 17. In keeping with this, the Court ruled in *Saldanha* that Article 12 applied to any discriminatory rule of this kind, if applied by the Austrian authorities after that country's accession to the Community. In such a case, the fact that the underlying transaction involving an exercise of one of the four freedoms– *e.g.* the importation of goods— occurred before accession is thus irrelevant.

No doubt this case law should be seen together with *Peralta* (see para. 6.23 above). See also para. 7.70 below. As to exports, see also Case C-412/97 *ED v Fenocchio* [1999] E.C.R. I-3845 (paras 6.91 and 7.110 below).

[70] Case 32/80 [1981] E.C.R. 251; [1982] 3 C.M.L.R. 46; see also Cases C-78 to 93/90 *Compagnie Commerciale de L'Ouest v Receveur Principal des Douanes* [1992] E.C.R. I-1847; C-17/91 *Lornoy v Belgium* [1992] E.C.R. I-6523; and C-228/98, see n.64 above.

[71] Para. 7.39 below.

[72] Paras 7.08 *et seq.* below.

[73] Cases 55/80 and 57/80 [1981] E.C.R. 147; [1981] 2 C.M.L.R. 44, para. 8.172 below.

[74] Cases 206, 207, 209 and 210/80 [1982] E.C.R. 2147 at 2171; para. 7.39 below.

[75] See also Case 82/77, see n.31 above. Some guidance is perhaps also to be derived from Case 73/79 *Commission v Italy* [1980] E.C.R. 1533; [1982] 1 C.M.L.R. 1, although that case concerned the relationship between Arts 87-88 and 90 [1985] E.C.R. 817; [1985] 3 C.M.L.R. 380; see also Case 248/84 *Germany v Commission* [1987] E.C.R. 4013.

stipulate that such aids are in principle incompatible with the common market, but lay down a number of exceptions to that rule[76] and give the Commission a wide discretion to accept a State aid in derogation of this principle. Consequently, the Court held that this principle of incompatibility did not have direct effect, whereas Article 28 did have such effect. In the light of this the Court ruled:

> "The effect of an interpretation of Article [28] which is so wide as to treat an aid as such within the meaning of Article [87] as being similar to a quantitative restriction referred to in Article [28] would be to alter the scope of Articles [87 and 88] of the Treaty and to interfere with the system adopted in the Treaty for the division of powers by means of the procedure for keeping aids under constant review as described in Article [88]."

Yet the Court at once proceeded to qualify this ruling as follows:

> "Nevertheless the position is different if it is possible when a system of aid is being analysed to separate those conditions or factors which, even though they form part of this system, may be regarded as not being necessary for the attainment of its object or for its proper functioning.
> In the latter case there are no reasons based on the division of powers under Articles [87] and [88] which permit the conclusion to be drawn that, if other provisions of the Treaty which have direct effect are infringed, those provisions may not be invoked before national courts simply because the factor in question is an aspect of aid."

It might have been preferable for the Court to follow the Advocate General and rule that the principle that an aid could not fall under Article 28 was unqualified: as Dashwood pointed out,[77] the test which the Court laid down lacked clarity and might prove very hard to apply. This was perhaps borne out by the Court's attempt to apply its severability test to the case in hand; it ruled that Article 28 would apply to that aspect of an:

> "arrangement whereby aid is granted to traders who obtain supplies of imported products through a State agency but is withheld when the products are imported direct, if this distinction is not clearly necessary for attainment of the objective of the said aid or for its proper functioning."

6.29 The approach followed by the Court in *Commission v Ireland* ("Buy Irish")[78] differs sharply from this, although there is no direct conflict between the two judgments. In its defence, Ireland had argued that the campaign was to be judged on the basis of Articles 87 and 88 and not Article 28. The Court gave this argument short shrift: "The fact that a substantial part of the campaign is

---

[76] Thus, an aid may fall outside Art. 87(1) altogether on the grounds that it is too insignificant to "affect trade between Member States"; Cases 296 and 318/82 *Netherlands v Commission* [1985] E.C.R. 809. In contrast, Arts 28 and 29 are not subject to any *de minimis* rule: para. 6.17–6.18.

[77] [1977] E.L.Rev. 376; contra Schramme, "Rapport entre les measures d'effet equivalent a des restrictions quantitatives et les aides nationales" (1985) R.T.D.E. 487.

[78] Case 249/81, see n.13 above.

financed by the Irish Government and that Articles [87 and 88] of the Treaty may be applicable to financing of that kind does not mean that the campaign itself may escape the prohibitions laid down in Article [28]." The Court also went on to observe that "in any case, if the Irish Government considered that such financing amounted to aid within the meaning of Articles [87 and 88] it ought to have notified the aid to the Commission in accordance with Article [88(3)]."

6.30   The problem arose once again in *Commission v France* (tax benefit for newspapers).[79] That case concerned legislation granting a tax advantage to newspaper publishers on condition that the publications were printed in France. Once again the Commission brought proceedings for the breach of Article 28 and the defendant Member State maintained that the relevant provision was in fact Article 87. Once again this argument was dismissed. The Court began by pointing out, as it had done in the "Buy Irish" case, that the scheme had never been notified to the Commission. Second, it ruled that "Articles [87 and 89] cannot, as is clear from a long line of cases decided by the Court, be used to frustrate the rules of the Treaty on the free movement of goods or the rules on the repeal of discriminatory tax provisions. According to those cases, provisions relating to the free movement of goods, the repeal of discriminatory tax provisions and aid have a common objective, namely to ensure the free movement of goods between Member States under normal conditions of competition." It concluded from this that "the mere fact that a national measure may possibly be defined as an aid within the meaning of Article [87] is therefore not an adequate reason for exempting it from the prohibition contained in Article [28]", and went on to find for the Commission.

Essentially the same reasoning was applied in *Commission v Italy*,[80] where State subsidies for the purchase of national vehicles were held to contravene Article 28. There the Court rejected the application in even stronger terms, stating: "Article [87] may *in no case* be used to frustrate the rules of the Treaty on the free movement of goods."[81] The Court repeated this statement in *Du Pont de Nemours v Unita Sanitaria Locale*,[82] where an Italian measure requiring authorities to purchase at least 30 per cent of their supplies from industrial and agricultural undertakings established in the southern part of the country was held to fall under Article 28, not Article 87.

6.31   It is not unfair to say that the law on the relationship between Articles 28 and 87 continues to be in a considerable state of uncertainty. Yet this is an inherently vexed issue which does not permit of any easy answer. At all events, it is notable that in *France* and *Italy* the contested measure was severable from the aid itself: in *France* the Commission did not object to the tax advantage, but to the condition attached to it; and in *Italy* also the Commission's sole objection

---

[79] Case 18/84 [1985] E.C.R. I-3339; [1986] 1 C.M.L.R. 605; para. 2.37 above.
[80] See n.14 above.
[81] Emphasis added.
[82] Case C-21/88 [1990] E.C.R. I-889, paras 6.95 and 7.16 below.

was to the condition of origin attached to the subsidy. Thus even on the *Iannelli* test, both of the measures in issue in those two cases would fall under Article 28. The *Buy Irish* case was different in that there the publicity campaign in favour of Irish goods was not a condition or an element of a broader measure.

Also, in these three infringement proceedings the Court was no doubt influenced by the unattractive nature of the defence concerned: by arguing that the contested measures fell outside Article 28 because they constituted State aids within the meaning of Article 87, when they had failed to notify them, the Member States were seeking to profit by their own wrong. No such considerations were present in *Iannelli*. Accordingly, Flynn[83] and Marenco[84] may well be right in suggesting that *Iannelli* has not been reversed.

6.32   As regards internal taxation, in *Fink-Frucht v Hauptzollamt München*[85] the Court held that one and the same national provision could not fall to be considered under both Article 28 and Article 90. This was subsequently confirmed in *Iannelli*.[86] Furthermore, in *Bergandi v Directeur-Général des Impôts*[87] it was held that a restriction of a fiscal nature was to be considered under Article 90 alone and not under Article 28.

In *Commission v Denmark*[88] (registration tax for cars) the Commission maintained that the defendant State had infringed Article 90 by imposing such a high duty on private motor cars that the free movement of goods was impeded. There is no Danish production of cars. There was thus no similar or competing domestic production. The Court found that in these circumstances Article 90 did not apply, but it added:

" ... the only possibility of appraising an adverse effect of that kind on the free movement of goods is by reference to the general rules contained in Article [28] et seq. of the Treaty."

Subsequently, Tesauro A.G. sought to explain that ruling by stating that this case displayed two specific features:

"first, the tax at issue escaped the prohibition in Article [90] in that there was no domestic production whatsoever which competed with or was similar to the taxed imported product; secondly, it was necessary to establish whether, in such circumstances, the amount of tax was so great as to impede the movement of goods within the Community."[89]

---

[83] [1987] E.L.Rev. 131 (case note).
[84] "La giurisprudenza comunitaria sulle misure di effetto equivalente a una restrizione quantitativa (1984-1986)" [1988] Il Foro Italiano IV 166.
[85] Case 27/67 [1968] E.C.R. 223; [1968] C.M.L.R. 228.
[86] See also *Dounias* (see n.64 above), para. 39
[87] [1988] E.C.R. 1343; see also *Compagnie Commerciale de l'Ouest* and *Lornoy* (see n.64 above).
[88] Case C-47/88 [1990] E.C.R. I-4509.
[89] *Compagnie Commerciale de l'Ouest* (see n.64 above) at 1865.

He concluded that the ruling in *Denmark* was confined to its own facts.[90]

6.33 The Treaty as originally worded required the Member States to "authorise, in the currency of the Member State in which the creditor or the beneficiary resides, any payments connected with the movement of goods, services or capital" as and when those movements themselves were liberalised (Article 106(1)).[91] This provision is now to be found in a modified form in Article 56(2).[92] Despite the existence of this provision, the Court has generally held that restrictions on current payments for imports of goods fall foul of Article 28.[93]

As will be suggested in paragraph 8.34 below, the exceptions to the free movement of capital set out in the new Article 58 (ex 73D) would appear to apply in this context, but they are subsumed within the recognised grounds of justification discussed in Chapter VIII.

6.34 It is appropriate at this stage to turn to the relationship between Articles 28 and 29 on the one hand and Articles 81 and 82 (ex 85 and 86) on the other.[94] We noticed in an earlier Chapter[95] how in principle Articles 28 and 29 cover State measures, whereas Articles 81 and 82 relate to the agreements and practices of private undertakings.

The similarities between the two sets of provisions are striking: both prohibit restrictions on imports (or exports, as the case may be), subject to a justification clause (Articles 30 and 81(3)). Yet there are notable differences. As the Court pointed out in *Van de Haar*,[96] Articles 28 and 81 pursue quite different aims from one another and, while the latter is subject to a *de minimis* rule, the former is not. Consequently, although a comparison between the two sets of provisions will yield results of great practical importance, the reader well versed in competition law should not be lulled into thinking that the principles which he

---

[90] A new case raising the question as to the compatibility with Article 28 of the Danish car registration tax, albeit in an amended form, is currently pending before the Court: Case C-383/01 *De Danske Bilimportører v Ministry of Fiscal Affairs.*

[91] Paras 2.05 and 2.06 above.

[92] Given its position in the Treaty and its wording, this provision is ambiguous, since it could be taken as covering only current payments connected with capital movements. However, the Court has held that it also relates to current payments for goods and services: Case C-163/94 *Saenz de Lera* [1995] E.C.R. I-4821, para. 17.

[93] Cases 95/81 *Commission v Italy* [1982] E.C.R. 2187 (paras 7.39 and 8.34 below); and 124/85 *Commission v Greece* [1986] E.C.R. 3935; [1988] 2 C.M.L.R. 518. The ruling in Case C-358/93 *Bordessa* ([1995] E.C.R. I-361, para. 14) is anomalous in this regard.

[94] This question has spawned a large number of learned articles: Matthies, "Die Verantwortung der Mitgliedstaaten fur den freien Warenverkehr im Gemeinsamen Markt" (1977) Festschrift für Ipsen 669 at 672 *et seq.*; Mortelmans, "Towards Convergence in the Application of the Rules on Free Movement and on Competition" (2001) 38 C.M.L.Rev. 613; Stuyck, "Libre circulation et concurrence : les deux piliers du Marché commun" in *Mélanges en l'honneur de Michel Waelbroeck* (1999) vol. 2 p. 1478; and VerLoren van Themaat, "Zum Verhältnis zwischen Artikel 30 und Artikel 85 EWG-Vertrag" (1976) Festschrift für Gunther 373; "De artikelen 30-36 van het EWG-Vertrag" (1980) R.M. Themis 4/5, 378 at 399; "Gaat de Luxemburgse rechtspraak over de vier vrijheden en die over het mededingingsrecht uiteenlopen ?" [1998] S.E.W. 398.

[95] Paras 4.26 *et seq.* above.

[96] See n.34 above.

knows can quite simply be applied unaltered to State measures under Articles 28 to 30.

Can the two sets of provisions apply to one and the same set of circumstances? The ruling in *GB-Inno v ATAB*[97] suggests that a national measure may simultaneously be caught by Article 28 (or Article 29) and Article 82, read with Articles 3(1)(g) (formerly 3(g)) and 10 (ex 5). Indeed, the Court held there that "a national measure which has the effect of facilitating the abuse of a dominant position capable of affecting trade between Member States will generally be incompatible with Articles [28 and 29]."[98]

It seems clear that the same would apply to national measures facilitating the conclusion of agreements contrary to Article 81, especially as the Court also held in that judgment that Member States may not enact measures enabling private undertakings to escape from the constraints imposed by Articles 81 to 89 (ex 94) of the Treaty. In addition, if Articles 28 and 29 cover measures facilitating agreements or abuses by undertakings contrary to Article 81 and 82, then *a fortiori* Articles 28 and 29 must apply to measures requiring such agreements or abuses. At all events, it is now plain that a State measure will only fall foul of Articles 3(1)(g), 10 and 81 read together if it requires or encourages undertakings to enter into agreements or concerted practices contrary to Article 81, or reinforces the effect of such agreement or connected practices. The imposition of trade restrictions in another form will not contravene these provisions.[99]

C. "Indistinctly Applicable" Measures under Article 28

6.35 To what extent does Article 28 cover measures applying in the same way to domestic and imported goods ("indistinctly applicable" measures)? Since the position of the Court, the Commission and the various legal commentators on these questions has evolved with time, it is appropriate to follow a chronological approach.

---

[97] Case 13/77 [1977] E.C.R. 2115; [1978] 1 C.M.L.R. 283.

[98] See also the A.G. in Case 82/77, see n.31 above, at 47; and Cases 5/79 *Buys* [1979] E.C.R. 3203; [1980] 2 C.M.L.R. 99; and C-179/90 *Merci Convenzionali v Siderurgica Gabrielli* [1991] E.C.R. I-5889 (see para. 9.06 below).

[99] See, *e.g.* Cases 5/79 *Buys*, see n.98 above; *Van de Haar*, see n.34 above, (noted by Marenco [1984] R.T.D.E. 527); and 231/83 *Leclerc* [1985] 2 C.M.L.R. 524; also generally Cases 229/83 *Leclerc v Au Blé Vert* [1985] E.C.R. 17; [1985] 2 C.M.L.R. 286; 267/86 *Van Eycke v ASPA* [1988] E.C.R. 4769; C-2/91 *Meng* [1993] E.C.R. I-5751; C-185/91 *Bundesanstalt für den Güterfernverkehr v Reiff* [1993] E.C.R. I-5801; and C-245/91 *Ohra Schadeverzekeringen* [1993] E.C.R. I-5851; *Leclerc-Siplec* (see n.36 above); C-35/96 *Commission v Italy* (customs agents) [1998] E.C.R. I-3851; C-9/99 *Echirolles Distribution v Association du Dauphiné* [2000] E.C.R. I-8207; and C-35/99 *Arduino* (judgment of February 19, 2002); Reich, "The November Revolution of the European Court of Justice: *Keck, Meng* and *Audi* Revisited" (1994) C.M.L.Rev. 459; D. Waelbroeck, "Application des règles de concurrence du Traité de Rome a l'autorité publique" [1987] R.M.C. 25; and M. Waelbroeck, "Les rapports entre les règles sur la libre circulation des machandises et les règles de concurrence applicables aux entreprises dans la CEE", [1987] Liber Amicorum Pierre Pescatore at 781.

(i) The Initial period

6.36 The Commission encountered the problem of "indistinctly applicable" measures at a very early stage. The first case concerned fertilisers.[100] By a Belgian Royal Decree of 1961 only ammonium nitrate containing at least 22 per cent nitrogen could be sold in Belgium, be it domestically produced or imported ammonium nitrate. The normal nitrogen content in the Community was 20.5 per cent. This meant that producers of ammonium nitrate in other Member States were faced with the choice of making a special production for Belgium or stopping exports to that country. The Belgian authorities were unable to show any convincing reason for this measure and it was clear that it was designed to protect Belgian producers. The Commission prevailed upon the Belgian authorities to repeal the measure.

6.37 Perhaps more telling to the non-scientist was the French blanket case. A French Ministerial Decree of 1968 provided that only blankets of a particular size could be sold in France. It was no accident that the decreed sizes were those already applied by French producers. This meant that blanket manufacturers in other Member States were obliged to stop exporting to France or to have a special production for the French market, with all the resulting expense, whereas French manufacturers continued to produce as before. The French Government was unable to show that the measure was justified on any grounds known to Community law, since its object was clearly to protect French manufacturers. France therefore bowed to pressure from the Commission and repealed the Decree. This case shows with the utmost clarity how an "indistinctly applicable" measure can be blatantly protectionist in its effects.

6.38 In the light of these cases, the Commission set out a twofold definition of measures of equivalent effect under Article 28 in Directive 70/50[101]:

(a) overtly discriminatory ("distinctly applicable") measures: those which apply to imported products only and make importation more costly or more difficult, and those which impose on imported products a condition differing from that required for domestic products and more difficult to satisfy (Article 2 of the Directive);

(b) "indistinctly applicable" measures, those which are equally applicable to domestic and imported products alike. Such measures were to be governed by Article 3, which reads:

> "This directive also covers measures governing the marketing of products which deal, in particular, with shape, size, weight, composition, presentation, identification or putting up and which are equally applicable to domestic and

---

[100] Written question 118/66 ([1966] J.O. 901 at 903).
[101] Para. 6.04 above; prior to this directive, the Commission also gave indications of its views in its answers to written question 118/66, n.100 above; written questions 64/67 ([1967] J.O. 169/11) and 185/67 ([1968] J.O. C5/5).

imported products, where the restrictive effect of such measures on the free movement of goods exceeds the effects intrinsic to trade rules.

This is the case, in particular, where:

— the restrictive effects on the free movement of goods are out of proportion to their purpose;
— the same objective can be attained by other means which are less of a hindrance to trade."

Thus, while overtly discriminatory measures were automatically considered to be measures of equivalent effect, there was a presumption that "indistinctly applicable" measures were compatible with Article 28.

The Directive was expressed to apply without prejudice to Article 30: Article 5(2).

6.39 In the early days, the views of legal authors as to the concept of measures of equivalent effect could be divided into three categories[102]:

(a) the narrow definition (Seidel, Graf, Marx and to a certain extent also Meier);

(b) the wide definition (VerLoren van Themaat, Waelbroeck);

(c) the intermediate approach, some of whose proponents supported Directive 70/50 (Beraud, Dona-Viscardini), while others criticised that Directive (Ulmer, Steindorff).

6.40 According to the narrow view, only "distinctly applicable" measures[103] fell to be considered as measures of equivalent effect under Article 28. Seidel,[104] the first author to take this approach, relied on an analogy with quotas. Graf[105] reached this conclusion on the basis of a comparison between the four freedoms, while Marx[106] based his theory on an analysis of Article 94 (ex 100) EC. Meier's[107] initial approach was particularly restrictive: according to him, only those measures which operated at the frontier were measures of equivalent

---

[102]The views of the authors listed here have evolved over the years in accordance with changing events, in particular the Court's case law. For summaries of the various views during this period, see Ehlermann in Groeben, Boeckh and Thiesing, *Kommentar zum EWG-Vertrag* (1974), Vol. 1, 263; Waelbroeck, *Les réglementations, nationales de prix et le droit communautaire* (1975), 23 *et seq.*; Meij and Winter, "Measures having an effect equivalent to quatitative restrictions" [1976] C.M.L.Rev. 79; van Gerven, "The Recent Case-law of the Court of Justice concerning Articles 30 and 36 of the EEC Treaty" [1977] C.M.L.Rev. 5; Ehlermann, "Das Verbot der Massnahmen gleicher Wirkung in der Rechtsprechung des Gerichtshofes" [1977] Festschrift für Ipsen 579; Veelken, "Massnahmen gleicher Wirkung wie mengenmässige Beschränkungen" (1977) EuR 311; VerLoren van Themaat, "De artikelen 30–36 van het EEG-Verdrag", *op. cit.* n.94 above.

[103]*i.e.* measures applying only to imports, or imposing a greater burden on them; see para. 6.35 above.

[104]"Der EWG-rechtliche Begriff der 'Maßnahmen gleicher Wirkung wie eine mengennässige Beschränkung'" [1976] N.J.W. 2081.

[105]*op. cit.* n.10 above.

[106]*Funktion und Grenzen der Rechtsangleichung nach Art. 100 EWG-Vertrag* (1976), in particular at 84 *et seq.*

[107]In Ehle and Meier, *EWG-Warenverkehr* (1971), 158 *et seq.*

effect. Measures applying at a later stage, and in particular at the point of sale, fell outside Article 28 altogether in his view.

The overwhelming disadvantage of this school of thought was that it would lead to Article 28 being circumvented simply by careful drafting of national legislation. In any case, it became untenable with the ruling in *Dassonville*.[108]

6.41 According to VerLoren van Themaat[109] and M. Waelbroeck,[110] the proponents of the wide definition, Article 28 did not apply only to measures discriminating against imports. In their view, all measures restricting interstate trade were prohibited by Article 28, unless they were justified under Article 30 or were governed by other provisions of the Treaty. In support of this view, they pointed to the wide formulation of Article 28, which makes no mention of discrimination. Meij and Winter,[111] who adhered to this theory in a qualified form, also criticised Article 3 of Directive 70/50 on the grounds that it purported to deprive Article 30 of its proper scope by using the test of justification to decide whether a measure fell under Article 28 in the first place.

On the other hand, the effect of this wide definition of measures of equivalent effect was to overstretch Article 30, which only applies to measures pursuing goals of a non-economic nature.[112] In consequence, Waelbroeck[113] added the rider that to come under Article 28 a measure must have a direct causal effect on imports or on the marketing or use of an imported product, so that economic policy measures affecting such matters as interest rates and incomes[114] fall outside Article 28. However, as has been pointed out,[115] the test of directness is no easier to apply than that of discrimination. Nor does it accord with the *Dassonville*[116] formula, according to which measures capable of hindering intra-Community trade "directly or indirectly, actually or potentially" constitute measures of equivalent effect. Similarly, Meij and Winter sought to overcome the same difficulty by putting forward the view that the concept of measures of equivalent effect only covered "trading rules". However, as they themselves admitted, it is not clear what is meant by "trading rules".[117]

6.42 The intermediate approach was followed by those authors[118] who advocated the definition laid down by Directive 70/50. A second form of inter-

---

[108]See n.47 above.
[109]"Bevat art. 30 van het EEG-Verdrag slechts een non-diskriminatie-beginsel ten aanzien van invoebeperkingen?" (1967) 15 S.E.W. 632; see also his comments on Directives 70/32 and 70/50 in (1970) 18 S.E.W. 258.
[110]*Le droit de la Communauté économique européenne* (1970) Vol. 1, 102.
[111]*op. cit.* n.102 above.
[112]See para. 8.32 below.
[113]*op. cit.* n.99 above, at p. 19 *et seq.*
[114]See para. 7.99 below.
[115]Van Gerven, *op. cit.* n.102 above, at p. 9.
[116]See para. 6.22 above.
[117]In addition, the Court does not always use the term "trading rules"; see para. 6.20 above.
[118]Béraud, "Les mesures d'effet équivalent au sens des articles 30 et suivants du Traité de Rome" [1968] R.T.D.E. 265; Dona, "Les mesures d'effet équivalent à des restrictions quantitatives" [1973] R.M.C. 224; Mattera, "Libre circulation des marchandises et articles 30 à 36 du Traité CEE" [1976] R.M.C. 500.

mediate approach was adopted by Steindorff,[119] who stated that the concept of measures of equivalent effect only applied to discriminatory measures. However, unlike the proponents of the narrow definition, he considered that discrimination in this context covered not only discrimination of form but also discrimination of substance. This meant that one must look behind a measure which was not discriminatory "on its face" to see whether it was discriminatory in practice. Unfortunately, the practical difficulties of applying such a test are very considerable[120] since it may involve consideration of complicated statistical data. What is more, on this test a measure may constantly oscillate between being discriminatory and not being discriminatory.[121]

This prompted Ulmer[122] to suggest yet another intermediate position. He criticised the test of discrimination, claiming that it was often hard to determine what was meant by this concept and thus to apply the test. He gave as an example the requirement that goods of a certain kind, domestic and imported, bear an indication of origin likely to reduce the attractiveness of the imported product for consumers. Furthermore, the test could not be applied at all to measures concerning products for which no national production existed. His solution was to suggest that the test set out in Article 3 of the Directive was to be applied to all measures, whether discriminatory or not.

(ii) Cassis de Dijon

6.43   Ulmer's view may have influenced the Advocate General and the Court in the leading case of *REWE-Zentral v Bundesmonopolverwaltung für Branntwein*[123] (commonly known as the *"Cassis de Dijon"* case). The plaintiffs, who sought to import the French blackcurrant-based drink known as "Cassis de Dijon", contested the validity of a provision of German law requiring spirits to have a minimum alcohol content. Cassis de Dijon, which in France had a content of between 15 per cent and 20 per cent, fell into the category of products required to have 25 per cent alcohol under the German provision. The German court

---

[119] In "Dienstfreiheit und Versicherungsaufsicht im Gemeinsamen Market" (1971), 79 at 82.
[120] Peter Ulmer, "Zum Verbot mittelbarer Einfuhrbeschränkungen im EWG-Vertrag" [1973] G.R.U.R.Int. 502 at 507.
[121] With respect to one category of measures, namely certain price controls, the Court has always applied the test of discrimination of substance: para. 7.75 *et seq.* below. The result is that it is extremely difficult to determine whether a given maximum price control is compatible with Art. 28 or not; see also para. 6.63 below.
[122] *op. cit.* n.120 above.
[123] Case 120/78 [1979] E.C.R. 649; [1979] 3 C.M.L.R. 494; case notes, inter alia, by Millarg [1979] EuR 420; Deringer and Sedemund [1979 N.J.W. 1079; Oliver [1980] C.M.L.Rev. 109; Wyatt [1981] E.L.Rev. 185; see also Capelli, "Les malentendus provoqués par l'arrêt 'Cassis de Dijon'" [1981] R.M.C. 421; Dashwood, "Cassis de Dijon: A major step in the liberalization of trade" (1981) 9 E.I.P.R. 268; Masclet, "Les articles 30, 36 et 100 du Traité CEE à la lumière de l'arrêt 'Cassis de Dijon' [1980] R.T.D.E. 64; Mattera "L'arrêt 'Cassis de Dijon'": une nouvelle approche pour la réalisation et le bon fonctionnement du marché intérieur" [1980] R.M.C. 505; Meier, "Zur Kombination von nationalen Lebensmittel-Begriffsbestimmungen und Vorschriften zum Schutz des Verbrauchers gegen Irreführungen als Rechtfertigungsgründe nach Art. 36 EWGV" [1980] W.R.P. 59; Meier, "Kennzeichnung statt Verkehrsverbote–Die Rechtsprechung als Schrittmacher des Lebensmittelrechts" (1980) 94 Schriftenreihe des Bundes für Lebensmittelrecht und Lebensmittelkunde, 47; VerLoren van Themaat, *op. cit.* n.94 above.

referred a question on the compatibility of such a measure with Article 28.

Capotorti A.G.'s conclusions are of particular interest, since they cast some light on certain aspects of the Court's judgment. He rejected the presumption contained in Directive 70/50 that "indistinctly applicable" measures were compatible with Article 28. In his view this presumption was based on an "attitude of prudence" which ceased to be justified after the end of the transitional period. On the other hand, he considered that consumer protection, though it did not expressly figure in the heads of justification in Article 30, did in fact fall under that provision. Applying both Article 30 EC and Article 3 of the Directive, he found that a minimum alcohol requirement constituted an unjustified restriction on imports contrary to Article 28.

6.44 The Court's starting point was that "in the absence of common rules relating to the production and marketing of alcohol" it is for the Member States to regulate these matters on their own territory.[124] Thereupon the Court stated:

> "Obstacles to movement within the Community resulting from disparities between the national laws relating to the marketing of the products in question must be accepted in so far as those provisions may be recognised as being necessary in order to satisfy mandatory requirements relating in particular to the effectiveness of fiscal supervision, the protection of public health, the fairness of commercial transactions and the defence of the consumer."[125]

It is clear from the words "in particular" that the "mandatory requirements" listed are merely examples. The list given in the judgment is therefore not exhaustive.[126] For the reasons set out in paragraphs 8.03 to 8.10 below, the better view is that the "mandatory requirements" are to be treated on a par with the grounds of justification set out expressly in Article 30.

The Court then proceeded to reject the German Government's arguments to the effect that the restriction in question was justified on the grounds of public health and consumer protection. In particular, as regards consumer protection, it held that a reasonable labelling requirement would constitute an adequate guarantee for the consumer so that the imposition of a minimum alcohol requirement for drinks intended for human consumption constituted a measure of equivalent effect contrary to Article 28, if it applied to the importation of alcoholic beverages lawfully produced and marketed in another Member State.

6.45 This ruling constituted a major landmark in the Court's case law on Article 28, especially as it has been confirmed in a long series of subsequent judgments.[127] On the other hand it would be wrong to describe *"Cassis de*

---

[124] On this part of the judgment see para. 12.108 below.

[125] Para. 8 of the judgment.

[126] See paras 8.158 *et seq.* below.

[127] See paras 7.28 *et seq.* below. Also to underline the importance of this ruling the Commission took the unusual step of issuing a Communication, setting out the consequences flowing from that ruling ([1980] O.J. C256/2).

Dijon" as a "revolutionary" judgment. Rather it has brought together in a new form strands that were to be found in various earlier cases.[128]

6.46   At all events, the first case to confirm *"Cassis"* was *Gilli and Andres*.[129] Since then, the ruling in *"Cassis"* has been reiterated and applied on countless occasions, notable examples including *Commission v Germany* (beer)[130] and *Commission v France* (substitute milk powder).[131] The latter case is particularly striking since the measure held to be unlawful there could not in any sense be regarded as protecting a typical national product: the sale of substitute milk powder was not permitted in any form or under any designation. The situation was therefore wholly different from that in *"Cassis de Dijon"* since the measure contested in that case required imports to be brought into line with German products, thereby putting the latter at an advantage; and while the avowed aim of the ban on substitute milk powder was to protect the dairy sector, milk could scarcely be regarded as a typically French product, especially as the substitutes are normally produced in other Member States with a sizeable dairy industry.

Another particularly important ruling following *"Cassis"* was *Cinéthèque v Fédération Nationale des Cinémas Français*.[132] That case concerned a prohibition on the sale or rental of video cassettes of any film within one year of that film being authorised for showing in cinemas. The Advocate General took the view that, since that measure was "indistinctly applicable" and not "protectionist", it fell outside Article 28. The Court took the opposite view. It accepted that the measure did "not have the purpose of regulating trade patterns" and its effect was "not to favour national production as against the production of other Member States, but to encourage cinematographic production as such". Yet it found that despite this the measure fell foul of Article 28, unless it was justified.[133]

6.47   However, given the vast body of cases concerning indistinctly applicable measures decided since *"Cassis"*, it is scarcely surprising to find a small number of judgments which diverge from it. In this connection the following three cases should be noted:

Oebel[134] concerned, *inter alia*, a prohibition on the delivery of bread during the night. One of the reasons given by the Court for holding this restriction to be compatible with Article 28 was that it applied "to the same extent to all producers, wherever they are established." Similarly, the defendant in *Blesgen*[135] had been charged with holding in stock on premises adjoining his hotel spirits with a view to selling them in that hotel, contrary to Belgian law; spirits were

---

[128] Case 13/77, n.97 above; see para. 7.80 below; Case 82/77, see n.31 above; see para. 7.82 below.
[129] Case 788/79 [1980] E.C.R. 2071 at 2078; [1981] 1 C.M.L.R. 146 at 154.
[130] Case 178/84 [1988] 1 C.M.L.R. 780.
[131] Case 216/84 [1988] E.C.R. 793.
[132] Cases 60 and 61/84 [1985] E.C.R. 2605; [1986] 1 C.M.L.R. 365.
[133] Admittedly, the Court then took the unprecedented and questionable step of holding the measure to be justified, without saying on what grounds: para. 8.36 below.
[134] Case 155/80 [1981] E.C.R. 3147.
[135] Case 75/81, see n.54 above.

defined under that legislation as drinks with an alcoholic strength exceeding 22 degrees at a temperature of 15 degrees centigrade. The defendant's plea that such a law infringed Article 30 was rejected primarily on the grounds that "the restrictions placed on the sale of the spirits in question make no distinction whatsoever based on their nature or origin. Such a legislative measure has therefore in fact no connection with the importation of the products and for that reason is not of such a nature as to impede trade between Member States". Finally, in *Directeur-Général des Impôts v Forest*[136] nationally imposed flour-milling quotas were held to fall outside Article 30, when the quotas applied in the same way to imported and to domestic wheat.

6.48 In 1984 Marenco[137] mounted an attack on the view that non-discriminatory measures may be caught by Article 28. In his view discrimination was the very essence of measures of equivalent effect, although he defined discrimination fairly widely to cover "indistinctly applicable" measures which required manufacturers of other Member States to institute a special production for exports to the offending State. By this means he sought to bring the *"Cassis de Dijon"* line of cases within his theory.

(iii) The situation in the late 1980s

6.49 It is appropriate to pause briefly in this "narrative" to describe the situation as it stood at the end of the 1980s. At that time, all restrictions on imports not falling within the scope of other Treaty articles were deemed to be caught by Article 28, regardless of whether they discriminated against imports. This was said to be subject to the following exceptions:

(a) as regards price controls, it appeared that discrimination was the determining criterion[138];

(b) a small body of other judgments, which appeared to be at variance with *"Cassis de Dijon"* unequivocally applied the test of discrimination[139]; and

(c) the idea was also mooted that the effect of certain measures on imports might be regarded as so remote or so tenuous that they were not caught by Article 28 at all. "Indistinctly applicable" legislation on shop opening hours was given as a possible example of such legislation.

As regards (c), it became clear that the test of remoteness is not appropriate to

---

[136] Case 148/85 [1986] E.C.R. 3349; [1988] 2 C.M.L.R. 577.
[137] "Pour une interprétation traditionnelle de la notion de mesure d'effet équivalent à une restriction quantitative" [1984] C.D.E. 291. For a much attenuated form of this theory see M. Waelbroeck, "Mesures d'effet equivalent, discrimination formelle et matérielle dans la jurisprudence de la Cour de Justice" Liber Amicorum; Frédéric Dumon and Defalque, "Le concept de discrimination en matière de libre circulation des marchandises" [1987] C.D.E. 471.
[138] See paras 7.75 *et seq.* below.
[139] See para. 6.47 above.

overcome this problem: in *Torfaen v B&Q*,[140] the first Sunday trading case, the defendant do-it-yourself store provided evidence to show that it had lost sales of millions of pounds worth of imports as a result of the contested restriction.

With the exception of *Cinéthèque* there was then no judgment in which the Court applied Article 28 to a non-discriminatory measure far removed from imports. The overstretching of Article 28 had yet to begin.

(iv) The overstretching of Article 28

6.50 In 1989 White published a seminal article[141] advocating a wholly novel criterion for keeping the concept of measures of equivalent effect within its proper bounds. To use his own words, this article sought to propose a definition of the concept of measures which "encompasses all those measures which hinder the establishment of the Common Market but does not also cover those measures in respect of which Member States can safely be allowed to take divergent paths without endangering this objective". In his view, the *Dassonville* formula could not be taken literally, as it was too broad. This formula and "*Cassis de Dijon*", he claimed, should only be applied to restrictions on the characteristics of products (*e.g.* their composition, size, shape, weight, presentation, denomination and labelling). The rationale for this was that such restrictions prevent the product "from benefiting in the importing Member State from the advantages arising out of its production in the different legal and economic environment prevailing in the other Member State". In contrast, restrictions on the circumstances in which goods may be sold (*i.e.* by whom, where, when or how goods may be sold or used or at what price they may be sold) only fall within the concept of measures of equivalent effect if they discriminate against imports, he suggested. Measures falling within the latter category would include restrictions on Sunday trading, advertising and sales promotion techniques (clearance sales, special offers, etc.) and price controls.

This approach has much to commend it. However, it in effect breaks down when restrictions on the circumstances in which a product may be sold are so severe as to amount to a virtual prohibition on its sale. White himself conceded that this would be a problem, giving as an example a measure permitting the sale of cigarettes on Christmas Day only. Such severe restrictions must in his view be assimilated to a total ban on sale.

6.51 Mortelmans[142] was broadly in sympathy with White, while claiming that the latter author went too far: "this criterion has too many loopholes. This view excludes far too many national rules from the scope of Article [28], particularly rules on how goods may be sold or used or at what price they may be sold."

Mortelmans then went on to say that, while he endorsed White's views about measures relating to the characteristics of products, indistinctly applicable rules

---

[140] See n.15 above.
[141] "In Search of the Limits to Article 30 of the EEC Treaty" [1989] C.M.L.Rev. 235.
[142] "Article 30 of the EEC Treaty and Legislation Relating to Market Circumstances: Time to Consider a New Definition?" [1991] C.M.L.Rev. 115.

on the circumstances of sale should only be caught by Article 28 if they have no "territorial element". He regarded the latter type of measure (such as restrictions on door-to-door selling) as posing a threat to the internal market. In contrast, indistinctly applicable rules on "market circumstances relating to a fixed location", such as Sunday trading restrictions, fell outside Article 28, he argued.

It is not clear, however, that the distinction between itinerant sales and sales at a fixed location is of any consequence, since in any event by definition the sale is expected to occur within the territory of the host State. He concluded by proposing an interesting "rule of thumb" for the borderline cases which are bound to arise. These must be considered as falling under Article 28, he maintained, even adapting a Latin maxim for the occasion: "*in dubio pro communitate*".

6.52   At all events, White's theory was propounded to the Court by the Commission in *Torfaen v B&Q*, the first case on Sunday trading legislation.[143] It fell on deaf ears.

After a very thorough review of the case law, van Gerven A.G. reached the conclusion that a restriction on Sunday trading did not constitute a measure of equivalent effect within the meaning of Article 28 at all, unless it discriminated against imports in some way or "screened off" the domestic market. For the concept of "screening off", which was of an economic rather than a legal nature, he drew on ideas developed in relation to Article 81 of the Treaty. A sales ban and similarly severe measures would be regarded as automatically "screening off" the domestic market. He continued:

> "If the national rule at issue merely increases the difficulty in penetrating the national market, the prohibition in Article [28] is applicable only if it appears from the entire legal and economic context that the economic interweaving of national markets sought by the Treaty is thereby threatened. In such a case, the compartmentalisation of the market should be made sufficiently probable by a number of quantitative factors which show that the application of the rule makes it more difficult to penetrate the market, thereby rendering the market so inaccessible (expensive, unprofitable) that it must be feared that the majority of imported goods will disappear from the market."[144]

One can only agree with Mortelmans[145] that this approach would have failed to "provide the courts with a clear and decisive guideline on which to base their judgments", since it would have required them to have regard to "the entire legal and economic context". In short, this approach was not consonant with the principle of legal certainty.

The Court's judgment rejected the Advocate General's approach in terms which were both terse and delphic. It first pointed out that the case related to a measure which applied in the same way to national and imported goods, but

---

[143] See n.15 above.
[144] at 3878.
[145] *op. cit.* n.142 above, at 127.

found that, in view of its earlier ruling in *Cinéthèque*, this did not prevent it constituting a measure of equivalent effect. Thus it was contrary to Article 28 unless it could be justified. It then continued:

" ... the Court has already stated in its judgment of 14 July 1981 in Case 155/80 *Oebel* ([1981] E.C.R. 1993) that national rules governing the hours of work, delivery and sale in the bread and confectionery industry constitute a legitimate part of economic and social policy, consistent with the objectives of public interest pursued by the Treaty.

The same consideration must apply as regards national rules governing the opening hours of retail premises. Such rules reflect certain political and economic choices in so far as their purpose is to ensure that working and non-working hours are so arranged as to accord with national or regional socio-cultural characteristics, and that, in the present state of Community law, is a matter for the Member States. Furthermore, such rules are not designed to govern the patterns of trade between Member States.

Secondly, it is necessary to ascertain whether the effects of such national rules exceed what is necessary to achieve the aim in view ... [T]he prohibition laid down in Article [28] covers national measures governing the marketing of products where the restrictive effect of such measures on the free movement of goods exceeds the effect intrinsic to trade rules.

The question whether the effects of specific national rules do in fact remain within that limit is a question of fact to be determined by the national court.

... Article [28] of the Treaty must therefore be interpreted as meaning that the prohibition which it lays down does not apply to national rules prohibiting retailers from opening their premises on Sunday where the restrictive effects of Community trade which may result therefrom do not exceed the effects intrinsic to rules of that kind."

It would not be an understatement to say that this judgment failed to give adequate guidance to the national court. Not surprisingly, a host of conflicting judgments from a whole range of courts in England and Wales ensued[146]; the ruling also produced a storm of hostile comment.[147] The controversy was only laid to rest when the Court held such legislation to be justified.[148]

6.53 To complicate matters still further, the Court followed a radically different approach in *Quietlynn v Southend Borough Council*.[149] Quietlynn, which had been prosecuted for running a sex shop without a licence contrary to English law, argued that the legislation concerned fell foul of Article 28. The Court rejected this argument in the following terms:

"First, it must be noted that national legislation prohibiting the sale of sex articles from unlicensed sex establishments applied without distinction to imported and domestic products. It thus does not constitute an absolute prohibition on the sale of the products in question, but merely a rule regarding their distribution, regulating the outlets through which the products may be marketed. In principle, therefore, the

---

[146]See Arnull, "What shall we do on Sunday?" [1991] E.L.Rev. 112; Jarvis, "The Sunday Trading Episode: In Defence of the Euro-Defence" (1995) 44 I.C.L.Q. 451; and Oliver, "Sunday Trading and Article 30 of the Treaty of Rome" [1991] I.L.J. 298.

[147]Arnull, *op. cit.* n.146; Gormley case note [1990] C.M.L.Rev. 141; Mortelmans, *op. cit.* n.142 above.

[148]Cases C-312/89 *CGT v Conforama* [1991] E.C.R. I-997; C-332/89 *Marchandise* [1991] E.C.R. I-1027; C-169/191 *Stoke-on-Trent v B&Q* [1992] E.C.R. 6635, para. 8.164 below.

[149]Case C-23/89 see n.54 above; also Case C-350/89 *Sheptonhurst v Newham Borough Council* [1991] E.C.R. I-2387.

marketing of products imported from other Member States is not rendered any more difficult that than of domestic products.''

After referring to *Oebel*[150] and *Blesgen*[151] the Court continued:

"It must also be pointed out that the provisions prohibiting the sale of sex articles from unlicensed sex establishments have in fact no connection with intra-Community trade, since the products covered by the Act may be marketed through licensed sex establishments and other channels, that is to say through shops in which sex articles account for only an insignificant proportion of sales which are therefore not required to be licensed, or by mail order. Moreover, those provisions are not intended to regulate trade in goods within the Community and they are therefore not of such a nature as to impede trade between Member States.''

While few would quibble with the view that the legislation contested in *Quietlynn* should not properly be caught by Article 28 at all, the Court's statement that the licensing requirement did not restrict imports because the products concerned could be marketed through other channels is far from convincing: surely the fact that the contested licensing requirements did not render sales totally impossible is beside the point; by making sales more difficult, it constituted a restriction.

Quietlynn also gave greater prominence to the line of cases including *Oebel*, *Blesgen* and *Forest*. This latter group comprised only a handful of judgments, but the glaring contradiction between them and the majority of decisions was highlighted dramatically by the two judgments in *Torfaen* and *Quietlynn*. [152]

(v) Keck and its aftermath

6.54 Then came the dramatic judgment in *Keck and Mithouard*.[153] The defendants there were prosecuted for selling goods below their purchase price, contrary to the provisions of French law. The French court hearing the case asked whether such legislation was contrary to the Treaty.

Legislation prohibiting traders from selling goods at a loss is widespread in the Member States and is frequently regarded as serving to prevent unfair competition. The Court might easily have upheld the provisions in question on these grounds, given that the prevention of unfair competition is one of the recognised requirements justifying restrictions on imports.[154] However, the

---

[150] See n.134 above.

[151] See n.135 above.

[152] For analyses during this period see Chalmers, "Free Movement of Goods within the European Community: an Unhealthy Addiction to Scotch Whisky?" [1993] I.C.L.Q. 269; Gormley, "Actually or Potentially, Directly or Indirectly? Obstacles to the Free Movement of Goods" [1990] Y.E.L. 197; Matthies "Artikel Art. 30 E.G.–Vertrag nach Keck" in *Festschrift für Everling*; Steiner, "Drawing the Line: Uses and Abuses of Article 30 EEC" [1992] C.M.L.Rev. 749; Wils, "The Search for the Rule in Article 30 EEC: Much Ado about Nothing?" [1993] E.L.Rev. 475.

[153] See n.16 above.

[154] Admittedly, in the first of his two Opinions in this case, the A.G. found that this legislation was unlawful because it extended to cases where it could not be justified on these grounds. However, he reversed this position in his second Opinion. He was called upon to deliver two Opinions because after the initial hearing before a Chamber, it was decided to transfer this case to the full Court consisting of all 13 judges.

Court chose instead to seize this opportunity to reverse part of its earlier case law. The Court's decision to effect a major change in its jurisprudence was no doubt influenced in part by the Opinion of Tesauro A.G. in *Hünermund v Landesapothekerkammer Baden-Württemberg*,[155] in which he did not mince his words about the contradictions and inconsistencies in the Court's case law on the scope of Article 28 and invited the Court to redraw the boundaries of that provision.

In *Keck*, after setting out the *Dassonville* formula, the Court stated:

"12 It is not the purpose of national legislation imposing a general prohibition on resale at a loss to regulate trade in goods between Member States.

13 Such legislation may, admittedly, restrict the volume of sales, and hence the volume of sales of products from other Member States, in so far as it deprives traders of a method of sales promotion. But the question remains whether such a possibility is sufficient to characterise the legislation in question as a measure having equivalent effect to a quantitative restriction on imports.

14 In view of the increasing tendency of traders to invoke Article [28] of the Treaty as a means of challenging any rules whose effect is to limit their commercial freedom even where such rules are not aimed at products from other Member States, the Court considers it necessary to re-examine and clarify its case law on this matter.

15 In 'Cassis de Dijon' (Case 120/78 *Rewe-Zentral v Bundesmonopolverwaltung für Branntwein* [1978] E.C.R. 649) it was held that, in the absence of harmonisation of legislation, measures of equivalent effect prohibited by Article 30 include obstacles to the free movement of goods where they are the consequence of applying rules that lay down requirements to be met by goods (such as requirements as to designation, form, size, weight, composition, presentation, labelling, packaging) to goods from other Member States where they are lawfully manufactured and marketed, even if those rules apply without distinction to all products unless their application can be justified by a public interest objective taking precedence over the free movement of goods.

16 However, contrary to what has previously been decided, the application to products from other Member States of national provisions restricting or prohibiting certain selling arrangements is not such as to hinder directly or indirectly, actually or potentially, trade between Member States within the meaning of the *Dassonville* judgment (Case 8/74 [1974] E.C.R. 837), provided that those provisions apply to all affected traders operating within the national territory and provided that they affect in the same manner, in law and in fact, the marketing of domestic products and of those from other Member States.

17 Where those conditions are fulfilled, the application of such rules to the sale of products from another Member State meeting the requirements laid down by that State is not by nature such as to prevent their access to the market or to impede access any more than it impedes the access of domestic products. Such rules therefore fall outside the scope of Article [28] of the Treaty."

6.55 This ruling, in which the Court largely accepted White's theory,[156] entails a partial reversal of the earlier law, as the Court expressly acknowledged in

---

[155] Case C-292/92 see n.43 above. However, it should not be thought that the Court necessarily took over every part of the Opinion. Thus, it seems clear that it declined to endorse the suggestion in para. 22 of the Opinion that measures with a specific effect on imports are caught by Article 28: D. Waelbroeck, "L'arrêt Keck et Mithouard: les conséquences pratiques" [1994] J.T.D.E. 160.
[156] n.141 above.

paragraph 16 ("contrary to what has previously been decided"). It has given rise to a vast body of literature, much of which is highly critical.[157]

Despite this criticism, the Court has persistently adhered to the *Keck* approach. It is the Court's very tenacity in continuing to apply that ruling which has enabled it to ensure a high degree of legal certainty in this area of the law. Indeed, while *Keck* itself was not a model of clarity,[158] it has been greatly clarified by the subsequent case law.[159]

6.56 At the heart of the judgment lies the distinction between:

— "rules that lay down requirements to be met by goods" (paragraph 15 of the judgment in *Keck*); and

— "selling arrangements" (paragraph 16 of that judgment).

This distinction is of crucial importance: measures in the first category continue to be subject to the previous case law (*i.e.* "*Cassis de Dijon*") and are thus considered to fall *per se* within the scope of Article 28 without there being any need to consider whether they are also discriminatory. Only those in the second category are subject to a discrimination test.[160] Measures falling with the first category relate to the inherent characteristics of products and are therefore

---

[157] Writing articles about Keck became a cottage industry in its own right. Apart from those referred to in other footnotes in this section, see: Ackermann, "Warenverkehrsfreiheit und 'Verkaufsmodalitäten'" [1994] R.I.W. 189; Basedow, "Keck on the facts" [1994] EuZW 225; Becker, "Von Dassonville über Cassis zu Keck" [1994] EuR 162; Gormley, "Reasoning Renounced? The Remarkable Judgment in Keck and Mithouard" [1994] E.B.L.R. 63; Higgins "The Free and Not So Free Movement of Goods Since *Keck*" 1997 I.J.E.L. 166; Lüder "Die Grenzen der Keck-Rechtsprechung" [1996] EuZW 615; Martinez, Lage editorial in Gaceta Juridica de la CEE, December 1993; Moore, case note [1994] E.L.Rev. 195; Mortelmans casenote [1994] S.E.W. 120; Müller-Graff, *op.cit.* (see n.54 above) at 720-729; Schilling, "Rechtsfragen zu Art. 30 E.G.V." [1994] EuR 50; Schwintowski "Freier Warenverkehr im europäischen Binnenmarkt—eine Fundamentalkritik an der Rechtsprechung des EuGH au Art. 28 EGV" [2000] RabelZ 38; Todino and Lüder, "La jurisprudence 'Keck' en matière de publicité: vers un marché unique inachevé?" [1995] R.M.U.E. I-171; Wainwright and Melgar, "Bilan de l'article 30 après vingt ans de jurisprudence: de Dassonville à Keck et Mithouard" [1994] R.M.C. 533; Weyer, "Die Rechtsprechung zum freien Warenverkehr: Dassonville–Cassis de Dijon–Keck" [1994] Deutsches Zeitschrift für Wirtschaftsrecht 90.

[158] Even a member of the Court conceded this: Judge Joliet, "La libre circulation des marchandises: l'arrêt Keck et Mithouard dans les nouvelles orientations de la jurisprudence" [1994] J.T.D.E. 145.

[159] This has surely taken much of the steam out of those hostile comments based on the lack of clarity of the ruling in *Keck* (*e.g.* Mattera, "De l'arrêt 'Dassonville' à l'arrêt 'Keck': l'obscure clarté d'une jurisprudence riche en principes novateurs et en contradictions" [1994] R.M.U.E. 117; Reich, *op.cit.* (n.99 above), and Stuyck casenote [1994] C.D.E. 435).

[160] Nic Shuibne ("The Free Movement of Goods and Article 28 EC: An Evolving Framework" [2002] E.L.Rev. 408) appears to suggest that even product-bound measures are subject to a discrimination test, albeit a very wide one. This idea harks back to Marenco (para. 6.48 above). However, it is submitted that there is little room left for this theory today. For example, an indistinctly applicable prohibition on the use of a particular food additive will not usually constitute even a covert form of discrimination. Quite apart from that, discrimination does not enter into the *reasoning* when determining the legality of product-bound measures: once it is established that they restrict imports, it is only necessary to consider whether they are justified.

widely known as "product-bound". In contrast, those in the second category relate to matters extrinsic to the goods themselves.

Examples of measures held to be "product-bound" are set out in paragraph 15 of *Keck*, namely: requirements as to designation, form, size, weight, composition, presentation, labelling, packaging.[161]

The concept of "selling arrangements", which the Court had not attempted to define in *Keck* itself, has now been held to cover the following categories of measure:

— restrictions on when goods may be sold[162];

— restrictions on where or by whom goods may be sold[163];

— advertising restrictions[164]; and

— price controls,[165] although these were already subject to a discrimination test prior to *Keck*.[166]

It now seems plain from the post-*Keck* case law that the two categories of measure are mutually exclusive, although this was not clear from that judgement itself. Similarly, all types of "selling arrangements" would now appear to fall within the second category, despite the fact that the ruling in *Keck* speaks only of "certain selling arrangements". When any doubt exists as to whether a measure is "product-bound" or relates to a "selling arrangement", the Court tends to incline towards the former;[167] this has not been formulated as a principle, but it certainly appears to be the Court's practice.

6.57   At the same time, it is plain that some measures—such as import controls and discrimination in the award of public contracts—cannot reasonably be

---

[161] The rationale behind treating restrictions as to designation as product-bound is no doubt that the name of the product must appear on the packaging. See generally Case C-315/92 *Verband Sozialer Wettbewerb v Estée Lauder* [1994] E.C.R. I-317 (ban on the sale of a cosmetic product under the name "Clinique").

[162] Cases C-401-2/92 *'t Heukske v Boermans* [1994] E.C.R. I-2199; C-69/93 *Punto Casa v Capena* [1994] E.C.R. I-2355 and Joined Cases C-418-421 & 460-464,/93 9-15/94, 23-4 & 332/94 *Semeraro and others* [1996] E.C.R. I-2975.

[163] Case C-319/92 *Commission v Greece* (processed milk for infants) [1995] E.C.R. I-1621; and C-254/98. see n.50 above.

[164] *Hünermund* (see n.43 above); *Leclerc-Siplec* (see n.36 above); Case C-34/95 *Konsumenten-ombudsmannen v De Agostini* [1997] E.C.R. I-3843, *Gourmet International* (see n.52 above).

[165] Case C-63/94 *Belgapom v ITM Belgium* [1995] E.C.R. I-2467.

[166] Paras 6.49 above and 7.75 *et seq.* below.

[167] Cases C-470/93 *Verein gegen Unwesen im Handel v Mars* [1995] E.C.R. I-1923; and *Vereinigte Familiapress* (n.49 above). *Mars* concerned a prohibition on the sale of ice-cream bars with wrapping papers bearing the symbols "+ 10%"; this could have been treated either as a labelling requirement (a product-bound measure) or as advertising (a "selling arrangement"). *Familiapress* related to a prohibition on the sale of periodicals containing games or competitions for prizes; again this could have been categorised as a restriction on the content of the periodicals (a product-bound measure) or as a restriction on promotion (a "selling arrangement"). In both cases, the Court found that the measures in issue were to be treated as product-bound.

described either as "product-bound" or as "selling arrangements".[168] To what extent discrimination would have to be shown before measures of this sort are to be regarded as falling within Article 28 is unclear, although it is necessarily present in the two examples given here. While this is not a major difficulty, this matter remains to be clarified.

6.58   What is meant by the requirement in paragraph 16 of the ruling in *Keck* that measures relating to "selling arrangements" must "apply to all affected traders operating within the national territory", if they are to fall outside Article 28? This is far from clear. Indeed, it is hard to avoid the impression that, by introducing this requirement in its judgment in *Keck*, the Court has inadvertently strayed into the fields of establishment and services which are governed by Articles 43 and 49 respectively. In any case, the following passage from the Opinion of van Gerven A.G. in *Boermans* has done little to clarify this issue:

> "the wording used has to be interpreted as meaning that, in order to fall outside the prohibition set out in Article [28] of the EC Treaty, the national measures may in no respect impede the access of traders from other Member States to the relevant market more than they impede the access of domestic traders. In contrast, Article [28] of the EC Treaty does not preclude different treatment of categories of domestic economic operators (for example, importers and manufacturers established and carrying out their activities in the Member State), provided, at least, that the measures in question do not affect the marketing of domestic and imported products differently (this is the aspect covered by the [next] condition). The national prohibition of resale at a loss which gave rise to the judgment in *Keck and Mithouard* itself involved such a difference in treatment, since it applied to retailers but not to manufacturers. I therefore interpret the judgment as meaning that, although the prohibition of resale at a loss was not applicable to national retailers and manufacturers alike, it nevertheless satisfied [this] condition ... ".[169]

The Advocate General went on to apply this interpretation in his Opinion in *Punto Casa*.[170] It was argued that the contested restrictions on Sunday trading affected large stores more severely than other categories of trader. In the light of his Opinion in *Boermans*, he was able to reject the suggestion that the legislation contested there fell foul of Article 28 by reason of this circumstance. One can only regret that the Court in *Punto Casa* did not see fit to allude to this issue at all.

Since then, there has been a dearth of authority as to the meaning of this limb of the judgment in *Keck*. The Court has referred to it on occasion,[171] so

---

[168] A further example is the obligation on traders to compile statistics on imports: see Case C-114/96 *Kieffer* [1997] E.C.R. I-3629.

In contrast, any suggestion that outright import bans also fall within this residual category is surely misconceived. Such bans are quantitative restrictions pure and simple, and are therefore not in issue: like *Dassonville* and *Cassis de Dijon* before it, *Keck* is only concerned with measures of equivalent effect.

[169] See n.153 above, para. 21 of the Opinion.

[170] See n.162 above.

[171] *De Agostini* (see n.164 above), para. 41; Case C-6/98 *ARD v Pro Sieben Media* [1999] E.C.R. I)7599, para. 48.

that it would be premature to treat it as a dead letter. Yet the Court has failed to shed further light on its true meaning.

6.59 At all events, the Court attaches far greater importance to the second condition in paragraph 16 ("provided that they affect in the same manner, in law and in fact, the marketing of domestic products and of those from other Member States").

Discrimination "in law" is a concept which should give rise to no difficulty: it occurs when measures are discriminatory on their face.[172] In contrast, the concept of discrimination "in fact" is more complex. Initially, the Court construed this concept relatively narrowly: *Commission v Greece* (processed milk for infants).[173] However, in more recent cases Court's interpretation of this concept has been strikingly broad.

6.60 In the latter case, the Court found that the concept of *de facto* discrimination ought not to depend on data which may vary over time, since otherwise a measure could constantly oscillate between falling within and outside Article 28.

Mention should also be made of the assertion of the Advocate General in the same case that a measure applying to goods which are not produced in the Member State concerned necessarily falls more heavily on imports in fact. This approach may be regarded as unduly simplistic, since it would automatically catch harmless measures within the net of Article 28, merely because the goods concerned are not produced in the State. Accordingly, the Court rejected this approach, describing as "purely fortuitous" the circumstance that no national production existed. Indeed, the Court arguably went to the other extreme, finding that a measure could only be said to discriminate against imports "in fact" if it protected similar or competing national products.

6.61 A broad interpretation of the concept of *de facto* discrimination is to be found in two cases relating to far-reaching advertising restrictions which did not discriminate against imports on their face: *De Agostini*[174] and *Gourmet International.*[175]

De Agostini concerned a Swedish law prohibiting advertising on television directed at children. Following the Opinion of Jacobs A.G. in that case, the Court held:

---

[172] Case C-320/93 *Lucien Ortscheit v Eurim-Pharm* [1994] E.C.R. I-5243 was arguably such a case: under the legislation in issue there, pharmaceuticals which were not authorised in Germany could be imported in small quantities under certain circumstances but could not be advertised there. Since this advertising ban applied only to imported products, the Court found that it was caught by Article 28. Even if such a measure is not to be regarded as discrimination in law, it must on any view constitute discrimination in fact.

[173] See n.163 above (para. 17 of the judgment). For a further example of a limited application to the concept of discrimination "in fact" see Semeraro, n.162 above especially at paras 18 and 24.

[174] See n.164 above.

[175] See n.52 above.

" ... it cannot be excluded that an outright ban, applying in one Member State, of a type of promotion for a product which is lawfully sold there might have a greater impact on products from other Member States.

Although the efficacy of the various types of promotion is a question of fact to be determined in principle by the referring court, it is to be noted that in its observations De Agostini stated that television advertising was the only effective form of promotion enabling it to penetrate the Swedish market since it had no other advertising methods for reaching children and their parents.

Consequently, an outright ban on advertising aimed at children less than 12 years of age and of misleading advertising, as provided for by the Swedish legislation, is not covered by Article [28] of the Treaty, unless it is shown that the ban does not affect in the same way, in fact and in law, the marketing of national products and of products from other Member States."[176]

Similarly, *Gourmet International* related to Swedish legislation prohibiting the advertising of alcoholic products, subject only to limited exceptions. Following Jacobs A.G. once again, the Court ruled on an analysis of this legislation that, although it did not discriminate against imports on its face, it did so in fact. On this point, the Court recalled point 17 of its judgment in *Keck*. A more detailed discussion of that judgment is set out at paragraph 7.45 below.

As we shall see below, the Court was undoubtedly influenced by the Opinions of Jacobs A.G. in *Leclerc-Siplec*.

6.62   This question also arose in *Schutzverband gegen unlauteren Wettbewerb v TK-Heimdienst.*[177] This case concerned Austrian legislation under which bakers, butchers and grocers could make sales on rounds in an administrative district ("*Verwaltungsbezirk*") only if they also traded from a permanent establishment in that district or an adjacent municipality, where they offered for sale the same goods as on their rounds. While the Court found that such legislation related to selling arrangements, it also ruled that it did not affect in the same manner the marketing of domestic products and those from other Member States, saying:

"Such legislation imposes an obligation on bakers, butchers and grocers who already have a permanent establishment in another Member State and who wish to sell their goods on rounds in a particular administrative district such as an Austrian Verwaltungsbezirk to set up or purchase another permanent establishment in that administrative district or in an adjacent municipality, whilst local economic operators already meet the requirement as to a permanent establishment. Consequently, in order for goods from other Member States to enjoy the same access to the market of the Member State of importation as domestic goods, they have to bear additional costs ...

That conclusion is not affected by the fact that, in each part of the national territory, the legislation affects both the sale of products from other parts of the national territory and the sale of products imported from other Member States (see Joined Cases C-277/91, C-318/91 and C-319/91 *Ligur Carni and Others* [1993] E.C.R. I-6621, paragraph 37). For a national measure to be categorised as discriminatory or protective for the purposes of the rules on the free movement of goods, it is not necessary for it to have the effect of favouring national products as a whole or of placing only imported products at a disadvantage and not national products (see Joined Cases C-1/

---

[176]Paras 42-4 of the judgment.
[177]Case C-254/98 see n.50 above, noted by Spaventa, [2000] C.M.L.Rev. 1265.

90 and C-176/90 *Aragonesa de Publicidad and Publivía* [1991] E.C.R. I-4151, paragraph 24).

That being so, it is of no consequence whether, as the Schutzverband contends, the national legislation in question also applies to economic operators with a permanent establishment in an adjacent municipality in another Member State. Even if it did, it would not cease to be restrictive merely because in part of the territory of the Member State concerned, namely the border area, it affects the marketing of national products and that of products from other Member States in the same manner."[178]

Once again, it is plain that the Court has adopted a wide definition of the concept of *de facto* discrimination.

6.63 Clearly, the Court in *De Agostini, Gourmet International* and *TK-Heimdienst* was at pains to temper what Weatherill has referred to as the "rigid formalism" of *Keck*.[179] That is certainly welcome, since the scope of Article 28 should obviously not be unduly narrow. However, there are two clear dangers here.

First, if the concept *de facto* discrimination is defined too broadly, the distinction between product-bound measures and those relating to selling arrangements is at risk of breaking down altogether; in which case the *Keck* approach would be in tatters. Some would say that this has already occurred.

Second, reversing what appeared to be its position in *Greece* (processed milk for infants), the Court in *De Agostini* seems implicitly to have accepted the use of statistics in determining *de facto* discrimination, since it has ruled that an outright ban on advertising certain products on television would fall within Article 28, if it could be shown to have a "greater impact on products from other Member States". The inference to be drawn from *Gourmet International* is much the same.

Reliance on statistical data can lead to perverse results, as the legality of a measure might vary from month to month.[180] The dangers of introducing a case by case economic assessment and thus the use of statistics into Articles 28 to 30—a virtually statistics-free zone until very recently—are plain enough.[181] One need only consider the Court's case law on indirect sex discrimination under Article 141 (ex 119) EC, where the Court has been at pains to stress that some statistics may not constitute a valid basis for assessing discrimination in that they may not cover enough individuals, they may illustrate purely fortuitous or short-term phenomena or may not be significant.[182] By the same token, the Court has insisted that a measure will only constitute indirect discrimination under Article

---

[178] Paras 26 to 28 of the judgment.
[179] "After *Keck*: Some Thoughts on How to Clarify the Clarify the Clarification" [1996] C.M.L.Rev. 885 at 886.
[180] Or should this be evaluated on an annual basis? Another nice question.
[181] Price controls have always constituted an exception (see paras 7.75 *et seq.* below); this may largely explain why this case law has been notoriously difficult to apply in practice. Leaving aside price controls, it was probably in *Vereinigte Familiapress* (see n.49 above) that the Court first expressly authorised reliance of statistics in this area of the law; and it was for a most unusual purpose, namely to determine whether an import restriction was justified for the protection of the diversity of the press.
[182] Cases C-127/92 *Enderby v Frenchay Health Authority* [1993] E.C.R. I-5535; and C-167/97 *Regina v Secretary of State for Employment Ex p. Seymour-Smith* [1999] E.C.R. I-666.

141, if the statistics available indicate that its effects are "considerably" different as between the men and women concerned, or if "the statistical evidence [reveals] a lesser but persistent and relatively constant disparity over a long period between men and women".[183] This terminology is hardly very precise!

In short, if undue importance is attached to statistical data, then the case law will cease to be "rule-based" and its application will become dependent on complex economic data, which could fluctuate over time. This would not be conducive to legal certainty and the task of national judges would become correspondingly harder.[184]

6.64 Returning to the *Keck* judgment itself, the reference in paragraph 12 to the purpose of the measure when deciding whether it constitutes a restriction caught by Article 28 appears to be at variance with the *Dassonville* formula: as we noticed at paragraph 6.21, that formula speaks of "direct or indirect, actual or potential" hindrances to interstate trade without any mention of their purpose. Yet this is not the first time that the Court has referred to this criterion.[185] According to van Gerven A.G.'s Opinion in *Boermans*,[186] this paragraph of the judgment is to be taken to mean that, where the purpose of an indistinctly applicable measure is to "regulate" trade in goods between Member States, then that constitutes an indication that it does in fact do so.

6.65 At first sight, there appears to be a direct contradiction between paragraph 13 of the judgment ("Such legislation may, admittedly, restrict the volume of sales, and hence the volume of sales of products from other Member States ... ") and paragraph 16 ("the application to products from other Member States of national provisions restricting or prohibiting certain selling arrangements is not such as to hinder directly or indirectly, actually or potentially, trade between Member States within the meaning of the *Dassonville* judgment ... "). Logic would suggest that, if a measure may restrict the volume of imports, then it constitutes at least a potential hindrance to trade. At all events, in paragraph 17 the Court sought to explain the reasoning behind the ruling, and thus in effect to reconcile the statements in paragraphs 13 and 16.

6.66 Turning to paragraph 17 of *Keck*, what is one to make of the statement that non-discriminatory measures relating to "selling arrangements" are not "by nature such as to prevent ... access to the market" of the Member State concerned. As von Wilmowsky has pointed out,[187] this is a legal fiction. Indeed, it is somewhat akin to a *de minimis* rule in that it involves tolerance of measures

---

[183] *Seymour-Smith.*

[184] On the national case law in this area, see Jarvis, *The Application of EC Law by National Courts: the Free Movement of Goods* (1998); and Lichtenwalder, *Die Anwendung von Art. 30 EGV in der mitgliedstaatlichen Rechtsprechung* (1995).

[185] *Krantz, Motorradcenter* and *Quietlynn* (all mentioned at n.54 above). All these rulings were the prelude to the *Peralta* line of case law (para. 6.23 above).

[186] Para. 22.

[187] "Ausnahmebereiche gegenüber EG-Grundfreiheiten ?" [1996] EuR 362 at 368; see also Weatherill, *op. cit.*, at 894.

which restrict imports in some way. Yet there are two important differences between the two approaches:

— while a *de minimis* rule entails the evaluation of complex economic data, the Court's approach is "rule-based" and thus far easier for national courts to apply; and

— the *de minimis* test entails tolerating restrictions which may have harsh effects on a group of traders or consumers, just because that group is small; in contrast, the Court's approach could only very rarely, if ever, produce such an unfortunate result.[188]

6.67   The most eloquent and authoritative assault ever mounted on the reasoning in *Keck* was that of Jacobs A.G. in *Leclerc-Siplec v TF1 Publicité*,[189] which concerned a French prohibition on advertising a wide range of products on television, the apparent purpose being to protect the advertising revenues of France's regional daily press. Applying the tests laid down in *Keck*, he found that the contested legislation fell outside Article 28. However, he took the opportunity to set out a detailed critical analysis of that ruling, and proposed an alternative approach (although he admitted that that approach led to the same result in the case in point). He gave two reasons for finding the reasoning in *Keck* to be unsatisfactory:

"First, it is inappropriate to make rigid distinctions between different categories of rules, and to apply different tests depending on the category to which particular rules belong. The severity of the restriction imposed by different rules is merely one of degree. Measures affecting selling arrangements may create extremely serious obstacles to imports. For example, a rule permitting certain products to be sold only in a handful of small shops in a Member State would be almost as restrictive as an outright ban on importation and marketing. The point is particularly well illustrated by restrictions on advertising: the type of restriction in issue in Hünermund may have had little impact on trade between Member States, but it is difficult to contend that, for example, a total ban on advertising a particular product which can lawfully be sold could fall outside Article [28] ... .[I]t would be more appropriate to measure restrictions against a single test formulated in the light of the purpose of Article [28].
    Secondly, the exclusion from the scope of Article [28] of measures which 'affect in the same manner, in law and in fact, the marketing of domestic products and those from other Member States' amounts to introducing, in relation to restrictions on selling arrangements, a test of discrimination. That test, however, seems inappropriate. The central concern of the Treaty provisions on the free movement of goods is to prevent unjustified obstacles to trade between Member States. If an obstacle to inter-State trade exists, it cannot cease to exist simply because an identical obstacle affects domestic trade ... .
    ... [F]rom the point of view of the Treaty's concern to establish a single market, discrimination is not a helpful criterion: from that point of view, the fact that a Member State imposes similar restrictions on the marketing of domestic products is simply irrelevant. The adverse effect on the Community market is in no way alleviated; nor is the adverse effect on the economies of the other Member States, and so on the

---

[188]See para. 6.18 above.
[189]See n.36 above.

Community economy. Indeed the application of the discrimination test would lead to the fragmentation of the Community market .... Restrictions on trade should not be tested against local conditions which happen to prevail in each Member State, but against the aim of access to the Community market. A discrimination test is therefore inconsistent as a matter of principle with the aims of the Treaty."

On a different note, the Advocate General attached considerable importance to the role of advertising: since most products are little known outside their own Member States, he regarded advertising as crucial if traders are to penetrate other markets. Thus "measures that prohibit or severely restrict advertising tend inevitably to protect domestic manufacturers and to disadvantage manufacturers located in other Member States".[190]

Surely it is no accident that two of the post-*Keck* cases in which the Court has defined the scope of Article 28 most widely relate to advertising: *De Agostini* and *Gourmet International.* Moreover, Jacobs A.G. appeared in both cases.

6.68 It must be acknowledged that there is considerable force in the Advocate General's comments in *Leclerc-Siplec*, not least as regards the importance of advertising. Nevertheless, the fact remains that he was unable to propose a more satisfactory test. In his view, the appropriate test was whether there is a substantial restriction on access to the market of the Member State concerned. Yet, as explained at paragraphs 6.17 and 6.18 above, that amounts to a *de minimis* test, but the Court has always refused to countenance a such a test in relation to Article 28. Moreover, it comes perilously close to the test of whether measures "screen off" the national market propounded by van Gerven A.G. in *Torfaen* – a test which, as was noted at paragraph 6.52, is scarcely conducive to legal certainty.

The case for *Keck* is not that it is perfect, but that every other approach which has been tried or suggested to date has greater shortcomings. Whether the Court were to revert to the exorbitant view that all restrictions on imports are caught by Article 28 regardless of discrimination, or whether it were to adopt the "substantial restriction" on access test, great legal uncertainty would ensue; and legal certainty is surely of the essence if national courts are to apply Article 28 effectively. Despite all its imperfections, the approach in *Keck* involves a "rule-based" test which is reasonably clear and precise.

(vi) Conclusion on this section

6.69 The ruling in *Keck* was a welcome attempt to bring the scope of Article 28 back within reasonable bounds and to restore a degree of legal certainty to this area of the law. While the Court has continued to abide steadfastly by the

---

[190] The importance of advertising for market integration has also been stressed by a number of authors: Thus Reich, *op.cit.* (see n.99 above) at 471 noted "today's marketing mix derives from a uniform concept of product presentation, advertising and sales promotion". Similarly, Steindorff, "Unvollkommener Binnenmarkt" (1994) Z.H.R. 149 stressed the importance of advertising to enable producers to penetrate the markets of other Member States, where the products are unknown.

approach laid down in *Keck*, it is submitted that these criticisms have not gone unheeded. The Court has, it is suggested, responded in two ways:

— when a measure could be considered either as product-bound or as a selling arrangement, the Court has preferred the former[191]; and

— as regards selling arrangements, the Court has interpreted as widely as it could the concept of discrimination in law or in fact.[192]

By steadfastly continuing to apply and to clarify *Keck* despite the barrage of criticism, the Court has indeed ensured a high degree of legal certainty and stability in this area of the law. At the same time, the Court has rightly not been insensitive to such criticism and has cast the scope of Article 28 as widely as possible within the confines of *Keck*.

Having said that, it is manifest that, if the concept of "discrimination in law or in fact" is defined too widely, then the distinction between product-bound measures and those relating to "selling arrangments" will disappear in practice and the entire *Keck* approach will collapse. Also, great caution must be exercised in the use of statistics to establish discrimination.

In addition, it should be recalled that in recent years the Court has also avoided an exorbitant application of Article 28 by excluding from its scope those measures which are too remote to affect the free movement of goods: the *Peralta* line of case law.[193]

D. The Principle of Equivalence or Mutual Recognition

6.70 In the penultimate ground of its judgment in *"Cassis de Dijon"* the Court ruled that:

> "There is ... no valid reason why, provided that they have been lawfully produced and marketed in one of the Member States, alcoholic beverages should not be introduced into any other Member State; the sale of such products may not be subject to a legal prohibition on the marketing of beverages with an alcoholic content lower than the limit set by national rules."

Consequently, in the operative part of its judgment, the Court ruled that a measure of the kind in question was contrary to Article 28 "where the importation of alcoholic beverages lawfully produced and marketed in another Member State is concerned".[194]

The Court spelt out more clearly the principle of equivalence—also known as the principle of mutual recognition - in its subsequent ruling in *Fietje*.[195] There,

---

[191] See para. 6.56 above.
[192] See paras 6.59 *et seq.* above.
[193] Para. 6.23 above.
[194] See also, *e.g.* para. 6.46, Case 788/79, see n.129 above; and Case 130/80 *Keldermann* [1981] E.C.R. 527.
[195] See n.32 above.

the Court held in effect that the obligation to declare the nature of goods on their label was, in principle, justified on consumer protection grounds. However, it added that:

"There is no longer any need for such protection if the details given on the original label of the imported product have as their content information on the nature of the product and that content includes at least the same information and is just as capable of being understood by the consumers in the importing State as the description prescribed by the rules of that State."

The Court also made the point very clearly in *Commission v France* (woodworking machines)[196] when it held that a Member State:

"is not entitled to prevent the marketing of a product originating in another Member State which provides a level of protection of the health and life of humans equivalent to that which the national rules are intended to ensure or establish. It is therefore contrary to the principle of proportionality for national rules to require such imported products to comply strictly and exactly with the provisions or technical requirements laid down for products manufactured in the Member States in question when those imported products afford users the same level of protection."[197]

6.71 The Commission attached particular importance to this matter in its Communication[198] on "*Cassis de Dijon*". It drew the conclusion that this passage was of general application, asserting that:

"Any product imported from another Member State must in principle be admitted to the territory of the importing Member State if it has been lawfully produced, that is, conforms to rules and processes of manufacture that are customarily and traditionally accepted in the exporting country, and is marketed in the territory in the latter ...

The principles decided by the Court imply that a Member State may not in principle prohibit the sale in its territory of a product lawfully produced according to technical or quality requirements which differ from those imposed on its domestic products. Where a product 'suitably and satisfactorily' fulfils the legitimate objective of a Member State's own rules (public safety, protection of the consumer or the environment, etc.) the importing country cannot justify prohibiting its sale in its territory by claiming that the way it fulfils the objective is different from that imposed on domestic products."

6.72 This calls for a number of comments:

(a) Although "*Cassis de Dijon*" spoke of goods lawfully produced *and* marketed in another Member State, La Pergola A.G. took the view in the *foie gras* case that it suffices for goods to be lawfully produced *or* marketed there.[199] While he did not set out detailed reasons in support of this conclusion, it is true

---

[196] Case 188/84 [1986] E.C.R. 419.
[197] See also the passage quoted at para. 7.15 below from the Order in Case 45/87R *Commission v Ireland* (Dundalk Water Supply) [1987] E.C.R. 1369; [1987] 2 C.M.L.R. 563.
[198] See n.127 above.
[199] n.53 above, at 6210.

that there is no good reason why the test should be cumulative.[200]

6.73   (b) The judgments do not define what is meant by lawful marketing in the Member State of production. Nor does the Commission's Communication. Presumably it will be enough if, on production, the goods are lawfully sold for export. There would appear to be no need for an initial sale entirely within the producing Member State before the goods are sold for export.[201]

6.74   (c) As the Commission pointed out in its Communication, even if a product is lawfully produced and marketed in a Member State, it may not be sold within another Member State which has higher standards than the Member State of production—provided always that those higher standards are justified as being necessary to satisfy mandatory requirements. Thus if the optimal standard for a given product is 100 and the importing Member State requires 80, then it may justifiably prohibit the sale of goods conforming to the standard of only 70 imposed by the producing Member State. The same applies *a fortiori* if the producing Member State imposes no minimum standards at all. However, as already explained,[202] there is always a rebuttable presumption that the higher standard is not necessary.

On the other hand, if two Member States both require a standard of 80 but lay down different means of reaching that result, then each must permit the sale of the other's product. Since it will not always be clear whether two standards are in fact equivalent, Member States are under a duty to take active steps[203] to establish whether this is so.

6.75   (d) What is important in this context is not whether the producing Member State imposes a standard equivalent to that of the importing Member State. What matters rather is whether the product in question in fact meets a standard equivalent to that of the importing Member State—assuming that the product was lawfully produced in the Member State of production. This is illustrated by *Fietje* which in essence concerned the compatibility with Articles 28 to 30 of the obligation to indicate the denomination "liqueur" on goods of a particular kind. The Court found that such a requirement fell foul of Article 28 if the goods in fact bore a label containing information of equivalent value to the consumer. The Court did not state that it was necessary to look into the legislation of the producing Member State to consider whether it required such labelling.

---

[200]The A.G. relied on two judgments in support of his proposition, namely: Cases 59/82 *Schutzverband v Weinvertriebs* [1983] E.C.R. 1217, para. 12; and C-131/93, see n.32 above, para. 10. However, it is respectfully suggested that these rulings do not provide unequivocal support for his view.

[201]Mattera, "L'article 30 du Traité CEE la jurisprudence 'Cassis de Dijon' et le principe de la reconnaissance mutuelle" [1992] R.M.U.E. 13 at 46. See also Gormley, "Prohibiting Restrictions on Trade within the EEC" (1985) at 48, the requirement is in truth that the goods must be lawfully produced or marketed in the exporting Member State.

[202]Para. 6.70 above.

[203]See generally Case 104/75 *De Peijper* [1976] E.C.R. 613.

6.76 Does the mention in *"Cassis de Dijon"* of goods lawfully produced and marketed in a Member State mean that the principle of equivalence does not apply to goods originating in a third State but in free circulation in the Community? In view of the immense importance of this question, it is extraordinary that the Court has never been called upon to rule on it.[204]

It is submitted that goods originating in third States may in fact benefit from the principle of equivalence. Indirect authority for this proposition may be found in *Co-Frutta v Amministrazione delle Finanze dello Stato*.[205] One of the questions which arose there was whether Article 90 applies to all products coming from other Member States, including those which originate in third countries but are in free circulation in the Community. This was a vexed question, since Article 90 merely speaks of "products of other Member States". The Court found that Article 90 did extend to such products. It deduced this from the fact that the Community forms the basis for a customs union; and that as a result Article 23(2) of the Treaty requires third country products in free circulation to be "definitively and wholly assimilated" to products originating in Member States.[206] What is more, the Court made it plain that it is of no consequence in which third country the goods originate: the Court declined the invitation of the national court to rule on the relevance of the GATT, thereby implicitly ruling that Article 90 applied despite the fact that the country of origin of the goods in question, Colombia, was not a full member of the organisation.[207]

The same reasoning can be applied here. Let us take the following example: a product is manufactured in a third country and is then put in free circulation in France, whereupon it is imported into Germany[208]; the product complies with the relevant French standard, but not with the German one, although the two are equivalent. If a restrictive view of the principle of equivalence is taken, then the product cannot be marketed in Germany, even if it can be sold in France. The unity of the single market is thus undermined. The harmful effects of this restrictive approach would be felt by the Community itself, quite apart from the obvious adverse effects of its trade relations with the third country concerned. Accordingly, on the basis of an analogy with *Co-Frutta* it is suggested that in such circumstances the principle of equivalence also works for the benefit of third country goods.

As we noticed in paragraph 6.72 above, La Pergola A.G. suggested in *"foie gras"* that, to benefit from the principle of equivalence, goods need only have been lawfully produced or marketed in a Member State. If that is so, then this problem is automatically solved.

Moreover, the outcome should be the same, if the goods are put into free

---

[204] There is also a dearth of authority on this point in the legal literature, but see Bruha, "Normen und Standards im Warenverkehr mit Drittstaaten" in *EG und Drittstaatsbeziehungen nach 1992* (1991) at 83.

[205] Case 193/85 [1987] E.C.R. 2085.

[206] See paras 2.15 *et seq.* above.

[207] As to the Court's case law on GATT, see para. 1.02.

[208] This is quite different from the case where restrictions are imposed on direct imports into the Community–a subject which falls outside the scope of this book.

circulation in, say, Belgium, which has no equivalent standard and are imported indirectly from there into Germany—provided that they always conform to the standard of one Member State (*e.g.* France), which is equivalent to the German standard.

6.77 What are the practical consequences of the principle of equivalence? Potentially they are enormous. Mattera[209] sees this ruling as a step away from the faceless world of Euro-bread, Euro-beer and Euro-toys. Instead, local specialities from every Member State can in principle be bought and sold in their traditional form all over the Community. This gives the consumer a wide range of products to choose from.

On the other hand, this ruling has been criticised on the grounds that it will result in lowering of standards.[210] Yet, as has just been explained, the effect of the ruling is that a Member State may prohibit the sale of goods complying with a lower standard than its own, provided the higher standard is justified. Thus, for instance, it cannot seriously be argued that the judgment in *Gilli*—in which the Court held that the prohibition in a Member State on the sale of cider vinegar was contrary to Article 28—resulted in any lowering of standards. The case law shows that the Court consistently upholds measures which are genuinely justified on, say, consumer protection grounds.[211]

6.78 The ruling in *Commission v France* (foie gras)[212] has triggered a new spate of activity with respect to the principle of equivalence. For the first time, it was held there that France had breached Article 28 by laying down a standard for goods sold as *foie gras* products, because the contested decree did not contain a mutual recognition clause. This has led Mattera[213] to conclude that Member States are under a general obligation to insert such a clause into their legislation.

This theory is being tested in another action brought by the Commission against France[214]; the Opinion of Mischo A.G. has already been delivered but the judgment is still awaited. This case concerns two French decrees which relate to a broad range of food products and food additives. The Commission alleges *inter alia* that those decrees infringe Article 28, because they do not contain a mutual recognition clause.

The Advocate General has advised the Court to dismiss this claim, on the following grounds[215]:

---

[209] *op. cit.* n.201 above at p. 50.

[210] Seidel, "Die Sogenannte Cassis-de-Dijon Rechtsprechung des Europäischen Gerichtshofes und der Schutz von Herkunftsangaben in der Europäischen Gemeinschaft" [1984] G.R.U.R.Int. 80.

[211] See paras 8.125 *et seq.* below, and see Judge Everling, "Die Cassis de Dijon Rechtsprechung des EuGH und ihre Auswirkungen auf die Ernährungswirtschaft" (1987) 10 Schriftenreihe des Bundes für Lebensmittelrecht und Lebensmittelkunde.

[212] n.53 above.

[213] *op.cit.*, n.53 above; see also González Vaqué, "Faut-il insérer des clauses de reconnaissance mutuelle dans les législations internes ?" [1999] J.T.D.E. 87.

[214] Case 24/00 *Commission v France* (pending); see also paras 78 and 79 of Mischo A.G.'s Opinion in Case C-95/01 C *Greenham and Abel* (pending).

[215] Paras 40 *et seq.* of the Opinion.

— First, he maintained that it is not sustained by the wording of the *foie gras* ruling: in the body of the judgment, the Court remarked that the contested French legislation did not permit the marketing of an imported product which did not "fully" comply with the legislation of the host State.[216] In the light of this passage, he found that the *foie gras* judgment fell short of requiring mutual recognition clauses across the board.

— Second, he noted that, while the *foie gras* case merely related to consumer protection, the present proceedings concerned public health. However, it is submitted that this distinction seems somewhat questionable, given that the principle of equivalence has always been applied by the Court to all the grounds of justification, including public health.[217]

— Third, he sought to distinguish *foie gras* on the basis that the decree in issue in that case concerned a limited class of products, which was not the case here. However, with respect one might have some doubts as to whether this is a workable distinction in law.

— Last, he maintained that a general clause to the effect that "equivalent products" would be permissible would create more difficulties than it would solve. Here one must acknowledge that he has a point: such a clause would not be fully conducive to legal certainty.

The Court's judgment is eagerly awaited. What it is called upon to do is to reconcile two fundamental principles of Community law, which in this instance appear to conflict: the principle of the free movement of goods (of which the principle of equivalence forms part) and the principle of legal certainty.[218] [219] Plainly, this is no easy matter.

IV. MEASURES OF EQUIVALENT EFFECT ON EXPORTS

6.79 Before examining the concept of measures of equivalent effect falling under Article 29, it is as well to consider why Member States impose restrictions on exports at all. A Member State will normally be moved to take such action by one or more of the following motives:

— a desire to ensure supplies[220];

— the protection of jobs in processing industries (in this case the export

---

[216] Para. 18 of the judgment.

[217] See, *e.g. Commission v France* (woodworking machines) (n.196 above).

[218] On legal certainty, see para. 12.29 below.

[219] Another Commission initiative following the "*foie gras*" judgment was its Communication entitled "Mutual Recognition in the Context of the Follow-up to the Action Plan for the Single Market" (COM(1999) 299 final); discussed by González Vaqué, "Marché intérieur : renforcer l'efficacité de la reconnaissance mutuelle" [1999] J.T.D.E. 230; see also the Council Resolution of October 28, 1999 on mutual recognition ([2000] O.J. C141/5).

[220] As in Case 68/76 *Commission v France* (export licences for potatoes) [1977] E.C.R. 515; see para. 7.102 below.

restriction will cover the raw material or component part, but not the finished product)[221];

— the prevention of parallel exports (so that manufacturers established in the Member State in question will be able to obtain higher profits in their export trade);

— the maintenance of the quality of exports[222];

— the preservation of works of art for the nation.[223]

6.80 The timetable for the abolition of such measures is that set out in paragraphs 5.01 to 5.04 and 6.03 *et seq.* above.

Parts II and IIIB of this Chapter apply *mutatis mutandis* to Article 29. In so far as discrimination is relevant here, it is discrimination against goods intended for export in favour of goods intended for the domestic market. This applies whether these goods were produced in the Member State in question or are merely in free circulation there; it is clear that the prohibition in Article 29 applies to re-exports.[224] Like measures of equivalent effect on imports, such measures relating to exports may take effect at the border but do not necessarily do so. Classic examples are: export licences[225]; measures which lower the value of a product intended for export or increase its cost; and measures which discourage the sale of products for export. Once again, a measure will not fall under Article 29 if it is caught by another prohibition in the Treaty, such as Article 23, 87 or 90.

6.81 As we have noticed in Section IIIC above, a measure restricting imports may fall under Article 28, even if it applies to domestic and imported products in the same way. The fundamental question concerning Article 29 is: can measures fall within the concept of measures of equivalent effect under Article 29, even if they apply in the same way to exports and to goods intended for the domestic market? In other words, does a measure restricting exports fall under Article 29 even if it does not discriminate against exports? At first sight, there would appear to be no obstacle to Article 29 covering this type of measure, especially as the *Dassonville* formula does not purport to be limited to measures of equivalent effect on imports.[226] Nevertheless, on closer examination the problem becomes more complex.

6.82 In *Groenveld v Produktschap voor Vee en Vlees*,[227] which concerned a prohi-

---

[221] Cases C-203/96 *Chemische Afvalstoffen Dusseldorp v Minister van Milieubeheer* [1998] E.C.R. I-4075; and C-209/98 *FFAD v Københavns Kommune* [2000] E.C.R. I-3743; see para. 7.113 below.
[222] Case 53/76 *Procureur de la République v Bouhelier* [1977] E.C.R. 197; see para. 7.103 below.
[223] Measures adopted for the latter motive will often be justified under Art. 30; see paras 8.115 *et seq.* below.
[224] Restrictions on re-exports may infringe both Art. 28 and Art. 29.
[225] Paras 7.102 *et seq.* below.
[226] The *Dassonville* formula (para. 6.20 above) was incorporated (albeit in rather an oblique way) in para. 16 of the judgment in *Bouhelier* (see n.222 above) at 205.
[227] Case 15/79 [1979] E.C.R. 3409; [1981] 1 C.M.L.R. 207.

bition on producing horse meat, the Court held that Article 29:

> "concerns national measures which have as their specific object or effect the restriction of patterns of exports and thereby the establishment of a difference between the domestic trade of a Member State and its export trade in such a way as to provide a particular advantage for national production or for the domestic market of the State in question at the expense of the production or of the trade of other Member States."

Even since then, the Court has found that Article 29 applies exclusively to measures having the specific object or effect of restricting exports.[228] Accordingly, that provision does not catch measures applying in the same way to goods intended for export and to goods intended for the domestic market.

6.83   What is the rationale behind the Court's relatively restrictive approach to Article 29? If that provision were to extend to all barriers to exports regardless of discrimination or protective intent, it would cover a large number of restrictions on production such as planning regulations for factories, which are far removed from interstate trade. This would surely be exorbitant—particularly as restrictions on movements of goods which are purely internal to a Member State are not caught by any of the prohibitions in the Treaty, as explained in Part VII of this Chapter. Also, if the net of Article 29 were cast so wide, it would catch measures which are properly the preserve of Article 43 (ex 52) EC on the freedom of establishment. Furthermore, States rarely have any incentive to restrict exports. Export restrictions –especially those applicable at the production rather the marketing stage—are thus of a fundamentally different nature from import restrictions. According to the prevailing body of opinion,[229] the Court is therefore correct in construing Article 29 more narrowly than Article 28, at least as regards restrictions on production.

True, in *Oebel*[230] Capotorti A.G. endorsed the converse, "unitary" approach whereby the scope of Article 29 is as broad as that of Article 28[231]; but that was over 20 years ago. It should also be mentioned that in recent years the Court has applied the unitary approach to the free movement of workers[232] and of services.[233] In other words, it has construed Articles 39 (ex 48) in the same way with respect to restrictions on outgoing workers as with incoming workers; and the same has occurred with respect to services under Article 43 EC. These rulings have some relevance to Article 29 because, as we noticed in paragraph 1.12 above, the case law on the four freedoms has been converging in recent years;

---

[228] The ruling in *Bouhelier* see (n.222 above) appears to constitute an exception to this.

[229] *e.g.* Defalque, *Commentaire Mégret—Le droit de la CEE* (2nd ed., 1992) Vol. 1 at 268; Müller-Graff, commentary on Article 34 (old numbering) in Groeben, Thiesing, Ehlermann, *op. cit.* (see n.54 above) at 770–772; VerLoren van Themaat, "De artikelen 30-36 van het EEG-verdrag" [1980] RM Themis 4/5 378.

[230] See n.134 above.

[231] This statement was supported by Mattera, *Le marché unique européen: Ses règles, son fonctionnement* (2nd ed., 1990) at 516 *et seq.*

[232] Cases Case C-415/93 *Union Royale Belge des Sociétés de Football Association v Bosman* [1995] E.C.R. I-4921; and C-18/95 *Terhoeve* [1999] E.C.R. I-345.

[233] Case C-384/93 *Alpine Investments v Ministerie van Financiën* [1995] E.C.R. I-1141.

and the analogy between goods and services is especially close. Nevertheless, it seems clear that in this instance different considerations apply to the free movement of goods.

6.84 The situation is perhaps somewhat different with respect to restrictions which take effect at the marketing stage. In previous editions of this book, the idea was mooted that measures of that kind might be subject to the "*Cassis de Dijon*" test rather than a test along the lines of that in *Groenveld*.[234] This suggestion has not found favour with the Court, which treats such export restrictions in the same way as restrictions on production.[235] However, it was recently endorsed by Jacobs A.G. in *Alpine Investments*.[236] This issue will be considered further below.

6.85 Having discussed the general issues of principle, it is appropriate at this juncture to return to an examination of the case law on Article 29.

The Court has repeated the rather cumbersome formula in *Groenveld* on a number of occasions.[237] However, since *Oebel*[238] it has delivered a series of judgments in which the final words of that formula ("at the expense of the production or of the trade of the other Member States") have been omitted.[239] To complicate matters further, in *Belgium v Spain* (Rioja) the Court recently came up with yet another formula, saying that Article 29 applied to measures which have "the effect of specifically restricting patterns of exports ... and thereby of establishing a difference of treatment between trade within a Member State and its export trade".[240] Yet within a matter of days it reverted to the *Oebel* formula in *FFAD v Københavns Kommune*.[241] What can account for this surprising lack of consistency?

6.86 At all events, the new "*Rioja*" test is welcome, as it is clearly preferable to that in *Groenveld* and *Oebel*. In reality, whatever test it purports to apply, the Court merely checks whether the contested measure has the specific object or effect of restricting exports as opposed to goods intended for the domestic market. Thus the Court itself treats most clauses of the *Groenveld* and *Oebel* tests as no more than surplus verbiage, implicitly recognising that:

— There is no objective reason why it need be shown that the measure provides "a particular advantage for national production or for the

---

[234] See also Defalque, *op. cit.* at 268.
[235] See Case C-339/89 *Alsthom Atlantique v Sulzer* [1991] E.C.R. I-107 (provision imposing liability for latent defects on vendor); Case C-80/92, see n.26 above.
[236] See n.233 above, at 1156-7.
[237] Cases C-9/89 *Spain v Council* [1990] E.C.R. I-1383 (para. 21); and *Alsthom Atlantique* (para. 14).
[238] See n.134 above.
[239] Cases C-47/90 *Delhaize v Promalvin* [1992] E.C.R. I-3669, para. 12; Case C-80/92 para. 24; *Dusseldorp* (see n.221 below) para. 40; and *FFAD* (n.221 above), para. 34.
[240] Case C-388/95 [2000] E.C.R. I-3123, para. 41.
[241] See n.221 above, para. 34 of the judgment.

domestic market of the State in question" (*Oebel*)[242]; and

— There is still less reason to establish in addition that this occurs "at the expense of the production or of the trade of other Member States" (*Groenveld*).

Accordingly, it is to be hoped that in future the Court will apply the "*Rioja*" test in all cases. True, that test does not mention the "specific object" of the measure, but no doubt a protectionist effect may be inferred from a protectionist intent; and even the *Dassonville* formula does not refer to the object of the measure.[243]

In any case, it seems clear that the scope of Article 29 is not confined to national measures which discriminate against exports on their face: *de facto* discrimination will suffice, as the measure will then have the "specific effect" of restricting exports.

6.87 Even though it was not followed in *FFAD*, the ruling in "*Rioja*" shows that the Court is not deaf to criticism that the *Groenveld* and *Oebel* tests are too narrow. That criticism emanates both from certain Advocates General and from a number of authors. Before examining the statements by the Advocates General and the literature, it should be stressed that these authorities would require a further change in the case law beyond the change in form effected in "*Rioja*"—but only with respect to restrictions on marketing.

6.88 In *Delhaize v Promalvin*,[244] Gulmann A.G. briefly remarked that the existing test was too narrow, although it is not clear how broad he believed the proper scope of Article 29 to be.

As already mentioned, Jacobs A.G. stated in *Alpine Investments* that the *Groenveld* test was inappropriate for restrictions on marketing. The facts of that case were that the Dutch authorities prohibited the practice known as "cold calling" whereby financial services are offered to individuals by means of unsolicited telephone calls. This ban applied in the same way to calls made to potential clients within the Netherlands as to those made to individuals outside the country. The plaintiffs maintained that this restriction fell foul of Article 49, in so far as it related to telephone calls to other Member States. Accordingly, the Advocate General only considered Article 29 by way of analogy. In any case, the following passage of his Opinion is particularly noteworthy:

"It may be doubted ... whether the case law of the Court under Article [29] applies to rules of the exporting State concerning the marketing of goods. A Member State may prohibit traders established in its territory from using a marketing technique in order to sell their products in that State. However, it does not follow that it is entitled to prohibit them from using that marketing technique in order to sell their products in

---

[242] Müller-Graff, *op. cit.* at n.54; Van Calster, "Export restrictions—a Watershed for Article 30" [2000] E.L.Rev. 335 at 336.
[243] The words "object or effect" are drawn from Art. 81 of the Treaty.
[244] See n.239 above, at 3699.

other Member States. Clearly, a trader cannot be required by the exporting Member State to abstain from using in another Member State a form of advertising which is prohibited in the exporting State but is permitted in the other Member State in order to market his products in the latter, unless there is good reason for the prohibition."[245]

This passage must be understood in the context of the same Advocate General's assault on *Keck* in relation to advertising and promotion—which has largely failed to sway the Court.[246] Let us imagine that a Member State imposed a blanket ban on advertising certain goods and that that ban was applicable to imports, exports and domestic goods marketed within the Member State. It would be paradoxical if that ban were caught by Article 29 but not Article 28.

6.89   Turning to the literature, Roth[247] has championed a reassessment of the Court's approach to Article 29 which is more balanced than the unitary approach. While acknowledging that Member States have little incentive to restrict exports, he questions whether they should be entitled to do so at all. He rightly points out that the *Groenveld* test, which focuses exclusively on the relationship between the potential exporter and the authorities of his Member State, is out of keeping with the Court's more recent emphasis on the right of the recipient to import goods into his home State.[248] He therefore advocates a new definition of measures of equivalent effect under Article 29, which would embrace all marketing restrictions as well as product-bound measures applying to exports (such as rules relating to their composition or presentation), whether or not they specifically aim to discriminate against exports or have that effect.[249] On this view, Member States must exempt goods intended for export from such restrictions, subject of course to justification. In contrast, measures relating to the conditions in which goods are produced—such a rules of labour or environmental law, or town planning legislation—would continue to be governed by a test based on discrimination.

While this approach has much to commend it, it should be recalled that in *Alpine Investments* the Court held that "maintaining the reputation of the national financial sector may ... constitute an imperative reason of public interest capable of justifying restrictions on the freedom to provide financial services"; the ban on "cold calling" both within the Netherlands and to other Member States was therefore held to be justified. No doubt, restrictions on exports of goods could be justified on the same grounds.[250] This would clearly reduce the impact of the reform advocated by Roth.

---

[245] at 1157.
[246] Paras 6.67 *et seq.* above.
[247] "Wettbewerb der Mitgliedstaaten oder Wettbewerb der Hersteller ?—Plädoyer für eine Neubestimmung des Art. 34 EGV" [1995] Z.H.R. 78; see also Müller-Graff, *op.cit.* at 772.
[248] Cases 215/87 *Schumacher v Hauptzollamt Frankfurt* [1989] E.C.R. 617 (goods ordered by a consumer by mail from another Member State); C-62/90 *Commission v Germany* [1992] E.C.R. I-2575; and Case C-120/95 *Decker v Caisse de Maladie des Employés Privés* [1998] E.C.R. I-1831.
[249] This is akin to the test in *Keck.* See para. 6.00 above.
[250] See para. 8.170 below.

6.90 The situation can be summarised as follows: while the new "*Rioja*" test is to be warmly welcomed, there may be a need for the Court to widen the test so as to catch restrictions imposed on exports at the marketing stage, including product-bound restrictions. On the other hand, there is now broad consensus that restrictions on production should only fall within Article 29 if they specifically affect exports as opposed to goods intended for the domestic market.

6.91 On another point, in *ED v Fenocchio*[251] the Court held that the possibility that traders would be deterred by the contested measure from selling goods to purchasers established in other Member States "too uncertain and indirect for the national provision to be regarded as liable to hinder trade between Member States".[252] The Court has thus transposed its *Peralta* line of case law[253] from Article 28 to Article 29.

6.92 Last, do the "mandatory requirements" laid down in "*Cassis de Dijon*"[254] apply to measures of equivalent effect on exports? In his observations in *Groenveld* and *Oebel*, Capotorti A.G. propounded the view that the "mandatory requirements" did apply to export restrictions.[255] Moreover, the Court in *Oebel* more or less implied this to be so.[256] Indeed, there is every reason to suppose than an export restriction justified on, say, environmental grounds will be compatible with Article 29, even though the protection of the environment constitutes a "mandatory requirement" rather than a ground of justification set out expressly in Article 30. The ruling in *Chemische Afvalstoffen Dusseldorp v Minister van Milieubeheer*[257] appears to acknowledge this implicitly.

It is difficult to see how the Court could find room for the "mandatory requirements" to apply to export restrictions if:

— it continued to cling to the notion that the "mandatory requirements" do not apply to "distinctly applicable" measures[258]; and

— the concept of measures of equivalent effect under Article 29 only covers measures discriminating against exports ("distinctly applicable" measures).

However, as explained at paragraphs 8.03 to 8.10 below, recent case law— notably *Dusseldorp* – suggests that the Court is now moving away from its traditional categorisation of the "mandatory requirements" towards an acceptance that they should be treated in the same way as the grounds of justification

---

[251] See n.69 above; see para. 7.110 below.
[252] Para. 11 of the judgment.
[253] Para. 6.23 above.
[254] See n.123 above.
[255] However, he took the view that *Cassis de Dijon* could quite generally be applied *mutatis mutandis* to Art. 29 so that "indistinctly applicable" measures fell under that provision. As we have seen, the Court held otherwise in *Groenveld* and *Oebel*.
[256] Para. 8.163 below.
[257] See n.221 above, para. 44 of the judgment; see para. 8.09 below.
[258] Para. 8.07.

expressly set out in Article 30. On that view, which has been advocated in this book since its very first edition, export restrictions caught by Article 29 can be justified by the "mandatory requirements".

V. *DE FACTO* HARMONISATION

6.93 We noticed in an earlier part of this Chapter[259] how the Court held in the *"Cassis de Dijon"* case that, in the absence of a mandatory requirement, a Member State is bound to admit goods lawfully produced and marketed in another Member State. If all the Member States impose precisely the same technical standard for a particular product, then goods not complying with that standard cannot be lawfully produced or marketed in any Member State of the Community. There will then be no restriction on imports or exports between Member States, so that neither Article 28 nor Article 29 will be infringed. It is submitted that, as regards technical standards, *de facto* harmonisation is compatible with Articles 28 to 30.[260]

To take one example, should all Member States require a particular drink to have an alcoholic content of at least 15 per cent, there will be no infringement of Articles 28 to 30, simply because there will be no restrictions on imports or exports between Member States. This will be so whether or not Member States have acted in concert. It will be otherwise, however, if one single Member State imposes a different minimum alcohol requirement, or none at all: trade between that State and the others will then be restricted. This shows that *de facto* harmonisation is no lasting substitute for Community legislation.[261]

6.94 However, it must not be overlooked that, as a general rule, if all Member States enact the same restriction, they will all be infringing Article 28. Thus, for instance, if they all subject imports of a certain product to unnecessary import controls, then they are all committing an infringement. Only technical standards cease to constitute import restrictions once they are adopted by all the Member States.

VI. DISCRIMINATION AND REGIONAL RESTRICTIONS

6.95 As mentioned in paragraph 4.03, measures adopted by regional or local authorities, however small, may fall foul of Articles 28 and 29. It may also happen that central government imposes an export restriction applying only to part of the national territory.

What then is the situation if, for example, a restriction were to be imposed on

---

[259] Paras 6.70 *et seq.* above.
[260] In a rather different context, Case 89/76 *Commission v Netherlands* [1977] E.C.R. 1355; [1978] 3 C.M.L.R. 630, which concerned phytosanitary controls on exports, shows that the Court attaches importance to *de facto* harmonisation.
[261] See Ch. XII.

goods entering Northern Ireland from any source? It could be argued that in such a case, no discrimination arises because some domestic goods also suffer discrimination. However, the Court ruled otherwise in *Du Pont de Nemours*[262] where it held:

"products originating in other Member States suffer discrimination in comparison with products manufactured in the Member State in question, with the result that the normal course of intra-Community trade is hindered.

That conclusion is not affected by the fact that the restrictive effects of a preferential system of the kind at issue are borne in the same measure both by products manufactured by undertakings from the Member State in question which are not situated in the region covered by the preferential system and by products manufactured by undertakings established in other Member States.

It must be emphasised in the first place that, although not all the products of the Member State in question benefit by comparison with products from abroad, the fact remains that all the products benefiting by the preferential system are domestic products; secondly, the fact that the restrictive effect exercised by a State measure on imports does not benefit all domestic products but only some cannot exempt the measure in question from the prohibition set out in Article [28]."

Precisely the same applies in relation to Article 29, as is clearly shown by the ruling in *Delhaize v Promalvin*[263]: the requirement of bottling Rioja wine in the region of that name discriminated against all bottlers in other Member States, even though Spanish bottlers outside that region were similarly disfavoured.

VII. "PURELY NATIONAL" MEASURES; REVERSE DISCRIMINATION

6.96 Do Articles 28 and 29 prohibit restrictive national measures relating to goods which affect neither imports nor exports? Similarly, can a domestic producer supplying only the domestic market invoke either of these provisions against a measure on the grounds that the measure also restricts imports or exports? For example:

— can a producer of goods in a Member State invoke Articles 28 or 29 against a restriction on sale in that Member State in respect of goods put on the national market?

— can an importer of goods originating in England, Scotland or Wales rely on Article 28 with respect to a restriction on importing those goods to Northern Ireland?

The result should be the same whether the measure complained of applies only

---

[262] See n.76 above at 920; confirmed in *Aragonesa de Publicidad,* see n.12 above, and *Ligur Carni,* para. 6.56, see n.56 above.
[263] See n.239 above; see in particular para. 29 of the A.G.'s Opinion; see also Case C-388/95 (n.240 above).

to national goods or applies also to goods from other Member States.

6.97   Article 3 of the Treaty lists among the activities of the Community "(a) the prohibition, *as between Member States*, of customs duties and quantitative restrictions on the import and export of goods, and of all other measures having equivalent effect ... [and] (c) an internal market characterised by the abolition, *as between Member States*, of obstacles to the free movement of goods, persons, services and capital".[264] In keeping with that, restrictions on imports "between Member States" are prohibited by Article 28, while those on exports "between Member States" are prohibited by Article 29.

What is more, Article 14(2) states: "The internal market shall comprise an area without internal frontiers in which the free movement of goods, persons, services and capital is ensured *in accordance with the provisions of this Treaty*".[265] Since no provisions of the Treaty appear to prohibit restrictions on movements of goods within Member States, the conclusion should be that such restrictions are compatible with the Treaty.[266]

In short, one will search the Treaty in vain for any provision to the effect that restrictions on the movement of goods **within** Member States are prohibited. The draftsmen of the Treaty plainly took the view that it is no business of the Community to prevent Member States from imposing restrictions on trade in goods and services within their own territory. This result appears to reflect the principle of subsidiarity,[267] even before that concept become part of Community law.

In the light of these considerations, the view has been taken in the previous editions of this book that "purely national" measures are not caught by these provisions at all; and that, by the same token, there is no bar to Member States practising reverse discrimination (*i.e.* treating their domestic products less favourably than imports).

That was also the stance initially adopted by the Court.

6.98   The matter first arose directly in *Waterkeyn*.[268] This case constituted the sequel to *Commission v France*,[269] where the Court had held that "by subjecting advertising in respect of alcoholic beverages to discriminatory rules and thereby maintaining obstacles to the freedom of intra-Community trade, the French Republic has failed to fulfil its obligations under Article [28] of the EEC Treaty." It had reached this conclusion notwithstanding the fact that a minority

---

[264] emphasis added.

[265] emphasis added; on this provision, see paras 12.13 *et seq.* below.

[266] True, Article 3(g) provides for "a system ensuring that competition in the internal market is not distorted", and this wording covers restrictions *within* the Member States. Yet surely this paragraph only concerns competition between undertakings within the meaning of Arts 81 and 82, and not competition in the broadest sense. In any event, Art. 3(g) would constitute a most slender basis for the view that restrictions on the free movement of goods are contrary to Arts 28 and 29, given that it would run counter to the clear wording of the latter provisions. On the combined application of Art. 10 (ex 5) EC with Art. 81 or 82, see paras 6.33–6.34 above.

[267] See paras 12.04 *et seq.* below.

[268] Cases 314-316/81 and 83/82 [1982] E.C.R. 4337; [1983] 2 C.M.L.R. 145.

[269] Case 152/78 [1980] E.C.R. 2299; [1981] 2 C.M.L.R. 743.

of French-produced alcoholic drinks was subject to the more severe restrictions on categories of drink which were typically imported. The principal question which arose in *Waterkeyn* was whether the Court had ruled the legislation to be contrary to Article 28 only in so far as it applied to imports, or whether its ruling also extended to domestically produced drinks. In answer to a request for a preliminary ruling, the Court held that its earlier ruling was limited to imports. It is clear from the wording of the judgment that the result flows from the nature of Article 28 itself rather than merely from the terms of the earlier ruling.

6.99 This was confirmed in *Oosthoek's Uitgeversmaatschappij*,[270] which related to Dutch legislation prohibiting the promotion of sales by means of free gifts, subject to certain immaterial exceptions. The defendants in the main case were prosecuted for seeking to induce the public to buy their encyclopaedias in this way. Some of these encyclopaedias had been produced in Belgium, while others had been produced in the Netherlands. As regards the second category, the Court held:

> "the application of the Netherlands legislation to the sale in the Netherlands of encyclopaedias produced in that country is in no way linked to the importation or exportation of goods and does not therefore fall within the scope of Articles [28 and 29] of the EEC Treaty."

6.100 As regards Article 28, the position is stated most clearly of all in *Cognet*.[271] The defendant had been charged with selling books at a 20 per cent discount, contrary to French law. Following the Court's ruling in *Leclerc v Au Blé Vert*,[272] that law had been amended so as to provide for an exemption for all books imported from another Member State where they had been marketed. This exemption extended to books published in France and exported before being re-imported into France. The accused maintained that the law discriminated against French books put directly on the French market and was therefore contrary to Community law. The Court rejected this view in the following terms:

> "Article [28] of the EEC Treaty does not forbid such a difference of treatment. The purpose of that provision is to eliminate obstacles to the importation of goods and not to ensure that goods of national origin always enjoy the same treatment as imported or re-imported goods. The absence of restrictions as regards the selling price of re-imported books does not prejudice the sale of such books. A difference in treatment between goods which is not capable of restricting imports or of prejudicing the marketing of imported or re-imported goods does not fall within the prohibition contained in Article [29]."[273]

---

[270] Case 286/81 [1982] E.C.R. 4575; [1983] 3 C.M.L.R. 428.
[271] Case 355/85 [1986] E.C.R. 3231; [1987] 3 C.M.L.R. 942
[272] See n.36 above.
[273] See also, Case 98/86 *Mathot* [1987] E.C.R. 809; [1988] 1 C.M.L.R. 411. (The Court followed the same approach with regard to services: Cases 52/79 *Procureur du Roi v Debauve* [1980] E.C.R. 833; and C-70/95 *Sodemare v Lombardy* [1997] E.C.R. I-3395).

6.101   This case law was, however, tempered by the Court's readiness to decide a question on the interpretation of Article 28 in relation to national legislation, even though the main case concerned goods produced in the same Member State: *Smanor*.[274] The Court held there that it was "for the national courts, within the system established by Article [234] of the Treaty, to weigh the relevance of the questions which they refer to the Court ... ". This ruling did not in any sense affect the scope of Articles 28 and 29, but related exclusively to the Court's jurisdiction under Article 234.

6.102   One objection which could perhaps be levelled at this body of case law is that it required the concept of the domestic products of a Member State to be defined. Yet there appears to be no reason for declining to apply by analogy the principles laid down in the Community Regulations on origin.[275] Apart from that minor difficulty, it is submitted that this case law was clear and consistent, and faithfully reflected the language of the Treaty.

Nevertheless, in a series of recent rulings the Court has now progressively distanced itself from its traditional position.

6.103   This trend began in *Lancry v Direction Générale des Douanes*.[276] In that case the Court held invalid a Council Decision purporting to authorise a levy on imports into the French overseas departments. One of the questions which arose was whether this levy (known as the *octroi de mer*) could be lawfully imposed on goods originating in other parts of France. Tesauro A.G. came out unreservedly in favour of the traditional view that the Treaty had no bearing on this matter, since the transaction was internal to a Member State. To rule otherwise, he said, would be to call in question "the settled case law of several decades on wholly internal situations, not only as regards the Customs Union and the movement of goods, but also as regards services and free movement of persons".[277]

He acknowledged that it was anomalous that in a common market Member States could erect internal borders to trade in their own goods, but pointed out that in practice this problem was unlikely to arise, as reverse discrimination is never attractive to Member States.

Despite the cogency of this reasoning, the Court espoused the opposite view, thereby muddying the waters in an area of law that had hitherto been pellucidly clear. It did so in the following terms:

"26 In the *Legros* judgment, the Court noted (at paragraph 16) that a charge levied at a regional frontier by reason of the fact that goods are brought into one region of a Member State undermines the unity of the Community customs territory and constitutes an obstacle of free movement of goods at least as serious as a charge levied at a national frontier on products entering a Member State as a whole.
27 The unity of the Community customs territory is undermined by the establish-

---

[274] Case 298/87 [1988] E.C.R. 4489, para. 9.
[275] See para. 2.13 above.
[276] Case C-363/93 [1994] E.C.R. I-3957; see paras 3.04 and 4.20 above.
[277] Para. 27 of the Opinion.

ment of a regional customs frontier just the same, whether the products on which a charge is levied by reason of the fact that they cross a frontier are domestic products or come from other Member States.

28 Furthermore, the obstacle to the free movement of goods created by the imposition on domestic products of a charge levied by reason of their crossing that frontier is no less serious than that created by the collection of a charge of the same kind on products from another Member State.

29 Since the very principle of a customs union covers all trade in goods, as provided for by Article [23] of the Treaty, it requires the free movement of goods generally, as opposed to inter-State trade alone, to be ensured within the union. Although Article [23] *et seq.* makes express reference only to trade between Member States, that is because it was assumed that there were no charges exhibiting the features of a customs duty in existence within the Member States. Since the absence of such charges is an essential precondition for the attainment of a customs union covering all trade in goods, it follows that they are likewise prohibited by Article [23] *et seq.*

30 Secondly, the situation does not appear to be of a kind where all the components are wholly confined to one Member State. As the French Government has correctly pointed out, the levying of charges exhibiting the features of dock dues could be classified as a purely internal situation only if the dues were levied exclusively on products from the same Member State. It is not disputed that the dock dues apply to all products entering the overseas department concerned, irrespective of their origin. It would accordingly be inconsistent to hold, on the one hand, that dock dues constitute charges having equivalent effect in so far as they are levied on goods from other Member States and to concede, on the other, that dock dues constitute charges having equivalent effect where they are levied on goods from metropolitan France.

31 Finally, since charges such as dock dues are imposed on all goods alike, it would be very difficult, if not impossible, in practical terms, to distinguish between products of domestic origin and products originating in other Member States. For example, a product manufactured in the Member State concerned but containing parts from another Member State, or a product imported into the State and later shipped to an overseas department, should not be described as domestic products. That would make it necessary to establish in every case, even in the case of deliveries of products from the same State, whether such products in fact originated in another Member State of that Community. The process of verification would give rise to administrative procedures and further delays which would in themselves constitute obstacles to the free movement of goods.''[278]

Arguably, the fall-out from this case was confined to restrictions having the effect of dividing up the territory of a Member State. In relation to this category of barrier to trade, since the abolition of border controls between Member States at the end of 1992,[279] it may indeed have become "very difficult, if not impossible, in practical terms to distinguish between products of domestic origin and products originating in other Member States".[280] Even so, why did the Court not simply apply its traditional approach, leaving it to the French authorities to sort out practical problems of this nature? If these problems are indeed insuperable, then it is for the Member States to draw the inevitable consequences and abolish such restrictions altogether.

---

[278] The Fifth Chamber of the Court confirmed this ruling in Case C-485-486/93 *Simitzi v Kos* [1995] E.C.R. I-2665, which related to trade between the Dodecanese to other parts of Greece. Unlike *Lancry*, this case concerned "exports" from the region, as well as "imports" into it.

[279] Paras 12.12 *et seq.* below.

[280] Para. 31 of the judgment.

Although *Lancry* concerned the compatibility of an "import" tax with Article 23, it seemed clear from the outset that the reasoning set out there would apply equally to Articles 28 and 29,[281] at least as regards quantitative restrictions and other restrictions taking effect at the "border" (*e.g.* import licences, controls, etc.).

6.104 The waters were muddied further by the Court's ruling in *Pistre*.[282] Unlike the measure in issue in *Lancry*, the restriction before the Court in this case did not create divisions between different parts of the territory of a Member State. The case concerned French legislation laying down stringent conditions for marketing cooked meat as a "mountain" product. One of these conditions was that the product should originate in various specified parts of France, so that imported goods could never be sold under this description. The measure was thus distinctly applicable. However, this was of no immediate concern to the defendants, who were prosecuted for improperly selling as "mountain" products French goods which did not meet the conditions laid down in the legislation.

Since the goods in question in the main case were French and there was no factual link with any other Member State, Jacobs A.G. strongly urged the Court to decline the request of the Court of Cassation to rule on whether such legislation infringed Article 28. As he pointed out, it is "well established that Article [28] is not infringed in purely internal situations." After a thorough discussion of the issues raised, he concluded: " ... such issues can and should only be addressed in a factual context which genuinely raises them". He gave particular consideration to the argument to the effect that a ruling might be necessary so as to enable the French courts to establish whether reverse discrimination against domestic products contrary to national law was present; but he was not swayed by it, since in his view the overriding consideration was that such questions should not be decided *in abstracto*.[283]

However, the Court found otherwise, saying:

---

[281] Keppenne and van Ypersele, "Vers une application du droit communautaire à des obstacles à la libre circulation des marchandises à l'intérieur d'un Etat membre" [1994] J.T.D.E. 179; Slotboom, "L'application du Traité CE au commerce intraétatique ? Le cas de l'octroi de mer" [1996] C.D.E. 9 at 16; Weyer, "Freier Warenverkehr, rein innerstaatliche Sachverhalte und umgekehrte Diskriminierung" [1998] EuR 435 at 439. It is well established that restrictions on imports into part of the territory of a Member State may fall under Art. 28 (see para. 6.95 above).

[282] Case C-321/94 [1997] E.C.R. I-2343; see Mortelmans, "The Common Market, the Internal Market and the Single Market, What's in a Market ?" [1998] C.M.L.Rev. 101 at 134; Rochard, "Dispositions de la loi "montagne" et principe communautaire de libre circulation des produits" [1998] R.T.D.E. 237.

[283] This reasoning is close to that in the same A.G.'s Opinion in Cases C-28/95 *Leur-Bloem v Inspecteur der Belastingen* [1997] E.C.R. I-4161; and Case C-130/95 *Giloy v Hautzollamt Frankfurt am Main-Ost* [1997] E.C.R. I-4291. In these cases, the Court had to decide whether it enjoyed jurisdiction to interpret Community legislation, which was not applicable as such in the main cases but which the Member States concerned had chosen in their legislation to apply by analogy to other circumstances. Jacobs A.G. urged the Court to decline jurisdiction on the grounds that no question of Community law arose to be decided. However, this plea fell on deaf ears, and the Court accepted jurisdiction in both cases.

" ... whilst the application of a national measure having no actual link to the importation of goods does not fall within the ambit of Article [28] of the Treaty ... , Article [28] cannot be considered inapplicable simply because all the facts of the specific case before the national court are confined to a single Member State.

In such a situation, the application of the national measure may also have effects on the free movement of goods between Member States, in particular when the measure in question facilitates the marketing of goods of domestic origin to the detriment of imported goods. In such circumstances, the application of the measure, even if restricted to domestic producers, in itself creates and maintains a difference of treatment between those two categories of goods, hindering, at least potentially, intra-Community trade."[284]

Most authors see this ruling as opening up Article 28 to purely internal measures.[285] Indeed, it has even been described as a "conceptual revolution".[286] However, at the time it seemed possible to lend a less dramatic interpretation to this judgment, reading it as simply confirming *Smanor* without more; on this view, the Court left the national court to decide whether to extend the principles of Article 28 to domestic products (*e.g.* on the basis of a national principle of equality).[287] The ruling in *TK-Heimdienst*[288] might have been regarded as confirming that view, although La Pergola A.G. expressly declared in that case that Article 28 does apply to purely internal situations.[289]

6.105 Then came the recent ruling in *Guimont*.[290] The defendant there was accused of selling as "Emmenthal" (a generic name) cheese produced in France, although it did not have a "hard, dry rind" of the kind required by French legislation. The French Government, supported by Denmark, contended that Article 28 was thus inapplicable, given that the national legislation concerned applied exclusively to domestic production. Once again, the Advocate General urged the Court to endorse this reasoning. Nevertheless, the Court rejected France's argument, in the following terms:

"19 Mr Guimont, the German, Netherlands and Austrian Governments and the Commission argue that, according to the Court's case law, Article [28] cannot be considered inapplicable simply because all the facts of the specific case before the national court are confined to a single Member State (Joined Cases C-321/94 to C-324/94 *Pistre and Others* [1997] E.C.R. I-2343, paragraph 44).

20 In regard to that argument, it should be noted that the *Pistre* judgment con-

---

[284] The same occurred in C-159/00 *Sapod Audic v Eco-Emballages*, where the Court in its judgment of June 6, 2002 declined to follow Jacobs A.G.'s Opinion (see especially para. 72 thereof).

[285] Simon and Lagondet, "Libre circulation des marchandises et situations purement internes : chronique d'une mort annoncée" Europe—Edition du Juris-Classeur July 1997 p. 7; Tagaras, "Règles communautaires de libre circulation, discriminations à rebours et situations dites 'purement internes' " in *Melanges en hommage à Michel Waelbroeck* (1999) Vol. II, p. 1499; Weyer, *op. cit.*

[286] Simon and Lagondet, *op. cit.* at 8-II. See also generally Gaja, "Les discriminations à rebours : un revirement souhaitable" in *Mélanges en l'honneur de Michel Waelbroeck* (1999) Vol. 2 p. 993.

[287] See Oliver, "Some Further Reflections on the Scope of Articles 28-30 (ex 30-36) EC" [1999] C.M.L.Rev. 783 at 787; Spaventa, *op. cit.* at n.177 above.

[288] See n.50 above; see Spaventa, *op. cit.*

[289] Para. 8 of the Opinion.

[290] Case C-448/98 [2000] E.C.R. I-10663.

cerned a situation where the national rule in question was not applicable without distinction but created direct discrimination against goods imported from other Member States.

21 As for a rule such as that at issue in the main proceedings, which, according to its wording, applies without distinction to national and imported products and is designed to impose certain production conditions on producers in order to permit them to market their products under a certain designation, it is clear from the Court's case law that such a rule falls under Article [28] of the Treaty only in so far as it applies to situations that are linked to the importation of goods in intra-Community trade (Case 286/81 *Oosthoek's Uitgeversmaatschappij* [1982] E.C.R. 4575, paragraph 9; *Mathot*, paragraphs 3 and 7 to 9).

22 However, that finding does not mean that there is no need to reply to the question referred to the Court for a preliminary ruling in this case. In principle, it is for the national courts alone to determine, having regard to the particular features of each case, both the need for a preliminary ruling in order to enable them to give their judgment and the relevance of the questions which they refer to the Court. A reference for a preliminary ruling from a national court may be rejected only if it is quite obvious that the interpretation of Community law sought by that court bears no relation to the actual nature of the case or the subject-matter of the main action (Case C-281/98 *Angonese v Cassa di Risparmio di Bolzano* [2000] E.C.R. I-4139, paragraph 18).

23 In this case, it is not obvious that the interpretation of Community law requested is not necessary for the national court. Such a reply might be useful to it if its national law were to require, in proceedings such as those in this case, that a national producer must be allowed to enjoy the same rights as those which a producer of another Member State would derive from Community law in the same situation."

The Court's conclusion was that Article 28 precludes a Member State from applying a rule of the kind in question to "products imported from another Member State". Thus the Court did not in practice require the national court to apply Article 28 to domestic products.

Nevertheless, the surprising and delphic pronouncement in paragraphs 20 and 21 is not easy to fathom. How can it be relevant to determine whether a measure is distinctly or indistinctly applicable, when we are dealing with domestic products in any event ?

6.106 Surely the Court's traditional approach, as reflected in *Waterkeyn, Oosthoek* and *Cognet*, is preferable on grounds of legal certainty and of consistency with the wording of the Treaty. Thus it is by no means surprising to find the various Advocates General in *Lancry, Pistre* and *Guimont* exhorting the Court to hold true to that approach. It is submitted that those three recent judgments create more problems than they solve.

Plainly, to this extent the "single market" established by the Treaty falls short of the ideal laid down in *Gaston Schul v Inspecteur der Invoerrechten*[291] where the Court held: "the concept of the common market ... involves the elimination of all obstacles to intra-Community trade in order to merge the national markets into a single market bringing about conditions as close as possible to those of a genuine internal market". Yet it is scarcely open to the Court to ignore the clear

---

[291] Case 15/81 [1982] E.C.R. 1409 at 1431-2.

wording of the Treaty. Quite apart from that, the words "as close as possible" clearly indicate that the "single market" is not perfect.

6.107   At all events, a common market organisation may widen the prohibitions contained in Articles 28 and 29 so as to prohibit even "purely national" measures.[292] This is a consequence of the common agricultural policy, not of Articles 28 and 29. Other forms of Community legislation may also have this effect.

VIII. ABUSE OF RIGHTS

6.108   In *Leclerc v Au Blé Vert*,[293] which concerned resale price maintenance for books, the Court ruled that Article 28 could not be invoked with respect to goods "exported for the sole purpose of re-importation in order to circumvent legislation of the type at issue". This appears to be the only instance of the concept of abuse of rights being applied to Article 28, although in other areas it has come to the fore in recent years.[294] It would seem that this concept has not been applied to Article 29 at all, and indeed it is hard to imagine circumstances in which reliance on that provision could be regarded as abusive, especially since it is more limited in scope than Article 28. Having said that, the concept of abuse of right has made an appearance in the case law relating to Article 30.[295]

This contrasts with the case law on the free provision of services, in which the concept has played a prominent role.[296] Thus in *TV10 v Commissariaat Voor de Media*[297] a Dutch television company had established itself in Luxembourg with the aim of broadcasting to the Netherlands without having to observe certain provisions of Dutch law. The Court held that in these circumstances the establishment in Luxembourg constituted an abuse; and that the company could therefore be treated as being established in the Netherlands, so that it could not rely on Articles 49 and 50 (ex 59 and 60) EC. If one were to transpose this situation to the free movement of goods, it would involve a manufacturer leaving his own Member State, setting up his factory in another Member State

---

[292] Para. 10.16 below.

[293] See n.99 above.

[294] See Cases C-206/94 *Brennet v Paletta* [1996] E.C.R. I-2357; C-367/96 *Kefalas v Greece* [1998] E.C.R. I-2843 (noted by Triantafyllou [1999] C.M.L.Rev. 157); C-212/97 *Centros v Erhvervs-og Selskatbsstyrelsen* [1999] E.C.R. I-1459; C-373/97 *Diamantis v Greece* [2000] E.C.R. I-1705; and C-110/99 *Emsland-Stärke v HZA Hamburg-Jonas* [2000] E.C.R. I-11569, especially paras 52-54; Article 4(3) of Regulation 2988/95 on the protection of the European Communities' financial interests ([1995] O.J. L312/1); Neville Brown, "Is There a General Principle of Abuse of Rights in European Community Law ?" in *Essays in Honour of Henry Schermers* (1994) Vol. II-511; and Triantafyllou, "L'interdiction des abus de droit en tant que principe général du droit communautaire" [2002] C.D.E. (forthcoming).

[295] Para. 8.17 below.

[296] Cases 33/74 *van Binsbergen v Bedrijfsvereniging Metaalnijverheid* [1974] E.C.R. 1299; C-148/91 *Veronica Omroep Organisatie v Commissariaat voor de Media* [1993] E.C.R. I-487; and C-23/93 *TV10 v Commissariaat Voor de Media* [1994] E.C.R. 4795; but see Jacobs A.G. in *De Agostini* (see n.164 above) at pp. 3858-9.

[297] See n.296 above.

and exporting back to his home State—all just to circumvent some national legislation which was inconvenient to him. Since this would necessarily mean manufacturing the goods in the second Member State and given the considerable expense involved in moving a factory, it seems unlikely that the entire operation could be treated as a sham, as happened in *TV10*.

IX. ARTICLE 10 READ WITH ARTICLES 28 AND 29

6.109   In its ground-breaking judgment in *Commission v France*,[298] the Court was called upon for the first time to rule on whether a Member State is liable for its inaction in the face of restrictions on imports emanating from third parties. The Commission claimed that, by failing for more than a decade to take adequate measures against the consistent and frequent violent action and protest movements by farmers aimed at preventing imports of agricultural products, France had infringed Article 10 (ex 5) EC read with Article 28. In particular, the farmers' action took the form of the interception of lorries transporting those products, the destruction of their loads and violence towards drivers as well as threats to wholesalers and retailers and damaging goods on display. After stressing the fundamental importance of the free movement of goods, the Court stated:

> "Article [28] therefore requires the Member States not merely themselves to abstain from adopting measures or engaging in conduct liable to constitute an obstacle to trade but also, when read with Article [10] of the Treaty, to take all necessary and appropriate measures to ensure that that fundamental freedom is respected on their territory."[299]

While acknowledging that public order and internal security were the exclusive preserve of the Member States and that they "unquestionably enjoy a margin of discretion in determining what measures are most appropriate in this regard",[300] the Court nevertheless made it clear that it was responsible for determining, in cases brought before it, whether the Member State concerned had indeed taken the appropriate measures to ensure the free movement of goods. On a detailed analysis of the facts, which were not contested in any event, the Court found:

> "In the light of all the foregoing factors, the Court, while not discounting the difficulties faced by the competent authorities in dealing with situations of the type in question in this case, cannot but find that, having regard to the frequency and seriousness of the incidents cited by the Commission, the measures adopted by the French Government were manifestly inadequate to ensure freedom of intra-Community trade in agricultural products on its territory by preventing and effectively dis-

---

[298] Case C-265/95, see n.41 above; noted by Jarvis, [1998] C.M.L.Rev. 1371; Muylle, [1998] E.L.Rev. 467; Schwarze, [1998] EuR 53.
[299] Para. 32 of the judgment.
[300] Para. 33.

suading the perpetrators of the offences in question from committing and repeating them."[301]

In addition, the Court held that France had adduced "no concrete evidence proving the existence of a danger to public order with which it could not cope".[302] The Court therefore concluded:

> "Having regard to all the foregoing considerations, it must be concluded that in the present case the French Government has manifestly and persistently abstained from adopting appropriate and adequate measures to put an end to the acts of vandalism which jeopardise the free movement on its territory of certain agricultural products originating in other Member States and to prevent the recurrence of such acts."[303]

Accordingly, it upheld the Commission's request for a declaration that the defendant had breached Articles 10 and 28.[304]

Plainly, the Court did not reach this conclusion lightly: the whole thrust of its judgment was that only "manifest and persistent" abstentions on the part of a Member State will render it liable under these provisions.

It is strongly arguable that the principles laid down in this judgment would also apply where the State fails to take action against a long-running "buy national" campaign organised by private interests.[305] In any case, it seems clear that the principles laid down in this ruling can be directly transposed to export restrictions created by third parties, for which a Member State may be similarly liable under Article 10 read with Article 29.

Following this judgment, the Council enacted Regulation 2679/98 on the functioning of the internal market in relation to the free movement of goods among the Member States,[306] which will be considered at length at paragraphs 12.96 *et seq.* below.

X. BURDEN OF PROOF

6.110 It is axiomatic that, where the Commission brings infringement proceedings against a Member State for breach of Article 28 or 29, it bears the burden of proving that part of its case.[307] Logically, the same must apply to any party alleging that a breach of one of these articles has been committed, regardless of which court is hearing the case. Thereupon the burden shifts to the Member State or other party which contending that the restriction is justified under Article 30.[308]

---

[301] Para. 52.
[302] Para. 57.
[303] Para. 65.
[304] In accordance with the Commission's application, the Court also ruled that France had breached Art. 10 read with the Regulations establishing the common organisations of the market in those products.
[305] See also generally the Opinion of Jacobs A.G. in Case C-112/00 (see n.36 above).
[306] [1998] O.J. L337/8.
[307] Case C-160/94 *Commission v Spain* (electricity monopoly) [1997] E.C.R. I-5851.
[308] See para. 8.11 below.

CHAPTER VII

Measures of Equivalent Effect: II

7.01 In the previous Chapter we considered the general principles relating to measures of equivalent effect. The purpose of the present Chapter is to consider specific measures with a view to establishing whether or not they constitute measures of equivalent effect under Article 28 or 29, as the case may be. It will be seen that the Court's case law on measures of equivalent effect under Articles 28 and 29 is quite remarkable for its breadth and depth of application. Articles 28 and 29 will be examined in turn.

As we saw in the previous Chapter, the compatibility of a national measure with Article 28 or 29 must be tested in two stages, by asking two fundamental questions:

1. Does this measure constitute a measure of equivalent effect falling under Article 28 or Article 29?

2. If so, is it justified under Article 30 or the "mandatory requirements"?

This Chapter is concerned with the first of these two questions, while the second is dealt with in the following Chapter. However, it has not been found possible to avoid mentioning Article 30 altogether here.

7.02 Furthermore, it should be pointed out that a large number of the Court's rulings discussed here concern agricultural products falling under a common market organisation.[1] As will be explained later in this book,[2] it is not clear whether rulings of this kind are in fact interpretations of the common market organisation in question rather than of Articles 28 and 29. This means that it is uncertain whether such rulings apply to all products.

---

[1] On the meaning of this concept of common market organisations, see para. 10.01 below.
[2] Paras 10.08 *et seq.* below.

I. MEASURES OF EQUIVALENT EFFECT UNDER ARTICLE 28

Import Licences

7.03 The obligation to obtain an import licence or permit from the importing Member State before importing goods is a clear example of a measure of equivalent effect.[3] In one of the first cases on Article 28 to come before it, *International Fruit Company v Produktschap voor Groenten en Fruit*,[4] the Court decided that this held good even where licences were granted automatically and the Member State concerned did not purport to reserve the right to withhold a licence. It did so in the following terms:

"Apart from the exceptions for which provision is made by Community law itself [Articles 28 and 29] preclude the application to intra-Community trade of a national provision which requires, even purely as a formality, import or export licences or any other similar procedure."

The reason clearly is that even automatic licences can give rise to delay and abuse on the part of the importing Member State. The effect of this ruling was implicitly to strike down Article 2(2) of Commission Directive 70/50,[5] in so far as this provision suggests that a mere formality is compatible with Article 28.

This ruling has been confirmed in a number of subsequent cases, notably *Donckerwolcke v Procureur de la République*,[6] which show that such measures constitute measures of equivalent effect rather than quantitative restrictions.[7]

Import Inspections and Controls

7.04 The obligation to submit imports or exports to veterinary, sanitary, phytosanitary or similar inspections or controls constitutes a measure of equivalent effect within the meaning of Articles 28 and 29 respectively. This was established with respect to phytosanitary controls on apple imports (designed to track down the formidable San José scale insect) in *Rewe-Zentralfinanz v Land-wirtschaftskammer*[8] and with respect to veterinary and public health inspections on veal imports in *Simmenthal v Minister for Finance*.[9] Frequently inspections will be justified under Article 30 on the grounds of the protection of the health and life of humans, animals or plants, as the case may be.[10]

---

[3] Case C–189/95 *Franzén* [1997] E.C.R. I-5909, paras 67–71.
[4] Cases 51-54/71 [1971] E.C.R. 1107.
[5] [1970] J.O. L13/29. See paras 6.04 and 6.06 and Annex II to this book.
[6] Case 41/76 [1976] E.C.R. 1921; [1977] 2 C.M.L.R. 535. For a further example, see Case C–304/88 *Commission v Belgium* (live cattle) [1990] E.C.R. I-2801. The following cases concern export licences: Case 53/76 *Bouhelier* [1977] E.C.R. 197; [1977] 1 C.M.L.R. 436; Case 68/76 *Commission v France* [1977] E.C.R. 515; [1977] 2 C.M.L.R. 161.
[7] As to justification, see paras 8.70, 8.110 and 8.111 below.
[8] Case 4/75 [1975] E.C.R. 843; [1977] 1 C.M.L.R. 599.
[9] Case 35/76 [1876] E.C.R. 1871; [1977] 2 C.M.L.R. 1.
[10] Paras 8.71 and 8.113 below.

With effect from January 1, 1993,[11] it is now clear that customs controls are also measures having equivalent effect and are therefore prohibited by Articles 28 and 29.[12] As a result, a Member State may only carry out controls at its internal borders to the same extent as it does within its own territory. However, in exceptional cases, Member States will be able to rely on Article 30.

In the rare cases where such inspections and controls are still lawful under Article 30, Member States may not unduly restrict the number of border posts where goods to be inspected may cross into their territory,[13] and they must carry out those inspections as promptly as possible.[14]

The Obligation to Produce Certificates

7.05   We are concerned here with the requirement that an importer produce certain types of certificate on importation, whether furnished by the authorities of an exporting Member State or by any other public or private body outside the importing Member State. This is to be distinguished from the case of import licences granted by the importing Member State itself, which was discussed in paragraph 7.03 below.

The first major case on Article 28, *Procureur du Roi v Dassonville*,[15] was concerned with this type of measure. That case concerned a Belgian Royal Decree of 1934 prohibiting the importation into Belgium of spirits bearing a designation of origin officially recognised by the Belgian Government without an official document certifying their entitlement to such designation. The designation of origin "Scotch Whisky" had been duly adopted by the Belgian Government. In 1970 (before the United Kingdom joined the Community) the defendants in the main case were parallel importers who had imported into Belgium various quantities of Scotch whisky from France, where they were in free circulation. They were charged with forging the official certificates of authenticity. In a reference for a preliminary ruling the Brussels court asked the Court of Justice, *inter alia*, whether measures of this kind were compatible with Article 28. In its reference the Brussels court pointed out that the effect of the Belgian provisions was to make imports of whisky from France impossible, since France did not require such certificates of authenticity.

The Court replied as follows:

"All trading rules enacted by Member States which are capable of hindering, directly or indirectly, actually or potentially, intra-Community trade are to be considered as

---

[11] Art. 14 (ex 7A) EC, a provision inserted into the EC Treaty by the Single European Act required the dissolution of internal border controls by that date.

[12] Prior to that date, customs and other border controls and formalities were considered to be lawful so long as they did not exceed the "normal requirements inherent in the crossing of the frontier by any goods, whatever their nature": Case C–186/88 *Commission v Germany* (poultry) [1989] E.C.R. I-3997 at 4012.

[13] Cases 132/80 *United Foods v Belgian State* [1981] E.C.R. 945; [1982] 1 C.M.L.R. 273; and C128/89 *Commission v Italy* (grapefruit) [1990] E.C.R. I-3239; see para. 8.113 below.

[14] Case 42/82 *Commission v France* (Italian wine) [1983] E.C.R. 1013; [1984] 1 C.M.L.R. 160. See also Case C–105/94 *Celestini v Saar-Sektkellerei Faber* [1997] E.C.R. I-2971.

[15] Case 8/74 [1974] E.C.R. 837; [1974] 2 C.M.L.R. 436.

measures having an effect equivalent to quantitative restrictions.

In the absence of a Community system guaranteeing for consumers the authenticity of a product's designation of origin, if a Member State takes measures to prevent unfair practices in this connection, it is however subject to the condition that these measures should be reasonable and that the means of proof required should not act as a hindrance to trade between Member States and should, in consequence, be accessible to all Community nationals.

Even without having to examine whether or not such measures are covered by Article [30], they must not, in any case, by virtue of the principle expressed in the second sentence of that Article, constitute a means of arbitrary discrimination or a disguised restriction on trade between Member States.

That may be the case with formalities, required by a Member State for the purpose of proving the origin of a product, which only direct importers are really in a position to satisfy without facing serious difficulties.

Consequently, the requirement by a Member State of a certificate of authenticity which is less easily obtainable by importers of an authentic product which has been put into free circulation in a regular manner in another Member State than by importers of the same product coming directly from the country of origin constitutes a measure having an effect equivalent to a quantitative restriction as prohibited by the Treaty."

7.06 It is clear from this passage that Article 28 prohibits not only restrictions on imports as such, but also measures discriminating in favour of direct imports against indirect imports. As already explained, the facts in *Dassonville* arose before the United Kingdom had acceded to the Community, so that this principle manifestly applies even where the country of origin is not a Member State.[16]

7.07 Indeed, the wording of this passage suggests that the requirement that imports be accompanied by a certificate of authenticity is not in itself a measure of equivalent effect. The wording suggests, rather, that this requirement only constituted a measure of equivalent effect because the certificates were harder to obtain for indirect imports than for goods coming directly from the country of origin.

However, this is merely due to the fact that *Dassonville* was the first major judgment of the Court on Article 28 and the Court's case law has evolved considerably since then. That the obligation to produce a certificate on importation in itself constitutes a measure of equivalent effect is shown by later cases. In particular, in *Denkavit Futtermittel v Minister für Ernährung*[17] concerning imports of animal feed the Court held that:

---

[16] In the subsequent Case 2/78 *Commission v Belgium* [1979] E.C.R. 1761 the Court dismissed the Commission's infringement proceedings in relation to certain "liberalising measures" introduced with respect to imports of Scotch whisky into Belgium on the grounds that the alleged difficulties under those measures in obtaining certificates for indirect imports were not unreasonable. That test is open to criticism and it is doubtful that it would be followed today. The better approach is to determine whether the measure in question hinders, directly or indirectly, imports from other Member States.

[17] Case 251/78 [1979] E.C.R. 3369; [1980] 3 C.M.L.R. 513; see also Case 53/76 (n.6 above), as regards exports.

"the concept of a measure having an effect equivalent to a quantitative restriction ... applies to the obligation to produce a certificate to the effect that the imported feeding-stuffs have undergone specified treatment in the exporting country."

It is clear, then, that any requirement to produce a document on importation constitutes a measure of equivalent effect under Article 28.[18] This applies whatever the nature of the document, be it a certificate of authenticity or origin, or a sanitary, veterinary or phytosanitary certificate. Inasmuch as such requirements do fall under Article 28, they will frequently be justified under Article 30, particularly on health grounds.

Certain Sanctions or Fines

7.08   There are three ways in which fines or other sanctions imposed for an offence under national law with respect to imported goods may fall under Article 28[19]:

(a) It is clear that a sanction attached to a restriction on imports will be contrary to Article 28 if the restriction itself is: *Procureur de la République v Rivoira*.[20]

(b) It is also evident that criminal penalties discriminating against imported goods are contrary to Article 28: *Cayrol v Rivoira*.[21] This may occur where national law either lays down no penalties, or lighter penalties, for offences relating to domestic goods.[22]

(c) Lastly there is a measure of equivalent effect under Article 28 when a Member State imposes a penalty for a customs irregularity, if that penalty is disproportionately high, at least where the Member State is not entitled to prohibit the importation of the goods in question.[23]

7.09   This last point was established in *Donckerwolcke v Procureur de la République*[24] and in *Cayrol v Rivoira*. In each case criminal proceedings had been brought against persons who had imported goods into France and falsely declared them to originate in a Member State. However, although the goods

---

[18] Case C–205/89 *Commission v Greece* [1991] E.C.R. I-1361 (para. 8.75 below). Similar restrictions operating at a later stage (*e.g.* sale) also constitute measures of equivalent effect: para. 7.28 below.

[19] See generally the 1992 FIDE Report on "Enforcement of Community Law by Sanctions and Remedies".

[20] Case 179/78 [1979] E.C.R. 1147; [1979] 3 C.M.L.R. 456, para. 14 of judgment.

[21] Case 52/77 [1977] E.C.R. 2261; [1978] 2 C.M.L.R. 253, para. 5 of judgment.

[22] See also Cases C–276/91 *Commission v France* (VAT) [1993] E.C.R. I-4413 (Art. 90 (ex 95)); C–224/00 *Commission v Italy* (traffic offences) [2002] E.C.R. I-2965 (Art. 122 (ex 6)); C–378/97 *Wijsenbeek* [1999] E.C.R. I-6207 at para. 44 (free movement of persons).

[23] Interestingly enough, this principle has echoes of clause 20 of Magna Carta 1215, which provided: "For a trivial offence, a man shall be fined only in proportion to the degree of his offence, and for a serious offence correspondingly ...".

[24] Case 41/76 (see n.6 above); see generally Case 65/79 *Procureur de la République v Chatain* [1980] E.C.R. 1345; [1981] 3 C.M.L.R. 418. For an application of the same principle in the context of the free movement of persons, see Case C–378/97 (n.22 above).

were in free circulation in the Community, they had in fact originated in a third country. The object of the reference was to ascertain whether the requirement of a declaration of origin imposed by the French authorities, and connected measures, were contrary to Article 28. As regards penalties, the Court held:

"The fact that the importer did not comply with the obligation to declare the real origin of the goods cannot give rise to the application of penalties which are disproportionate taking account of the purely administrative nature of the contravention ...

In general terms any administrative or penal measure which goes beyond what is strictly necessary for the purposes of enabling the importing Member State to obtain reasonably complete and accurate information on the movement of goods falling within specific measures of commercial policy[25] must be regarded as a measure having an effect equivalent to a quantitative restriction prohibited by the Treaty."

The same applies to other customs offences, or contraventions of other purely administrative rules. This is perhaps the only case where proportionality is part of the test for the application of Articles 28 and 29 rather than Article 30.[26]

In *Donckerwolcke* and *Cayrol* the Court gave two examples of sanctions which are excessive for offences of this kind: first, seizure of the goods, and, secondly, any pecuniary penalty fixed according to the value of the goods.

7.10   In *Procureur de la République v Rivoira* the Court held that the criminal penalties concerned "cannot be applied without regard being had to the fact that the present case did not concern prohibited imports". This appeared to suggest that a sanction will only be caught by Article 28 on the grounds of disproportionality where the Member State is entitled to prohibit or restrict the imports concerned.

However, in *Aimé Richardt*,[27] where the Court found that Luxembourg was entitled to subject the transit of strategic material to a special authorisation on external security grounds, it ruled that:

"a measure involving seizure or confiscation may be considered disproportionate to the objective pursued, and thus incompatible with Article 30 of the Treaty, in a case where the return of the goods to the Member State of origin could suffice.

However, it is for the national court to determine whether the system established complies with the principle of proportionality, taking account of all the elements of each case, such as the nature of the goods capable of endangering the security of the State, the circumstances in which the breach was committed and whether or not the trader seeking to effect the transit and holding documents for that purpose issued by another Member State was acting in good faith."

What is not clear is whether this ruling is intended to open the door to a general right to challenge disproportionate sanctions in all cases where imports may be prohibited.

---

[25] The phrase "specific measures of commercial policy" would appear to be a reference to Art. 134 (ex 115); see para. 9.28 below.
[26] As to the principle of proportionality in Art. 30, see paras 8.12 *et seq.*
[27] Case C–367/89 [1991] E.C.R. I-4621.

At all events, it is hard to imagine how any penalties falling under Article 28 could be justified under Article 30.[28]

The Obligation to make a Declaration of Origin

7.11 In certain circumstances the requirement that the importer make a declaration of origin is contrary to Article 28. This was laid down in the *Donckerwolcke* judgment, already discussed, where the Court held:

> "The requirement by the importing Member State of the indication of the country of origin on the customs declaration document for products in free circulation ... does not in itself constitute a measure of equivalent effect ... if the goods in question are covered by measures of commercial policy adopted by that State in conformity with the Treaty.
>   Such a requirement would, however, fall under the prohibition contained in Article [28] of the Treaty if the importer were required to declare, with regard to origin, something other than what he knows or may reasonably be expected to know ... ."

This was confirmed in *Cayrol v Rivoira* and *Procureur de la République v Rivoira*, both of which have also been discussed.

At least since January 1, 1993, when Article 14 (ex 7A) of the Treaty took effect, all obligations to make a declaration of origin constitute measures of equivalent effect.[29] The qualifications in *Donckerwolcke*, which related to the now moribund Article 134 (ex 115), no longer apply.

Measures Restricting the use of Imported Products or Requiring the use of Domestic Products

7.12 Directive 66/683,[30] based on Article 33(7),[31] required Member States to abolish measures which

(a) partially or totally prohibited the use of an imported product;

(b) required the partial or total use of a domestic product;

(c) subjected the entitlement to a benefit, other than an aid within the meaning of Article 87 (ex 92) of the Treaty, to the total or partial use of a national product.[32]

In addition, Article 2(3)(k) of Directive 70/50 defined as measures of equivalent effect those measures which "require ... the purchase of domestic products only."

---

[28] See Case 155/82 *Commission v Belgium* [1983] E.C.R. 531 and Case 247/81 *Commission v Germany* (pharmaceuticals) [1984] E.C.R. 1111 and discussion of these cases at para 8.85.
[29] Para. 7.04 above.
[30] [1966] J.O. 3748, para. 6.04 above.
[31] Art. 33(7) was deleted from the Treaty on the entry into force of the Treaty of Amsterdam.
[32] Dir. 66/683 itself exempted certain products from its operation, but those exemptions ceased to have effect at the end of the transitional period; para. 6.05 above.

A provision of this kind was in issue in *Peureux v Directeur des Services Fiscaux.*[33] The plaintiffs wished to distil some oranges steeped in alcohol, which they had imported from Italy, where they were in free circulation. The defendant contested their right to do this on the basis of a provision in the *Code Général des Impôts* stating that: "distillation of all imported raw material with the exception of fresh fruit other than apples, pears or grapes shall be prohibited." On a reference from a French court under Article 234 (ex 177), the Court found that such a measure constituted a measure of equivalent effect contrary to Article 28.

Also in *Campus Oil v Minister for Industry and Energy*[34] the requirement that importers of petroleum products purchase a specific proportion of their supplies from the one remaining oil refinery in Ireland was held to constitute a measure of equivalent effect.[35]

Type Approval

7.13 Similarly, rules making goods subject to type approval before sale or use constitute measures of equivalent effect: *Commission v France* (postal franking machines)[36]; *Commission v France* (woodworking machines)[37] and *Radiosistemi v Prefetto di Genova* (radio equipment).[38]

Such requirements will frequently be justified on public health or other grounds.[39] In *RTT v GB-Inno*[40] it was held that a requirement of this kind might be justified even if the authority responsible for granting type approval (in this instance the national telephone company) itself markets competing goods. This was held to be subject to the proviso that it must be possible to challenge the decisions of that authority before the courts; but that proviso would not appear to add anything to the general rule that the Member States must make the necessary remedies and procedures available for the enforcement of rights flowing from directly applicable provisions of Community law.[41]

Discrimination in Public Supply Contracts

7.14 Any measure by which public authorities discriminate against imported goods in the award of public supply contracts is a measure of equivalent effect contrary to Article 28. Such measures were the subject of Commission Directive

---

[33] Case 119/78 [1979] E.C.R. 975; [1980] 3 C.M.L.R. 337.
[34] Case 72/83 [1984] E.C.R. 2727; [1984] 3 C.M.L.R. 544; see paras. 8.29, 8.33 and 8.53 below.
[35] See also Case C–137/91 *Commission v Greece* (cash registers) [1992] E.C.R. I-4023; Case C–379/98 *PreussenElektra v Schleswag* [2001] E.C.R. I-2099 at paras 70–71 and; Case C–398/98 *Commission v Greece* (petroleum products) [2001] E.C.R. I-7915 at paras 26–27.
[36] Case 21/84 [1985] E.C.R. 1355.
[37] Case 188/84 [1986] E.C.R. 419.
[38] Joined Cases C–388 and 429/00 [2002] E.C.R. I-nyr (judgment of June 20, 2002).
[39] See para. 8.93 below.
[40] Case C–18/88 [1991] E.C.R. I-5941. In the same case such a system was held to contravene Art. 81 (ex 86) read with Art. 86 (ex 90). See also Cases C–46/90 *Lagauche* [1993] E.C.R. I-5267; and C–314/93 *Rouffeteau* [1994] E.C.R I-3257.
[41] See para. 8.77 below.

70/32[42] based on Article 33(7) of the Treaty.[43] That directive prohibited measures relating to the supply of goods to the State, regional or local authorities and other legal persons governed by public law,

(a) which totally or partially prohibited the use of an imported product; or

(b) which required the total or partial use of domestic products or granted domestic products a preference other than an aid under Article 87 (ex 92); or

(c) made the supply of imported products more difficult or onerous.

Foremost among such measures—though not specifically mentioned in the directive—are those by which the public authorities of a Member State award a contract to a tenderer offering goods manufactured within that state, thus discriminating against another tenderer offering imported goods at more favourable terms.[44] Such infringements of Article 28 are rife, but difficult to prove. Since 1977, Article 28 has also been supplemented by the public procurement directives, which are considered at paragraphs 12.99 to 12.102 below.

7.15 The first case on the incompatibility of this type of measure with Article 28 was *Commission v Ireland*.[45] This case concerned a contract to be concluded by Dundalk Urban District Council for the construction of a water main. The invitation to tender stipulated that all asbestos cement pressure pipes must be certified as complying with the relevant Irish standard. In fact, only one manufacturer had obtained such approval for its pipes and this was an Irish company. Consequently a tender for pipes manufactured in Spain was not considered. The Commission, which maintained that this was contrary, *inter alia*, to Article 28, sought an interim order to ensure that no contract was concluded for the work pending either final judgment or a settlement between the Commission and Ireland. In a key passage of his Order the President stated:

> "Although it would seem normal that in a public works contract such as that at issue the materials to be used may be required to comply with a certain technical standard, even a national standard, in order to ensure that they are appropriate and safe, such a technical standard cannot, without creating prima facie a barrier to trade which is contrary to Article [28] of the EEC Treaty, have the effect of excluding, without so much as an examination, any tender based on another technical standard recognised in another Member State as providing equivalent guarantees of safety, performance and reliability."

The application for interim measures was rejected on the grounds that the balance of interests was weighted in favour of the defendants. However, in its final judgment the Court confirmed that the contested measure infringed

---

[42] [1970] J.O. L13/1, para. 6.04 above.
[43] Art. 33(7) was deleted from the EC Treaty on the entry into force of the Treaty of Amsterdam.
[44] The concept of a "measure" for the purposes of Art. 28 is a wide one: paras 6.11 *et seq.* above.
[45] Case 45/87R, [1987] E.C.R. 1369; [1987] 2 C.M.L.R. 563; Case 45/87 [1988] E.C.R. 4929.

Article 28. To comply with that provision it would have sufficed, it held, to stipulate in the invitation to tender that pipes conforming to standards equivalent to the Irish standards would be accepted.

7.16 A different kind of public procurement restriction was in issue in *Du Pont de Nemours Italiana v United Sanitare Locale*.[46] That case concerned an Italian measure requiring authorities to purchase 30 per cent of their supplies from industrial and agricultural undertakings established in southern Italy. The Court condemned this measure as an infringement of Article 28; it could not be justified on any grounds known to Community law.[47]

7.17 Another judgment relating to this type of restriction concerned the celebrated case of the contract to build a bridge over part of the Great Belt dividing the Danish islands of Funen and Seeland.[48] An invitation to tender was put out by a wholly owned subsidiary of the Danish state, according to which Danish materials were to be used for the project insofar as possible. The Danish Government had conceded that this clause infringed Article 28 and indeed the Court had little difficulty in finding the existence of such an infringement.

Denmark had argued that it had complied with Community law by eliminating the offending clause shortly before signing a contract with a syndicate of companies (and before receiving the reasoned opinion). The Court rejected this argument, since the tender procedure had been carried out on the basis of that clause.

7.18 A less serious restriction was in issue in *Commission v Netherlands*.[49] The public procurement directives prohibit public authorities from publishing specifications for a contract which mention goods of a specific make or source. However, they provide an exception where the desired product cannot otherwise be described with sufficient precision. In that case, the brand name may appear in the specifications followed by the words "or equivalent".

The Dutch authorities had published contract specifications for a "UNIX" installation, which is the name of computer software developed by ITT's Bell Laboratories (of the USA). The words "or equivalent" did not appear in the specifications. It was common ground between the parties that "UNIX" was a brand name.

The Court held that the Netherlands had infringed Article 28 as well as the public procurement directives. It is also interesting to note the Advocate General's observation that it was no defence that the contract had in fact been awarded to a tenderer offering an equivalent product, because the mere fact of publishing specifications in these terms might deter potential tenderers with equivalent products to offer.

---

[46] Case C–21/88 [1990] E.C.R. I-889, see para. 6.30 above.
[47] See also generally the Commission Communication on the regional and social aspects of public procurement ([1989] O.J. C311/7); and Case 31/87 *Beentjes v Netherlands* [1988] E.C.R. 4635.
[48] Case C–243/89 *Commission v Denmark* [1993] E.C.R. I-3353.
[49] Case C–359/93 [1995] E.C.R. I-157; see para. 12.100 below.

Incitement to Purchase Domestic Products

7.19 Article 2(3)(k) of Directive 70/50 defined as measures of equivalent effect, *inter alia*, those measures which "encourage ... or give preference to the purchase of domestic products only".[50]

The *locus classicus* on this type of measure is *Commission v Ireland* ("Buy Irish").[51] This case concerned a campaign run by the Irish Government and designed to encourage all classes of purchaser within Ireland, be they end consumers, industrialists or state bodies, to buy Irish goods in preference to imported goods. This campaign took a variety of forms, the main one being a wide-ranging advertising campaign in which purchasers were asked to give preference to goods bearing the Guaranteed Irish symbol. Other forms of promotion were also used such as the compilation and distribution to industrialists at trade fairs and elsewhere of catalogues of producers of particular types of product. There was also a "Sell Irish" campaign, mounted with the aim of persuading shops to stock and sell Irish goods in preference to imported goods. There was no real doubt that the campaign was attributable to the state.[52] Accordingly, the Court upheld the Commission's contention that the campaign taken as a whole infringed Article 28. In so doing the Court stressed the distinction between the "Buy Irish" campaign and

> "advertising by private or public undertakings or by a group of undertakings, to encourage people to buy goods produced by these undertakings. Regardless of the means used to implement it, the campaign is a reflection of the Irish Government's considered intention to substitute domestic products for imported products on the Irish market and thereby to check the flow of imports from other Member States."

7.20 Light was shed on the scope and meaning of the "Buy Irish" judgment by the ruling in *Apple and Pear Development Council v Lewis*.[53] The plaintiff body was set up by statutory instrument with the principal function of promoting apples and pears in England and Wales. This included advertising on television (with the use of such slogans as "Polish up your English") and in the press and in stores. It concentrated to a considerable extent on varieties grown in England and Wales, such as Cox and Bramley apples and Conference pears. The Court held that Article 28 did not prevent a body such as the Development Council

---

[50] On the other hand, measures by which a Member State promotes the sale or advertises its own products outside its own territory are in themselves entirely compatible with Art. 28. Such measures in no way restrict trade between Member States. On the contrary, they promote exports. Such measures may, however, fall foul of other provisions such as Art. 87 (ex 92) *et seq.*, EC.

[51] Case 249/81 [1982] E.C.R. 4005; [1983] 2 C.M.L.R. 104; paras 6.06 and 6.11 above.

[52] Para. 4.05 above.

[53] Case 222/82 [1983] E.C.R. 4083; [1984] 3 C.M.L.R. 733. This case was also decided on the basis of Council Reg. 1035/72 establishing the common market organisation for fruit and vegetables. However, there is no reason to believe that the Court would have reached a different result had it decided the case on the basis of Art. 28 alone, or had the products concerned not been subject to a common market organisation.

"from drawing attention, in its publicity, to the specific qualities of fruit produced within the Member State in question or from organising campaigns to promote the sale of certain varieties, mentioning their particular properties, even if those varieties are typical of national production; on the other hand, it would be contrary to Article [28] of the Treaty for such a body to engage in publicity intended to discourage the purchase of products from other Member States or to disparage those products in the eyes of consumers, or to advise consumers to purchase domestic products solely by reason of their national origin."

7.21 In view of the importance of this matter, the Commission published "Guidelines for Member States' involvement in promotion of agricultural and fisheries products".[54] It is not possible to reproduce these guidelines in full here, but the following passages are worthy of note:

"Identification of the producing country by word or symbol may be made providing that a reasonable balance between references, on the one hand to the qualities and varieties of the product and, on the other hand, its national origin is kept. The references to national origin should be subsidiary to the main message put over to consumers by the campaign and not constitute the principal reason why consumers are being advised to buy the product .... .
References to quality control should only be made where the product is subjected to a genuine and objective system of control of its qualities."

No such guidelines exist for industrial products.

7.22 National legislation which had the effect of encouraging the purchase of domestic products arose in a different context in *Schmit*.[55] In that case, French legislation allowed motor vehicles which had been manufactured in France and which were intended for the home market during the second half of any calendar year to be held out as falling under the model-year date of the following calendar year. By contrast, vehicles imported or re-imported into France through parallel channels did not benefit from that advantage since such vehicles had to be marketed under the model-year date applied in the Member State from which they were imported, which generally corresponded to the calendar year of sale or the date of first registration. In those circumstances, the Court found that the French rules were likely to discourage the sale of vehicles imported or reimported into France through unofficial channels and thus had the effect of impeding imports, contrary to Article 28.[56]

Similarly, in *Aher-Waggon*,[57] German legislation which made the first registration in national territory of aircraft previously registered in another Member State conditional upon compliance with strict noise standards, while exempting from those standards aircraft which obtained registration in Germany before

---

[54] [1986] O.J. C272/4.
[55] Case C–240/95 [1996] E.C.R. I-3179.
[56] On parallel imports, see also para. 2.27 above. See also Case C–314/98 *Snellers Auto's v Algemeen Directeur van de Dienst Wegverkeer* [2000] E.C.R. I-8633.
[57] Case C–389/96 [1998] E.C.R. I-4473, noted by Jans, (1998) Milieu en Recht Jur. 314.

those standards were implemented, was equally held to fall within the prohibition in Article 28.

The Obligation to appoint a Representative in the Importing Member State

7.23   Article 2(3)(g) of Directive 70/50 defined as measures of equivalent effect under Article 28 those measures which "make access of imported products to the domestic market conditional upon having an agent or representative in the territory of the importing Member State". *Commission v Belgium*[58] concerned legislation making the sale of certain pesticides and phytopharmaceutical products in Belgium subject to authorisation from the Belgian Government. It was further provided that such authorisation could only be obtained by a person established in Belgium who had responsibility for the marketing of one of those products as producer, importer, proprietor or concessionaire. Only the latter provision was impugned by the Commission. The Court held that the obligation to appoint a representative within the importing Member State fell within Article 28 and was not justified under Article 30.[59] This ruling was subsequently confirmed in *Commission v Germany*,[60] which related to pharmaceuticals.

7.24   In the last edition of this book, it was suggested that this case law has not been affected by the ruling in *Keck*[61]: even if such measures were to be regarded as restrictions on certain "selling arrangements" of the variety contemplated in paragraph 16 of that judgment, they are overtly discriminatory and thus continue to fall squarely within Article 28. This is so, it was claimed, whether or not they are framed in such a way as to apply equally to domestic manufacturers, since they are by definition automatically present on the territory. This view was confirmed by the Court in *TK-Heimdienst Sass*.[62] In that case, Austrian legislation prohibited butchers, bakers and grocers from making sales on rounds in a particular administrative district if they did not also carry on business in a permanent establishment situated in that administrative district or in an adjacent municipality where they also sold goods offered for sale on rounds. The Court held that such legislation constituted a "selling arrangement" within *Keck* "in that it lays down the geographical areas in which each of the operators concerned may sell his goods by that method".[63] However, referring to paragraph 16 of *Keck*, the Court held that the Austrian rule did not affect in the same manner the marketing of domestic products and that of products from other

---

[58]   Case 155/82 [1983] E.C.R. 531; [1983] 2 C.M.L.R. 556.
[59]   Para. 8.85 below.
[60]   Case 247/81 [1984] E.C.R. 1111; [1985] 1 C.M.L.R. 640.
[61]   Cases C–267 and 268/91 [1993] E.C.R. I-6079; [1993] 1 C.M.L.R. 101.
[62]   Case C–254/98 [2000] E.C.R. I-151, noted by Spaventa (2000) C.M.L.Rev. 1265 and Temmink (2001) S.E.W. 27.
[63]   Para. 24 of the judgment.

Member States and therefore fell within the prohibition in Article 28. The Court held:

> "Such legislation imposes an obligation on bakers, butchers and grocers who already have a permanent establishment in another Member State and who wish to sell their goods on rounds in a particular administrative district ... to set up or purchase another permanent establishment in that administrative district or in an adjacent municipality, whilst local economic operators already meet the requirement as to a permanent establishment. Consequently, in order for goods from other Member States to enjoy the same access to the market of the Member State of importation as domestic goods, they have to bear additional costs."[64]

The Court went on to find that the restriction to the free movement of goods could not be justified.[65]

Rules imposing Liability on the Importer

7.25 *Wurmser*[66] was concerned with a rule of French law whereby the person responsible for placing the product on the national market for the first time was criminally liable for any misdescription of the goods; for French goods this person would be the manufacturer, whereas with respect to imports, it was the distributor. The Court held that this rule fell within Article 28, since distributors might be deterred from dealing in imports for fear of incurring such liability. It went on to hold, however, that it might be justified in certain circumstances.

Import Monopolies

7.26 It was previously thought that, where a state monopoly enjoyed the exclusive right to import goods and to market imports, only Article 31 (ex 37) was infringed. However, in *Commission v Greece*[67] (oil and petroleum monopoly) an exclusive import right was held to contravene Article 28 as well. The Advocate General also considered that an exclusive marketing right fell foul of both Articles 28 and 31. In *France v Commission*[68] (telecommunications) the Court confirmed that both types of exclusive right were contrary to Article 28. This state of affairs has changed in recent years and Article 31 has enjoyed something of a renaissance as a provision with independent force.[69] Regrettably, the demarcation (if any) between Articles 28 to 30 on the one hand and Article 31

---

[64] Para. 26 of the judgment.
[65] This aspect of the judgment is discussed further at para 8.105.
[66] Case 25/88 [1989] E.C.R. 1105; see para. 8.86 below.
[67] Case C–347/88 [1990] E.C.R. I-4747; see para. 11.18 below; also see generally paras 9.04 *et seq.*
[68] Case C–202/88 [1991] E.C.R. I-1223.
[69] Case C–189/95 (n. 3 above), noted by Mortelmans (1998) S.E.W. 30 and Slot (1998) C.M.L.Rev. 1183. Cases C–157/94 *Commission v Netherlands* [1997] E.C.R. I-5699; C–158/94 *Commission v Italy* [1997] E.C.R. I-5789; C–159/94 *Commission v France* [1997] E.C.R. I-5815; and C–160/94 *Commission v Spain* [1997] E.C.R. I-5851.

on the other, remains unclear.[70] This case law is not affected by *Keck*, since measures of this kind are inherently discriminatory.

7.27   In the last edition of this book, it was suggested that restrictions of this kind could only be justified in highly exceptional circumstances, if at all. The ruling in *Franzén*,[71] insofar as it concerned the import licencing system linked to the Swedish alcohol monopoly, now appears to have confirmed this.[72] However, it now seems that in certain circumstances import monopolies may fall within the exemption of Article 86(2) (ex 90(2)).[73]

The Prohibition on the Sale of Goods

7.28   It has always been clear that a prohibition on sale applying to imported goods only was a measure of equivalent effect under Article 28. Thus Article 2(3) of Directive 70/50 defined as measures of equivalent effect measures which:

"(j) ... subject imported products to conditions which are different from those of domestic products and more difficult to satisfy;

(k) hinder the purchase by private individuals of imported products only...."

Thus a prohibition on or injunction against[74] the selling of imported goods covered by intellectual property rights constitutes a measure of equivalent effect within the meaning of Article 28, although it might be justified under Article 30.[75]

However, the *"Cassis de Dijon"* judgment[76] showed that all measures including "indistinctly applicable measures" prohibiting the sale of a product containing particular ingredients are measures of equivalent effect under Article 28–though they will frequently be justified under Article 30. As the reader will be aware, the Court held in that case that the imposition of a minimum alcohol requirement with respect to drinks was contrary to Article 28.[77] That judgment has been considered at length in the previous Chapter and requires no further comment here.

7.29   The Court had occasion to build on that ruling in *Gilli and Andres*.[78] An Italian decree prohibited the sale in Italy of all vinegar, be it domestic or

---

[70] See detailed discussion at 11.19 below.
[71] Case C–189/95 (n.3 above).
[72] See para. 8.95 below.
[73] Cases C–157/94, C–158/94 and C–160/94 (n. 69 above); see para 9.12 below.
[74] With respect to an injunction, see Case C–349/95 *Loendersloot* [1997] E.C.R. I-6227 at para. 16. See also Case C–313/94 *Graffione v Ditta Fransa* [1996] E.C.R. I-6039 at para. 16.
[75] See paras 8.172 *et seq.* below.
[76] Case 120/78 [1979] E.C.R. 649; [1979] 3 C.M.L.R. 494.
[77] As to minimum alcohol requirements, see also Case 182/84 *Miro* [1985] E.C.R. 3731; [1986] 3 C.M.L.R. 545.
[78] Case 788/79 [1980] E.C.R. 2071, [1981] 1 C.M.L.R. 146.

imported, other than wine vinegar. Since the product concerned constitutes no health hazard, it was clear that the sole object of the decree was to protect Italian wine products. The defendants were charged before the Italian courts with contravening the decree by selling quantities of cider vinegar imported from Germany, whereupon a reference for a preliminary ruling was made asking the Court whether this decree was compatible with Article 28. As the Court pointed out, it was undisputed that cider vinegar was harmless to health and that the vinegar in issue in the main proceedings was provided with a sufficiently clear label indicating that it was cider vinegar, thus avoiding any possibility of the consumer's confusing it with wine vinegar. It continued:

> "Thus there is no factor justifying any restrictions on the importation of the product in question from the point of view either of the protection of public health or of the fairness of commercial transactions or of the defence of the consumer.
> It appears therefore that a unilateral requirement, imposed by the rules of a Member State, prohibiting the putting on the market of vinegars not produced from the acetic fermentation of wine constitutes an obstacle to trade which is incompatible with the provisions of Article [28] of the Treaty."

This judgment was confirmed in *Commission v Italy*.[79]

7.30 The case of *Officer van Justitie v Koninklijke Kaasfabriek Eyssen*[80] concerned a prohibition on the use of a preservative called nisin in processed cheese sold in the Netherlands. In criminal proceedings brought against a manufacturer for having in stock with a view to sale quantities of cheese containing nisin, the national court asked the Court in effect whether the measure at issue was justified under Article 30. After pointing out that other Member States permitted the use of nisin either without limit or subject to certain maximum limits, the Court stated:

> "In view of this disparity of rules it cannot be disputed that the prohibition by certain Member States of the marketing on their territory of processed cheese containing added nisin is of such a nature as to affect imports of that product from other Member States where, conversely, the addition of nisin is wholly or partially permitted and that it for that reason constitutes a measure having an effect equivalent to a quantitative restriction."

The Court found, however, that the measure in question was justified on grounds of public health under Article 30.[81]

7.31 The reference in *Kelderman*[82] concerned the Dutch *Broodbesluit*, which stipulated that all bread sold in the Netherlands must contain a proportion of dry matter falling within fixed bands. The defendants were charged with selling in the Netherlands brioches from France containing a quantity of dry matter

---

[79] Case 193/80 [1981] E.C.R. 3019.
[80] Case 53/80 [1981] E.C.R. 409; [1982] 2 C.M.L.R. 20.
[81] Para. 8.76 below.
[82] Case 130/80 [1981] E.C.R. 527.

falling outside the permitted limits. Since the Court found that the measure of the kind in question was not necessary to fulfil any mandatory requirement such as the protection of public health or consumer protection, it held that it was contrary to Article 28.[83]

7.32 In *Frans-Nederlandse Maatschappij voor Biologische Producten*,[84] the Court was asked whether a prohibition on the sale of plant protection products without prior Government approval was compatible with Article 28 insofar as it applied to a product imported from another Member State where it had received such approval. Once again, the national legislation applied in the same way to domestic products and to imports. It is clear from the judgment that a measure of this kind will be contrary to Article 28 in certain circumstances discussed more fully in paragraph 8.80 below.

7.33 In *Industrie Diensten Groep v Beele*,[85] the Court found that the prohibition on the sale of imported or domestically produced goods constituting a slavish imitation of other goods already on the national market of the Member State concerned was in principle a measure of equivalent effect under Article 28. The Court went on to find, however, that such a prohibition was, under certain circumstances set out in the next Chapter,[86] justified on the grounds of consumer protection and the prevention of unfair competition.

7.34 Other measures in this category which have been held to infringe Article 28, subject to their being justified, include:

— a ban on the sale of beer exceeding the nationally prescribed acidity level[87];

— a ban on the sale of beer made from ingredients other than barley, malt and hops[88];

— a ban on the sale of substitute milk powder (i.e. "coffee whitener" not based on milk products)[89];

— a prohibition on the sale of pasta made wholly or partly from soft wheat[90];

---

[83] For similar cases concerning the salt content in bread, see Case C–17/93 *Van der Veldt* [1994] E.C.R. I-3537 and as regards moisture and ash content see Case C–358/95 *Morellato v USL* [1997] E.C.R. I-1431.

[84] Case 272/80 [1981] E.C.R. 3277; [1982] 2 C.M.L.R. 497. See also Cases C–293/94 *Brandsma* [1996] E.C.R. I-3159; C–400/96 *Harpegnies* [1998] E.C.R. I-5121; and C–473/98 *Kemikaliein-spektionen v Toolex Alpha* [2000] E.C.R. I-5681.

[85] Case 6/81 [1982] E.C.R. 707; [1982] 3 C.M.L.R. 102.

[86] See para. 8.152 below.

[87] Case 94/82 *De Kikvorsch* [1983] E.C.R. 947; [1984] 2 C.M.L.R. 323.

[88] Case 176/84 *Commission v Greece* [1987] E.C.R. 1193; [1988] 1 C.M.L.R. 813.

[89] Cases 216/84 *Commission v France* [1988] E.C.R. 793; and 76/86 *Commission v Germany* [1989] E.C.R. 1021.

[90] Cases 407/85 *Drei Glocken v USL* [1988] E.C.R. 4233; and 90/86 *Zoni* [1988] E.C.R. 4285.

— a ban on the sale of cheese having less than a prescribed minimum fat content.[91]

7.35 This case law is not affected by the ruling in *Keck*[92] since in paragraph 15 of that judgment the Court expressly preserved the *"Cassis de Dijon"* decision which concerned indistinctly applicable restrictions as to the composition of products.

Requirements as to the Presentation and Labelling of Products

7.36 Article 2(3)(j) of Directive 70/50 defined as measures of equivalent effect under Article 28 measures which "subject imported products only to conditions, in respect in particular of shape, size, weight, composition, presentation, identification or putting up … .". It follows from the *"Cassis de Dijon"* ruling[93] that all obstacles to the sale of imported goods constitute measures of equivalent effect under Article 28, subject to the application of Article 30.

An "indistinctly applicable" measure relating to the presentation of goods fell to be considered in *Fietje*.[94] The defendant was charged with marketing in the Netherlands an apple-based drink containing 25 per cent alcohol which did not bear the legend "liqueur" as required by the Dutch *Likeurbesluit*. The Court held that the measure was contrary to Article 28 in certain circumstances discussed more fully in the following Chapter of this book.[95]

7.37 Similar measures which have been held contrary to Article 28, subject to their being justified, include:

— an "indistinctly applicable" ban on the sale of silver-plated articles without the requisite hallmarks[96];

— an "indistinctly applicable" requirement that margarine be sold in cubic packaging so as to distinguish it from butter[97];

— a ban on the sale of *pétillant de raisin* (a drink with a 3 per cent alcohol content) in bottles of a type associated with champagne.[98]

7.38 This case law has not been affected by the ruling in *Keck*. Indeed, requirements as to presentation, labelling and packaging are expressly mentioned in paragraph 15 of that judgment as being amongst the measures to

---

[91] Case C–196/89 *Nespoli* [1990] E.C.R. I-3647.
[92] Cases C–267 and 288/91 (n.61 above)
[93] Case 120/78 (n.76 above).
[94] Case 27/80 [1980] E.C.R. 3839; [1981] 3 C.M.L.R. 722.
[95] Para. 8.130 below.
[96] Case 220/81 *Robertson* [1982] E.C.R. 2349; [1983] 1 C.M.L.R. 556. See also Cases C–293/93 *Houtwipper* [1994] E.C.R. I-4249; and C–30/99 *Commission v Ireland* [2001] E.C.R. I-4619; para 8.140 below.
[97] Case 261/81 *Rau v De Smedt* [1982] E.C.R. 3961; [1983] 2 C.M.L.R. 496.
[98] Case 179/85 *Commission v Germany* [1988] 1 C.M.L.R. 135, para. 8.150 below.

which "*Cassis de Dijon*" still applies. Thus in *Verband Sozialer Wettbewerb v Clinique Laboratories*[99] the Court held that a German prohibition on marketing a particular cosmetic product under the name "Clinique" (in spite of the fact that the same product was freely marketed under that name in other Member States) was prohibited by Article 28 since "the undertaking in question is obliged in the Member State alone to market its products under a different name and to bear additional packaging and advertising costs".[100] Similarly, in *Verein gegen Unwesen im Handel v. Mars*[101] the application of national unfair competition legislation which in effect required repackaging of ice cream bars that were lawfully marketed in other Member States was held to be incompatible with Article 28.[102]

Conditions of Payment, Obligatory Deposits and Guarantees and Restrictions on Credit

7.39   Article 2(3) of Directive 70/50 defined as measures of equivalent effect measures which:

> "(h)   lay down conditions of payment in respect of imported products only ...
>
> (i)   require, for imports only, the giving of guarantees or making of payments on account."

The Court has held that a restriction on the payment for goods is, like the actual supply of the goods, an essential element of an import or export transaction.[103] Therefore, measures which restrict such payment are equivalent in effect to a quantitative restriction "since their application precludes the making of payments in consideration of the supply of goods".[104]

The term "guarantees" in Article 2(3)(i) of Directive 70/50 is clearly used to cover deposits.[105] The view that the obligation to pay an import deposit constitutes a measure of equivalent effect was upheld in *Commission v Italy*.[106] That case involved Italian legislation making advance payments for imports subject to the lodging of a deposit which would be forfeited to the state if the goods were not imported within the period prescribed. The Court held:

> "although the measures in question were enacted for the purpose of preventing currency speculation, they do not constitute specific rules for the attainment of that objective but general rules dealing with the intra-Community transactions as a whole

---

[99] Case C–315/92 [1994] E.C.R. I-317.
[100] Para. 19 of the judgment.
[101] Case C–470/93 [1995] E.C.R. I-1923.
[102] See also Case C–368/95 *Vereinigte Familiapress Zeitungsverlags-und vertriebs v Heinrich Bauer Verlag* [1997] E.C.R. I-3689.
[103] C–124/95 *R. v H.M. Treasury and Bank of England Ex p. Centro-Com* [1997] E.C.R. I-81 at para. 41.
[104] *ibid.* at para. 42.
[105] See also Art. 38 of the Act of Accession of Greece and Case 58/83 *Commission v Greece* (payments for imports in cash) [1984] E.C.R. 2027; [1986] 1 C.M.L.R. 673.
[106] Case 95/81 [1982] E.C.R. 2187, incorporated by reference in Cases 206, 207, 209 and 210/80 *Orlandi v Ministry of Foreign Trade* [1982] E.C.R. 2147; see paras 6.33 above and 8.34 below.

where payment is made in advance. In fact, insofar as the Italian Government extends its rules to cover payments made by letters of credit and similar documents, the financial method usually employed for imports of goods in certain commercial sectors, it is dealing with a means of payment normally employed in international trade. The measures in question thus affect not only speculative operations but normal commercial transactions, and since their effect is to render imports more difficult or burdensome than internal transactions, they produce restrictive effects on the free movement of goods. For these reasons and insofar as they produce these effects, the measures at issue are contrary to Article [28]."

Similarly, restrictions on credit for imported goods constitute measures of equivalent effect. Thus *Commission v Greece*[107] concerned a circular which required the main credit institution in the Greek agricultural sector to refrain from granting loans for the purchase of certain agricultural machinery, in the absence of a certificate from the Ministry stating that such machinery was manufactured in Greece. This measure was held to contravene Article 28.

7.40 Nevertheless, in *Commission v Italy* the Court made it clear that:

"the Member States remain free to employ all means of ensuring that payments made abroad relate exclusively to genuine transactions, subject always to the condition that such means do not hinder the freedom of intra-Community trade as defined in the Treaty."

This was presumably an implied reference to Article 5 of the first capital directive,[108] which provided for certain exceptions to the free movement of capital. That directive was replaced by Directive 88/361,[109] Article 4 of which contained similar exceptions. On December 31, 1993 that directive in turn lapsed, together with Articles 67 to 73 of the Treaty, which were replaced by the new Articles 56 to 60 (ex 73B to 73G) introduced by the Treaty of Maastricht. Exceptions of the kind originally found in Article 5 of the first directive are now enshrined in Article 58 (ex 73D), which, *inter alia*, empowers the Member States to take the necessary measures to prevent that evasion. Consequently, it would seem clear that, in cases involving payment for goods, Article 58, which in any event corresponds to grounds of justification recognised by the Court in relation to the free movement of goods, is to be applied by analogy.[110]

Accordingly, the judgment in *Bordessa*[111] is of the utmost interest in this context. The Court held there that Directive 88/361 precluded Member States from subjecting exports of coins, bank notes or bearer cheques to a system of prior authorisation, although they were entitled to require such capital exports to be notified beforehand so that effective controls could be carried out at that stage. Since the Court also held that Article 4 of that Directive was reproduced in the new Article 58 of the Treaty, it seems clear that this ruling is still good law

---

[107] Case 192/84 [1985] E.C.R. 3967; [1988] 1 C.M.L.R. 420.
[108] Directive of May 11, 1960 ([1960] O.J. Spec. Ed. 921), as amended. See para. 2.05 above.
[109] [1988] O.J. L178/5.
[110] See para. 8.34 below.
[111] Case C–358/93 [1995] E.C.R. I-361; noted by Jarvis (1995) E.L.Rev. 514; see paras 2.05 and 8.34.

today. In any event, it appears inconceivable that provisions introduced by the Treaty of Maastricht—which provides for economic and monetary union—could be regarded as broadening pre-existing exceptions to free movement.

Discriminatory Restrictions on Advertising and Promotion

7.41 Article 2(3)(m) of Directive 70/50 defined as measures of equivalent effect on imports measures which "prohibit or limit publicity in respect of imported products only, or totally or partially confine publicity to domestic products only."[112]

Prior to *Keck*, the Court repeatedly held that even indistinctly applicable advertising restrictions were caught by Article 28. Thus, in *Oosthoek's Uitgeversmaatschappij*[113] a ban on the promotion of sales by means of free gifts was held to constitute a measure of equivalent effect contrary to Article 28 in the absence of justification. Similarly, in *GB-Inno v Confédération du Commerce Luxembourgeois*[114] and *Schutzverband gegen Unwesen in der Wirtschaft v Yves Rocher*,[115] restrictions on advertising temporary price reductions were held to constitute measures of equivalent effect. The Court ruled to the same effect in *Aragonesa de Publicidad v Departamento de Sanidad*[116] which concerned restrictions on advertising alcoholic drinks. All these measures were indistinctly applicable.

7.42 Insofar as indistinctly applicable measures are concerned, this case law was reversed by *Keck*. As is plain from *Hünermund v Landesapothekerkammer Baden-Württemberg*[117] and *Leclerc-Siplec v TFI Publicité*,[118] restrictions on advertising and promotion are to be regarded as "selling arrangements" of the kind referred to in paragraph 16 of the judgment in *Keck*.[119] Consequently, such measures only fall within Article 28 if they discriminate against imports in law or in fact.

7.43 However, Jacobs A.G.'s Opinion in *Leclerc-Siplec* marked the beginning of a trend away from the narrow interpretation of Article 28 in relation to advertising. He stressed the importance of advertising in a passage that deserves to be reproduced here in full:

---

[112] On advertising see generally Drijber "Les communications commerciales au carrefour de la dérégulation et de la régulation" (2002) Cahiers de Droit Européen (forthcoming); Greaves, "Advertising restrictions and the free movement of goods and services" (1998) 23 E.L.Rev. 305; Schwarze (ed.), *Werbung und Werbeverbote im Lichte des europäischen Gemeinschaftsrechts* (Nomos Verlag, Baden-Baden, 1998); especially C. Timmermans, "Werbung und Grundfreiheiten" at p. 26.

[113] Case 286/81 [1982] E.C.R. 4547; [1983] 3 C.M.L.R. 428; see para. 8.143 below.

[114] Case C–362/88 [1990] E.C.R. I-667; see paras 2.30 and 8.127.

[115] Case C–126/91 [1993] E.C.R. I-2361.

[116] Cases C–1/90 and C–176/90 [1991] E.C.R. I-4151.

[117] Case C–292/92 [1993] E.C.R. I-6787 (ban on advertising "parapharmaceutical" products outside the confines of pharmacies).

[118] Case C–412/93 [1995] E.C.R. I-179 (restriction on television advertising of goods). See also Case C–6/98 *ARD v PRO Sieben Media* [1999] E.C.R. I-7599 at paras 45-46.

[119] See paras 6.54 *et seq.*

"In a developed market economy based on free competition the role of advertising is fundamental. Advertising is the means by which manufacturers and distributors of goods, and providers of services, seek to persuade consumers that their goods or services are worth buying. . . .

Advertising plays a particularly important part in the launching of new products. It is by means of advertising that consumers can be induced to abandon their existing brand loyalties and make a sample purchase of a different manufacturer's goods. Without advertising consumers would tend to go on buying the goods that they are familiar with and it would be difficult for manufacturers to persuade retailers to stock unknown brands that could not be promoted by means of advertising. Without advertising it would be much easier for established manufacturers to retain their existing market share, because prospective market entrants would find it difficult to gain a foothold. In short, advertising injects greater fluidity and mobility into the economy and enhances competitiveness. A ban on advertising tends to crystallize existing patterns of consumption, to ossify markets and to preserve the status quo.

These findings have important implications for the basic freedoms created by Community law. In markets that are still, notwithstanding the process of economic integration initiated by the Treaty, to a large extent divided and compartmentalized along the lines of national frontiers, it is likely that the established brands will predominantly belong to domestic producers. Without advertising it would be extremely difficult for a manufacturer located in one Member State to penetrate the market in another Member State where his products have not previously been sold and so enjoy no reputation among consumers. Thus measures that prohibit or severely restrict advertising tend inevitably to protect domestic manufacturers and to disadvantage manufacturers located in other Member States. Such measures prevent the inter-penetration of markets and are inimical to the very concept of a single market. The Court should therefore be extremely vigilant when appraising the compatibility with Community law of restrictions on advertising.

The recognition that freedom to advertise is an essential corollary to the fundamental freedoms created by the Treaty does not of course mean that Member States are prevented from regulating and restricting advertising. On the contrary, Article [30], supplemented by the case law on 'mandatory requirements', provides ample scope for Member States to subject advertising to reasonable restrictions. These may be based *inter alia* on the protection of health, public morality, consumer protection and fair trading, and protection of the environment. There is thus no reason to fear that by recognizing a general principle of freedom to advertise the Court will deprive Member States of the power to curb the worst excesses of the advertising industry."[120]

7.44   Clearly, the Court has been influenced by that Opinion, as witnessed by its rigorous application, in cases subsequent to *Leclerc-Siplec,* of the proviso set out in paragraph 16 of *Keck,* whereby "selling arrangements" only fall outside the scope of Article 28 if they affect "in the same manner, in law and in fact, the marketing of domestic products and those from other Member States". In *KO v De Agostini,*[121] the Court applied that proviso to Swedish legislation prohibiting advertising on television directed at children. The Court held:

" . . . it cannot be excluded that an outright ban, applying in one Member State, of a type of promotion for a product which is lawfully sold there might have a greater impact on products from other Member States.

---

[120] Paras 19 to 22 of the Opinion. See also Steindorff, "Unvollkommener Binnenmarkt" [1994] Z.H.R. 149.
[121] Case C–34-36/95 [1997] E.C.R. I-3843, noted by Stuyck [1997] C.M.L.Rev. 1445.

Although the efficacy of the various types of promotion is a question of fact to be determined in principle by the referring court, it is to be noted that in its observations De Agostini stated that television advertising was the only effective form of promotion enabling it to penetrate the Swedish market since it had no other advertising methods for reaching children and their parents.

Consequently, an outright ban on advertising aimed at children less than 12 years of age and of misleading advertising, as provided for by the Swedish legislation, is not covered by Article [28] of the Treaty, unless it is shown that the ban does not affect in the same way, in fact and in law, the marketing of national products and of products from other Member States."[122]

7.45 The Court left that question for the national court to determine on the facts.[123] In *KO v Gourmet International*,[124] and in the context of a ban on the advertising of alcoholic beverages, the Court itself applied the *Keck* proviso to the facts of the case. In that case, the Court concluded that the prohibition on advertising affected the marketing of products from other Member States more heavily than the marketing of domestic products for two principal reasons. First, the Court concluded that:

"in the case of products like alcoholic beverages, the consumption of which is linked to traditional social practices and to local habits and customs, a prohibition of all advertising directed at consumers in the form of advertisements in the press, on the radio and on television, the direct mailing of unsolicited material or the placing of posters on the public highway is liable to impede access to the market by products from other Member States more than it impedes access by domestic products, with which consumers are instantly more familiar."[125]

Second, the Court observed that the Swedish legislation did not prohibit the promotion of alcoholic beverages in articles forming part of the editorial content of a publication. In that regard, the Court held that "for various, principally cultural, reasons, domestic producers have easier access to that means of advertising than their competitors established in other Member States" and the latter was therefore liable to "increase the imbalance inherent in the absolute prohibition on direct advertising".[126]

7.46 Likewise, in *Lucien Ortscheit v Eurim-Pharm*[127] pharmaceuticals which were not generally authorised for sale in Germany could be imported in small quantities under certain circumstances, but could not be advertised there. Given that this prohibition on advertising applied to imported goods alone, the Court had no difficulty in finding that it fell within Article 28.

7.47 In any event, it should also be recalled that in certain instances adver-

---

[122] Paras 42–44 of the judgment.
[123] In Case C–6/98 *ARD v PRO Sieben Media* [1999] E.C.R. I-7599, the Court itself held that proviso in para. 16 of *Keck* were "clearly satisfied": see para. 48 of the judgment.
[124] Case C–405/98 [2001] E.C.R. I-1795, noted by Stuyck [2001] C.D.E. 683.
[125] Para. 21 of the judgment.
[126] Para. 24 of the judgment.
[127] Case C–320/93 [1994] E.C.R I-5243.

tising restrictions are not so far removed from restrictions on labelling[128] and the latter are specifically mentioned in paragraph 15 of *Keck* as falling within the category of measures which constitute measures of equivalent effect, even if they are indistinctly applicable. Indeed, in *Verein gegen Unwesen im Handel v Mars*[129] the Court endorsed Léger A.G.'s view that a restriction on placing certain advertisements on chocolate wrappers related to the presentation of the product and therefore fell within the class of measures described in paragraph 15 of *Keck*. Similarly, in *Familiapress v Heinrich Bauer*,[130] legislation prohibiting the sale of magazines and periodicals containing games or competitions for prizes was held to bear on the actual content of the products in so far at the competitions formed an integral part of the magazine and the legislation in question would require traders established in other Member States to alter the contents of the periodical. Thus, where a restriction applies to advertising appearing on or in the product itself, it falls within paragraph 15.

Requirements that Goods be sold by Qualified Persons or Licensed Traders

7.48 In *Delattre*[131] an indistinctly applicable measure granting dispensing pharmacists the exclusive right to sell medicinal and "para-medical" products was held to constitute a measure of equivalent effect. The Court ruled to the same effect in *Laboratoire de Prothèses Oculaires v Union Nationale de Syndicats d'Opticiens de France*[132] with regard to an indistinctly applicable measure conferring on qualified opticians the sole right to sell contact lenses.

As explained above,[133] since the judgment in *Keck*,[134] national rules requiring that goods be sold only by qualified or licensed persons are considered to be "selling arrangements" and accordingly outside the scope of Article 28 altogether. Thus, in *Commission v Greece* national legislation requiring processed milk for infants to be sold exclusively through pharmacists' shops was held to be a "selling arrangement".[135]

Discriminatory Restrictions on the Time and Place where Goods may be sold

7.49 In *Buet*[136] an indistinctly applicable ban on doorstep selling was held to fall within Article 28. Yet even before *Keck*[137] it was not entirely free from doubt

---

[128] See para. 26 of the judgment in Case C–241/89 *SARPP v Chambre Syndicale des raffineurs de sucre* [1990] E.C.R. I-4695.
[129] Case C–470/93 [1995] E.C.R. I-1923.
[130] Case C–368/95 [1997] E.C.R. I-3689, noted by Bavasso [1998] C.M.L.Rev. 1413.
[131] Case C–369/88 [1991] E.C.R. I-1487; see also Case C–60/89 *Monteil* [1991] E.C.R. I-1547.
[132] Case C–271/92 [1993] E.C.R. I-2899.
[133] Para. 6.56.
[134] Case C–267 and 268/91 (n.61 above).
[135] Case C–391/92 [1995] E.C.R. I-1621.
[136] Case 382/87 [1989] E.C.R. 1235, see para. 8.144 below.
[137] Cases C–267 and 268/91 (n.61 above).

whether indistinctly applicable measures of this kind were indeed to be regarded as measures of equivalent effect.[138] Now it is clear that restrictions of this kind are only to be so regarded if they discriminate against imports in law or in fact: the Court in *Tankstation 't Heukske v Boermans*[139] established that restrictions on the place where goods may be sold constitute "selling arrangements" of the kind which, according to *Keck*, only fall within Article 28 if they are discriminatory. Similarly, in *Banchero*[140] Italian legislation which reserved the retail sale of tobacco products to authorised distributors was held to constitute a "selling arrangement" and thus outside the scope of Article 28.[141]

7.50   A similar pattern is to be observed as regards restrictions on the time at which goods may be sold. In *Torfaen v B&Q*,[142] it was held that even an indistinctly applicable restriction on Sunday trading was caught by Article 28, subject to justification. Once again, there was earlier case law which suggested that such measures fell outside that provision altogether.[143] However, since *Keck*, that judgment is no longer good law: as the Court confirmed in *Boermans*, restrictions on the time when goods may be sold also constitute "selling arrangements" of the type referred to in paragraph 16 of the judgment in *Keck*. Thus, in that case and in *Punto Casa v Capena*[144] and *Semeraro*,[145] indistinctly applicable restrictions on Sunday trading were held to fall outside Article 28.

Restrictions or Requirements on Stocking Goods

7.51   Article 2(3)(n) of Commission Directive 70/50 defined as measures of equivalent effect under Article 28 measures which

> "prohibit, limit or require stocking in respect of imported goods only; totally or partially confine the use of stocking facilities to domestic products only, or make the stocking of imported products subject to conditions which are different from those required for domestic products and more difficult to satisfy."

Eggers v Freie Hansestadt Bremen[146] concerned a measure requiring goods to be stocked. There the Court in effect held to be contrary to Article 28 a German measure providing that wine-based spirits could only bear certain designations

---

[138] Cases 75/81 *Blesgen v Belgium* [1982] E.C.R. 1211; [1983] C.M.L.R. 431 (para. 6.47 above); and C–23/89 *Quietlynn v Southend BC* [1990] E.C.R. I-3059 (para. 6.53 above).

[139] Cases 401-2/92 [1994] E.C.R. I-2199; see also Case C–391/92 *Commission v Greece* [1995] E.C.R. I-1621, where a requirement that certain baby foods be sold only in pharmacies was held to constitute a "selling arrangement" (see para. 6.56 above).

[140] Case C–387/93 [1995] E.C.R. I-4663.

[141] For the position in *Banchero* as regards Art. 31 (ex 37), see para 11.11.

[142] Case C–145/88 [1989] E.C.R. 3851, see also Cases C–312/89 *CGT v Conforama* [1991] E.C.R. I-997; C–332/89 *Marchandise* [1991] E.C.R. I-1027; and C–169/91 *Stoke on Trent v B&Q* [1992] E.C.R. I-6635.

[143] Case 155/80 *Oebel* [1981] E.C.R 1993, [1983] 1 C.M.L.R. 390; see para. 6.47 above.

[144] Case C–69/93 [1994] E.C.R. I-2355.

[145] Joined Cases C–418-421/93, 460-464/93, 9-15/94, 23-24/94 & 332/94 [1996] E.C.R. I-2975.

[146] Case 13/78 [1978] E.C.R. 1935; [1979] 1 C.M.L.R. 562.

of quality if they were stored for at least six months on German territory. This case will be discussed more fully at paragraph 7.59 below.

7.52 In *Commission v Greece*,[147] Greek legislation which offered to companies that marketed petroleum products in Greece the possibility of transferring to refineries their obligation to store petroleum only if they obtained a significant part of their supplies from refineries established in Greece was held to breach Article 28 and was not justified for the protection of public security under Article 30 because the same objectives could have been achieved by less restrictive means.

Reference back to the Law of the Exporting Member State

7.53 Article 2(3)(p) of Directive 70/50 defined as measures of equivalent effect measures which "prescribe that imported products are to conform, totally or partially, to rules other than those of the importing country." The Court has had occasion to rule on such a measure, in *Schutzverband gegen Unwesen in der Wirtschaft v Weinvertriebs*.[148] That case concerned a provision of German law prohibiting the importation of wine-based drinks unless they conformed to the requirements of the state of production and they could be sold there for human consumption in an unaltered state. According to Italian law, vermouth sold in Italy was to have an alcohol content of at least 16 per cent. It followed that Italian-made vermouth could only be imported into Germany if it met that requirement. Yet there were two anomalies: the Italian regulation did not apply to vermouth produced in Italy and exported; and German law did not lay down any minimum alcohol requirement for German-made vermouth. In view of the latter anomaly the measure was thus blatantly discriminatory. The Court therefore held that it constituted a measure of equivalent effect which could not be justified on consumer protection grounds, since it was distinctly applicable.[149]

The Abusive Reservation of Appellations of Origin or Indications of Source

7.54 Article 2(3)(s) of Directive 70/50 defined as measures of equivalent effect contrary to Article 28 measures which "confine names which are not indicative of origin or source to domestic products only." The French text reads: "qui ... réservent aux seuls produits nationaux des dénominations ne constituant pas des appellations d'origine ou des indications de provenance." The terms "appellations d'origine" and "indications de provenance" are terms of art in French law and that of certain other Member States, but there is no equivalent term in English law.

---

[147] Case C–398/98 [2001] E.C.R. I-7915.
[148] Case 59/82 [1983] E.C.R. 1217; [1984] 1 C.M.L.R. 319.
[149] See paras 8.03 *et seq.* below.

Commission v Germany[150] concerned measures of this type. A German statute provided that in addition to other conditions, the appellation *Sekt* could only be used to describe a German sparkling wine or sparkling foreign wine if German was an official language throughout the whole of the country of production.[151] What is more, the appellation *Prädikatssekt* could only describe a *Sekt* containing at least 60 per cent of German grapes. Again, the appellation *Weinbrand* was reserved to a certain type of German spirit and to similar foreign products if German was the official language throughout the whole of the country of production. On the other hand, sparkling wines and spirits produced in countries in which German was not such an official language were, in principle, compelled to use less prestigious appellations.

The Court upheld the Commission's contention that the reservation of these prestigious denominations to goods of such origin was contrary to Article 28.

7.55 *Prantl*[152] concerned an indirect indication of origin, namely a German measure reserving the right to market wines in bottles of a particular shape known as *Bocksbeutel* to wines from particular regions of Germany. Although the Court accepted that the shape of the bottle constituted an indirect indication of geographical origin, it held that it was contrary to Article 28 to prohibit the sale in Germany of wine from the Italian Tyrol in such bottles, when this accorded with the "fair and traditional" usage of that region.

7.56 Again, *Exportur v LOR*[153] related to an agreement between France and Spain on the mutual protection of appellations of origin and indications of provenance. This agreement reserved the denominations *Turron de Alicante* and *Turron de Jijona* (denoting a type of sweet) to products from Spain. It expressly precluded this restriction being circumvented by the use of accompanying words such as "type", "style" and so forth. The defendants produced and sold in Perpignan in France products under the names "touron Alicante", "touron Jijona", "touron catalan type Alicante" and "touron catalan type Jijona". The question arose as to whether they could be enjoined from doing so pursuant to the Franco-Spanish agreement. The Court found that such a restriction constituted a measure of equivalent effect but was justified under Article 30.

7.57 Finally, in *Pistre*,[154] French legislation which restricted the use of the description "mountain" to products prepared on national territory from domestic raw materials was held to infringe Article 28.

7.58 This case law is not affected by the ruling in *Keck*,[155] since requirements

---

[150]Case 12/74 [1975] E.C.R. 181; [1975] 1 C.M.L.R. 340.
[151]This "language clause" was apparently designed to cover Austrian *Sekt* and *Weinbrand*: Warner A. G. [1975] E.C.R. at 204; [1975] 1 C.M.L.R. 340 at 346.
[152]Case 16/83 [1984] E.C.R. 1299, [1985] 2 C.M.L.R. 238.
[153]Case C–3/91 [1992] E.C.R. I-5529. See also Case C–87/97 *Consorzio per la Tutela del Formagio Gorgonzola v Käserei Champignon Hofmeister* [1999] E.C.R. I-1301 at para. 20.
[154]Joined Cases C–321–24/94 [1997] E.C.R. I-2343, noted by Rochard [1998] R.T.D.E. 237.
[155]Cases C–267 and 268/91 (n.61 above).

relating to designation are explicitly mentioned in the category of measures to which *"Cassis de Dijon"* continues to apply (paragraph 15 of the judgment). Thus such requirements still constitute measures of equivalent effect, whether they are distinctly or indistinctly applicable. This case law is examined in greater depth at paragraphs 8.237 *et seq.* below.

Abusive Restrictions on the use of Generic Terms

7.59 *Eggers v Freie Hansestadt Bremen*[156] concerned the compatibility with Article 28 of a German statutory provision according to which spirits from wine could be designated as *Qualitätsbranntwein aus Wein* (high quality spirits made from wine) or as *Weinbrand* (brandy) only if:

— at least 85 per cent of the alcoholic content was derived from home-produced wine distillate; and

— the whole of the wine distillate used had been kept for at least six months in oaken casks in the factory where the distillate produced on national territory had been manufactured.

The Court held:

"In order to be effective the prohibition on the reserving of certain designations (other than those indicative of origin or source), and in particular designations of quality, for domestic products only must extend to measures which distinguish between domestic products according to whether or not the raw materials or the semi-finished products from which they are manufactured have been produced or treated on national territory and which reserve for goods derived from semi-finished products, treated on national territory, special designations such as to give them an advantage in the opinion of the traders or consumers concerned.

In fact in a market which, as far as possible, must present the features of a single market, entitlement to a designation of quality for a product can—except in the case of the rules applicable to registered designations of origin and indications of origin—only depend upon the intrinsic objective characteristics governing the quality of the product compared with a similar product of inferior quality and not on the geographical locality where a particular production stage took place.

It follows from all the foregoing considerations that a national measure which makes the right to use a designation of quality for a domestic product subject to the condition that the semi-finished product from which it was manufactured was either produced or treated on national territory and refuses to allow the use of that designation simply because the semi-finished product was imported from another Member State, is a measure having an effect equivalent to a quantitative restriction.

The fact that the use of that designation of quality is optional does not mean that it ceased to be an unjustified obstacle to trade if the use of that designation promotes or is likely to promote the marketing of the product concerned as compared with products which do not benefit from its use."

7.60 In *Commission v Italy*[157] the Court was concerned, *inter alia*, with a national

---

[156] Case 13/78 (n.146 above).
[157] Case 193/80 (n.79 above).

measure prohibiting the use of the term *aceto* (vinegar) in Italy for vinegar other than wine vinegar.[158] The effect of this measure, which was clearly designed to protect Italian wine producers, was to make all vinegar other than wine vinegar virtually unsaleable in that country. Nevertheless, it is important to note that, unlike the measures at issue in the *Eggers* case, this particular measure applied in the same way to domestic products and to imports. The Italian Government sought to show that, for the Italian consumer, the term *aceto* had come to designate only wine vinegar, to the exclusion of all other vinegars. However, the Court found, by reference to the definition given in the relevant heading of the Common Customs Tariff, that the term was in fact a generic one, covering various different types of vinegar. The Court held that, where a generic term such as this refers to a number of different varieties of product, the reservation of that term to one of those varieties only constitutes a measure of equivalent effect contrary to Article 28.

On the other hand, the Court recognised that the Italian consumer might have become conditioned by the contested measure to think of *aceto* as covering only wine vinegar. The Italian Government could therefore adopt other, less restrictive measures to protect the consumer, such as a requirement that the precise nature of the product be set out on a label affixed to the product. But the Court stressed that such a requirement would have to apply in the same way to all varieties of vinegar, including wine vinegar.[159]

7.61 *Miro*[160] was in a sense the sequel to *"Cassis de Dijon"*.[161] Whereas the earlier case concerned a complete ban on the sale of certain drinks containing less than the stipulated minimum alcohol content, *Miro* concerned a measure linking the right to use a generic name to the respect of a minimum alcohol requirement. Under Dutch law the use of the name *jenever* (gin) was permitted only for products with an alcohol content of at least 35 per cent. The defendants imported from Belgium quantities of gin with an alcohol content of only 30 per cent, gin of this type having been produced in Belgium for many years. No minimum alcohol content for gin was prescribed in Belgian law at the relevant time. The defendants were charged with possessing with a view to sale bottles with labels bearing the word *jenever*, even though those labels also stated that the alcohol content was 30 per cent. The Court found this to be a restriction on imports which, not being justified,[162] was contrary to Article 28.

7.62 *Commission v Germany* (beer)[163] was in many ways similar to *Commission v Italy* (vinegar). The Court found there that it was contrary to Article 28 for the

---

[158] As to the prohibition on the sale of such vinegar, see para. 7.29 above.

[159] See also Case 281/83 *Commission v Italy* (failure to implement the ruling in Case 193/80) E.C.R. 3397; [1987] 1 C.M.L.R. 865, and para. 8.136 below.

[160] Case 182/84 (n.77 above).

[161] Case 120/78 (n.76 above).

[162] See Ch. VIII below.

[163] Case 178/84 [1988] 1 C.M.L.R. 780, noted by Rabe (1987) EuR 253; and see Brouwer, "Free movement of foodstuffs and quality requirements; has the Commission got it wrong?" (1988) C.M.L.Rev. 237; see paras 8.149 and 8.153 below.

defendant to restrict the use of the designation "beer" to products made from a prescribed range of raw materials. Once again, the contested restriction applied in the same way to imported goods as to domestic production, but such raw materials as rice and maize which are frequently used for manufacturing beer in other Member States were precluded. The defendant had argued that the "Italian vinegar" case should be distinguished on the grounds the measure in issue in that case had made it impossible for Member States with no vines to sell domestically produced vinegar in Italy, whereas all Member States could produce barley (a permitted raw material) and could therefore comply with the German rules. As Slynn A.G. pointed out, this difference was of no consequence whatsoever.

The Court held that the contested restriction was not justified on consumer protection grounds, at least when such raw materials as rice and maize, frequently used for the manufacture of beer in other Member States, were precluded. The Court gave two grounds for this finding. First, the Member State must not crystallise consumer habits so as to consolidate an advantage acquired by national industries concerned to comply with them. Second, "beer" was a generic term in the other Member States and in Community law (as shown by the relevant Common Customs Tariff heading). Even in German legislation—indeed in other provisions of the very statute in issue—the word "beer" was used to denote certain drinks not conforming to the German requirements. Thus the Court rejected the defendant Government's claim that "beer" was not a generic term.

7.63   *Smanor*[164] was concerned with French legislation prohibiting the use of the term "yoghourt" for deep-frozen yoghourt, even in conjunction with another word indicating that the product was deep-frozen; under French law this product could only be sold as "deep-frozen fermented milk". Such legislation was held to be contrary to Article 28 where the labelling made it clear that the product was deep-frozen, unless its characteristics were not those which a consumer would be led to expect from the use of the denomination "yoghourt". The *Codex Alimentarius* adopted by the FAO and the World Health Organisation showed that the principal characteristic of products sold as "yoghourt" was that they contained large quantities of living lacto-bacillae. Thus the measure was contrary to Article 28 unless the deep-frozen product was substantially different from fresh yoghourt, notably as regards the numbers of such bacillae. This was a matter for the national court to decide.

Subsequently, in its Communication on the names under which foodstuffs are sold,[165] the Commission deduced from this judgment that a Member State may prohibit the sale of "a product, which has undergone treatment and no longer contains live bacteria, as 'yoghourt' or by any other name containing a reference to yoghourt. Such a reference could mislead the consumer as to the

---

[164] Case 298/87 [1988] E.C.R. 4489.
[165] [1991] O.J. C270/2.

real nature of the product which could not be overcome by additional corrective labelling".

7.64   Like *Miro*, *Deserbais*[166] was highly reminiscent of "*Cassis de Dijon*". The case related to the minimum fat content of Edam cheese. It was common ground that this name had become generic. The defendant was prosecuted for importing quantities of German Edam into France and marketing it there under this name, although its fat content of 34.3 per cent was below the minimum required in France (40 per cent). The cheese had been lawfully produced and marketed in Germany, and the consumer's attention was drawn to the fat content by the labelling.

In these circumstances, the Court held that the French restriction was contrary to Article 28, adding:

> "The question may arise whether the same rule must be applied where a product presented under a particular name is so different, as regards its composition or production, from the products generally known by that name in the Community that it cannot be regarded as falling within the same category. However, no situation of that kind arises in the circumstances described by the national court in this case."

The Court subsequently ruled to the same effect in *Commission v Italy*[167] which concerned a prohibition on the use of the very designation "cheese" for products with less than a prescribed minimum fat content.[168]

7.65   In *Commission v France*,[169] French legislation relating to preparations containing *foie gras* as a base was at issue. The legislation in question reserved certain trade descriptions to products possessing particular qualities without including a mutual recognition clause for products coming from other Member States which were compatible with the rules enacted by those states. In other words, the French legislation had the effect of prohibiting the marketing under a given trade description of a product which complied fully with the rules laid down by another Member State but which did not fully satisfy the requirements imposed by the French legislation. On the facts of that case, the evidence was that no other Member State had in fact enacted specific rules concerning preparations with *foie gras* as a base. The Commission thus relied on a potential (as opposed to an actual) effect on trade between Member States. Unlike the Advocate General, the Court held that notwithstanding the fact that no rules had in fact been laid down by other Member States, the French legislation was at least potentially capable of hindering inter-state trade.

7.66   Finally, an infringement of Article 28 could also occur in the following manner: Member State A reserves the right to use a particular designation

---

[166] Case 286/86 [1988] E.C.R. 4907.
[167] Case C–210/89 [1990] E.C.R. I-3697.
[168] See also Case C–448/98 *Guimont* [2000] E.C.R. I-10663 at para. 26, which concerned a prohibition on the marketing of cheese without rind under the designation "Ementhal".
[169] Case C–184/96 [1998] E.C.R. I-6197, noted by Mattera [1998] R.M.U.E. 113.

within its territory to the products of Member State B, whereas in reality the products of other Member States should also be entitled to the use of that designation. Such a restriction would not be justified under Article 30, since it would constitute arbitrary discrimination.

7.67   As already mentioned, this case law is not affected by the ruling in *Keck*,[170] since requirements relating to designation are explicitly mentioned in the category of measures to which "*Cassis de Dijon*" continues to apply (paragraph 15 of the judgment). Thus such requirements still constitute measures of equivalent effect, whether they are distinctly or indistinctly applicable. The reader is also referred to para. 8.135 below.

Obligatory Origin Marking

7.68   A measure requiring the origin of goods to be marked on them constitutes a measure of equivalent effect. On the other hand, it is clear that it is perfectly lawful for traders to indicate the origin of their goods of their own accord should they so wish.

The first case on this type of measure to be decided by the Court of Justice was *Commission v Ireland*.[171] It concerned two Irish statutory instruments prohibiting the importation into and sale in Ireland of certain categories of metal article bearing certain motifs, unless they were marked with a word or words indicating that they were manufactured outside the Republic. The list of articles included not only jewellery but also such objects as buckles, dress-combs and key-rings. The motifs ranged from those with specifically Irish associations to thatched cottages. There was no corresponding origin marking requirement with respect to such goods manufactured within the state. Consequently, the measures in question were "distinctly applicable".

The Commission brought infringement proceedings against Ireland with respect to these measures. It claimed that the obligation to mark the origin on goods was only justified if this was necessary to avoid the purchaser being misled as to the true origin of a product bearing a false or misleading indication. It pointed out that it will be more important for the purchaser to know whether a product is or is not of a particular origin where such origin implies a certain quality, basic materials or process of manufacture or a particular place in the folklore or tradition of the region in question.[172]

The Commission claimed that the metal articles covered by the Irish measures did not fall within these conditions and thus the measures were not justified on the grounds of consumer protection, the prevention of unfair competition or any other grounds. The Commission added that even if the statutory instruments had applied in the same way to Irish goods, they would still not have been justified.

---

[170] Cases C–267 and 268/91 (n. 61 above).
[171] Case 113/80 [1981] E.C.R. 1625; [1982] 1 C.M.L.R. 706.
[172] See generally para. 7.54 above.

While finding for the Commission in the case before it, the Court saw no need to rule on all those points. Having noted that most of the products in question were souvenirs, it ruled:

"The essential characteristic of the souvenirs in question is that they constitute a pictorial reminder of the place visited, which does not by itself mean that a souvenir, as defined in the [Irish] Orders, must necessarily be manufactured in the country of origin, ... it is important to note that the interests of consumers and fair trading would be adequately safeguarded if it were left to domestic manufacturers to take appropriate steps such as affixing, if they so wish, their mark of origin to their own products or packaging."

Consequently, it held that the measures at issue infringed Article 28.

7.69 Unlike the Irish case, *Commission v United Kingdom*[173] concerned a measure which purported to apply in the same way to imports and to domestic products. The measure related to four categories of goods, namely clothing and textiles, domestic electrical appliances, footwear and cutlery. Subject to certain exceptions, it prohibited the retail sale of such goods unless they were marked with or accompanied by an indication of origin.

In contrast to the Advocate General, the Court found that this legislation constituted a measure of equivalent effect. First, the Court pointed out that, although its requirements could be satisfied by indicating the origin on a notice accompanying the goods, evidence showed that in practice retailers insisted that the origin of the goods should be marked on the goods themselves by the manufacturer. Secondly:

"it has to be recognised that the purpose of indications of origin or origin marking is to enable consumers to distinguish between domestic and imported products and that this enables them to assert any prejudices which they may have against foreign products. As the Court has had the occasion to emphasise in various contexts, the Treaty, by establishing a common market and progressively approximating the economic policies of the Member States, seeks to unite national markets in a single market having the characteristics of a domestic market. Within such a market, the origin marking requirement not only makes the marketing in a Member State of goods produced in other Member States in the sectors in question more difficult; it also has the effect of slowing down economic interpenetration in the Community by handicapping the sale of goods produced as a result of a division of labour between Member States."

In view of these considerations, the Court concluded that the contested provisions were liable to "have the effect of increasing the production costs of imported goods and making it more difficult to sell them on the United Kingdom market."

The Court then went on to reject the United Kingdom's defence based on consumer protection:

---

[173] Case 207/83 [1985] E.C.R. 1201; [1985] 2 C.M.L.R. 259.

"The requirements relating to the indication of origin of goods are applicable without distinction to domestic and imported products only in form because, by their very nature, they are intended to enable the consumer to distinguish between those categories of products, which may thus prompt him to give his preference to national products ....[T]he fact that United Kingdom consumers associate a product's quality with its national origin does not appear to have been a consideration which prompted the United Kingdom Government when it suggested to the Commission that, as far as the Member States of the Community were concerned, it was prepared to accept the indication 'Made in the European Community'. Besides, if the national origin of goods brings certain qualities to the minds of consumers, it is in manufacturers' interests to indicate it themselves on the goods or on their packaging and it is not necessary to compel them to do so. In that case, the protection of consumers is sufficiently guaranteed by rules which enable the use of false indication of origin to be prohibited. Such rules are not called in question by the EEC Treaty."

The Court did not specify whether there are exceptional circumstances in which a Member State can go beyond merely prohibiting false (or misleading) indications or origin and require an indication of origin.[174]

Discriminatory Rules of Procedure and Evidence

7.70   It was established in *Procureur-Général v Arnaud*[175] that a rule of procedure can constitute an infringement of Article 28. The reference arose out of a series of prosecutions of French wine traders for illegal enrichment ("over-alcoholisation") of certain quantities of red wine. The French *Code du Vin* created a rebuttable presumption of over-alcoholisation of wine if the proportion of alcohol to reduced extract was in excess of a certain figure. The *Cour d'Appel* of Bordeaux asked, *inter alia*, whether this presumption was compatible with the Regulations setting up a common market organisation in wine, which included a provision prohibiting quantitative restrictions and measures of equivalent effect.

The Court replied that a rebuttable presumption of this kind was compatible with Article 28 unless its application could put at a disadvantage wines from other Member States as where, for example, the presumption was harder to rebut in the case of wines from other Member States.[176] There is every reason to suppose that the same ruling would apply to industrial products and to agricultural products not covered by a common market organisation.

Language Requirements

7.71   In *Fietje*[177] it was held that a Member State may not require labelling to be

---

[174] See para. 8.127 below.
[175] Cases 89/74, 1819/75 [1975] E.C.R. 1023; [1975] 2 C.M.L.R. 490; see also Cases 1014/75 *Lahaille* [1975] E.C.R. 1053.
[176] See also Case 202/82 *Commission v France* (pasta) [1984] E.C.R. 933; [1985] 2 C.M.L.R. 185.
[177] Case 27/80 (n.94 above). See also Cases C–369/89 *Piageme v Peeters* [1991] E.C.R. I-2971; C–51/93 *Meyhui v Schott Zwiesel Glaswerke* [1994] E.C.R. I-3879; C–85/94 *Piageme v Peeters* [1995] E.C.R. I-2955; C–385/96 *Goerres* [1998] E.C.R. I-4431; C–33/97 *Colim v Bigg's Continent Noord* [1999] E.C.R. I-3175; and C–169/99 *Hans Schwarzkopf* [2001] E.C.R. I-5901 and paras 8.130 *et seq.* below.

in its language where the information contained on the original label in another language is equally comprehensible to consumers in that state.

The same principle surely applies to documents directed not at consumers, but at officials of the importing state. Thus the Commission has stated[178] that a French official circular requiring all customs documents to be in French was contrary to Article 28. Presumably the same applies to documents required for the type approval of products. Yet there are undoubtedly cases in which such a requirement may be justified, albeit that no criterion for assessing such justification appears to be readily available. In relation to customs documents the Commission has stated[179] that "a translation of such documents can only be demanded in cases where there are serious doubts about what they contain or they are not understood at all", but this is a subjective test not susceptible to proof.

Restrictions on Health Care Coverage

7.72 *Duphar v Netherlands*[180] must rank amongst the most difficult cases on Article 28 which the Court has had to decide. It concerned a list of pharmaceutical products drawn up by the Dutch authorities which did not qualify for reimbursement out of the State social security fund, in view of their allegedly excessive cost. Each of these excluded products could, it was said, be replaced by another product which was equally effective and less costly. Under the scheme national products and imports were treated in the same way. The plaintiffs were pharmaceutical companies which claimed that the scheme was contrary, *inter alia*, to Article 28.

Plainly such a scheme may actually or potentially, directly or indirectly, impede imports. Yet its object was to reduce State spending. While this objective is wholly unobjectionable in itself, it is of a purely economic nature and thus cannot be justified under Article 30.[181]

Mancini A.G. considered that the contested measure constituted a measure of equivalent effect under Article 28, since it discouraged the purchase of the products concerned so as to cause a fall in imports. However, in his view the scheme was justified on public health grounds under Article 30. He conceded that its immediate aim was to reduce public expenditure but stressed that its ultimate purpose was to protect public health. He regarded it as contradictory and hypocritical to acknowledge the importance of the protection of public health, while at the same time denying the Member States the means for ensuring proper health care. It might be that the measure in issue in the main case was disproportionately restrictive having regard to the end to be achieved, but that was for the national court to determine. At the same time he wholly rejected the Commission's suggestion that the improvement of the financial

---

[178] Written questions 1744/82 ([1983] O.J. C92/20); 2126/82 ([1983] O.J. C141/9), ([1983] O.J. C232/5); and 1032/83 ([1983] O.J. C359/11).
[179] Written question 1032/83 (see n.178 above).
[180] Case 238/82 [1984] E.C.R. 523; [1985] 1 C.M.L.R. 256.
[181] See para. 8.32 below.

management of a public sickness insurance scheme be regarded as a "mandatory requirement" justifying measures applying to imports and domestic goods
in the same way under the terms of "*Cassis de Dijon.*"[182] If this were to be
accepted as justification, then it was only a short step to extending that principle
to all types of public or social expenditure.

The Court also found that such a scheme might in certain circumstances be
lawful, but reached that result by a different route. It began by stressing that in
other Member States only those pharmaceuticals on the official list qualified for
reimbursement, all other products being excluded. In the Netherlands, on the
other hand, the converse applied: all products were subject to reimbursement
except those specifically excluded. Next, it rejected the Dutch Government's
argument to the effect that this provision could be equated with that of a private
body purchasing goods on the market. Despite this, the Court acknowledged
that "social security institutions are substituted for consumers as regards
responsibility for the payment of medical expenses." Accordingly, even though
it might restrict imports, such legislation was held to fall outside Article 28 if
certain conditions were satisfied. These conditions were as follows: the exclu-
sionary lists must be drawn up in accordance with objective criteria without
reference to the origin of the products (*e.g.* the existence on the market of
other, less expensive products having the same therapeutic effect or the fact
that a product may be purchased without a prescription); they must be verifiable by any importer; and it must be possible to amend the lists whenever
compliance with the specific criteria so required.

On the other hand, the Court held that, if these conditions were not met,
then the measure was caught by Article 28 and was not justified under Article
30. That provision could not "justify a measure whose primary objective is
budgetary in as much as it is intended to reduce the operating costs of a sickness
insurance scheme".[183]

7.73 While the Court's judgment will have been widely welcomed in its result,
the reasoning was questionable. In particular, the basis upon which the Court
decided that the legislation fell outside Article 28 even though imports were
restricted was left decidedly unclear.[184] It is to be expected that the Court would
now avoid such unsatisfactory reasoning in view of the fact that it has recently
grasped the nettle by recognising the preservation of the financial balance of
social security systems as a mandatory requirement and therefore as a possible

---

[182] Case 120/78 (n.76 above).

[183] After the judgement in *Duphar* the Council enacted Dir. 89/105 [1989] O.J. 40/8 relating to the
transparency of measures regulating the pricing of medicinal products for human use and their
inclusion in the scope of national health insurance systems. Art. 7 provides that a decision to
place a product on a blacklist "shall contain a statement of reasons based on objective and
verifiable criteria". See also the Commission's communication on the subject ([1986] O.J. C310/
7) as well as its more general communication on the pharmaceutical industry (Com. (93) 718)
and Thompson, "The Single Market for Pharmaceuticals" (1994) at 9.

[184] See para. 20 of the judgment.

head of justification for restrictions to the free movement of goods.[185] Indeed, in *Geraets-Smits*,[186] a case concerning the freedom to provide services, the Court has already had occasion to incorporate the conditions that it laid down in *Duphar* into its analysis of this justification under the mandatory require-ments.[187] Accordingly, such measures which restrict imports will fall within Article 28 and the analysis has now shifted to considering whether that restriction may be justified for the preservation of the financial balance of social security systems.[188]

7.74 A more straighforward case was *Decker v Caisse de Maladie des Employés Privés*[189]: in that case, national rules made reimbursement of costs incurred to purchase medical products (*in casu* spectacles) in other Member States subject to prior authorisation, whereas costs incurred in the state of insurance were not subject to that authorisation. This scheme was held to be incompatible with Article 28. The Court held that the rules in question had the effect of encouraging persons insured under the social security scheme in that Member State (*in casu* Luxembourg) to purchase their spectacles from, and to have them assembled by, opticians established in Luxembourg rather than in other Member States.

Certain Price Controls

7.75 The term "price controls" is used here to cover the following range of measures: price freezes, minimum and maximum prices, minimum and max-imum profit margins and resale price maintenance. Countless variants and combinations of these types of measure have been imposed by the different Member States with respect to various products, although price controls are less widespread today.[190]

Furthermore, price controls generally form an integral part of the economic policies of the Member States. As it originally stood, the Treaty largely left intact

---

[185] See Case C–120/95 *Decker v Caisse de maladie des employés privés* [1998] E.C.R. I-1831 at para. 39. As to services, see Cases C–158/96 *Kohll v Union des Caisses de Maladie* [1998] E.C.R. I-1931 at para. 41; and C–157/99 *Geraets-Smits v Stichting Ziekenfonds* [2001] E.C.R. I-5473 at para. 72. See further discussion at paras 8.166 *et seq.*

[186] Case C–157/99 (n.185 above).

[187] See paras 86 to 90 of the judgment.

[188] See further discussion at paras 8.166 *et seq.*

[189] Case C–120/95 (n.185 above). Noted by Huglo (1998) R.T.D.E. 584 and Stuyck (1999) S.E.W. 259.

[190] This no doubt explains why most of the case law and literature on price controls date from the 1970s and 1980s. As to the literature, see Capelli, *Controllo dei Prezzi e Normativa Comunitaria* (1981); Galmot and Biancarelli, "Les réglementations nationales en matière de prix au regard du droit communautaire" [1985] R.T.D.E. 269; Mattera, *Le marché unique européen: ses règles, son fonctionnement* (1990) Chap VI; Matthies, "Die Verantwortung der Mitgliedsstaaten für den freien Warenverkehr in Gemeinsamen Markt" in *Festschrift für Ipsen* (1977); Mestmäcker, *Vereinbarkeit von Preisregelungen auf dem Arzneimittelmarkt mit dem Recht der Europäischen Wirtschaftsgemeinschaft* (1980) (summary in English); Sabiani, "L'incidence de droit de la Communauté Economique Européenne sur la réglementation française des prix" (1975) R.T.D.E. 470 and 633; Waelbroeck, *Les réglementations nationales de prix et le droit communautaire* (1975); Winkel, "Die Vereinbarkeit staatlicher Preislenkungsmassnahmen mit dem EWGVertrag" (1976) N.J.W. 2048.

the right of each Member State to take the economic policy measures which it deemed necessary under Articles 103(1) (now 99(1)), 104 (now 101) and 145 (now 202). This explains why the Court has trodden more warily with regard to price controls than with respect to other types of measure falling under Article 28. It would have been rash indeed to have held that all price controls automatically constitute measures of equivalent effect.

Although the provisions of the Treaty of Maastricht imposed a new discipline on the Member States with a view to Economic and Monetary Union, those states still retain a certain freedom of manoeuvre under such provisions as Articles 98 (ex 102A) and 99 (ex 103).[191] These provisions apply to all the Member States, including those which do not participate in the euro.

7.76 At all events, the Commission in Article 2(3) of Directive 70/50 defined as measures of equivalent effect measures which:

"(a) lay down, for imported products only, minimum or maximum prices below or above which imports are prohibited, reduced or made subject to conditions liable to hinder importation; or

(b) lay down less favourable prices for imported products than for domestic products; or

(c) fix profit margins or any other price components for imported products only or fix these differently for domestic products and for imported products, to the detriment of the latter; or

(d) preclude any increase in the price of the imported product corresponding to the supplementary costs and charges inherent in importation; or

(e) fix the prices of products solely on the basis of the cost price or the quality of domestic products at such a level as to create a hindrance to importation."

This has now been supplemented by a body of case law of the Court, much of which concerns products not subject to a common market organisation.[192]

7.77 The first cases in which the Court ruled on the compatibility of price

---

[191] All the cases discussed in paras 7.75 to 7.90 were decided prior to the Maastricht Treaty.
[192] The Court's case law on the compatibility of national price controls with the common market organisations and in particular the provisions of those organisations relating to price formation falls outside the scope of this book (see paras 10.06 *et seq.*). This case law includes: Case 31/74 *Galli* [1975] E.C.R. 47; [1975] 1 C.M.L.R. 211; Case 154/77 *Dechmann* [1978] E.C.R. 1573; [1979] 2 C.M.L.R. 1; Case 223/78 *Grosoli* [1979] E.C.R. 2621; Case 10/79 *Toffoli* [1979] E.C.R. 3301; Cases 95-96/79 *Kefer and Delmelle* [1980] E.C.R. 103; Case 216/86 *Antonini* [1987] E.C.R 2919; Berardis, "The common organisation of agricultural markets and national price regulations" (1980) C.M.L.Rev. 539; Colinet and Maresceau, "Interprétation et application du droit communautaire dans le domaine des réglementations des prix des produits agricoles de l'arrêt Dechmann à l'arrêt KeferDelmelle" (1980) C.D.E. 507.

controls with Article 28 were the two parallel cases of *Tasca*[193] and *SADAM v Comitato Interministeriale dei Prezzi*,[194] both involving maximum prices for sugar fixed by the Italian authorities. In each case the national court asked whether such maximum prices were compatible with Article 28 and with Regulation 1009/67 establishing a Common Market organisation for sugar.[195] As regards Article 28 the Court replied in each case:

"Article [28] of the Treaty prohibits in trade between Member States all measures having an effect equivalent to quantitative restrictions and this prohibition is repeated in Article 35 of Regulation No. 1009/67 as regards the market in sugar. For the purposes of this prohibition it is sufficient that the measures in question are likely to constitute an obstacle, directly or indirectly, actually or potentially, to imports between Member States. Although a maximum price applicable without distinction to domestic and imported products does not in itself constitute a measure having an effect equivalent to a quantitative restriction, it may have such an effect, however, when it is fixed at a level such that the sale of imported products becomes, if not impossible, more difficult than that of domestic products. A maximum price, in any event insofar as it applies to imported products, constitutes therefore a measure having an effect equivalent to a quantitative restriction, especially when it is fixed at such a low level that, having regard to the general situation of imported products compared with that of domestic products, dealers wishing to import the products in question into the Member State concerned can do so only at a loss."

7.78 It would appear[196] that the measures which the Court describes in this passage as applying in the same way to imports and to domestic products (and thus "indistinctly applicable") in fact fall under Article 2(3)(d) and (e) of Directive 70/50, since the objection to these measures is that they fail to take account of the special position of imports. Yet Article 2(3) of Directive 70/50 covers "distinctly applicable" measures only. This shows how precarious is the distinction between "distinctly applicable" and "indistinctly applicable" measures.

More curious is the fact that the passage quoted from the *Tasca* and *SADAM* judgments appears to contradict itself. On the one hand, the Court states that a maximum price applying to domestic products and to imports in the same way does not in itself constitute a measure of equivalent effect, but only does so when it makes the sale of imported products more difficult than that of domestic products. On the other hand, in the following sentence the Court holds that a maximum price does constitute a measure of equivalent effect "especially when ... ." There appears to be no way of reconciling these two statements. However, as will be seen below, subsequent judgments such as *GB-Inno v ATAB* and *Danis* follow the former line: maximum prices applying in the same way to domestic products and to imports do not in themselves constitute measures of equivalent effect.

---

[193]Case 65/75 [1976] E.C.R. 291; [1977] 2 C.M.L.R. 183.
[194]Cases 8890/75 [1976] E.C.R. 323; [1977] 2 C.M.L.R. 183.
[195][1967] O.J. Spec.Ed. 304.
[196]Winkel, *op. cit.* n.190 above, at 2051.

7.79 The Court also held in *SADAM* that a Member State could not rely on the former Article 103 to justify a maximum consumer price controls contrary to Article 28 (the new Articles 99 and 100 inserted by the Treaty of Maastricht broadly correspond to that provision).[197] There is every reason to think that this ruling applies to all products, even those not covered by a common market organisation; and that it applies to all price controls. On this view these provisions can never be relied on to justify a price control falling under Article 28.

7.80 This brings us to *GB-Inno v ATAB*[198] itself. By Belgian law, excise duty on Belgian or imported manufactured tobacco was to be calculated on the basis of the price appearing on the tax label; furthermore this price, freely chosen by the manufacturer or the importer as the case may be, was the compulsory selling price to the consumer. This measure was therefore at once broadly equivalent to a minimum and a maximum price control. In an action in which it was accused of selling below this price, GB-Inno, a major Belgian supermarket chain, claimed that this system was contrary to a number of provisions of Community law, including Article 28. The national court asked four questions, the third of which concerned the compatibility of such a measure with Article 28.

Before the answers to those questions, the Court's judgment contains a section entitled "general observations". In this section the Court pointed out that the prohibition on selling cigarettes above the price used for calculating the tax was essential to make the tax workable.[199] This could not be said of the prohibition on selling below this price, which was designed rather to protect small retailers against destructive competition from supermarkets. It also noted that, while in theory there was nothing to prevent a retailer from determining his own price by obtaining tobacco products with appropriate labels, this required the co-operation of the manufacturer or importer and of the Belgian tax authorities, and this co-operation might be difficult to obtain.

In answer to the third question the Court held:

"Although a maximum price applicable without distinction to domestic and imported products does not in itself constitute a measure having an effect equivalent to a quantitative restriction, it may have such an effect, however, when it is fixed at such a level that the sale of imported products becomes, if not impossible, more difficult than that of domestic product.

On the other hand, a system whereby the prices are freely chosen by the manufacturer or the importer as the case may be and imposed on the consumer by a national legislative measure, and whereby no distinction is made between domestic products and imported products, generally has exclusively internal effects.

However, the possibility cannot be excluded that in certain cases such a system may be capable of affecting intra-Community trade."

The Court therefore concluded that, even taking into account the inherent barriers to trade due to differences in the tax systems of the Member States, it

---

[197] See paras 9.14 *et seq.* below.
[198] Case 13/77 [1977] E.C.R. 2115; [1978] 1 C.M.L.R. 283.
[199] See para. 8.122 below.

was possible that such a system might hinder, directly or indirectly, actually or potentially, imports between Member States. This was for the national court to assess.[200]

7.81 The Court subsequently extended this case law to price freezes, in *Openbaar Ministerie v Danis*.[201] The defendants in the main case were traders in animal feedstuffs accused of increasing their prices without notifying the Belgian Minister of Economic Affairs as required by a Belgian Ministerial Order. That Order provided that all price increases were to be notified to the Minister at least two months before they took effect and that the Minister could extend this period. The Belgian court consequently asked the Court of Justice whether such a scheme was compatible with Article 28.

After repeating the *Dassonville* formula the Court stated:

"National rules of this kind, even if they are confined to requiring the producer or importer to 'notify' proposed price increases before they are applied, have the effect of a price freeze, since the prices quoted by the producer prior to his notification are, in fact, 'frozen' for at least the duration of the waiting period.

Whilst rules imposing a price freeze which are applicable equally to national products and to imported products do not amount in themselves to a measure having an effect equivalent to a quantitative restriction, they may in fact produce such an effect when prices are at such a level that the marketing of imported products becomes either impossible or more difficult than the marketing of national products. That is especially the case where national rules, while preventing the increased prices of imported products from being passed on in sale prices, freeze prices at a level so low that–taking into account the general situation of imported products in relation to that of national products–traders wishing to import the products in question into the Member State concerned can do so only at a loss, or, having regard to the level at which prices for national products are frozen, are impelled to give preference to the latter products."

7.82 Lastly, the Court has also had occasion to rule on the compatibility with Article 28 of minimum prices and minimum profit margins, in *van Tiggele*.[202] There the defendant was charged before a Dutch court with having sold spirits below minimum prices fixed by the Dutch authorities. Different rules applied to three different types of spirit:

(a) for "new hollands gin" and *vieux*, the retail price had to be the manufacturer's catalogue price per unit (if any) plus 0.60 Fl. per unit and VAT, the total of which could in no case be lower than 11.25 Fl. per litre;

(b) for "old hollands gin" the minimum retail price was fixed at 11.25 Fl. per litre;

---

[200] See also Cases 177178/82 *Van de Haar* [1984] E.C.R. 1797; [1985] 2 C.M.L.R. 566.
[201] Cases 1620/79 [1979] E.C.R. 3327; [1980] 3 C.M.L.R. 492. See also Case 5/79 *Buys* [1979] E.C.R. 3203; [1980] 2 C.M.L.R. 493.
[202] Case 82/77 [1978] E.C.R. 25; [1978] 2 C.M.L.R. 528.

(c) for other spirits, the minimum retail price was the actual purchase price plus VAT.

The Court replied to the question put by the Dutch court as follows:

> "Whilst national price-control rules applicable without distinction to domestic products and imported products cannot in general [hinder, directly or indirectly, actually or potentially imports between Member States], they may do so in specific cases.
>
> Thus imports may be impeded in particular when a national authority fixes prices or profit margins at such a level that imported products are placed at a disadvantage in relation to identical domestic products either because they cannot profitably be marketed in the conditions laid down or because the competitive advantage conferred by lower cost prices is cancelled out ... ."

Applying this test the Court found, first, that a prohibition on retail sales below the purchase price paid by the retailer "cannot produce effects detrimental to the marketing of imported products alone" and therefore did not infringe Article 28. Secondly, the fixing of a minimum profit margin at a specific amount rather than as a percentage of the cost price, is "likewise incapable of producing an adverse effect on imported products which may be cheaper as in the present case where the amount of the profit margin constitutes a relatively significant part of the final retail price". Thirdly, as regards minimum prices the Court took the view that:

> "this is not so in the case of a minimum price fixed at a specific amount which, although applicable without distinction to domestic products and imported products, is capable of having an adverse effect on the marketing of the latter insofar as it prevents their lower cost price from being reflected in the retail selling price."

7.83 The law relating to fixed profit margins was clarified by the judgment in *Commission v Italy*.[203] Although that case was decided on the basis of Article 31 (ex 37) alone, it drew on and applied earlier case law relating to Article 28. Accordingly, there is every reason to believe that the Court's ruling would have been the same had it been based on Article 28. Italy had a state monopoly in the production and distribution of tobacco products. The right to carry out retail sales of these products was limited to tobacconists approved by the tax authorities, of whom there were admittedly some 80,000. The Commission claimed that the provision of Italian law whereby these retailers always took 8 per cent of the retail value of their sales infringed Article 31, even though the price was freely determined by the manufacturer. In its view the effect of this provision was to put Italian products, by definition manufactured by the state monopoly, at an advantage over imports.

After rehearsing the principles laid down in *Tasca, van Tiggele* and *Danis*, the Court stated:

> "In the present case, the rules in dispute do not affect the freedom of producers to fix

[203] Case 78/82 [1983] E.C.R. 1955.

the retail price of their products. Competition may be freely pursued in the essential field of retail prices. Foreign producers of tobacco products are free either to take advantage of more competitive production costs or to pass on higher production costs in their entirety. It is not contested that the uniform margin represents an adequate remuneration to tobacconists for the retailing of tobacco products, whether they be imported or domestic products.''

Consequently the action was dismissed.

As already mentioned, in *Van Tiggele* the Court had held that:

"the fixing of the minimum profit at a specific amount, and not as a percentage of the cost price, applicable without distinction to domestic products and imported products is ... incapable of producing an adverse effect on imported products which may be cheaper, as in the present case where the amount of the profit margin constitutes a relatively significant part of the final retail price."

Taking the two cases together, one might be tempted to think that all kinds of measure restricting profit margins fall outside Article 28—were it not for the ruling in *Roelstraete*, discussed below.

7.84 *Roussel v Netherlands*[204] concerned maximum prices. This case arose against the background of considerably higher prices for pharmaceuticals in the Netherlands than in certain other Member States, where they were kept artificially low by state price controls. This meant that companies manufacturing pharmaceuticals in the low-price Member States were able to make substantial profits on their sales in the Netherlands. This was resented by the Dutch Government, because 80 per cent of the pharmaceuticals purchased in the Netherlands were imported and it bore the lion's share of the cost through its sickness insurance scheme. Until June 1982 it fixed maximum profit margins annually by reference to the prices charged in the preceding year. That system applied to domestic and imported products in the same way. In June 1982 it adopted a new system of price controls with the avowed aim of reducing the profits made on imported pharmaceuticals from the low-price Member States. The new legislation laid down maximum profit margins for imported pharmaceuticals calculated on the basis of the factory gate price of each product in the Member State of production, though such factors as transport costs and VAT were also taken into account. On the other hand, the old legislation continued to apply to pharmaceuticals produced in the Netherlands. The result of this legislative change was that the maximum prices for Dutch pharmaceuticals remained unchanged, whereas imports were now to be sold at drastically reduced prices. A number of pharmaceutical companies brought an action against the Dutch Government, claiming that the new legislation infringed Article 28, whereupon the national court requested the Court of Justice to rule on the point.

The Court held that such legislation was contrary to Article 28. There was a presumption that price controls applying to imports and domestic goods in the

---

[204]Case 181/82 [1983] E.C.R. 3849; [1985] 1 C.M.L.R. 834.

same way did not constitute a measure of equivalent effect. However, that presumption did not apply here because the legislation applied to imports in a different way and put them at a disadvantage.[205] Although factory gate prices were the starting point of the calculation in both cases, in the low price Member States factory gate prices were kept artificially low as a result of pressure from the governments concerned, whereas in the Netherlands there was no such pressure. The Court did not advert to the problem of justification at all. However, it did briefly remark that Member States were entitled to take measures to reduce inflation and to limit increases in the cost of pharmaceuticals, provided that imports were not put at a disadvantage.[206]

7.85 *Leclerc v Au Blé Vert*[207] concerned resale price maintenance for books. The French law in issue, generally known as the "loi Lang," required publishers to fix the retail price at which retailers were obliged to sell, subject to the possibility of granting discounts of no more than 5 per cent of that price. The price of imported books was to be fixed by the importer instead, the principal distributor being deemed to be the importer. Where books published in France were reimported, the retail price was to be no lower than that fixed by the publisher. The provision in question applied to all books intended for retail sale in France, whatever their origin. The law contained a number of exceptions, none of which were relevant to the proceedings. Leclerc was a chain of supermarket stores which had been prohibited by injunction from selling at more than 5 per cent below the fixed retail price. Although the French legislation also banned sales at prices higher than that fixed by the publisher or importer, this was not in issue.

As to Articles 28 to 30, the Court began by rejecting the French Government's contention that the legislation treated imported and domestically produced books in the same way. The law transferred the responsibility for fixing retail prices to the principal distributor who was at a different stage of the commercial process from the publisher. This made it impossible for any other importer of the same book to charge the retail price in France that he considered adequate in the light of the cost price in the state in which it was published. Such a provision therefore created separate rules for imported books which were liable to impede trade between Member States. Accordingly, it constituted a measure of equivalent effect.

This analysis is in direct contrast to that in *GB-Inno*.[208] That case also concerned resale price maintenance, with the price of the domestic product being determined by the manufacturer and the price of the imported product by the importer. The Court ruled that the prohibition on selling above the price on

---

[205] For another price control which was more onerous as regards imports, see Cases 80 and 159/85 *Nederlandse Bakkerij Stichting v Edah* [1988] E.C.R. 3359; [1988] 2 C.M.L.R. 113.

[206] Other discriminatory maximum price regimes for pharmaceuticals were held to be contrary to Art. 28 in Cases 56/87 *Commission v Italy* [1988] E.C.R. 2919; and C–249/88 *Commission v Belgium* [1991] E.C.R. I-1275.

[207] Case 229/83 [1985] E.C.R. 1; [1985] 2 C.M.L.R. 524.

[208] Para. 7.80 above.

the tax label freely chosen by the manufacturer or importer made no distinction between domestic and imported products. Yet it could surely not be suggested that such a regime is "indistinctly applicable", insofar as it prohibits retail sales above the price chosen by the manufacturer or importer, but "distinctly applicable" insofar as it prevents the retailer from selling below that price. This demonstrates once again how frail is the differentiation between "distinctly applicable" and "indistinctly applicable" measures.

At all events, as regards reimports of goods published in France the Court held that "a provision requiring such books to be sold at the retail price fixed by the publisher does not make a distinction between domestic and imported books."[209]

The Court then went on to rule that the measures could not be justified on consumer protection grounds, since this was a mandatory requirement and could not therefore justify measures of the kind in issue, in effect because they were distinctly applicable.[210] The Court did not stop to explain why this should be so as regards reimports, given that it had just held the measure to be indistinctly applicable with respect to them. Thus the measure was held to contravene Article 28 insofar as it affected both imports and reimports. However, the Court found that it was otherwise "where it is established that the books in question were exported for the sole purpose of reimportation in order to circumvent legislation of the type at issue."[211]

The question which arises in the aftermath of *Leclerc* is this: can a Member State (State A) lawfully extend its resale price maintenance legislation to imports by requiring the retail price fixed by the manufacturer in the exporting Member State (State B) to be observed? This puts him on the same footing as the manufacturer in the importing Member State (State A) and thus appears at first sight to be an attractive solution. Yet it is by no means free of difficulty, since it prevents parallel importers from taking advantage of the lower prices that might be available in State B.[212]

7.86 In *Cullet v Leclerc*,[213] which related to petrol, the Court expanded on its ruling in *van Tiggele* on minimum prices. Put shortly, minimum prices for petrol were held to contravene Article 28 when they were fixed on the basis of national ex-refinery prices only, thereby depriving imported products of any competitive advantage. This ruling can scarcely be said to break new ground.[214]

7.87 Maximum profit margins were considered by the Court for the first time in relation to Article 28, in *Roelstraete*.[215] The case related to pork, beef and veal and indeed the Court was primarily concerned with the common market

---

[209] See, however, paras 2.27 and 6.108.
[210] See paras 8.03 *et seq.* above.
[211] Para. 2.28 above.
[212] As to parallel imports, see generally para. 2.28 above.
[213] Case 231/83 [1985] E.C.R. 315; [1985] 2 C.M.L.R. 524.
[214] See also Case C–287/89 *Commission v Belgium* (manufactured tobacco) [1991] E.C.R. I-2233.
[215] Case 116/84 [1985] E.C.R. 1705; [1986] 3 C.M.L.R. 562.

organisations for those products.[216] As regards Article 28, it was held to be contrary to that provision for a Member State to fix a gross profit margin at a single amount applicable both to the domestic product and to imports, without making any allowance for the costs of importation. In such circumstances the net profit of a retailer who has imported his products from other Member States is reduced by an amount corresponding to the import costs and is therefore lower than the profit which he can make by buying his products on the national market. Such a system discourages imports.[217] This judgment is to be contrasted with the Court's rulings on other types of fixed profit margins in *van Tiggele* and *Commission v Italy.*[218]

7.88　It is submitted that the main principles laid down in this series of cases may be summarised as follows:

(a) A maximum price or price freeze applicable without distinction to domestic and imported products does not necessarily constitute a measure of equivalent effect.

(b) However, such measures do constitute measures of equivalent effect when prices are fixed or frozen at such a level that the marketing of imported products becomes either impossible or more difficult than the marketing of national products. This is particularly the case when prices are fixed at a level so low that—taking into account the general situation of imported products in relation to that of national products—traders wishing to import the products in question can only do so at a loss.

(c) A prohibition on retail sales at a loss does not constitute a measure of equivalent effect.

(d) The fixing of a minimum profit margin at a specific amount rather than as a percentage of the cost price does not constitute a measure of equivalent effect either. The same applies to a fixed retail profit margin which is a proportion of the retail price freely determined by the manufacturer at least when it constitutes adequate remuneration for the retailers.

(e) In contrast, a maximum gross profit margin which is fixed at a single amount applicable both to domestic products and to imports and which fails to make allowances for the costs of importation is caught by Article 28.

(f) A minimum price fixed at a specific amount which, although applicable without distinction to domestic and imported products, can restrict

---

[216]The judgment was in part a clarification of the earlier ruling in *Kefer and Delmelle* (Cases 95-96/79; see n.192 above) which did not mention Art. 28.
[217]See also Case 188/86 *Lefevre* [1987] E.C.R. 2963.
[218]See paras 7.82 and 7.83 above.

imports by preventing their lower cost price from being reflected in the retail selling price, is a measure of equivalent effect.

(g) Resale price maintenance probably falls within Article 28 whenever the retail price of imported goods is fixed by the importer.

7.89 In 1986 the Commission published a Communication[219] on price controls for medical products. This Communication consists largely of a summary of the case law, but it also contains some fresh points of note. Thus, the section entitled "Determination of Prices" begins:

"The general principles to be observed here are grouped around two main aspects: realistic prices and transparency of prices. Each product must be able to have its own price, calculated on the basis of its real cost using a transparent method of calculation."

7.90 What is meant by the "general situation of imported products compared to that of domestic products" which, the Court has repeatedly said, must be considered in judging whether a maximum price is set too low? According to Mestmäcker,[220] one must look at the market prices of the product in question in other Member States, add to them the costs of exporting and deduct the costs spared by exporting. This means that transport costs must be considered. The same applies to currency fluctuations. It follows that, since currencies can fluctuate considerably from day to day, a given price control can suddenly cease to be compatible with Article 28.[221]

In the Communication referred to in the preceding paragraph the Commission appears to have gone further, saying:

"If, when new products are placed on the market, Member States can justify asking firms for information to enable them to assess the components of the prices that such firms propose to charge, they must then allow pharmaceutical firms to take account of the various elements making up the cost of the products (research, raw materials, processing, advertising, transport, expenses and charges inherent in importing, etc.)."

The same calculations must be made in deciding whether a particular minimum price restriction is such as to cancel out the competitive advantage of imports.

7.91 On a different note, as mentioned earlier,[222] price controls are the one type of measure which was subject to a test of *de facto* discrimination even before the ruling in *Keck*. Now there can be little doubt that they constitute "selling arrangements" under that judgment and are thus still subject to that test.

---

[219] [1986] O.J. C310/7. This is now supplemented by Council Directive 89/105 [1989] O.J. C40/8, but this relates essentially to questions of procedure.

[220] *op. cit.* n.190 above, at p. 53.

[221] It could perhaps be argued that the uncertainty created for potential importers would in itself make such a price control a measure of equivalent effect. The impact of currency fluctuations has, of course, been reduced as regards trade between Member States participating in Economic and Monetary Union.

[222] Paras 6.49 and 6.50 above.

Indeed, this view appears to be supported by the judgment in *Groupement national des négociants en pommes de terre de Belgigue v I.T.M. Belgium.*[223]

7.92 Finally, can price controls ever be justified under Article 30 on the mandatory requirements? It is submitted that they can only very rarely be so justified even though the grounds of justification have been extended. This is because Article 30 is "directed to eventualities of a non-economic kind."[224] *Campus Oil*[225] was an exceptional case, where the price at which petroleum products had to be purchased was in effect incidental to the purchasing obligation; in these circumstances the Court took the view that it might be justified if certain conditions were fulfilled.

Restrictions on Goods in Transit

7.93 *Monsees*[226] concerned Austrian legislation laying down short maximum journey times and distances for the transport of animals for slaughter and providing that all such transport in Austria must end at the nearest suitable abattoir in order for the animals to be killed. Such legislation was held to constitute an obstacle to international transport as regards journeys to or from Austria and transit through that country. As such, the Austrian legislation was held to be a measure having an effect equivalent to a quantitative restriction prohibited by Article 28.

7.94 *Commission v France*[227] related to a different type of restriction on goods in transit. French legislation empowered customs authorities, on an application from the proprietor of the right in designs of spare parts for motor vehicles, to detain spare parts in transit through French territory for a 10-day period, during which the applicant could refer the matter to the competent national courts. This was held to infringe Article 28. The Court ruled that it was "bound to conclude that such detention, which delays the movement of goods and, if the competent court rules that they are to be confiscated, may block their movement completely, has the effect of restricting the free movement of goods".[228]

II. MEASURES FALLING OUTSIDE ARTICLE 28

7.95 In addition to the cases already mentioned, the following types of measure have been held to be compatible with Article 28 (without falling under any other provision of the Treaty).

---

[223] Case C–63/94 [1995] E.C.R. I-2467.
[224] See para. 8.32 below on the old Art. 99 (ex 103).
[225] Case 72/83 (n.34 above); see para. 8.29 below.
[226] Case C–350/97 [1999] E.C.R. I-2921.
[227] Case C–23/99 [2000] E.C.R. I-7653.
[228] Para. 22 of the judgment.

7.96   (a) In *Kramer*,[229] the Court was asked to rule on the compatibility of fishing conservation quotas with Articles 28 and 29 and the common market organisation for fish.[230] The Court replied as follows:

> "National regulations such as those forming the subject-matter of the present proceedings on the one hand and the prohibition laid down in Article [28] *et seq.* of the Treaty on the other hand relate to different stages of the economic process, that is to say, to production and to marketing respectively.
>
> The answer to the question whether a measure limiting agricultural production impedes trade between Member States depends on the global system established by the basic Community rules in the sector concerned and on the objectives of those rules. In this connection, the nature and the circumstances of 'production' of the product in question, fish in the present case, should also be taken into consideration. Measures for the conservation of the resources of the sea through fixing catch quotas and limiting the fishing effort, whilst restricting 'production' in the short term, are aimed precisely at preventing such 'production' from being marked by a fall which would seriously jeopardise supplies to customers. Therefore, the fact that such measures have the effect, for a short time, of reducing the quantities that the States concerned are able to exchange between themselves cannot lead to these measures being classified among those prohibited by the Treaty, the decisive factor being that in the long term these measures are necessary to ensure a steady, optimum yield for fishing."

While this ruling is obviously of the utmost importance to the fisheries sector, it may well not apply to any other products.

7.97   (b) *Directeur Général des Impôts v Forest*[231] concerned a system of flour-milling quotas under which each mill held certain quotas. The Court's ruling in relation to Article 28 was in the following terms:

> "It must be pointed out that even though a restriction on the quantities of wheat which may be milled may prevent millers from buying wheat, millers are free to buy imported wheat to cover part or all of their requirements. It therefore appears that such a system of quotas at the level of flour production in fact has no effect on wheat imports and is not likely to impede trade between Member States.
>
> It follows that such legislation cannot be regarded as a measure having equivalent effect to a quantitative restriction on imports for the purposes of Article [28] of the EEC Treaty."

It is possible that such measures will now be regarded as "selling arrangements" of the kind contemplated in paragraph 16 of the judgment in *Keck*.[232]

7.98   (c) *Motorradcenter v Baskiciogullari*[233] concerned the obligation on the seller under German law to divulge all relevant information to the prospective purchaser. This rule was indistinctly applicable. The Court held that such an

---

[229] Cases 3, 4 and 6/76 [1976] E.C.R. 1279, [1976] 2 C.M.L.R. 440.
[230] See paras 10.06 *et seq.* below.
[231] Case 148/85 [1986] E.C.R. 449; [1988] 2 C.M.L.R. 577.
[232] Cases C–267 and 268/91 (n.61 above).
[233] Case C–93/92 [1993] E.C.R. I-500.

obligation could not restrict imports and therefore fell outside Article 28.[234]

It so happened that the Motorradcenter sold motorcycles which were parallel imports. The case concerned their failure to inform the defendant that she might have difficulty having her motorcycle repaired by official distributors, because it was a parallel import. When she discovered this, Frau Baskiciogullari refused to take delivery of the motorcycle. The Court rightly pointed out that in this case the restriction on parallel imports resulted from the conduct of the official distributors, not as such from the obligation to inform prospective purchasers.

7.99 (d) A deflationary economic policy consisting of keeping interest rates and the national currency high and/or an incomes policy is designed to slow down the economy as a whole and thus one of its effects will be to reduce imports. Yet it is submitted that such measures probably do not fall under Article 28. This is probably because these matters fall within other provisions of the Treaty, although the new provisions inserted into the Treaty of Rome by the Treaty of Maastricht impose a new discipline on the Member States in the context of Economic and Monetary Union, the Member States still retain a certain freedom of manoeuvre by virtue of such provisions as Articles 98 and 99.[235] Only a specific economic policy measure singling out certain categories of product could constitute a restriction caught by one of the prohibitions in the Treaty.[236]

7.100 (e) In a series of cases, the Court has held that measures fall outside Article 28 on the grounds that they were indistinctly applicable and that the possibility of their affecting imports was too "uncertain and indirect":

— In *Peralta*[237] Italian legislation prohibited vessels flying the Italian flag from discharging harmful chemical substances on the high seas. It was argued that that prohibition had the effect of requiring Italian vessels to carry costly equipment which requirement might in turn have made the importation of such chemicals into Italy more expensive.

— In *Centro Servizi*[238] Italian legislation provided for road-haulage tariffs to be approved and brought into force by the state on the basis of proposals submitted by a national committee. It was argued that the practical effect of that requirement was to make transportation in Italy more expensive.

— In *DIP*[239] Italian legislation made the opening of new shops subject to the grant of a licence issued by the mayor on the mandatory opinion of a

---

[234] See para. 6.53.
[235] Para. 7.75 above.
[236] See Case 6/69 *Commission v France* [1969] E.C.R. 523; [1970] C.M.L.R. 43, where a preferential rediscount rate for exports was held to have been an unlawful state aid.
[237] Case C–379/92 [1994] E.C.R. I-3453.
[238] Case C–96/94 [1995] E.C.R. I-2883.
[239] Case C–140-2/94 [1995] E.C.R. I-3257.

municipal committee. It was argued that such legislation had the effect of restricting the importation of goods from other Member States.

— In *Esso Española*[240] the regional authority of the Canary Islands required all petroleum product wholesalers wishing to extend their activities to the that territory to supply a certain number of islands in the archipelago.

— In *Corsica Ferries*[241] Italian legislation required shipping companies which were established in other Member States and whose vessels made port stops in Italian ports to have recourse to the services of local mooring groups holding exclusive concessions, at a charge higher than the actual cost of the service provided.

— In *BASF v Präsident des Deutschen Patentamts*,[242] German legislation (based on the Convention on the Grant of European Patents) required patent holders to file a translation of the specifications of their European patents with the German Patent Office and in the German language failing which the patent would be deemed to be void *ab initio* in Germany.

In the above cases, the mantra recited by the Court was (allowing for immaterial variations) as follows:

"legislation such as that at issue in the main proceedings makes no distinction according to the origin of the goods transported, its purpose is not to regulate trade in goods with other Member States and the restrictive effects which it might have no the free movement of goods are too uncertain and indirect for the obligation which it imposes to be regarded as being capable of hindering trade between Member States."[243]

It is submitted that the effect of this line of cases is that the measures concerned did not even constitute an indirect or a potential restraint on imports within the terms of the *Dassonville* formula. Accordingly, the better view of these cases is that they did not introduce a separate rule of remoteness, still less a *de minimis* test into Article 28.[244]

III. MEASURES OF EQUIVALENT EFFECT UNDER ARTICLE 29

7.101 As we saw in the previous Chapter,[245] some of the principles governing measures of equivalent effect on imports under Article 28 apply *mutatis mutandis* to measures of equivalent effect on exports under Article 29. However, as we

---

[240] Case C–134/94 [1995] E.C.R. I-4223.
[241] Case C–266/96 [1998] E.C.R. I-3949.
[242] Case C–44/98 [1999] E.C.R. I-6269.
[243] See *Peralta* (n.237 above) at para. 24; *Centro Servizi* (n.238 above) at para. 41; *DIP* (n.239 above) at para. 29; *Esso Española* (n.240 above) at para. 24; *Corsica Ferries* (n.241 above) at para. 31; and *BASF* (n.242 above) at para 21.
[244] See detailed discussion of this point at para. 6.23.
[245] Paras 6.79 *et seq.*

noticed,[246] the Court has held that discrimination is a necessary element in concluding that a particular measure is a measure having equivalent effect to an export restriction under Article 29, which is not necessarily the case with respect to Article 28. Discrimination in the context of Article 29 is practised in favour of goods intended for the national market against goods intended for export. Some of the cases on export restrictions that are interpretations of common market organisations rather than Article 29 will be considered in Chapter X.[247]

Export Licences, Controls and Certificates

7.102 This type of measure arose for consideration in *Commission v France*.[248] As a result of the sharp drop in potato production in Europe, the French Government subjected exports of potatoes to the production of an export certificate endorsed by a Government body bearing the acronym FORMA. Citing its ruling in the *International Fruit Company* case[249] the Court held:

"even if in connection with intra-Community trade the FORMA granted its endorsement without delay and for all quantities requested and even if the object of the measures was merely to ascertain the intentions of the exporters, it must be held to be a measure having an effect equivalent to a quantitative restriction on imports."

7.103 The measure at issue in *Procureur de la République v Bouhelier*[250] was somewhat more complex. Exporters of particular categories of watches were required either to obtain an export licence or to obtain a certificate attesting that the watches were of a given quality. No such requirements were laid down for watches sold within France. The certificates were issued by a technical body recognised by the French Government.

The Court held that the obligation to obtain an export licence was contrary to Article 29,[251] as was the obligation to obtain a certificate of quality. What is more, the latter obligation could not be justified since it constituted arbitrary discrimination.[252]

7.104 In *Jongeneel Kaas v Netherlands*[253] the Court stated that a national rule requiring producers to place on cheese a control stamp attesting compliance with national rules on quality was compatible with Article 29, provided that the requirement applied in the same way to domestic production marketed in the Member State concerned and to goods intended for export. The same held good for inspections and inspection documents. On the other hand, to require

---

[246] Para. 6.82 above.
[247] Paras 10.12 *et seq.* below.
[248] Case 68/76 (see n.6 above).
[249] Cases 51–54/71 (see n.4 above).
[250] Case 53/76 (n.6 above).
[251] This was confirmed in Case C–5/94 *R. v MAFF Ex p. Hedley Lomas* [1996] E.C.R. I-2553 at para. 17, where the refusal of export licences was also held to constitute a quantitative restriction on exports contrary to Art. 29.
[252] Para. 8.12 below.
[253] Case 237/82 [1984] E.C.R. 483; [1985] 2 C.M.L.R. 53; see paras 10.12 *et seq.* below.

inspection documents for exports only was contrary to Article 29. In support of the latter proposition the Court cited its earlier judgment in *Bouhelier*.

The judgment in *Jongeneel Kaas* confirms that *Bouhelier* is still good law after *Groenveld v Produktschaap voor Vee en Vlees*,[254] as indeed it would have to be if Article 29 were not to be deprived of its meaning.[255]

7.105 In *Bundesanstalt für Landwirtschaft und Ernährung v Deutsches Milch-Kontor*[256] the Court held that, since inspections carried out systematically by the exporting Member State and intended to verify the composition and quality of skimmed-milk powder were not provided for by the relevant Community legislation, they constituted measures having equivalent effect to quantitative restrictions on exports in trade between Member States prohibited by Article 29. The Court held that that conclusion was not affected by the fact that the inspections of the goods concerned were carried out not at the frontier but within the country, since they were conducted with a view to the subsequent export of those goods. The Court held:

> "It would run counter to the sense and purpose of Article [29] to take the view that only restrictions occurring at or close to the frontier are capable of coming within its scope. If that were in fact the case, it would be easy to circumvent the prohibition contained in that provision by moving the place in which the restriction occurs to another location."[257]

7.106 Any border controls on exports within the Community must be regarded as falling within Article 29 since January 1, 1993 by virtue of Article 14 (ex 7A) of the Treaty. This is of course subject to the application of Article 30 (including the mandatory requirements).[258] The reader is referred to paragraph 7.04 and Chapter XII for a more detailed discussion of this issue.

Local Bottling Requirements

7.107 One type of export restriction which had been the subject of controversy for many years came before the Court in *Delhaize v Promalvin*.[259] That case concerned Spanish legislation prohibiting Spanish quality wine from being transported in bulk outside the Rioja region, thereby ensuring that it was bottled in its region of production. Failure to comply with this rule entailed loss of the right to sell the product as a quality wine (*"denomination de origen calificada"*). The Court found that such a measure fell within Article 29.[260]

---

[254] Case 15/79 [1979] E.C.R. 3409; [1981] 1 C.M.L.R. 207; para. 6.82 above.
[255] For a further case on export documents, see Case 15/83 *Denkavit Nederland v Hoofdproduktschap voor Akkerbouwprodukten* [1984] E.C.R. 2171.
[256] Case C–272/95 [1997] E.C.R. I-1905.
[257] Para. 31 of the judgment.
[258] But see para. 6.92 above.
[259] Case C–47/90 [1992] E.C.R. I-3669.
[260] See also Case C–388/95 *Belgium v Spain* [2000] E.C.R. I-3123, where however the Court altered its position as to justification; see para 8.245 below.

Export Monopolies

7.108 We noticed in paragraph 7.26 that import monopolies fall under Article 28, even though they may also be covered by Article 31. Similarly, in *Commission v Greece*,[261] an export monopoly for maize was held to be incompatible with Article 29. As noted at para 7.26 above, the demarcation (if any) between Articles 28 to 30 on the one hand, and Article 31 on the other, is unclear.[262]

Discriminatory Conditions of Insurance

7.109 *Haug-Adrion v Frankfurter Versicherungs-AG*[263] was a somewhat unusual case. The plaintiff bought a car in Germany and exported it to Belgium where he lived. For this purpose he obtained insurance coverage for third-party liability from the defendants under conditions approved by the public authorities. Under these conditions companies were permitted not to grant a no-claims bonus for cars fitted with customs plates (i.e., cars intended for export). The defendant took advantage of this possibility. The plaintiff claimed that the relevant condition discriminated against exports and thus fell foul of Article 29. The Court rejected this view. After rehearsing the *Groenveld* formula[264] it held:

> "National rules such as those in question in the main proceedings do not fall within that category; they merely authorise insurance companies to take into account in their tariff conditions particular circumstances in which vehicles are used which increase or diminish the insurance risk, such as, for example, the use of vehicles registered under customs plates.
>
> Quite apart from the fact that the enactment of such rules in a Member State in no way prohibits insurers in that State from granting a bonus in respect of vehicles registered under customs plates, there is nothing to suggest that a tariff condition such as that at issue in the main proceedings, covered by such rules, gives any advantage whatever to national products or to the domestic market of the Member State concerned."

One might have thought that the granting of less favourable terms for exports, when officially approved by the state, was indeed a restriction on exports contrary to Article 29 even after *Groenveld*.

Discriminatory Rules of Procedure

7.110 In *ED v Italo Fenocchio*[265] the Court found that by restricting recourse to the procedure in the Italian Code of Civil Procedure for obtaining summary payment orders to cases where service on the debtor is to be effected in another Member State did not breach Article 29. The Court acknowledged that the

---

[261] Case C–110/89 [1991] E.C.R. I-2659.
[262] See detailed discussion at para. 11.19 below.
[263] Case 251/83 [1984] E.C.R. 4277, [1985] 3 C.M.L.R. 266.
[264] See para. 7.114 below at n. 276. See also para. 6.82.
[265] Case C–412/97 [1999] E.C.R. I-3845.

effect of the Italian provision was to subject traders to different procedural rules according to whether they supplied goods within Italy or exported them to other Member States. However, it held that "the possibility that nationals would therefore hesitate to sell goods to purchasers established in other Member States is too uncertain and indirect for the national provision to be regarded as liable to hinder trade between Member States".[266]

Obligation to land Fish in Flag State

7.111   R. v Ministry of Agriculture, Fisheries and Food, ex p. Jaderow[267] was one of a series of cases concerned with restrictions placed by the United Kingdom on Spanish fishermen fishing on British vessels and thus on British quotas (a practice widely known as "quota-hopping"). The measure in issue in that case was a condition attached to a fishing licence which required the vessel to operate out of the United Kingdom, the Isle of Man or the Channel Islands. That general condition was upheld by the Court as being compatible with the various provisions applicable to fishing quotas.

However, one of the ways in which this general condition could be satisfied was by the vessel landing 50 per cent of its catch in those territories. Mischo A.G. had no hesitation in saying that such a measure fell foul of Article 29, recalling that under Article 4(2)(f) of Council Regulation 802/68 on the origin of goods,[268] fish were deemed to originate in the country of the flag of the vessel which caught them. In his view, the measure "has a real and specific effect on exports which it affects directly and in a discriminatory way". In contrast the Court, without deciding the point, simply said that the test was lawful in view of the requirements of the Common Fisheries Policy and also because the vessel could establish by other means that it satisfied the general condition mentioned above.

An alternative method of establishing that a vessel was operating from a British port was to show that it was present in such a port on at least four occasions at 15-day intervals within each six-month period. Such a test was likewise condemned by the Advocate General as being contrary to Article 29, but upheld by the Court on the same grounds "provided that the frequency required does not hinder normal fishing operations or does not in practice entail the necessity to land a proportion of catches when calls are made at those ports."

7.112   The sequel to *Jaderow* was *Spain v Commission*,[269] where the applicant attacked a Commission Regulation which, *inter alia*, imposed restrictions on

---

[266] Para. 11 of the judgment. See also para 7.100 above in relation to the application of Art. 28 to similar measures.

[267] Case C–216/87 [1989] E.C.R. I-4509; see also Case C–279/89 *Commission v United Kingdom* [1992] E.C.R. I-5785.

[268] [1968] O.J.Spec.Ed. (I) 165, now replaced by Art. 23(2)(f) of Council Reg. 2913/92 establishing the Common Customs Code ([1992] O.J. L302/1). See para. 2.13 above.

[269] Case C–9/89 [1990] E.C.R. I-1383.

fishing vessels that contravened the conservation or control measures laid down pursuant to the Treaty. The restriction consisted in a ban on landing or transhipping catches outside the flag state unless a certificate of control issued by that state was kept on board. This measure—which only applied to a very small number of recalcitrant vessels—was likewise held to fall outside Article 29. Even if the Court had not reached that conclusion, it would no doubt have had regard to the strong public policy arguments in favour of this measure, which was in effect a form of sanction.

Providing a Particular Advantage for National Processors

7.113 In *Dusseldorp*[270] the Court held that a Dutch long-term environmental plan which prohibited export of waste for recovery unless the processing of that waste (*in casu* oil filters) abroad was superior to that performed in the Netherlands infringed Article 29. The Court simply held that it was "plain that the object and effect of such a provision is to restrict exports and to provide a particular advantage for national production".[271]

Similarly, in *FFAD v Københavns Kommune*[272] the Court held that a system for the collection and receipt of non-hazardous building waste for recovery under which a limited number of undertakings were authorised to process waste produced in the municipality in question would only be compatible with Article 29 so long as waste producers were able, both in principle and in practice, to export such waste.[273]

Restrictions on Production

7.114 The first case to come before the Court concerning the compatibility with Article 29 of a restriction on the production of goods not covered by a common market organisation[274] was *Groenveld*.[275] On a reference under Article 234 (ex 177) the Court was asked to rule on the compatibility with Article 29 of a Dutch measure prohibiting a manufacturer of processed meat products from having in stock and processing horsemeat. The plaintiffs wished to begin the manufacture of horsemeat sausages and consequently sought a determination by the courts as to the validity of this measure. The unusual aspects of the Dutch regulation were that:

— butchers dealing in horsemeat were entitled to manufacture horsemeat sausages provided they sold them directly to consumers and not to middlemen;

---

[270] Case C–203/96 [1998] E.C.R. I-4075, noted by Notaro (1999) C.M.L.Rev. 1309; and Van Calster (1999) E.L.Rev. 178.
[271] Para. 42 of the judgment.
[272] Case C–209/98 [2000] E.C.R. I-3743.
[273] See paras 34 to 43 of the judgment.
[274] For cases on products covered by such organisations, see paras 10.06 *et seq.* below.
[275] Case 15/79 (see n.254 above).

— the import and export of horsemeat sausages were not in themselves prohibited so that traders could import them, either from Member States or third countries, and re-export them either to Member States or third countries.

The defendant body stated that it had adopted these rules in view of the strong aversion felt in the United Kingdom, the United States and the Federal Republic of Germany to the consumption of horsemeat by human beings. The mere fact that British consumers might think that Dutch exports of processed meat might contain horsemeat would seriously harm Dutch exports. Furthermore, the defendant claimed that it was practically impossible to detect the presence of horsemeat in processed meat products, and this is why it found it necessary to prohibit manufacturers of such products from having in stock or processing horsemeat.

The Court was swayed by these arguments. It set out the test for finding a breach of Article 29 as follows[276]:

"[Article 29] concerns national measures which have as their specific object or effect the restriction of patterns of exports and thereby the establishment of a difference in treatment between the domestic trade of a member State and its export trade in such a way as to provide a particular advantage for national production or for the domestic market of the State in question at the expense of the production or of the trade of other Member States."

The Court then held that that test was not satisfied in this case because the prohibition in question:

"applied objectively to the production of goods of a certain kind without drawing a distinction depending on whether such goods are intended for the national market or for export.
    The foregoing appreciation is not affected by the circumstance that the regulation in question has as its objective *inter alia* the safeguarding of the reputation of the national production of meat products in certain export markets within the Community and in non-member countries where there are obstacles of a psychological or legislative nature to the consumption of horsemeat where the same prohibition is applied identically to the product in the domestic market of the State in question. The objective nature of that prohibition is not modified by the fact that the regulation in force in the Netherlands permits the retail sale of horsemeat by butchers. In fact that concession at a level of local trade does not have the effect of bringing about a prohibition at the level of industrial manufacture of the same product regardless of its destination."

The Court concluded that a prohibition of the kind in question was compatible with Article 29.

7.115 The Court repeated and applied the test for Article 29 set down in

---

[276]See also para. 6.82 above.

Groenveld in *Oebel*[277] and found that a prohibition on night baking applying in the same way to goods intended for the domestic market and to goods intended for export was not a measure of equivalent effect within the meaning of Article 29.

Similarly, the Court ruled in *Holdijk*[278] that national legislation laying down minimum standards for enclosures for fattening calves, which does not make any distinction as to whether the animals or their meat are intended for the national market or for exports, is compatible with Article 29. Likewise, in *Jongeneel Kaas*,[279] minimum standards for cheese which made no distinction as to whether the cheese was intended for the domestic market or for export, were also held to be compatible with Article 29.

[277] Case 155/80 (see n.143 above).
[278] Cases 141-143/81 [1982] E.C.R. 1299; [1983] 2 C.M.L.R. 635.
[279] Case 237/82 (n.253 above).

CHAPTER VIII

The Main Exception: Article 30 EC Including the "Mandatory Requirements"

8.01   Article 30 (ex 36) of the Treaty of Rome reads:

"The provisions of Articles 28 and 29 shall not preclude prohibitions or restrictions on imports, exports or goods in transit justified on grounds of public morality, public policy or public security; the protection of health and life of humans, animals or plants; the protection of national treasures possessing artistic, historic or archaeological value; or the protection of industrial and commercial property. Such prohibitions or restrictions shall not, however, constitute a means of arbitrary discrimination or a disguised restriction on trade between Member States."[1]

The wording of this provision shows that it applies both to quantitative restrictions and to measures of equivalent effect. Furthermore, it covers the latter whether they are "distinctly" or "indistinctly" applicable.[2] Equally, it applies both to import restrictions and to export restrictions. Moreover, it is also clear from the wording of Article 30 that, subject to certain limits, it merely entitles the Member States to exercise certain powers: it does not oblige them to do so.

As the Court held in *Bauhuis v Netherlands*,[3] Article 30 "constitutes a derogation from the basic rule that all obstacles to the free movement of goods between Member States shall be eliminated and must be interpreted strictly". As explained in paragraph 9.01 below, it shares this trait with the other exceptions to the prohibition on restrictions on the free movement of goods between Member States.

---

[1] This provision is clearly modelled on the considerably lengthier Art. XX of GATT, which begins: "Subject to the requirement that such measures are not applied in a manner which would constitute a means of arbitrary or unjustifiable discrimination between countries where the same conditions prevail, or a disguised restriction on international trade, nothing in this Agreement shall be construed to prevent the adoption or enforcement by any contracting party of measures: (a) necessary to protect public morals; (b) necessary to protect human, animal or plant life or health ... etc."
However, the exceptions allowed by the two Articles are not all identical: in particular, Art. XX includes a number of specific exceptions such as restrictions on the import or export of gold or silver and restrictions on the products of prison labour, which are not to be found in Art. 30 EC.
[2] For this terminology, see paras 6.35 *et seq.* above.
[3] Case 46/76 [1977] E.C.R. 5.

8.02   To be justified under Article 30, national provisions:

— must fall within one of the grounds of justification covered by the first sentence of Article 30; and

— must not constitute arbitrary discrimination nor a disguised restriction on trade between Member States and must be justified.

Although it is somewhat artificial to separate the two conditions, it is necessary to do so here. It is appropriate to start with the second condition. However, even before doing that, it is necessary to explain why it is appropriate to consider that the "mandatory requirements" are subsumed within this provision.

I. THE STATUS OF THE "MANDATORY REQUIREMENTS"

8.03   In Chapter VI,[4] we discussed how the Court in *"Cassis de Dijon"*[5] and subsequent cases has recognised a series of "mandatory requirements" in addition to the grounds of justification expressly set out in Article 30. For the reasons explained below, the better view is that the "mandatory requirements" fall under that provision, despite the Court's traditional view that they were subsumed within Article 28.

The "mandatory requirements" recognised so far are: the prevention of tax evasion, consumer protection, the prevention of unfair competition, the protection of the environment, the improvement of working conditions, the maintenance of press diversity, and possibly the preservation of the financial balance of the social security system and the protection of national or regional culture; but the list is not closed.

In this Chapter, we shall continue to use the term "mandatory requirements", although the Court has recently developed a fondness for some even more cumbersome terms such as "overriding requirements of general public importance"[6] and "overriding requirement justifying a restriction on the free movement of goods".[7]

8.04   One question left open by *"Cassis de Dijon"* was the relationship between the "mandatory requirements" laid down by that judgment and Article 30, which is not mentioned at all in the judgment. Two schools of thought evolved on this matter:

(a) According to the first view, the "mandatory requirements" are to be weighed up within Article 28, not Article 30. Moreover, only "indistinctly

---

[4] Paras 6.43 *et seq.* above.
[5] Case 120/78 *Rewe-Zentral v Bundesmonopolverwaltung für Branntwein* [1979] E.C.R. 649; [1979] 3 C.M.L.R. 494.
[6] Case C-34/95 *Konsumentombudsmannen v De Agostini* [1997] E.C.R. I-3843, para. 46.
[7] C-368/95 *Vereinigte Familiapress v Heinrich Bauer Verlag* [1997] E.C.R. I-3689, para. 18.

applicable" measures may qualify, so that "distinctly applicable" measures may only be justified on the grounds expressly set out in Article 30. On this view, therefore, "indistinctly applicable measures" are granted more favourable treatment in that the "mandatory requirements" apply to them alone.

(b) According to the second view, the "mandatory requirements" are regarded as being subsumed under Article 30, on the grounds that they constitute additions to the list of grounds of justification expressly set out in Article 30. On this view, the mandatory requirements are subject to precisely the same tests as the latter grounds.

8.05 In support of the first theory, it should be said that the Court has repeatedly held that Article 30 must be interpreted narrowly since it constitutes an exception to a fundamental principle of Community law.[8]

Yet it is submitted that that is outweighed by the following considerations:

(a) The second view avoids the undue harshness resulting from the first theory with respect to "distinctly applicable" measures necessary on such grounds as consumer protection. According to the first theory, even though they are necessary, such measures are quite simply prohibited. According to the second theory, they are considered to fall under Article 28, but may be justified under Article 30. Since the Court has now accepted that consumer protection may justify restrictions otherwise prohibited by Article 28, does it make sense to approach it differently from, say, plant health merely because in 1957 (when the Treaty of Rome was first drafted) consumer protection did not yet arouse much passion? Indeed, it is hard to see why, in appropriate cases, even quantitative restrictions should not benefit from the "mandatory requirements". In this context, it should not be forgotten that any abuses may be adequately policed by means of a rigorous application of the proportionality principle.

(b) It always seemed clear that the "mandatory requirements" have the same properties as the grounds of justification in Article 30. As van Gerven A.G. remarked in *Aragonesa de Publicidad v Departamento de Sanidad*,[9] "... the conditions governing the applicability of the *Cassis de Dijon* doctrine and of Article [30] are the same (absence of harmonisation, examination of the criteria of necessity and proportionality, prohibition of arbitrary discrimination or disguised restriction on trade)."

8.06 For these reasons, the second approach has been firmly and consistently advocated in this book since its very first edition, which appeared in 1982. This is despite the fact that, as we shall see, the Court had already chosen to follow

---

[8] Para. 8.01 above.
[9] Cases C-1 and 176/90 [1991] E.C.R. I-4151 at 4177.

the other approach, which was also backed by most commentators for many years.[10]

More recently, a further factor has come into play which confirms that the second approach is to be preferred. As has already been noted, the Court's approach in applying all four freedoms has "converged" in recent years.[11] That convergence, however, simply underlines the anomalies inherent in the Court's traditional approach, given that the grounds of justification set out in Article 30 are more numerous than under Article 46(1) (ex 56(1)). For example, the protection of industrial and commercial property is a ground of justification expressly referred to in Article 30, while it is only a mandatory requirement with respect to services.[12] The distortions between the freedoms created by the Court's traditional approach are obvious.

8.07 The *locus classicus* on the Court's traditional approach is the ruling in *Commission v Ireland*.[13] That case arose out of proceedings brought by the Commission under Article 226 (ex 169) of the Treaty with respect to two Irish Orders requiring certain metal objects to bear an origin marking. The Orders only applied to imported goods and were thus "distinctly applicable". The Irish Government contended that these measures were justified on the grounds of consumer protection, a "mandatory requirement". Thus the question whether the "mandatory requirements" applied to "distinctly applicable" measures was squarely posed. The Court ruled in the following terms:

> "The orders concerned in the present case are not measures which are applicable to domestic products and to imported products without distinction, but rather a set of rules which apply only to imported products and are therefore discriminatory in nature, with the result that the measures in issue are not covered by the decisions cited above which relate exclusively to provisions that regulate in a uniform manner the marketing of domestic products and imported products."

Yet the Court then proceeded to rule that it was "necessary to consider whether

---

[10] Among the numerous authors supporting the first approach, the following should be mentioned: Ahlfeld, *Zwingende Erfordernisse im Sinne der Cassis-Rechtsprechung des Europäischen Gerichtshofs zu Art. 30 EGV* (1997) passim; Hatzopoulos, "Exigences essentielles, impératives ou impérieuses: *une théorie, des théories, ou pas de théorie du tout?*" [1998] R.T.D.E. 191; Mattera, *Le marché unique européen—Ses règles, son fonctionnement* (2nd ed., 1990) at 274; Judge Touffait, "Les entraves techniques à la libre circulation des marchandises" (1982) 37 *Recueil Dalloz-Sirey*, and VerLoren van Themaat, "La libre circulation des marchandises après l'arrêt 'Cassis de Dijon'" [1982] C.D.E. 123.
　　Those who have advocated the second approach have included: Barnard, "Fitting the remaining pieces into the goods and persons jigsaw" (2001) 26 E.L. Rev. 35 at 54; Masclet, "Les articles 30, 36 et 100 du traité CEE à la lumière de l'arrêt 'Cassis de Dijon'" [1980] R.T.D.E. 64; Roth "Diskriminierende Regelungen des Warenverkehrs und Rechtfertigung durch die 'zwingende Erfordernisse' des Allgemeininteresses" [2000] W.R.P. 979; von Wilmovsky, "Waste Disposal in the Internal Market: the State of Play after the ECJ's Ruling on the Walloon Import Ban" (1993) 30 C.M.L. Rev. 541 and; and Weiler, "The Constitution of the Market Place", in Craig and De Búrca, *The Evolution of EU Law*, (Oxford, 1999) at 366.
[11] See para. 1.12 above.
[12] See Case 62/79 *Coditel v Ciné Vog* [1980] E.C.R. 833. See Oliver, "Goods and Services: Two Freedoms Compared" in *Mélanges en homage à Michel Waelbroeck* (1999) at 1403.
[13] Case 113/80 [1982] E.C.R. 1625; [1982] 1 C.M.L.R. 706.

the contested measures are indeed discriminatory or whether they constitute discrimination in appearance only." It then examined the measures to see if they were justified on consumer protection grounds (and found that they were not). This appears to go back on the passage of this judgment just quoted. The idea that a "distinctly applicable" measure may be justified on the grounds of consumer protection was put out by the door and let in through the window! Despite its lack of logic, this reasoning has been systematically applied by the Court until recently.

8.08 What is more, the Court has on occasion had recourse to some far-fetched—not to say exotic—devices so as to maintain the façade that the "mandatory requirements" apply only to "indistinctly applicable measures". Thus the Court has been driven to holding the following measures to be "indistinctly applicable" so as to be able to consider the "mandatory require-ments" at all: a German statutory provision to the effect that only wines from certain specific regions of Germany could be marketed in bottles of a particular shape[14]; legislation prohibiting the importation and marketing of meat pro-ducts containing non-meat ingredients[15]; and a measure prohibiting the use of the letter R in a circle (which indicates that a name constitutes a registered trade mark), unless such registration had occurred in the Member States in question.[16]

Perhaps the most striking example occurred in *Commission v Belgium*[17] (waste disposal), which concerned a blatantly discriminatory ban on imports of waste into Wallonia from other Member States. The defendant State relied on the protection of the environment, a "mandatory requirement". The Court in effect ruled that this ban was to be treated as "indistinctly applicable" by virtue of Article 174(2) (ex 130R(2)) of the Treaty, which stipulated that priority should be given to rectifying environmental problems at source; it followed that it was for each local authority in principle to ensure the treatment and destruction of its own waste. Thus the contested measure was held to be justified on environmental grounds despite being manifestly discriminatory.

The foregoing cases demonstrate that it is possible for circumstances to arise in which it will be wholly warranted to treat imports more harshly than domestic products not just on the grounds set out in Article 30 but also under any of the mandatory requirements.

8.09 In a move which deserves a most warm welcome, Jacobs A.G. has criticised the Court's traditional approach on at least two occasions. In *Chemische Afval-stoffen Dusseldorp v Minister van Milieubeheer*,[18] referring to the last edition of this book, he acknowledged that the Court had been "obliged to adopt rather tortuous reasoning" in the cases just mentioned and most particularly in the

---

[14] Case 16/83 *Prantl* [1984] E.C.R. 1299; [1985] 2 C.M.L.R. 238.
[15] Case 274/87 *Commission v Germany* [1989] E.C.R. 229.
[16] Case C-238/89 *Pall v Dahlhausen* [1990] E.C.R. I-4827.
[17] Case C-2/90 [1992] E.C.R. I-4431, para. 8.160 below.
[18] C-203/96 [1998] E.C.R. I-4075 at paras 89–90.

Walloon Waste case. In *PreussenElektra v Schleswag*,[19] the same Advocate General went further, saying that "the reasoning in *Walloon Waste* is flawed' and that "it is desirable that even directly discriminatory measures can sometimes be justified on grounds of environmental protection", the latter being a "mandatory requirement".[20] He then added: "In view of the fundamental importance for the analysis of Article 30 of the Treaty of the question whether directly discriminatory measures can be justified by imperative requirements, the Court should, in my view, clarify its position in order to provide the necessary legal certainty".[21]

Without expressly renouncing its earlier position, the Court has grudgingly moved in this direction. The Court first appeared to reverse its traditional position, albeit tacitly, in *Konsumentenombudsmannen v De Agostini*,[22] which was decided even before the Advocate General's Opinion in *Dusseldorp*. In *De Agostini*, the Court considered whether a measure which discriminated against imports (the outright ban on advertising certain products on television which was held to have a greater impact on products from other Member States than on domestic products) could be justified under the mandatory requirements (the protection of consumers). Likewise, in *Decker v Caisse de maladie des employés privés*,[23] the Court considered whether a "distinctly applicable" Luxembourg rule requiring the prior authorisation of the purchase of glasses from another Member State could be justified under one of the mandatory requirements (the preservation of the financial balance of the social security system). Yet again, in *PreussenElektra*, blatantly discriminatory legislation on wind energy was held to be justified for the protection of the environment (a mandatory requirement).[24]

While this development must surely be applauded, it is a pity that the Court has not yet shown the courage to disown its earlier approach expressly, as this would undoubtedly be in the interests of legal certainty.

8.10   In short, the view consistently espoused in all the previous editions of this book has been gaining ground in recent years. Thus there is every reason to treat the "mandatory requirements" in this Chapter. Each of the individual "mandatory requirements" will therefore be considered below, immediately before the section on industrial and commercial property which will be treated last in view of its considerable length.[25]

---

[19] C-379/98 [2001] E.C.R. I-2099.
[20] Paras 225 and 226 of the Opinion respectively.
[21] Para. 229 of the Opinion.
[22] C-34/95, see n. 6 above.
[23] C-120/95 [1998] E.C.R. I-1831; see also the parallel judgment in Case C-158/96 *Kohll v Union des Caisses de Maladie* [1998] E.C.R. I-1931, which related to services under Article 49.
[24] See also C-389/96 *Aher-Waggon* [1998] E.C.R. I-4473.
[25] Whether Art. 30 should be amended to include the "mandatory requirements" expressly is another matter. Arguably, the wisest course is not to do so, since this might stifle the future development of the case law.
    A radical overhaul of Art. 30 has been called for by Mortelmans in his thought-provoking article entitled "Excepties bij non-tarifaire intracommunautaire belemmeringen: assimilatie in het nieuwe EG-Verdrag?" ([1997] S.E.W. 182). Mortelmans points out that the exceptions to the free

II. THE BURDEN OF PROOF

8.11   Common sense suggests that the burden of proving that a measure falls under Article 28 or Article 29 rests on the party alleging that this is so.[26] Thereafter, in keeping with the principle that Article 30 constitutes a derogation from a fundamental rule of Community law,[27] a national authority relying on that provision bears the burden of proving that contentious measures are justified under that provision: *Denkavit Futtermittel v Minister of Agriculture.*[28] It is submitted that this ruling cannot be limited to national authorities, so that any party seeking to rely on Article 30 bears the burden of proof. Indeed, it is submitted that the Court made the same point in relation to the "mandatory requirements" in *Gilli and Andres,*[29] when it held:

> "It is only where national rules . . . may be justified as being necessary in order to satisfy imperative requirements relating in particular to the protection of public health, the fairness of commercial transactions and the defence of the consumer that they may constitute an exception to the requirements arising under Article [28]."

However, at least in infringement proceedings brought by the Commission against Member States under Article 226 (ex 169), that is not the end of the matter: if the Member State makes out a convincing case on the justification, then the burden shifts once again to the Commission.[30] In proceedings before national courts, however, it is submitted that the burden of proving that a State measure restricting intra-Community trade is justified under Article 30 rests with and remains with the Member State concerned and is a matter for the national court.[31]

---

movement of goods (and other Treaty freedoms) have developed and accumulated in a haphazard fashion and have never been categorised on any rational basis. He argues for a distinction to be drawn (by amendment to the Treaty) between general-interest exceptions (*e.g.* for the protection of public morality, public policy, public security, public health, the environment, the coherence of fiscal policy, language and plurality of the press) and specific-interest exceptions (*e.g.* for the protection of consumers or intellectual property right owners). The former concern society as a whole, whereas the latter only seek to protect one group at the expense of another. According to his view, it should only be possible to invoke specific-interest exceptions if the measure in question is indistinctly applicable. It is questionable whether a major *substantive* alteration of Art. 30 is desirable.

[26] Para. 6.110 above.
[27] Para. 8.01 above.
[28] Case 251/78 [1979] E.C.R. 3369; [1980] 3 C.M.L.R. 513.
[29] Case 788/79 [1980] E.C.R. 2071; [1981] 1 C.M.L.R. 146.
[30] See, *e.g.* Cases 178/84 *Commission v Germany (beer)* [1987] E.C.R. 1227; [1988] 1 C.M.L.R. 780; C-55/99 *Commission v France (medical reagents)* [2000] E.C.R. I-11499.
[31] See C-510/99 *Tridon* [2001] E.C.R. I-7777 at para. 58. A possible exception is the case of "industrial and commercial property" in Art. 30, at least when that justification arises in national legal proceedings between two private parties. See generally, Jarvis, *Application of EC Law by National Courts: The Free Movement of Goods* (Oxford, 1998) at pp. 337–40. See further para. 8.220 below.

III. PROPORTIONALITY AND NON-DISCRIMINATION

"Arbitrary Discrimination"

8.12   The use in Article 30 of the word "arbitrary", which might otherwise be thought to be superfluous, is no doubt due to the fact that the term "arbitrary discrimination" appears in Article XX of GATT, on which Article 30 was modelled. Such discrimination can take the following forms:

(a) The most obvious is discrimination against imports in favour of domestic products, either by applying a restriction to imported products only or by applying a greater restriction with respect to imported products. An example is *Commission v France*[32] where advertising restrictions on alcoholic drinks were framed in such a way as to fall more heavily on imports. The Court held that, even though in principle advertising restrictions on alcoholic drinks would be justified under Article 30 on public health grounds, the particular measures in question were not so justified because they constituted arbitrary discrimination—even though some domestically produced drinks were caught by the heavier restrictions.[33]

(b) Conversely, a restriction falling solely or more heavily on exports, to the exclusion of products intended for the domestic market also constitutes arbitrary discrimination. Thus in *Bouhelier*[34] the requirement to obtain certificates of quality for exports of watches was held to constitute arbitrary discrimination, since no corresponding obligation existed as regards watches intended for the domestic market.[35]

(c) *Dassonville*[36] shows that discrimination between imports coming directly from the State of production on the one hand, and indirect imports on the other, will constitute arbitrary discrimination.[37] The *Dassonville* case itself shows that this holds good even where the goods were produced outside the Community (at the material time the United Kingdom had not yet acceded to the Community).

(d) It can be deduced from the *De Peijper*[38] case discussed below that discrimination against parallel imports will also constitute arbitrary discrimination.

---

[32] Case 152/78 [1980] E.C.R. 2299; [1981] 2 C.M.L.R. 743.

[33] Similarly, see Case 121/85 *Conegate v H.M. Customs and Excise Commissioners* [1986] E.C.R. 1007; [1986] 1 C.M.L.R. 739, para. 8.44 below. In contrast, for an anomalous judgment in which the Court's reasoning is hard to fathom, see Case C-389/96, see n.24 at para. 8.161 below.

[34] Case 53/76 [1977] E.C.R. 197; [1977] 1 C.M.L.R. 436.

[35] It is true that Art. 30 was not expressly mentioned, but the mere use of the words "arbitrary discrimination" in the judgment can be taken as an implied reference to that provision.

[36] Case 8/74 [1974] E.C.R. 837; [1974] 2 C.M.L.R. 436.

[37] See paras 7.05 *et seq.* above.

[38] Case 104/75 [1976] E.C.R. 613; [1976] 2 C.M.L.R. 271. See also C-267 and 268/95 *Merck v Primecrown* [1996] E.C.R. I-6285; and Joined Cases C-427, 429 and 436/93 *Bristol-Myers Squibb v Paranova A/S* [1996] E.C.R. I-3457.

(e) Finally, where Member State A discriminates in favour of goods coming from or originating in Member State B as against those coming from or originating in Member State C, that is also arbitrary discrimination.[39]

8.13 However, there will be no arbitrary discrimination in any of these cases if the difference of treatment is objectively justified. In a quite different context in *Italy v Commission*[40] the Court defined the principle of non-discrimination under the Treaty as follows:

> "The different treatment of non-comparable situations does not lead automatically to the conclusion that there is discrimination. An appearance of discrimination in form may therefore correspond in fact to an absence of discrimination in substance. Discrimination in substance would consist in treating either similar situations differently or different situations identically."

Also, in *Rewe-Zentralfinanz v Landwirtschaftskammer*[41] the Court was asked, *inter alia*, whether the obligation to submit imports of apples to phytosanitary controls constituted arbitrary discrimination under Article 30, when no corresponding requirement existed with respect to domestically produced apples. The Court replied that:

> "The different treatment of imported and domestic products, based on the need to prevent the spread of the harmful organism could not, however, be regarded as arbitrary discrimination if effective measures are taken in order to prevent the distribution of contaminated domestic products and if there is reason to believe, in particular on the basis of previous experience, that there is a risk of the harmful organism's spreading if no inspection is held on importation."

8.14 There may also be highly exceptional cases, it would seem, in which the less favourable treatment of imports is not warranted in itself but must nevertheless be accepted as being justified under Article 30, because an equally effective and non-discriminatory means of achieving the desired protection cannot be devised. This appears to be the implicit message of the recent ruling in *Konsumentombudsmannen v Gourmet International Products*.[42] That case concerned a stringent, though not absolute, ban on advertising alcoholic drinks in Sweden. Although the provision concerned was not discriminatory on its face,

---

[39] An extremely limited exception to this rule is contained in Art. 306 (ex 233) EC; see para. 9.44 below. In contrast, it would seem clear that the "closer co-operation" which Member States may establish between themselves on the basis of Art. 43 (ex K.15) TEU may not involve restrictions on trade between Member States: paragraph 1(e) of that provision makes it clear that such measures may not "affect the '*acquis communautaire*'". Indeed, Art. 11(1)(e) EC expressly provides that, if such co-operation is carried out under the auspices of the EC institutions and according to EC procedures, then it must not "constitute a discrimination or a restriction of trade between Member States" and must not "distort the conditions of competition between the latter". See generally Tuytschaever, *Differentiation in European Law* (1999).

[40] Case 13/63 [1963] E.C.R. 165; [1963] C.M.L.R. 289; the case concerned Art. 226 EC which was deleted during the re-numbering and re-organisation of the Treaty on the entry into force of the Treaty of Amsterdam.

[41] Case 4/75 [1975] E.C.R. 843; [1977] 1 C.M.L.R. 599.

[42] Case C-405/98 [2001] E.C.R. I-1795.

the Court found that in the light of the particular circumstances the legislation taken as a whole in fact fell more heavily on products from other Member States. This was in part because it authorised advertising at the point of sale, where in practice the State retail alcohol monopoly only distributed its own magazine. At all events, for present purposes the important point is that the Court by no means ruled out the possibility that a restriction such as that in issue in the main case might be justified under Article 30 on public health grounds; it left this question for the referring court in Sweden to decide. It should be noted, however, that the Court took particular care to stress that it saw no evidence of any protectionist intent on the part of the Swedish authorities.

8.15   On a different but related point, the Court held in *Procureur du Roi v Debauve*[43] that "differences, which are due to natural phenomena, cannot be described as 'discrimination' within the meaning of the Treaty; the latter regards only differences in treatment arising from human activity." Although this case concerned services rather than goods, it is submitted that this particular part of the judgment is of general application. The case involved the prosecution of a number of individuals and undertakings engaged in the diffusion in Belgium of cable television from other Member States for infringing the prohibition on television advertising in Belgium. One of the questions referred by the Belgian court for a preliminary ruling was whether a prohibition of this kind constituted "discrimination based on the geographical locality of the foreign broadcasting station which would be able to transmit advertisements only within its natural receiving zone [inside Belgian territory], as these zones may, because of the differences in density of population, be of very different interest from the advertising point of view". The point of this question was that, even if the prohibition on television advertising in Belgium covered retransmission by cable television of broadcasts of other Member States, nevertheless broadcasting networks in neighbouring countries could not avoid reaching certain frontier districts of Belgium. The Court, however, reached the conclusion that this would not constitute discrimination.

8.16   What if the laws of some of the constituent parts of a Member State are less restrictive than the measures applying to imports into the entire territory of that Member State? This was essentially one of the issues in *R. v Henn and Darby*,[44] which concerned the offence of importing "indecent or obscene articles" into the United Kingdom. That offence covered certain categories of article which might lawfully be sold in some, but not all, constituent parts of the United Kingdom. On this point the Court held that:

> "the fact that certain differences existing between the laws enforced in the different constituent parts of a Member State does not thereby prevent that State from applying

---

[43] Case 52/79 [1980] E.C.R. 881; [1981] 2 C.M.L.R. 362; see para. 2.04 above.
[44] Case 34/79 [1979] E.C.R. 3795; [1980] 1 C.M.L.R. 246.

a unitary concept in regard to prohibitions on imports imposed on grounds of public morality, on trade with other Member States."

Later passages of the judgment could perhaps be taken as implied acceptance by the Court of the Advocate General's view[45] that "where the Member State concerned is so constituted that there are variations in the laws of different parts of it, that in my opinion is a factor—it may be an important factor—to be taken into account in applying the test [of whether more restrictive treatment of imports is reasonable.]" This judgment will be more closely examined under the "public morality" heading below.

"Disguised Restriction"

8.17   In *Henn and Darby*[46] the Court stated that the second sentence of Article 30 "is designed to prevent restrictions on trade based on the grounds mentioned in the first sentence of Article [30] from being diverted from their proper purpose and used in such a way as either to create discrimination in respect of goods originating in other Member States or indirectly to protect certain national products".[47] Thus the Court has introduced into Article 30 the concept of abuse of right.[48] This may presumably be taken as an interpretation of the words "disguised restriction on trade between Member States".

The Court built on this ruling in *Commission v United Kingdom*.[49] This case concerned a ban on imports into the United Kingdom of poultry products, eggs and egg products from those Member States (including France) which did not have a policy of slaughtering flocks infected with Newcastle disease. The United Kingdom sought to justify this ban on animal health grounds. However, the Court found that the real purpose of this provision was to protect domestic production. It deduced this from a number of facts. First of all, for some months prior to the introduction of the ban the United Kingdom Government had been subject to pressure from domestic poultry producers to block imports. This was well documented in the British press. Secondly, the ban was announced on August 27, 1981 and came into effect on September 1, 1981. It was thus introduced so hastily that the Commission and the Member States were neither consulted nor even informed in good time. This timing also had the effect of excluding French Christmas turkeys from the British market for the 1981 season. Thirdly, when France sought to comply with the new British requirement, the United Kingdom refused to take cognisance of it, adding a further requirement which France did not meet. The Court concluded that the import ban constituted a disguised restriction on imports.

The view that a measure is not justified under Article 30 merely because it is

---

[45] At 3831 (E.C.R.), 265 (C.M.L.R.). On arbitrary discrimination and restrictions only to part of a Member State, see also Cases C-1/90 and 176/90 *Aragonesa de Publicidad v Departamento de Sanidad* [1991] E.C.R. I-4151 and para. 6.95 above.
[46] See n.44 above.
[47] See also C-405/98, See n.42 above at para. 32.
[48] See para. 6.106 above
[49] Case 40/82 [1982] E.C.R. 2793; [1982] 2 C.M.L.R. 497.

enacted for protectionist reasons would clearly lead to questionable results. It would mean that, even where a measure was in itself undoubtedly justified under Article 30 it could nevertheless he held to fall outside the protection of that provision on the grounds that the Member State concerned had acted out of the wrong motives. Not only would this create considerable legal uncertainty, but it would also have the undesirable result that measures would be unlawful even though they were objectively justified. However, the Court avoided this pitfall: it held in effect that, since the import ban constituted a disguised restriction on trade between Member States, the presumption that it was not justified under Article 30 was increased. In the event it found that the ban was not so justified.

There is some difficulty in reconciling this reasoning with the language of Article 30 which suggests that, if a measure is caught by the second sentence, it cannot be justified. Thus it appears preferable to regard protectionist moves as evidence that a measure is not justified. This appears to be the approach followed by the Court in *Commission v France ("Italian wine")*.[50]

"Justified"

8.18 According to the principle of proportionality a measure may not restrict trade between Member States more than is necessary to achieve its legitimate object. As regards the Community institutions, this principle is now enshrined in the Protocol on the application of the principles of subsidiarity and proportionality, which was concluded at the same time as the Treaty of Amsterdam but is annexed to the EC Treaty.[51] With respect to Article 30, this principle was clearly set out by the Court in *De Peijper*[52] as follows:

> "It emerges from Article [30] that national rules or practices which do restrict imports of pharmaceutical products or are capable of doing so are only compatible with the Treaty to the extent to which they are necessary for the effective protection of health and life of humans.
>
> National rules or practices do not fall within the exception specified in Article [30] if the health and life of humans can [be] as effectively protected by measures which do not restrict intra-Community trade so much."

The Court made the same point in a different way in *Eggers v Freie Hansestadt Bremen*[53] when it held:

> "Article [30] is an exception to the fundamental principle of the free movement of goods and must, therefore, be interpreted in such a way that its scope is not extended any further than is *necessary*[54] for the protection of those interests which it is intended to secure."

---

[50] Case 42/82 [1983] E.C.R. 1013; [1984] 1 C.M.L.R. 160.
[51] See para. 12.10 below.
[52] See n.38 above.
[53] Case 13/78 [1978] E.C.R. 1935; [1979] 1 C.M.L.R. 562; para. 7.59 above.
[54] The italics are those of the author.

It is submitted that the Court was making the same point once again in "*Cassis de Dijon*"[55] when it held: "Obstacles to movement within the Community ... must be accepted insofar as those provisions may be recognised as being necessary in order to satisfy mandatory requirements."

8.19   Moreover, the Court also held in the *De Peijper* case that:

"Article [30] cannot be relied on to justify rules or practices which, even though they are beneficial, contain restrictions which are explained primarily by concern to lighten the administration's burden or reduce public expenditure, unless, in the absence of the said rules or practices, this burden or expenditure clearly would exceed the limits of what can reasonably be required."[56]

8.20   In accordance with the principle of equivalence,[57] if the optimal standard for a given product is 100 and two Member States both require a standard of 80 but lay down different means of reaching that result, then each must permit the sale of the other's product. What matters is not whether the Member State in which the product is produced imposes a standard equivalent to the Member State of importation, but whether the product in question in fact meets a standard required by the importing Member State. The Commission attached particular importance to this matter in its Communication on "*Cassis de Dijon*"[58] where it stated:

"The principles decided by the Court imply that a Member State may not in principle prohibit the sale in its territory of a product lawfully produced according to technical or quality requirements which differ from those imposed on its domestic products. Where a product 'suitably and satisfactorily' fulfils the legitimate objective of a Member State's own rules (public safety, protection of the consumer or the environment, etc.) the importing country cannot justify prohibiting its sale in its territory by claiming that the way it fulfils the objective is different from that imposed on domestic products."

8.21   Each Member State is free to choose its own level of protection within the limits set by Article 30. The provision is thus purely permissive. Consequently, in *MacQuen v Grandvision Belgium*, a case relating to the freedom of establishment, the Court stated: "... the fact that one Member State imposes less strict rules than another Member State does not mean that the latter's rules are disproportionate and hence incompatible with Community law".[59] In the same case, the Court then added: "The mere fact that a Member State has chosen a system of protection different from that adopted by another Member State cannot affect the appraisal as to the need for and proportionality of the

---

[55] See n.5 above.
[56] See also para. 8.59 below. This ruling has been confirmed on a number of occasions: see, *e.g.* Case C-128/89 *Commission v Italy (checks on grapefruit)* [1990] E.C.R. I-3239.
[57] See 6.70.
[58] [1980] O.J. C256/2.
[59] Case C-108/96 [2001] E.C.R. I-837, para. 33, citing two earlier cases on services (Cases C-384/93 *Alpine Investments v Minister van Financiën* [1995] E.C.R. I-1141, para. 51; and C-3/95 *Reisebüro Broede v Sandker* [1996] E.C.R. I-6511, para. 42).

provisions adopted".[60] With respect, the latter statement goes too far, since it suggests that no account whatever is to be taken of the measures adopted in other Member States.[61] Measures adopted in other Member States may be relevant in demonstrating that there are alternative means of achieving the same level of protection which are less restrictive of trade.

8.22 It was suggested above[62] that, where the Member State is proved to have acted out of protectionist motives, that is evidence that the measure concerned is not justified. The ruling in *Commission v France ("Italian wine")*[63] appears to constitute authority for this proposition.

Quite apart from statements made by the authorities of the Member State concerned, the following have been taken by the Court to show the existence of protectionist motives[64]: pressure from domestic producers to restrict imports; the sudden introduction of a measure without consultation of the Commission or the other Member States; and inconsistent or erratic action.

8.23 As we noticed in Chapter VI,[65] Articles 28 and 29 are subject to no *de minimis* exception. In *Bluhme*, which concerned a measure limited to a few small islands in Denmark, the Advocate General stated: "In assessing the proportionality of [the contested measure], the national court should also bear in mind its limited geographical scope. The restriction on the exercise of Community-law rights in Denmark is correspondingly reduced."[66]

Perhaps this statement is merely intended to mean that the principle of proportionality requires a restriction to be strictly limited to the geographical area affected. That proposition is incontrovertible. However, if the Advocate General intended to suggest that the courts should view more favourably restrictions having a limited geographical scope, then that is a cause for concern. Since the volume of goods affected is irrelevant when it comes to determining whether a restriction falls under Articles 28 or 29 in the first place, it is difficult to see why one should have regard to this matter when weighing up the possible justification of that restriction. Surely, having driven the *de minimis* principle out of this area of the law by the door, there is no reason to let it in through the window. Otherwise, restrictions adopted by Luxembourg would be more likely to be justified than identical restrictions imposed by a large Member State such as France, merely because of the difference in scale.[67] Moreover, the Advocate's General's suggestion overlooks the formidable practical problems posed by a *de minimis* rule, which were discussed in Chapter VI.

At all events, the Court in *Bluhme* made no comment on the Advocate Gen-

---

[60] Para. 34 of the judgment, referring to Case C-67/98 *Zenatti* [1999] E.C.R. I-7289, para. 34.
[61] See also para. 8.66 below.
[62] Para. 8.17.
[63] Case 42/82, see n.50 above.
[64] See Cases 40/82, see n.49 above; and 42/82, see n.50 above.
[65] Paras 6.17 *et seq.*
[66] C-67/97 [1998] E.C.R. I-8033 at 8051.
[67] It may also happen that, for technical or scientific reasons, a measure applied to a large territory is justified only with respect to *part* of that territory; but that is another matter.

eral's suggestion. The better view, it is submitted, is therefore that, when weighing up the possible justification of a restriction, its geographical scope is to be regarded as a neutral factor.

8.24 The fact that victims of a breach by a Member State of the free movement of goods provisions have been provided with compensation cannot be used by that Member State to justify that breach. This unsurprising proposition was laid down in *Commission v France*[68] where the Court held that "even though compensation can provide reparation for at least part of the loss or damage sustained by the economic operators concerned, the provision of such compensation does not mean that the Member State has fulfilled its obligations."[69]

8.25 Next, what if imports are subject to restrictions justified under Article 30 but the public authorities are empowered to relax the restrictions in individual cases?

In *Denkavit Futtermittel*[70] the Court ruled as follows:

"Article [30] of the Treaty cannot be interpreted as meaning that it forbids in principle a national authority, which has imposed by a general rule veterinary and public health restrictions on imports..., from providing that it will be possible to derogate therefrom by individual measures left to the discretion of the administration if such derogations assist the simplification of the restrictions imposed by the general rules and if this power of derogation does not[71] give rise to arbitrary discrimination between traders of different Member States.

Nevertheless it does not automatically follow that each of the conditions to which the national authority subjects the grant of authorization itself complies with what is permitted by Article [30]. It is in each case for the national courts ... to determine whether these conditions are necessary to attain the objective which Article [30] allows to be sought..."

This approach was later confirmed by the Court in *Fietje*,[72] where it held:

"in the case of a measure justified on grounds recognised by the Treaty, the Treaty does not forbid in principle provision being made for the possibility of granting derogations therefrom by individual decisions left to the discretion of the administration. However, exceptions must not lead to the favouring of domestic products because this would constitute arbitrary discrimination against or a disguised restriction on products imported from other Member States."

On the other hand, held the Court in *Denkavit Futtermittel*, if the individual dispensation "only made possible a relaxation of a general supervisory system which went beyond what Article [30] permits it would be necessary to consider it

---

[68] C-265/95 [1997] E.C.R. I-6959.
[69] Para. 60 of the judgment.
[70] See n.28 above.
[71] The word "not" is missing from the English text but it is clear from the sense and from other language texts that it should be there.
[72] Case 27/80 [1980] E.C.R. 3839; [1981] 3 C.M.L.R. 722.

on its own merits in the light of the exceptions permitted by Article [30] ..."[73]

8.26 The proportionality of national provisions that require prior adminis-trative authorisation before imported goods (or services) may be marketed on the territory of a Member State was dealt with in *Canal Satélite Digital v Admin-istracíon General del Estado*.[74] That case concerned Spanish legislation that required undertakings wishing to market equipment, decoders or digital transmission and reception systems for television signals by satellite to register as an operator of conditional-access broadcasting services. The Court set down four considerations that must be taken into account when determining whether such national legislation complies with the principle of proportionality:

(a) the prior administrative authorisation scheme must be based on objec-tive, non-discriminatory criteria which are known in advance, in such a way as to circumscribe the exercise of the national authorities' discretion, so that it is not used arbitrarily[75];

(b) any such scheme must not essentially duplicate controls that have already been carried out in the context of other procedures, either in the same State or in another Member State[76];

(c) a prior authorisation procedure will be necessary only where subsequent control must be regarded as being too late to be genuinely effective and to enable it to achieve the aim pursued[77]; and

(d) a prior authorisation procedure will not be proportionate if, on account of its duration and the costs to which it gives rise, it is such as to deter the operators concerned from pursuing their business plan.[78]

IV. EXTRA-TERRITORIAL APPLICATION OF ARTICLE 30

8.27 Can a Member State rely on Article 30 to impose its own standards or morals unilaterally on other Member States? The earliest authority on this point appears to be the Opinion of Trabucchi A.G. in *Dassonville*, according to which this provision entitles Member States to derogate from the prohibition on quantitative restrictions and measures of equivalent effect "only for the purpose of the protection of their own interests and not for the protection of the interests of other States".[79]

---

[73] See also Case 82/77 *van Tiggele* [1978] E.C.R. 25; [1978] 2 C.M.L.R. 528; para. 7.82 above.
[74] C-390/99 [2002] E.C.R. I-607.
[75] Para. 35 of the judgment.
[76] Paras 36–8 of the judgment.
[77] Paras 39–40 of the judgment.
[78] Paras 41–2 of the judgment.
[79] See n.36 above at 860. See also Written question 375/77 ([1977] O. J. C265/8): the Commission took the view that a Member State, which bans cruelty in the rearing and slaughtering of poultry (*e.g.* a ban on battery rearing), may not ban imports from other Member States applying less stringent rules. In particular, such an import ban would not be justified on the grounds of public

This view was forcefully endorsed by Léger A.G. in *R. v Ministry of Agriculture Ex p. Hedley Lomas*[80] and in *R. v Minister of Agriculture Ex p. Compassion in World Farming*.[81] In both cases, he concluded that the United Kingdom was not entitled to restrict the export of live animals to other Member States on the grounds that the methods of slaughter or rearing in those States did not comply with the Community's animal welfare legislation.[82] In *Hedley Lomas* he based this view on the considerations that "the principle of mutual confidence prohibits a Member State from adopting unilaterally a measure based on Article [30] for protecting animals within the territory of another Member State" and furthermore that "only the Member State within whose territory the protective measure must be adopted is in a position to ensure that the measure is strictly necessary and to check that it is being complied with".

This interpretation would appear to be confirmed by the Court's only—and very brief—ruling on the issue. This occurred in *Alpine Investments v Minister van Financiën*,[83] which concerned the free movement of services. That case concerned the practice known as "cold calling", whereby providers of financial services contact individuals without their prior consent to offer them such services. Dutch legislation banned companies established in the Netherlands from "cold calling" potential clients in other Member States. The Court held that "the protection of consumers in other Member States is not, as such, a matter for the Netherlands authorities", although it went on to find the prohibition justified on other grounds.[84]

As Roth points out,[85] the provisions in the EC Treaty on the four freedoms are to be read in the light of the Treaty of European Union. What is now Article 6(3) of that Treaty provides: "The Union shall respect the national identities of its Member States." To allow one Member States to impose its values on others by means of trade restrictions runs counter to the rule in Article 6(3). True, that paragraph is not one of the provisions listed in Article 46 TEU, which confers jurisdiction on the Court; but that surely does not deprive the Court of the power to take cognisance of that provision.[86]

To judge from Jacobs A.G.'s Opinion in *Werner v Germany*,[87] there appears to be one major exception to this rule, however. That case related not to Article 30 itself, but to the corresponding provision in the Community legislation on

---

morality, since "any affront to public morals ... would occur solely in the country where the cruel treatment takes place and can be witnessed by the local population, and not in the importing country".

[80] Case C-5/94 [1996] E.C.R. I-2553.

[81] Case C-1/96 [1998] E.C.R. I-1251. See Van Calster, "Export Restrictions – A Watershed for Article 30" [2000] E.L.Rev. 335.

[82] See also Van Gerven A.G. in Case C-169/89 *Gourmetterie van Den Burg* [1990] E.C.R. I-2143 at 2155.

[83] See n.59 above.

[84] See para. 43 of the judgment, and para. 8.170 below.

[85] "Altruistische Interessenwahrnehmung im Binnenmarkt" in *Festschrift für Wolfgang Fikentscher* (1998) 723 at 732.

[86] The Court has been known to take cognisance of treaties which were not part of Community law: Cases 89/76 *Commission v Netherlands* [1977] E.C.R. 1355; [1978] 3 C.M.L.R. 630; and 44/84 *Hurd v Jones* [1986] E.C.R. 29. Similarly, the Court has not been deterred from continuing to develop its case law on fundamental rights by the terms of Article 46 (see para. 8.39 below).

[87] Case C-70/94 [1995] E.C.R. I-3189.

restrictions on exports to third countries—a provision which, he considered, was to be interpreted "in much the same way" as Article 30. The question arose whether, on the basis of this provision, Member States could restrict exports of arms. The Advocate General found that such action was lawful where human health and life is at stake, adding that the contrary view would be "indefensible" given that such restrictions might avoid "a great deal of bloodshed".[88] It seems difficult to imagine the Court taking issue with this interpretation, except conceivably where the health risk is trivial in nature.

In short, altruism has its limits in the eyes of the law: despite the absence of a clear ruling from the Court on the point, it seems clear that Member States may not rely on this provision to impose their standards or morals on others, save where human health and life are at stake. Having said that, it should be recalled that only those restrictions which discriminate against exports in favour of goods sold on the domestic market are caught by Article 29 in the first place[89]; thus it is unnecessary to consider the justification of bans on selling goods of a particular composition which apply to both categories of product in the same way.

For the sake of clarity, it should be stressed that we are concerned here only with the cases in which Member States act to protect interests other than their own. Thus different considerations apply where a Member State imposes restrictions on exports so as to protect its own commercial reputation in other markets.[90]

Equally, we are concerned here only with the unilateral acts of Member States: it is quite another matter for two or more Member States to co-operate amongst themselves so as to grant each other certain protection. In that event, as Roth points out, there is no question of one Member State imposing its values on another contrary to the latter's wishes; and no conflict with Article 6(3) TEU therefore arises. Thus in *Exportur v LOR*, which related to a convention concluded by France and Spain for the mutual protection of certain geographical denominations, it was held that "where the protection afforded by a State to names indicating regions or places in its territory is justified under Article [30] of the Treaty, that provision does not preclude such protection from being extended to the territory of another Member State".[91] In that case, there was no suggestion that the convention concerned in any way restricted trade in the goods of Member States other than France and Spain.

V. THE RELATIONSHIP BETWEEN ARTICLE 30 AND COMMUNITY LEGISLATION

8.28   The Court held in *Simmenthal v Italian Minister of Finance*[92] that:

---

[88] See points 39 and 59 of his Opinion.
[89] Paras 6.79 to 6.92 above.
[90] See para. 8.170 below.
[91] C-3/91 [1992] E.C.R. I-5529, para. 38 of the judgment.
[92] Case 35/76 [1976] E.C.R. 1871; [1977] 2 C.M.L.R. 1.

"Article [30] is not designed to reserve certain matters to the exclusive jurisdiction of Member States but permits national laws to derogate from the principle of the free movement of goods to the extent to which such derogation is and continues to be justified for the attainment of the objectives referred to in that Article."

The question referred by the national court was whether systematic veterinary and public health checks on meat imports into Italy from another Member State were compatible with Articles 28 and 30. The Court found that certain Community directives harmonising health checks in the exporting Member State rendered systematic import checks unnecessary, so that they were no longer justified under Article 30.[93]

In the subsequent cases of *Tedeschi v Denkavit*,[94] *Ratti*,[95] and *Denkavit Futtermittel*[96] the Court repeated the passage quoted above, adding:

"Where ... Community directives provide for the harmonisation of the measures necessary to ensure the protection of animal and human health and establish Community procedures to check that they are observed, recourse to Article [30] is no longer justified and the appropriate checks must be carried out and the measures of protection adopted within the framework outlined by the harmonising directive."[97]

8.29 This is not to say that every directive necessarily provides exhaustive guarantees such as to oust the application of Article 30.[98] It is a question of the wording of each directive whether the guarantees which it provides are exhaustive. Thus in the *Rewe-Zentralfinanz*[99] case concerning phytosanitary controls on apple imports to check for San José scale insects, the Court found that recourse could still be had by Member States to Article 30 in spite of the existence of a Directive on the control of that very insect; this was because that Directive expressly authorised the Member States to adopt such stricter provisions as might prove necessary.[100]

---

[93] See further discussion of this question at paras 12.103 *et seq.*

[94] Case 5/77 [1977] E.C.R. 1555; [1978] 1 C.M.L.R. 1.

[95] Case 148/78 [1979] E.C.R. 1629; [1980] 1 C.M.L.R. 96.

[96] See n.28 above.

[97] This passage is in fact taken from the *Tedeschi* case; there are insignificant textual differences between the three judgments; see also Cases 28/84 *Commission v Germany (compound feeding stuffs)* [1985] E.C.R. 3097; C-323/93 *Centre d'insémination de la Crespelle v Coopérative d'élevage* [1994] E.C.R. I-5077; and C-473/98 *Kemikalieinspektionen v Toolex Alpha* [2000] E.C.R. I-5681 at para. 25. Furthermore, between the adoption of a Directive and the date set for its implementation, it is a breach of Arts 10 (ex 5) and 249 (ex 189) for Member States to take "any measures liable seriously to compromise the result prescribed": Case C-129/96 *Inter-Environnement Wallonie v Région Wallonne* [1997] E.C.R. I-7411 at para. 45.

[98] Even a Regulation setting up a common organisation of the market may fail to oust Art. 30 in the absence of express wording: Written question 468/80 ([1980] O. J. C302/3) concerning a ban on growing hemp. However, this will only occur in highly exceptional circumstances.

[99] See n.41 above. See also Case 73/84 *Denkavit Futtermittel v Land Nordrhein-Westfalen* [1985] E.C.R. 103; [1986] 2 C.M.L.R. 482 and *Toolex* (n.97 above) at paras 26–33.

[100] See also, *e.g.* Case 406/85 *Gofette* [1987] E.C.R. 2525. In its judgment in Case C-1/00 *Commission v France (BSE)* [2001] E.C.R. I-9989, the Court first found that, by refusing to lift the ban on beef imports from the United Kingdom, the defendant had infringed various Decisions of the Council and the Commission; the Court then went on to rule that the Commission had failed to "offer any justification for finding a separate infringement of Article 28 EC" (para. 138 of the judgment).

In this context the ruling in *Campus Oil v Minister for Industry and Energy*[101] is of some concern. This case concerned a requirement that importers of petroleum products into Ireland purchase a specified proportion of their supplies from the one remaining Irish refinery. Ireland maintained that it was necessary to keep the refinery in operation so as to guarantee supplies, particularly in the event of a crisis. Yet the Community had adopted legislation[102] designed to meet this very problem, and this required Member States, *inter alia*, to maintain minimum stocks of petroleum products of at least 90 days' average consumption. While acknowledging that this legislation provided "certain guarantees" in this regard to a Member State with no or virtually no crude oil of its own, the Court considered that it did not afford "an unconditional assurance that supplies will in any event be maintained at least at a level sufficient to meet its minimum needs"; it therefore found that this legislation did not preclude a Member State from relying on Article 30. Read literally this ruling appears alarming: it is difficult to imagine that any measure can give an unconditional assurance that the interest in question will be protected in all circumstances. Indeed, the "unconditional assurance" test is at variance with the Court's case law on Article 30, which requires the Member States to admit imports affording less than absolute guarantees with regard to health and safety.

8.30   The Single European Act inserted into the Treaty of Rome three provisions which specifically empower the Member States to introduce measures which are more stringent than those provided for in Community legislation. Thus, a Member State may opt out of legislation enacted under Article 95 (ex 100A) by invoking the controversial paragraph 4 of that Article, but only after notifying its own measure to the Commission and receiving the latter's approval.[103] Member States may also go beyond Community legislation adopted under Article 138 (ex 118A) regarding "improvements, especially in the working environment, as regards the health and safety of workers" (Article 138(3)); and the same applies to legislation on the environment (Article 176 (ex 130T)). Under Articles 138(3) and 176 Member States need not submit their measures to the Commission for approval, or even notify them.

8.31   Finally, directives cannot extend the powers enjoyed by the Member States under Article 30. This was held in *De Peijper*,[104] which concerned the formalities laid down by the Dutch authorities for giving approval to pharmaceutical products imported from other Member States. Having ruled that formalities of this kind might constitute measures of equivalent effect, the Court went on to consider the contention of the British, Danish and Dutch Governments that such measures were necessary to comply with the Council Directives

---

[101] Case 72/83 [1984] E.C.R. 2727; [1984] 3 C.M.L.R. 544; see para. 8.33.
[102] Council Dir. 68/414 ([1968] II O. J. Spec. Ed. 586) as amended by Council Dir. 72/425 ([1972] J.O. L291/154); Council Dir. 73/238 ([1973] O.J. L228/1); and Council Dir. 77/186 ([1977] O.J. L61/23) and 77/706 ([1977] O.J. L292/9).
[103] Paras 12.45 *et seq.*
[104] See n.38 above.

on the approximation of national provisions relating to proprietary medicinal products.[105] The Court rejected this contention on the grounds that "the sole aim of these directives is to harmonise national provisions in this field; they do not and cannot aim at extending the very considerable powers left to Member States in the field of public health by Article [30]." This is merely a particular manifestation of the general rule discussed earlier in this book to the effect that Community legislation may not create undue barriers to trade between Member States.[106]

VI. THE GROUNDS OF JUSTIFICATION

General

8.32 In *Commission v Italy*,[107] the first case on Article 30, the Court held that this provision is "directed to eventualities of a non-economic kind". The importance of this rule cannot be sufficiently stressed: if it were otherwise, a coach and horses would be driven through the very principle of the free movement of goods. Thus it is by no means surprising to find the Court reaffirming this rule on numerous occasions.[108] It follows that such objects as the promotion of employment or investment, curbing inflation and controlling the balance of payments fall outside Article 30. Similarly in *Sandoz*[109] the Court held that it could not under any circumstances be justified under Article 30 for the authorities of a Member State to refuse to authorise the sale of a product on the ground that there was no demand for it. Again, in *Evans Medical*[110] it ruled that a restriction could not be justified by "a Member State's wish to safeguard the survival of an undertaking."

8.33 In *Campus Oil*[111] Ireland argued that the requirement that importers of petroleum products purchase a specified proportion of their needs from the one remaining Irish refinery was justified for the purpose of ensuring essential supplies, particularly in the event of a crisis, although Ireland has no crude oil of its own. At the same time, this requirement plainly served to keep the refinery in operation and was thus of economic benefit to Ireland. The two aims were

---

[105] Dir. 65/65 ([1965] O.J. Spec. Ed. 20); Dirs 75/318 and 75/319 ([1975] O.J. L147/13).
[106] Paras 4.10 *et seq.*
[107] Case 7/61 [1961] E.C.R. 317 at 329; [1962] C.M.L.R. 39.
[108] *e.g.* Cases 95/81 *Commission v Italy (import deposits)* [1982] E.C.R. 2187; 288/83 *Commission v Ireland (Cyprus potatoes)* [1985] E.C.R. 1761; [1985] 3 C.M.L.R. 152; C-324/93 *R. v Secretary of State for the Home Department, Ex p. Evans Medical* [1995] E.C.R. I-563; C-265/95, see n.68 above at para. 62; C-120/95 *Decker v Caisse de maladie des employés privés* [1998] E.C.R. I-1831 at para. 39, see n.23 above; C-203/96 see n.18 above at para. 44; C-254/98 *TK-Heimdienst Sass GmbH* [2000] E.C.R. I-151 at para. 33; for a difficult case see, however Case 238/82 *Duphar v Netherlands* [1984] E.C.R. 523 at para. 23; [1985] 1 C.M.L.R. 256, see para. 7.72 above.
[109] Case 174/82 [1983] E.C.R. 2445; [1984] 3 C.M.L.R. 43.
[110] See n.108 above, para. 36 of the judgment.
[111] See n.101 above. See also Case 118/86 *Nertsvoederfabriek Nederland* [1987] E.C.R. 3883; and C-398/98 *Commission v Greece* [2001] E.C.R. I-7915 at para. 30.

indissociable. After confirming that "Article [30] refers to matters of a non-economic nature", the Court went on:

> "However in the light of the seriousness of the consequences that an interruption in supplies of petroleum products may have for a country's existence, the aim of ensuring a minimum supply of petroleum products at all times is to be regarded as transcending purely economic considerations and thus as capable of constituting an objective covered by the concept of public security."[112]

This may apply whenever a measure is based equally on economic grounds and on grounds which are admissible under Article 30. However, when the economic purpose is predominant, the measure cannot be justified.[113]

8.34   The Court has, it is true, accepted that a Member State may take limited measures to prevent imports being used to speculate in currency or for the purposes of tax fraud.[114] In *Commission v Italy*[115] the defendant argued that legislation making the advance payment for imports subject to the lodging of a deposit was justified for preventing currency speculation. Although the Court dismissed this argument, it accepted that "the Member States remain free to employ all means of ensuring that payments made abroad relate exclusively to genuine transactions, subject always to the condition that such means do not hinder the freedom of intra-Community trade as defined in the Treaty". The Court appeared to go further in *Commission v Greece*,[116] where the defendant maintained that a ban on the import of certain cuts of meat was justified to prevent unlawful exports of capital. This argument was dismissed on the grounds that "measures which, as in this case, impede intra-Community trade more than is necessary cannot come within the scope of the power which the Member States continue to have with regard to the control of transfers of foreign currency". Unlike the judgment in *Commission v Italy*, this passage necessarily implies that limited restrictions on genuine imports may be justified for these purposes.

This corresponds to an exception in the old directives on the freedom of capital which has now been replaced by Article 58 (ex 73D).[117] In view of the case law referred to, it would seem clear that by an analogy with that provision a Member State may require persons exporting large quantities of bank notes or coins to declare such exports, even if they constitute payment for imports.[118] However, the justification for such a measure would not be purely economic but would be subsumed within one of the recognised grounds of justification, particularly public policy, public security and the prevention of tax fraud.

---

[112] Para. 35 of the judgment.

[113] In any case, the existence of an economic incentive for the Member State to adopt the measure will be evidence that it is not justified: para. 8.17 above.

[114] See also para. 8.46 below.

[115] Case 95/81, see n.108 above; see para. 7.39 above.

[116] Case 124/85 [1986] E.C.R. 3935; [1988] 2 C.M.L.R. 518.

[117] Paras 2.05, and 7.40 above.

[118] Case C-358/93 *Bordessa* [1995] E.C.R. I-361; see para. 7.40 above and note by Jarvis, "Free Movement of Capital Comes of Age" [1995] E.L.Rev. 514.

Accordingly this is not an exception to the rule referred to in paragraph 8.32.

8.35 The first four grounds of justification are similar to the exceptions to the free movement of workers, the freedom of establishment and the free provision of services as regards public policy, public security and public health (Articles 39(3), 46(1) and 55 respectively).[119] It is probable that the same meaning should be given to those terms in Article 30 as in the equivalent Articles, although this is not necessarily so. Certain disparities will be due to the inherent differences between movements of goods on the one hand and persons and services on the other. Other differences may be due to the fact that the list of grounds in Article 30 is more detailed, so that the term "public policy" can be interpreted more narrowly.

8.36 *Cinéthèque v Fédération Nationale des Cinémas Français*[120] is probably the only case in which the Court has held a restriction falling under Article 28 or Article 29 to be justified without specifying the grounds of justification. The case concerned national legislation providing that, within one year of the authorisation to show a film, no video cassettes of that film could be sold or hired for private showing unless either: (a) a dispensation had been granted by the competent authorities; or (b) the film was not being shown at all in the cinemas during that period. Production of video cassettes in France during the one-year period was not forbidden, nor was there any ban on imports. The alleged aim of this legislation was to protect the film industry, although it was clearly also highly beneficial to cinema owners. The Court found that such legislation was contrary to Article 28 unless it was justified. As to justification it said simply this:

"...a national system which, in order to encourage the creation of cinematographic works irrespective of their origin, gives priority, for a limited initial period, to the distribution of such works through the cinema, is so justified."

This case was undoubtedly one of considerable difficulty. Yet the practice of ruling a restriction to be justified, without specifying under what head of justification it falls, is scarcely conducive to legal certainty and is therefore to be regretted.

8.37 On another point, in *Commission v France*[121] the defendant Member State argued that its ban on the sale of substitute milk powder was justified in view of the Community's vast surpluses of milk and milk powder: to allow substitutes

---

[119]See generally para. 1.12 above. On the relationship between the Treaty provisions on goods and services as regards justification, see Oliver, "Goods and Services: Two Freedoms Compared" in *Mélanges en homage à Michel Waelbroeck*, (1999) at 1400 *et seq.*
  On workers see in particular Dir. 64/221 ([1964] J.O. 850); Case 41/74 *Van Duyn v Home Office* [1974] E.C.R. 1337; [1975] 1 C.M.L.R. 1; Case 30/77 *R. v Bouchereau* [1977] E.C.R. 1999; [1977] 2 C.M.L.R. 800; on services see in particular Directive 64/221 already referred to and Case 52/79, see n.43 above; [1981] 2 C.M.L.R. 362; Case 62/79 *Coditel v Ciné Vog Films* [1980] E.C.R. 883; [1981] 2 C.M.L.R. 362.
[120]Cases 60 and 61/84 [1985] E.C.R. 2605; [1986] 1 C.M.L.R. 365.
[121]Case 216/84 [1988] E.C.R. 793; see also Case 76/86 *Commission v Germany* [1989] E.C.R. 1021.

would, it claimed, undermine the common agricultural policy. The Court gave this argument short shrift, stating that, even if national measures bolstered a common policy, they could not run counter to one of the fundamental principles of the Community such as the free movement of goods, unless they were justified on grounds recognised in Community law.[122]

Fundamental Rights

8.38   Must the courts have regard to fundamental rights, and in particular the European Convention on Human Rights, when construing Article 30? The Court's case law on this subject is neatly resumed in the following passage from *ERT v DEP*:

> "41 ... fundamental rights form an integral part of the general principles of law, the observance of which it ensures. For that purpose the Court draws inspiration from the constitutional traditions common to the Member States and from the guidelines supplied by international treaties for the protection of human rights on which the Member States have collaborated or of which they are signatories (see, in particular, the judgment in Case C-4/73 *Nold v Commission* [1974] ECR 491, paragraph 13). The European Convention on Human Rights has special significance in that respect (see in particular Case C-222/84 *Johnston v Chief Constable of the Royal Ulster Constabulary* [1986] ECR 1651, paragraph 18). It follows that, as the Court held in its judgment in Case C-5/88 *Wachauf v Federal Republic of Germany* [1989] E.C.R. 2609, paragraph 19, the Community cannot accept measures which are incompatible with observance of the human rights thus recognized and guaranteed.
>
> 42 ... the Court ... has no power to examine the compatibility with the European Convention on Human Rights of national rules which do not fall within the scope of Community law. On the other hand, where such rules do fall within the scope of Community law, and reference is made to the Court for a preliminary ruling, it must provide all the criteria of interpretation needed by the national court to determine whether those rules are compatible with the fundamental rights the observance of which the Court ensures and which derive in particular from the European Convention on Human Rights.
>
> 43 ... Thus the national rules in question can fall under the exceptions provided for by the combined provisions of Articles [46 and 55] only if they are compatible with the fundamental rights the observance of which is ensured by the Court."[123]

Moreover, while the Court has fallen short of ruling that the Convention binds the Community as such, it has has made frequent reference to the case law of the European Court of Human Rights.[124] It should also be noted that in *Wachauf v Germany*,[125] a case concerning national legislation adopted pursuant to the Community milk quota Regulations, the Court held that human rights

---

[122] See also Cases 407/85 *Drei Glocken v USL* [1988] E.C.R. 4233; and 90/86 *Zoni* [1988] E.C.R. 4285 (prohibition on the sale of pasta made wholly or partly from soft wheat contrary to Article 28).

[123] Case C-260/89 [1991] E.C.R. I-2925; see also Cases C-288/89 *Stichting Collectieve Antennevoorziening Gouda v Commissariaat voor de Media* [1991] E.C.R. I-4007; and C-159/90 *SPUC v Grogan* [1991] E.C.R. I-4685; Opinion 2/94 [1996] E.C.R. I-1759 at para. 33; and C-299/95 *Kremzow v Austria* [1997] E.C.R. I-2629 at para. 14.

[124] Cases C-13/94 *P v S and Cornwall County Council* [1996] E.C.R. I-2143; *Familiapress* (see n.7 above) para. 26; and C-249/96 *Grant v South West Trains Ltd* [1998] E.C.R. I-621 at paras 43–5.

[125] Case 5/88 [1989] E.C.R. 2609.

were among the general principles of law to be observed by Member States when implementing Community law.

In line with this case law, the judgment in *Rutili v Minister for the Interior*[126] strongly suggested that Article 39(3) is to be read in the light of the Convention; this is of particular relevance since, as mentioned in paragraph 8.35, Article 39(3) is analogous to Article 30. Consequently, it was by no means surprising to find Warner A.G. in *Henn and Darby*[127] referring to a judgment of the European Court of Human Rights for assistance in interpreting the public morality exception in Article 30.

Slynn A.G. expressed the same view in *Cinéthèque*[128] where the claimants had contended that the contested provision was in breach of the principle of the freedom of expression enshrined in Article 10 of the Convention and therefore incompatible with Community law. However, the Court bluntly refused to entertain the claimant's argument based on the Convention, dismissing it in the following terms:

"Although it is true that it is the duty of this Court to ensure observance of fundamental rights in the field of Community law, it has no power to examine the compatibility with the European Convention of national legislation which concerns, as in
this case, an area which falls within the jurisdiction of the national legislators".[129]

The Court's refusal to have any regard to the Convention in *Cinéthèque* was at variance with its earlier case law, notably *Rutili*. Fortunately the earlier case law was subsequently confirmed in *ERT v DEP*, which has been quoted above.

ERT v DEP related to services but in *Familiapress*[130] the Court confirmed that the same principle applied equally under Article 30, saying:

"...where a Member State relies on overriding requirements to justify rules which are
likely to obstruct the exercise of the free movement of goods, such justification must
also be interpreted in the light of the general principles of law and in particular of
fundamental rights."[131]

Accordingly, it is now beyond doubt that regard must indeed be had to the Convention when interpreting Article 30.[132] What is more, the better view is that the same applies to the whole body of fundamental rights as applied by the Court to the Community institutions, although there is a dearth of authority on this point.

---

[126] Case 36/75 [1975] E.C.R. 1205.
[127] See n.44 above.
[128] See n.120 above.
[129] at 2627.
[130] See n.7 above. Noted by Bavasso (1998) 35 C.M.L. Rev. 1413.
[131] Para. 24 of the judgment.
[132] In an extra-judicial pronouncement, Jacobs A.G. has pointed out: "Once it has been established
that a restriction is justified from the perspective of Community law, the restriction might still be
caught as infringing fundamental rights. But that would be a matter for national law, or possibly
the European Convention on Human Rights, not for Community law." ("Human Rights in the
European Union" (2001) 26 E.L. Rev. 331 at 336).

8.39 Endorsement of the Court's case law on fundamental rights from the highest political levels is to be found in the Treaties of Maastricht and Amsterdam. Article 6(2) (ex F(2)) TEU provides:

> "The Union shall respect fundamental rights as guaranteed by the European Convention for the Protection of Human Rights and Fundamental Freedoms signed in Rome on 4 November 1950 and as they result from the constitutional traditions common to the Member States, as general principles of Community law."

The Union is "founded on the European Communities" (Article 1 (ex A) TEU). Moreover, by virtue of Article 46(d) (ex L) TEU, the Court's jurisdiction extends (since the Treaty of Amsterdam) to "Article 6(2) with regard to action of the institutions, insofar as the Court has jurisdiction under the Treaties establishing the European Communities and under this Treaty". The fact that this provision does not cover the acts of Member States will not deter the Court from continuing to develop its case law on fundamental rights in relation to Article 30.[133]

While the principles laid down by the Court have been given greater force by being enshrined in the Treaty, the words "as general principles of law" would appear to indicate that Article 6(2) TEU has not altered the basis on which the Convention is applied by the Court, namely as a source of inspiration but not as a binding instrument. That view is bolstered by the reference to the "constitutional traditions common to the Member States" which is an inherently vague concept; it is scarcely conceivable that such "traditions" could bind the Court in the same way as a legal text.[134]

8.40 In addition, cognisance must now be taken of the Charter of Fundamental Rights of the European Union, which was solemnly proclaimed by the European Parliament, the Council and the Commission in December 2000.[135]

---

[133] Prior to the entry into force of the Treaty of Amsterdam, Article F(2) TEU was entirely excluded from the Court's jurisdiction as defined by Article L, but the Court carried on regardless: see, *e.g. Familiapress* (see n.7 above). This was logical, given that the Treaties had previously contained no human rights provisions at all. In Case C-84/95 *Bosphorus Hava v Minister for Transport* [1996] E.C.R. I-3956 at pp. 3971–2, Jacobs A.G. said: "Article F(2) ... gives Treaty expression to the Court's case law. Article F(2) appears in Title I of the Treaty, and therefore does not fall within the jurisdiction of the Court in so far as it extends to the Union Treaty as a whole. In relation to the EC Treaty, it confirms and consolidates the Court's case law, underlining the paramount importance of respect for fundamental rights". Literature on these provisions includes: Albors-Llorens, "Changes in the Jurisdiction of the European Court of Justice under the Treaty of Amsterdam" (1998) C.M.L. Rev. 1273; Alston (ed.) "The EU and Human Rights" (1999); Colvin and Noorlander, "Human Rights and Accountability after the Treaty of Amsterdam" [1998] E.H.R.L.R. 191; Gallagher, "The Treaty of Amsterdam and Fundamental Rights" [1998] I.J.E.L. 21; Lenaerts, "Respect for Fundamental Rights as a Constitutional Principle of the European Union" [1999–2000] Columbia Journal of European Law 1; Louis, "Le traité d'Amsterdam: une occasion perdue ?" (1997) 2 R.M.U.E. 5; Oliver, "Fundamental Rights in European Union Law after the Treaty of Amsterdam" in *Liber Amicorum in Honour of Lord Slynn of Hadley* vol. I p. 319; and Wachsmann, "Le traité d'Amsterdam: les droits de l'homme" [1997] R.T.D.E. 883.

[134] The Court has held that Art. 6(2) TEU does not create a positive competence for the Community to accede to the European Convention on Human Rights: Opinion 2/94, see n.123 above.

[135] [2000] O.J. C364/1; see De Búrca, "The Drafting of the European Charter of Fundamental Rights" [2001] E.L.Rev. 126; Dutheil de la Rochère, "La Charte des Droits Fondamentaux de

In *R v Secretary of State for Trade and Industry and BECTU*,[136] Tizzano A.G. stated that the Charter is not "formally" binding and is principally devoted to a reaffirmation of rights already enshrined in other instruments.[137] Nevertheless, he found that:

> "in proceedings concerned with the nature and scope of a fundamental right, the relevant statements of the Charter cannot be ignored; in particular, we cannot ignore its clear purpose of serving, where its provisions so allow, as a substantive point of reference for all those involved—Member States, institutions, natural and legal persons—in the Community context. Accordingly, I consider that the Charter provides us with the most reliable and definitive confirmation of the fact that the right to paid annual leave [the right in issue in those proceedings] constitutes a fundamental right."[138]

Similarly, in *Booker Aquaculture v Scottish Ministers* Mischo A.G. has stated:

> "I know that the Charter is not legally binding, but it is worthwhile referring to it given that it constitutes the expression, at the highest level, of a democratically established political consensus on what must today be considered as the catalogue of fundamental rights guaranteed by the Community legal order."[139]

As to the Court of First Instance, its practice has been inconsistent. In *Mannesmann v Commission*,[140] it declined to apply the Charter to acts which occurred prior to its adoption. Yet in *max-mobil v Commission*,[141] the same Court appeared to find no difficulty in doing precisely that. In the latter case, the Court obviously wished to distance itself from its ruling in *Mannesmann*, however, it was careful to couch its invocation of the Charter (Articles 41 and 47) as merely confirming the constitutional traditions of the Member States. In any event, as Lenaerts and De Smijter have put it, the Charter is "part of the *acquis communautaire*, even if it is not part of the Treaties on which the Union is founded".[142]

Since the Charter is so recent, the Court has not yet had time to consider its possible impact on Article 30. However, it should be noted that, according to Article 51, its provisions are addressed not only to the "institutions and bodies of the Union," but also to the Member States, albeit "only when they are implementing Union law". In view of this wording, the question arises as to

---

l'Union européenne : quelle valeur ajoutée, quel avenir? " [2000] R.M.C. 674; Jacobs, "Human Rights in the European Union" (2001) 26 E.L. Rev. 331 at 338–40; Lenaerts and De Smijter, "A 'Bill of Rights' for the European Union" [2001] C.M.L.Rev. 273; Magiera, "Die Grundrechtcharta der Europäischen Union" [2000] D.Ö.. 1017; Schwarze, "Der Grundrechtsschutz für Unternehmen in der Europäischen Grundrechtcharta" [2001] EuZW 517; Vitorino, "La Charte des droits fondamentaux de l'Union européenne" [2001] R.D.U.E. 27; also editorial comments [2001] C.M.L. Rev. 1.

[136] Case C-173/99 [2001] E.C.R I-4881.

[137] Perhaps more disparagingly, Lenaerts and De Smijter (*op. cit.* at p. 281) describe the Charter as a "handy catalogue of the fundamental rights recognised at present".

[138] Paras 27 and 28 of the Opinion.

[139] Cases C-20 and 64/00, Opinion of September 20, 2001, point 126.

[140] Case T-112/98 [2001] E.C.R. II-729, para. 76

[141] Case T-54/99 [2002] E.C.R. II-313, paras 48 and 57.

[142] *op.cit.* p. 299

whether the Charter applies to Member States only when they implement Community legislation,[143] or whether it also extends to other acts of Member States falling "within the scope of Community law" (the expression used in *ERT*). It would appear that the language of Article 51 reflects the "emerging reluctance" of the Member States to commit themselves to observing the Charter beyond the field of Community legislation.[144] Nevertheless, having regard in particular to the non-binding character of the Charter, it would seem reasonable to construe Article 51 broadly enough to cover acts allegedly adopted within the scope of the exception in Article 30 of the Treaty.

Public Morality

8.41   The first judgment of the Court of Justice on public morality under Article 30 was *Henn and Darby*.[145] At its simplest the Court's decision in this case means that a Member State may rely on this provision to prohibit imports of pornographic material when there is no lawful trade in such goods within its territory. Yet on closer examination it proves more complex.

The facts were that the defendants were convicted of importing into the United Kingdom a lorry-load of pornographic films and magazines originating in Denmark, contrary to s.42 of the Customs Consolidation Act 1876. The object of the reference was primarily to ascertain whether this provision was compatible with Articles 28 and 30.

As to whether such a measure was justified on the grounds of public morality within the meaning of Article 30, the Court ruled:

> "In principle, it is for each Member State to determine in accordance with its own scale of values and in the form selected by it the requirements of public morality in its territory. In any event, it cannot be disputed that the statutory provisions applied by the United Kingdom in regard to the importation of articles having an indecent or obscene character come within the powers reserved to the Member States by the first sentence of Article [30]."

The use of the words "in principle" indicates that the Member States may only exercise their discretion within the boundaries of a Community-wide concept of public morality. This is much the same as the Court's rulings on the concept of public policy in Article 39(3) in *Van Duyn v Home Office and R. v Bouchereau*[146] where it held:

> "the concept of public policy in the context of the Community and where, in particular, it is used as a justification for derogating from the fundamental principle of freedom of movement for workers, must be interpreted strictly, so that its scope cannot be determined unilaterally by each Member State without being subject to control by the institutions of the Community. Nevertheless the particular circumstances justifying recourse to the concept of public policy may vary from one country

---

[143] As in *Wachauf v Germany* (n.125 above).
[144] De Búrca, *op. cit.* pp. 136–137.
[145] See n.44 above.
[146] See n.119 above.

to another, and it is therefore necessary in this matter to allow the competent national authorities an area of discretion within the limits imposed by the Treaty.''[147]

As will be clear from the passage quoted above, in *Henn and Darby* the Court did not seek to define the boundaries of the concept of public morality.

8.42 So much for the general principle. However, the picture in *Henn and Darby* itself was complicated by the fact that s.42 of the Customs Consolidation Act 1876 was more restrictive than the laws applying within the United Kingdom in three respects:

(a) in no part of the United Kingdom was it a criminal offence merely to possess pornographic material otherwise than with a view to sale, yet such possession at a point of entry into the United Kingdom contravened section 42;

(b) whereas section 42 prohibited the importation of indecent and obscene articles (standard A), in England and Wales only the sale of "obscene" material was prohibited, while "indecent" material could be sold (standard B); thus articles which were merely "indecent" without being so offensive as to be considered "obscene" could be sold within England and Wales but could not be imported into any part of the United Kingdom;

(c) again as far as articles sold within England and Wales were concerned, the Obscene Publications Acts 1959 and 1964 excepted from the provisions of those Acts obscene articles when their publication was, despite their obscenity, "justified as being for the public good on the ground that it is in the interests of science, literature, art or learning, or of other objects of general concern." No equivalent defence existed under the Customs Consolidation Act.

The object of the fifth and sixth questions posed by the House of Lords was in effect to ascertain whether the import prohibition could be justified under Article 30. The Court held that such a prohibition was justified, in the following terms:

"[The second sentence of Article 30] is designed to prevent restrictions on trade based on the grounds mentioned in the first sentence of Article [30] from being diverted from their proper purpose and used in such a way as either to create discrimination in respect of goods originating in other Member States or indirectly to protect certain national products. That is not the purport of a prohibition such as that in force in the United Kingdom, on the importation of articles which are of an indecent or obscene character. Whatever may be the differences between the laws on this subject in force in the different constituent parts of the United Kingdom, and notwithstanding the fact that they contain certain exceptions of limited scope, these

---

[147] The parallel with the *Van Duyn* and *Bouchereau* cases was made by the A.G. in *Henn and Darby* at p. 3828 (E.C.R.).

laws, taken as a whole, have as their purpose the prohibition, or at least, the restraining, of the manufacture and marketing of publications or articles of an indecent or obscene character. In these circumstances it is permissible to conclude, on a comprehensive view, that there is no lawful trade in such goods in the United Kingdom. A prohibition on imports which may in certain respects be more strict than some of the laws applied within the United Kingdom cannot therefore be regarded as amounting to a measure designed to give indirect protection to some national product or aimed at creating arbitrary discrimination between goods of this type depending on whether they are produced within the national territory or another Member State."

8.43   The statement that there was no lawful trade in indecent or obscene articles within the United Kingdom lies at the core of this argument, but is factually incorrect: in most parts of the United Kingdom there was in fact lawful trade in articles which were indecent but not obscene and in obscene articles justified "for the public good".

The approach followed by the Advocate General appears to be more in keeping both with the facts and with the previous case law of the Court. In his view the test must in each case be whether any element of discrimination inherent in the prohibition or restriction on imports under consideration is in all the circumstances proportionate to its legitimate purpose. To prevent, to guard against or to reduce the likelihood of breaches of the domestic laws of the Member State concerned was a legitimate purpose. The Advocate General pointed out that in the present case there was probably no discrimination since (1) the articles appeared so obscene and unmeritorious that it was probably a criminal offence to sell them in any part of the United Kingdom, and (2) a man who imports in bulk plainly does so with a view to sale. Yet in so far as there was discrimination it might well be arbitrary within the meaning of Article 30:

> "I doubt if the application of that test [of proportionality] would justify the prohibition of the importation into the United Kingdom of a book that was lawfully on sale in English bookshops. Clearly it would be unreasonable and disproportionate to forbid the importation of such a book just because of the risk that it might be ... put on sale in Scotland or the Isle of Man. Those very same risks flow from the publication of the book in England."

8.44   Light was shed on the judgment in *Henn and Darby* by the ruling in *Conegate v H.M. Customs and Excise.*[148] Conegate had attempted to import from Germany various consignments of "inflatable dolls which were clearly of a sexual nature" and other erotic items. These were seized by the United Kingdom customs authorities as being "indecent and obscene" articles whose importation was prohibited under s.42 of the Customs Consolidation Act 1876, the provision which had also been in issue in the earlier case. There was no absolute ban on the manufacture and sale of such articles within the United Kingdom, although there was a total ban on their sale in the Isle of Man. In England and Wales they were only subject to three lesser restrictions: they could not be sent through the post; they could not be displayed in public; and in areas

---

[148] n.33 above.

where local authorities had chosen to subject sex shops to licences, they could only be sold in licensed sex shops, and in any event only to persons of 18 years of age or over. The situation in Northern Ireland was broadly similar. As for Scotland, there was a dispute between the parties as to whether such goods could be freely sold there.

The Court held that a Member State could not rely on the public morality exception in Article 30 in order to prohibit the importation of goods from other Member States when its legislation contained no prohibition on the manufacture or marketing of the same goods on its territory. It continued:

> "However, the question whether or not such a prohibition exists in a State comprised of different constituent parts which have their own internal legislation can be resolved only by taking into consideration all the relevant legislation. Although it is not necessary, for the purpose of the application of the abovementioned rule, that the manufacture and marketing of the products whose importation has been prohibited should be prohibited in the territory of all the constituent parts, it must at least be possible to conclude from the applicable rules, taken as a whole, that their purpose is, in substance, to prohibit the manufacture and marketing of those products."

On the basis of the three limited restrictions in force within England and Wales, the Court therefore in effect concluded that the goods could be lawfully marketed within the United Kingdom and that their importation could thus not be prohibited. In effect, the import ban constituted arbitrary discrimination within the meaning of the last sentence of Article 30.

8.45 Further guidance as to the meaning of the public morality exception is perhaps to be derived from the Opinion of van Gerven A.G. in *Torfaen v B & Q*.[149] The Torfaen Borough Council argued, *inter alia*, that a restriction on Sunday trading might be justified on these grounds, given that some members of the population would have religious objections to this practice. The Advocate General rejected this suggestion, since in his view the prevention of offence to religious convictions did not fall within the concept of the protection of public morality. The Court decided the case on other grounds.

8.46 Although it concerned services, the following passage from the judgment in *H.M. Customs and Excise v Schindler*[150] is worthy of note:

> "Given the peculiar nature of lotteries, which has been stressed by many Member States [the considerations of public interest] are such as to justify restrictions, as regards Article [49 (ex 59)] of the Treaty, which may go so far as to prohibit lotteries in a Member State.
>
> First of all, it is not possible to disregard the moral, religious or cultural aspects of lotteries, like other types of gambling, in all the Member States. The general tendency of the Member States is to restrict, or even prohibit, the practice of gambling and to

---

[149] Case C-145/88 [1989] E.C.R. I-3851.
[150] Case C-275/92 [1994] E.C.R. I-1039, paras 59 and 60 of the judgment. For subsequent cases on lotteries, see *Familiapress* (n.7 above); and Cases C-124/97 *Läärä* [1999] E.C.R. I-6067; and C-67/98 *Zenatti*, see n.60 above.

prevent it from being a source of private profit. Secondly, lotteries involve a high risk of crime or fraud, given the size of the amounts which can be staked and of the winnings which they can hold out to the players, particularly when they are operated on a large scale. Thirdly, they are an incitement to spend which may have damaging individual and social consequences. A final ground which is not without relevance, although it cannot in itself be regarded as an objective justification, is that lotteries may make a significant contribution to the financing of benevolent or public interest activities such as social works, charitable works, sport or culture."

It is not clear whether the reference to religious consideration is to be taken as a rejection of the view expressed by the Advocate General in *Torfaen*.

8.47 Public morality also arose in *R. v Minister of Agriculture, Fisheries and Food, Ex p. Compassion in World Farming Ltd.*[151] That case concerned judicial review proceedings brought by Compassion in World Farming against the refusal of the respondent Minister to prohibit or restrict, on the basis of Article 30, the export from the United Kingdom of calves for rearing in veal crates. The case was thus unusual in that it was private parties, rather than the Member State, who were arguing that Article 30 could be relied upon to restrict the free movement of goods. Both its Advocate General and the Court held that reliance on Article 30 in order to restrict the export of calves to other Member States for reasons relating to the protection of health of animals was precluded because those matters had been the subject of exhaustive harmonisation legislation at Community level.[152] However, no such legislation existed as regards public morality and the question therefore arose as to whether this ground of justification could be invoked.

Léger A.G. approached the question on the basis that Article 30 could not be relied on by Member States in order to ensure protection of an interest safeguarded in that Article outside its own national territory.[153] On this footing, export restrictions could only be justified if the acts or practices in question offended against public morality in the State of exportation (*in casu* the United Kingdom). In this regard, the Advocate General concluded that:

"... the fact that a Member State should consider that harm unjustifiably caused to the life or health of domestic animals, even for economic purposes, through the use of a particular rearing method is a matter of public morality in that State does not appear to be manifestly contrary to Article [30]".

The question of the proportionality of the measure should, according to the Advocate General, be left to the national court.

The Court, by contrast, did not deal with the question of whether Article 30 could be applied to safeguard interests on the territory of other Member States. It simply remarked that recourse to the public morality justification "by drawing attention to the views and reactions of a section of national public opinion

---

[151] Case C-1/96 [1998] E.C.R. I-1251.
[152] The Directive in question was Directive 91/629 laying down minimum standards for the protection of calves ([1991] O.J. L340/28).
[153] See para. 8.27 above.

which believes that the system put in place by the Directive does not adequately protect animal health" was, in reality, not to invoke public morality as a separate justification but rather to invoke an aspect of the justification relating to the protection of animal health which it had concluded was the subject of the harmonising Directive.

Public Policy

8.48 Public policy being of a more general nature than the other grounds of justification in Article 30, it presumably only comes into play when the other grounds are not in point. This can be deduced from *Campus Oil*[154] where the Court without giving reasons held that public security, and not public policy, was the applicable head of justification.[155]

With respect to the public policy exception to the free movement of workers the Court held in *Bouchereau*[156] that "recourse by a national authority to the concept of public policy presupposes ... the existence ... of a genuine and sufficiently serious threat to the requirements of public policy affecting one of the fundamental interests of society".[157]

An echo of that ruling is to be found in *R. v Thompson, Johnson and Woodiwiss*.[158] That case concerned a prohibition on the import and export of certain coins into and out of the United Kingdom. The Court found that only one of the three categories of coin in issue was to be regarded as goods under Community law: the British silver alloy half-crowns minted before 1947 which, although no longer legal tender, could be exchanged at the Bank of England and were protected from destruction by persons other than the State. In its fourth and final question the Court of Appeal asked, *inter alia*, whether the prohibition on the export of such coins was justified on the grounds of public policy under Article 30. In its submissions to the Court the United Kingdom Government put forward three reasons for the prohibition on the export of these coins:

(a) to ensure that there was no shortage of current coins for use by the public;

(b) to ensure that any profit resulting from any increase in the value of the silver content of the coins would accrue to the United Kingdom, since it had minted them;

(c) to prevent the destruction of United Kingdom coins occurring outside its

---

[154] See n.101 above; see ground 33 of the judgment and Slynn A. G. at p. 2764 (E.C.R.).
[155] Case note by Mortelmans [1984] C.M.L. Rev. 687 at 705.
[156] See n.119 above.
[157] "Public policy" does not necessarily have the same meaning under Art. 30: see para. 8.35 above. However, see Opinion of Léger A.G. in *Compassion in World Farming Ltd* at para. 108 where the same passage from *Bouchereau* was "transposed to the field of free movement of goods".
[158] Case 7/78 [1978] E.C.R. 2247; [1979] 1 C.M.L.R. 47.

jurisdiction, it being a criminal offence to destroy coins of the realm within the United Kingdom.

The Court was clearly swayed by these arguments, since it ruled:

"It is for the Member States to mint their own coinage and to protect it from destruction. A ban on exporting such coins with a view to preventing their being melted down or destroyed in another Member State is justified on grounds of public policy within the meaning of Article [30] of the Treaty, because it stems from the need to protect the right to mint coinage which is traditionally regarded as involving the fundamental interests of the State."

It would be erroneous to regard this as a retreat from the Court's earlier ruling to the effect that Article 30 does not justify measures of economic protection[159]: the judgment is in fact based on the assertion that the State enjoyed a right akin to a property right in the coins. The protection of a property right is a very different matter from the protection of the economy as a whole. In any case, the earlier ruling has since been reaffirmed on a number of occasions.[160]

8.49 Public policy (as well as public security) was relied on by France in *Cullet v Leclerc*.[161] It was claimed that the contested price controls on petroleum products were necessary to avert unrest on the part of retailers. This argument was rejected by VerLoren van Themaat A.G. in the following forthright terms:

"the acceptance of civil disturbances as justification for encroachments upon the free movement of goods would, as is apparent from experiences of the last year, ... have unacceptably drastic consequences. If road-blocks and other effective weapons of interest groups which feel threatened by the importation and sale at competitive prices of certain cheap products or services, or by immigrant workers or foreign businesses, were accepted as justification, the existence of the four fundamental freedoms of the Treaty could no longer be relied upon. Private interest groups would then, in the place of the Treaty and Community institutions, determine the scope of those freedoms. In such cases, the concept of public policy requires, rather, effective action on the part of the authorities to deal with such disturbances."

The Court refrained from ruling on the general issue raised, but remarked cryptically:

"the French Government has not shown that it would be unable, using the means at its disposal, to deal with the consequences which an amendment of the rules in question in accordance with the principles set out above would have upon public order and security."

8.50 The views of the Advocate General in *Cullet* were echoed by Léger A.G. in *Compassion in World Farming*[162] which related to the refusal of the United

---

[159] See para. 8.32 above.
[160] See para. 8.32 above; see also para. 8.34.
[161] Case 231/83 [1985] E.C.R. 305; [1985] 2 C.M.L.R. 524.
[162] See n.81 above.

Kingdom Government to prohibit or restrict, on the basis of Article 30, the export from the United Kingdom of calves for rearing in veal crates. The order for reference explained that the veal crate system had produced a strong public response in the United Kingdom. Léger A.G. rejected any justification based on public policy and remarked:

> "...it would seem to me to be dangerous for a Community principle—in this case, freedom of movement for goods—to be called in question on the ground that its application provokes a social reaction, if there are no other reasons for limiting its application."[163]

The Court has, however, maintained the approach that it adopted in *Cullet v Leclerc* in *Commission v France*[164] in which the Commission sought *inter alia* a declaration that, by failing to take all necessary and proportionate measures in order to prevent the free movement of fruit and vegetables from being obstructed by actions by private individuals, France had failed to fulfil its obligations under Article 28 in conjunction with Article 10 EC. The Court held that, while Member States "retain exclusive competence as regards the maintenance of public order and the safeguarding of internal security",[165] "[a]pprehension of internal difficulties cannot justify a failure by a Member State to apply Community law correctly".[166] The Court then stated:

> "It is for the Member State concerned, unless it can show that action on its part would have consequences for public order with which it could not cope by using the means at its disposal, to adopt all appropriate measures to guarantee the full scope and effect of Community law so as to ensure its proper implementation in the interest of all economic operators.
>   In the present case the French Government has adduced no concrete evidence proving the existence of a danger to public order with which it could not cope."[167]

As in *Cullet v Leclerc*, the Court thus appears to have left the door open to a plea of public policy in extreme cases, provided that the risk is clearly proven.

8.51 One might have expected the Court to have applied the public policy exception to matters such as the prevention of tax evasion and the maintenance of the diversity of the press.[168] This has not happened. Instead, the Court has chosen a more complicated path, since it has found these interests to constitute separate "mandatory requirements", and they will therefore be treated below under the appropriate headings.

---

[163] Para. 111 of the Opinion.
[164] C-265/95, see n.68 above, noted by Jarvis, [1998] C.M.L. Rev. 1371; Meier, [1998] EuZW 87; Muylle, [1998] E.L. Rev. 467; Schwarze, [1998] EuR 53.
[165] Para. 33 of the judgment. See also, to the same effect, C-394/97 *Sami Heinonen* [1999] E.C.R. I-3599 at para. 43.
[166] Para. 55 of the judgment.
[167] Paras 56 and 57 of the judgment.
[168] See as regards the diversity of the press Jacobs A.G., "Human rights in the European Union" (see n.132 above) at p. 336.

Public Security

8.52   This limb of Article 30 covers both internal security (*e.g.* crime detection and prevention and the regulation of traffic) and external security: *Aimé Richardt*.[169] When construing this head of justification, one must not overlook Articles 296 (ex 223) and 297 (ex 224), which are considered in Chapter IX.[170]

8.53   Public security was in issue in *Campus Oil*.[171] Slynn A.G. expressed the view that the maintenance of essential oil supplies fell within "public security," since it was vital to the stability and cohesion of the life of the modern State. "Public security" in Article 30 was not limited to external military security which largely fell to be dealt with under Articles 296 to 298; nor was it limited to the maintenance of law and order within the State, although it might include this.

The Advocate General pointed out that the Irish court had so far made only a few of the necessary findings of fact. Accordingly, he implied that the Court should confine itself to giving guidance to the Irish court as to the considerations to be taken into account in deciding whether the contested measure was in fact justified on public security grounds. He thereafter kept within the limits which he had set himself. In particular, he refrained from deciding whether any restrictions under Article 28 were justified to maintain in operation a refinery such as the one at Whitegate. He concluded that the Court should rule along the lines that:

> "such legislation will be justified under Article [30] on the grounds of public security, and thereby not precluded by Article [28], if it is necessary other than on economic grounds, to maintain essential services and supplies. It will not be necessary for this purpose where the requisite oil supplies can be ensured by other means which are less restrictive of imports, such as the keeping of stocks."

The Court held that the maintenance of essential oil supplies was covered by the public security exception, since not only a country's economy but "above all its institutions, its essential public services and the survival of its inhabitants" depended upon it.[172] However, the Court did not give any general indication as to the meaning of "public security" in Article 30 or its relationship with Articles 296 to 298.[173]

---

[169] Case C-367/89 [1991] E.C.R. I-4621, para. 8.55 below. That ruling was confirmed in C-423/98 *Albore* [2000] E.C.R. I-5965; casenote by Hatzopoulos [2001] C.M.L. Rev. 455.

[170] See also paras 9.31 *et seq.* above.

[171] See n.101 above.

[172] In the context of the freedom to provide services, the Court has accepted in principle, citing its judgment in *Campus Oil*, the possibility that the maintenance of an essential treatment facility or medical service on national territory could be justified under Article 46 (ex 56) for *inter alia* "the survival of the population": C-158/96, see n. 23 above at para. 51. On the facts, however, the Court concluded that the national rules in question, which restricted movement to receive medical services in other Member States, was not indispensible for the maintenance of an essential treatment facility or medical service on national territory.

[173] In the context of the free movement of capital, the Court has held that public security (in Art. 56 EC) may be relied on "if there is a genuine and sufficiently serious threat to a fundamental interest of society": C-483/99 *Commission v France* [2002] E.C.R. I-nyr (judgment of June 4, 2002) at para. 48.

Unlike the Advocate General, the Court appeared not to regard the absence of crucial findings of fact by the referring court as any form of constraint. It therefore proceeded to rule that it was justified on public security grounds for a Member State with no crude oil of its own to keep a refinery in operation, a point which the Advocate General had left open. The submission had been put forward by the claimants and the Commission that a refinery would be of no assistance in a crisis, since no crude oil would be available. That argument was dismissed. Instead, the Court was swayed by the argument that the fact of having refinery capacity in its territory enables the State concerned to enter into long-term contracts with the oil-producing countries for the supply of crude oil to its refinery which offer a better guarantee of supplies in the event of a crisis. The Court's ruling on this point virtually determined the outcome of the case.

Having regard to the principle of proportionality, the Court went on to hold that compulsory sales were only justified if the refinery's output could not be freely disposed of at competitive prices. Even then, the quantities of petroleum products covered by such a system must not exceed the minimum supply requirements without which the public security of the State concerned would be affected; nor must they exceed the level of production necessary to keep the refinery's production capacity available in the event of a crisis and to enable it to continue to refine at all times the crude oil covered by long-term contracts concluded by the State. These were matters for the national judge to determine.

As to the price, the Court held that, if compulsory sales were justified, this could be fixed by the competent minister on the basis of the costs incurred in the operation of the refinery. Arguably, this matter is purely economic. Never before had the Court held any form of price control to be justified under Article 30. Yet in *Campus Oil* the price was inextricably bound up with the compulsory purchasing requirement. This judgment, which might be regarded as a serious blow for the prospects of creating a common energy policy, did not go uncriticised.[174]

8.54 The principle laid down in *Campus Oil* that the aim of ensuring the minimum supply of petroleum products at all times could fall within the public security exception was confirmed in *Commission v Greece*.[175] The defendant relied on this exception in relation to a provision requiring companies to submit their annual procurement programmes for petroleum products for approval by the State which had the power to compel the companies to amend these programmes. (This provision must be seen as an exception to the State's virtual monopoly over the importation and distribution of these products.)

---

[174] Thus Gormley, *Prohibiting Restrictions on trade within the EEC* (1985) at 139, pointed to the excessively vague nature of the expression "essential public services" which the Court failed to define. Marenco, "La giurisprudenza communitaria sulle misure di effetto equivalente a una restrizione quantitativa (1984–1986)" [1988] Il Foro Italiano IV 166 questioned whether the maintenance of a refinery in Ireland was necessary to refine oil covered by long-term contracts; in his view, Ireland could ensure supplies equally well by having such oil refined in refineries not situated on Irish soil. Both authors expressed surprise at the Court giving its blessing under Art. 30 to such an apparently protectionist measure (Gormley at 139).
[175] Case C-347/88 [1990] E.C.R. I-4747.

The Court found expressly that the contested provision contributed towards ensuring that the country was supplied with these products at all times. The information contained in those programmes permitted the Greek authorities to establish the extent to which the country's minimum requirements for petroleum products could be covered by the operations of distribution companies in the event of a crisis; and to determine how to guarantee a permanent minimum supply.

However, Greece had failed to prove that the measure was essential to achieve these ends, particularly as the production capacity of its two public sector refineries exceeded the country's minimum needs in a period of crisis. Accordingly, the measure was not justified under Article 30.[176]

8.55   In *Aimé Richardt*,[177] the Court dealt with the issue of trade in strategically sensitive goods. The facts of that case occurred in 1985. The defendant had contracted to export a piece of computer technology known as a microetch from France to the Soviet Union. The consignment was to have been transported directly from Paris to Moscow but the flight was cancelled and the goods were dispatched by air to Luxembourg, where they were to be loaded onto another plane bound for Moscow. However, they were seized by the Luxembourg authorities pursuant to measures taken by Cocom (Co-ordinating Committee for Multilateral Export Controls). This body, which was not an international organisation and whose existence was not based on any formal treaty, controlled exports of strategically sensitive goods to certain third countries. Its members included the United States and all the Member States of the Community except Ireland, which in practice abided by its decisions. The Luxembourg court hearing criminal charges against M. Richardt asked whether the refusal to authorise transit without a special export licence was compatible with Council Regulation 222/77 on Community transit.[178]

The Court turned at once to Article 30, which was incorporated by reference into that Regulation.[179] After recalling its judgment in *Campus Oil* and the principle of proportionality, it found that the concept of public security covered both internal and external threats to the State. Thus the import, export and transit of goods which could be used for strategic purposes may affect public security in this sense. Accordingly, Member States could subject the transit of such goods to special authorisation.

---

[176] See also C-398/98 *Commission v Greece*, n.111 above, concerning legislation which offered to companies that marketed petroleum products in Greece the possibility of transferring their obligation to store petroleum to refineries on condition that if they obtained a significant part of their supplies from refineries established in Greece. This measure was held not to be justified for the protection of public security because the same objectives could have been achieved by less restrictive means.

[177] See n.169 above.

[178] [1977] O.J. L38/1.

[179] Jacobs A.G. considered that Reg. 222/77 was not in point at all, since it only related to movements of goods between two points in the Community, whereas this case concerned exports from the Community to a third country. Although his approach appears to be the better view, this issue need not detain us here.

8.56 The Court's conclusions in *Aimé Richardt* have been applied in the context of foreign and security policy considerations and Regulation 2603/69[180] establishing common rules for exports to non-Member States in particular. Article 11 of that Regulation provides for exceptions to such exports for reasons, *inter alia*, of public security. In *Leifer*[181] and *Werner v Germany*,[182] which concerned German legislation requiring a special licence for the export of dual-use goods, the Court drew an explicit parallel between that provision and Article 30 EC and held that:

> "... the risk of a serious disturbance to foreign relations or to peaceful coexistence of nations may affect the security of a Member State.

Although it is for the national court to decide whether Article 11 of the Regulation, as interpreted by the Court of Justice, applies to the facts and measures which it is called on to appraise, it should, however, be observed that it is common ground that the exportation of goods capable of being used for military purposes to a country at war with another country may affect the public security of a Member State within the meaning referred to above."[183]

In *Aimé Richardt*, the Court did not consider whether the restriction in that case met the proportionality test, an omission which attracted criticism.[184] However, in *Leifer*, the Court was forced to grapple in some detail with the proportionality test. This is because the national court had asked whether a Member State could impose on applicants for an export licence the burden of proving that dual-use goods are for civil use, to refuse a licence if the goods are objectively suitable for military use and to impose criminal penalties for breaches of the licensing procedure. The Court replied that it was for the national court to determine, in accordance with the principle of proportionality, whether or not the above requirements could be justified but added:

> "However, depending on the circumstances, the competent national authorities have a certain degree of discretion when adopting measures which they consider to be necessary in order to guarantee public security in a Member State. .. When the export of dual-use goods involves a threat to the public security of a Member State, those measures may include a requirement that an applicant for an export licence show that the goods are for civil use and also, having regard to specific circumstances such as *inter alia* the political situation in the country of destination, that a licence be refused if those goods are objectively suitable for military use."

Finally, with respect to the criminal penalties, the Court held that Community

---

[180] [1969] O.J. English Sp. Ed. (II), p. 590 as last amended by Reg. 3918/91 [1991] O.J. L372/31.
[181] C-83/94 [1995] E.C.R. I-3231.
[182] See n.87 above.
[183] Paras 27 and 28 of the judgment in *Werner* and paras 28 and 29 of the judgment in *Leifer*. See also C-124/95 *R. v HM Treasury and Bank of England Ex p. Centro-Com Srl* [1997] E.C.R. I-81 at para. 44.
[184] Govaere and Eeckhout, "On dual use goods and dualist case law: the Aimé Richardt judgment on export controls" [1992] C.M.L. Rev. 941; the Court did consider proportionality in relation to the sanction imposed, but that is a different matter.

law does not preclude national rules from making the failure to comply with the licensing procedure a matter subject to penalties, provided that the penalties laid down are not disproportionate to the public security aim pursued.[185]

8.57 Another highly important case on the public security exception is *Albore*.[186] Although that case concerned the free movement of capital, the judgment appears equally applicable to the other freedoms, as confirmed by the Court's reliance on its earlier ruling in *Aimé Richardt*.[187] The case related to discriminatory national legislation on the obligation to seek an administrative authorisation for any purchase of real property in an area of the country designated as being of military importance. The Court held that such legislation could only be justified and proportionate if it were demonstrated that non-discriminatory treatment of the nationals of all the Member States would expose the military interest of the Member State concerned to "real, specific and serious risks which could not be countered by less restrictive procedures".[188]

8.58 Certain restrictions on the movements of firearms are laid down by Council Directive 91/477 on control of the acquisition and possession of weapons when moving between Member States.[189]

A Community regime for the control of exports of "dual-use items and technology" is now provided for in Council Regulation 1334/2000.[190] Like its predecessor,[191] this Regulation is based on Article 133 (ex 113) EC and was designed to cover problems of the kind which arose in *Aimé Richardt*. It provides for a regime for the export from the Community of "dual-use items" which are defined as "items, including software and technology, which can be used for both civil and military purposes, and shall include all goods which can be used for both non-explosive uses and assisting in any way in the manufacture of nuclear weapons or other nuclear explosive devices".[192] Nevertheless, the preamble to the Regulation makes express reference to Article 30 of the Treaty and to the right retained by Member States, pending a greater degree of har-

---

[185] For a further application of the proportionality principle in the context of public security exception in Article 11 of Regulation 2603/69, see *Ex p. Centro-Com*, see n.183 above at paras 51 and 52.

[186] See n.169 above.

[187] Indeed, this ruling has even been hailed as a supreme example of the convergence of the four freedoms in the Court's case law: Hatzopoulos (see n.169 above).

[188] Para. 22 of the judgment.

[189] [1991] O.J. L256/51 with correction at [1993] O.J. L54/22; see Collet "Le développement des actions communautaires dans le domaine des matériels de guerre, des armes et des munitions" [1990] R.T.D.E. 75; "L'Europe des armes, une double démarche" [1992] R.T.D.E. 105.

[190] [2000] O.J. L159/1, as amended. See Karpenstein, "Die neue Dual-use-Verordnung" [2000] EuZW 677.

[191] Council Reg. 3381/94 [1994] O.J. L 367/1 as amended by Council Reg. 837/95 ([1995] O.J. L90/1) and Council Decision 94/942 [1994] O.J. L 367/8; see Jestaedt and von Behr, "Die EG-Verordnung zur Harmonisierung der Exportkontrollen von zivil und militärisch verwendbaren Gütern" [1995] EuZW 137.

[192] Regulation 1334/2000 is broader in scope than its predecessor which simply applied to "goods which can be used for both civil and military purposes". In particular Reg. 1334/2000 also controls the transmission of software and technology by means of electronic media, fax or telephone to destinations outside the Community.

monisation, to carry out controls on transfers of dual-use items within the Community in order to safeguard public policy or public security.

The Protection of Human Health and Life

(a) General principles

(i) The importance of this ground; the precautionary principle

8.59 It seems scarcely necessary to repeat here the Court's ruling in *De Peijper*[193] that "national rules or practices do not fall within the exception specified in Article 30 if the health and life of humans can [be] as effectively protected by measures which do not restrict intra-Community trade so much." This is the rule of proportionality which applies to Article 30 generally[194] and indeed to all exceptions to the principle of the free movement of goods.[195] It follows that a Member State:

> "is not entitled to prevent the marketing of a product originating in another Member State which provides a level of protection of the health and life of humans equivalent to that which the national rules are intended to ensure or establish. It is therefore contrary to the principle of proportionality for national rules to require such imported products to comply strictly and exactly with the provisions or technical requirements laid down for products manufactured in the Member State in question when those imported products afford users the same level of protection."[196]

In line with this, the Court has held that the importing Member State must take account of tests or controls carried out in the exporting Member State providing equivalent guarantees and evidenced by certificates. The importing Member State may not systematically duplicate those controls, but may carry out spot checks as well as tests designed to detect damage or disease which might have occurred after the inspection in the exporting State.[197]

8.60 At the same time, the Court also ruled in *De Peijper* that the "health and the life of humans rank first among the property or interests protected by Article 30 and it is for the Member States, within the limits imposed by the Treaty, to decide what degree of protection they intend to assure, and in particular how strict the checks to be carried out are to be".[198] The Court has

---

[193] See n.38 above.
[194] See para. 8.18 above.
[195] See para. 9.01 below.
[196] See also Case 188/84 *Commission v France (woodworking machines)* [1986] E.C.R. 419; see generally paras 6.70 *et seq.* above.
[197] These principles were formulated in more qualified terms in the past: *e.g.* Case 132/80 *United Foods v Belgian State* [1981] E.C.R. 995; [1982] 1 C.M.L.R. 273; 124/81 *Commission v United Kingdom (UHT milk)* [1983] E.C.R. 203; [1983] 2 C.M.L.R. 1. More recently, however, it has become clear that these principles apply in every case: see, *e.g.* Case 228/91 *Commission v Italy (fish)* [1993] E.C.R. I-2701; and C-105/94 *Celestini v Saar-Sektkellerei Faber* [1997] E.C.R. I-2971 at paras 34 to 36.
[198] See also to similar effect Cases C-293/94 *Brandsma* [1996] E.C.R. I-3159 at para. 11; C-400/96 *Harpegnies* [1998] E.C.R. I-5121 at para. 33 and *Toolex* (see n.97 above) at para. 38.

consistently shown great caution in applying this exception, upholding the right of Member States to take steps to guard against a risk of this kind, however slight and uncertain, so long as that risk is genuine. This is illustrated by a number of judgments discussed below.[199]

8.61   The Court's traditionally cautious approach to matters of public health has been confirmed in recent years by its endorsement of the precautionary principle. This principle, which is now widely accepted internationally, should not be thought of as a wholly new departure in the case law.[200] On the contrary, it is firmly rooted in a number of judgments going back to the very beginning of the case law on the public health exception in Article 30.

The only explicit reference in the EC Treaty to the precautionary principle is to be found in the provisions relating to the Community policy on the environment and dates from the Treaty of Maastricht: Article 174(2) (ex 130R(2)) lists this principle amongst those which are to constitute the basis of that policy.

This principle also applies in the field of public health. So much is apparent from the Court's judgment on the validity of the Commission's decision banning the exportation of beef from the United Kingdom to reduce the risk of BSE transmission. In *United Kingdom v Commission*, the Court held:

"Where there is uncertainty as to the *existence or extent* of risks to human health, the institutions may take protective measures without having to wait until the reality and seriousness of those risks become fully apparent.

That approach is borne out by Article [174(1)] of the EC Treaty, according to which the Community policy on the environment is to pursue the objective *inter alia* of protecting human health. Article [174(2)] provides that that policy is to aim at a high level of protection and is to be based in particular on the principles that preventive action should be taken and that environmental protection requirements must be integrated into the definition and implementation of other Community policies".[201] (*emphasis added*)

---

[199] e.g. Cases 53/80 *Officier van Justitie v Koninklijke Kaasfabriek Eyssen* [1981] E.C.R. 409; [1982] C.M.L.R. 20, para. 8.76 below; 272/80 *Frans-Nederlandse Maatschappij voor Biologische Producten* [1981] E.C.R. 3277; [1982] 2 C.M.L.R. 497, para. 8.80 below; 94/83 *Heijn* [1984] E.C.R. 3263; and 97/83 *Melkunie* [1984] E.C.R. 2367; [1986] 2 C.M.L.R. 318, paras 8.81 and 8.83 below.

[200] This is stressed by Gonzaléz Vaqué, Ehring and Jacquet, "Le principe de précaution dans la législation communautaire et nationale relative à la protection de la santé" [1999] R.M.U.E. 1/79. For a wide-ranging review of this principle in Community and international law, see Alemano, "Le principe de précaution en droit communautaire" [2001] R.D.U.E. 917; Christoforou, "The Origins, Content and Role of the Precautionary Principle in European Community Law" in *Le principe de précaution: Aspects de droit international et communautaire* (2002); and De Sadeleer, "Le statut juridique du principe de précaution en droit communautaire : du slogan à la règle" [2001] C.D.E. 91.

[201] Case C-180/96 [1998] E.C.R. I-2265, paras 99 and 100 of the judgment. See also C-157/96 *R. v Minister for Agriculture, Fisheries and Food Ex p. NFU* [1998] E.C.R. I-2211 at para. 63; T-199/96 *Laboratoires pharmaceutiques Bergaderm v Commission* [1998] E.C.R. II-2805 at para. 66. On the precautionary principle generally, see Orders of the President of the CFI in Cases T-13/99R *Pfizer v Commission* [1999] E.C.R. II-1961; T-70/99R *Alpharma v Commission* [1999] E.C.R. II-2027; Case C-6/99 *Greenpeace France v Commission* (genetically modified organisms) [2000] E.C.R. I-1651 (see also paras 69 *et seq.* of Mischo A.G.'s Opinion in that case) and Cases T-13/99 *Pfizer Animal Health v Council*; and T-70/99 *Alpharma v Council* (judgment of September 11, 2002).

As this passage clearly shows, the precautionary principle allows action to be taken not only where the extent of the risk is uncertain, but also where its very existence is uncertain—provided, of course, that there is a sound scientific basis for believing that the risk might exist.

8.62 An especially striking pronouncement in this context is that of the President of the Court of First Instance in his interim Order in *National Farmers' Union v Commission*,[202] another case concerning the ban on exporting beef from the United Kingdom during the BSE crisis where he stated:

> "...the protection of public health ... is based on requirements of a higher order which have to do with the protection of human rights and which underpin the entire legal system of the Community ... When implementing the principle of the free movement of goods, the Community institutions must therefore take into account the requirements related in particular to the protection of the health and life of humans, which may entail, it necessary, the adoption of appropriate measures to ensure proper protection of public health."

That the right to life is a fundamental right—indeed the most fundamental of all—is scarcely new.[203] Surely it is entirely logical to extend this rule so as to treat public health protection as also being a matter of fundamental rights, even though the individual can scarcely enjoy an enforceable right to have a particular product prohibited on public health grounds. The apparent paradox that the public health exception is more important than the free movement of goods is resolved by the principle of proportionality.[204]

8.63 This case law is reflected in the new wording of Article 152(1) (ex 129(1)) EC as amended by the Treaty of Amsterdam, which provides for common action in the field of public health. The first subparagraph of that provision now reads: "A high level of health protection shall be ensured in the definition and implementation of *all* Community policies and activities." (emphasis added)[205]

8.64 According to the Commission's Communication on the precautionary principle,[206] this principle applies in the fields of environmental protection and human, animal and plant health. It covers "those specific circumstances where scientific evidence is insufficient, inconclusive or uncertain and there are

---

[202] Case T-76/96R [1996] E.C.R. II-815, para. 75.

[203] See Art. 3 of the 1948 Universal Declaration of Human Rights, Art. 6 of the 1966 International Covenant on Civil and Political Rights, Art. 2 of the 1950 European Convention on Human Rights and, more recently, Art. 2 of the Charter of Fundamental Rights of the European Union (see n.135 above).

[204] As to whether the free movement of goods can be characterised as a fundamental right, see para. 1.13 above. As to conflicting priorities, see generally Weiler, *The Constitution of Europe* (1999) Ch. 2 "Fundamental Rights and Fundamental Boundaries: on the Conflict of Standards and Values in the Protection of Human Rights in the European Legal Space".

[205] Emphasis added. See para. 12.63 below.

[206] COM (2000) 1.

indications through preliminary objective scientific evaluation that there are reasonable grounds for concern that the potentially dangerous effects on the environment, human, animal or plant health may be inconsistent with the chosen level of protection".

The Communication also states that measures taken pursuant to this principle should be applied according to the general principles of proportionality and non-discrimination, be consistent with "the measures already adopted in similar circumstances or using similar approaches", and be based on an examination of the benefits and costs of action or lack of action and examination of scientific developments. In addition, the Communication stresses that such measures are provisional in nature, and may only be maintained "as long as the scientific data remain incomplete, imprecise or inconclusive and as long as the risk is considered too high to be imposed on society"; thus scientific research must be continued "with a view to obtaining more complete data". The Communication also sets out the approach to be followed in risk assessment.

Finally, the approach of the Community institutions to this principle is encapsulated in Article 7 of Regulation 178/2002 of the European Parliament and the Council laying down the general principles and requirements of food law, establishing the European Food Authority and laying down procedures in matters of food safety.[207] That provision, entitled "Precautionary principle", is drafted in the following terms:

> "1. In specific circumstances where, following an assessment of available information, the possibility of harmful effects on health is identified but scientific uncertainty persists, provisional risk management measures necessary to ensure the high level of health protection chosen in the Community may be adopted, pending further scientific information for a more comprehensive risk assessment.
>
> 2. Measures adopted on the basis of paragraph 1 shall be proportionate and no more restrictive of trade than is required to achieve the high level of health protection chosen in the Community, regard being had to technical and economic feasibility and other factors regarded as legitimate in the matter under consideration. The measures shall be reviewed within a reasonable period of time, depending on the nature of the risk to life or health identified and the type of scientific information needed to clarify the scientific uncertainty and to conduct a more comprehensive risk assessment."

(ii) The burden of proof; evidence

8.65   As we noticed in paragraph 8.11 above, the burden of proving that a restriction is justified on public health grounds is borne by the party making that claim. However, once that party makes out a convincing case on the justification, then the burden shifts once again to the other party. Indeed, as explained in paragraph 8.77 below, the Court has gone so far as to uphold, albeit subject to conditions, the system of "positive lists" for additives whereby those substances are presumed to be harmful until the contrary is proved; but such a scheme can only be lawful with respect to "substances deemed 'a priori' hazardous".[208]

---

[207] [2002] O.J. L31/1.
[208] Point 6.4 of the Commission's Communication on the precautionary principle.

8.66 Any attempt to give a full account of the Court's handling of evidence of public health risks would be impossible within the present confines. Plainly, this is a highly delicate task, since the Court is composed of lawyers, not scientists; and while human lives may be at stake, there is also a real danger of protectionist measures being adopted under the cloak of public health.

Nevertheless, it should be pointed out that, in evaluating these matters, the Court has consistently paid particular attention to recommendations and studies emanating from other international organisations such as the World Health Organisation and the Food and Agricultural Organisation.[209] The Court will also have regard to the practices of other Member States and comparable third countries. Having said that, as mentioned in paragraph 8.21 above, each State is entitled to decide on the level of protection which it wishes to ensure, so that it is by no means decisive that States other than that involved in the legal proceedings concerned impose less stringent requirements.[210]

What is more, as explained in paragraph 8.22 above, evidence of protectionist intent may be relied on as an indication that the contested measure is not justified.

(iii) Public health and the "mandatory requirements"

8.67 It will be recalled that in "*Cassis de Dijon*"[211] the Court held that public health constituted a "mandatory requirement", even though it is expressly listed amongst the grounds of justification in Article 30. In *Aragonesa de Publicidad*[212] the Court held that public health is to be considered under Article 30 alone. In any case, as van Gerven A.G. remarked, this question has "little if any practical import", since the conditions governing the "mandatory requirements" are the same as for the grounds of justification set out in Article 30.[213] Indeed, as we noticed in paragraphs 8.03 to 8.10 above, the better view is that the "mandatory requirements" are subsumed within Article 30 altogether.

(b) Specific restrictions

8.68 At this juncture it is appropriate to break down the case law into categories according to the nature of the measures concerned. However, these categories are by no means watertight and indeed the judgments contain many express references to cases considered in other categories.

When considering public health, it should be borne in mind that there is a

---

[209] See, *e.g. Commission v Germany* (beer) n.30 above at paras 44 and 52; Cases C-13 and 113/91 *Debus* [1992] E.C.R. I-3617; *Toolex* (n.97 above) at para. 43. The same applies with regard to other grounds of justification: Case 298/87 *Smanor* [1988] E.C.R. 4489, para. 8.146 below.

[210] Conversely, simply because other Member States impose similar restrictions will not necessarily mean that a restriction is justified: C-265/95, see n.68 above at para. 63 and C-217/99 *Commission v Belgium* [2000] E.C.R. I-10251 at paras 19–20.

[211] See n.5 above.

[212] See n.9 above

[213] at 4177.

large body of relevant Community legislation; where it provides exhaustive guarantees, such legislation ousts Article 30 in accordance with the rule discussed earlier in the Chapter.[214]

(i) Re-treatment in the importing Member State

8.69   *Commission v United Kingdom*[215] was concerned, *inter alia*, with the requirement that imported ultra-heat treated milk undergo the heat treatment process a second time in the United Kingdom. This was tantamount to a total ban on imports, since it rendered them economically prohibitive. Although there were disparities between the laws of the Member States regarding such heat treatment, the Court found that in fact these disparities were limited. Moreover, the Court referred to other technical factors which ensured that UHT milk produced in the various Member States was of similar quality as regards health. Accordingly, it sufficed to require imported UHT milk to meet such conditions as were absolutely necessary and this could be evidenced by certificates issued by the exporting Member State. While this case turned in part on the technical data concerned, it is hard to imagine such a re-treatment requirement ever being justified.

(ii) Import licences

8.70   In *Commission v Belgium*,[216] which concerned an import licensing system for live animals, the Court held:

> "a system requiring prior import authorisations constitutes a measure which is disproportionate in relation to the objective of protecting the health and life of humans and animals. It is clear from the Court's judgment in Case 124/81 *Commission v United Kingdom*, cited above, that a Member State may adopt measures less restrictive than a system of prior import authorisations in order to protect those interests, by confining itself to obtaining the information which is of use to it, for example, by means of declarations signed by the importers, accompanied if necessary by the appropriate certificates issued by the exporting Member State."

The Court therefore ruled that the measure was not justified under Article 30.[217] It is not easy to imagine cases in which imposition of import licences may be justified: a system of import declarations or certificates will always, or nearly always, suffice.

(iii) Import controls and inspections

8.71   In the absence of a reasonable suspicion in relation to a specific consignment, an importing Member State may not duplicate checks relating to a

---

[214] See para. 8.28 above.
[215] Case 124/81, see n.197 above.
[216] Case C-304/88 [1990] E.C.R. I-2901 at 2816.
[217] See also C-77/97 *Österreichische Unilever v Smithkline Beecham Markenartikel* [1999] E.C.R. I-431.

particular disease or harmful substance carried out by the exporting Member State and evidenced by the appropriate certificates, except by way of spot or random checks.[218]

This rule is subject to the condition that the controls carried out in the exporting State present equivalent guarantees, but in the light of the case law discussed here it would seem that the Court would only regard that condition as not met in an extreme case where the control in the exporting State was manifestly inadequate. In addition, the importing State is entitled to check that the goods have not become damaged or diseased since the inspections were effected in the exporting Member State.[219]

8.72 What if the goods are not accompanied by health certificates? It follows from *Commission v Italy (fish)*[220] that in these circumstances systematic controls are justified to deter any disease or disorder presenting a genuine risk to public health.

8.73 On a related point, in *Commission v France*[221] the Court held that, in the absence of reasonable suspicion of fraud or irregularity, the importing Member State was not justified in detaining consignments of wine until the analysis was complete. The reasons given by the Court for this ruling were that it was not always the practice of the French authorities to detain French wine during the analysis of a sample; and that the Community provisions on wine enabled a consignment to be located once the results of the analysis were known.

8.74 Finally, even when import inspections are justified, it is not clear to what extent a Member State may limit the number of entry points where such inspections may be conducted—or whether it may do so at all. This issue is discussed in relation to animal and plant health at paragraph 8.113 below.

(iv) Certificates

8.75 It will be apparent from the preceding paragraphs that the requirement that imports be covered by health certificates issued in the exporting Member State will be justified—provided that the importing Member State is entitled to prescribe the health standards to which the certificates relate. In *Commission v Greece*[222] the requirement of such certificates for imports of pasteurised butter was held to be unlawful, since it was not warranted on any scientific basis.

---

[218] Para. 8.59 above.
[219] *ibid.*
[220] See n.197 above.
[221] Case 42/82, see n.50 above.
[222] C-205/89 [1991] E.C.R. I-1361.

(v) Additives and vitamins

8.76   The first case on additives was *Officier van Justitie v Koninklijke Kaasfabriek Eyssen.*[223] The case arose out of a prosecution before the Dutch courts of a Dutch company manufacturing processed cheese both for the home market and for export. The defendant was charged with having in stock with a view to sale quantities of cheese containing a preservative known as nisin. Dutch regulations forbade the use of nisin in processed cheese sold on the home market, although they laid down an exemption with respect to exports. Reliable studies showed that nisin was not necessarily harmful in itself, but only became so when consumed in excessive quantities. However, it had not yet been established what the acceptable daily intake was. In view of this, a number of Member States permitted the use of nisin up to certain specified limits, and the United Kingdom and France even permitted its use without limit. Nevertheless, the Court held that the ban imposed by the Dutch authorities was justified on public health grounds. In reaching this conclusion the Court cited the fact that the acceptable daily intake had not yet been established, that such intake depended not only on one particular product but on the entire dietary habits of an individual, and that such habits varied from one Member State to another. Given such varying dietary habits, the specific exemption with respect to exports did not render the measure in issue arbitrarily discriminatory.[224]

8.77   In a series of subsequent cases culminating in *Commission v Germany (beer),*[225] the Commission has built on this ruling, while at the same time addressing itself to the problem of positive lists. That case concerned a blanket prohibition imposed by Germany on all additives in beer, including those approved for use in beer by other Member States. The Court reaffirmed that, insofar as scientific opinion is uncertain and in the absence of harmonisation, it is for the Member States to decide what degree of health protection they intend to achieve.[226]

For the first time, the Court was required to consider the legality of the system of "positive lists" is justified under Article 30. This is the system applied throughout the Western world, whereby additives are presumed to be harmful until the contrary is proved; unless an additive figures on the list of permitted additives established by legislation, its use is prohibited. At first sight, the system of positive lists runs counter to the rebuttable presumption that a restriction is

---

[223] Case 53/80 see n.199 above.

[224] Meier has nevertheless suggested ([1983] R.I.W. 864) that the existence of such an exemption for exports is evidence that such a restriction is not justified.

[225] n.30 above noted by Rabe [1987] EuR 253; see also Cases 174/82 *Sandoz,* see n.109 above; 227/82 *Van Bennekom* [1983] E.C.R. 3883; 247/84 *Motte* [1985] E.C.R. 3887; 304/84 *Muller* [1986] E.C.R. 1511; 176/84 *Commission v Greece (beer)* [1987] E.C.R. 1193; [1988] 1 C.M.L.R. 813; C-42/90 *Bellon* [1990] E.C.R. I-4863; C-95/89 *Commission v Italy (nitrate in cheese)* [1992] E.C.R. I-4545; C-293/89 *Commission v Greece (nitrate in cheese)* [1992] E.C.R. I-4577; and C-344/90 *Commission v France (nitrate in cheese)* [1992] E.C.R. I-4719.

[226] Nowadays, it would be appropriate to add that this should also be subject to a judicious application of the precautionary principle: see paras 8.61–8.64 above.

not justified under Article 30.[227]

The Member States are entitled to make the sale of foodstuffs containing additives subject to an authorisation procedure for each additive, it being understood that authorisations are granted *erga omnes* for use in particular foodstuffs or in all foodstuffs or for other specific uses. However, where goods containing an additive approved in another Member State are exported from that State, the importing Member State is bound to do the following:

(a) It must authorise the use of that additive, if (i) international scientific data (particularly those compiled by scientific committees operating under the auspices of the Community and the FAO) show it to be harmless to individuals with the dietary habits of its population and (ii) if it meets a genuine technical or other need[228];

(b) It must make readily available to companies an administrative procedure for seeking a general authorisation for the use of particular additives, which procedure can be concluded within a reasonable time.[229] (As to this procedure, it may be assumed that, although the Court did not repeat it, the following statement in *Sandoz*[230] is still good law: "although the national authorities may, insofar as they do not have it themselves, ask the importer to produce the information in his possession relating to the composition of the product and the technical or nutritional reasons for adding vitamins they must themselves assess, in the light of all the relevant information, whether authorisation must be granted pursuant to Community law." It follows from this passage that the Member State is under a positive duty to take active steps to establish whether the additive is harmful.);

(c) It must ensure that an action may be brought before the courts with respect to a refusal to grant an authorisation.[231] The Court stressed that

---

[227] See paras 8.11 and 8.65 above.

[228] In *Sandoz*, which concerned added vitamins, the Court held that a nutritional need would also suffice, while in *Motte* and *Muller* it implied that an economic need would suffice. The judgment in *Motte* also suggests that, as regards flavouring or colouring matters, an organoleptic or psychological need will qualify.

[229] In C-24/00 *Commission v France* [2002] E.C.R. I-nyr, Mischo A.G. was of the opinion that an administrative procedure that is alleged to exist in practice (but which is not formally written down) did not satisfy this requirement. The case is pending before the Court.

[230] See n.109 above, see also *Frans-Nederlandse Maatschappij voor Biologische Producten*, n.199 above and para. 8.80 below.

[231] It is not clear how this differs from the general duty on Member States to make judicial remedies available for the enforcement of directly applicable Community rights: see *e.g.* Cases 33/76 *Rewe-Zentralfinanz v Landwirtschaftskammer für das Saarland* [1976] E.C.R. 1989; [1977] 1 C.M.L.R. 533; 45/76 *Comet v Produktschap voor Siergewassen* [1976] E.C.R. 2043; [1977] 1 C.M.L.R. 533; 222/84 *Johnston v R.U.C.* [1986] E.C.R. 1651; and 222/86 *Heylens v Union nationale des entraîneurs* [1987] E.C.R. 4097; Biondi, "The European Court of Justice and Certain National Procedural Limitations: not Such a Tough Relationship" [1999] C.M.L. Rev. 1271; De Schutter, "Fonctions de juger et droits fondamentaux: transformation du contrôle juridictionnel dans les ordres juridiques américain et européen" (1999) (especially Ch. III.2); Harlow, "Access to Justice as a Human Right: the European Convention and the European Union" in Alston (ed.) *The EU and Human Rights* (19990; Picod, "Le droit au juge en droit communautaire" in Rideau, (ed.) *Le droit*

in such proceedings the Member State bears the burden of showing that the restriction is indeed justified under Article 30 on public health grounds.

8.78 In *Commission v Germany (beer)*, the Court went on to rule that Germany had not satisfied these conditions and that the contested legislation was thus not justified. It had simply imposed a blanket prohibition on the use of all the additives in beer authorised in other Member States, without regard to the dietary habits of its population. What is more, it had not provided for any procedure whereby companies could obtain approval for particular additives. The fact that some of the additives concerned were permitted in Germany for all or nearly all other drinks was also evidence that the ban was not justified.

The Court also rejected the defendant's interpretation of the concept of technical need. Germany had argued that there was no technical need for the additives concerned since German beer was manufactured without them. Instead, the Court held that the question whether a technical need for a particular additive existed had to be determined in the light of the following factors: the raw materials actually used; the views of the authorities of the Member State where the product was legally produced and marketed; and the results of international scientific research. The Court thus dismissed Germany's suggestion that there was no technical need for an additive just because alternative ingredients were available.

8.79 The ruling in the "beer" case contrasts with that in *Motte*[232] which concerned certain colouring agents used in potted lumpfish roe imported into Belgium. Those colourants were authorised for the same use in lumpfish roe in Germany, from where the product had been exported, and they were authorised in Belgium as ingredients in other foodstuffs. However, the Belgian authorities had not authorised their use in lumpfish roe. An administrative procedure existed whereby traders could seek official approval for the use of the additives concerned in the product, but no such application had ever been made. In these circumstances, the Court held that the contested restriction was justified, rejecting the Commission's arguments to the contrary.

(vi) Prohibited pesticides

8.80 *Frans-Nederlandse Maatschappij voor Biologische Producten*[233] concerned a fungicide used for disinfecting sugar vats. This product had not been approved

au juge dans l'Union européenne (1998); Prechal, "Community Law in National Courts: the Lessons from *van Schijndel*" [1998] C.M.L. Rev. 681; Rideau, "Le rôle de l'Union européenne en matière de protection des droits de l'homme" (1997) p. 139; Schockweiler, "L'accès à la justice dans l'ordre juridique communautaire" [1996] J.T.D.E. 1; Struys, "Le droit communautaire et l'application des règles procédurales nationales" [2000] J.T.D.E. 49; Van Gerven, "Of Rights, Remedies and Procedures" [2000] C.M.L. Rev 501.
[232] See n.225 above.
[233] See n.199 above. See also, with respect to biocidal products, C-293/94 *Brandsma*, see n.198 above; and C-400/96 *Harpegnies*, see n.198 above.

in the Netherlands, but it had been imported from France where it had been approved after scientific tests similar to those which the Dutch authorities would have carried out. As to the lawfulness of an importing Member State prohibiting sales of a product in such circumstances, the Court ruled as follows:

"It follows from Article [28] in conjunction with Article [30] of the Treaty that a Member State is not prohibited from requiring plant protection products to be subject to prior approval, even if those products have already been approved in another Member State. The authorities of the importing State are however not entitled unnecessarily to require technical or chemical analyses or laboratory tests when the same analyses or tests have already been carried out in another Member State and the results are available to those authorities or may at their request be placed at their disposal."

The crucial question is clearly what is meant by "unnecessarily".

8.81 Thereafter, in *Heijn*[234] the Court was asked to rule on the lawfulness of a national measure prescribing a maximum permitted level of residue of a particular pesticide on apples. The Court held that Member States must take account of the fact the pesticides are substances which are both necessary to agriculture and dangerous to health. They could regulate the presence of residues of pesticides in foodstuffs in a way which could vary from one country to another according to the climate, the normal diet of the population and its state of health. The Court did, however, enter the proviso that the authorities of the importing Member State were "obliged to review the prescribed maximum level if it appears to them that the reasons which led to its being fixed have changed, for example, as a result of the discovery of a new use for such and such a pesticide".

This ruling was confirmed in *Mirepoix*,[235] although the Court did add that a review would also be necessary in the event of further information becoming available through scientific research. This case concerned a total ban on the treatment of onions with a particular pesticide, whereas *Heijn* had merely concerned a permitted maximum level of residues. The Commission therefore invited the Court to distinguish *Heijn* on these grounds, but the Court declined.

8.82 Plainly, according to these judgments the Member States enjoy greater freedom to prohibit or restrict the use of particular pesticides than they do in relation to additives and vitamins according to the judgments relating to those products. Yet it seems reasonable to suppose that *Heijn* and *Mirepoix* have been superseded, at least in part, by the latter body of case law and in particular the "beer" case. For instance, there appears to be no reason why Member States should not be required to make available an administrative procedure for the authorisation of particular pesticides. In any case, whether or not *Heijn* and

[234] See n.199 above.
[235] Case 54/85 [1986] E.C.R. 1067; [1987] 2 C.M.L.R. 44.

Mirepoix are still good law, an effective judicial remedy must always be available to contest a Member State's refusal to approve a particular product.[236]

(vii) Maximum levels of bacteria

8.83   *Melkunie*[237] related to a national measure fixing the maximum permissible level of active non-pathogenic micro-organisms in milk. As one would expect, the Court held that it was justified on health grounds for Member States to impose restrictions of this kind. More significant is its ruling that Member States may fix the maximum level sufficiently low to take account of (a) the needs of particularly sensitive consumers and (b) the fact that after purchase, consumers may store the product in less than ideal conditions. The Court made no mention whatever of any obligation on Member States to review their maximum permitted levels in particular circumstances. Nevertheless, the Court's case law on additives and vitamins is surely applicable here now.

(viii) The prohibition of harmless foodstuffs

8.84   The sale of a particular category of foodstuffs may not be prohibited solely because it is of limited nutritional value. This was established in *Commission v France (substitute milk powder)*,[238] where the Court also pointed out that apart from substitute milk powder there were many products having little nutritional value on the market and these were not subject to any restriction on sale in the defendant Member State.

(ix) The obligation to appoint a representative in the importing Member State

8.85   *Commission v Belgium*[239] concerned a provision whereby approval for the sale of certain pesticides and phyto-pharmaceutical products in Belgium could only be granted to a person established there with responsibility for the sale of the product concerned as producer, importer, proprietor or concessionaire. It was common ground between the parties that some or all of the products concerned were toxic. The Commission nevertheless contested the Belgian Government's view that the requirement that the person concerned be established in Belgium was justified on public health grounds. The Court upheld the Commission's view.

First, the Belgian Government argued that it was necessary for a person responsible for the product concerned to be established on Belgian territory for the proper completion of the approval formalities, the enforcement of the rules on labelling, the verification of the conformity of the product marketed with the product approved and the availability of information in the event of an accident

---

[236] See n.231 above.
[237] See n.199 above.
[238] See n.121 above, see also Case 274/87, n.15 above.
[239] Case 155/82 [1983] E.C.R. 531; [1983] 2 C.M.L.R. 566.

or a complaint. The Court took the view that these matters could be fully satisfied by appropriate administrative measures taken when the application was examined and the approval granted, without its being necessary to require the establishment of a representative on the national territory.

The Belgian Government claimed, secondly, that it was necessary to ensure that a person was present on national territory to be prosecuted for any contravention of public health legislation. The Court held that, while criminal sanctions may have a deterrent effect, the effect was not increased by the requirement concerned. The Court thus appears to have accepted the view expressed by Rozès A.G. that responsible persons in other Member States could equally well be prosecuted by the Belgian authorities.

This ruling was confirmed in *Commission v Germany (pharmaceuticals)*[240] where the Court added that "the possibility that the authorisation might be suspended or revoked is an incentive to the manufacturers and the person responsible for placing products on the market to comply with the rules in force." Unfortunately, this case law has now been thrown into some doubt by the ruling in *Wurmser*,[241] which is discussed below.

(x) Rules imposing liability on the importer

8.86 In *Wurmser*[242] the Court was required to rule on whether a French measure imposing criminal liability on the distributor for the misdescription of imported goods was justified, although such liability was borne by the manufacturer with respect to domestic goods.

The Court rejected the suggestion of the Commission and the defendants in the main case that the manufacturer could perfectly well be prosecuted before the French courts. Its reasoning was as follows:

> "even when the criminal law of the Member State of importation provides for such a possibility, its application pre-supposes that exports to that State are carried out by the manufacturer himself and not by a trader independent of him. Moreover, as Community law stands at present, there is no obligation to enforce a criminal sentence imposed by the courts of another Member State. In those circumstances, the possibility of imposing criminal liability on a foreign manufacturer who has not carried out the same verification as is required of a domestic manufacturer cannot suffice to achieve the objective pursued by a provision such as that at issue in the main proceedings."

This reasoning does not sit well with the case law on the obligation to appoint a representative in the importing Member State, where the Court in effect reached the opposite conclusion.

At all events, the Court went on to rule that this requirement was justified so long as the distributor was able to discharge his responsibility by producing a certificate issued by the authorities of the Member State of production or by a laboratory authorised by those authorities to issue such certificates. The dis-

---

[240] Case 247/81 [1984] E.C.R. 1111; [1985] 1 C.M.L.R. 640.
[241] Case 25/88 [1989] E.C.R. 1105.
[242] See n.241 above.

tributor could not "as a general rule" be required to have the product analysed, since "such an obligation would impose on the importer a burden considerably greater than that imposed on a domestic manufacturer, who himself has control of the composition of the product, and it would often be disproportionate to the objective to be achieved."

(xi) Requirements that goods be sold by qualified persons only

8.87   In *Laboratoire de prothèses oculaires v Union nationale des syndicats d'opticiens de France*[243] a measure restricting the right to sell contact lenses and certain related products to qualified opticians was held to be justified on public health grounds.

The situation in *Delattre*[244] was more complex. That case concerned a measure granting to dispensing pharmacists the exclusive right to sell medicinal and "para-pharmaceutical" products. As to medicinal products,[245] the restriction was held to be justified on public health grounds, save as regards those products for which it could be shown that their use would not involve any serious danger to public health and "whose inclusion within the pharmacists' monopoly would seem manifestly disproportionate". With respect to "para-pharmaceutical" products the danger to public health must be established on a case-by-case basis.

In effect, then, the general presumption that measures are not justified under Article 30 was held to be reversed as regards medicinal products, but not with respect to "para-pharmaceutical" products.

(xii) Restrictions on parallel imports of pharmaceuticals

8.88   The above-mentioned ruling in *De Peijper* arose out of criminal proceedings brought before the Dutch courts against a parallel importer accused of contravening Dutch public health legislation by supplying pharmacies in the Netherlands with pharmaceutical products imported from the United Kingdom without the consent of the Dutch authorities, and with failing to have in his possession certain documents connected with these products. Having ruled that measures restricting parallel imports were measures of equivalent effect within the meaning of Article 28, the Court went on to consider the compatibility of rules of the kind in question with Article 30. In this connection, the Court held in the operative part of its judgment that:

> "Given a factual situation such as that described in the first question national rules or practices which make it possible for a manufacturer of the pharmaceutical product in question and his duly appointed representatives, simply by refusing to produce the documents relating to the medicinal preparation in general or to a specific batch of

---

[243] Case C-271/92 [1993] E.C.R. I-2899. As already mentioned (para. 7.48) it seems that such a measure is no longer to be regarded as falling under Article 28 at all, following *Keck*.

[244] Case C-369/88 [1991] E.C.R. I-1487. See also Case C-60/89 *Monteil* [1991] E.C.R. I-1547.

[245] The term "medicinal product" is defined by Article 1 of Council Directive 65/65 on proprietary medicinal products as amended ([1965–66] O.J. Eng. Spec. Ed. p. 20). That provision has been interpreted by the Court in a number of judgments, including *Delattre* itself.

that preparation, to enjoy a monopoly of the importing and marketing of the product must be regarded as being unnecessarily restrictive and cannot therefore come within the exceptions specified in Article [30] of the Treaty, unless it is clearly proved that any other rules or practices would obviously be beyond the means which can reasonably be expected of an administration operating in a normal manner."

In the grounds of its judgment the Court did in fact suggest two methods by which such restrictions might be lessened: Member States might compel the manufacturer or his duly appointed representative to deliver up the necessary information, and "simple co-operation between the authorities of the Member States would enable them to obtain on a reciprocal basis the documents necessary for checking certain largely standardised and widely distributed products."[246] The Court continued:

"Taking into account all these possible ways of obtaining information the national public health authorities must consider whether the effective protection of health and life of humans justifies a presumption of the non-conformity of an imported batch with the description of the medicinal preparation, or whether on the contrary it would not be sufficient to lay down a presumption of conformity with the result that, in appropriate cases, it would be for the administration to rebut this presumption."

What if there were minor differences in composition between the "official" and the parallel imports? This was in effect the second question put by the national court, which indicated that the differences might be so minor that it was likely that they were deliberately created by the manufacturer with a view to preventing parallel imports. The Court replied in the following terms:

"It is only if the information or documents to be produced by the manufacturer or his duly appointed importer show that there are several variants of the medicinal preparation and that the differences between these variants have a therapeutic effect that there would be any justification for treating the variants as different medicinal preparations for the purpose of authorising the relevant document, it being understood that the answer to the first question remains valid as regards each of the authorisation procedures which have become necessary."[247]

(xiii) Imports of pharmaceuticals and medical products for personal use

8.89   The claimant in *Schumacher v HZA Frankfurt*[248] challenged the legality of a provision of German law which prohibited him, as an unauthorised person, from importing for his own consumption pharmaceuticals lawfully purchased from a pharmacy in Strasbourg, even though no prescription was required for the product concerned in Germany. Only wholesalers, pharmaceutical companies and pharmacists were authorised to import pharmaceuticals into Germany. The Court held that such a restriction was not justified: since the product had

---

[246] See also C-94/98 *R. v The Licensing Authority ex parte Rhône-Poulenc* [1999] E.C.R. I-8789 at para. 46.
[247] See also *R. v The Licensing Authority ex parte Rhône-Poulenc*, see n. 246 above at para. 45.
[248] Case 215/87 [1989] E.C.R. 617.

been bought in a pharmacy in another Member State, the individual enjoyed guarantees in terms of proper information, advice and product quality which were equivalent to those available in Germany. This conclusion was all the more compelling in that professional qualifications for pharmacists had been harmonised by Community law.

In *Commission v Germany*[249] the Court was called upon to rule on the lawfulness of a similar restriction applying to products available only on prescription within the defendant State, which had been lawfully purchased from a pharmacy in another Member State pursuant to a prescription dispensed by a doctor established there. Since by definition the marketing of the product must have been authorised by the State of sale, and since professional qualifications for doctors had been harmonised by Community legislation, the Court concluded that such a restriction was not justified.

The Court was not swayed by the German Government's argument that its nationals might not know how to use medicines acquired in this way, since the instructions might not be in German. This difficulty could be overcome by information given orally by the prescribing medical practitioner.[250]

Equally, the Court saw no merit in the defendant's contention that, in order to check whether a product was not being imported in quantities exceeding the personal requirements of the patient, its agents would have to inspect incoming consignments, thus violating his medical secrecy. While stressing that the protection of privacy (including medical secrecy) was a fundamental right, the Court found that Germany had failed to show that it was impossible to carry out such inspections without infringing these rights.

8.90   In *Decker v Caisse de maladie des employés privés*[251] the Court had the opportunity to make a similar finding with respect to spectacles with corrective lenses purchased from an optician established in another Member State. In that case, under Luxembourg rules, a social security institution in Luxembourg refused to reimburse an insured person on a flat-rate basis for the cost of a pair of spectacles with corrective lenses purchased from an optician established in another Member State, on the ground that prior authorisation was required for the purchase of any medical product abroad. Having found that such rules were a barrier to the free movement of goods prohibited by Article 28, the Court rejected the argument that the restriction was justified on the ground of public health provided for in Article 30 by observing that the conditions for the taking up and pursuing regulated professions had been harmonised under Community law which meant "... that the purchase of a pair of spectacles from an optician established in another Member State provides guarantees equivalent to those afforded on the sale of a pair of spectacles by an optician established in the national territory."[252]

[249] Case C-62/90 [1992] E.C.R. I-2575.
[250] As to language requirements, see para. 8.130 below.
[251] C-120/95, see n.23 above; see also the parallel judgment in Case C-158/96, see n.23 above, which related to services under Art. 49.
[252] Para. 43 of the judgment.

(xiv) The obligation to repackage pharmaceuticals prior to importation

8.91 *Freistaat Bayern v Eurim-Pharm*[253] related to pharmaceuticals marketed in another Member State and imported by a parallel importer into Germany. The products themselves complied with German legislation, but their packaging did not. However, it was the parallel importer's intention to repackage the goods prior to marketing them, and indeed it held a specific licence from the German authorities to do so. The question which arose for decision was whether the importer could be required to repackage the goods before they entered German territory. Having regard to the Community legislation relating to pharmaceuticals, the Court found that such a requirement was not justified.

(xv) Ban on the substitution of identical pharmaceutical products

8.92 *R. v Royal Pharmaceutical Society of Great Britain*[254] concerned a ban by the defendants on pharmacists substituting, except in cases of emergency, one product for another product specifically named in a prescription, even where the quality and the therapeutic effects of the two products are the same. This measure had a devastating effect on parallel imports. The Court nevertheless upheld the restriction on the following grounds:

"the rules concerning the relationship between doctors and pharmacists and in particular those rules relating to the attending doctor's freedom to prescribe any product he chooses and to any possibility which the pharmacist may have to dispense a medicinal product other than that prescribed in the prescription are part of the national public health system. As long as those matters have not been regulated by Community legislation, it is for the Member States, within the limits laid down in Article [30], to decide on the degree to which they wish to protect human health and life and how that degree of protection is to be achieved.

There is no evidence in this case to justify a conclusion by the Court that a rule prohibiting pharmacists from substituting another medicinal product for one designated by name in the prescription, even if the other product has the same therapeutic effect, goes beyond what is necessary to achieve the objective in view, which is to leave the entire responsibility for the treatment of the patient in the hands of the doctor treating him. In particular, the Court finds itself unable to discount the reasons, based on psychosomatic phenomena, for which, according to the observations submitted by the Pharmaceutical Society of Great Britain and by the governments of several Member States, a specific proprietary medicinal product might be prescribed rather than a generic product or any other proprietary medicinal product having the same therapeutic effect."[255]

Not everyone will be convinced by this reasoning which appears to be based more on psychological than on objective considerations.

---

[253] Case C-347/89 [1991] E.C.R. I-1747.
[254] Cases 266–7/87 [1989] E.C.R. 1295.
[255] at 1328–9.

(xvi) Type approval for machines used at work

8.93 In *Commission v France*[256] the Court ruled that the French safety requirements for woodworking machines were justified on public health grounds, although they were stricter than those prevailing in other Member States. The French legislation was based on the idea that the users of machines must be protected from their own mistakes and that the machine must be so designed as to limit the user's intervention to the absolute minimum. In other Member States, the predominant approach to the problem was different. In Germany in particular the basic principle was that the worker should receive thorough and continuing training so as to be capable of responding correctly if a machine did not function properly.

The Court stated that it was "contrary to the principle of proportionality for national rules to require such imported products to comply strictly and exactly with the provisions or technical requirements laid down for products manufactured in the Member State in question when those imported products afford users the same level of protection". However, it found that the Commission had failed to prove that imported woodworking machines did in fact protect users equally well; the German approach to accident prevention had not been shown to be as satisfactory as the French approach. The Commission had put in statistics showing that the machines manufactured according to the specifications of other Member States did not cause more accidents than machines made to French standards. Nevertheless, in the Court's view such statistics could not establish by themselves that the French approach did not provide greater protection to users since they left out of account other factors such as "the extensive training of users". One can deduce from this that a Member State is not required to grant type approval for dangerous machines which can only be used safely after extensive training, if machines meeting the specifications laid down by that State do not require such training. Yet the Court cannot be taken to have given its blessing to national rules which exploit users' habits so as to give an advantage to domestic manufacturers.[257]

The Court also held that it was lawful for the defendant to require applicants for type approval to transport their machines to France for testing.

(xvii) Roadworthiness tests

8.94 *Schloh v Auto Contrôle Technique*[258] concerned the requirement that imported cars undergo a roadworthiness test prior to their registration, the cars concerned not being of a category covered by any relevant Community Directive. The Court held that such a requirement was not justified on health grounds in respect of unused cars covered by a certificate of conformity to the

---

[256] Case 188/84, see n.196 above.
[257] See Case 178/84, see n.30 above.
[258] Case 50/85 [1987] 1 C.M.L.R. 450, on car registration; see also Case 406/85, see n.100 above; and C-314/98 *Snellers Auto's v Algemeen Directeur van de Dienst Wegverkeer* [2000] E.C.R. I-8633 at para. 55.

vehicle types approved in the importing Member States. In contrast, it found that it was justified on these grounds as regards used cars, provided that cars originating in the importing Member State were treated in the same way.

(xviii) Restrictions on importation and sale of alcoholic beverages

8.95 The accession of Sweden and Finland to the European Union in 1994 has brought with it challenges to the provisions in force in those States which restrict the importation, sale and consumption of alcoholic drinks. In *Franzén*,[259] the Court analysed the Swedish monopoly on the retail of alcoholic beverages against the provisions of Article 31.[260] However, other provisions in the Swedish legislation, although not regulating the functioning of the monopoly itself, nevertheless had a direct bearing on its operation. Such provisions fell to be analysed against the provisions of Articles 28 to 30. For example, it was a requirement for the retail monopoly in question to obtain supplies of alcoholic beverages only from holders of production or wholesale licences. The grant of the latter licences was the subject of restrictive conditions which included the provision by traders of sufficient personal and financial guarantees to carry on the activities in question, the availability of storage capacity in Sweden and the payment of substantial fees for the licences. The Court held that such requirements were contrary to Article 28. The Swedish Government had however invoked the protection of public health as a justification for the restriction. The Court accepted that "the protection of human health against the harmful effects of alcohol ... is indisputably one of the grounds which may justify derogation from Article [28] of the Treaty".[261] However, the Court rejected the justification on the facts because "the Swedish Government has not established that the licensing system set up by the Law on Alcohol, in particular as regards the conditions relating to storage capacity and the high fees and charges which licence-holders are required to pay, was proportionate to the public health aim pursued or that this aim could not have been attained by measures less restrictive of intra-Community trade."[262]

(xix) Restrictions on advertising and sales promotion[263]

8.96 Following the Court's ruling in *Keck*,[264] advertising restrictions will normally fall within the category of "selling arranagements" and will frequently fall outside the scope of Article 28. However, it will be recalled that the Court has become more vigilant in policing advertising restrictions by means of a more rigorous application of the second proviso set down by the Court in *Keck*.[265] As

---

[259] C-189/95 [1997] E.C.R. I-5909.
[260] See discussion in Ch. XI.
[261] Para. 76 of the judgment. See also, with respect to Reg. 3285/94 on common rules for imports ([1994] O.J. L349/53), C-394/97, see n.165 above at para. 33.
[262] *ibid.* See also *Gourmet International* discussed at 8.100 below.
[263] See also paras 7.41 *et seq.*
[264] See paras 6.54 *et seq.*
[265] See further discussion at para. 6.61.

such the justification for such advertising restrictions remains a point of considerable importance.[266]

8.97 In many cases, restrictions imposed by Member States on methods of advertising will fall to be considered under the head of consumer protection.[267] However, public health issues also arise.

In *Commission v France (alcohol advertising)*[268] the Court recognised that national legislation restricting advertising in respect of alcoholic beverages may in principle be justified by concern relating to the protection of public health. The Court stated that "it is in fact undeniable that advertising acts as an encouragement to consumption" and therefore that there is a connection between the control of advertising in respect of alcoholic drinks and the campaign against alcoholism.[269] On the facts of that case, however, the Court found that the French restriction was not justified because it gave rise to arbitrary discrimination in that it authorised advertising in respect of certain national products whilst advertising in respect of products having comparable characteristics but originating in other Member States was restricted or entirely prohibited.[270]

8.98 In *Aragonesa de Publicidad*,[271] a restriction on the advertising of beverages having an alcoholic strength of more than 23 degrees in the media, on streets and highways, in cinemas and on public transport was held to be justified for the protection of public health. In reaching the conclusion that the restriction was proportionate to the objective pursued in that case, the Court was influenced by the following factors: the restriction applied only to beverages having an alcoholic strength of more than 23 degrees; and advertising was restricted in places particularly frequented by motorists and young persons which, the Court said, were two categories of the population in regard to which the campaign against alcoholism is of "quite special importance".[272]

8.99 The Court has also decided two cases relating to the more stringent restrictions on advertising alcoholic drinks in Sweden, where those products are subject to a State retail monopoly.

In the first of these cases, *Franzén*,[273] this question was only considered in passing, since the Court was primarily concerned with the legality of the monopoly itself. On the advertising restriction, the Court simply held: ". . . the

---

[266] See generally, Drijber, "Les communications commerciales au carrefour de la dérégulation et de la régulation" [2002] C.D.E. (forthcoming); Greaves, "Advertising Restrictions and the Free Movement of Goods and Services" (1998) 23 E.L. Rev. 305; Schwarze (ed.) *Werbung und Werbeverbote im Lichte des europäischen Gemeinschaftsrechts* (1998, Baden-Baden Nomos Verlag), especially C. Timmermans "Werbung und Grundfreiheiten" at p. 26.

[267] See paras 8.125 *et seq* below.

[268] Case 152/78, see n.32 above.

[269] Para. 17 of the judgment. On this point, see also *Aragonesa de Publicidad* (n.9 above) at para. 15.

[270] Para. 18 of the judgment.

[271] See n.9 above.

[272] Paras 17 and 18 of the judgment.

[273] Case C-189/95, see n.259 above; see paras 7.27 and 11.14.

method of promotion used by the monopoly applies independently of the products' origin and is not in itself apt to put at a disadvantage, in fact or in law, beverages imported from other Member States in relation to those produced on national territory".[274]

8.100 However, in *Gourmet International*[275] the Court specifically concentrated on the advertising restriction and reached a different conclusion. It is important to stress that this legislation was far more stringent than that in *Aragonesa de Publicidad*, since it applied to all drinks with an alcohol content of more than 2.25 per cent. Moreover, this ban was subject to a questionable exception for advertising at the point of retail sale: by definition, the only retail outlets were those of the State monopoly which, it was found, only distributed its own magazine at those outlets. This might be thought to have introduced an inherent element of discrimination into the legislation.

In his Opinion, Jacobs A.G. stated clearly that "justification under Article [30] is in principle available for measures to reduce alcohol consumption".[276] Thus various restrictions on alcohol advertising (*e.g.* as regards children and young people, and for drinks with a higher alcohol content) must be regarded as justified; and he endorsed the earlier ruling in *Aragonesa de Publicidad*. Nevertheless, he was "not convinced" that "it is either necessary or effective, in the light of the aim of reducing lawful alcohol consumption by adults, to impose a ban on all commercial advertising of alcoholic beverages in all media directed at the general public, bearing in mind that [under the Swedish legislation] such advertisements must in any event display 'particular moderation' ".[277] Having said that, he took the view that the proportionality of the ban should be decided by the national court.

While the Court also concluded that this matter should be left to the Swedish court, its approach was generally more guarded. Indeed, it found that there was no evidence before it to suggest that the public health grounds relied upon by the Swedish authorities had been diverted from their purpose and used in such a way as to discriminate against goods originating in other Member States or to protect certain national products indirectly.[278] The Court then concluded:

> "the decision as to whether the prohibition on advertising at issue in the main pro-
> ceedings is proportionate, and in particular as to whether the objective sought might
> be achieved by less extensive prohibitions or restrictions or by prohibitions or
> restrictions having less effect on intra-Community trade, calls for an analysis of the
> circumstances of law and of fact which characterise the situation in the Member State
> concerned, which the national court is in a better position than the Court of Justice to
> carry out."[279]

---

[274] Para. 64 of the judgment.
[275] C-405/98, see n.42 above.
[276] Para. 41 of the Opinion.
[277] Para. 57 of the Opinion.
[278] Para. 32 of the judgment.
[279] Para. 33 of the judgment.

8.101   In *Ortscheit v Eurim-Pharm Arzneimittel*[280] a German prohibition of advertising of medicinal products was at issue. Under German law, medicinal products that had not been authorised by the competent body in Germany could nevertheless be imported from another Member State in response to an individual order, if the product in question had been lawfully put into circulation in the other Member State. However, advertising of such products, even in publications aimed at doctors and pharmacists, was prohibited. The Court held that this prohibition was justified for the protection of public health. It reasoned that:

> "If medicinal products which were not authorised in Germany could be advertised there, there would be a danger that manufacturers would obtain authorisation for their medicinal products in a Member State imposing fewer requirements and then import them into Germany on the basis of individual orders which they would have encouraged by advertising campaigns."[281]

Accordingly, the prohibition on advertising was held to be justified because it was necessary to prevent systematic circumvention of the general requirement for national authorisation before medicinal products could be put on the market in Germany.

8.102   The relationship between advertising restrictions and the protection of public health was recently dealt with by Fennelly A.G. in his Opinion in *Germany v Parliament and Council*.[282] That case concerned the successful challenge by Germany of the tobacco advertising Directive.[283] The Court annulled that Directive on the principal ground that Article 95 (ex 100A) did not provide an appropriate legal basis for the Directive.[284] Among the further grounds of challenge, dealt with by the Advocate General but not the Court, were the claims that the Directive infringed the principle of proportionality and constituted a breach of fundamental rights. The Advocate General found that the Directive was "an ineffective means of achieving the objectives that it pursued" and, for that reason, infringed the principle of proportionality.[285] He also took the view that the provisions of the Directive constituted a interference with the rights to property and to pursue a professional activity, albeit on the basis of a very cursory consideration of this issue.[286]

On the question of freedom of expression, Fennelly A.G. noted (on the hypothesis that the Directive was lawful and proportionate) that the protection of health is one of the grounds on which Article 10(2) of the European Convention on Human Rights expressly permits the imposition of restrictions on

---

[280] C-320/93 [1994] E.C.R. I-5243.
[281] Para. 19 of the judgment.
[282] C-376/98 [2000] E.C.R. I-8419, see paras 12.41 and 12.63 below.
[283] Directive 98/43 on the approximation of the laws, regulations and administrative provisions of the Member States relating to the advertising and sponsorship of tobacco products: [1998] O.J. L213/9.
[284] See further para. 12.41 below.
[285] See para. 149 of the Opinion.
[286] See para. 151 of the Opinion.

freedom of expression prohibited by Article 10(1). Citing judgments of the European Court of Human Rights,[287] he noted that that Court treated the freedom of commercial expression as less important than other forms of expression. He then concluded:

> "Where it is established that a Community measure restricts freedom of commercial expression ... the Community legislator should also be obliged to satisfy the Court that it had reasonable grounds for adopting the measure in question in the public interest. In concrete terms, it should supply coherent evidence that the measure will be effective in achieving the public interest objective invoked – in these cases, a reduction in tobacco consumption relative to the level which would otherwise have obtained—and that less restrictive measures would not have been equally effective".[288]

As to the nature of the "coherent evidence" that must be supplied, he stated:

> "...the Community should not be prevented from acting in the public interest simply because justification of its action necessarily depends, not on 'hard' scientific studies, but on evidence of a social scientific character, which predicts, on the basis of past behaviour, the future responses of consumers to changes in their level of exposure to promotional material. Furthermore, where the Community legislator can show that it acted upon the basis of reputable specialist studies in the field, the fact that other apparently reputable studies have reached a contrary conclusion does not, in itself, show that that legislator did not have reasonable grounds for acting".[289]

On the evidence, Fennelly A.G. concluded that the Community legislator had reasonable grounds for adopting the measure in question in the public interest and that less restrictive measures would not have been equally effective.[290] He also concluded that the comprehensive prohibition on advertising in the Directive was proportionate to the restriction on freedom of expression.[291]

On the other hand, he reached the opposite conclusion with respect to the ban on advertising diversification products (non-tobacco goods and services which bear brands or other distinguishing features associated with tobacco products). This finding was simply based on the failure of the Community legislator to adduce any evidence that the advertising of such products has any effect on tobacco consumption, and is thus limited to the circumstances of those particular proceedings.

Insofar as it relates to proportionality and the rights to property and to pursue a professional activity, this Opinion was based on the premises that the Directive imposed restrictions that did not "correspond to the internal market objectives which were necessary for its lawful adoption"[292] and that "health protection

---

[287] *Sunday Times v United Kingdom* [1979] Series A, No 30; *Observer and Guardian v United Kingdom* [1991] Series A, No 216, para. 59; *Markt Intern v Germany* [1989] Series A, No 165, para. 37 and *Groppera v Switzerland* [1990] Series A, No 173, para. 73.
[288] Para. 159 of the Opinion.
[289] Para. 160 of the Opinion.
[290] Paras 163 and 164 of the Opinion.
[291] Paras. 175 of the Opinion.
[292] Para. 151 of the Opinion.

cannot function independently as an objective".[293] Accordingly, that part of the Opinion cannot be transposed to Article 30. While the same cannot be said of his finding that the restriction on the freedom of commercial expression was justified with regard to tobacco products, the Advocate General arguably failed to give sufficient weight to the protection of public health: whereas he rightly treated freedom of expression as a fundamental right, he appeared to regard public health as a merely technical objective. It is a pity that he omitted any consideration of the statement of the President of the Court of First Instance in the *National Farmers' Union case*—which admittedly has yet to be endorsed by the Court of Justice—that protection of public health must itself be considered as a fundamental right.[294]

(xx) Labelling requirements

8.103   Measures requiring products to be labelled in a language that is easily understood by consumers are usually enacted for the protection of those consumers. As such, the justification for such measures (when they restrict intra-Community trade) is usually to be found in consumer protection.[295] However, where the product in question is potentially dangerous, justification might also be found in the protection of public health. This was the case in *Schwarzkopf*,[296] which concerned a requirement that the outer packaging of certain hair dyes intended for professional (as opposed to private) users contain a warning in a language understood by those users as to the safe use of those products. The Court held that the requirement was justified for the protection of public health, without even mentioning the protection of consumers. It held that the warning would be of "no practical use unless it is given in a language which can be understood by the persons for whom it is intended".[297] It held, however, that it would be otherwise where the information could be effectively conveyed by the use of pictogrammes or signs other than words.

(xxi) Restrictions on noise pollution

8.104   In *Aher-Waggon v Germany*, which related to the registration of aircraft, the Court held that restrictions on noise pollution "may be justified by considerations of public health" as well as protection of the environment.[298]

---

[293] Para. 149 of the Opinion.
[294] Case T-76/96R (see n.202 above). However, in his Opinion of September 10, 2002 in Case C-491/01 R *(on the application of British American Tobacco and Imperial Tobacco) v Secretary of State for Health* (pending) Geelhoed A.G. gave greater weight to public health.
[295] See detailed discussion of language requirements as an aspect of consumer protection at para. 8.130 below.
[296] C-169/99 [2001] E.C.R. I-5901. See also Case C-491/01 *British American Tobacco* (n.294 above).
[297] Para. 40 of the judgment.
[298] See n.24 above, para. 19; as mentioned in that footnote, it is surprising that the restriction in issue there was not held to constitute arbitrary discrimination.

(xxii) Miscellaneous

8.105 There are many other cases in which the Court has found a restriction not to be justified on public health grounds. Examples[299] include:

— a minimum alcohol requirement: *"Cassis de Dijon"*[300];
— a prohibition on the importation of meat-based products manufactured in one Member State from animals slaughtered in another Member State: *Commission v Germany*[301];
— a prohibition on the importation and sale of vinegar other than wine vinegar: *Gilli and Andres*[302];
— a prohibition on the sale of bread containing more than a certain quantity of (a) dry matter: *Kelderman*[303]; (b) salt: *Van der Veldt*[304]; or (c) moisture and ash: *Morellato v USL*[305];
— a territorial restriction on the sale on rounds of baker's, butcher's and grocer's wares: *TK-Heimdienst Sass.*[306] If the purpose was to prevent the deterioration of the goods, then that objective could be attained by rules on refrigerating equipment in the vehicles used.

Animals and plants

8.106 The principles relating to the health and life of animals[307] and plants[308] are essentially the same as those relating to human life and health—with the obvious and fundamental difference that human health and life are more important.[309] The reader should therefore have regard to paragraphs 8.59 to 8.105 above. The term "plants" must be taken to cover plants and trees and their produce generally.

Various categories of animal and plant protection may be distinguished, including:

— the protection of rare or endangered species;
— the prevention of animal or plant diseases, in particular where those diseases may have harmful consequences for breeders or other persons with a commercial interest; and
— animal welfare.

The factors to be weighed up in respect of each of these different categories may be markedly different.

---

[299] See also Case 36/76 *Simmenthal*, see n. 92 above; Case 46/76 see n.3 above see; Case 152/78 see n. 32 above.
[300] See n. 5 above.
[301] Case 153/78 [1979] E.C.R. 2555; [1980] 1 C.M.L.R. 198.
[302] See n.29 above.
[303] Case 130/80 [1981] E.C.R. 527.
[304] C-17/93 [1994] E.C.R. I-3537.
[305] C-358/95 [1997] E.C.R. I-1431.
[306] C-254/98, see n. 108 above.
[307] See, *e.g.* Case 35/76, n.92 above; Case 46/76, see n.3 above; Case 251/78, see n.28 above.
[308] See Case 4/75, n.41 above; Case 89/76, see n.86 above; [1978] 3 C.M.L.R. 630.
[309] Para. 8.60 above.

(i) The protection of rare and endangered species

8.107   An important judgment on the protection of rare or endangered species was delivered in *Gourmetterie van den Burg*.[310] The accused was convicted of importing into the Netherlands and/or possessing and/or selling a "dead red grouse" (*lagopus lagopus scoticus*). The hapless bird had been imported from the United Kingdom, to which the species is native. This bird does not live in the wild in the Netherlands.

Since the red grouse is not a migratory bird and was not classified as an endangered species under the relevant Community legislation, the Court held that the measure was not justified under Article 30. Unfortunately, it gave no indication as to what principles would apply in the absence of Community legislation.

8.108   Another highly important case on the protection of rare and endangered species is *Bluhme*.[311] That case concerned criminal proceedings for the infringement of Danish legislation prohibiting the keeping on the island of Læsø of bees other than those of the subspecies *Apis mellifera mellifera* (Læsø brown bee). Given the recessive nature of the Læsø brown bee's genes, the Danish legislation in question had been introduced in order to prevent the disappearance of the Læsø brown bee as a result of their mating with golden bees. The Court held that the Danish legislation in question constituted a quantitative restriction prohibited by Article 28[312] but that that restriction was justified for the protection of the life of animals under Article 30. In particular, the Court held that:

> "...measures to preserve an indigenous animal population with distinct characteristics contribute to the maintenance of biodiversity by ensuring the survival of the population concerned. By so doing, they are aimed at protecting the life of those animals and are capable of being justified under Article [30] of the Treaty.

From the point of view of such conservation of biodiversity, it is immaterial whether the object of protection is a separate subspecies, a distinct strain within any given species or merely a local colony, so long as the populations in question have characteristics distinguishing them from others and are therefore judged worthy of protection either to shelter them from a risk of extinction that is more or less imminent, or, even in the absence of such risk, on account of a scientific or other interest in preserving the pure population at the location concerned."[313]

Furthermore, the Court went on to hold that the Danish legislation was necessary and proportionate to its aim and that it was not possible to achieve the same result by less stringent measures. In so holding, the Court had regard, and

---

[310] See n.82 above. See also C-149/94 *Vergy* [1996] E.C.R. I-299; and C-510/99, see n. 31 above.
[311] See n.66 above.
[312] See para. 8.23.
[313] Paras 33 and 34 of the judgment.

made express reference, to the Convention on Biological Diversity signed at Rio de Janeiro on June 5, 1992.[314]

(ii) The prevention of disease

8.109 A ban on the importation of poultrymeat, poultry products and most eggs and egg products from all countries which did not prohibit vaccination against Newcastle disease (a poultry disease) was held not to be justified in *Commission v United Kingdom*[315] and *Commission v Ireland*.[316] For several decades Ireland and Northern Ireland had had a policy of prohibiting such vaccination, coupled with a requirement to slaughter any infected flocks. All imports from countries which permitted vaccination were banned. The thinking behind this policy was that vaccination might mask the disease, so that vaccinated birds might in fact be infected by field virus. Quite suddenly, in August 1981, Great Britain switched to this system with effect from September 1, 1981. This meant that without warning all Member States other than Denmark and Ireland were deprived of the possibility of exporting the products concerned to Great Britain. In particular, this change had the effect of excluding French turkey products from the lucrative Christmas market in Great Britain.

As regards Great Britain the Court had no difficulty in finding that the ban was not justified, especially in view of various factors indicating that the true purpose of the switch to a non-vaccination policy was to protect domestic production, notably from French imports.[317]

The question was more complex in relation to Ireland and Northern Ireland, since these factors were not present and those parts of the Community had particularly good records with respect to Newcastle disease. The Court nevertheless found that even there the ban was unjustified. This was in the first place because internationally accepted statistics showed a steady reduction in outbreaks within the Community in recent years, so that the incidence of the disease had become relatively limited. Under these circumstances the risk of flocks being infected by field virus, which had entered vaccinated birds and remained active in the carcases of those birds, was extremely slight. That risk could not justify a complete ban on imports from countries which permitted vaccination. Moreover, the "prohibition of imports of carcases and poultrymeat is in any event out of proportion to the aim pursued where those imports come from a country in which no outbreak of Newcastle disease has been detected over a number of years and where, moreover, it is established that the carcases and meat in question are of unvaccinated birds".

The rulings concerning Ireland and Northern Ireland are particularly significant in view of their good record and of the long-standing nature of the

---

[314] Para. 36 of the judgment. On endangered species, see also Case C-510/99, n.31 above.
[315] Case 40/82, see n.45 above; [1982] 3 C.M.L.R. 497 (Great Britain); and [1984] E.C.R. 283.
[316] Case 74/82, see n.109 above.
[317] See para. 8.17 above.

import ban. They indicate that in the absence of specific grounds of suspicion a blanket prohibition of this kind will rarely, if ever, be justified.[318]

8.110   The question whether import licences could be justified on animal health grounds first arose in *Commission v United Kingdom (UHT milk and cream)*.[319] The defendant maintained that a system of individual import licences applying to each consignment of ultra-heat treated milk or cream was justified, notably because these products might be imported before an outbreak of foot-and-mouth disease in the exporting region had become known; in such cases it was essential to be able to trace a consignment and destroy it, and this could only be done by means of specific import licences. The Commission contested this view. It regarded import licences as creating uncertainty for importers and a risk of delay without constituting a real health guarantee for the importing Member State. A less restrictive solution which was also more satisfactory from the health point of view was the requirement that imports of the products concerned be accompanied by a certificate made out by a veterinary surgeon officially approved by the exporting Member State showing that the requisite health standards were met—provided of course that these health standards were themselves justified. It was for this reason that a system of health certificates issued by the exporting Member State was laid down in the Community's own veterinary directives. The Commission therefore considered that import licences were more restrictive than was necessary to protect animal health and were therefore not justified. However, it did not rule out the possibility of there being other cases in which an import licensing system was justified.

The Advocate General gave only qualified approval to the Commission's position. He found that import licences were justified provided that they were issued immediately and automatically, subject to production on importation of certificates attesting to UHT treatment in the exporting country, and provided that no more stringent requirements were imposed as regards those certificates than applied to the UHT treatment of milk produced within the United Kingdom.

On the other hand the Court endorsed the Commission's position, in the following terms:

> "Even though the United Kingdom maintained at the hearing that current administrative practice permits licences to be issued promptly and automatically, a system requiring the issue of an administrative authorisation necessarily involves the exercise of a certain degree of discretion and creates legal uncertainty for traders. It results in an impediment to intra-Community trade which, in the present case, could be eliminated without prejudice to the effectiveness of the protection of animal health and without increasing the administrative or financial burden imposed by the pursuit of that objective. That result could be achieved if the United Kingdom authorities abandoned the practice of issuing licences and confined themselves to obtaining the information which is of use to them, for example, by means of declarations signed by the importers, accompanied if necessary by the appropriate certificate."

---

[318] See also Case C-131/93 *Commission v Germany* (crayfish) [1994] E.C.R. I-3303.
[319] See n.215 above.

However, the Court made it clear that its ruling was confined to the case in hand.

8.111 In the two cases discussed in paragraph 8.109 the Court confirmed that the question whether specific import licences could be justified on animal health grounds was indeed to be decided on a case-by-case basis. The criterion to be applied was "the relationship between, on the one hand, the inconvenience caused by the administrative and financial burdens imposed under such a system and, on the other hand, the dangers and risks for animal health resulting from the imports in question". Applying this criterion the Court found that specific import licences for certain poultry and egg products were justified on animal health grounds in relation to Ireland and Northern Ireland, but not as regards Great Britain. The reason given was the exceptionally high health standards of Irish and Northern Irish flocks over recent years, which were not matched by flocks in Great Britain.

Lastly, it should be noted that in the *Newcastle disease* cases the Commission expressly excluded "open general licences" from the scope of its application. By this it meant licences which (a) are published and open to all importers (b) require no further authorisation from the authorities of the importing Member State, and (c) are subject to no other condition. The Commission's position is possibly vindicated by the ruling in *Denkavit Futtermittel v Land Nordrhein-Westfalen*[320] where a licence to import an unlimited amount of feedingstuffs was held to be justified when it was subject only to the requirement to produce a copy of that licence with each consignment together with a veterinary certificate from the exporting Member State, which was valid for one year, to the effect that the goods had undergone a specified process.

8.112 Although in the cases discussed above the Court stressed that this matter must be decided on a case-by-case basis, it appears to have abandoned this approach in *Commission v Belgium (live animals)*.[321] In the light of that judgment, it would appear that import declarations or certificates will suffice in every, or nearly every, case. Accordingly, import licences will only be justified in highly exceptional circumstances, if at all.

8.113 Finally, there remains the problem of import controls. As already mentioned, subject perhaps to very limited exceptions, in the absence of a reasonable suspicion in relation to a specific consignment an importing Member State may not duplicate controls carried out to protect human health by the exporting Member State, although the importing State may make random checks or spot checks. This must apply *a fortiori* to animals or plant health checks.

Nevertheless, in *REWE-Zentrale v Direktor der Landwirtschaftskammer Rhein-*

---

[320] See n.99 above.
[321] See n.216 above.

land[322] the Court rejected the argument that Council Directive 77/93 on protective measures against the introduction into the Member States of harmful organisms of plants or plant products contravened Article 28 in that it permitted an importing Member State to subject as many as one-third of all consignments of plants and plant products to phytosanitary controls. The Court found that the Community institutions had not exceeded the discretionary power conferred by Articles 43 and 100 (now Articles 37 and 94) on which the Directive was based, since harmonisation could properly be effected in stages and national obstacles to trade be abolished gradually. This necessarily implies that the contested provision may in time cease to be valid. Indeed, Slynn A.G., who took the same view as the Court, said as much.

Assuming that such controls are justified, to what extent can Member States limit the points of entry for goods subject to controls? In Case *Commission v Italy*[323] a ban on importing grapefruit overland on these grounds was held to be unlawful. Given that border controls have been admissible only in exceptional circumstances since the end of 1992,[324] one would think that such restrictions will not normally be justified.

(iii) Animal welfare

8.114   In *Holdijk*,[325] which concerned national legislation prescribing the conditions and minimum size of enclosures for fattening calves, the Court held that this matter is covered by Article 30; it follows that the "protection of the health and life of animals" extends to animal welfare.[326]

Among the instruments concluded at Amsterdam is the new Protocol on protection and welfare of animals which reads: "In formulating and implementing the Community's agriculture, transport, internal market and research policies, the Community and the Member States shall pay full regard to the welfare requirements of animals, while respecting the legislative or administrative provisions and customs of the Member States relating in particular to religious rites, cultural traditions and regional heritage".[327] That Protocol replaces a declaration on the same subject adopted by the Intergovernmental Conference at the time of signature of the Treaty of Maastricht.

---

[322] Case 37/83 [1984] E.C.R. 1229; [1985] 2 C.M.L.R. 586.
[323] C-128/89, see n.56 above; see also *United Foods* (n.197 above).
[324] Paras 6.10 and 7.04.
[325] Cases 141–143/81 [1982] E.C.R. 1299 at 1314; [1983] 2 C.M.L.R. 635 at 650.
[326] See also *Hedley Lomas* (para. 80 above); *Compassion in World Farming* (para. 81 above); and C-350/97 *Monsees v Unabhängiger Verwaltungssenat für Kärnten* [1999] E.C.R. I-2921.
[327] See case C-189/01 *Jippes v Minister of Agriculture* [2001] E.C.R. I-5689, especially para. 73.

The Protection of National Treasures Possessing Artistic, Historic or Archaeological Value

8.115 Normally this head of justification[328] will be relied on to justify restrictions on exports; indeed it will rarely, if ever, be invoked to prevent imports. So it is that the only case concerning this ground of justification to come before the Court of Justice, *Commission v Italy*,[329] involved an export restriction on art treasures. However, as already explained,[330] that restriction took the form of an export tax and the Court held that Article 30 could not be relied on to justify a tax. In view of this, neither the Court nor the Advocate General found it necessary to interpret this limb of Article 30. Nor is there any other case law on the subject.

8.116 In the absence of such case law, the obvious question is whether or not the definition of the concept of "national treasures" should be left to each Member State to define (subject to the second sentence in Article 30) or whether the Court should develop a Community-wide definition of that concept. It is submitted that a Community-wide definition is both necessary and desirable given that national legislation controlling the export of works of art varies widely from one Member State to another.[331] Accordingly, the approach which the Court has adopted towards the "public morality" justification in Article 30 where the Court has held that it is "in principle" for each Member State to determine the requirements of public morality in its territory,[332] should not be followed in this context.

8.117 Regard must now be had to Council Directive 93/7 on the return of cultural objects unlawfully removed from the territory of another Member State,[333] which was adopted in view of the abolition of controls at the Community's internal borders. Where "cultural objects classified as national

---

[328] See Biondi "The Merchant, the Thief and the Citizen: The Circulation of Works of Art Within the European Union" (1997) 34 C.M.L. Rev. 1173; Mattera "La libre circulation des oeuvres d'art à l'intérieur de la Communauté et la protection des trésors nationaux ayant une valeur artistique, historique ou archéologique" [1993] R.M.U.E. 9; von Plehwe "European Union and the Free Movement of Cultural Goods" (1995) 20 E.L. Rev. 431; Voudouri, "Circulation et protection des biens culturels dans l'Europe sans frontières" [1994] Rev. Dr. Pub. 479.

[329] Case 7/68 [1968] E.C.R. 423; [1969] C.M.L.R. 1.

[330] Para. 2.03 above.

[331] See, for example, Polonsky and Canat, "The British and French Systems of Control of the Export of Works of Art" (1996) 45 I.C.L.Q. 557.

[332] See para. 8.41 above.

[333] [1993] O.J. L74/74 as amended by Dirs 96/100 ([1997] O.J. L60/59) and 2001/38 ([2001] O.J. L187/43). This Directive is to be read with Council Reg. 3911/92 on the export of cultural goods ([1992] O.J. L395/1) as amended by Council Reg. 974/2001 ([2001] O.J. L137/10), which requires licences for the export of such goods to third countries. That Regulation was implemented by Commission Reg. 752/93 ([1993] O.J. L77/24). See De Ceuster, "Les règles communautaires en matière de restitution de biens culturels ayant quitté illicitement le territoire d'un Etat membre" [1993] R.M.U.E. 33; and Margue, "La protection des trésors nationaux dans le cadre du marché commun" [1992] R.M.C. 905 and "L'exportation des biens culturels dans le cadre du Grand Marché" [1993] R.M.U.E. 89.

treasures within the meaning of Article [30]" are unlawfully removed from one Member State to another on or after January 1, 1993, the former State may secure their return thanks to the provisions of this Directive.

The "cultural objects" to which the directive applies are items which are (a) "classified, before or after [their] unlawful removal from the territory of a Member State, among the 'national treasures possessing artistic, historic or archaeological value' under national legislation or administrative procedures within the meaning of Article [30] of the Treaty" and (b) either belong to one of the categories listed in the annexe to the directive or form part of "public collections listed in the inventories of museums, archives or libraries' conservation collection" or "the inventories of ecclesiastical institutions".

The annexe to the Directive contains a heterogeneous list, including: pictures and paintings executed entirely by hand on any medium and on any material, provided that they are at least 50 years old, do not belong to their "originators" and are worth at least €150,000; sculptures, subject to the same conditions save that the minimum requisite value is €50,000; books more than 100 years old, singly or in collections, with a value of at least €50,000; "means of transport" more than 75 years old and having a minimum value of at least €50,000; watercolour, gouache and pastel pictures executed entirely by hand; and "archives and any elements thereof, of any kind, on any medium, comprising elements more than 50 years old" regardless of value.[334]

The preamble to the Directive specifically states that:

> "the Annex to this Directive is .. not intended to define objects which rank as 'national treasures' within the meaning of the said Article [30], but merely categories of object which may be classified as such and may accordingly be covered by the return procedure introduced by this Directive...".

Yet in practice it is likely that the Court will use the annexe to the Directive as an aid to the interpretation of the words "national treasures possessing artistic, historic or archaeological value" in Article 30.

8.118   The following questions arise in this connection:

(a) What is meant by a "treasure"? Clearly the use of this term indicates that the work must be of special importance.[335] If an item satisfies this standard on historical or archaeological grounds, then it need have no artistic merit. If not, then it must be decided whether it is of sufficient artistic merit to be described as an artistic treasure. This is a type of decision which a court is not well equipped to make, so that it must inevitably rely to a considerable extent on expert evidence. When the expert witnesses agree, this matter will be relatively

---

[334] According to Dir. 2001/38 (see n.333 above), for the Member States which do not have the euro as their currency, the rate of exchange from the euro shall be that applicable on December 31, 2001, but that shall be reviewed every two years.

[335] It is true that there is some difference between the French, English, Danish and Greek language versions on the one hand and the Italian, Spanish, Portuguese and Dutch versions on the other. The latter do not speak of "treasures" but only of "artistic heritage". See further Voudouri n.328 above at 486.

straightforward but it will be an almost intractable problem in the face of contradictory evidence.

Mattera points out[336] that it is only in exceptional circumstances that works by contemporary artists will satisfy this test. As already mentioned, Directive 93/7 suggests a solution to their problem by laying down conditions as to the age, ownership and value of paintings and sculptures.

8.119 (b) Does the use of the term "national treasures" exclude objects of artistic, historical or archaeological value only to a region of a Member State? At a time of growing interest in regional culture, it does not seem possible to exclude such objects from the protection of Article 30.[337] It seems fitting to apply the maxim that the greater includes the lesser: the reference to national treasures must be taken to include regional treasures.

8.120 (c) Does this limb of Article 30 only cover objects which are products of the civilisation or culture of the Member State concerned? Where an item is an historical or archaeological treasure without being an artistic treasure, then it would seem that a Member State can only retain it if it has such value to that Member State. On this view, the Netherlands could not prevent the exportation of an item of historical or archaeological importance only to Italy (a Member State) or Peru (a third country).

8.121 However, the situation may be different where artistic treasures are concerned; if so, the United Kingdom may prevent the export to another Member State of a Titian or a Ming vase. On this reading "national treasures" is taken to refer to art treasures belonging to the nation and not to treasures of national art. In favour of this view one might rely on the practical consideration that once Member States are required to let such works of art out of their clutches, then they may often disappear from the Community altogether; the cultural loss would then be borne by the entire Community. Ranged against this practical view is the formidable argument that Article 30, as an exception to a fundamental rule of the Treaty, must be interpreted restrictively.[338]

At all events, it seems clear that, even if the narrower construction is to be placed on the term "national treasures", the place where an object was created and the nationality of its creator are of no consequence. Rather the decisive question is whether the object forms part of the culture and civilisation of the Member State.[339]

The Prevention of Tax Evasion

8.122 This is the first of the three "mandatory requirements" added by the

---

[336] See n.328 above.
[337] Mattera, *op. cit.* n.328 above, at 24. See generally para. 8.168.
[338] Gormley (*op. cit.* n.174 above at 183) considers that the narrower interpretation would frustrate the purpose of this ground of justification.
[339] Mattera, *op. cit.* at 23.

Court in the *"Cassis de Dijon"*[340] case where it is described as "the effectiveness of fiscal supervision". As mentioned in paragraph 8.51 above, the more straightforward approach might have been simply to treat this interest as being covered by the public policy exception.

At all events, it is probable that the mention of this ground of justification is a reference to the earlier case of *GB-Inno v ATAB*.[341] That case arose out of the prosecution of a Belgian supermarket chain, GB-Inno, for selling cigarettes below the price appearing on the tax label, contrary to Belgian law. The Belgian Court of Cassation asked the Court of Justice whether this provision was compatible with, *inter alia*, Article 28. In what amounted to an *obiter dictum* the Court stated:

> "In a system in which, as in Belgium, the basis of assessment to excise duty and to VAT is the retail selling price, a prohibition on selling tobacco products at a price higher than the retail selling price appearing on the tax label constitutes an essential fiscal guarantee, designed to prevent producers and importers from undervaluing their products at the time of paying the taxes."

8.123   The Court had occasion to consider this ground of justification once again in *Carciati*.[342] The facts were that one Herr Fink, a German national, had entrusted a car registered in Germany to the defendant for him to use in Italy on his frequent business visits. Since the defendant was resident in Italy, he was charged with having in his possession and using within Italian customs territory a car registered abroad in infringement of the provisions governing temporary importation. The Italian court therefore referred to the Court of Justice the question whether the Italian provisions governing the matter were compatible with "the Community rules in relation to the free movement of goods". The Italian provisions were essentially dictated by the New York Customs Convention of 1954, to which all Member States were party, and by Community VAT directives. In the light of this, the Court held that:

> "Member States retain broad powers to take action in respect of temporary importation, specifically for the purpose of preventing tax frauds. It follows that if the measures adopted to that end are not excessive, they are compatible with the principle of the free movement of goods.
>
>   As regards the prohibition imposed by a Member State on persons resident in its territory on the use of vehicles imported temporarily tax-free, it is an effective way of preventing tax frauds and ensuring that taxes are paid in the country of destination of the goods."

Although neither the reference nor the judgment mentions Articles 28 to 30, they refer generally to the Treaty provisions on the free movement of goods so that they are of relevance here.

---

[340] See n.5 above.
[341] Case 13/77 [1977] E.C.R. 2115; [1978] 1 C.M.L.R. 283. Para. 7.80 above.
[342] Case 823/79 [1980] E.C.R. 2773; [1981] 2 C.M.L.R. 193; see also Case 159/78 *Commission v Italy (customs agents)* [1979] E.C.R. 3247; [1980] 3 C.M.L.R. 446.

8.124 The facts of *Abbink*[343] were quite different. The defendant in the main case was primarily resident in the Netherlands, but he also resided in Saarbrücken in Germany, where he worked for the wholesale florists owned by his son. Every week he went back and forth between the two places, buying flowers on the Dutch market and exporting them to Saarbrücken. One day when he was on his way back to Germany he was questioned by the Dutch police about his use of a company car with a German registration plate. Since he was resident in the Netherlands, this led to his being charged with driving a foreign-registered car there without paying Dutch tax on it.

After the material facts arose, the Council passed Directive 83/182[344] on tax exemptions within the Community for certain means of transport temporarily imported into one Member State from another. That Directive relaxed the restrictions concerned to some extent. However, it did not apply to vehicles intended for transporting goods. Thus, even if it had been in force at the material time, it would have been of no avail to the defendant.

At all events, the court at Arnhem made a reference for a preliminary ruling asking whether such a measure was compatible with the Treaty provisions on the free movement of goods, even where the car was driven without any intention of evading tax. It was clear that the question as worded could only be answered in the negative. Unfortunately, the Dutch court did not ask any question about the fact that the vehicle was being used by the defendant in the course of his employment exporting goods to another Member State, where his employers were established.

In its submissions the Commission stressed that measures of this kind caused very considerable problems to frontier workers who have no intention of evading tax.[345] It illustrated this by reference to various complaints which it had received from such persons. In extreme cases the prohibition on a person driving a temporarily imported vehicle in the Member State in which he resides led to such persons having to give up their jobs altogether. For instance, a person cannot deliver goods to his own Member State in a foreign-registered lorry. The Commission took the view that in circumstances such as those in *Abbink* the prohibition in question was contrary to Article 29, since it was more restrictive than necessary to prevent tax evasion.

The Advocate General went some way with the Commission. In his view *Carciati* was not the last word on the matter. However, he rejected the broad view advocated by the Commission. He concentrated instead on the fact that the product concerned, namely flowers, was an agricultural product governed by a common market organisation. His conclusion was that in relation to such a product a measure of this kind was contrary to Article 32(2) (ex 38(2)) read with Article 29 when it could be proved that the vehicle was being used for exporting the goods concerned. Yet it is submitted with respect that nothing should turn on the fact that the goods concerned were agricultural goods

---

[343] Case 134/83 [1984] E.C.R. 4097; [1986] 1 C.M.L.R. 579.
[344] [1983] O.J. L105/59.
[345] See also its answer to Written question 22/82 ([1982] O.J. C262/1).

covered by a common market organisation; this fact does not appear to have any bearing on the measure concerned.

The five-judge chamber of the Court that decided the case relied on the narrow wording of the question, without giving any guidance on the wider problem. Citing *Carciati*, it held that the prohibition on residents of a Member State driving within that State cars which had been temporarily imported there and thus had not been subject to VAT there was compatible with the Treaty provisions on the free movement of goods, even where the persons concerned did not intend to evade tax. An opportunity for the Court to rule on this major obstacle to the free movement of goods was thus lost.[346]

Consumer Protection

8.125 While this ground of justification[347] is generally linked to the prevention of unfair competition, this is not necessarily so. Nevertheless, the two grounds of justification are so closely interlinked that, to gain a complete picture of this area of the law, the reader would be well advised to peruse paragraphs 8.148 to 8.157 below.

Greater emphasis has been placed on consumer protection by the EC Treaty since the Treaty of Maastricht inserted a new provision on the matter (Article 153 (ex 129a)). The first paragraph of that article requires the Community to "promote the interests of consumers and to ensure a high level of consumer protection", including "their right to information". The second paragraph of that article provides for the integration of consumer protection requirements into other Community policies and activities.

(i) General

8.126 It now seems clear that a person purchasing a product for the purposes of his business may be a "consumer" for these purposes. In *Denkavit Futtermittel v Land Baden-Württemberg*[348] a labelling requirement for animal feed was held to be justified, *inter alia*, on consumer protection grounds (the "consumers" were not the livestock, but the farmers !).

---

[346] But see the important judgments in Cases 249/84 *Ministère Public v Profant* [1985] E.C.R. 3237; [1986] 2 C.M.L.R. 378; and 127/86 *Ledoux* [1988] E.C.R. 3741, neither of which concerned goods. See also Case C-451/99 *Cura Anlagen v Auto Service Leasing* [2002] E.C.R. I-3193, para. 2.44 above. With respect to Dir. 83/182 on tax exemptions within the Community for certain means of transport temporarily imported into one Member State from another (see n.344 above) and its direct effect in particular, see C-389/95 *Klattner v Greek State* [1997] E.C.R. I-2719.

[347] See the 1982 FIDE Report on "Consumer Protection and the Common market"; Brouwer, "Free Movement of Foodstuffs and Quality Requirements: Has the Commission got it Wrong?" [1988] C.M.L. Rev. 237; Mortelmans and Watson, "The Notion of Consumer in Community Law: A Lottery?" in Lonbay (ed.) *Enhancing the Legal Position of the European Consumer* (1996) and Weatherill, *EC Consumer Law and Policy*, (1997).

[348] Case C-39/90 [1991] E.C.R. I-3069.

8.127 In *GB-Inno v Confédération du commerce luxembourgeois*[349] it was held that an import restriction which involved denying information to the consumer could not be justified on consumer protection grounds. The case concerned legislation which prohibited the distribution of publicity on temporary price reductions which stated the duration of the special offer or contained any reference to previous prices.

Conversely, it goes virtually without saying that a ban on false or misleading information is justified on consumer protection grounds. Thus, in *De Kik-vorsch*[350] the Court was concerned with a provision of Dutch law which made it an offence to state the specific strength of the original wort of beer on the packaging. The Dutch Government maintained that this prohibition was necessary to prevent the consumer confusing that information with the alcohol content, which was required to be stated on the packaging. The Court held that, if this was so, the prohibition was justified on consumer protection grounds. By the same token, it emerges clearly from the judgment in *Commission v United Kingdom*[351] that the Member States may prohibit false or misleading indications of origin.

8.128 What might be termed the "golden rule" is the principle that the sale of a product should never be prohibited when the consumer will be sufficiently protected by adequate labelling requirements.[352] Thus in *"Cassis de Dijon"* itself the Court ruled that one cannot:

> "regard the mandatory fixing of minimum alcohol contents as being an essential guarantee of the fairness of commercial transactions, since it is a simple matter to ensure that suitable information is conveyed to the purchaser requiring the display of an indication ... of the alcohol content on the packaging of products."

Similarly in *Gilli and Andres*,[353] where the defendants had been prosecuted for importing apple vinegar contrary to Italian law, the Court held that the national prohibition in question was not justified on the grounds of consumer protection because "the receptacles containing [the] vinegar are provided with a sufficiently clear label indicating that it is in fact apple vinegar, thus avoiding any possibility of the consumers confusing it with wine vinegar." Likewise, in *Rau v De Smedt*[354] the requirement that margarine be sold in cubic packaging to

---

[349] Case C-362/88 [1990] E.C.R. I-667; see also Case C-126/91 *Schutzverband gegen Unwesen in der Wirtschaft v Yves Rocher* [1993] E.C.R. I-2361.
[350] Case 94/82 [1983] E.C.R. 947; [1984] 2 C.M.L.R. 323.
[351] Case 207/83 [1985] E.C.R. 1201; [1985] 2 C.M.L.R. 259, para. 7.69 above.
[352] On labelling, see generally Dir. 2000/13 of the Parliament and the Council labelling, presentation and advertising of foodstuffs ([2000] O.J. L109/29). For criticism of the adequacy of labelling as an alternative means of consumer protection, see MacMaoláin, "Free movement of foodstuffs, quality requirements and consumer protection: have the Court and the Commission both got it wrong?" [2001] E.L. Rev. 413.
[353] See n.29 above; see also Case 130/80, see n.303 above. For a recent example, see C-448/98 *Guimont* [2000] E.C.R. I-10663 where it was held that the fact that Emmenthal cheese had been matured without a rind could be communicated to consumers through appropriate labelling rather than prohibiting the use of the Emmenthal designation at all.
[354] Case 261/81 [1982] E.C.R. 3961; [1983] 2 C.M.L.R. 496.

distinguish it from butter was held to be unjustified, since adequate labelling would suffice.

The same principle has been held to be applicable to products such as beer which are not necessarily sold to the consumer in packaged form: the requisite labelling can perfectly well appear on the barrel or tap, if draft beer is consumed at the point of sale.[355] Yet in *Commission v France (substitute milk products)*[356] the Court recognised that there were difficulties about giving detailed information to consumers about foodstuffs consumed in restaurants. However, it held that, since detailed information was not given about other products consumed in restaurants, it would not be justified to single out substitute milk products and impose specific requirements of this kind in relation to them. On the other hand, in *Drei Glocken v USL and Zoni*,[357] the Court appeared to suggest that Italy would be entitled to require restaurants to inform customers that their pasta was based on soft wheat.

8.129 Equally, the sale of a product under a particular designation may not be prohibited where adequate labelling would suffice. In *Commission v Italy*[358] the Court held that, while it was contrary to Article 28 to reserve the use of the term *aceto* (vinegar) to wine vinegar, it would be justified to require the exact nature of the product to be set out on a label affixed to that product. However, the Court stated that such a labelling requirement would only be justified if it applied to wine vinegar in the same way as to other types of vinegar. It is significant that on this point the Court did not follow the Advocate General's approach: he took the view that Italy was justified in prohibiting the use of the word *aceto* used alone as a description of vinegar not derived from wine, but that it was unjustified in prohibiting the use of that word coupled with another word or words indicating that the product is derived from a substance other than wine, such as cider or malt. The Court was clearly at pains to ensure that the same treatment should be accorded to wine vinegar (the "typically Italian" product) and other types of vinegar.[359]

(ii) Language requirements

8.130 It should by no means be thought that all labelling requirements are necessarily justified, as is shown by *Fietje*.[360] The defendant in the main case was a trader, who had sold in the Netherlands an alcoholic drink imported from Germany bearing the label in German "Berentzen Appel-Aus Apfel mit Weizenkorn 25 vol. %". He was prosecuted for not indicating the word likeur or liqueur on the bottles as required by Dutch law; drinks with a specified alcohol and sugar content were required to bear this indication. In reply to a reference

---

[355] Case 178/84, see n.30 above.
[356] See n.121 above.
[357] See n.122 above.
[358] Case 193/80 [1981] E.C.R. 3019.
[359] See also Case 281/83 *Commission v Italy* [1985] E.C.R. 3397; [1987] 1 C.M.L.R. 865.
[360] See n.72 above.

by the Dutch court as to the compatibility of such a measure with Article 28, the Court ruled:

> "If national rules relating to a given product include the obligation to use a description that is sufficiently precise to inform the purchaser of the nature of the product and to enable it to be distinguished from products with which it might be confused, it may well be necessary, in order to give consumers effective protection, to extend this obligation to imported products also, even in such a way as to make necessary the alteration of the original labels of some of these products...
>
> However, there is no longer any need for such protection if the details given on the original label of the imported product have as their content information on the nature of the product and that content includes at least the same information, and is just as capable of being understood by consumers in the importing State, as the description prescribed by the rules of that State. In the context of Article [234 of the EC] Treaty, the making of the findings of fact necessary in order to establish whether there is such equivalence is a matter for the national court."

It emerges from this passage that a Member State will not always be justified in requiring all labelling to be in its own language: if the particular words appearing on the label are just as comprehensible to the consumer of that Member State as the equivalent words in his own language, then the requirement is not justified.

8.131   The question of language requirements arose again in *Piageme v Peeters*.[361] The defendant company sold in Flanders imported bottled water labelled only in French or German. This ran counter to a Belgian Royal Decree which required food products sold in Flemish territory to be labelled in Dutch, albeit not exclusively so. The company argued that this Decree was incompatible with Article 28 and with Article 14 of Council Directive 79/112 on the labelling of foodstuffs,[362] according to which goods must be labelled in "a language easily understood by purchasers".

The Court found that goods might be labelled in a language easily understood by the consumer for the purposes of Article 14 of the Directive without necessarily being in the language of the region of sale. If that were the case, it would be contrary to that provision to require the goods to be labelled in the local language as well. It is not entirely clear from the judgment whether in these circumstances a non-exclusive labelling requirement would also fall foul of Article 28, but in the light of *Fietje* it would seem that it would do so. At all events, the Court naturally left it to the referring court to decide whether labels in French or German would be readily comprehensible to the Flemish consumer. Moreover, it remarked *obiter* that it would be contrary to Article 28 to require goods to be labelled exclusively in the language of the region of sale.

Subsequently the Commission set out its thinking on this area of the law in a

---

[361] Case C-369/89 [1991] E.C.R. I-2971.
[362] [1979] O.J. L33/1.

"Communication concerning the use of languages in the marketing of food-stuffs in the light of the judgment in the *Peeters* case".[363]

8.132 The judgments in *Fietje* and *Piageme* appeared to have been reversed by the ruling in *Meyhui v Schott Zwiesel Glaswerke*.[364] In this case the Court was asked by a Belgian court to rule on the validity of a provision in an annexe to Council Directive 69/493[365] on the approximation of laws relating to crystal glass. The annexe divided crystal glass products into four categories, indicating that for categories 1 and 2 any of the specified descriptions might be freely used, regardless of the country of destination. In contrast, for categories 3 and 4 it specified that: "Only the description in the language or languages of the country in which the goods are marketed may be used." Category 1 and 2 products were of higher quality than products in categories 3 and 4. Meyhui, a glass trader based in Kortrijk in the Dutch-speaking part of Belgium, imported Category 3 products sold by Schott, a German company. Schott's practice was to indicate the specified description in English, French and German. It refused to accede to Meyhui's request that Dutch, French and German (Belgium's official languages) be used instead, claiming that the relevant provision of the Directive was contrary to Article 28.

It is never an easy matter for the Court to assess the linguistic ability of the average consumer in a given Member State. Consequently, in *Fietje* and *Piageme* it treated this as a question to be decided by the national court, confining itself to laying down the principles to be applied. However, in this case the Court was unable to follow this course, since it alone has jurisdiction to find that a provision of Community law is contrary to the Treaty.[366] This may go some way to explain the rather surprising ruling delivered by the Court in this case.

Let us first consider the Opinion of Gulmann A.G. He pointed out that there were two aspects to the contested provision: the requirement to use the language or languages of the country concerned; and the prohibition on using any other language in addition. Applying the earlier case law, he found that the first aspect was warranted in some cases, but not in others: it must be justified to require a French category 3 product (*cristallin* in French) to be sold under the Dutch name (*sonoorglas*) in the Netherlands as the two words were so different; but the French, Italian, Spanish and Portuguese names for the category 4 product (*verre sonore, vetro sonoro, vidrio sonoro and vidro sonoro* respectively) were so close that they could be used interchangeably. As to the prohibition on the use of other languages, this was particularly onerous for traders. The Council had thought that the consumer would be misled if the name of the product was

---

[363] [1993] O.J. C345/3; see Gonzalez Vaque and Pirotte, "La communication interprétative de la Commission concernant l'emploi des langues pour la commercialisation des denrées alimentaires à la suite de l'arrêt Peeters" [1994] R.M.U.E. 25. A second reference was made in *Piageme v Peeters* (Case C-85/94 [1995] E.C.R. I-2955) but the judgment casts no light on the application of Articles 28 and 30. See also Cases C-385/96 *Goerres* [1998] E.C.R. I-4431; and C-366/98 *Geffroy* [2000] E.C.R. I-6579.

[364] Case C-51/93 [1994] E.C.R. I-3879.

[365] [1969] O.J. Eng. Spec. Ed. (II) 599.

[366] Case 314/85 *Foto-Frost v HZA Lübeck-Ost* [1987] E.C.R. 4199.

indicated not only in his own language, but in others as well. Yet this was not necessarily the case.

Although the task of weighing up all these elements was not easy, on balance the Advocate General concluded that the offending provision as a whole was invalid, since it must be possible to find a rule which took greater account of the requirements of the free movement of goods, while still giving adequate protection to the consumer.

The Court found otherwise. After stating that, in view of their higher lead-oxide content, category 1 and 2 products were of a higher quality, it went on:

"It may accordingly be considered that, in the case of the first two categories, consumers are adequately protected by the fact that in all the descriptions adopted by the directive (cristal supérieur 30 per cent, cristallo superiore 30 per cent, hochbleikristall 30 per cent, volloodkristal 30 per cent, full lead crystal 30 per cent, krystal 30 per cent, ... cristal superior 30 per cent, cristal de chumbo superior 30 per cent, cristal au plomb 24 per cent, cristallo al piombo 24 per cent, bleikristall 24 per cent, loodkristal 24 per cent, lead crystal 24 per cent, krystal 24 per cent, ... cristal al plomo 24 per cent, cristal de chumbo 24 per cent) the word 'crystal' is easily recognizable and, moreover, is always accompanied by an indication of the percentage of lead.

In the case of the lower two categories, on the other hand (cristallin, vetro sonoro superiore, kristallglass, kristallynglas, sonoorglas, crystal glass, crystallin, vidrio sonoro superior, vidro sonoro superior, verre sonore, vetro sonoro, vidrio sonoro, vidro sonoro, ...), the difference in the quality of the glass used is not easily discernible to the average consumer for whom the purchase of crystal glass products is not a frequent occurrence. It is therefore necessary for him to be given the clearest information possible as to what he is buying so that he does not confuse a product in categories 3 and 4 with a product in the higher categories and consequently that he does not pay too much.

The fact that consumers in a Member State in which the products are marketed are to be informed in the language or languages of that country is therefore an appropriate means of protection. In this regard it should be held that the hypothesis referred to by the national court that another language may be easily comprehensible to the purchase is of only marginal importance.

Finally, the measure chosen by the Community legislature in order to protect consumers does not appear disproportionate to the goal pursued. There is nothing in the file to suggest that there might conceivably be some different measures which could achieve the same goal while being less constrictive for producers.

It is apparent from the foregoing that the requirement that "Only the description in the language or languages of the country in which the goods are marketed may be used" is necessary for the protection of consumers and the Council has, therefore, not exceeded the limits of its discretion in the framework of its powers of harmonization by adopting the explanatory notes in question (see in particular Case 37/83 REWE-Zentrale v Landwirtschaftskammer Rheinland [1984] E.C.R. 1229, paragraph 20)."[367]

Following the Court's judgment in *Meyhui* the principles laid down in *Fietje* and *Piageme* appeared to be in tatters. Indeed, the Court even went so far as to give its blessing to the most restrictive type of measure, namely a ban on the use of additional languages together with that or those of the State of sale. Perhaps the best explanation for the judgment in *Meyhui* is that, as we noticed in

---

[367] Paras 17 to 21.

Chapter IV, the Court tends to allow the Commission and the Council more latitude as regards the justification for restrictions on trade than is the case with national legislation.[368] However it is true that there is nothing in this ruling to suggest that it would not apply equally to national measures.

8.133 Fortunately, the approach which the Court adopted before *Meyhui* has more recently been reaffirmed in *Colim v Bigg's Continent Noord.*[369] In that case, one of the questions that the Belgian court referred for a preliminary ruling was whether, where no specific Community rules exist, Member States are entitled to require all or part of the information appearing on the product to be given in the language of the area in which it is sold or in another language which may be readily understood by consumers in that area. The Court responded by underlining the importance of the purchaser or end-user being able to understand information which can be communicated by words alone subject, of course, to compliance with the principle of proportionality. The Court then held:

> "It follows, first, that a measure requiring the use of a language which consumers can readily understand must not exclude the possible use of other means of informing them, such as designs, symbols or pictograms. It is for the national court to determine in each case whether what appears on the labelling is such as to give consumers full information.
>
> Second, a measure of that kind must be restricted to the information made mandatory by the Member State concerned. Decisions as to the availability, in the language of the consumer, of information which, in the view of that State, need not be made mandatory must be left to the trader responsible for marketing the product, who may have it translated if he wishes."[370]

8.134 It would appear therefore, that the Court's previous case law remains intact. At all events, it is probable that the ruling in *Meyhui* does not affect the judgment in *Commission v Germany (pharmaceuticals).*[371] As we noticed at paragraph 8.89, it was held there that Germany could not prevent individuals importing pharmaceuticals for their own needs, even if a prescription was required for their purchase in Germany where they had been lawfully acquired in another Member State under a prescription issued by a doctor established there. The Court found that it was irrelevant that the instructions for use might not be in German, since the prescribing doctor in the other Member State concerned could give the necessary explanations to the patient. In the light of that circumstance, this case differs from the normal language requirement.

(iii) Generic names

8.135 We noticed at paragraphs 7.59 *et seq.* above that abusive restrictions on

---

[368] Paras 4.10 *et seq.* above.
[369] C-33/97 [1999] E.C.R. I-3175.
[370] Paras 41 and 42 of the judgment.
[371] See n.249 above.

the use of generic names are contrary to Article 28. Precisely because they are abusive, such measures cannot be justified on consumer protection grounds— as the Court held in the cases discussed in the paragraphs referred to.

(iv) Geographical denominations

8.136 Prior to the judgments in *Delhaize v Promalvin*[372] and *Exportur v LOR*[373] the protection of such denominations was treated under the heading of consumer protection and the prevention of unfair competition. Thanks to those judgments, geographical denominations are now regarded as industrial and commercial property. Consequently they will be considered at paragraphs 8.237 *et seq.* below.

(v) Other names

8.137 In *Verband Sozialer Wettbewerb v Estée Lauder*[374] the Court was called upon to consider a German prohibition on marketing a particular cosmetic product under the name "Clinique", the basis for this measure being the fear that consumers might mistakenly believe that the product had medicinal properties. The use of this name for the product was lawful in other countries. The Advocate General urged the Court not to decide this question itself, since in his view this would involve the Court overstepping the bounds of its jurisdiction under Article 234 of the Treaty; instead it should confine itself to setting out the criteria to be applied by the national court. However, the Court found that this restriction was not justified on consumer protection grounds, having regard to the following considerations:

> "the range of cosmetic products manufactured by the Estée Lauder company is sold in the Federal Republic of Germany exclusively in perfumeries and cosmetic departments of large stores, and therefore none of those products is available in pharmacies. It is not disputed that those products are presented as cosmetic products and not as medicinal products. It is not suggested that, apart from the name of the products, this presentation does not comply with the rules applicable to cosmetic products. Finally, according to the very wording of the question referred, those products are ordinarily marketed in other countries under the name "Clinique" and the use of that name apparently does not mislead consumers."[375]

8.138 The Court was concerned *inter alia* with the use of the trade descriptions "hollandaise" and "béarnaise" sauce in *Commission v Germany*.[376] German legislation required products which had not been manufactured in accordance with the traditional German recipe (that is, products manufactured with vegetable fats rather than eggs and butter) to carry an additional statement indi-

---

[372] Case C-47/90 [1992] E.C.R. I-3669.
[373] Case C-3/91, see n. 91 above.
[374] Case C-135/92 [1994] E.C.R. I-317.
[375] As to trade marks, see paras 8.186 *et seq.* and 8.221 *et seq.* below.
[376] C-51/94 [1995] E.C.R. I-3599. See also C-184/96 *Commission v France (foie gras)* [1998] E.C.R. I-6197 at paras 19 to 22.

cating that they had not been made in accordance with that traditional recipe. The German Government contended that the requirement was justified for the protection of consumers. The Court disagreed on the facts before it. Thus, while the Court accepted that in certain cases the requirement that an additional statement accompany the trade description is necessary to avoid consumer confusion, "consumers whose purchasing decisions depend on the composition of the products in question will first read the list of ingredients". Thus the Court concluded that "[e]ven though consumers may sometimes be misled, that risk remains minimal and cannot therefore justify the hindrance to the free movement of goods created by the requirements at issue".[377]

(vi) Distinctive symbols

8.139 *Pall v Dahlhausen*[378] concerned the right to use the letter "R" in a circle to indicate that the name of the product is a registered trade mark. This practice first started in the United States of America, where it was expressly provided for by statute. The practice became widespread throughout the Community, although there was no statutory basis for it in any Member State.

The defendants marketed in Germany blood filters imported from Italy. Both the filters themselves and their packaging bore the trade mark "Miropore" followed by the letter "R" in a circle. The claimants sought to prohibit the use of this symbol pursuant to the German law on unfair trading on the grounds that, although the mark had been registered in Italy, it had not been registered in Germany. In German law the use of this symbol was regarded as misleading the consumer and thus as constituting unfair trading, unless the product was registered in Germany.

The claimants maintained that this restriction was justified both on consumer protection grounds and for the prevention of unfair competition. It was not open to them to rely on the industrial property exception in Article 30, since they were not questioning the defendants' right to use the "Miropore" trade mark itself.

The Court rejected the claimants' argument based on consumer protection, in the following terms:

"Firstly, it has not been established that in practice the symbol (R) is generally used and understood as indicating that the trade mark is registered in the country in which the product is marketed.

Secondly, even assuming that consumers, or some of them, might be misled on that point, such a risk cannot justify so considerable an obstacle to the free movement of goods, since consumers are more interested in the qualities of a product than in the place of registration of the trade mark."

---

[377] Para. 34 of the judgment.
[378] Case C-238/89, see n. 16 above, also discussed at para. 8.156 below.

(vii) Hallmarking

8.140 The same approach was followed in *Robertson*[379] which concerned a process analogous to labelling, namely hallmarking. The Belgian provision in question required silver-plated articles to bear hallmarks of a particular type. Although Belgium was the only Member State to require silver-plated ware to be hallmarked, the Court found such a requirement to be justified. However, this was subject to the qualification that:

> "there is no longer the need for such protection where articles of that kind are imported from another Member State in which they have been lawfully marketed, if they are already hallmarked in accordance with the legislation of that State, on condition however that the indications provided by the hallmarks prescribed by that State, in whatever form, contain information which includes indications equivalent to those provided by the hallmarks prescribed by the Member State of importation and intelligible to consumers of that State.
>
> It is for the national court to make the findings of fact needed for the purposes of determining whether or not such equivalence exists."

It has been suggested[380] that in the light of this passage the importing Member State may require the article to bear relevant information in the form of a hallmark rather than any other form.

8.141 A further case relating to hallmarking was *Houtwipper*.[381] The Court there found that the obligation to stamp a hallmark on jewellery in gold and silver indicating its content was justified as protecting the consumer and preventing unfair competition, since otherwise it was impossible for the consumer to ascertain, by touching or looking at an item, what its precise gold or silver content was. It went on to confirm its ruling in *Robertson* that an equivalent hallmark from another Member State must suffice.

Next, the Court considered whether it was justified to require the hallmarking to be effected by an independent body (as in the Netherlands, the relevant State in that case, and a number of other Member States) rather than by the producer or importer himself, as occurred in the remaining Member States. Tesauro A.G. had taken the view that it was justified to extend this requirement to goods imported from Member States where the producer could hallmark his own goods, in view of the risks of fraud involved. Unfortunately, the Court's ruling was not wholly clear on this point. In contrast, the Court made it plain that it was not open to the Dutch authorities to refuse to recognise hallmarking effected by an independent body in another Member State.

Finally, the Court held that it was not justified for the Dutch to require the date to be indicated on imports. In most instances this was of no interest to the

---

[379] Case 220/81 [1982] E.C.R. 2349; [1983] 1 C.M.L.R. 556.
[380] Case note by D. Waelbroeck, [1983] C.D.E. 241.
[381] Case C-293/93 [1994] E.C.R. I-4249.

consumer, and in any event there was nothing to prevent such information being supplied on a voluntary basis. Moreover, where goods were hallmarked by an independent body, the year indicated would be that of the hallmarking, which would not necessarily correspond with the date of manufacture.

8.142 Yet another ruling concerning hallmarking was delivered in proceedings brought by the Commission against Ireland.[382] A number of features of the Irish system were challenged by the Commission. Amongst them was rule prohibiting the marketing in Ireland of precious metals that did not comply with Irish standards of fineness but which nevertheless bore an indication of fineness for the metal in question in parts per thousand. The Court held that the rule could not be justified because "a consumer familiar with the Irish system of indicating standards of fineness for articles of precious metal is given equivalent and intelligible information by a hallmark struck on an article of precious metal from another Member State which indicates the standard of fineness in parts per thousand".[383] Likewise, the Court rejected the justification for a rule that the aricle of precious metal must bear a mark of a sponsor registered in Ireland. The Court accepted the Commission's argument that the identification of the person responsible for an article of precious metal is possible if that article bears a sponsor's mark struck in accordance with the legislation of another Member State.[384]

(viii) Restrictions on advertising and sales promotion[385]

8.143 Advertising restrictions can in some circumstances be justified on consumer protection grounds. In *Oosthoek's Uitgeversmaatschappij*[386] it was held that:

> "the offering of free gifts as a means of sales promotion may mislead consumers as to the real prices of certain products and distort the conditions on which genuine competition is based. Legislation which restricts or even prohibits such commercial practices for that reason is therefore capable of contributing to consumer protection and fair trading."

8.144 In *Buet*[387] the Court held that a prohibition on sales of language teaching materials by door-to-door canvassing was justified on consumer protection grounds. Such canvassing exposed "the potential customer to the risk of making an ill-considered purchase". Moreover, with this kind of product "the potential purchaser often belongs to a category of people who are ... particu-

---

[382] C-30/99 *Commission v Ireland* [2001] E.C.R. I-4619. See also C-84/00 *Commission v France* [2001] E.C.R. I-4553. In the latter case however, the French Government had simply not put forward any justification for the restriction to trade (see para. 26 of the judgment).
[383] Para. 33 of the judgment.
[384] Paras 51-5 of the judgment.
[385] See also paras 7.4 and 8.96.
[386] Case 286/81 [1982] E.C.R. 4575; [1983] 3 C.M.L.R. 428.
[387] Case 382/87 [1989] E.C.R. 1235.

larly vulnerable". The Court found that giving purchasers a right of cancellation would not be an adequate alternative.[388]

8.145 *De Agostini*[389] is the only case to deal with the protection of children as a special category of consumers. This reference for a preliminary ruling concerned Swedish legislation which prohibited television advertising aimed at children under 12 years of age. Noting that children are a particularly vulnerable group of consumers, Jacobs A.G. rejected the Commission's suggestion that the ban was disproportionate: in his view, it was not obvious that the alternative measures advocated by the Commission (rules as to content and quality of such advertisements or an obligation to indicate the price of costly items) were an adequate substitute. In contrast, the Court of Justice left the point open, so that it fell to the Swedish court to decide whether the restriction was justified.[390]

(ix) Assessing the consumer's understanding[391]

8.146 When deciding whether a practice is liable to confuse the consumer, what yardstick is to be used: the understanding of the average consumer of the importing State, or that of the average Community consumer? The Court's case law is unclear on this point, and indeed the answer may vary according to the type of practice concerned.

Thus, in *Fietje* the Court stated unequivocally that, as regards a label in another Community language, one must have regard to the linguistic ability of the average consumer of the importing State. Indeed, it could scarcely be otherwise: any attempt to apply a Community-wide criterion in determining whether a Dutchman can understand a particular label in German would surely be doomed to failure. It is submitted that the same would generally apply to cases which turn on the associations evoked by particular words in the language of the importing State. Thus in *Graffione v Ditta Fransa*,[392] in deciding whether or not the trade mark "Cottonelle" applied to toilet paper and disposable handkerchiefs might induce a consumer wrongly to believe that the products under that mark contained cotton, the Court acknowledged that "it is possible that because of linguistic, cultural and social differences between Member States a trade mark which is not liable to mislead a consumer in one Member

---

[388] See also C-362/88, see n. 349 above; C-126/91 *Schutzverband gegen Unwesen in der Wirtschaft v Yves Rocher* [1993] E.C.R. I-2361; C-315/92 *Verband Sozialer Wettbewerb v Estée Lauder* [1994] E.C.R. I-330; and Case C-470/93 *Mars* [1995] E.C.R. I-1923. See also Dir. 84/450 relating to the approximation of the laws, regulations and administrative provisions of the Member States concerning misleading advertising ([1984] O.J. L 250/17), as amended; the Commission's Green Paper on Consumer Protection (COM(2001)531 final) and the Commission's Proposal for a Regulation of the EP and the Council concerning sales promotion in the internal market (COM(2001) 546 final).

[389] See n.22 and para. 7.44 above.

[390] See paras 45 and 46 of the judgment.

[391] For a comprehensive review of the case law in this area, see Weatherill, "Recent case law concerning the free movement of goods: Mapping the frontiers of market deregulation" (1999) 36 C.M.L. Rev 51 at 54–70.

[392] C-313/94 [1996] E.C.R. I-6039.

State may be liable to do so in another".[393] In *Smanor*,[394] however, the Court determined the meaning of the word "yoghourt" to the French consumer on the basis of the *Codex Alimentarius* adopted by the FAO and the World Health Organisation; yet this term is particularly international in nature. Another exception was *Estée Lauder*,[395] where the Court determined that the German consumer was not likely to be misled into thinking that a cosmetic sold under the name "Clinique" had therapeutic qualities.

In a series of cases the Court has held that adequate labelling would afford sufficient protection to the consumer.[396] In each of these cases the Court has not considered the ability of consumers in the State concerned to understand clear labels in their own language, but has—rightly, it is submitted—assumed that consumers throughout the Community are alike in this respect. Furthermore, in *Commission v Germany (beer)*[397] the Court stated that Member States may not crystallise the habits of consumers so as to consolidate an advantage acquired by national industries; thus it was not justified to prohibit the sale as "beer" of a product containing rice or maize merely because this was traditionally prohibited in Germany. This is in effect why the Court is not impressed by opinion polls.[398]

There is no inherent contradiction between these two lines of case law. Certain matters, particularly those connected with a particular language, are inherently related to the understanding of consumers in a particular Member State, while others are not. By its very nature, the Court is inevitably less well equipped than a national court to rule on cases falling within the former category. However, it is submitted that even in cases which concern matters inherently related to the understanding of consumers in a particular Member State, the risk to consumers must nevertheless be "sufficiently serious"[399] and be subject, in general terms, to an emerging Community concept of "the average consumer—reasonably well informed and reasonably observant and circumspect".[400]

---

[393] Para. 22 of the judgment. However, it may be noted that the Court was quick to qualify this by stating at para. 24 that "the risk of misleading consumers cannot override the requirements of the free movements and so justify barriers to trade, unless that risk is sufficiently serious". It is submitted that this, to a certain extent, reimposes a Community-wide objectivity. See also, C-220/98 *Estée Lauder Cosmetics v Lancaster Group* [2000] E.C.R. I-117 where the Court again referred to "social, cultural and linguistic factors" (para. 29) particular to one Member State, but qualified this by a reference to "the average consumer—reasonably well informed and reasonably observant and circumspect" (para. 30). Again, it is submitted that this reimposes a degree of Community-wide objectivity.

[394] See n. 209 above.

[395] Case C-135/92, See n. 374 above, para. 8.137 above.

[396] Para. 8.128 above.

[397] See n.30 above.

[398] See para. 8.239 below. However, with respect to cosmetic products, the Court has expressly stated that the national courts may, in determining whether or not labelling was liable to mislead consumers, "consider it necessary to commission an expert opinion or survey of public opinion in order to clarify whether or not a promotional description or statement is misleading": *Estée Lauder Cosmetics GmbH v Lancaster Group GmbH*, n.393 above at para. 31.

[399] *Graffione v Ditta Fransa*, n.392 above at para. 24.

[400] *Estée Lauder Cosmetics v Lancaster Group*, n.393 above at para. 30. See also Cases C-470/93 *Verein gegen Unwesen v Mars* [1995] E.C.R. I-1923 at para. 24; C-3/99 *Cidrerie Ruwet v Bulmer* [2000] E.C.R. I-8749 at para. 53.

(x) Criticism deflected

8.147   The charge has been levelled against the judgment in *"Cassis de Dijon"* and the subsequent decisions that they have resulted in a lowering of quality standards.[401] However, this is not necessarily so.[402] The Court has held that certain particular restrictions (*e.g.* a minimum alcohol requirement, a prohibition on the sale of cider vinegar and a prohibition on the sale of bread containing a certain proportion of dry matter)[403] were not justified on consumer protection grounds or any other grounds. Moreover, in each case the products concerned were traditional products of another Member State. Yet the Court has not gone so far as to rule out the possibility for a Member State to prohibit the sale of a product on quality grounds, as distinct from health grounds. Nevertheless, it is arguable that there will always be a sufficient guarantee for the consumer if the sale of low quality products is banned under a given designation rather than if their sale is banned altogether. For example, on this view there is no necessity to prohibit outright the sale of "orange juice" containing only 2 per cent orange, since it is enough to ban its sale under that name.

The Prevention of Unfair Competition

8.148   The term "prevention of unfair competition" is used here as being more appropriate than the expression "the fairness of commercial transactions" used in the *"Cassis de Dijon"*[404] case. Indeed, "unfair competition" was used in *Commission v Germany (Sekt/Weinbrand)*[405]. Perhaps the best guidance on the meaning of this concept can be drawn from Article 10*bis* inserted into the Paris Convention for the Protection of Industrial Property of 1883.[406] This provision reads as follows:

"(1)   The countries of the Union are bound to assure the nationals of such countries effective protection against unfair competition;

(2)   Any act of competition contrary to honest practices in industrial or commercial matters constitutes an act of unfair competition;

(3)   The following in particular shall be prohibited:

1)   all acts of such a nature as to create confusion by any means whatever with the establishment, the goods, or the industrial or commercial activities of a competitor;

---

[401] See para. 6.77 above.
[402] *ibid.*
[403] See paras 7.28 *et seq.* above.
[404] See n.5 above.
[405] Case 12/74 [1975] E.C.R. 181; [1975] 1 C.M.L.R. 340.
[406] In principle the Treaty of Rome prevails over the Convention as between Member States: see paras 9.45 *et seq.* below. Consequently, the Paris Convention (last amended at Stockholm in 1967) only gives guidance on this matter, rather than being binding as between Member States.

> 2) false allegations in the course of trade of such a nature as to discredit the establishment, the goods, or the industrial or commercial activities of a competitor;
>
> 3) indications or allegations the use of which in the course of trade is liable to mislead the public as to the nature, the manufacturing process, the characteristics, the suitability for their purpose, or the quantity, of the goods."[407]

The concept of unfair competition therefore broadly corresponds to practices actionable in English law for passing off or slander of title.[408] As has already been pointed out, these matters go hand in hand with consumer protection, so that this section should be read together with paragraphs 8.125 to 8.147 above.

However, especially in view of the provision of the Paris Convention quoted above, there are also links between unfair competition and intellectual property law. This is particularly the case where, as in the English action for passing off, a party seeks to prevent specific actions of a competitor by relying on his own prior activity or right.

Although the Court of Justice has never labelled such forms of unfair competition law "intellectual property" or "industrial and commercial property", there remains the possibility that it might do so in the future.[409] The Court should tread with extreme caution in this regard, given that intellectual property current enjoys a higher status and thus greater protection than the prevention of unfair competition. Such a step would be highly questionable if it were to result in the Court giving the Member States as much leeway in determining their laws on unfair competition as with respect to intellectual property[410]: as demonstrated by some of the cases discussed below, some national laws on unfair competition are extremely far-reaching.

8.149 It would seem that where a Member State prohibits the sale of goods having a particular content or presentation so as to prevent them from benefiting from some advantageous provision of its own law, then this ground of justification is not in point. The ruling in *Miro*[411] appears to be authority for this proposition. In that case the Dutch Government sought to justify its prohibition on the use of the name "jenever" for drinks with an alcohol content of less than 35 per cent on the grounds, *inter alia*, that such a product would attract a lower rate of tax and excise duties. This would, it submitted, confer an unfair price advantage on such products. The Court dismissed this argument on the grounds that:

---

[407] See Bodenhausen's *Guide to the Paris Convention* (1968).

[408] For a comparative study, see Ulmer's series of volumes entitled *La répression de la concurrence déloyale dans les Etats membres de la Communauté économique européenne*, (1967).

[409] As explained at para. 8.172 below, the term "intellectual property" is generally to be preferred, although Article 30 speaks of "industrial and commercial property".

[410] See paras 8.183 *et seq.* below.

[411] Case 182/84 [1985] E.C.R. 3731; [1986] 3 C.M.L.R. 545.

"such differences in taxes and excise duties charged under national legislation are part of the objective conditions of competition of which every trader may freely take advantage, provided that purchasers are given information so that they can freely make their choice on the basis of the quality and price of the products."

This wording suggests that the same principle might perhaps apply where the legislation conferring the advantage is not that of the importing Member State.[412]

8.150 The Court in effect stated in *Commission v Germany*[413] that a measure might only be justified on the grounds of unfair competition if it was simultaneously justified on the grounds of consumer protection; the Court appears to have retreated from that unduly restrictive position. Yet the fact remains that the prevention of unfair competition is often so closely linked to that of consumer protection as to stand or fall with it: if there is no danger of the consumer being misled, then frequently unfair competition is not likely to occur.[414]

8.151 However, in *Dansk Supermarked v Imerco*[415] the question of unfair competition did arise independently of consumer protection. The facts were that Imerco, a syndicate of Danish ironmongers, had a dinner service made in the United Kingdom to celebrate its 50th anniversary. Each item of the service was decorated with pictures of Danish royal castles and bore Imerco's name and a legend referring to its 50th anniversary. The exclusive right to sell this service was reserved to members of the syndicate. It was agreed between Imerco and the British manufacturer that "seconds"—which amounted to about 20 per cent of production because of the criteria chosen—could be sold on the British market, but should on no account be exported to Denmark or to other Scandinavian countries. However, Dansk Supermarked acquired some such "seconds" on the British market and proceeded to sell them in Denmark, whereupon Imerco brought an action against it before the Danish courts. The action reached the Supreme Court of Denmark which put a question to the Court asking in effect whether it was compatible with Article 30 to prevent such imports on the grounds of copyright protection, trade mark protection or the prevention of unfair competition.

The Court replied with respect to unfair competition as follows:

"In order to reply to that question it must first of all be remarked that Community law does not in principle have the effect of preventing the application in a Member State to goods imported from other Member States of the provisions on marketing in force in the State of importation. It follows that the marketing of imported goods may be prohibited if the conditions on which they are sold constitute an infringement of the marketing usages considered proper and fair in the Member State of importation.

It must nevertheless be emphasised, as the Court of Justice has stressed in another

---

[412] Slynn A.G. rejected the argument on other grounds, namely that it was of an entirely economic nature (see para. 8.32 above).
[413] See n.405 above.
[414] *e.g.* Case 12/74, n.405 above; Case 120/78, see n.5 above.
[415] Case 58/80 [1981] E.C.R. 181; [1981] 3 C.M.L.R. 590.

context in its judgment of November 25, 1971 (Case 22/71 *Béguelin* [1971] E.C.R. 949; [1972] C.M.L.R. 81), that the actual fact of the importation of goods which have been lawfully marketed in another Member State cannot be considered as an improper or unfair act since that description may be attached only to offer or exposure for sale on the basis of circumstances distinct from the importation itself..."

It therefore found that Article 28 of the Treaty must be interpreted as meaning:

"That the importation into a Member State of goods lawfully marketed in another Member State cannot as such be classified as an improper or unfair commercial practice, without prejudice however to the possible application of legislation of the State of importation against such practices on the ground of the circumstances or methods of offering such goods for sale as distinct from the actual fact of importation..."

This last proviso appears to relate to a point made by the Advocate General: he took the view that, although in principle sales of "seconds" could not be prevented on the grounds of unfair competition, it would be otherwise if they held themselves out to the consumer as being of first quality.

8.152 The prevention of unfair competition was also in point in *Industrie Diensten Groep v Beele*.[416] There, the appellants in the main case had imported certain cable conduits into the Netherlands for a number of years. The Dutch patent had now expired and the respondents had begun to market in the Netherlands other cable conduits imported from Germany, which bore a striking resemblance to those imported by the appellants. The appellants alleged before the Dutch courts that the respondents' goods constituted slavish imitation of their own, and thus sought an injunction preventing the respondents from marketing their products in the Netherlands. In English law, this would have amounted to an action for passing off. In its reference for a preliminary ruling, the Dutch court asked the Court of Justice in essence whether it would be contrary to Articles 28 to 30 to grant such an injunction, stating that the similarity between the two products was greater than necessary.

Citing Article *10bis* of the Paris Convention, the Court replied that it was justified on the grounds of the prevention of unfair competition and on consumer protection grounds to prohibit the sale of imported goods which were "for no compelling reason practically identical to the products imitated" and caused unnecessary confusion. On the latter point, the Court stressed that "the judgment of the national court shows that the question whether or not such imitation is necessary was considered not only from the technical point of view, but also from the economic and commercial point of view".

---

[416] Case 6/81 [1982] E.C.R. 707; [1982] 3 C.M.L.R. 102.

8.153 This ground of justification also arose in *Miro*.[417] Under Dutch law, "gin" was defined as a drink with an alcohol content of at least 35 per cent. It was prohibited to use the name jenever or other related designations for products with a lower alcohol content. The defendants imported from Belgium quantities of gin with an alcohol content of 30 per cent. Such gin had been produced in Belgium for many years. At the material time Belgium imposed no alcohol requirement for this product. The alcohol content was clearly indicated on the label, but the name jenever was also used. The defendants, who were charged with the offence of possessing stocks of bottles so labelled with a view to sale, claimed that the relevant provisions of Dutch law infringed Article 28.

Referring, *inter alia*, to *Prantl*,[418] the Advocate General reached the conclusion that the measure was not justified. However, he expressly left open the question as to what would be the position of gin containing a mere 15 per cent alcohol, a point which had been raised by the Dutch Government.

The Court also found on the basis of *Prantl* that the measure was not justified, subject to the condition that "the purchaser is provided with proper information." In reaching this conclusion, the Court more or less directly applied the "fair and traditional" test first laid down in *Prantl*. It did not rule on the hypothetical problem of gin having a far lower alcohol content.

8.154 In *Prantl* it was held that the sale of wine in bottles of a particular shape "fairly and traditionally" used in a region of Italy could not be prohibited in Germany, although bottles of a similar shape had been used for centuries for wines of certain German regions. This "fair and traditional" test is the source of some concern. The time-honoured criterion laid down in *"Cassis de Dijon"* is that the goods must have been "lawfully produced and marketed" in another Member State.[419] This criterion is more satisfactory than the "fair and traditional" test on two counts. First of all, it is far more conducive to legal certainty: whether marketing and production are lawful is a question of law, while "fair" and "traditional" are largely subjective terms.[420] Secondly, the requirement of "traditional" usage will prevent imports of new products—scarcely a desirable result. What is more, it is surely undesirable that the two tests should coexist alongside each other.

In these circumstances the judgment in *Commission v Germany*[421] is of particular interest. *Pétillant de raisin* is a product which has been made in France since 1956 from partially fermented grape juice and has always been marketed in bottles similar in shape to that of the traditional champagne-type bottle with a wired mushroom-shaped stopper; its alcoholic strength does not exceed 3 per cent. Under German legislation its sale in such bottles was prohibited. This was

---

[417] See n.411 above. Consumer protection was not in point since the referring court had found that the label gave rise to no confusion. In a sense, that court thereby pre-empted discussion on the central issue raised by the case.
[418] Case 16/83, See n.14 above; [1985] 1 C.M.L.R. 688, para. 8.154 below.
[419] Paras 6.70 *et seq.* above.
[420] Brouwer, *op. cit.* n.347 above, at 253.
[421] Case 179/85 [1986] E.C.R. 3879; [1988] 1 C.M.L.R. 135.

anomalous because under the legislation the use of such bottles was not in fact reserved for champagne and sparkling wines: cider and certain sparkling drinks made from fruit juice could also be sold in bottles of this kind.

Slynn A.G. considered that the restriction was not justified, since the labelling was sufficient. As to the "fair and traditional" test he had this to say:

"whereas the 'fair and traditional usage' test may be appropriate in a case like *Prantl* where the question of indirect designation of origin arose, it does not seem to me that it has to be established in every case. If it did, the development and marketing of new products would be stifled. The appropriate test in a case like the present is in my view stated in *Cassis de Dijon*—whether the product was 'lawfully produced and marketed' in one Member State. If it is, it may be marketed in another Member State subject to mandatory requirements of the kind indicated in *Cassis de Dijon* and subject to the provisions of Article [30] of the Treaty. I should in any event accept that the sale of a product for thirty years in a particular container was capable of amounting to a fair and traditional usage."

The Court also found that the labelling sufficed. It continued:

"As regards the Federal Government's arguments concerning fair trading, it must be borne in mind, as is clear from the documents and oral arguments submitted to the Court, that:

(i)   since production began in 1956, *pétillant de raisin* has been lawfully and continuously marketed in France and other Member States in its original presentation consisting of the traditional champagne-type bottle with its traditional stopper. It cannot therefore be maintained that such a presentation is used on the German market for unfair trading purposes or to exploit the good name of other products;

(ii) in any event, the traditional champagne-type bottle with its traditional stopper has been used for a long time in the Member States to bottle not only champagne and sparkling wine but also a number of other beverages such as cider or drinks made from fruit juice without conferring on their manufacturers an exclusive right to use that type of presentation and without affecting fair trading;

(iii) the German legislation itself allows the traditional champagne-type bottle to be used to bottle not only sparkling wines but also sparkling drinks made from fruit or berries.

Therefore, the marketing of *pétillant de raisin* on the German market in the bottle in which it has been continuously and lawfully marketed since it came onto the market 30 years ago must be regarded as satisfying the requirements arising from the need to have regard on all sides for the fair and traditional practices observed in the various Member States, and it is not necessary to consider whether the presentation in question is technically or economically necessary for the producer."

This ruling watered down the test of "fair and traditional" usage to a considerable extent. It remains to be seen whether this test is to continue and, if so, what its function is to be.

8.155 Another interesting case was *Kohl v Ringelhan & Rennett*,[422] which con-

---

[422] Case 177/83 [1984] E.C.R. 3651; [1985] 3 C.M.L.R. 340.

cerned the right to use the distinctive sign consisting of the letters "r + r" in white against a contrasting background. That sign has been used by the German firm Ringelhan & Rennett, which had set up the defendant company as its subsidiary in France in 1971. The German company had gone bankrupt in 1982. The defendant company had been taken over by a third party. The claimant was a competing company which brought an action before the German courts claiming that the defendant was not entitled to use the distinctive sign in Germany without indicating that it no longer had any economic or legal connection with its former parent. The claimant relied on the German law of unfair competition. The national court made a reference for a preliminary ruling on this matter on the basis that the use of the distinctive sign by the defendant was lawful in France.

The Court began by pointing out that the claimant company did not itself claim the right to use the distinctive sign in question. It merely contended that the use of this sign by the defendant gave a misleading impression to the public that its products emanated from, or were connected with, the bankrupt company. This was why industrial and commercial property was not directly raised in the case: even if the right to use the sign constituted industrial and commercial property, the plaintiff was unable to rely on it.

Next, the Court went on to consider whether the measure at issue was "indistinctly applicable". It found that it was not. The reason for prohibiting the use of the sign was that it misled the public into thinking that the goods were of German origin, when in fact they were imported from France. Thus there was discrimination against imported goods. Accordingly, the measure could not be justified on the grounds of the prevention of unfair competition (or consumer protection).[423]

8.156 The Court was to build on the latter ruling in *Pall v Dahlhausen*,[424] where it stated:

"It has also been argued that the use of the symbol (R) in a State in which the trade mark is not registered should be regarded as unfair competition vis-à-vis competitors and that, if the registration of a trade mark in any Member State is sufficient to justify the use of the symbol at issue, manufacturers could elect to register their trade marks in the States with the least demanding requirements.

That argument must be rejected. Firstly, prudent economic operators with an interest in knowing whether or not a trade mark is registered can determine the legal situation concerning the trade mark in question at the public register. Secondly, the principal aim of a person registering a trade mark in a particular State is to obtain legal protection in that State. The symbol (R), like other symbols which indicate that a trade mark is registered, is, in relation to that legal protection, which constitutes the object of the registration, of an ancillary or supplementary nature."

8.157 Finally, it should be noted that the Court is, in principle, willing to turn the prevention of unfair competition on its head: the very reason why an

---

[423] See paras 8.125 *et seq.* above.
[424] See n.378 above.

imported product allegedly gives rise to unfair competition may also provide the domestic producer with a potential marketing advantage. It will be recalled that in *Commission v Germany*[425] German legislation required use of the trade descriptions "hollandaise" and "béarnaise" sauce for products which had not been manufactured in accordance with the traditional German recipe (which required the use of eggs and butter) to carry an additional statement to that effect. The German Government contended that the latter requirement was justified for the prevention of unfair competition because the use of ingredients such as vegetable fats, which are less expensive than eggs and butter, enabled manufacturers of imported products to enjoy a competitive advantage. The Court did not accept this argument, pointing out *inter alia* that it was "open to producers to draw the attention of [consumers who are heedful of the composition of a product] to the fact that traditional ingredients are used".[426] In other words, rather than requiring the imported product to carry an additional statement indicating that it was not made in accordance with the traditional German recipe, it was open for products which were made using that traditional recipe, to draw consumers' attention to that fact thereby, in effect, "neutralising" the alleged competitive advantage enjoyed by the imported product.[427]

The Protection of the Environment

8.158 Frequently, measures that are justified on environmental grounds will be justified in any event on the grounds of the protection of the health and life of human beings, animals or plants.[428] However, this will not always be so. Confirming earlier indications in the case law,[429] the Court first recognised the protection of the environment as a ground of justification in *Commission v Denmark*.[430]

It should be recalled that the precautionary principle applies to the protection of the environment. Indeed, the only mention of this principle in the EC Treaty is to be found in the title on environmental policy (Article 174(2)). For a full examination of that principle, the reader is referred to paragraphs 8.61 to 8.64 above.

The importance of environmental protection is further underscored by the

---

[425] See n.376 above.
[426] Para. 36 of the judgment.
[427] See also, Case 178/84, see n.30 above. Following the Court's judgment in that case, it was similarly open to German beer producers to draw the attention of consumers to the fact that their beer had been brewed in accordance with the *Reinheitsgebot*.
[428] See, for example, *Aher-Waggon* (see n.24) where it was held that legislation on noise standards for aircraft "may be justified by considerations of public health and environmental protection" (at para. 19). See also C-203/96 see n.18 above, (paras. 44–48); and Case C-209/98 *FFAD v Københavns Kommune* [2000] E.C.R. I-3743 at paras 45–7.
[429] Cases 3–4/76 *Kramer* [1987] E.C.R. 1279 at 1325; [1976] C.M.L.R. 440; 240/83 *Procureur de la République v ADBHU* [1985] E.C.R. 532 (paras 13 and 15 of the judgment); and 54/85 *Mirepoix*, (see n.235 above).
[430] Case 302/86 [1988] E.C.R. 4607, para. 8 of the judgment. For more recent examples, see Cases C-284/95 *Safety Hi-Tech v S & T* [1998] E.C.R. I-4301 at paras 64–66; C-341/95 *Bettati v Safety Hi-Tech* [1998] E.C.R. I-4355 at paras 62–64; and C-314/98 *Snellers Auto's v Algemeen Directeur van de Dienst Wegverkeer* [2000] E.C.R. I-8633 at paras 49–60.

Treaty of Amsterdam, which introduced into Part I of the EC Treaty ("Principles") a new Article 6 drafted in the following terms: "Environmental protection requirements must be integrated into the definition and implementation of the Community policies and activities referred to in Article 3, in particular with a view to promoting sustainable development."[431]

8.159 In *Commission v Denmark*, the Commission maintained that Danish legislation requiring beer and soft beverages to be sold in reusable containers and made subject to a deposit was contrary to Article 28. The Court dismissed this claim on the grounds that this requirement was necessary on environmental grounds to ensure that containers were in fact reused. It was therefore proportionate to the aim of protecting the environment.

In contrast, the Court found for the Commission as regards the Danish requirement that only containers conforming to types approved by the Danish authorities could be used, although each producer was entitled to sell no more than 3,000 hectolitres of beer or soft beverages per year in unapproved containers. The Court stressed the expense which this measure imposed on foreign producers, since they would have to use special containers for their sales to Denmark. It found that this specific measure was disproportionate and thus not justified.[432]

8.160 The protection of the environment also arose in *Commission v Belgium*.[433] The Region of Wallonia had imposed a ban on imports of waste from outside its borders. The legislation provided that exceptions could be made in accordance with agreements to be concluded with other regions of Belgium (Brussels and Flanders), but no such exceptions could be made for waste from other Member States. The Commission relied both on Council Directive 84/631 on the supervision and control within the European Community of the transfrontier shipment of hazardous waste[434] and (with respect to refuse not covered by that directive) on Article 28.

---

[431] See para. 12.24 below; also C-379/98 see n.19 above at para. 76; and Wasmeier, "The integration of environmental protection as a general rule for interpreting Community law" (2001) 38 C.M.L. Rev 159. It is something of a paradox that the insertion of the new Article 6 into the Treaty gives the impression that the Treaty accords greater weight to the protection of the environment than it does to the protection of public health. See also, generally, Bär and Kraemer, "European Environmental Policy after Amsterdam" (1998) 10 J.E.L. at 315; Jans, *European Environmental Law* (2000, 2nd Ed.); Müller-Graf, "Umweltschutz und Grundfreiheiten" in *Handbuch zum Europäischen und Deutschen Umweltrecht* (ed. Rengeling) 1998 vol. 1 p. 222; and Scheuing, "Regulierung und Marktfreiheit im Europäischen Umweltrecht" (2001) EuR 1.

[432] For the surprising claim that this point of judgment was reversed when the Single European Act introduced Art. 174 (ex 130R) into the Treaty, see Krämer, "Environmental Protection and Article 30 EEC Treaty" (1993) 30 C.M.L. Rev. 111.

Two cases on the more recent Danish legislation on containers for drink are currently pending: Cases C-233/99 *Hansen* and C-246/99 *Commission v Denmark*.

[433] Case C-2/90, see n.17 above, noted by Gerardin [1993] E.L. Rev. 144; Sevenster, *Milieubeleid en Gemeenschapsrecht* (1992) at 319; and von Wilmovsky [1993] C.M.L. Rev. 541; see also the latter's book *Abfallwirtschaft im Binnenmarkt* (1990).

[434] [1984] O.J. L326/31, subsequently amended. Following the judgment this Directive was replaced by Council Reg. 259/93 on the supervision and control of shipments of waste within, into and out of the European Community ([1993] O.J. L30/1). The validity of the legal basis of this Reg. (Art. 175 (ex 130S)) was upheld in Case C-187/93 *Parliament v Council* [1994] E.C.R. I-2874.

The directive layed down the administrative procedures to be followed for the transactions in question and the Court therefore found that it precluded a ban such as that imposed by Wallonia.

As to Article 28, the Court found that the case was justified on environmental grounds. It avoided alluding to the Commission's argument that waste produced in other Member States was no more harmful than that originating in Wallonia. Instead, it referred to the argument as to quantity: Belgium had claimed that exceptionally large imports of waste into the region had created an environmental danger, and the Commission had not contested this claim.

Finally, it referred to its traditional case law to the effect that mandatory requirements can only justify indistinctly applicable measures.[435] This difficulty was particulary acute in this case since the contested import ban constituted a quantitative restriction pure and simple, not a measure of equivalent effect. However, the Court overcame this problem by referring to Article 174(2) (ex 130R(2)) which lays down as one of the planks of the Community's environmental policy the rule that "environmental damage should as a priority be rectified at source".[436] Accordingly, it held, refuse was to be disposed of as near as possible to its place of origin. Moreover, the same principle was enshrined in the Basle Convention of 1989 on the control of transboundary movements of hazardous wastes and their disposal, which had been signed by the Community.

Thus the Court ruled that the ban was unlawful as regards the hazardous waste covered by Directive 84/631, but justified on environmental grounds as regards other, less harmful types of waste.

Is this really inconsistent? The Court's conclusion may perhaps be warranted given the absence of Community legislation ensuring guarantees for the transfrontier shipment of less hazardous waste. Yet it should be recalled that, even in the absence of Community legislation, it is incumbent on Member States to take all reasonable steps to minimise import restrictions; this includes administrative co-operation with one another.[437]

8.161 In *Aher-Waggon v Germany*[438] the Court held that legislation on noise standards for aircraft "may be justified by considerations of public health and environmental protection".[439] The German legislation in question made the first registration in national territory of aircraft previously registered in another Member State conditional upon compliance with noise standards stricter than those in Directive 80/51,[440] while exempting from those standards aircraft which obtained registration in national territory before that Directive was implemented. The Court's conclusion that the German legislation was pro-

---

[435] Paras 8.03 *et seq* above.
[436] See also *FFAD* (see n.428 above) at paras 48–9.
[437] Para. 8.80 above.
[438] See n.24 above.
[439] Para. 19 of the judgment.
[440] Directive on the limitation of noise emissions from subsonic aircraft [1980] O.J. L 18/26 (as amended by Dir. 83/206 [1983] O.J. L117/15).

portionate is open to criticism. In so concluding, the Court noted first, that limiting noise emissions from aircraft is "the most effective and convenient means of combating the noise pollution which they generate".[441] Secondly, the Court observed that the restriction applied to all aircraft irrespective of their origin and did not prevent aircraft registered in another Member State from being used in Germany.[442] Thirdly, the Court noted that aircraft which had been registered in Germany before the Directive was implemented would have to comply with the stricter noise standards when they underwent technical modification or when they were withdrawn from service.[443] Finally, the Court stated that the German authorities were entitled to consider that "the number of aircraft not meeting the stricter noise standards was necessarily going to fall and, therefore, that the overall level of noise pollution could not fail to diminish gradually".[444]

The Court's reasoning is opaque and the conclusion is at least open to question. The German legislation restricted intra-Community trade and its effect was arbitrary: aircraft imported from another Member State had to comply with more onerous standards than those registered in Germany before the Directive was implemented. The fact that it applied to all aircraft irrespective of their origin therefore misses the point. In addition, the arbitrary effect was no less on account of the fact that it would diminish over time and in the future.

8.162 A further baffling ruling on the environmental exception is that in *PreussenElektra v Schleswag*.[445] That case concerned German legislation that obliged electricity suppliers to purchase all electricity produced from renewable energy sources from producers of renewable energy within the respective supply area of each undertaking concerned. The Court had no difficulty in concluding that such a discriminatory measure breached Article 28 because it excluded the possibility for traders to obtain supplies from producers situated in other Member States. However, the Court's analysis of whether the measure could be justified is idiosyncratic to say the least.

The Court began by pointing out that "in order to determine whether such a purchase obligation is nevertheless compatible with Article [28] of the Treaty, account must be taken, first, of the aim of the provision in question, and, second, of the particular features of the electricity market".[446] The Court then noted that the growth in the use of renewable energy sources was among the environmental objectives of several international instruments and Community

---

[441] Para. 21 of the judgment.
[442] Para. 22 of the judgment.
[443] Para. 23 of the judgment.
[444] Para. 24 of the judgment.
[445] See n.19 above.
[446] Para. 72 of the judgment.

decisions.[447] After that, the Court stated that "it should be noted that that policy is also designed to protect the health and life of humans, animals and plants".[448] Next, the Court recalled that Article 6 of the Treaty requires the Community to integrate environmental protection in the definition and implementation of other policies. Also, the Court noted that the recitals to Directive 96/92 concerning common rules for the internal market in electricity[449] refer to the need to give priority to the production of electricity from renewable sources.[450] None of these general statements give rise to any controversy.

However, the Court then turned to specific considerations. "The nature of electricity", it held, "is such that, once it has been allowed into the transmission or distribution system, it is difficult to determine its origin and in particular the source of energy from which it is produced".[451] Finally, the Court added its support to the view of the Commission in its proposal for a Directive on the promotion of electricity from renewable sources, that "the implementation in each Member State of a system of certificates of origin for electricity produced from renewable sources, capable of being the subject of mutual recognition, was essential in order to make trade in that type of electricity both reliable and possible in practice".[452] At the end of that rather disparate list, the Court then simply concluded that "having regard to all the above considerations, ... in the current state of Community law concerning the electricity market, legislation [such as that in issue] is not incompatible with Article [28] of the Treaty".[453]

As will be evident, the Court's reasoning is not easy to follow. The considerations set out do not lead ineluctably to the conclusion reached. The only reason advanced by the Court that in any way supports that conclusion is that "the particular features of the electricity market", namely that "once [electricity] has been allowed into the transmission or distribution system, it is difficult to determine its origin and in particular the source of energy from which it is produced" justifies the discriminatory rule obliging electricity suppliers to purchase all electricity produced from renewable energy sources from producers of renewable energy within the respective supply area. However, that conclusion is difficult to reconcile with the Court's well-established "mutual recognition" case law in circumstances where the German provision in question did not even give importers of renewable energy the opportunity to provide a

---

[447] The Court referred to the United Nations Framework Convention on Climate Change, approved on behalf of the Community by Council Decision 94/69 ([1994] O.J. L33/11), and the Protocol of the third conference of the parties to that Convention, done in Kyoto on December 11, 1997, signed by the European Community and its Member States on April 29, 1998 (see Council Resolution 98/C 198/01 on renewable sources of energy ([1998] O.J. C198/1), and Decision No 646/2000/EC of the European Parliament and of the Council adopting a multiannual programme for the promotion of renewable energy sources in the Community (Altener) (1998 to 2002) ([2000] O.J. L79/1)).
[448] Para. 75 of the judgment.
[449] [1997] O.J. L27/20.
[450] Paras 77–8 of the judgment.
[451] Para. 79 of the judgment.
[452] Para. 80 of the judgment.
[453] Para. 81 of the judgment.

certificate from the Member State of production proving that the electricity was produced from renewable sources.[454]

Finally, the Court's judgment is baffling in its result. As Jacobs A.G. said, it is hard to see why "electricity from renewable resources produced in another Member State would not contribute to the reduction of gas emissions in Germany to the same extent as electricity from renewable resources produced in Germany".[455] Indeed, the production of electricity from renewable sources in one Member State will contribute to the reduction of emissions in other Member States, since it reduces the production of electricity from conventional energy sources in that Member State. In short, the Court's judgment in *PreussenElektra* is questionable both in its reasoning and in its result.[456]

The Improvement of Working Conditions

8.163 Health and safety at work fall under the heading of public health in Article 30, but the improvement of working conditions constitutes a "mandatory requirement" even in the absence of any health considerations. This emerges from *Oebel*,[457] which concerned national legislation prohibiting the baking of bread at night. The Advocate General found that such a measure was justified on the grounds that it served to improve working conditions. In so doing he referred to Article 117 of the Treaty (before amendment by the Treaty of Amsterdam), which began[458]: "Member States agree upon the need to promote improved working conditions and an improved standard of living for workers...".[459]

Although the Court found that a measure of this kind fell outside Articles 28 and 29 altogether, it indirectly confirmed the Advocate General's finding on this point, by stating that the prohibition on night baking was a legitimate economic and social policy decision aimed at improving working conditions in a manifestly sensitive sector, and thus was compatible with the objects of general interest recognised by the Treaty.

Article 117 (now Article 136) was not referred to by the Court. What is more, the Court's observations on this point were confined to the promotion of

---

[454] See, example, Case 272/80 *Frans-Nederlandse Maatschappij voor Biologische Producten*, see n.199 above. Moreover, as Baquero Cruz and Castillo de la Torre point out in their casenote ([2001] E.L. Rev. 489), this aspect of the judgment is difficult to reconcile with Case C-213/96 *Outokumpu* [1998] E.C.R. I-1777 at para. 41 where the fact that Finnish legislation did "not even give the importer the opportunity of demonstrating that the electricity imported by him has been produced by a particular method" was fatal to the Finnish Government's attempts to justify discriminatory internal taxation in that case. See also note by Goossens and Emmerechts, [2001] C.M.L. Rev. 1007.

[455] Para. 236 of his Opinion.

[456] See, *contra*, Drijber, [2001] S.E.W. 400 at 402 who claims that extending the measure to benefit imports was not politically feasible and thus that the German measure was better than no measure. Further, Drijber praises the Court for its reluctance to interfere with or jeopardise the evolution of Community legislation in this field.

[457] Case 155/80 [1981] E.C.R. 1993; [1983] 1 C.M.L.R. 390.

[458] Art. 117 in its amended form is now at Article 136 EC.

[459] Art. 136 (ex 117) now provides that "the Community and the Member States ... shall have as their objectives the promotion of ... improved living and working conditions...".

improved working conditions. The promotion of an improved standard of living for workers, also mentioned in Article 117 (now Article 136), is not referred to in the judgment. It is submitted that this is simply because the promotion of an improved standard of living is a goal of a purely economic nature and therefore cannot justify restrictions on imports and exports.[460]

8.164 This exception was also held to apply to measures prohibiting shops from employing staff on Sundays.[461] However, since it has now been held that indistinctly applicable restrictions on Sunday trading fall outside Article 28 altogether,[462] that ruling is only of historical interest today.

The Maintenance of the Diversity of the Press

8.165 *Vereinigte Familiapress v Heinrich Bauer Verlag*[463] concerned Austrian legislation prohibiting the sale in Austria of periodicals containing games or competitions for prizes. Having held that such legislation was capable of infringing Article 28, the Court accepted that the aim of the national legislation in question was to maintain press diversity and that this was capable of constituting a mandatory requirement for the purposes of Article 28. It added that press diversity helped to safeguard freedom of expression, as protected by Article 10 of the European Convention on Human Rights and Fundamental Freedoms "which is one of the fundamental rights guaranteed by the Community legal order".[464] As mentioned in paragraph 8.51 above, the more straightforward approach might have been simply to treat this interest as being covered by the public policy exception, but the Court did not do so.

Whether or not the Austrian legislation was proportionate to the legitimate aim was left to the referring national court. No doubt, the Court's reasoning would apply equally to measures designed to create greater press diversity rather than merely maintain such diversity. Finally, it seems safe to assume that that reasoning also applies to media other than the press.

The Preservation of the Financial Balance of Social Security Systems

8.166 According to the ruling in *Decker*, "it cannot be excluded that the risk of seriously undermining the social security system may constitute an overriding reason in the general interest capable of justifying a barrier" to the free

---

[460] As to the "working environment", see now also Art. 138 (ex 118A) inserted into the Treaty by the Single European Act ([1987] O.J. L169/1), discussed at para. 12.61 below.
[461] Cases C-312/89 *CGT v Conforama* [1991] E.C.R. I-997; C-332/89 *Marchandise* [1991] E.C.R. I-1027; C-169/91 *Stoke on Trent v B&Q* [1992] E.C.R. I-6635.
[462] Cases C-69/93 *Punto Casa v Capena* [1994] E.C.R. I-2355; and C-401–2/92 *Tankstation 't Heukske v Boermans* [1994] E.C.R. I-2199; see para. 6.56 above.
[463] C-368/95, see n.7 above.
[464] Para. 18 of the judgment.

movement of goods.[465] This cautious language reflects the Court's obvious reluctance to decide the point, since such a purpose is not far removed from "aims of an economic nature" which "cannot justify a barrier to the fundamental principle of the free movement of goods".[466] As explained in paragraph 7.72 above, the Court had already indulged in some rather public and contorted soul-searching on the same issue in *Duphar v Netherlands*.[467] In contrast, in his Opinion in *Decker*, Tesauro A.G. was more forthright, clearly espousing the view that this did constitute a valid ground of justification. No doubt, the Court found rather strained his conclusion from an analysis of the case law that "economic aims are indeed justifiable, where far from being an end in themselves, they are crucial to the operation of the system in question, or affect interests of vital importance to the State".[468]

At all events, in the circumstances of *Decker*, the Court found it unnecessary to decide the point. The facts were that the plaintiff in the main case, a resident of Luxembourg, was seeking reimbursement from a health care fund in that Member State for spectacles acquired in Belgium. The defendant refused to cover those expenses on the grounds that Mr Decker had failed to request prior authorisation for the purchase of a medical product abroad, as required by Luxembourg law. His claim was merely for the sum which he would have received had he purchased the spectacles in Luxembourg, and it was therefore held that the restriction could in any case not be warranted for the protection of the social security system.

8.167 The Court has now, in a case concerning the freedom to provide services, applied this justification in some considerable detail. *Geraets-Smits and Peerbooms*[469] concerned Dutch legislation which permitted the costs of medical treatment provided in a hospital in another Member State to be reimbursed under the Dutch sickness insurance scheme on condition that the person receiving the treatment had obtained prior authorisation for that treatment. Such prior authorisation could only be granted if two conditions were met: first, that the treatment in question was covered by the sickness insurance scheme in the Netherlands which required that the treatment be "normal within the professional circles concerned"; and secondly that adequate timely treatment could not be provided by a contracted care provider in the Netherlands.

In the light of its previous case law, it is not surprising that the Court found that the requirement to obtain prior authorisation was a restriction on the provision of services contrary to Article 49 (ex 59). However, the Court accepted the justification for the prior authorisation system on the grounds of the preservation of the financial balance of social security systems. In particular, the Court held:

---

[465] See n.23 above, para. 39 of the judgment. The same wording is to be found in para. 41 of the parallel judgment in *Kohll* (n.23 above) which related to services under Art. 49. See also C-157/99 *Geraets-Smits and Peerbooms v Stichting Ziekenfonds* [2001] E.C.R. I-5473 at paragraph 72.

[466] See para. 8.32 above.

[467] See n.108 above.

[468] at p.1865.

[469] See n.465 above.

"if insured persons were at liberty, regardless of the circumstances, to use the services of hospitals with which their sickness insurance fund had no contractual arrangements, whether they were situated in the Netherlands or in another Member State, all the planning which goes into the contractual system in an effort to guarantee a rationalised, stable, balanced and accessible supply of hospital services would be jeopardised at a stroke."[470]

That was not, however, the end of the matter since the Court added that the two conditions attached to the grant of authorisation had also to satisfy the proportionality requirement. As regards the condition that the proposed treatment be "normal", the Court held that that condition could only satisfy the proportionality requirement if what was "normal" was assessed in an individual case by reference to what is "sufficiently tried and tested by international medical science" as opposed to in the Netherlands medical community alone.[471] On the other hand, the Court indicated that the condition that adequate timely treatment could not be provided by a contracted care provider in the Netherlands was proportionate because:

"Were large numbers of insured persons to decide to be treated in other Member States even when the hospitals having contractual arrangements with their sickness insurance funds offer adequate identical or equivalent treatment, the consequent outflow of patients would be liable to put at risk the very principle of having contractual arrangements with hospitals and, consequently, undermine all the planning and rationalisation carried out in this vital sector in an effort to avoid the phenomena of hospital overcapacity, imbalance in the supply of hospital medical care and logistical and finacial wastage."[472]

Although the Court comes perilously close in this judgment to recognising aims of an economic nature to justify a barrier to one of the four Community law freedoms, the result is nevertheless one with which it is difficult to disagree.

Moreover, the Court continues to be coy about recognising the preservation of the financial balance of social security systems as a ground of justification at all, saying merely that this "cannot be excluded".[473] Nevertheless, the conclusion that in practice it does accept it as a ground of justification is hard to escape, given that the Court has proceeded to a thorough investigation of the application of this ground on each occasion.

The Promotion of National or Regional Culture

8.168 It has frequently been argued that the protection of culture constitutes a ground of justification for restrictions on imports or exports. The problem is most delicate. On the one hand, the protection of culture is obviously a worthy objective which should have its place in Community law and which is by no

---

[470] Para. 81 of the judgment.
[471] Para. 94 of the judgment.
[472] Para. 106 of the judgment.
[473] Para. 72 of the judgment.

means fully covered by the exception in Article 30 relating to "the protection of national treasures possessing artistic, historic or archaeological value." On the other hand, to bring whole sectors of commercial activity virtually outside Article 28 on the grounds that they involve the production of "cultural" goods would be unthinkable. Moreover, "culture" is notoriously difficult to define: to classify all books (let alone all films!) as "culture" would seem absurd. This no doubt explains why the Court has been reluctant to decide the point.[474]

8.169 However, a series of cases relating to services indicates that a restriction on imports or exports might be justified on such grounds, although even there the Court has yet to accept the protection of any form of "culture" as valid. Thus in *Commission v France (tourist guides)*[475] the Court was called upon to decide whether legislation requiring tourist guides to hold a diploma and obtain a licence was compatible with Article 49 (ex 59). France contended, *inter alia*, that this measure sought to ensure the protection of "general interests relating to the proper appreciation of places and things of historical interest and the widest possible dissemination of knowledge of artistic and cultural heritage of the country". The Court ruled that such interests could constitute a mandatory requirement, but that the restriction was disproportionate to this aim and thus unjustified. Similarly, in *Collectieve Antennevoorziening Gouda v Commissariaat voor de Media*,[476] which related to restrictions on broadcasting, it held that the ensurance of cultural pluralism could constitute such justification, particulary as it was linked to freedom of expression within the meaning of Article 10 of the European Convention of Human Rights.[477] Yet once again the Court found that the measure before it failed the proportionality test.[478] Most revealing of all is the judgment in *Federación de Distribuidores Cinematográficos v Spain*[479] where the defendant State claimed that the contested restriction on film distribution was justified on cultural grounds: without even accepting that the protection of culture could be a valid ground of justification, the Court held that in any case it was not in point, since the contested legislation discriminated in favour of all national films regardless of their content or quality.

Moreover, in *Bickel* the Court held that "of course" the protection of an "ethno-cultural minority"—*in casu* the German speakers of the Trentino-Alto Adige region of Italy—was a legitimate aim for the purposes of Article 12 of the Treaty.[480]

Finally, the Court will have to take cognisance of the Article 151 (ex 128)

---

[474] See in particular *Cinéthèque* (see n.120 above); the reference to "socio-cultural characteristics" in the Sunday trading cases (para. 8.164) has nothing to do with culture in this sense, but is rather a reference to custom and tradition.

[475] Case C-154/89 [1991] E.C.R. I-649; see also Cases C-180/89 *Commission v Italy (tourist guides)* [1991] E.C.R. I-709; and C-199/89 *Commission v Greece (tourist guides)* [1991] E.C.R. I-727.

[476] Case C-288/89, see n.123 above; and see Case C-353/89 *Commission v Netherlands (broadcasting)* [1991] E.C.R. I-4069.

[477] Para. 8.38 above.

[478] See, however, Case C-148/91 *Veronica Omroep Organisatie v Commissariaat voor de Media* [1993] E.C.R. 487 but the judgment really turned on an abuse of rights.

[479] Case C-17/92 [1993] E.C.R. I-2239.

[480] Case C-274/96 [1998] E.C.R. I-7637, para. 30.

relating to culture inserted into the EC Treaty by the Treaty of Maastricht. Paragraph 1 requires the Community to "contribute to the flowering of the cultures of the Member States, while respecting their national and regional diversity and at the same time bringing the common cultural heritage to the fore". Paragraph 4 of that provision reads: "The Community shall take cultural aspects into account in its action under other provisions of the Treaty, in particular in order to protect the diversity of its cultures."[481]

Protection of Commercial Reputation

8.170   In *Alpine Investments*,[482] it was held that a Member State was entitled to impose restrictions on "exports" of its services so as to safeguard the commercial reputation of its industry. The case concerned a Dutch prohibition on providers of financial services contacting individuals in other Member States without their prior consent to offer them such services ("cold calling"). The Court ruled: "Maintaining the good reputation of the national financial sector may ... constitute an imperative reason of public interest capable of justifying restrictions on the freedom to provide financial services." Consequently, this ban was found to be compatible with Article 49 of the Treaty. Precisely the same reasoning can be expected to apply under Article 30. Having said that, the issue is unlikely to arise frequently in view of the Court's narrow construction of Article 29.[483] It will be recalled that under the latter Article national measures will breach Article 29 only if they establish a difference between domestic trade of a Member State and its export trade in such a way as to provide a particular advantage for national production. Such measures are likely, by their very nature, to give rise to arbitrary discrimination. As such, they will invariably fall foul of the second sentence of Article 30.[484]

Other Possible Grounds

8.171   The categories of "mandatory requirements" are still not closed. It follows that still further grounds may be added, provided that they are "directed to eventualities of a non-economic kind".[485] Conceivably, in *RTT v GB-Inno*[486] the Court intended to create a new "mandatory requirement". In that case, which concerned standards for telephone equipment to be connected to the public network, the Court held that such measures might be justified, *inter alia*, for "the protection of the public network and its proper functioning".

---

[481] Similar provisions are to be found in Arts 152 (ex 129) (Public Health) and 174(2) (ex 130R(2)) (Environment). In addition, the Treaty of Maastricht amended Art. 92(3)(d) (now 87(3)(d)) EC so as to empower the Commission to authorise State aid granted to "promote culture and heritage conservation".

[482] See n.59 above.

[483] See paras 6.79 to 6.92 above.

[484] See para. 8.12 above and Case 53/76 *Procureur de la République v Bouhelier* [1977] E.C.R. 197, see n.34 above at para. 15.

[485] Para. 8.32 above.

[486] Case C-18/88 [1991] E.C.R. I-5941.

Industrial and Commercial Property

(a) Introduction

8.172 Although Article 30 uses the terminology "industrial and commercial property", it is now clear that this is not intended to draw a distinction between industrial property rights (such as patents, trade marks, designs and plant breeds) and copyright and neighbouring rights. The initial doubts as to whether the expression covered copyright were finally dispelled in 1981 by the judgment of the Court in *Membran v GEMA*,[487] where it was held that Article 30 "includes the protection conferred by copyright, especially when exploited commercially in the form of licences capable of affecting distribution in the various Member States of goods incorporating the protected literary or artistic work." What is more, Article 17(2) of the Charter of Fundamental Rights of the European Union[488] is worded as follows: "*Intellectual property* shall be protected" (emphasis added). Accordingly, the more widely accepted term "intellectual property" will be preferred to "industrial and commercial property" for the remainder of the Chapter.

The Court has also held, in *Delhaize v Promalvin*,[489] that appellations of origin constitute "industrial and commercial property" under Article 30, although Gulmann A.G. had pointed out that it was unnecessary to decide the point. In *Exportur v LOR*[490] the Court extended this to cover indications of source. Therefore, the categories of "industrial and commercial property" are not closed. In particular, it remains unclear whether general unfair competition rules would fall within the category.[491] In any case, indications of origin are subject to different rules from other categories of intellectual property and will therefore be considered separately at the very end of this Chapter.

8.173 The Court has defined the "specific subject matter" of each type of intellectual property in a series of cases. Before considering the application of Article 30 to intellectual property it is worth summarising these definitions in order to clarify what is covered by the various types of intellectual property.

For patents, the specific subject matter is "the guarantee that the patentee, to reward the creative effort of the inventor, has the exclusive right to use an invention with a view to manufacturing industrial products and putting them into circulation for the first time, either directly or by grant of licences to third parties, as well as to oppose infringements."[492]

For trade marks, it is "the guarantee that the owner of the trade mark has the

---

[487] Cases 55/80 and 57/80 [1981] E.C.R. 147; [1981] 2 C.M.L.R. 44, noted by Alexander (1981) C.M.L.Rev. 422.
[488] n.135 above.
[489] n.372 above.
[490] n.373 above.
[491] See para. 8.148 above.
[492] Case 15/74 *Centrafarm v Sterling Drug* [1973] E.C.R. 1147; [1974] 2 C.M.L.R. 480, para.9.

exclusive right to use that trade mark, for the purpose of putting products protected by the trade mark into circulation for the first time, and is therefore intended to protect him against competitors wishing to take advantage of the status and reputation of the trade mark by selling products illegally bearing that trade mark."[493] It also includes "the right ... of preventing any use of the trade mark which is likely to impair the guarantee of origin", which is the consumer's guarantee that "a trade marked product which is sold to him has not been subject at a previous stage of marketing to interference by a third person, without the authorisation of the proprietor of the trade mark, such as to affect the original condition of the product."[494] The owner also has a legitimate interest, related to the specific subject of the trade mark right, in preventing damage to the reputation of his trade mark.[495]

For designs, the specific subject matter is "the right of the proprietor of a protected design to prevent third parties from manufacturing and selling or importing, without its consent, products incorporating the design".[496]

Finally, although it did not use the term "specific subject matter", the Court has said that copyright includes moral rights (such as "the right of an author to claim authorship of the work and to object to any distortion, mutilation or other alteration thereof, or any other action in relation to the said work which would be prejudicial to his honour or reputation") and "other rights, notably the right to exploit commercially the marketing of the protected work, particularly in the form of licences granted in return for payment of royalties."[497] Some types of copyright will include other rights: in *Coditel v Ciné Vog Films* the Court held that the essential function of copyright in films includes "the right of a copyright owner and his assigns to require fees for any showing of a film".[498]

8.174 The first cases[499] on intellectual property to come before the Court related to Articles 81 and 82, not least because the prohibitions in Article 28 on quantitative restrictions on imports and measures of equivalent effect did not come into effect until 1968 and 1970 respectively.[500] Although Article 30 had come to be relied on by the Court as an aid to the interpretation of Articles 81 and 82,[501] it was not until the Court's landmark decision in *Deutsche Grammophon v Metro*[502] introduced the concept of exhaustion that the Court applied Articles

---

[493] Case 16/74 *Centrafarm v Winthrop* [1974] E.C.R. 1183; [1974] 2 C.M.L.R. 480.
[494] Case 102/77 *Hoffman-La Roche v Centrafarm* [1978] E.C.R. 1139; [1978] 3 C.M.L.R. 217, para.7.
[495] Cases C-427/93, C-429/93 and C-436/93 *Bristol-Myers Squibb v Paranova* [1996] E.C.R. I-3457 (presentation of repackaged goods); Case C-337/95 *Parfums Christian Dior v Evora* [1997] E.C.R. I-6013 (advertising). The extent of this legitimate interest remains unclear: in *Bristol-Myers Squibb* the Court talked of damage to reputation, while in *Christian Dior* it spoke of *serious* damage.
[496] Case 238/87 *Volvo v Veng* [1988] E.C.R. 6211; [1989] 4 C.M.L.R. 122, para.8.
[497] Cases 55 and 57/80 *Music-Vertrieb*, above n.487, paras 11–12.
[498] Case 62/79, see n.119 above; [1981] 2 C.M.L.R. 362.
[499] Cases 56/64 and 58/64 *Consten and Grundig v Commission* [1966] E.C.R. 299; [1966] C.M.L.R. 418; Case 24/67 *Parke, Davis v Centrafarm* [1968] E.C.R. 55; [1968] C.M.L.R. 47; Case 40/70 *Sirena v Eda*, [1979] E.C.R. 3169; [1971] C.M.L.R. 260.
[500] Paras 5.01 *et seq.* and 6.02 *et seq.* above.
[501] Case 40/70, see n.499 above.
[502] Case 78/70 [1971] E.C.R. 487; [1971] C.M.L.R. 631.

28 to 30 to industrial property rights quite independently of the Treaty provisions on competition.

However, one issue which the Court first dealt with under the competition provisions before expanding its reasoning into free movement was the meaning of Article 295 (ex 222), which states: "This Treaty shall in no way prejudice the rules in Member States governing the system of property ownership." It appears that this is intended to indicate that nationalisation is compatible with the Treaty, and is not designed to exclude questions of property from the scope of the Treaty altogether.[503] The Court has nevertheless had to grapple with this problem from the very beginning. Since *Consten and Grundig v Commission*[504] the Court has overcome Article 295 by drawing a distinction between the existence and exercise of intellectual property rights: Community law, it has held, does not affect the existence of such rights, only their exercise.

The distinction between existence and exercise of rights is open to criticism[505] in that a right can scarcely be said to exist if it cannot be exercised. Moreover, as we shall notice shortly, the Court has in fact called into question national legislation on intellectual property where it is discriminatory or otherwise flouts fundamental principles of Community law. A further criticism is that if it is true that Community law only affects the *exercise* (as opposed to existence) of intellectual property rights, this is at odds with the fact that Articles 28 to 30 EC are addressed to measures "enacted by Member States" and not to the acts of individuals.[506]

As Gulmann A.G. has said,[507] the distinction between the existence and exercise of rights has "no independent significance for the solution of specific questions of delimitation". Instead, one must look for guidance to the Court's definitions of the specific subject-matter of the various categories of intellectual property. However, even these definitions cannot constitute an objective limit to Article 30. At the root there is clearly a policy question as to how widely the Court is willing to interpret the second sentence of Article 30 in order to restrict the grant by Member States of intellectual property rights.

8.175 The position is perhaps most elegantly summarised in the following passage of the judgment in *Commission v United Kingdom* (compulsory patent licences)[508]:

---

[503] See para. 8.179 below.
[504] Cases 56/64 and 58/64, see n.499 above.
[505] See generally Beier "Gewerblicher Rechtsschutz und freier Warenverkehr im Europäischen Binnenmarkt und im Verkehr mit Drittstaaten" [1989] G.R.U.R. Int. 603 at 609; Friden, "Recent Developments in EEC Intellectual Property Law: the Distinction between Existence and Exercise Revisited" (1989) C.M.L.Rev. 193; Marenco and Banks, "Intellectual Property and the Community Rules on Free Movement: Discrimination Unearthed" [1990] E.L.Rev. 224; Rothnie, *Parallel Imports* (1993) at p. 374.
[506] See paras 4.26 to 4.42 above.
[507] Case C-9/93 *Internationale Heiztechnik v Ideal Standard* [1994] E.C.R. I 2789, para. 32 of the Opinion.
[508] Case C-30/90 [1992] E.C.R. I 829 at 865; see para. 8.193 below.

"Article [295] cannot be interpreted as reserving to the national legislature, in relation to industrial and commercial property, the power to adopt measures which would adversely affect the principle of free movement of goods within the common market as provided for and regulated by the Treaty.

First, the prohibitions and restrictions on imports justified on grounds of the protection of industrial and commercial property are allowed by Article [30] of the Treaty only subject to the express proviso that they do not constitute a means of arbitrary discrimination or a disguised restriction on trade between Member States.

Secondly, as the Court has consistently held, Article [30] only admits derogations from the fundamental principle of the free movement of goods within the common market to the extent to which such derogations are justified for the purpose of safeguarding rights which constitute the specific subject-matter of such property (Case C-10/89 *CNL-SUCAL HAG* [1990] E.C.R. I-3711 [*Hag II*], paragraph 12)."

On this point one should also have regard to the trenchant comment of Jacobs A.G. in *Phil Collins v Imtrat*,[509] dismissing the suggestion that Article 7 EEC (now Article 12 EC) did not apply to intellectual property in view of Article 295. That comment is discussed at paragraph 8.179 below.

(b) Other provisions relating to intellectual property

8.176 Other than Articles 28 to 30 (and 49 in relation to services), the Community provisions relating to intellectual property fall into five groups:

(a) Community legislation;

(b) International agreements between the Community (sometimes with the participation of the Member States) and third countries;

(c) Article 12: Non-Discrimination;

(d) Articles 81 and 82: Competition; and

(e) Article 17(2) of the Charter of Fundamental Rights of the European Union.

Although these other aspects do not fall within the scope of this book, in order to understand the intricacies of this area one cannot avoid mentioning them briefly.

(i) Community legislation

8.177 It is appropriate to begin with the measures adopted by the Community and under Community auspices to harmonise and co-ordinate intellectual property law. Such provisions fall into two categories; some harmonise national law, while others create distinct Community intellectual property rights.[510]

---

[509] Cases C-92/92 and 326/92 [1993] E.C.R. I 51445; see Mestmäcker, "Schutz der ausübenden Künstler und EWG-Diskriminierungsverbot" [1993] G.R.U.R. Int. 532; Dworkin in [1994] E.I.P.R. 187; Flynn in [1995] C.M.L.R. 997; and Gaster in [1996] R.I.D.A. 261.
[510] In para. 59 of Opinion 1/94 [1994] E.C.R. I-5267 the Court indicated that Arts 94 and 95 were the

Community instruments relating to patents which have come into force include Council Regulation 1768/92 concerning the creation of a supplementary protection certificate for medicinal products,[511] Regulation 1610/96 concerning such certificates for plant protection products[512] and Directive 98/44 on the legal protection of biotechnological inventions.[513] In addition, the Commission has submitted proposals for Directives harmonising the protection of inventions by utility model[514] and the patentability of computer-implemented inventions.[515]

As regards a Community Patent, the first Community Patent Convention ("CPC")[516] was signed by the Member States in Luxembourg in 1975. It was intended to interlock with the international patent system created by the European Patent Convention ("EPC") signed at Munich in 1973, which now covers the fifteen Member States along with Bulgaria, Cyprus, the Czech Republic, Estonia, Liechtenstein, Monaco, the Slovak Republic, Switzerland and Turkey and which entered into force in 1977. The CPC was developed as an international agreement outside the scope of the EC Treaty because, at the time, the Community was not deemed to be competent in the field of patents. Nonetheless, the CPC was expressed to be subject to the EC Treaty by Article 93 of the Convention and, by virtue of Article 5, the Court of Justice was to have jurisdiction in respect of it. Its essential object was to enable an applicant to obtain a single patent applying throughout the Community without prejudice to the right of the Member States to grant national patents. In addition, it contained a small number of provisions harmonising aspects of national patent laws. This convention never entered into force for want of ratification by all the Member States.[517] Nonetheless, the Court has been willing to use it as a guide to the interpretation of other Community provisions, including Article 30 EC.[518]

The views on the Community's competence have of course evolved, and now the CPC may be superseded following the Commission's proposal for a Regulation on the Community Patent.[519] This proposal aims to create a single

---

appropriate legal basis for the former category of legislation while Art. 308 was the appropriate basis for the latter. It is by no means clear, however, why Art. 94 should be relevant today, given that none of the matters listed in Art. 95(2) are in point. This ruling was applied in Case C-350/92 *Spain v Council* [1995] E.C.R. I-1985 where the Court rejected Spain's argument that the contested Regulation was not validly based on Art. 95.

[511] [1992] O.J. L182/1. This Directive was unsuccesfully challenged for lack of competence in Case C-350/92 *Spain v Council*, see n.510 above.

[512] [1996] O.J. L198/30.

[513] [1998] O.J. L213/13. This Directive was unsuccessfully challenged in Case C-377/98 *Netherlands v Parliament and Council* [2001] E.C.R. I-7079, see para. 12.41 below.

[514] COM(99)0309 final ([2000] O.J. C248E/56).

[515] COM(2002)92 final ([2002] O.J. C151E/129).

[516] [1976] O.J. L17/1.

[517] See also the second CPC signed at Luxembourg in 1989: [1989] O.J. L401/1 which never came into force either for want of ratification by the (then) twelve Member States.

[518] Case 288/82 *Duijnstee v Goderbauer* [1983] E.C.R. 3663; [1985] 1 C.M.L.R. 765, para. 27; see also Cases 19/84 *Pharmon v Hoechst* [1985] E.C.R. 2281; [1985] 3 C.M.L.R. 775; C-30/90 *Commission v United Kingdom*, see n.508 above; and C-316/95 *Generics v Smith Kline & French Laboratories* [1997] E.C.R. I-3929 at para. 20.

[519] COM (2000) 412 final ([2000] O.J. C337E/278). See O. Bossung, "Rückführung des europäischen Patentrechts in die Europäische Union" [1995] G.R.U.R. Int. 923, in English in [1996] I.I.C. 287.

Community patent co-existing with the current national patent systems and with the EPC. Patents applied for under the procedure in the EPC are in practice a bundle of national patents which are granted by the European Patent Office in Munich following a central search and examination procedure.[520] By contrast, the proposed Community patent is intended to create a single and uniform title, valid throughout the Community and independently of national patents.

With respect to trade marks, more progress has been made: the Council has adopted both its First Directive on the harmonisation of national trade mark law,[521] and Regulation 40/94 introducing the Community trade mark.[522]

As for design rights, the Community has adopted Directive 98/71[523] harmonising the legal protection of designs and Council Regulation 6/2002 on a Community Design.[524]

In relation to copyright and neighbouring rights, several Directives have been forthcoming: Directive 91/250[525] on the legal protection of computer programs; Directive 92/100[526] on rental and lending rights and certain rights related to copyright; Directive 93/98[527] harmonising the term of protection of copyright and certain related rights[528]; and Directive 96/9 on the legal protection of databases.[529] A more general harmonisation effort has led to Directive 2001/29 on copyright and related rights in the information society[530] and

---

[520] However, note that these patents can still be annulled nationally and, in Case C-44/98 *BASF v Präsident des Deutschen Patentamts* [1999] E.C.R. I-6269, the ECJ held that Art. 28 was not infringed by a rule that failure to file a German translation of a non-German-language patent granted by the EPO within three months would render the German patent void.

[521] Dir. 89/104 ([1989] O.J. L30/1). The deadline for implementing that Directive was extended until December 31, 1992 by Dir. 92/10 ([1992] O.J.L6/35). See Brun, "Le futur systéme communautaire des marques commerciales – coexistence des marques communautaire et nationales" [1990] R.M.C. 507; Kunz-Hallstein, "Perspektiven der Angleichung des nationalen Markenrechts in der EWG" [1992] G.R.U.R. Int. 81; Rosini and Roche, "Trade Marks in Europe 1992 and Beyond" [1991] E.I.P.R. 404.

[522] [1994] O.J. L11/1, as amended by Council Reg. 3288/94 ([1994] O.J. L349/83). See also Reg. 2868/95 implementing Reg. 40/94 [1995] O.J. L303/1; and Reg. 216/96 laying down the rule of procedure of the Boards of Appeal of the Office for Harmonization in the Internal Market [1996] O.J. L28/11. See also the proposal for a Regulation amending Reg. 40/94 to give effect to the accession of the European Community to the Protocol relating to the Madrid Agreement concerning the international registration of marks adopted at Madrid on June 27, 1989: COM (96) 372 final.

[523] [1998] O.J. L289/28.

[524] [2002] O.J. L3/1.

[525] [1991] O.J. L122/42.

[526] [1992] O.J. L346/61; see Reinbothe and von Lewinski, *The E.C. Directive on Rental and Lending Rights and on Piracy* (1993). A challenge to the validity of Article 1(1) of the Directive was dismissed by the Court in C-200/96 *Metronome Musik GmbH v Music Point Hokamp* [1998] E.C.R. I-1953.

[527] [1993] O.J. L290/9.

[528] The Council also adopted Dir. 93/83 on copyright and related rights applicable to satellite broadcasting and cable retransmission ([1993] O.J. L248/15), but that concerns services, not goods.

[529] [1996] O.J. L77/20. Aside from harmonising national provisions relating to copyright protection in databases whose selection and organisation is original and can therefore be considered to from works, this Directive has also created a new right *sui generis* in databases which constitute substantial investment. This right allows the holder to prevent the unauthorised extraction and reuse of (substantial parts of) the contents of the database.

[530] [2001] O.J. L 167/10.

Directive 2001/84 on the resale right for the benefit of the author of an original work of art.[531]

In addition, the Council has enacted a variety of other measures: Regulation 2100/94[532] on Community plant variety rights, Regulation 2081/92[533] on the protection of geographical indications and designations of origin for agricultural products and foodstuffs[534] and Council Directive 87/54[535] which provides for *sui generis* rights in semi-conductors.

Mention should also be made of Regulation 3295/94[536] on counterfeit and pirated goods infringing certain intellectual property rights. This Regulation lays down a Community procedure to deal with such goods when they enter or leave the Community.[537] However, it does not affect the free movement of goods within the Community.[538]

(ii) International agreements

8.178 Furthermore, the Community and/or the Member States have concluded a number of treaties with third countries containing provisions—usually of a general nature—relating to industrial property.[539] By definition, these provisions usually have no bearing on trade between Member States, and are therefore not in point here. However, it would be wrong not to mention the Agreement on trade-related aspects of intellectual property rights[540] (TRIPS),

---

[531] [2001] O.J. L 272/32.

[532] [1994] O.J. L227/1. See also Reg. 1238/95 establishing implementing rules for the application of Reg. 2100/94 as regards the fees payable to the Community Plant Variety Office [1995] O.J. L121/31 (amended by Reg. 329/00 [2000] O.J. L37/19) and Reg. 1239/95 establishing implementing rules for the application of Reg. 2100/94 as regards proceedings before the Community Plant Variety Office [1995] O.J. L121/37.

[533] [1992] O.J. L208/1, as last amended by Commission Reg. 2796/2000 ([2000] O.J. L324/26); see para. 8.248 below.

[534] See also Reg. 1610/96 concerning the creation of a supplementary protection certificate for plant protection products: [1996] O.J. L198/30.

[535] [1987] O.J. L24/36.

[536] [1994] O.J. L341/8, as amended by Reg. 241/1999 [1999] O.J. L27/1.

[537] In Case C-383/98 *Polo/Lauren v Dwidua Langgeng Pratama* [2000] E.C.R. I-2519 the Court held that the Regulation covers goods which are merely in transit through the Community under the external transit procedure; see para. 8.196 below.

[538] The Commission has set out an action plan to deal with counterfeiting and piracy within the internal market: COM(2000) 789 final. However, the proposed Directive detailed in the action plan was still being prepared at the time of writing.

[539] These include treaties which cover industrial property law (Paris Convention 1883), copyright and neighbouring rights (Berne Convention 1886; WIPO Copyright Treaty 1996; Rome Convention 1961; Geneva Convention 1971; WIPO Performances and Phonograms Treaty 1996), trade marks (Madrid Agreement 1891) and patents (Patent Law Treaty 2000). In Case C-13/00 *Commission v Ireland* (judgment of March 19, 2002), the Court held that "there can be no doubt that the provisions of the Berne Convention cover an area which comes in large measure within the scope of Community competence" (para. 16 of the judgment).

[540] [1994] O.J. L336/213; see Opinion 1/94, see n.510 above; see Bronckers, "The Impact of TRIPS: Intellectual Property Protection in the Developing Countries" (1994) C.M.L. Rev. 1245; Drexl, "Nach GATT und WIPO: Das TRIPs Abkommen und seine Anwendung in der Europäischen Gemeinschaft" (1994) G.R.U.R. Int. 777; Worthy, "Intellectual Property Protection after GATT" [1994] E.I.P.R. 195. Like the CPC, the Court has been willing to use the TRIPS agreement as a guide to the interpretation of the Community provisions: see C-316/95 *Generics v Smith Kline & French Laboratories*, see n.518 above at para. 20 and C-200/96 *Metronome Musik v Music Point Hokamp*, n.526 above at para. 25.

one of the fruits of the Uruguay Round which required some changes to Community law.[541] Although the provisions of TRIPS do not create directly effective rights in the Member States,[542] in cases where the Community has legislated in a field covered by TRIPS the Court will interpret both the applicability and substance of Article 50 of the TRIPS agreement.[543] In such cases national courts must apply national rules on provisional measures as far as possible in the light of the wording and purpose of the article.[544]

Less well known is Protocol 28 to the EEA Agreement,[545] which contains a number of important provisions relating to intellectual property. In particular, Article 5 requires the Member States and the participating EFTA countries to accede to seven major multilateral conventions in this field, including the Paris Convention for the Protection of Industrial Property (as last amended by the Stockholm Act 1967) and the Berne Convention for the Protection of Literary and Artistic Works (as last amended by the Paris Act 1971).[546]

(iii) Article 12: non-discrimination

8.179 The judgment in *Phil Collins* is of considerable importance and, although specifically concerned with Article 12 (ex 6), has broad implications for intellectual property within the Treaty as a whole. The plaintiff there was a singer and composer of British nationality, who gave a concert in California in 1983; the concert was recorded without his consent and Imtrat then sold reproductions of that recording in Germany. Phil Collins wished to enforce his performer's rights by obtaining an injunction restraining Imtrat from marketing such recordings in Germany and requiring it to deliver copies in its possession to a court bailiff. Had he been a German national, his action would undoubtedly have succeeded; but under German law only German nationals were entitled to bring such an action, given that the recording had taken place outside Germany.[547] The Court was therefore asked whether such discrimination was compatible with Article 12. It should be noted that Articles 28 and 30

---

[541] See, for example, Council Reg. 3288/94 [1994] O.J. L349/83, amending Reg. 40/94 on the Community Trade Mark.

[542] Cases C-300/98 and C-392/98 *Christian Dior v Tuk Consultancy* [2000] E.C.R. I-11307, para.44.

[543] Case C-53/96 *Hermès v FHT Marketing Choice* [1998] E.C.R. I-3603, para.45; Case C-89/99 *Schieving-Nijstad v Robert Groeneveld* [2001] E.C.R. I-5851, para. 61.

[544] Case C-300/98 *Christian Dior*, above, para. 47. Para. 48 of the same case makes it clear that, where the Community has not legislated in the field, the question of the effect of TRIPS must be determined by the law of the Member State.

[545] [1994] O.J. LI/194. Art. 2 of the Protocol extends the principle of exhaustion (Rule 3 in para. 8.182 below) to the EEA. See generally Ch. XIII.

[546] In his Opinion in Case C-13/00 *Commission v Ireland*, see n.539 above, Mischo A.G. pointed out that the obligation is to accede to each convention as a whole, including those parts which do not fall under Community competence. Thus the Commission was entitled to bring proceedings pursuant to Article 226 EC with respect to Ireland's failure to accede to the Paris Act of the Berne Convention for the Protection of Literary and Artistic Works, even if that Act fell in part outside the scope of the Community's powers. The Court subsequently upheld that view.

[547] An exception was provided for recordings which had taken place in the territory of a Contracting Party to the 1961 Rome Convention on the Protection of Performers, but the United States was not party to this Convention.

were not in point, as trade between Member States was not involved.

The defendants argued that the grant of copyright and performing rights was not a matter for Community law at all, since it was the exclusive preserve of the Member States by virtue of Article 295. The Court pointed out, however, that it had repeatedly treated intellectual property rights, including copyright and neighbouring rights, as subject to the prohibitions enshrined in the Treaty, notably in Articles 28 and 49. This was despite the fact that the conditions for protecting such rights were primarily a matter for the Member States. Although the Court did not address Article 295 as such, one should note the response of Jacobs A.G. to the argument based on that provision: "That article ... clearly does not authorise Member States to grant intellectual property rights on a discriminatory basis. It might just as well be argued that a Member State could prohibit the nationals of other Member States from buying land for business use." At all events, the Court concluded that the grant of copyright and performing rights fell "within the scope of application" of the Treaty within the meaning of Article 12; and that an author or performer from another Member State or those claiming under them could therefore rely on that provision.

Second, the defendants denied that the contested measure constituted discrimination contrary to that provision, claiming that it was justified by disparities between national laws and by the fact that some Member States were still not party to the Rome Convention of 1961 for the Protection of Performers, Producers of Phonograms and Broadcasting Organisations, which provided for such protection on the basis of reciprocity. As might have been expected, the Court roundly rejected this argument, saying that these considerations in no way served to justify the measure.

Phil Collins is thus authority for two very simple but fundamental propositions: intellectual property, including copyright and neighbouring rights, falls within the scope of application of the Treaty[548]; and national laws governing the grant of such property may not discriminate between nationals of Member States. The reader may well be surprised that, as late as 1993, such elementary propositions were still being contested before the Court. However, even more recently the Court was asked to rule on the possible relevance of the circumstance that the author (*in casu* Puccini) had died before the EC Treaty applied to the Member State of which he was a national: *Land Hessen v Ricordi*.[549] Not surprisingly, the Court held that this circumstance did not preclude the application of the first paragraph of Article 12 EC, as copyright may be relied on not only by the author, also by those claiming under him.

(iv) Articles 81 and 82: competition

8.180 It is now appropriate to turn to Articles 81 and 82. As described above, neither Article prohibits the existence of intellectual property.[550] However, a

---

[548] See also Case C-13/00 *Commission v Ireland*, see n.539 and 546 above.
[549] Case C-360/00 (judgment of June 6, 2002).
[550] See above, para. 8.174.

considerable body of Commission Decisions and court judgments has been established on the compatibility of the exercise of industrial property rights with Articles 81 and 82. As competition law falls outside the scope of this book,[551] the following can only constitute a brief summary of the most important decisions.[552]

Article 81 prohibits agreements and concerted practices which are anti-competitive. The Court has held repeatedly[553] that the exercise of an industrial property right may fall foul of Article 81 when it constitutes "the subject, the means or the result of a restrictive practice". However, the mere unilateral enforcement of an intellectual property right cannot constitute an agreement or a concerted practice and so cannot fall foul of Article 81.[554] Examples of situations which could fall within the prohibition include: a party with an international trade mark registration allowing another party to register that trade mark in one Member State[555]; a combination of assignments of national trade marks to different users which would re-erect barriers between Member States[556]; an agreement between traders within the Community and those outside which would prevent the entry of products from third countries[557]; a patent licence containing a no-challenge clause where royalties are paid and the patented process is still used[558]; and an agreement between the owners of copyright not to grant licences to a third party.[559]

Article 82, on the other hand, prohibits monopolistic conduct. For it to be infringed, three elements must be present: the undertaking must have a dominant position in the market, it must abuse this position and this must be liable to affect trade between Member States.

The Court has held[560] that the ownership of an intellectual property right will not in itself imply a dominant position under Article 82. The question (as in all competition cases) is whether the intellectual property owner can "behave to an appreciable extent independently of its competitors, customers and ultimately of its consumers."[561] It remains an open question whether mere ownership of

---

[551] But see paras 4.26 et seq. and 6.33 et seq. above.
[552] For a full discussion, the reader is referred to: Faull & Nikpay, The E.C. Law of Competition (1999), Ch. 8; Anderman, E.C. Competition Law and Intellectual Property Rights (1998); Govaere, The Use and Abuse of Intellectual Property Rights in E.C. Law (1996), Ch. 5.
[553] e.g. Case 40/70, see n.499 above; Case 51/75 EMI Records v CBS United Kingdom [1976] E.C.R. 811; [1976] 2 C.M.L.R. 235.
[554] Article 81 only applies to "agreements between undertakings, decisions by associations of undertakings and concerted practices". The inapplicability of Article 81 to unilateral enforcement of intellectual property rights was noted, for instance, in Case 24/67 Parke, Davis v Centrafarm, n.499 above; and Case 78/70 Deutsche Grammophon, n.502 above.
[555] Cases 56/64 and 58/64 see n.499 above.
[556] Case 40/70 Sirena v Eda, see n.499 above.
[557] Case 51/75, see n.553 above.
[558] Case 65/86 Bayer v Süllhöfer [1988] E.C.R. 5249.
[559] Case T–504/93 Tiercé Ladbroke v Commission [1997] E.C.R. II-0923.
[560] e.g. Case 40/70, see n.499 above.
[561] Case 27/76 United Brands v Commission [1978] E.C.R. 207, para. 65.

intellectual property can lead to such a finding or what other factors are needed.[562]

Moreover, the Court at one stage held that "in so far as the exercise of a trade mark right is intended to prevent the importation into the protected territory of products bearing an identical mark, it does not constitute an abuse of a dominant position within the meaning of Article [82]".[563] This latter point, however, can no longer constitute good law, as more recently the Court of First Instance (basing itself on a decision of the Court of Justice) annulled a Commission decision that use of copyright to prevent parallel imports could not be abusive, stating that "whilst, as a rule, the enforcement of copyright by its holder, as in the case of the prohibition on importing certain products from outside the Community in to a Member State of the Community, is not in itself a breach of Article [82] of the Treaty, such enforcement may, *in exceptional circumstances*, involve abusive conduct."[564] It is submitted that, although both *Magill* and *Micro Leader* concerned copyright, this principle will cover any type of intellectual property.

It is therefore important to determine what is meant by "exceptional circumstances", in other words, what sort of exercise of an intellectual property right would constitute an abuse. In *Volvo v Veng*[565] the Court gave the following examples of conduct which would constitute an abuse: the arbitrary refusal to supply spare parts to independent repairers, the fixing of prices for spare parts at an unfair level; and a decision to discontinue the production of spare parts for a particular model even though many cars of that model are still in circulation. In that case, however, no such behaviour was found to have been adopted.

Most significantly, in *Magill* the Commission found that three television companies had abused their dominant position by refusing to allow Magill, the complainant company, to publish their programmes in a single magazine.[566] This finding was upheld by the Court of First Instance and, ignoring Gulmann A.G.'s opinion, the Court of Justice.[567] Both courts stressed that the refusal prevented the appearance of a new product, a comprehensive weekly guide to television programmes, for which there was potential consumer demand, and that there was no justification for the refusal.[568] This was the first case in which

---

[562] See the discussion of *IMS Health* below. This particular issue is discussed by Anderman, Ch. 12; and by Stothers, "The End of Exclusivity?: Abuse of Intellectual Property Rights in the EU" [2002] E.I.P.R. 86.

[563] Case 51/75, see n.553 above, para.37.

[564] Case T–198/98 *Micro Leader v Commission* [1999] E.C.R. II-3989, para. 56, emphasis added. This passage is based explicitly on Cases C-241/91P and C-242/91P *RTE and ITP v Commission* [1995] E.C.R. I-743 (*Magill*), discussed below.

[565] Case 238/87, see n.496 above.

[566] Commission Decision 89/205 in Case IV/31.851 *Magill TV Guide/ITP, BBC and* RTE [1989] O.J. L78/43.

[567] Cases T–69 *RTE v Commission* [1991] E.C.R. II 485; T–70/89 *BBC v Commission* [1991] E.C.R. II 575; and T–76/89 *ITP v Commission* [1991] E.C.R. II 575; on appeal Cases C-241/91P and 242/91P, see n.564 above.

[568] *ibid.*, Court of Justice paras 54–55.

the Court recognised the existence of an abuse of a dominant position through the exercise of an intellectual property right.

That decision has now been followed in the Commission's interim measures decision in *IMS Health*.[569] There the Commission found that IMS Health's system for dividing the German pharmaceutical sales market into 1860 "bricks" or geographical areas comprising four or more pharmacies, which enjoyed copyright, gave IMS Health a dominant position in the market. It then found that the refusal to licence this on reasonable terms constituted an abuse of that dominant position. However, this case can be distinguished from *Magill* in that there was no new product which was prevented from appearing. The decision was challenged before the Court of First Instance, which has suspended the measures pending a full hearing.[570] It is clear that one of the fundamental points in the full hearing will be the meaning of "exceptional circumstances".

(v)   Article 17(2) of the Charter

8.181   For completeness, Article 17(2) of the Charter of Fundamental Rights of the European Union[571] requires a brief mention here. Article 17 bears the title "right to property". Paragraph 2 provides: "Intellectual property shall be protected". This is subject to the general public interest exception in paragraph 52 of the Charter. As explained in paragraph 8.40 above, the precise status of the Charter remains unclear. In any case, it is doubtful whether Article 17(2) effects any change to Article 30 of the EC Treaty.

(c) *Intellectual property and Article 30*

8.182   The case law on the compatibility with Articles 28 to 30 of the exercise of intellectual property rights can be summarised in one general rule and three exceptions. However, special rules apply to geographical denominations.

General rule   Member States are free to legislate in the field of intellectual property unless and until it is harmonised, subject to the following exceptions.

Exception 1: Non-Discrimination   A Member State cannot discriminate in its legislation on grounds of nationality or place of manufacture.

Exception 2: Goods in Transit   A Member State may not prevent goods from passing through its territory, unless this entails the use of the intellectual property rights within that territory.

---

[569] Commission Decision in Case COMP D3/38.044 *NDC Health/IMS HEALTH: Interim Measures* of July 3, 2001 [2002] O.J. L59/18.

[570] Order of the President of the Court of First Instance in Case T–184/01R of October 26, 2001, [2001] E.C.R. II-3193, upheld by the ECJ on appeal in Case C-481/01(P)(R) *NDC Health v IMS Health*, Order of April 11, 2002, [2002] E.C.R. I-3401. The case has also gone directly to the Court of Justice from the German courts under Article 234, as Case C-418/01 *IMS Health v NDC Health*.

[571] n.135 above.

Exception 3: Community Exhaustion A Member State may not allow the owner of a right to prevent the import or sale of goods which have been lawfully distributed on the market of another Member State by the owner of that right, or with his consent.

These principles will now be examined in turn.

(i) General rule

8.183 As explained above, nearly all the cases on intellectual property state that the Treaty does not affect the existence of intellectual property rights granted pursuant to the legislation of a Member State, but only their exercise.[572] Accordingly, national legislation on the acquisition, transfer or extinction of such rights is lawful. While national legislation could in theory be so absurd as to fall outside the concept of industrial property in Article 30 altogether, the Court has consistently declined to make such a finding.

Parties have frequently sought to rely on Article 28 to cut back national intellectual property rights. Save for those cases which fit within the three exceptions, the Court has refused to interfere with national policy decisions. In particular, the Court has refused (a) to consider national conditions and procedures for grant of an intellectual property right; (b) to limit the breadth of trade mark rights by requiring a Community concept of confusion before this was harmonised; and (c) to require that intellectual property rights be restricted near the end of their term in order to allow free competition immediately on their expiry. Each of the foregoing examples will now be examined in turn.

Conditions and procedures for grant *Keurkoop v Nancy Kean Gifts*[573] was the first case in which a party challenged the conditions under which intellectual property is granted, rather than its application to imports from other Member States. Nancy Kean Gifts had registered the design of a handbag manufactured in Taiwan under the Uniform Benelux Law on Designs, even though it was not the author of the design and was not acting with the consent of the author. This was wholly compatible with the Uniform Law which simply provided that in such a case the author of the design could apply within five years to have the registration set aside in favour of himself. It was not open to any other person to contest the registration on the grounds that the person who had obtained it was neither the author nor acting with the author's consent. Keurkoop then began importing the handbag in question into the Netherlands, whereupon Nancy Kean Gifts brought an action against it before the Dutch courts. In its first question referred under Article 234 the Dutch court in effect asked whether such liberal provisions as to registration were justified under Article 30.

---

[572] Para. 8.174.
[573] Case 144/81 *Keurkoop v Nancy Kean Gifts* [1982] E.C.R. 2853.

The Court replied that "in the present state of Community law and in the absence of Community standardisation or of a harmonisation of laws the determination of the conditions and procedures under which protection is granted is a matter of national rules and, in this instance, for the common legislation established under a regional union between Belgium, Luxembourg and the Netherlands referred to in Article [306] of the Treaty."[574] Consequently, a provision of the kind in question was held to be compatible with Article 28.

8.184 *Nancy Kean* was confirmed in *Maxicar v Renault*[575] which related to the Italian law on registered design protection. The plaintiffs contended that, by extending the protection of such copyright to spare parts for cars having no original element and no intrinsic aesthetic value of their own, Italy had overstepped the bounds of intellectual property within the meaning of Article 30. As a result, they maintained, Italy had conferred an unjustified monopoly over spare parts to car manufacturers, which enabled them to eliminate competition from independent manufacturers of these products. The Court gave this argument short shrift. After repeating the central passage of its judgment in *Nancy Kean*, it added: "it is for the national legislature to determine which products qualify for protection, even if they form part of a unit already protected as such."[576]

8.185 The Court followed the same approach in *Thetford Corporation v Fiamma*.[577] The plaintiffs there, who owned United Kingdom patents for portable lavatories, sought to prevent the defendants from importing such lavatories from Italy. This invention had appeared in patent specifications filed more than 50 years previously, but the national legislation expressly stipulated that this constituted no bar to the valid grant of a patent. In these circumstances the defendants maintained that such a patent lacked the novelty or inventive step necessary for it to be covered by Article 30.

Like Mischo A.G., the Court dismissed the defendant's argument on the basis of *Nancy Kean*. Also rejected was the suggestion that *Nancy Kean* was to be distinguished on the grounds that patent law had been subject to a higher degree of harmonisation than registered design protection law. The Court pointed out that there was as yet no Community harmonisation of patent law, and found no relevant provision in any international convention.

Moreover, it went on to rule that the "50-year rule" did not constitute a disguised restriction on trade between Member States, since it "aimed to make it possible to give a reward, in the form of the grant of a patent, even in cases in

---

[574] *ibid.*, para.18.
[575] Case 53/87 [1988] E.C.R. 6039; see also Cases 238/87, see n.496 above; and C-38/98 *Renault v Maxicar* [2000] E.C.R. 2973 noted by Korah in [1988] E.I.P.R. 381.
[576] Para. 10 of the judgment.
[577] Case 35/87 [1988] E.C.R. 3585 noted by Bonet (1990) R.T.D.E. 713. In that case, the Court also rejected the suggestion that it was unlawful to grant an injunction prohibiting imports; the Court did not accept that damages were an adequate remedy.

which an 'old' invention was 'rediscovered'." In such cases the United Kingdom legislation was designed to prevent the existence of a former patent specification which had never been utilised or published from constituting a ground for revoking a patent which had been validly issued.

8.186 Breadth of trade mark rights: confusion The rule that confusion was to be determined by the national courts emerges from *Terrapin v Terranova*.[578] Terranova was a German company manufacturing dry plaster and other building materials in the Federal Republic under the "Terranova" trade mark. Terrapin was a British company manufacturing prefabricated houses in Britain under the trade mark "Terrapin" and exporting them to Germany under that mark. The trade marks were duly registered in Germany and the United Kingdom respectively and could be lawfully used there. There was no connection between the two companies or the two trade marks. An action was brought before the German courts in which the German company objected to the use of the "Terrapin" mark in Germany. The case reached the *Bundesgerichtshof*, which took the view that a risk of confusion existed, so that the sale of the imported goods under the "Terrapin" mark constituted an infringement under German law. It duly made a reference under Article 234 asking whether Articles 28 to 30 prohibited an import ban on such goods in these circumstances. After rehearsing the general principles already discussed here, the Court ruled as follows:

"In the present state of Community law an industrial or commercial property right legally acquired in a Member State may legally be used to prevent, under the first sentence of Article [30] of the Treaty, the import of products marketed under a name giving rise to confusion where the rights in question have been acquired by different and independent proprietors under different national laws. If in such a case the principle of the free movement of goods were to prevail over the protection given by the respective national laws, the specific objective of industrial and commercial property rights would be undermined. In the particular situation the requirements of the free movement of goods and the safeguarding of industrial and commercial property rights must be so reconciled that protection is ensured for the legitimate use of the rights conferred by national laws, coming within the prohibition on imports 'justified' within the meaning of Article 30 of the Treaty, but denied on the other hand in respect of any improper exercise of the same rights of such a nature as to maintain or effect artificial partitions within the common market."[579]

However, as will be discussed below, the Court also made it clear that the national court had to enquire whether the exercise of the national rights would constitute a means of arbitrary discrimination or a disguised restriction on trade between Member States. In particular, it held that the national court would have to consider "whether the rights in question are in fact exercised by the proprietor with the same strictness whatever the national origin of any possible infringer."[580] This will be discussed further below in exception (i).

---

[578] Case 119/75 [1976] E.C.R. 1039; [1976] 2 C.M.L.R. 482.
[579] *ibid.*, para.7.
[580] *ibid.*, para.4.

Plainly, the same approach applies to other forms of industrial property. Thus, in *Nancy Kean*[581] the Court ruled to the same effect in relation to protection in respect of a registered design.

8.187 An attempt to preclude Member States from applying an exorbitant concept of confusion was made by Jacobs A.G. in his seminal Opinion in *Hag II*,[582] in the following terms:

"the concept of confusingly similar marks must inevitably vary from one Member State to another and this can lead to a certain lack of reciprocity and to distortions of trade. For example, in *Terrapin v Terranova* the German courts found that there was a risk of confusion between the two marks. It is questionable whether an English court would take the same view. This could have the unfortunate consequence that the British manufacturer would be prevented from trading in Germany under his usual mark, while the German manufacturer would have unrestricted access to the British market. In fact, it appears that the German courts take a particularly broad view of the concept of confusingly similar marks, as is well illustrated by the facts of the proceeding before the Commission reported as *Tanabe Seiyaku Company v Bayer AG*, [1979] C.M.L.R. 2 at 80. In one notorious case (Bundespatentgericht [1973] G.R.U.R. 1975 74) the *Bundespatentgericht* held that the mark 'LUCKY WHIP' was liable to be confused with the mark 'Schöller-Nucki', a decision that seems to postulate a body of consumers afflicted with an acute form of dyslexia. It is against the background of that kind of national case law that the Court must consider whether to confirm and extend the approach adopted in *Terrapin v Terranova*."

In a subsequent passage he added:

"In my view, an unduly broad view of the concept of confusingly similar marks— exemplified in an extreme form in the 'LUCKY WHIP' decision—would run counter to Article [28] of the Treaty and would not be 'justified' under the first sentence of Article [30]. Moreover an excessively wide approach is prohibited by the second sentence of Article [30]. Reliance on a trade mark in order to exclude goods manufactured in another Member State where the risk of confusion between the marks is minimal would amount, if allowed by national courts, to a disguised restriction on trade between Member States..."

8.188 This plea fell on stony ground. In *Hag II* the Court did not consider this issue and subsequently in *Deutsche Renault v Audi*,[583] where the question could not be avoided, it resolutely adhered to its traditional approach. In that case the Court had to consider both the acquisition of intellectual property, discussed above, and its breadth through the concept of confusion. First, the Court had to determine whether it was consonant with Articles 28 and 30 for German law to grant to Audi protection of the word "quattro" for a four-wheel drive vehicle as a trade mark or related right. In other words, the Court was called upon to decide whether the grant of such protection to a word which merely designated the figure four in the language of another Member State fell within the concept

---

[581] Para. 8.183, see n.573 above.
[582] Case C-10/89 *CNL-SUCAL v Hag* [1990] E.C.R. I-3711 at 3740 and 3743.
[583] Case C-317/91 [1993] E.C.R. I 6227.

of intellectual property. Secondly, it had to determine whether such protection could extend, by reason of confusion, to preventing Deutsche Renault from using the name "Quadra" in Germany.

The Court followed the Advocate General and recognised that these two questions are in reality "two sides of the same coin" which must "be governed by a single, homogenous source of law—that is, at present, by national law".[584] Referring to its earlier case law, it held that the conditions under which such a name was protected were a matter for national law, subject to the limits laid down by the second sentence of Article 30. It went on to find that in this case the measure at issue was compatible with the latter sentence, for the following reasons: German law made the grant of trade mark protection to words denoting a numerical figure subject to strict rules, in particular that the word in question must have gained acceptance in the trade as a distinctive feature of the product concerned through use; and both the acquisition and scope of such protection was applied equally to producers from other Member States.

The Court then held that "Community law does not ... lay down any strict interpretative criterion for the concept of risk of confusion". It then went on to hold that, as the rules on confusion were not interpreted by the German courts in a discriminatory fashion, they did not constitute arbitrary discrimination nor a disguised restriction on intra-Community trade.

8.189 Since January 1, 1993 the "likelihood of confusion" of different trade marks has become a matter of Community law by virtue of Article 4 and 5 of the first trade mark Directive[585] (the material events in *Hag II* and *Deutsche Renault* occurred before that date).

One early example of the different approach post-harmonisation was seen in *SABEL v Puma*.[586] Article 4(1)(b) of the Directive provides that a "trade mark shall not be registered or, if registered, shall be liable to be declared invalid: ... if ... there exists a likelihood of confusion ... which includes the likelihood of association with the earlier trade mark". This provision left open the question of whether the purely associative nature of two trade marks is sufficient to assume that a risk of confusion exists (as was the case under Benelux trade-mark law[587]). In *SABEL v Puma*, the Court resolved the ambiguity by rejecting the Benelux approach and held that "the criterion of 'likelihood of confusion which includes the likelihood of association with the earlier mark' contained in Article 4(1)(b) of the Directive is to be interpreted as meaning that the mere association which the public might make between two trade marks as a result of their analogous semantic content is not in itself a sufficient ground for concluding that there is a likelihood of confusion within the meaning of the

---

[584] *ibid.*, para. 31.
[585] See n.521 above. Similar provisions are to be found in Arts 8 and 9 of Council Reg. 40/94 on the Community trade mark, See n.522 above.
[586] Case C-251/95 [1997] E.C.R. I-6191.
[587] See Art. 13A, Uniform Benelux Law on Trade Marks as interpreted by the Benelux Court of Justice in *Henri Jullien v Verschueren Norbert*, Jur. Benelux Court of Justice 1983, 36. ("Union").

term".[588] In other words, the Court has established that a "likelihood of association" between two trade marks will not constitute an infringement of trade
mark unless there is also a "likelihood of confusion" on the part of the public.[589]

However, the continuing relevance of the old law can be seen in the recent
opinion by Colomer A.G. in *Robelco v Robeco*.[590] The Advocate General said that,
for the purposes of Article 5(5) of the First Trade Mark Directive, which relates
to protection where a similar mark is used on dissimilar goods, the degree of
similarity of mark is a question for the Member States and not for the Community.

8.190 **Expiry of term** One particularly inventive attempt to cut down
national intellectual property rights came before the Court in *Generics v Smith
Kline & French Laboratories*.[591] Once a patent in respect of a manufacturing
process for a medicinal product has expired, a third party is of course free to
manufacture products using the process in question, and to apply to the
appropriate authority for permission to market that product. However, unless
that third party is entitled to submit samples of the medicinal product to the
appropriate authority before the patent expires there will, for obvious administrative reasons, be a delay between the expiry of the patent and the date on
which the third party receives actual authorisation to market that product in
question. In this case, the proprietor of such a patent attempted (shortly before
the patent expired) to rely on that patent to prevent the submission by a third
party of samples of a medicinal product (which had been manufactured using
the patented manufacturing process) in order to apply for marketing authorisation. The Court held that reliance by the proprietor of the patent in these
circumstances fell within the specific subject-matter of the patent right in so far
as such samples had been used without the direct or indirect consent of the
patentee.[592] Accordingly, in the absence of arbitrary discrimination or a disguised restriction on trade, a patent owner can rely on that patent right up to
the date of expiry, even if that means that in practice there will be a delay
between the expiry and the date on which a third party's products will reach the
market.

8.191 **Comment** Certain other matters relating to the grant, transfer and
extinction of intellectual property rights are governed by the other legislative
measures referred to in paragraph 8.177 above. However, the fact remains that

---

[588] Para. 26 of the judgment.
[589] See also on confusion Cases C-39/97 *Canon Kabushiki Kaisha v MGM* [1998] E.C.R. I-5507; C-342/
97 *Lloyd Schuhfabrik v Klijsen Handel* [1999] ECR I-3819; and C-425/98 *Marca Mode v Adidas* [2000]
E.C.R. I-4861.
[590] Case C-23/01 *NV Robelco v NV Robeco Groep*, Opinion of March 21, 2002. See also the opinion of
Tizzano A.G. in Case C-245/00 *SENA v. NOS*, Opinion of September 26, 2002, concerning the
interpretation of "equitable remuneration" in Article 8(2) of Directive 92/100 on rental and
lending rights.
[591] Case C-316/95, see n.518 above.
[592] Para. 20 of the judgment.

Community legislation is still silent on the bulk of such issues. Accordingly, the case law considered here continues to be of great importance.

Generally speaking, the Court's decision to steer clear of this minefield may well be warranted for reasons of principle: quite apart from the principles of subsidiarity and legal certainty, the Court must be wary of interfering with property rights more than is necessary, in view of Article 295 of the Treaty. What is more, the Court is by its very nature ill equipped to decide issues such as whether two marks are confusingly similar to the public in a particular Member State.

Nevertheless, there is plainly great force in the Advocate General's complaint in *Hag II* that a Member State grants very wide protection by treating the "LUCKY-WHIP" and "Schöller-Nucki" marks as being confusingly similar. Moreover, it should be recalled that in *Verband Sozialer Wettbewerb v Estée Lauder*,[593] the Court did not baulk from a finding that Germany was required to permit the sale of a cosmetic product under the name "Clinique" since, contrary to the German Government's submissions, that name would not give German consumers the erroneous impression that the product possessed medicinal qualities. The difference of approach is presumably due to the fact that in *Estée Lauder* intellectual property was not in issue.

(ii) Exception 1: non-discrimination

8.192 The Rule described above is subject to the overriding consideration that a Member State may not discriminate on the basis of nationality of the right-holder or the place of manufacture of the protected subject matter.

In paragraph 8.179 we noticed the ruling in *Phil Collins*, where the Court held that it was contrary to Article 12 EC for a Member State to discriminate against nationals of other Member States in the grant of industrial property rights. In that case, Articles 28 to 30 were not in point, since the recordings had been imported directly from the United States. Where Article 28 applies, it ousts Article 12, which is stated to be "without prejudice to any special provisions contained [within the Treaty]". Therefore, in this context we must look to Article 30.

On this basis, had the recordings in *Phil Collins* been imported from another Member State, the Court would undoubtedly have held the contested legislation to be contrary to Article 28 on the basis that it constituted arbitrary discrimination and/or a disguised restriction on trade between Member States within the meaning of the second sentence of Article 30. This emerges clearly from both *Thetford* and *Deutsche Renault*, although in neither case was such discrimination found to exist.

8.193 An equally blatant form of discrimination was in issue in *Commission v*

---

[593] See n.374 above.

United Kingdom.[594] These proceedings related to national provisions according to which a compulsory patent licence could be granted unless the patent was being worked to the full by manufacture within the territory of the defendant State. The Commission claimed that this measure constituted a significant deterrent to traders wishing to work their patent by importation into the United Kingdom and that the measure was therefore contrary to Articles 28 and 30. In its pleadings the Commission made it clear that it did not object to compulsory licences as such. Such measures were widespread in the Member States at that time, and indeed the Commission brought parallel proceedings against Italy.[595]

Both Van Gerven A.G. and the Court wholly endorsed the Commission's view. As in *Phil Collins,* they rejected the suggestion that Article 295 made legislation on the grant and transfer of industrial property rights the exclusive preserve of the Member States. That provision in no way prevented Articles 28 to 30 from applying to such measures. The essence of the Court's judgment is contained in the following passage:

> "Although the penalty for lack or insufficiency of exploitation of a patent may be regarded as the necessary counterpart to the territorial exclusivity conferred by the patent, there is no reason relating to the specific subject-matter of the patent to justify the discrimination inherent in the contested provisions between exploiting the patent in the form of production on the national territory and exploiting it by importation from the territory of other Member States.
>
> Such discrimination is in fact motivated not by the specific requirements of industrial and commercial property, but, as the defendant State moreover recognises, by the national legislature's concern to encourage domestic production.
>
> Such a consideration, the effect of which is to frustrate the objectives of the Community as laid down in particular in Article 2 and specified in Article 3 of the Treaty, cannot be accepted as a justification for a restriction on trade between Member States."[596]

8.194 Also, in *Terrapin v Terranova*[597] the Court held that the *proprietor* of an industrial property right must exercise it "with the same strictness whatever the national origin of any possible infringer". Discriminatory conduct of this variety, it held, would constitute arbitrary discrimination or a disguised restriction on trade between Member States. However, this part of the decision has not been repeated by the Court in any recent cases. It was mentioned by Tesauro A.G. in his Opinion in *Deutsche Renault v Audi,*[598] but the Court limited itself to

---

[594] Case C-30/90, see n.508 above; see Bonet, "Propriétés intellectuelles" (1993) R.T.D.E. 525 at 533; Cornish, "Intellectual Property" (1992) Y.E.L. 635 at 638. See also Case 434/85 *Allen and Hanbury's v Generics (UK)* [1988] E.C.R. 1245 and Case C-191/90 *Generics v Smith Kline and French Laboratories* [1992] E.C.R. I-5335, both of which concerned provisions of UK patent law which granted more favourable treatment to those who manufactured in the UK rather than in another Member State.

[595] Case C-235/89 [1992] E.C.R. I 777.

[596] This result reflects the provisions of the two successive Community Patent Conventions (para. 8.177 above), save that they contain optional transitional provisions. The Court pointed out that the defendant States could not rely on those transitional provisions as both Conventions were expressed to be subject to the Treaty of Rome.

[597] Case 119/75, see n. 578 above.

[598] Case C-317/91, see n.583 above, Opinion paras 24–25.

saying that "it does not appear from the documents before the Court that a manufacturer from another Member State is precluded from claiming the same [intellectual property protection] or that such protection varies according to whether or not the goods bearing that trade mark are of national or foreign origin".[599]

Terrapin v Terranova was decided in 1976 and it is by no means certain that the Court would adopt the same position today. As we noticed in Chapter 4, it now seems clear that Articles 28 to 30 do not impose obligations on private parties, so that those provisions leave them free, for instance, to boycott certain imports if they wish. The remedy against a private undertaking acting in a discriminatory fashion lies in competition law, under Article 81 (if in concert with another party) or Article 82 (if he holds a dominant position). Arguably, the situation contemplated in *Terrapin* is different, because intellectual property rights are created by the State; thus the Court's ruling may be understood to mean that Member States may not confer intellectual property rights entitling holders to discriminate in this way. Yet that contention may in turn be countered by the assertion that many other acts of private parties are ultimately founded on legislation or other State measures. Since there appears to be no reason to confine it to intellectual property, the Court's stance in *Terrapin* would clearly have far-reaching consequences, if confirmed today, imposing a general duty of non-discrimination on private undertakings acting within the Community. Accordingly, that path cannot be followed lightly.

Moreover, although the early cases on repackaging appeared to require the repackager to show that the owner was intending to divide the internal market, the Court confirmed in *Bristol-Myers Squibb v Paranova*[600] that this was not a prerequisite. Whether, as Jacobs A.G. suggested in his Opinion in *Pharmacia & Upjohn v Paranova*,[601] such intention still remains relevant remains unsettled. However, this may be a largely theoretical argument; it seems likely that, whenever there is such subjective intention, the parallel importer would more readily be able to show that repackaging was "necessary", as most recently defined by the ECJ in *Boehringer Ingelheim*.[602] Therefore, while the Court has not dealt with the question squarely, the relevance of subjective intention has, at the very least, been greatly diminished.

(iii) Exception 2: goods in transit

8.195 *Commission v France (spare parts in transit)*[603] concerned the use made by French customs authorities of legislation to detain spare parts which French law would regard as counterfeit but which had been lawfully manufactured in another Member State (such as Spain) and which were intended, following their transit through French territory, to be placed on the market in another

---

[599] *ibid.*, judgment para.27.
[600] Joined Cases C-427/93, 429/93 and 436/93 [1996] E.C.R. I-3457. See paras 8.221–228.
[601] C-379/97 *Pharmacia & Upjohn v Paranova* [1999] E.C.R. I-6927, para. 42.
[602] Case C-143/00 *Boehringer Ingelheim* [2002] E.C.R. I-3759, discussed below at para. 8.225.
[603] Case 23/99 [2000] E.C.R. I-7653, noted by Gonzalez Vaqué and Millerot [2001] R.D.U.E. 189.

Member State (such as Italy) where they could be lawfully marketed. This ban on transit was intended to protect the rights of holders of the French design right in these goods. The Court found that the detention of the spare parts by the French authorities constituted a restriction on the free movement of goods under Article 28. As to the question of justification, the French Government had submitted that the detention measures formed part of the specific subject-matter of design rights. This argument was rejected by the Court in the following terms:

> "Intra-Community transit ... consists in the transportation of goods from one Member State to another across the territory of one or more Member States and involves no use of the appearance of the protected design. ... [I]t does not, moreover, give rise to the payment of fees when the transportation is undertaken by a third person with the authorisation of the proprietor of the right. Intra-Community transit does not therefore form part of the specific subject-matter of the right of industrial and commercial property in designs.
>
> The putting into circulation referred to in [*inter alia* Case C-9/93 *Ideal Standard*] was not therefore the mere physical transportation of the goods but consisted in placing them on the market, that is to say the marketing of those goods. However, in this case, the product is marketed not in French territory, through which it only passes in transit, but in another Member State, where the product is not protected and may therefore be lawfully sold."[604]

Therefore, as they do not fall within the specific subject matter of intellectual property, intellectual property rights cannot be used to block the transport of goods between Member States. The key to this ruling is that no use was to be made of the intellectual property rights in France.

Furthermore, France contended that it was entitled to detain goods for up to 10 days so as to check whether they were indeed manufactured in another Member State and were merely in transit through French territory. The Court dismissed this argument in the following terms:

> "As regards the investigation of the origin and destination of the goods in transit, it should be possible for this to be carried out on the spot if the transporter is in possession of the relevant documents or if he can obtain them immediately. In any event, detention for up to 10 days is disproportionate in relation to the purpose of such an investigation and, accordingly, cannot be justified in regard to the purpose of protection of industrial and commercial property referred to in Article [30] of the Treaty."

8.196 To place this judgment in its context, it should be mentioned that the Court had already reached the opposite conclusion in *Polo/Lauren v Dwidua*,[605] where the goods were passing through the Community in external transit from one third country to another. On an analysis of Regulation 3295/94 on counterfeit and pirated goods,[606] the Court had held that the Austrian authorities were entitled to seize counterfeit goods originating in Indonesia and destined

---

[604] Paras 43 and 44 of the judgment.
[605] Case C-383/98, see n.537 above.
[606] See n.536 above.

for Poland. Having said that, it should be pointed out that there was no discussion before the Court as to whether the goods had been legally produced and marketed in Indonesia and would be legally marketed in Poland.

The defendant in *Commission v France* acknowledged that Regulation 3295/94 relates exclusively to trade between the Community and non-member countries, and thus does not concern trade between the Member States. Nevertheless, it argued that that Regulation would be undermined, if it were debarred from intercepting counterfeit goods from third countries put into free circulation by another Member State such as Spain with relatively "lax" intellectual property rules. On this point, the Court simply observed that "considerations concerning the effectiveness of Regulation 3295/94 cannot justify a breach of the rules of the Treaty relating to the free movement of goods within the Community".[607] Thus it is clear that France is equally prohibited from intercepting goods originating in third countries transiting through its territory, where those goods have been put into free circulation in the Community,[608] even though the actual proceedings related only to products manufactured in another Member State.[609]

(iv) Exception 3: exhaustion

8.197 The "exhaustion of rights" principle is a traditional concept of national intellectual property law. Its reasoning is so simple that it is typically taken for granted. Once an owner has sold a product which is protected by his intellectual property right, that particular product can generally be bought and sold freely on the national market (subject to any contractual restrictions). In other words, the intellectual property gives rights over the first sale market but not over the second hand market. Although it would be possible for a system to grant the owner rights over all sales, this does not typically happen within national systems.[610]

Difficulties arise, however, when the product is sold by the owner in one State and imported into another. Along with the right to prevent manufacture, intellectual property typically gives the right to prevent imports. Some jurisdictions traditionally ignore the prior sale abroad and say that the owner retains the right to prevent any such imports ("national exhaustion"). Other jurisdictions traditionally treat the sale abroad as no different from a sale within the national market and say that the owner thus has no right to prevent such imports ("international exhaustion"). Finally, some jurisdictions traditionally place themselves between the two camps and will allow imports under certain

---

[607] para. 31 of the judgment, and see also paras 48 to 53 of the A.G.'s Opinion. On the need for Community legislation to comply with the principle of the free movement of goods, see paras 4.10 to 4.25 above.

[608] See paras 2.15 *et seq.* above.

[609] See also Case C-115/02 *Administration des Douanes v Rioglass* (pending, [2002] O.J. C131/9).

[610] One key exception would be the moral right to object to derogatory treatment of a copyright work, which typically survives the sale of that work. Consider also the Artists' Resale Right under Dir. 2001/84, see n.531 above.

conditions (such as whether the products are of identical quality or whether there is reciprocity in allowing such imports).

8.198   These difficulties soon became an issue within the context of Article 30. The question which arose was whether Member States could continue to apply national exhaustion where a product had been put on the market in another Member State. In other words, the question was whether Member States could allow an intellectual property owner the right to block the import of a product which had been put on the market in another Member State by the owner or with his consent. As described below, the Court came to adopt a concept of Community exhaustion which mirrored the approach taken within a Member State and this concept has been adopted in the harmonisation legislation.

A further question, which did not arise within the context of Article 30 but which came to be dealt with in the harmonisation directives, was whether Member States should or should not apply international exhaustion. This issue will be dealt with at the end of the discussion on the concept of consent.

8.199   The Community exhaustion rule was first laid down in *Deutsche Gram-mophon v Metro.*[611] The facts were that Deutsche Grammophon had manu-factured certain records in Germany, which it had sold to its subsidiary Polydor in Paris and which then came into the hands of Metro. Deutsche Grammophon sought an injunction against Metro to prevent it from selling these records in Germany, claiming that this would be in breach of protection granted by Ger-man law to manufacturers of sound recordings, which protection is akin to copyright. The Hamburg court requested the Court of Justice to rule, *inter alia*, on whether the application of such a national law to exclude goods in these circumstances was contrary to Articles 10 and 81(1) of the Treaty. Article 10(2) imposes on the Member States a general obligation to "abstain from any measure which could jeopardise the attainment of the objectives of this Treaty."

The Court held that even if the exercise of an intellectual property right was not the subject, the means or the result of an agreement so as to fall under Article 81, its compatibility with the provisions of the Treaty on the free movement of goods must be examined and in particular its compatibility with Article 30. It continued:

"On the assumption that those provisions may be relevant to a right related to copyright, it is nevertheless clear from that Article that, although the Treaty does not affect the existence of rights recognised by the legislation of a Member State with regard to industrial and commercial property, the exercise of such rights may never-theless fall within the prohibitions laid down by the Treaty. Although it permits pro-hibitions or restrictions on the free movement of products, which are justified for the purpose of protecting industrial and commercial property, Article [30] only admits derogations from that freedom which constitute the specific subject-matter of such property.

If a right related to copyright is relied upon to prevent the marketing in a Member

---

[611] Case 78/70, see n.502 above. See also Cases 55/80 and 57/80 *Musik-Vertrieb Membran v GEMA*, see n.487 above.

State of products distributed by the holder of the right or with his consent on the territory of another Member State on the sole ground that such distribution did not take place on the national territory, such a prohibition which would legitimise the isolation of national markets, would be repugnant to the essential purpose of the Treaty, which is to unite national markets into a single market."[612]

This rule was then extended to the various forms of intellectual property, including patents,[613] trade marks,[614] design rights[615] and plant breeders rights.[616]

8.200　　This case law has consistently been given legislative form in provisions harmonising national intellectual property or providing for Community-based intellectual property: measures appear in the first[617] and second[618] Community Patent Conventions (which, as already mentioned, have not come into force); the proposed Community Patent Regulation[619]; the Trade Mark Directive[620] and Regulation[621]; the Design Directive[622] and Regulation[623]; the copyright Directives on software,[624] neighbouring rights[625] and the information society[626]; the Plant Variety Rights Regulation[627]; and the proposed Directive on the utility model.[628] Thus Article 7 of the Trade Mark Directive reads as follows:

"1. The trade mark shall not entitle the proprietor to prohibit its use in relation to goods which have been put on the market in the Community under that trade mark by the proprietor or with his consent.

2. Paragraph 1 shall not apply where there exist legitimate reasons for the proprietor to oppose further commercialisation of the goods, especially where the condition of the goods is changed or impaired after they have been put on the market."

For a period, there was some uncertainty as to the impact that this harmoni-

---

[612] Note that exhaustion only applies to copyright used to manufacture products: broadcasting, performance, rental and lending rights are not exhausted in the same way (see below, paras 8.230–8.236).

[613] Case 15/74 *Centrafarm v Sterling Drug*, n.492 above. For a national measure which apparently flouted the principles laid down in that case, see written question 1257/81 [1982] O.J. C53/5.

[614] Case 16/74, see n.493 above.

[615] Case 144/81, see n.573 above.

[616] Case 258/78 *Nungesser v Commission* [1982] E.C.R. 2015. This is indirect authority, as the case concerned only Art. 81, but it did state at para.33 that "the rules relating to trade in products, including competition law, must in principle be applied to the marketing of [protected seeds]". The Court went on to hold that plant breeders' rights were not "a species of commercial or industrial property right with characteristics of so special a nature as to require, in relation to the competition rules, a different treatment from other commercial or industrial property rights."

[617] See n.516 above, Arts 32 and 81.

[618] See n.517 above, Arts 28 and 76.

[619] See n.519 above, Art. 10.

[620] See n.521 above, Art. 7.

[621] See n.522 above, Art. 13.

[622] See n.523 above, Art. 15.

[623] See n.524 above, Art. 21.

[624] See n.525 above, Art. 4(c).

[625] See n.526 above, Art. 9(2).

[626] See n.530 above, Art. 4(2).

[627] See n.532 above, Art. 16. Note that this does allow the buyer to propagate a variety "unless such propagation was intended when the material was disposed of."

[628] See n.514 above, Art. 21.

sation was to have on the Court's case law on Article 30. Jacobs A.G. pointed out in *Hag II*[629] that Article 7 of the Trade Mark Directive did not purport to constitute an exhaustive codification of the prior case law on the exhaustion of trade mark rights. However, in *Bristol-Myers Squibb v Paranova*,[630] the Court rejected that view, finding instead that Article 7 of the Directive comprehensively regulated the question of the exhaustion of trade mark rights for products traded in the Community. As such "national rules on the subject must be assessed in the light of that Article [of the Directive]".[631] In the same case, the Court also held that the Directive must be interpreted in the light of the Treaty rules on the free movement of goods and in particular Article 30 EC.[632] In particular, it held:

> "Article 7 of the Directive, like Article [30] of the Treaty, is intended to reconcile the fundamental interest in protecting trade mark rights with the fundamental interest in the free movement of goods within the common market, so that those two provisions, which pursue the same result, must be interpreted in the same way."[633]

8.201 The concept of consent will now be considered in greater detail, followed by the particular cases of repackaging and advertising goods which have been imported from another Member State. Then copyright in broadcasting, performances, rental rights and lending rights, which are not subject to exhaustion rules, will be examined.

8.202 **The concept of consent** As discussed above, the "specific subject matter" of the main types of intellectual property is the right to be the first to market a product incorporating the intellectual property.[634] It is therefore necessary to consider in what circumstances an owner will be regarded as having marketed a product. This is normally described as the owner's "consent", although (as will be seen) the term is not always used in its standard sense.[635]

8.203 *(a) Sale by the owner within the EEA* Where the owner of intellectual property sells products in a Member State where he owns that intellectual property, or consents to another party doing so,[636] any parallel rights are exhausted in all other Member States.

---

[629] Case C-10/89, see n.582 above, at pp. 3744–6.

[630] Joined Cases C-427/93, 429/93 and 436/93, See n.600 above. On the same date the Court also handed down two further judgments, which were based on Art. 30 but decided in materially the same way, in C-232/94 *MPA Pharma v Rhône-Poulenc Pharma* [1996] E.C.R. I-3671; and Joined Cases C-71–73/94 *Eurim-Pharm Arzneimittel v Beiersdorf* [1996] E.C.R. I-3603.

[631] See *Bristol-Myers* at para. 26. See also Ch. 12. The fact that the provisions of a Directive (as opposed to those of the Treaty) are in place also gives rise to the further question of "horizontal" direct effect and the extent to which a national court is bound to interpret national provisions implementing the Directive as far as possible in the light of the wording and the purpose of the Directive: see *MPA Pharma* at para. 12 and *Beiersdorf* at para. 26.

[632] See *Bristol-Myers* at para. 27.

[633] See *Bristol-Myers* at para. 40.

[634] Para. 8.173 above.

[635] See in particular para. 8.218 below.

[636] See Case C-9/93, see n.507 above, para.38, discussed further in para. 8.212 below.

8.204 An intellectual property right will be exhausted in this way even if the owner does not hold a parallel right under the law of the Member State where the goods were marketed. This was established in *Merck v Stephar*.[637] There Merck held the patent in the Netherlands for a certain pharmaceutical product, which it also put on the market in Italy. That product was not covered by any patent in Italy, because at the material time pharmaceutical products could not be patented under Italian law. Stephar acquired quantities of this product on the Italian market and resold them in the Netherlands. The question which arose for decision was whether Merck could use its Dutch patent to prevent such imports.

On a reference from a Dutch court, the Court of Justice held in effect that a patent could not be used in this way, since it had been exhausted when the goods were put on the Italian market. If the holder of a patent in a product chose to market it in a Member State where it was not patentable, then he must bear the consequences.

This ruling manifestly applies to all forms of intellectual property. The result is that the owner of intellectual property in some, but not all, Member States must make a commercial decision on where to sell his products. On the one hand, he can compete freely on markets where he has no intellectual property, accepting the danger that the products which he sells there and which, lacking protection, will typically fetch a lower price will be freely imported into the countries where he does have protection. On the other hand, he can steer clear of such markets and avoid the risk of importation.

8.205 An exception to the rule in *Merck v Stephar* was contained in Article 47 of the Act of Accession[638] of Spain and Portugal, which is in the following terms:

"1. Notwithstanding Article 42, the holder, or his beneficiary, of a patent for a chemical or pharmaceutical product or a product relating to plant health, filed in a Member State at a time when a product patent could not be obtained in Spain for that product may rely upon the rights granted by that patent in order to prevent the import and marketing of that product in the present Member State or states where that product enjoys patent protection even if that product was put on the market in Spain for the first time by him or with his consent.
2. This right may be invoked for the products referred to in paragraph 1 until the end of the third year after Spain has made these products patentable."

Article 209 of the Act, which relates to Portugal, is in the same terms, *mutatis mutandis*.

Both Spain and Portugal enacted the envisaged legislation in 1992, and the transitional periods expired on December 31, 1994 in the case of Portugal and on October 6, 1995 in the case of Spain.[639] Pharmaceutical companies that had sold their products in those Member States before patent protection existed were subject to the cold winds of free movement of goods rules and the

---

[637] Case 187/80 [1981] E.C.R. 2063; [1981] 3 C.M.L.R. 463; compare Case 24/67 See n.499 above.
[638] [1985] O.J. L302/1; as to Art. 42, see paras 5.05 and 6.08 above.
[639] Cases C-267 and 268/95 *Merck v Primecrown* [1996] E.C.R. I-6285.

exhaustion of rights doctrine in particular. Parallel importers were quick to exploit the opportunity to purchase supplies of cheaper pharmaceutical products in Spain and Portugal and to export and market them in other Member States, making a tidy profit in the process. In the light of the Court's judgment in *Merck v Stephar*,[640] the pharmaceutical companies were not able to rely on their patents in other Member States to put a stop to the parallel imports: their products had been put on the Spanish and Portuguese markets by them or with their consent and, according the Court's reasoning in *Merck v Stephar*, they had to accept the consequences of their choice as regards the free movement of their products within the single market.

However, this did not stop one group of pharmaceutical companies from challenging the applicability of the *Merck v Stephar* ruling to the particular circumstances of this case. In *Merck v Primecrown*[641] the group argued before the English courts that they had a "legal or ethical" obligation to continue to market their products in Spain and Portugal (at prices fixed in accordance with national requirements) in order to satisfy the needs of patients in those Member States. The English High Court referred questions to the Court of Justice in effect asking the Court to re-consider its judgment in *Merck v Stephar*. Contrary to the Opinion of Fennelly A.G., the Court refused to do so. As to the fact that the (low) price at which the products had been marketed had been fixed by law in Spain and Portugal, the Court recalled that it was "well settled that distortions caused by different price legislation in a Member State must be remedied by measures taken by the Community authorities and not by the adoption by another Member State of measures incompatible with the rules on free movement of goods".[642] The Court did recognise, however, that where a patentee is legally bound to market his products in a Member State, he cannot be deemed to have given his consent to the marketing of the products concerned.[643] Thus, the patentee had to prove that there was a genuine and existing legal obligation to market the product concerned in the exporting Member State.[644] On the other hand, the Court rejected the argument that ethical obligations to market vitiated consent to the marketing of the products concerned, holding that "such considerations are not, in the absence of any legal obligation, such as to make it possible properly to identify the situations in which the patentee is deprived of his power to decide freely how he will market his product. Such considerations are ... difficult to apprehend and distinguish from commercial considerations".[645]

---

[640] See para. 8.204 above.
[641] See n.639 above.
[642] Para. 47 of the judgment.
[643] Case 19/84 *Pharmon v Hoechst*, see n.518 above.
[644] Para. 51 of the judgment.
[645] Para. 53 of the judgment. In a related development, Denmark, France, Germany and the UK sought the adoption of safeguard measures pursuant to Art. 379 of the Act of Accession against imports from Spain after the expiry of the exception in Art. 47. On December 20, 1995, the Commission refused to authorise those safeguard measures. A action for annulment of the Commission's decision (brought by three of the pharmaceutical companies concerned) was declared inadmissible by the Court of First Instance: T-60/96 *Merck v Commission* [1997] E.C.R. II-849.

8.206   *(b) Sale by a third party with no intellectual property rights* The important point in *Merck v Stephar* was that Merck had placed the goods on the Italian market itself. Had this been done by a third party without Merck's consent, then Merck could have prevented the goods being imported into the Netherlands. The third party would have been free to do so, given that Merck did not own a patent in Italy. However, because Merck could not have been said to "consent" to such a sale, Merck's rights in other Member States would not have been exhausted. This principle was clearly stated in *Centrafarm v Sterling Drug*[646] where the Court held:

> "an obstacle to the free movement of goods of this kind may be justified on the ground of protection of industrial property where such protection is invoked against a product coming from a Member State where it is not patentable and has been manufactured by third parties without the consent of the patentee..."

8.207   Precisely the same will occur when the industrial property rights in the exporting Member State have expired. This is clearly illustrated by *EMI Electrola v Patricia Im-und Export.*[647] There, sound recordings of musical works by a well-known British singer were marketed by the defendants in Denmark where the copyright had expired, and then exported to Germany where it was still valid; (in both countries the copyright period was 25 years, but it had started to run earlier in Denmark). At no stage did EMI, which owned the German copyright, consent to the marketing. EMI therefore sought to prevent the sale of the recordings in Germany. The Court held that the principle of exhaustion did not apply. The lawful marketing of the goods in Denmark was due:

> "not to an act or the consent of the copyright owner or his licensee, but to the expiry of the protection period provided for by the legislation of that Member State. The problem arising thus stems from the differences between national legislation regarding the period of protection afforded by copyright and by related rights, those differences concerning either the duration of the protection itself or the details thereof, such as the time when the protection period begins to run."

Since the restriction resulted from the very existence of intellectual property rights and since there was no evidence that the German legislation constituted arbitrary discrimination or a disguised restriction on trade between Member States, the Court upheld EMI's right to oppose the marketing of the recordings in Germany.[648] Thus, in the absence of consent on the part of the copyright holder, the general rule applied.[649]

---

[646] Case 15/74; see n.492 above; [1974] 2 C.M.L.R. 480, para. 11 of the judgment.

[647] Case 341/87 [1989] E.C.R. 79.

[648] It is a moot point whether this ruling would also apply to cases where the expiry of the industrial property right in the exporting Member State is attributable to the conduct of the holder (*e.g.* failure to renew a trade mark). Is such conduct tantamount to consent to marketing by a third party?

[649] To prevent this type of situation, the Commission made proposals which eventually led to Directive 93/98 harmonising the term of protection of copyright (see n.527 above).

8.208 As this case law clearly illustrates, the essence of the principle of exhaustion is the consent of the holder of the industrial property right to the initial marketing. This will typically be clear where the intellectual property owner in the importing Member State has no intellectual property rights in the exporting Member State, unless the person marketing in the exporting Member State can show some link to the owner. It may be less clear where the intellectual property owner in the importing Member State did in fact have intellectual property rights in the exporting Member State but chose not to exercise them. However, in such cases the Court is likely to follow the approach taken in *Silhouette* and *Davidoff*, discussed later, and require the parallel importer to show consent positively expressed to the marketing in the exporting Member State.[650]

8.209 *(c) Sale by a third party with its own intellectual property rights* In the 1970s, the Court was keen to go further than was described above and it introduced the "doctrine of common origin", holding that a trade mark right may not be relied on to prohibit the marketing in a Member State of goods lawfully produced in another Member State under an identical trade mark which has the same origin.[651] Although this line of case law has now been reversed,[652] it remains an important illustration of the tension between national intellectual property rights and the internal market.

8.210 The doctrine of common origin was introduced in *Hag I*.[653] The facts were that the trade marks in the name "Hag" for coffee were owned by one party in Belgium and Luxembourg and by an unconnected party in Germany. The ownership has been split as a result of sequestration in Belgium after World War II. Much later, the German owner began to market coffee under the mark in Luxembourg and the Luxembourg owner brought infringement proceedings. The Tribunal d'Arrondissement of Luxembourg asked the European Court under Article 234 whether this was contrary, *inter alia, to* Articles 28 to 30.

The Court held that "one cannot allow the holder of a trade mark to rely upon the exclusiveness of a trade mark right, which may be a consequence of territorial limitation of national legislations—with a view to prohibiting the marketing in a Member State of goods legally produced in another Member State under an identical trade mark having the same origin."

8.211 This doctrine attracted very considerable criticism.[654] Indeed, Leigh and Guy went as far as to say that "one is hard pressed to think of any objective

---

[650] See paras 8.217–8.218 below.
[651] Case 192/73 *Van Zuylen Frères v Hag (Hag I)* [1974] E.C.R. 731; [1974] 2 C.M.L.R. 127.
[652] Case C-10/89, see n.582 above.
[653] See n.651 above.
[654] *e.g.* Cornish, in the 1982 FIDE Report on "The Elimination of Non-Tariff Barriers with Particular Reference to Industrial Property Rights including Copyright" at 9.10; and *Intellectual Property: Patents, Copyright, Trade Marks and Allied Rights* (2nd ed., 1989) at 487; van Gerven and Gotzen, *ibid.* at 1.16; Gotzen, "Gewerbliche Schutzrechte und Urheberrecht in der Rechtsprechung des Europäischen Gerichtshofes zu Art. 30–36 des EWG-Vertrags" (1984) G.R.U.R. Int. 146 at 149.

justification for the Court's decision in the *Hag* case, at least as regards its answer to the first question referred to it".[655] However, the accidents of litigation ensured that no case directly raising the question of common origin came before the Court until *CNL-Sucal v Hag (Hag II)*.[656] The new case arose out of the same facts as *Hag I*, except that this time it was the German company that was seeking to prevent the Belgian product from being marketed in Germany. The *Bundesgerichtshof* (the German Federal Supreme Court) posed a series of questions, asking whether Articles 28 and 30 permitted this.

Although neither of the parties to the main case contested the ruling in *Hag I*, Jacobs A.G. mounted a direct attack on the previous judgment. In a most thorough Opinion, he analysed that ruling in minute detail and demonstrated the fallacy in its reasoning and in each and every argument which was or might have been advanced to support it.

The Advocate General's Opinion left the Court no honourable choice but to put *Hag I* out of its misery. This it proceeded to do, holding that "in a situation such as the present case, in which the mark originally had one sole proprietor and the single ownership was broken as a result of expropriation, each of the trade mark proprietors must be able to oppose the importation and marketing, in the Member State in which the trade mark belongs to him, of goods originating from the other proprietor, in so far as they are similar products bearing an identical mark or one which is liable to lead to confusion."

Hag I was thus reversed and the Belgian company was held to be entitled to exclude the German product bearing the mark from Belgium and Luxembourg, and *vice versa*. However, the terms of the judgment make it clear that no such mutual exclusivity can be enjoyed unless (a) the two marks are identical or confusingly similar and (b) the products are similar and (c) there are no legal or economic links between the parties.[657] The first two of these conditions are the normal requirements for establishing trade mark infringement, while the third condition is that for avoiding consent and thus exhaustion. Unless these three cumulative conditions are met, each of the two owners may market his products in the Member State of the other.

8.212 Only a handful of trade marks are thought to have been split in similar circumstances to the "Hag" mark. However, any doubts as to whether the *Hag II* judgment would be followed for marks which had been split voluntarily were then answered by the judgment in *Ideal Standard*.[658]

The American Standard group held the "Ideal Standard" trade mark in Germany and in France for sanitary fittings and heating equipment. In 1976 the French subsidiary of the group had become insolvent. A management agreement was concluded between the receivers and another French company, SGF,

---

[655] *The EEC and Intellectual Property* (1981), p.122.
[656] See n.582 above.
[657] Where such links do exist, the principle of exhaustion will apply and Arts 81 and 82 of the Treaty may also come into play.
[658] See n.507 above; Alexander (1995) C.M.L.Rev. 327; Jarvis [1995] E.L.Rev. 195; Lüder (1995) EuZW 15; Tritton [1994] E.I.P.R. 422.

whereby the latter carried on the production and sales activities of the insolvent company. In 1984 an agreement was reached whereby the French trade mark was assigned to SGF, which ultimately reassigned it to yet another French company, CICL. The latter company had no links of any kind with the American Standard group. Meanwhile, the German trade mark remained in the hands of American Standard's German subsidiary, Ideal Standard GmbH. However, that company had stopped manufacturing and marketing heating equipment in 1976, while retaining its sanitary fittings business.

Ideal Standard GmbH brought proceedings against Internationale Heiztechnik, the subsidiary of CICL, for marketing in Germany heating equipment bearing the "Ideal Standard" trade mark manufactured by the latter company in France.

Thus, the two wholly unrelated companies were using the same trade mark but Ideal Standard was manufacturing and marketing sanitary fittings, while IHT was in the heating equipment business.[659]

In an Opinion which left no stone unturned, Gulmann A.G. found that, having voluntarily divided the trade mark within the Community, the Ideal Standard group could not prevent agents of the French firm from marketing the latter's products in Germany. The essence of his assessment is contained in paragraph 102 of the Opinion, which reads:

> "A trade-mark proprietor who concludes a separate assignment for certain Member States has voluntarily relinquished the right to be the only one to market on Community territory products bearing the mark in question. In doing so he has in any case weakened the mark's distinguishing function for the consumer who travels across national borders, and his interest in being able to conclude a separate assignment for certain Member States whilst preserving the exclusive right to market within his own territory is not sufficiently compelling to justify in itself a partitioning of national markets contrary to one of the most essential purposes of the Treaty–the merging of the national markets into a single market."

In other words, having voluntarily split up his trade mark within the Community, the former owner must bear the consequences. This amounts to saying that, by assigning his trade mark in part of the Community, the owner consented to its production and marketing thereafter and that the principle of exhaustion of rights therefore applies.

He also dismissed the argument based on consumer protection according to which the consumer's guarantee as to the quality of the product would be undermined if the principle of the free movement of goods were to prevail. He pointed out first that this guarantee is weakened in any event for those consumers who chose to exercise their right of free movement and to sample the product in various Member States. In addition, he also showed that a trade mark does not give an absolute guarantee of quality "if only because it is open to the proprietor to change the quality. If a proprietor chooses to adapt the quality of his goods to different national markets, it will moreover follow from the

---

[659] Although the trade mark was split up as an indirect consequence of insolvency, the case was decided on the basis that the assignment was voluntary (see para. 44 of the judgment).

exhaustion principle that such goods may move freely between the markets in question."

The Court saw matters very differently. It took as its starting point Article 6(3) of the Paris Union Convention for the Protection of Industrial Property of 1883 as last revised at Stockholm in 1967, which provides "A mark duly registered in a country of the Union shall be regarded as independent of marks registered in other countries of the Union...". The Court continued: "That principle has led to recognition that a trade mark right may be assigned for one country without at the same time being assigned by its owner in other countries." One might wonder why the Court attached so much weight to this provision, given that the Treaty of Rome prevails as between Member States.[660] In any event, it has never been doubted that a trade mark owner can split his mark within the Community; the discussion concerns the consequences of his doing so.

Next, the Court went on to reaffirm its case law on the exhaustion of rights. However, in doing so it laid particular stress on the importance of quality control, saying:

"37. ..As was held in *Hag II* 'For the trade mark to be able to fulfil [its] role, it must offer a guarantee that all goods bearing it have been produced under the control of a single undertaking which is accountable for their quality' (paragraph 13) ...

"38 It must further be stressed that the decisive factor is the possibility of control over the quality of goods, not the actual exercise of that control. Accordingly, a national law allowing the licensor to oppose importation of the licensee's products on grounds of poor quality would be precluded as contrary to Articles [28] and [30]: if the licensor tolerates the manufacture of poor quality products, despite having contractual means of preventing it, he must bear the responsibility. Similarly, if the manufacture of products is decentralised within a group of companies and the subsidiaries in each of the Member States manufacture products whose quality is geared to the particularities of each national market, a national law which enabled one subsidiary of the group to oppose the marketing in the territory of that State of products manufactured by an affiliated company on grounds of those quality differences would also be precluded. Articles [28] and [30] require the group to bear the consequences of its choice."

As to the concept of consent, the Court stated:

"42 The Commission has submitted that by assigning in France the trade mark 'Ideal Standard' for heating equipment to a third company, the American Standard group gave implied consent to that third company, putting heating equipment into circulation in France bearing that trade mark. Because of that implied consent, it should not be possible to prohibit the marketing in Germany of heating equipment bearing the assigned trade mark.

43 That view must be rejected. The consent implicit in any assignment is not the consent required for application of the doctrine of exhaustion of rights. For that the owner of the right in the importing State must, directly or indirectly, be able to determine the products to which the trade mark may be affixed in the exporting State and to control their quality. That power is lost if, by assignment, control over the trade mark is surrendered to a third party having no economic link with the assignor."

---

[660] Art. 307 of the Treaty. See paras 9.45 *et seq.* below.

The Court then went on to dismiss a further argument against dividing up the market, as follows:

> "47 IHT in particular has submitted that the owner of a trade mark who assigns the trade mark in one Member State, while retaining it in others, must accept the consequences of the weakening of the identifying function of the trade mark flowing from that assignment. By a territorially limited assignment, the owner voluntarily renounces his position as the only person marketing goods bearing the trade mark in question in the Community.
>
> 48 That argument must be rejected. It fails to take account of the fact that since trade mark rights are territorial, the function of the trade mark is to be assessed by reference to a particular territory (paragraph 18 of *Hag II*)".

8.213 The ruling in *Ideal Standard* does not appear to have spurred owners of intellectual property rights to split up the common market by selling off national rights to third parties for a premium. Any attempt to retain economic links would risk a finding of consent (or an infringement of competition law under Article 81). On the other hand, a complete separation would result in the loss of a proportion of the owner's market without necessarily the compensation of being able to increase profits in the retained market.

8.214   *(d) Sale by a third party under a compulsory licence* In *Musik Vertrieb-Membran v GEMA*,[661] GEMA had argued that under the Copyright Act 1956 a compulsory licence was available in the United Kingdom to any manufacturer prepared to pay the royalty of 6.25 per cent to the copyright owner. It therefore claimed to be entitled to rely on German copyright to claim the difference between this and the normal German royalties, even though the products had been marketed with the owner's consent and not under such a compulsory licence. The Court rejected this argument, anticipating its decision in *Merck v Stephar* by stating that "in a common market distinguished by free movement of goods and freedom to provide services an author, acting directly or through his publisher, is free to choose the place, in any of the Member States, in which to put his work into circulation. He may make that choice according to his best interests, which involve not only the level of remuneration provided in the Member State in question but other factors such as, for example, the opportunities for distributing his work and the marketing facilities which are further enhanced by virtue of the free movement of goods within the Community."

8.215   On the other hand, the ruling in *Pharmon v Hoechst*[662] concerned goods which were actually produced by a third party under a compulsory patent licence. Hoechst owned a patent in the Netherlands and the United Kingdom in respect of a process for manufacturing medicine known as frusemide. In 1972, DDSA Pharmaceuticals obtained from the United Kingdom Patent Office

---

[661] Cases 55/80 and 57/80, see n.487 above.
[662] Case 19/84, see n. 518 above, noted by White (1986) C.M.L.Rev. 719; and see Burst and Kovar, "Les licences imposees et le droit communautaire" (1990) C.D.E. 251; and Demaret, *Patents, Territorial Restrictions and EEC Law* (1978).

a compulsory licence to exploit this invention under national patent law. By virtue of this provision the Comptroller-General of Patents was required to grant to any applicant a compulsory licence over any patent for foodstuffs, medicines or surgical instruments unless it appeared to him that there were good reasons for refusing the application. The purpose of this provision was to ensure that products could be obtained at the lowest possible price consistent with the patentee deriving a reasonable advantage from his patent rights. The licence in question could not be assigned, nor was it exclusive. Although a prohibition on exportation was attached to this licence, DDSA disregarded this and sold a large consignment of its frusemide tablets to Pharmon, a Dutch company. It would seem that Hoechst had never received royalties in respect of this consignment as it should have done. Pharmon intended to market these tablets in the Netherlands, but Hoechst obtained an injunction to restrain it from doing so.

Ultimately, these proceedings reached the Hoge Raad, which referred three questions for a preliminary ruling. By its first question it asked generally whether it was compatible with the Treaty provisions on the free movement of goods for a patent holder to exercise his rights under the legislation of a Member State to prevent supplies of a product being put into circulation, when those supplies had been manufactured in another Member State by a compulsory licensee under a parallel patent owned by the same patent holder in that Member State.

Mancini A.G. reached the conclusion that in principle such an exercise of rights was compatible with Articles 28 to 30. However, he put in the following proviso: it would be otherwise in his view where the patent holder had expressly or impliedly consented to the grant of the compulsory licence, whether before or after the product was marketed. This proviso was necessary because there might be links between the patent holder and the compulsory licensee. For instance, the compulsory licensee might be a subsidiary of the patent holder. He regarded *Merck v Stephar* as authority for the proposition that consent was of the essence in each case.

After setting out the facts and arguments the Court merely stated:

> "It is necessary to point out that where, as in this instance, the competent authorities of a Member State grant a third party a compulsory licence which allows him to carry out manufacturing and marketing operations which the patentee would normally have the right to prevent, the patentee cannot be deemed to have consented to the operation of that third party. Such a measure deprives the patent proprietor of his right to determine freely the conditions under which he markets his products.
>
> As the Court held most recently in its judgment of July 14, 1981 (*Merck v Stephar* cited above), the substance of a patent right lies essentially in according the inventor an exclusive right for first placing the product on the market so as to allow him to obtain the reward for his creative effort. It is therefore necessary to allow the patent proprietor to prevent the importation and marketing of products manufactured under a compulsory licence in order to protect the substance of his exclusive rights under his patent."

Regrettably, the Court did not put in the same proviso as the Advocate General. Nevertheless, in view of the subsequent case law, it seems clear that, if a case were to arise in which economic links existed between a patent holder and a compulsory licensee, the Court would not allow the common market to be divided.

8.216 *(e) Sale outside the EEA* At this stage it will come as no surprise to the reader to learn that Articles 28 to 30 only apply to restrictions on trade between Member States. This simple principle is the basis of the Court's ruling in the *EMI Records v CBS* cases.[663] Those cases concerned the "Columbia" trade mark, which until 1917 had belonged to the same undertaking both in Europe and the United States. However, by a series of transactions that trade mark had become vested in CBS as regards the United States and in the EMI group as regards every single Member State of the EEC. When CBS sought to import records into the Community bearing the Columbia trade mark, EMI commenced infringement proceedings before the British, German and Danish courts. Each of the three courts in question proceeded to make a reference under Article 234, asking in particular whether the sale of such goods could lawfully be prevented.

After pointing out that Article 28 only prohibited quantitative restrictions and measures of equivalent effect between Member States, the Court found that "the exercise of a trade mark right in order to prevent the marketing of products coming from a third country under an identical mark...does not affect the free movement of goods between Member States and thus does not come under the prohibitions set out in Article [28] *et seq.* of the Treaty." The Court added that it was not necessary to examine whether there was a common origin between the two Columbia trade marks, "since that question is relevant only in relation to considering whether within the Community there are opportunities for partitioning the market".[664]

The Court also held that Articles 28 to 30 did not entitle the holder of the trade mark in a third country to manufacture and then market his products within the Community either himself or through his subsidiaries established in the Community. As the Court pointed out, if it were otherwise a coach and horses would be driven through the protection of industrial and commercial property established by Article 30.

8.217 These decisions did not directly deal with the case of goods put on the market outside the EEA by the owner of the intellectual property right within the EEA. However, it was clear that, at that point in time, it was a question for national law whether to allow such imports ("international exhaustion") or whether to allow the owner the right to prevent such imports. In other words, national law determined whether sale outside the EEA would constitute consent to their sale within the EEA.

This situation has fundamentally changed following the entry into force of

---

[663] Case 51/75, see n.553 above; Case 86/75 [1976] E.C.R. 871; [1976] 2 C.M.L.R. 235; Case 96/75 [1976] E.C.R. 913; [1976] 2 C.M.L.R. 235. The ruling in each of the three cases is virtually identical.
[664] Nowadays, of course, since the common origin principle is defunct (see paras 8.210–8.212 above) it would not be necessary for the Court to add this remark.

the First Trade Mark Directive.[665] For many years, a heated debate took place concerning the question whether Article 7 of the Directive merely codified the Court's case law, in imposing Community exhaustion as opposed to national exhaustion, or whether it went further and prohibited the application of international exhaustion by Member States.[666] In *Silhouette International Schmied v Hartlauer*[667] the Court held that Article 7 of the First Trade Mark Directive had to be interpreted to the effect that rights conferred by the mark are exhausted only if the products had been put on the market in the Community with the consent of the trade mark owner and that the Directive does not leave it open to the Member States to provide in their domestic law for exhaustion of the rights conferred by the trade mark in respect of products put on the market outside the Community.[668]

8.218 *Silhouette* did not provide any indication as to the circumstances in which a trade mark owner would be regarded as consenting to parallel imports. In *Sebago v G-B Unic*,[669] the Court dealt with one specific example, holding that the rights conferred by a trade mark are exhausted only in respect of the individual items of the product which have been put on the market with the proprietor's consent. In other words, the proprietor may continue to prohibit the use of the mark on individual items which have been marketed in the EEA without his consent, even though he has given consent to the marketing of other, identical items in the EEA.

The Court has now clarified the concept of consent in *Davidoff v A&G Imports*.[670] The English High Court had referred three cases, which in essence asked whether consent could be implied, and if so in what circumstances. The Court held that "consent must be so expressed that an intention to renounce [the right to control initial marketing in the EEA] is unequivocally demonstrated". Although the Court said that this could be implied, it held that the burden lay on the parallel importer to show "consent positively expressed" and that consent could not be inferred from silence by the owner. There will now be very few situations where a national court can find that a trade mark owner has consented to import.

Although these judgments are based on the First Trade Mark Directive, they should apply equally to exhaustion of intellectual property rights under Article 30, insofar as national laws attempt to limit the concept of consent. However, the judgments will not prevent national law from laying down a wider concept of

---

[665] See n.521 above. The case law on consent has so far focussed on trade marks. However, there are similar provisions as to exhaustion in other Community legislation—see para. 8.200 above. It is likely that a similar approach to consent would be taken in respect of these other harmonised rights.

[666] See Beier in (1990) 21 I.I.C. 131, 157; and Rasmussen in [1995] E.I.P.R. 174.

[667] C-355/96 [1998] E.C.R. I-4799, noted by Gippini Fournier [1999] C.M.L.Rev. 807.

[668] Paras 18 and 26 of the judgment. Contrast the position taken by the EFTA Court in Case E-2/97 *Mag Instruments v California Trading Company Norway* ([1997] EFTA Court Reports 127); see para. 13.31 below.

[669] Case C-173/98 [1999] E.C.R. I-4103.

[670] Cases C-414/99–416/99 *Zino Davidoff v A&G Imports* [2001] E.C.R. I-8691, noted by Gross in [2002] E.I.P.R. 93.

consent where Article 30 applies directly, as the English High Court wished to do in *Davidoff.*

8.219   It should not be forgotten that trade mark owners in such circumstances will still be subject to the restraints of competition law.[671] *Javico*[672] concerned a case of goods exported from the EEA subject to contractual restrictions prohibiting reimportation. While holding that there was no infringement of Article 81 on the facts, the Court did say that there could be such an infringement where competition was limited within the Community, where there was a substantial price differential (even after customs duties and transport costs) and where the contract could affect trade between Member States.

It should be noted that the Court has not had to deal with a case where a product is sold by an intellectual property owner in a country outside the EEA, imported into a Member State where the owner does not have protection and then exported to a Member State where he does enjoy protection. As Gippini Fournier notes, the Court chose to avoid this question in *Phyteron International v Jean Bourdon.*[673] However, it is generally expected that the Court would apply the principles discussed above and allow the intellectual property owner to prevent the imports.[674]

8.220   One further question which remains unanswered is whether the burden of proving that the initial sale was in a Member State lies on the intellectual property owner or on the alleged infringer. This was recently at issue in *Van Doren & Q v Lifestyle Sports,*[675] in which Van Doren, enforcing the "Stussy" trade mark, claimed that the goods in question had only been sold in the USA, while Lifestyle claimed that they had been marketed in a Member State with the consent of Stussy Inc., the trade mark owner. Although the Court has yet to decide the case, the Advocate General has held that this is a matter for national procedural rules, so long as they do not (a) allow the owner of the mark to partition the national markets and to thus maintain the price differentials between Member States or (b) make it impossible or excessively difficult for the alleged infringer to prove his case by imposing unacceptable requirements, such as requiring him to reveal his supply sources where doing so would prevent him obtaining supplies from them in future.

8.221   **Repackaging**   A specific problem that arises with respect to the free movement of goods of trade-marked products is the extent to which parallel

---

[671] See also above, para. 8.180, particularly Case T-198/98, see n.564 above.

[672] Case C-306/96 *Javico International v Yves Saint Laurent Parfums* [1998] E.C.R. I-1983.

[673] Case C-352/95 [1997] E.C.R. I-1729, noted by Gippini Fournier (1998) 35 C.M.L.Rev. 947.

[674] Such a case may arise as a result of the decision of the Spanish Supreme Court in Case 779/1999, on September 22, 1999, that the Spanish trade mark rights in "Nike" were held by Cidesport, Nike's former distributor, rather than by the US company. Cidesport would therefore appear to be free to sell in Spain genuine Nike products which have been imported from outside the EEA, although Nike holds the trade marks in other Member States.

[675] Case C-244/00 *Van Doren & Q v Lifestyle Sports & Sportswear* (Opinion of Stix-Hackl A.G. of June 18, 2002), not yet reported.

importers may be permitted to repackage those products to make them suitable for the market of the importing Member State. This particularly arises with pharmaceutical products where (as a result of *inter alia* governmental health measures) there are often large price differentials between Member States. In many cases parallel importers will only be in a position to take full advantage of the opportunities offered by the single market if they are able to repackage the goods in question, to respect national rules on drug authorisation or to take national prescription practices into account.

Since Article 30 is silent on this point, it has fallen to the Court to define the precise circumstances in which parallel importers may repackage products without thereby interfering with the specific subject-matter and/or essential function of trade marks. The Court has performed this task in a series of cases beginning with *Hoffmann-La Roche v Centrafarm*.[676] There Centrafarm had acquired Valium tablets on the British market, where they had been marketed by Hoffmann-La Roche. It then repacked them, reaffixed Hoffmann-La Roche's trade mark to the new packages, and put them on the German market. The Hoffmann-La Roche group owned the mark concerned both in Britain and in Germany. The question posed by the German court was in essence whether it was compatible with the Treaty for the plaintiffs to rely on their German trade mark to prevent Centrafarm effecting parallel imports under these conditions.

The Court first repeated its definition of the specific subject-matter of trade marks already laid down in *Winthrop*. It continued:

"In order to answer the questions whether that exclusive right involves the right to prevent the trade mark being affixed by a third person after the product has been repackaged, regard must be had to the essential function of the trade mark, which is to guarantee the identity of the origin of the trade marked product to the consumer or ultimate user, by enabling him without any possibility of confusion to distinguish that product from products which have another origin. This guarantee of origin means that the consumer or ultimate user can be certain that a trade marked product which is sold to him has not been subject at a previous stage of marketing to interference by a third person, without the authorisation of the proprietor of the trade mark, such as to affect the original condition of the product. The right attributed to the proprietor of preventing any use of the trade mark which is likely to impair the guarantee of origin so understood is therefore part of the specific subject-matter of the trade mark right.

It is accordingly justified under the first sentence of Article [30] to recognise that the proprietor of a trade mark is entitled to prevent an importer of a trade marked product, following repackaging of that product, from affixing the trade mark to the new packaging without the authorisation of the proprietor."

The Court added, however, that the prevention of marketing repackaged products constitutes a disguised restriction on trade between Member States within the meaning of the second sentence of Article 30 where:

(1) it is established that the use of the trade mark right by the proprietor, having regard to the marketing system which he has adopted, will con-

---

[676] Case 102/77, see n.494 above, [1978] 3 C.M.L.R. 217.

tribute to the artificial partitioning of the markets between Member States; and

(2) it is shown that the repacking cannot adversely affect the original condition of the product; and

(3) the proprietor of the mark receives prior notice of the marketing of the repackaged product; and

(4) it is stated on the new packaging by whom the product has been repackaged.

In this connection, the Court expressly stated that "it is irrelevant in answering the legal question raised...that the question referred by the national court is exclusively concerned with medical products."

8.222   The Court has had the opportunity to expand upon and clarify its judgment in *Hoffmann-La Roche* in a series of subsequent judgments, culminating in its extremely important judgment in *Bristol-Myers Squibb v Paranova*[677] and further clarification in its judgment in *Boehringer Ingelheim*.[678] However, rather than leap frogging directly to these later judgments, it is instructive to track the development of the case law in a chronological fashion. In that regard, problems similar to those encountered in *Hoffmann-La Roche* were raised shortly after that case in *Centrafarm v American Home Products Corporation*.[679] American Home Products (AHP) owned the trade mark "Serenid D" in the United Kingdom and used it for a particular pharmaceutical product. AHP also owned the trade mark "Seresta" in the Benelux countries, which it used for a product which had the same therapeutic properties as "Serenid D" but presented certain minor differences such as a difference of taste. Centrafarm acquired quantities of the product on the British market, where it had been marketed by the AHP group. It removed the "Serenid D" mark, affixed the "Seresta" mark instead and then placed the product on the Dutch market. The question referred by the Dutch court was once again whether under the Treaty the trade mark holder could prevent such parallel imports.

The Court once more repeated its definition of the specific subject-matter of trade marks and added that the essential function is to guarantee the identity of the origin of the trade marked product to the consumer or ultimate user. It concluded:

"This guarantee of origin means that only the proprietor may confer an identity upon the product by affixing the mark. The guarantee of origin would in fact be jeopardised if it were permissible for a third party to affix the mark to the product, even to an original product ... The right granted to the proprietor to prohibit any unauthorised affixing of his mark to his product accordingly comes with the specific subject-matter of the trade mark."

---

[677] Joined Cases C-427/93, 429/93 and 436/93, see n. 600 above.
[678] Case C-143/00, see n. 602 above.
[679] Case 3/78 [1978] E.C.R. 1823; [1979] 1 C.M.L.R. 326.

The Court then considered whether the exercise of this right may constitute a disguised restriction on trade between Member States within the meaning of Article 30:

"In this connection it should be observed that it may be lawful for the manufacturer of a product to use in different Member States different marks for the same product.

Nevertheless, it is possible for such a practice to be followed by the proprietor of the marks as part of a system of marketing intended to partition the markets artificially.

In such case the prohibition by the proprietor of the unauthorised affixing of the mark by a third party constitutes a disguised restriction on trade for the purposes of the above mentioned provision.

It is for the national court to settle in each particular case whether the proprietor has followed the practice of using different marks for the same product for the purpose of partitioning the markets."[680]

As Caportorti A.G. put it,[681] a company which sells an identical product under different trade marks in different Member States must provide an "appropriate objective justification" for doing so.

8.223 Further refinements were added by *Pfizer v Eurim-Pharm*.[682] Eurim-Pharm was a parallel importer, which had imported into Germany quantities of Vibramycin, an antibiotic produced and marketed in Britain by the British subsidiary of Pfizer. The German trade marks "Vibramycin" and "Pfizer" were owned by Pfizer. It was the practice in Germany for doctors to prescribe packets of eight, 16 or 40 tablets, whereas in Britain they were sold in packets of 10 and 50. Consequently, to take account of German usage it was necessary for Eurim-Pharm to repack the tablets. However, it was possible for them to do this without tampering with or touching the tablets, because they were contained in blister-packs of five. So Eurim-Pharm simply removed the blister packs from their original packets and put them inside new packets. These new packets contained a window through which could be seen a label bearing the words "Vibramycin" and "Pfizer". The outer packing also stated that the tablets had been produced by Pfizer Ltd of Great Britain and that they had been repacked and imported by Eurim-Pharm. Also, Eurim-Pharm had obviously done its homework on the case law of the Court, because it took the trouble to inform Pfizer of what it was doing.

In the resulting action for trade mark infringement, the German court in its first question asked the Court of Justice whether a trade mark could be relied on to prevent such imports. The Court replied as follows:

"Article [30] of the Treaty must be interpreted as meaning that the proprietor of a trade mark may not rely on that right in order to prevent an importer from marketing a pharmaceutical product manufactured in another Member State by the subsidiary of the proprietor and bearing the latter's trade mark with his consent, where the importer, in repackaging the product, confined himself to replacing the external

---

[680] See also *Royal Pharmaceutical Society of Great Britain* (para. 8.92, n.254 above).
[681] At p. 1850.
[682] Case 1/81 [1981] E.C.R. 2913; [1982] 1 C.M.L.R. 406.

wrapping without touching the internal packaging and made the trade mark, affixed by the manufacturer to the internal packaging, visible through the new external wrapping, at the same time clearly indicating on the external wrapping that the product was manufactured by the subsidiary of the proprietor and repackaged by the importer."

In its second question, the national court asked whether, for the purpose of establishing that there is a disguised restriction on trade between Member States within the meaning of Article 30, it was necessary to prove an intention on the part of the trade mark owner to partition the common market or whether it was sufficient to prove that he exercised his trade mark rights in such a way that the common market was in fact partitioned. In other words, was the test a subjective or an objective one?

This question was obviously posed in the light of the *American Home Products* judgment, where the Court had concentrated on the subjective element, namely the trade mark owner's intention. Following the Commission, the Advocate General took the view that it was only in the special circumstances of the *American Home Products* case, where one person owned a different trade mark in each Member State concerned for the same product, that the test was subjective. If it were otherwise:

> "on the basis of the objective criterion adopted in the judgment in *Hoffman-La Roche v Centrafarm*, the proprietor of the parallel trade marks would ultimately find himself, in the light of Community law, in a position where he could never lawfully exercise his right. To avoid this excessively restrictive result, the Court took the view that in such circumstances it is not appropriate to speak of a disguised restriction on intra-Community trade except where the practice, adopted by or under the direction of the same proprietor, of using different trade marks for the same product in the various Member States is indicative of a plan to partition the markets."[683]

However, in other cases the correct test was, according to the Advocate General, an objective one. The Court ruled that, in view of its answer to the first question, it need not reply to the second question. However, as will be noted below, this was a question to which the Court was subsequently forced to return.

8.224 In *Bristol-Myers*, not only did the Court find that its existing case law continued to apply but it also took the opportunity to develop and clarify that case law significantly. The case concerned pharmaceutical products including those packaged as tablets or capsules in blister packs and those packaged in phials, ampoules and aerosols. In each instance, the products in question were packaged slightly differently or in different sizes in various Member States. These differences arose for a variety of reasons, which included compliance with national rules or practices, sickness insurance rules and established medical prescription practices. On the substance, the Court underlined the fact that trade marks constituted "an essential element in the system of undistorted

---

[683] At 2934–5.

competition which the Treaty is intended to establish"[684] and repeated its previous rulings as regards the specific subject-matter of trade marks and their "essential function". The Court then repeated the four criteria which it had laid down in *Hoffmann-La Roche* setting out, in effect, what a parallel importer must do in order to benefit from the free movement of repackaged goods. In so doing, the Court provided welcome clarification of the questions left unanswered by those criteria. For example, as to the first condition, namely that it be established that the use of the trade mark right by the owner contributes to the artificial partitioning of the markets between Member States, the Court held that this does not require the parallel importer to demonstrate that, by putting an identical product on the market in varying forms of packaging in different Member States, the trade mark owner deliberately sought to partition the markets between Member States. Thus the Court resolved the debate as to whether the test was objective or subjective by, in effect, concluding that it was objective. In other words, the only question that arises with respect to the first condition is whether the circumstances prevailing at the time of marketing made it *objectively* necessary to repackage and reaffix the trade mark or to replace the original trade mark by that of the importing Member State in order that the product in question could be placed on the market in that State by the parallel importer.[685]

In order to comply with the second condition, namely that the original condition of the product is not adversely affected, the Court clarified that that concept refers to the condition of the product *inside* the packaging. In practice this will be a matter for the national court to determine. However, the Court did remark that "the mere removal of blister packs, flasks, phials, ampoules or inhalers from their original external packaging and their replacement in new external packaging cannot affect the original condition of the product inside the packaging."[686] Moreover, the Court signalled that national courts should take a robust approach to claims of such adverse effect. This is evident from its response to the arguments put forward by the trade mark owners that blister packs coming originally from different packets and grouped together in single external packaging might have come from different production batches with different use-by dates, that products might have been stored for too long and

---

[684] See *Bristol-Myers* at para. 43. In so remarking, the Court has thus continued the process of recognising the competitive importance of trade marks to the functioning of the single market (on an equal footing with other intellectual property rights) which process began with its judgment in *Hag II* closely followed by that in *Ideal Standard* (see discussion at para. 8.212 below).

[685] In Case C-379/97, see n.601 above, it was confirmed that there is no difference between the position obtaining in Case 3/78, see n.679 above, where the parallel importer replaces the original trade mark used by the proprietor in the Member State of export by the trade mark which the proprietor uses in the Member State of import and that in *Bristol-Myers*, where the parallel importer repackages a trade-market product and reaffixes the same trade mark thereon. In both cases, the condition of artificial partitioning of the markets between Member States means that it is necessary to assess whether at the time of marketing it is objectively necessary either to replace the trade mark or reaffix the original trade mark (as the case may be) in order that the product in question may be marketed in that State by the parallel importer.

[686] See *Bristol-Myers* at para. 61.

that light-sensitive products might have been damaged by light during repackaging. To those arguments, the Court responded as follows:

> "It is not possible for each hypothetical risk or isolated error to suffice to confer on the trade mark owner the right to oppose any repackaging of pharmaceutical products in new external packaging."[687]

Next, the Court maintained the third and fourth conditions laid down in *Hoffmann-La Roche* and clarified not only that the proprietor of the mark must receive prior notice of the marketing of the repackaged product but also that the parallel importer must, on demand, supply the trade-mark proprietor with a specimen of the repackaged product before that product is put on sale. In addition, although the new packaging must state by whom the product has been repackaged, the Court made it clear that this did not mean that the parallel importer could also be required to state that the repackaging was carried out without the authorisation of the trade mark owner. Finally, the Court added what may in effect be regarded as a further, and fifth, condition to the list set out in *Hoffmann-La Roche*[688] to the effect that the presentation of the repackaged product must not be such as to be liable to damage the reputation of the trade mark and of its owners.[689] In other words, the packaging must not be defective, of poor quality, or untidy. This again will be a matter for the national courts, but the Court did add that the requirements to be met by the presentation of a repackaged pharmaceutical product will vary according to whether the product is sold to hospitals or, through pharmacies, to consumers.[690]

8.225   This case law was again subject to criticism in a recent reference from the English High Court, *Boehringer Ingelheim v Swingward*,[691] where the Court was asked to reconsider the first and third requirements (that repackaging be necessary and that notice be given to the trade mark owner). It has also been the subject of a reference from the *Landgericht* Köln, *Aventis Pharma Deutschland v Kohlpharma*,[692] where the Court was again required to clarify the concept of necessity.

In *Boehringer*, despite the criticism from the referring court, the ECJ once again upheld the *status quo*. However, it did take the opportunity to develop the concept of "necessity", holding that this would include the situation where "without such repackaging, effective access to the market concerned, or to a substantial part of that market, must be considered to be hindered as a result of strong resistance from a significant proportion of consumers to relabelled pharmaceutical products."[693] It further held that it was for the national court to consider whether the notice given allowed the trade mark owner a reasonable

---

[687] See *Bristol-Myers* at para. 63.
[688] See para. 8.221 above.
[689] See also n.495 above.
[690] See *Bristol-Myers* at para. 77.
[691] Case C-143/00, see n. 602 above. The first of these issues was also raised in Case C-443/99 *Merck, Sharp & Dohme v Paranova*, in which a similar judgment was given by the ECJ on the same day.
[692] Case C-433/00, judgment of September 19, 2002.
[693] Para. 54.

period of time to respond to the repackaging, suggesting that in the case itself 15 working days would seem sufficient.[694]

This approach was followed in the *Aventis* case, where the Court restricted itself to referring to its recent judgments.

8.226 In summary, the following criteria must now be satisfied for repackaging by a parallel importer to be admissible:

(i)   reliance on trade mark rights by the owner would contribute to the artificial partitioning of the markets between Member States (which will be the case where the repackaging is objectively necessary for the repackager to achieve effective access to the market or a substantial part of that market, including cases where such access is hindered as a result of strong resistance from a significant proportion of consumers to relabelled pharmaceutical products);

(ii) the repackaging cannot affect the original condition of the product inside the packaging;

(iii) the new packaging clearly states who repackaged the product and the name of the manufacturer;

(iv) the presentation of the repackaged product is not such as to be liable to damage the reputation of the trade mark and of its owner; and

(v)   the importer gives notice to the trade mark owner before the repackaged product is put on sale, and, on demand, supplies him with a specimen thereof, such notice and supply allowing the trade mark owner a reasonable time to react to the intended repackaging.

8.227 In principle, the above case law which defines with some precision the conditions under which repackaging by parallel importers must be carried out is of general application to all goods to which a trade mark is affixed. In other words, that case law is not restricted to the special case of pharmaceutical products. Although the latter was confirmed by the Court in *Loendersloot v George Ballantine*,[695] it is nevertheless apparent that, outside the field of pharmaceutical products, different considerations may apply. *Loendersloot* concerned parallel trade in alcoholic drinks, and whisky in particular. Before those goods had been marketed in the Netherlands, the parallel traders concerned relabelled the relevant bottles thereby removing the identification numbers placed by the trade mark owner on or underneath the labels and on the packaging of the bottles. Moreover, the traders removed from the original label both the English word "pure" and the name of the approved importer. The Court set out its by now well-developed case law on the circumstances in which parallel traders may repackage goods and rely on the free movement of goods irrespective of any

---

[694] Paras 67–68.
[695] C-349/95 [1997] E.C.R. I-6227 at para. 27.

infringement of national trade mark rights. However, the application of the first, third and fourth conditions[696] had to be specially adapted for application to the facts of this case. As to the first condition, namely that the trade mark owner's use of the trade mark contributes to artificial partitioning of the markets between Member States, it will be recalled that the Court has held that this will be the case where the repackaging undertaken by the importer is objectively necessary in order to market the product in the Member State of importation (without the need to establish the subjective intention of the trade mark owner to deliberately partition markets). In dealing with the application of this condition outside the field of pharmaceutical products the Court held:

> "...the task of the national courts, who have to assess whether the relabelling is necessary in order to prevent artificial partitioning of the markets between Member States, is different in cases such as that in the main proceedings and cases concerning the repackaging of pharmaceutical products. In the latter the national courts must consider whether circumstances in the markets of their own States make repackaging objectively necessary. In the present case, on the other hand, the national court must assess whether the relabelling is necessary to protect the sources of supply of the parallel trade and to enable the products to be marketed on the various markets of the Member States for which they are intended."[697]

There were two aspects to the application of those principles to the case in hand. First, the parallel importers had removed identification numbers from the bottles' labelling. On the one hand, the parallel traders argued that such measures were necessary because otherwise producers could and would be able to reconstruct the delivery chain with a view to preventing their distributors from supplying persons carrying on parallel trade. On the other hand, the producers argued that identification numbers were necessary (and often a legal obligation) to facilitate, for example, recall of faulty products and measures to combat counterfeiting. On this issue, the Court found for the producers and held that they could prevent the marketing of repackaged bottles if the identification numbers had been removed. The Court simply stated that in the latter circumstances, "there is no reason to limit the rights which the trade mark owner may rely on under Article [30] of the Treaty".[698] However, the Court's support of the producers' arguments on this issue was qualified by a reminder to the parallel traders that, should trade mark owners use identification numbers to combat parallel trade in his products, it is under the Treaty provisions on competition that they should seek protection.[699] In practice, however, it will no doubt be very difficult for a parallel trader to prove in civil proceedings that the trade mark owner has indeed used identification numbers on bottles to try to stifle parallel trade and that this breaches the competition rules.[700]

[696] See para. 8.226 above.
[697] Para. 38 of the judgment.
[698] Para. 42 of the judgment.
[699] Para. 43 of the judgment.
[700] See Case T–41/96 *Bayer v Commission ("Adalat")* [2000] E.C.R. II-3383, requiring proof of agreement in order to find an infringement under Article 81. See on competition in general para. 8.180 above.

The second (and less controversial) aspect to the application of the artificial partitioning of markets condition on the facts of this case concerned the removal by the parallel importer of the word "pure" and of the importer's name from labels. In this case, the Court held that relabelling would be necessary (and thus give rise to artificial partitioning of markets) if the use of the word "pure" and the name of the approved importer on the original labels would prevent the products in question from being marketed because it was contrary to the rules on labelling applicable in the Member State of destination.

Finally, it will be recalled that according to the third and fourth conditions, the proprietor of the trade mark must receive prior notice of the marketing of the repackaged product (and be provided with a sample of the repackaging on request) and the new packaging must state by whom the product has been repackaged. In effect, the Court held that in the circumstances of this case (as opposed to the case of pharmaceutical products) it was only necessary for the parallel importer to comply with the third condition, and even then restricted to the need to provide the proprietor of the mark with prior notice of the marketing of the repackaged product. In other words, the fourth condition, namely that the new packaging must state by whom the product has been repackaged, was dispensed within this case.

8.228   The Court's case law on repackaging, as might be expected with such a balancing act, has been attacked on all sides. Intellectual property owners complain that parallel importers are being permitted to usurp their rights when the real barrier to the internal market is due to measures taken by national governments. At the same time, parallel importers say that intellectual property owners are given excessive power to interfere in the market after the first sale.[701] The latter argument has found favour in the English High Court, as can be seen from its reference in *Boehringer* which attacked the use of trade mark rights where the specific subject matter of the trade mark was not affected by the repackaging. In response to this, the Court held that "the change brought about by any repackaging of a trade-marked pharmaceutical product [creates] by its very nature the risk of interference with the original condition of the product".[702] However, this area of law is very much still in the process of development.

8.229   Advertising   A further question which arises with regard to exhaustion is the following: where goods incorporating an intellectual property right have been put on the market in the Community by the owner or with his consent, does the consequent exhaustion of rights have the result that the owner may no longer restrict the use of the intellectual property in question when those goods are advertised by retailers? This question arose in *Parfums Christian Dior v Evora*[703] where products belonging to the market for luxury

---

[701] This tension is discussed in Stothers, "Are Parallel Imports Bad Medicine?" [2002] E.C.L.R. 417.
[702] Para. 34 of the judgment.
[703] C-337/95, see n. 495 above.

cosmetic products were imported by parallel importers into the Netherlands. Once imported, the packaging and bottles were used on advertising leaflets by a chain of chemists' shops for their promotion. Christian Dior sought to prevent such promotion on the grounds of trade mark and copyright infringement, claiming that it did not correspond to the luxurious and prestigious image of the goods. The Court held that once the trade mark owner had exhausted its rights by putting the products in question on the Community market itself or with its consent, a reseller was free not only to resell those goods, but also to make use of the trade mark in question in order "to bring to the public's attention the further commercialisation of those goods".[704] However, drawing on the Court's case law on repackaging generally, the Court added the proviso that the latter was only the case where, in the circumstances of an individual case, the use of the trade mark in the reseller's advertising does not seriously damage the reputation of the trade mark.[705] This was a question for the national court to apply but the Court did indicate that such damage could occur if a reseller allowed the trade mark to be seen in a context "which might seriously detract from the image which the trade mark owner has succeeded in creating around his trade mark".[706] The Court held that the owner could have no wider rights under its copyright. In practice therefore, the proprietor of a trade mark with a luxurious and prestigious reputation has considerable scope to exercise control over further commercialisation, even after his rights have been exhausted.

8.230 Copyright in broadcasting, performances, rental rights or lending rights Copyright and neighbouring rights are distinguished by the variety of ways in which such rights may be exploited. National and Community[707] legislation recognise copyright in sale, rental and performance of works. As mentioned above, the rules of exhaustion do not apply to the copyright in broadcasting, performances, rental rights or lending rights. These rights allow the owner the exclusive right to broadcast, perform, rent or lend his work, and are typically exploited by assigning the rights or by granting licences. They can therefore be distinguished from more normal copyright because they are rights to perform services and are not incorporated into goods. The question of a second-hand market is therefore not in issue.

8.231 *Coditel v Ciné Vog,*[708] therefore, concerned not the free movement of goods, but the free provision of services under Article 49 of the Treaty. That case related to the film rights for the film *Le Boucher*. The film rights are the part of copyright which gives the exclusive right to broadcast a film. In 1969 the owners of those rights assigned them with respect to Belgium to CinéVog, sti-

---

[704] Para. 38 of the judgment.
[705] Para. 46 of the judgment. On the word "serious", see n.495 above.
[706] Para. 47 of the judgment.
[707] See para. 8.177 above.
[708] Case 62/79 [1980] E.C.R. 833; [1981] 2 C.M.L.R. 362; see also the sequel, Case 262/81 *Coditel v Ciné-Vog* [1982] E.C.R. 3381; [1983] 1 C.M.L.R. 49, which concerned Art. 81.

pulating that the film was not to be shown on television in Belgium until 40 months after the first performance in that country. The owners then assigned the rights to broadcast the film in the Federal Republic of Germany to the German television broadcasting station. The Belgian cable television company, Coditel, picked up directly on its aerial the film *Le Boucher* broadcast on German television in January 1971, and retransmitted it directly in Belgium. Ciné Vog then brought an action for infringement before the Belgian courts.

On a reference under Article 234 the Court found in effect that Ciné Vog's copyright had been infringed, stating:

"A cinematographic film belongs to the category of literary and artistic works made available to the public by performances which may be infinitely repeated. In this respect the problems involved in the observance of copyright in relation to the requirements of the Treaty are not the same as those which arise in connection with literary and artistic works, the placing of which at the disposal of the public is inseparable from the circulation of the material form of the works, as in the case of books or records."

Consequently, it held that "the right of the copyright owner and his assigns to require fees for any showing of a film is part of the essential function of copyright in this type of literary and artistic work."

The Court continued:

"Whilst Article [49] of the Treaty prohibits restrictions upon freedom to provide services, it does not thereby encompass limits upon the exercise of certain economic activities which have their origin in the application of national legislation for the protection of intellectual property, save where such application constitutes a means of arbitrary discrimination or a disguised restriction on trade between Member States. Such would be the case if that application enabled parties to an assignment of copyright to create artificial barriers to trade between Member States."

Although this case concerned Article 49, the terminology used was borrowed from Article 30.[709] At all events, the Court found that the mere fact that the geographical limit of a particular assignment of performing rights coincided with national frontiers did not constitute either arbitrary discrimination or a disguised restriction on trade between Member States.

It concluded:

"The exclusive assignee of the performing right in a film for the whole of a Member State may therefore rely upon his right against cable television diffusion companies which have transmitted that film on their diffusion network having received it from a television broadcasting station established in another Member State, without thereby infringing Community law."

8.232 Therefore, it is clear that the principle of exhaustion as applied to other types of intellectual property (and to the copyright in physical works) does not

---

[709] See also to similar effect with respect to the freedom of establishment in Art. 43 EC Case C-255/97 *Pfeiffer Großhandel v Löwa Warenhandel* [1999] E.C.R. I-2835.

preclude the owner of performing rights from continuing to recover royalties since by definition royalties are due with respect to each performance of a work. This was expressly stated by the Court in *Ministère Public v Tournier*[710] where it held:

> "The problems in relation to the requirements of the Treaty, involved in the observance of copyright in musical words made available to the public through their performance are not the same as those which arise where the act of making a work available to the public is inseparable from the circulation of the physical medium on which it is recorded. In the former case the copyright owner and the persons claiming through him have a legitimate interest in calculating the fees due in respect of the authorisation to present the work on the basis of the actual or probable number of performances, as the Court held in Case 62/79 *Coditel v Cine Vog Films* [1980] E.C.R. 881."

8.233 The Court in *Tournier* also addressed the difficulty that both categories of right may exist in the same work, saying:

> "It is true that the present case raises the specific question of the distinction between the conditions applicable to those two situations, in so far as sound-recordings are products covered by the provisions on the free movement of goods contained in Article [28] *et seq.* of the Treaty but are also capable of being used for public performance of the musical work in question. In such circumstances, the requirements relating to the free movement of goods and the freedom to provide services and those deriving from the observance of copyright must be reconciled in such a way that the copyright owners, or the societies empowered to act as their agents, may invoke their exclusive rights in order to require the payment of royalties for music played in public by means of a sound recording, even though the marketing of that recording cannot give rise to the charging of any royalty in the country where the music is played in public."

8.234 In contrast, the question which arose in *Basset v SACEM*,[711] was whether the sale of a product in a Member State which did not recognise a particular performing right would exhaust the right in a Member State which did recognise it. Again, the Court made it clear that in such a case the right is not exhausted.

M. Basset was the owner of a French discotheque who had failed to pay the agreed royalties to the French collective copyright management society, SACEM. French law allowed the society to charge two fees for the public performance of musical works: one to cover the performing right and one to cover the copyright in the physical record, described in the case as the "supplementary mechanical reproduction fee". The latter fee was "supplementary" in that it had to be paid on top of the fee paid by the purchaser of a physical record for personal use. In a reference for a preliminary ruling the Court was asked whether it was compatible with Articles 28 and 30 to charge both fees in respect of sound recordings which had been manufactured and marketed in

---

[710] Case 395/87 [1989] E.C.R. 2521.
[711] Case 402/85 [1987] E.C.R. 1747; 3 C.M.L.R. 173.

another Member State which solely recognised royalties for the performing rights.

After pointing out that the French law concerned applied to imported goods in the same way as to domestic goods, the Court held:

> "disregarding the concepts used by French legislation and practice, the supplementary mechanical reproduction fee may thus be analysed as constituting part of the payment for an author's rights over the public performance of a recorded musical work. Moreover, the amount of that royalty, like that of the performance fee strictly so called, is calculated on the basis of the discotheque's turnover and not the number of records bought or played.
>
> It follows that, even if the charging of the fee in question were to be capable of having a restrictive effect on imports, it does not constitute a measure having equivalent effect prohibited under Article [28] of the Treaty inasmuch as it must be regarded as a normal exploitation of copyright and does not constitute a means of arbitrary discrimination or a disguised restriction on trade between Member States for the purposes of Article [30] of the Treaty."

One unusual feature of this ruling is that the charging of the "supplement" was held to fall outside Article 28 altogether rather than to be justified under Article 30. However, it is apparent that the basis for this was the fact that the use met the conditions of Article 30 and so little turns on this.

8.235 The two issues arose in reverse order in relation to lending and rental rights, but the result was the same. First the court ruled in *Warner Bros v Christiansen*,[712] which concerned lending rights for video cassettes which entitled their holder to a fee each time a video cassette was commercially rented. Video lending rights were provided for by Danish legislation, but were unknown in the United Kingdom. Warner Bros owned the British copyright in the film *Never say never again* which it had made in the United Kingdom. It ceded its video lending rights in Denmark to Metronome, the second plaintiff. Mr Christiansen, who owned a video rental business in Copenhagen, bought a cassette of the film in London and imported it into Denmark where he intended to rent it out. The plaintiffs sought an injunction from the Danish courts to prevent him from doing so. The Danish appeal court asked the Court to rule in effect whether Articles 28 to 30 permitted the owner of the video lending right to withhold his consent to the rental of cassettes in such circumstances.

The Court first held that the restriction on the rental of cassettes indirectly affected imports and thus fell under Article 28. However, it went on to rule that in the circumstances in question the measure was justified, thereby rejecting the Advocate General's views to the contrary based on *Musik-Vertrieb Membran v GEMA*. The Court pointed out that the Danish legislation applied in the same way whether the video cassettes were produced in Denmark or imported. Next, it stated that classic copyright did not give film makers remuneration in respect of the rental of video cassettes which was proportionate to the number of rentals or granted them a sufficient share in the rental market. Accordingly, video

---

[712] Case 158/86 [1988] E.C.R. 2605.

lending rights constituted industrial and commercial property within the meaning of Article 30. Finally, the Court rejected the analogy with *Musik-Vertrieb Membran* on the basis that the video lending right would be undermined if the owner was unable to exercise his right to authorise rentals of video cassettes marketed with his consent in another Member State where no lending rights existed.[713]

8.236 The question then arose of whether the holder of an exclusive rental right could prohibit copies of a film from being offered for rental in a Member State when the holder of that rental right has already authorised the offering of copies for rental under the parallel rental right within another Member State. In *Foreningen af danske Videogramdistributorer v Laserdisken*[714] the Court held that neither Articles 28 to 30 EC nor the rental right Directive[715] preclude the holder of an exclusive rental right to use that right in such circumstances. The Court reasoned that the principle of exhaustion of distribution rights where copyright works are offered for sale by the right holder or with his consent applies only where a product has been so distributed. However, literary and artistic works may also be the subject of commercial exploitation, whether by way of public performance or of the reproduction and marketing of the recordings made of them. Thus the Court held that by authorising the collection of royalties only on sales to private individuals and to persons hiring out video cassettes, it was impossible to guarantee to makers of films a remuneration which reflects the number of occasions on which the video cassettes are actually hired out and which secures for them a satisfactory share of the rental market.[716] The Court concluded:

> "The release into circulation of a picture and sound recording cannot therefore, by definition, render lawful other acts of exploitation of the protected work, such as rental, which are of a different nature from sale or any other lawful act of distribution. Just like the right to present a work by means of public performance, ... rental right remains one of the prerogatives of the author and producer notwithstanding sale of the physical recording...
> ... the exclusive right to hire out various copies of the work contained in a video film can by its very nature, be exploited by repeated and potentially unlimited transactions, each of which involves the right to remuneration. The specific right to authorise or prohibit rental would be rendered meaningless if it were held to be exhausted as soon as the object was first offered for rental."[717]

As a result of these judgments, it is difficult to imagine circumstances in which copyright in broadcasting or performances or rental or lending rights will ever be exhausted.

---

[713] The existence of such rights is now harmonised under Dir. 92/100, which was unsuccessfully challenged in Case C-200/96, see n.526 above.
[714] Case C-61/97 [1998] E.C.R. I-5171.
[715] See n.713 above.
[716] Paras 14 and 15 of the judgment.
[717] Paras 17 and 18 of the judgment.

(v) Geographical denominations

8.237 The expression "geographical denominations" may be used inter-changeably with "geographical indications". Both "indications of source" (*indications de provenance* in French) and "appellations of origin" (*appellations d'origine*) constitute geographical denominations. These expressions are terms of art in a number of Member States where they enjoy special protection.[718]

As the Court explained in *Exportur v LOR*,[719] indications of source serve to inform the consumer that a product comes from a particular place, region or country for which the product in question is renowned. Greater value is attached to appellations of origin which guarantee not only that a product has a particular geographical origin, but also that it possesses particular qualities or characteristics as a result of having been produced according to specific rules laid down by law for such products originating in the area concerned. Indications of source are protected by rules prohibiting misleading advertising or the improper exploitation of the reputation of others. Appellations of origin are granted more rigorous protection under specific national legislation. It is axiomatic that generic names can neither constitute indications of source nor *a fortiori* appellations of origin.

In addition to being covered by the Paris Convention for the Protection of Industrial Property of 1883, such denominations are protected respectively by the Madrid Arrangement concerning false and misleading indications of source of 1891 and the Lisbon Arrangement for the protection of appellations of origin of 1958. All three instruments were last revised in Stockholm in 1967.

One should also distinguish direct geographical indications (*i.e.* place names) from indirect geographical indications. The latter may involve the use of a name associated with a particular place, or the use of a particular symbol (such as the Eiffel Tower) or get-up or presentation (such as a wine bottle of a particular shape).

8.238 It was not until 1992 that the Court ruled that geographical denomi-nations could constitute industrial and commercial property within the mean-ing of Article 30, although as will be seen their characteristics differ in certain fundamental respects from most other forms of such property. Prior to that date, it had treated the protection of such denominations as forming part of consumer protection and the prevention of unfair competition.

8.239 The first case was *Commission v Germany*.[720] According to German leg-islation the appellation *Sekt* was reserved to sparkling wines from Germany and other countries where German was the official language throughout the whole territory (thus benefiting Austrian production). In addition, the appellation *Prädikatssekt* could only be used for *Sekt* containing at least 60 per cent of Ger-

---

[718] In addition, Arts 22 to 24 of the TRIPS Agreement, n.540 above contains provisions on geo-graphical indications.
[719] Para. 8.27, n.91 above; para. 11 of the judgment.
[720] Para. 8.148, n.405 above.

man grapes. The appellation *Weinbrand* was reserved to a certain type of spirits from Germany and other countries where German was the official language throughout the territory.

The Commission contended that the appellations *Sekt, Prädikatssekt* and *Weinbrand* were generic terms which the German authorities had attempted to transform into indirect indications of origin, at the same time requiring imported products to bear less attractive appellations. It therefore brought proceedings against the Federal Republic for infringement of Article 28 and, as regards sparkling wine, of the equivalent provision contained in Regulation 816/70 establishing the common market organisation in wine.[721] The Court found for the Commission. After citing Article 2(3)(s) of Directive 70/50[722] it held:

> "To the extent to which [appellations of origin and indirect indications of origin] are protected by law they must satisfy the objectives of such protection, in particular the need to ensure not only that the interests of the producers concerned are safeguarded against unfair competition, but also that consumers are protected against information which may mislead them.
>
> These appellations only fulfil their specific purpose if the product which they describe does in fact possess qualities and characteristics which are due to the fact that it originated in a specific geographical area.
>
> As regards indications of origin in particular, the geographical area of origin of a product must confer on it a specific quality and specific characteristic of such a nature as to distinguish it from all other products."

With reference to the appellations *Sekt* and *Weinbrand* the Court continued:

> "An area of origin which is defined on the basis either of the extent of national territory or a linguistic criterion cannot constitute a geographical area within the meaning referred to above, capable of justifying an indication of origin,[723] particularly as the products in question may be produced from grapes of indeterminate origin.
>
> In this instance, it is not disputed that the area of origin referred to by the legislation on wine products does not show homogeneous natural features which distinguish it in contrast to adjacent areas, as the natural characteristics of the basic products used in the manufacture of the product in question do not necessarily correspond to the line of the national frontier."

The Court went on to reject the argument to the effect that the products covered by the appellations *Sekt* and *Weinbrand* were different from all other products by virtue of their process of production:

> "In the case of wine products, the natural features of the area of origin, such as the grape from which these products are obtained, play an important role in determining their quality and their characteristics.
>
> Although the method of production used for such products may play some part in determining these characteristics, it is not alone decisive, independently of the quality of the grape used, in determining its origin.

---

[721] [1970] J.O. 99, now replaced by Reg. 822/87 ([1987] O.J. L84/1) as amended.
[722] Para. 6.04 above.
[723] See, however, the A.G. at p. 207.

Moreover, the method of production of a wine product constitutes a criterion which is all the less capable of being by itself sufficient [when] it is not linked with the use of a specific type of grape [so that] the method in question may be employed in other geographical areas."

Nor would the Court accept opinion polls put in evidence by the German Government, which were intended to show that the German consumer took the terms *Sekt* and *Weinbrand* to refer to German products only. This was not only because such data were inherently unreliable, but also because:

"the protection accorded by the indication of origin is only justifiable if the product concerned actually possesses characteristics which are capable of distinguishing it from the point of view of its geographical origin [so that] in the absence of such a condition this protection cannot be justified on the basis of the opinion of consumers such as may result from polls carried out on the basis of statistical criteria."

As regards the term *Prädikatssekt*, the Court ruled:

"as the legislation on wine products does not define the grapes which must be used in the production of *Prädikatssekt* with reference to their specific character but only on the basis of their national origin, the minimum percentage required does not necessarily imply that the product in question is actually of a special quality in comparison with *Sekt* and thus warrants the protection accorded to it."

Last, the measures in question were held to constitute arbitrary discrimination within the meaning of the second sentence of Article 30. The Court therefore concluded that these measures were contrary to Article 28 and, as regards sparkling wine, to Regulation 816/70.

8.240 Beier wrote a detailed critique[724] of this judgment. He agreed with the Court that the reservation of the national measures in question constituted measures of equivalent effect within the meaning of Article 28 without being justified under Article 30. Yet he would have reached this conclusion by a different route: in his opinion the terms *Sekt* and *Weinbrand* were not designations of origin or indications of origin at all, but purely generic names (like "potatoes" or "gloves"); seen in this light, the reservation of these terms to national products and the resulting use of less appealing terms for imported products could not possibly be justified under Article 30. On the other hand, the Court began by taking these terms as direct appellations of origin and then, finding that they were not justified, held that they were not appellations of origin after all. Had the Court followed the approach which he suggests, this unduly complicated and circuitous reasoning would have been bypassed. By this method, the Court would have avoided a number of pronouncements which Beier proceeded to criticise.

He singled out for particular criticism the Court's statement that designations

---

[724] "Das Schutzbedürfnis für Herkuntsangaben und Ursprungsbezeichnungen im Gemeinsamen Markt" (1977) G.R.U.R.. Int. 1 and (in English) in *Protection of Geographical Denominations of Goods and Services* (ed. Cohen Jehoram, 1980) at 18.

of origin and indication of origin "only fulfil their specific purpose if the product which they describe does in fact possess specific qualities and characteristics which are due to the fact that it originated in a specific geographical area." He asked whether such highly reputed appellations as "Brussels lace" and "Munich beer" could only be protected if it is shown that these products possess specific qualities or characteristics. In particular, he asked, to protect the term "Munich beer" would it be necessary to show that the same product could not be produced outside Munich by reason of the special qualities of Munich water?[725]

As we shall see, the Court has now brought its case law into line with Beier's thinking.

8.241   The next case was *Prantl*,[726] which concerned indirect geographical denominations. A German statutory provision stipulated that only wines from certain specified regions of Germany could be marketed in bottles of a particular shape known as *Bocksbeutel*. According to a tradition going back several centuries, wine from these regions was sold in these bottles which were of a squat and bulbous shape. The overwhelming majority of these wines are white. It so happened that red wine produced in the Italian Tyrol had been marketed, both in that region and elsewhere, in bottles of an almost identical shape for at least a century. The defendant in the main case was charged with selling or holding for sale quantities of Italian red wine in such bottles in contravention of the provision of German law referred to. The German court requested a preliminary ruling on whether such a provision was compatible with Articles 28 and 30 when applied to imports.

The Court found that such a measure could not be justified as preventing unfair competition (or on consumer protection grounds). Such grounds could not justify the prohibition on the sale of imported wines in bottles of a certain shape so as to protect an indirect designation of geographical origin without regard to the "fair and traditional practices observed in the various Member States". The offending Italian bottles, which were identical or virtually identical to the Bocksbeutel, met that test since they were traditionally used in certain regions of Italy.

Moreover, the Court went on to hold that there was no danger of the consumer's being misled, since the Community legislation on the labelling of quality wines was "particulary comprehensive" and thus ensured that such confusion was avoided.[727]

The Court described the Bocksbeutel bottle as an indirect indication of geographical origin; it was contended by the German Government that as such it was to be regarded as industrial and commercial property within the meaning of Article 30 and that the importation of similar bottles could therefore be precluded. The Court dismissed this argument in the following terms:

---

[725] See also Marenco (1975) *Diritto Comunitario de degli Scambi Internazionali* 358.
[726] Para. 8.154, n.418 above.
[727] See generally para. 8.128 above.

"In this regard it need merely be observed, without its being necessary to resolve these questions of law raised by that argument, that producers who traditionally use a bottle of a specific shape may not in any event successfully rely upon an industrial or commercial property right in order to prevent imports of wines originating in another Member State which have been bottled in identical or similar bottles in accordance with a fair and traditional practice in that State."

The Court thus declined to rule whether geographical denominations fell within the industrial and commercial property exception in Article 30, but preferred to decide the case on the basis of the rules relating to the prevention of unfair competition.

8.242 The ruling in *Delhaize v Promalvin*[728] represents a major turning point in the case law. Spanish legislation required quality Rioja wine to be bottled in the region. If it was transported in bulk from there and bottled elsewhere, it could not be so marketed as a quality wine (*denominación de origen calificada*).

Council Regulation 823/87[729] laying down special provisions relating to quality wines produced in specified regions empowered each Member State to specify its own rules in this regard. However, as the Court held, this did not entitle the Member States to breach Article 29.[730] It was at this point in its reasoning that the Court took a major step, by ruling that appellations of origin constituted industrial and commercial property within the meaning of Article 30. This was despite the fact that Gulmann A.G. found it unnecessary to decide the point.

One might question whether this categorisation is correct.[731] Plainly, appellations of origin share certain attributes with intellectual property: like trade marks they serve to protect the reputation of products manufactured by a select group of producers; and consequently producers outside the group are precluded from using them. On the other hand, they cannot be the subject of assignments, licences or exhaustion. Moreover, as explained in paragraph 8.247 below, it would appear that *Prantl* is still good law, so that designations of origin confer less protection than other forms of intellectual property. In any event, the fact that appellations of origin are covered by the Paris Convention scarcely seems conclusive, given that the same applies to the prevention of unfair competition.[732]

At all events, the Court then defined the specific function of appellations of origin as being to guarantee that the product concerned comes from certain geographical areas and possesses particular characteristics.

The Court found that the local bottling requirement was not necessary to ensure this. Such a rule did not guarantee either the quality or the specific characteristic of the wine. Nor was it necessary for control reasons, since it would suffice to provide that wine transported from the region in bulk be

---

[728] Para. 8.136, n.372 above.
[729] [1987] O.J. L84/59, as amended.
[730] Para. 4.14 above.
[731] See Stuyck, case note [1993] C.M.L.Rev. 847.
[732] Para. 8.148 above.

accompanied by the appropriate certificates. In consequence, the Court concluded that such a measure was contrary to Article 29.

8.243 The Court was to take the principles set out in *Delhaize v Promalvin* further in *Exportur v LOR*[733] This case concerned an agreement between France and Spain whereby the two countries undertook to protect each other's appellations of origin and "indications of source". The denominations *Turron de Alicante* and *Turron de Jijona* were reserved to sweets originating in Spain. Since the composition and characteristics of such sweets was in no way attributable to their place of manufacture, these names constituted indications of source, not appellations of origin. The use of accompanying words such as "type" and "style" to indicate that goods originated elsewhere was expressly precluded. The plaintiffs sought to prevent the defendants from continuing to produce this product in France and selling their wares as "touron Alicante", "touron Jijona", "touron catalan type Alicante" and "touron catalan type Jijona".

The Court confirmed its ruling in *Delhaize* to the effect that appellations of origin were covered by the exception relating to industrial and commercial property in Article 30; and extended it to include indications of source. This contrasts with the Opinion of Lenz A.G., which was delivered even before the judgment in *Delhaize*, to the effect that geographical designations do not fall within this concept, as they were not capable of being assigned or licensed.

In effect, the Court then reversed its ruling in the *Sekt/Weinbrand* case to the effect that denominations of origin could only be protected if the product concerned possessed specific qualities and characteristics by virtue of its origin. The Court stressed that denominations of origin might enjoy a considerable reputation even if this were not the case. Thus, as Brouwer has remarked[734] the essence of this judgment may be summarised with the words: "F. K. Beier has won!".

Next, the Court considered the defendants' arguments based on *Prantl*: they claimed to have used the denominations in question for their products fairly and traditionally, and therefore sought the benefit of the ruling in the earlier case. However, the Court distinguished *Prantl* on the grounds that there bottles of the shape concerned had been fairly and traditionally used in the exporting Member State, whereas here French producers were using the names of Spanish towns for their products.

Finally, the defendants contended that the designations in question had become generic. To this the Court replied that it would indeed not be justified under Article 30 to protect in France Spanish designations which had become generic in their own country.[735]

---

[733] Para. 8.136, n.373 above.
[734] Case note [1993] C.M.L.Rev. 1209 at 1217.
[735] For an example of a place name which has become generic (Edam cheese) see Case 286/86 *Deserbais* [1988] E.C.R. 4907. On the criteria for determining whether a name has become generic see also n.749 below.

8.244 Reaction to *Exportur* was mixed. Beier[736] was predictably jubilant since his cherished theory had been adopted by the Court. If he had any quibble with this judgment at all, it was that it failed to make it clear whether indirect indications of source (such as that in issue in *Prantl*) were covered by the exception for industrial and commercial property in Article 30. However, on balance he concluded that the Court did intend to include them within this exception.

Cornish[737] also gave it a cautious welcome as moving "away from the consumerist obsessions of the seventies towards a greater readiness to protect the values built up by traders". Nevertheless, he recognised the need to set limits to the scope of this newly accepted form of intellectual property, saying:

> "Community law must now seek to identify with some clarity the factors which raise a shared interest in a name to a level where it is worthy of protection as commercial property within Article [30]. These must include the number of enterprises claiming to share in the goodwill, the size of the area associated with the symbol, and the extent to which other traders may find their access to markets made more difficult."

Stuyck's assessment[738] was less charitable, since he claimed:

> "this ruling amounts to a collective monopoly of a certain geographical designation to the benefit of producers by reason of the mere fact that they are established in a certain geographical area, even though in reality products with identical characteristics could be produced anywhere (or at least in other places as well). Or to put it differently: the producers established in a particular area benefit from a kind of collective trade mark for which they have neither made a registration nor necessarily invested in the making of the reputation of that mark (and deserving for that reason the protection of goodwill)."

Brouwer supported this view, and added a further criticism:

> "A more immediate result of the judgment seems the fact that not only French and Spanish producers, but also producers in other Member States, when exporting to France, will have to abide by Spanish law and opinions as to whether the indications in question are to be protected. The situation in France (*i.e.* the view of the French public) is irrelevant. As a result, all Member States are (indirectly) bound by the bilateral Treaty between France and Spain, when exporting to these countries."[739]

8.245 Following the Court's ruling in *Delhaize v Promalvin*, the Spanish Government failed to amend or set aside the offending national legislation. The latter failure culminated in Belgium (supported by Denmark, the Netherlands, Finland and the United Kingdom) bringing proceedings under Article 227 (ex Article 170) EC against Spain. On its face, Belgium's application should have led to a straighforward finding that Spain had failed to take any appropriate measures to comply with the judgment in *Delhaize v Promalvin*. However, with the support of the Commission, Spain succeeded in convincing the Court to

---

[736] Case note [1993] G.R.U.R.Int. 76.
[737] "Intellectual Property" (1992) Y.E.L. 635 at 637.
[738] *op. cit.* n.731 above at 853.
[739] *op. cit.* n.734 above at 1225.

overturn the conclusion it reached in *Delhaize v Promalvin*.[740] The Court's essential reasoning as regards geographical denominations did not change. Rather, the Court was now persuaded that the Spanish rule did in fact guarantee the quality and the specific characteristic of Rioja wine. This time, the Court emphasised that the bottling process was an extremely important part of the production of wine and that its transportation in bulk may seriously damage its quality. Moreover, the Court agreed that bottlers within the region benefitted from specialised experience which included a deep understanding of the specific character of the wine in question. The Court's judgment in *Belgium v Spain* is consistent with a trend (described below) towards giving greater prominence to geographical denominations in the Community. Moreover, the change of heart was based more on fact than on principle. Nevertheless, the about turn is no less remarkable for either of the foregoing, and must be regarded as further emphasising the importance of this form of intellectual property.

8.246 In *Consorzio del Prosciutto di Parma v Asda Stores*,[741] a chain of British supermarkets is contesting the specifications for the protection of the designation of origin "Parma ham", insofar as they preclude the use of that designation for products sliced and packaged outside the Parma area. Alber A.G. distinguished *Belgium v Spain (Rioja)*, saying:

> "In the *Rioja* case, the Court came to the view that the bottling of wine in the region of production was a justified restriction on the free movement of goods since that was the best means of guaranteeing the quality of the bottled wine. It may be evident that the bottling of the wine in the region of production constitutes a commercially material characteristic, since consumers purchase wine primarily in bottles. In the case of ham, however, the situation is different. It is purchased by consumers either sliced—whether freshly by the retailer or pre-packaged—or by the piece or even as a whole ham. It is thus clear that the slicing of ham does not have a significance comparable to that of the bottling of wine. It is then even less the case that the place where slicing takes place can have a decisive influence on consumer choice. This supports the view that slicing in the region of production does not involve a commercially material characteristic."[742]

He also found that the contested restriction was not necessary to ensure quality control. Accordingly, he reached the conclusion that it was not justified.

In another Opinion delivered on the same day, Albers A.G. also made a finding to the same effect with respect to a requirement that the appellation of origin "grana padano" be used exclusively for cheese grated and packed in the region of origin.[743]

At the time of writing, judgment is awaited in both these cases.[744]

8.247 Since in *Exportur* the Court chose to distinguish *Prantl* rather to reverse it, it seems clear that geographical denominations are a weaker form of intel-

---

[740] Case C-388/95 *Belgium v Spain* [2000] E.C.R. I-3123.
[741] Case C-108/01, Opinion of April 25, 2002.
[742] Para. 85 of the Opinion.
[743] Case C-469/00 *Ravil v Bellon*.
[744] Both cases are also discussed further below at para. 8.249.

lectual property than patents, trade marks, copyright and plant breeders' rights and the like.

In *Prantl* it was held that two similar indirect geographical indications in fair and traditional use in two different Member States could both be employed throughout the territory of the Community. Presumably the same would apply to direct geographical denominations since the Court gave other reasons for not following *Prantl* (*i.e.* in distinguishing *Prantl* it did not invoke the fact that that case concerned only indirect indications of origin).

This is in direct contrast to the rule in *Terrapin v Terranova*, which governs other forms of intellectual property. As the reader will be aware, it was held there that, where two confusingly similar trade marks were lawfully acquired independently of one another in two different Member States, then each trade mark holder could preclude the other from marketing his goods in his territory. In other words, in the case in point the British manufacturer could be enjoined from selling his goods in Germany, and vice versa.[745]

8.248 Until 1992—the year which saw the landmark judgments in *Delhaize* and *Exportur*—Community legislation contained only isolated provisions on geographical denominations in specific sectors. In this context, Council Regulation 823/87[746] laying down special provisions relating to quality wines produced in specified regions is particularly worthy of note, as is Council Regulation 1576/89[747] laying down general rules on the definition, description and presentation of spirits.

This situation changed shortly before the judgment in *Exportur* when the Council adopted Regulation 2081/92 on the protection of geographical indications and designations of origin for agricultural products and foodstuffs.[748] Article 2(2)(a) confines designations of origin to goods "the quality or characteristics of which are essentially or exclusively due to a particular geographical environment with its inherent natural and human factors, and the production, processing and preparation of which take place in the defined geographical area". The definition of geographical indications in Article 2(2)(b) is broader: it suffices for the product to possess "a specific quality, reputation or other

---

[745] See paras 8.186 and 8.209–8.212 above.
[746] See n.729 above.
[747] [1989] O.J. L160/1.
[748] See n.533 above; see also Commission Reg. 2037/93 ([1993] O.J. L185/5) and the Commission's Communication on this subject ([1993] O.J. C273/4). See also Fettes, "Appellations d'origine et indications géographiques : le règlement 2081/92 et sa mise en oeuvre" [1997] R.M.U.E. 141; and Knaak, "Die Rechtsprechung des Europäischen Gerichtshofes zum Schutz geographischer Angaben und Ursprungsbezeichnungen nach der EG-Verordnung Nr. 2081/92" [2000] G.R.U.R.Int. 401.

This legislation is supplemented by Council Reg. 2082/92 on certificates of specific character for agricultural products and foodstuffs ([1992] O.J. L208/9) whereby the Commission is to administer a register of "certificates of specific character" of certain traditional products which may not benefit from Reg. 2081/92. See also Council Reg. 1107/96 on the regulation of geographical indications and designations of origin under the procedure laid down in Article 17 of Reg. 2081/92 ([1996] O.J. L148/1) as last amended by Reg. 564/2002 ([2002] O.J. L86/7). As to the procedure in Art. 17 of Reg. 2081/92, see Cases C-129 and 130/97 *Chiciak and Fol* [1998] E.C.R. I-3315 and C-269/99 *Kühne v Jütro* [2001] E.C.R. I-9517.

characteristics attributable to that geographical origin and the production and/ or processing and/or preparation of which takes place in the defined geographical area". The first subparagraph of Article 3(1) provides: "Names which have become generic may not be registered."[749]

Registration, which is effected by the Commission after a formal investigation (Article 6), confers exclusive rights (Article 13).[750] This Regulation does not apply to wine products or spirits (Article 1) since, as already mentioned, they are covered by separate legislation.

8.249 This Regulation has caused much ink to flow,[751] much of it critical. Beier and Knaak[752] have fired a volley of shots in its direction, and indeed question its very validity. The thrust of their sustained attack is that the Regulation does not go far enough to protect geographical denominations. Their principal contention is that there is a direct conflict between the Regulation and the *Exportur* judgment because the Regulation does not protect "quality— neutral" denominations (*i.e.* those relating to goods whose characteristics are not dependent on their place of manufacture). There is some support in the Court's judgment in *Pistre*[753] for Beier and Knaak's view that "quality-neutral"

---

[749]The following subparagraphs of this provision provide:

"For the purposes of this Regulation, a 'name that has become generic' means the name of an agricultural product or a foodstuff which, although it relates to the place or the region where this product or foodstuff was originally produced or marketed, has become the common name of an agricultural product or a foodstuff.

To establish whether or not a name has become generic, account shall be taken of all factors, in particular:

— the existing situation in the Member State in which the name originates and in areas of consumption;
— the existing situation in other Member States;
— the relevant national or Community laws."

In Cases C-289, 293 and 299/96 *Denmark, Germany and France v Commission* [1999] E.C.R. I-1541 the Court held that in registering the name "Feta" under the Regulation, the Commission had failed to take account of all the factors to which Article 3(1) refers.

[750]The exclusive rights in Art. 13 were the subject of the Court's judgment in C-87/97 *Consorzio per la Tutela del Formaggio Gorgonzola v Käserei Champignon Hofmeister* [1999] E.C.R. I-1301. In that case, the Court held that, subject to examining whether or not the registration of the trade mark "Cambozola" before the registration of the protected designation of origin "Gorgonzola" had been effected in good faith, the use of the name "Cambozola" may be deemed, for the purposes of Article 13(1)(b) of Reg. 2081/92, to evoke the designation of origin "Gorgonzola".

[751]Even prior to its adoption this proposal attracted a good deal of attention. See Kolia "Monopolising Names: EEC Proposals on the Protection of Trade Descriptions of Foodstuffs" [1992] E.I.P.R. 233 who expressed fears that the scheme would be protectionist, while Brouwer, "Community Protection of Geographical Indications and Specific Character as a Means of Enhancing Foodstuff Quality" (1991) C.M.L.Rev. 615 welcomed the proposal.

[752]"Der Schutz geographischer Herkunftsangaben in der Europäischen Gemeinschaft" [1992] G.R.U.R.Int. 411 (which appeared in English as "The Protection of Direct and Indirect Geographical Indications of Source in Germany and the European Community" [1994] I.I.C. 1) and "Der Schutz der geographischen Herkunftsangaben in der Europäischen Gemeinschaft—Die neueste Entwicklung" [1993] G.R.U.R.Int. 602. See also Tilmann, "Grundlage und Reichweite des Schutzes geographischer Herkunftsangaben nach der VO/EWG 2081/92" [1993] G.R.U.R.Int. 610. In his article on the case law relating to Reg. 2081/92 (see n.533 above, p. 407), Knaak describes that case law as "reassuring", while remarking that the Court has by definition not been in a position to remedy the "conceptional weaknesses" of this Regulation.

[753]C-321–324/94 [1997] E.C.R. I-2343.

denominations are not protected by the Regulation. That case concerned the indication of source "mountain" which was given protection under French legislation. The Court held:

"...the description 'mountain', cannot be regarded as covering a designation of origin or a geographical indication within the meaning of Regulation 2081/92. The description 'mountain' is quite general in character and transcends national frontiers, whereas, according to Article 2 of Regulation 2181/92, a direct link must exist between the quality or characteristics of the product and its specific geographical origin.

Nor, more generally, is the description 'mountain' an indication of provenance as defined by the Court in its case law on Articles [28] and [30] of the Treaty. According to that case law, an indication of provenance is intended to inform the consumer that a product bearing such an indication comes from a particular place, region or country (judgment in. .. *Exportur*)."[754]

Similarly, in "*Parma Ham*", Alber A.G. found that the slicing of ham in the region of production did not confer on it any particular characteristics and accordingly Regulation 2081/92 precluded specifications for that designation of origin from containing a requirement that that process be carried out in that region.[755] He reached the same conclusion with regard to a specification that the appellation "grana padano" could only be used for cheese grated and packed in the region of production.[756]

It seems therefore that the Court envisages that Article 2 of the Regulation can only apply where there is a "direct link" between "quality or characteristics" of the product and its "specific geographical origin". On its face, this would exclude the "quality neutral" characteristics identified by Beier and Knaak since such characteristics do not have a "direct link" with a "specific geographical origin". Moreover, the Court's reference in *Pistre* to quality neutral "indications of provenance" in *Exportur* is expressly tied to its more general case law on Articles 28 to 30 EC rather than to the provisions of the Regulation itself.

Nevertheless, it is submitted that the better view is that Beier and Knaak's concern overlooks Article 2(2)(b) of the Regulation, under which it suffices for a product to possess a "specific reputation" attributable to its geographical origin. Would Beier and Knaak wish to protect even those geographical indications enjoying no reputation at all? It is one thing for the Community to protect highly prestigious and recognised geographical indictions such as "Brussels lace" and "Swedish furniture" even if products having the same characteristics could equally well be produced elsewhere; it would be quite another for the Community to give protection to fanciful denominations such as "Brussels furniture" and "Swedish lace". Quite apart from these considerations, this charge seems to be at variance with the *Exportur* judgment itself where the Court attached importance to the reputation enjoyed by a denomi-

---

[754] Paras 35 and 36 of the judgment.
[755] Case C-108/01, see n.741 above.
[756] Case C-469/00, see n.743 above.

nation.[757] At all events Stuyck[758] and Salignon[759] find no contradiction between *Exportur* and the Regulation in this regard.

Beier and Knaak also complain that the Regulation applies exclusively to agricultural products and foodstuffs leaving industrial products "completely out of consideration". While one may or may not agree with this remark in policy terms, it cannot affect the validity of the Regulation. On the contrary, since it is based on Article 43 which relates only to agricultural products, it would have been unlawful to extend it to industrial goods.

Perhaps their most important criticism relates to the right to property. To deprive "owners" of geographical denominations of their use because they are not or cannot be registered would amount, they contend, to an unlawful deprivation of property, since the Court has recognised that geographical denominations constitute industrial and commercial property within the meaning of Article 30.[760]

In a quite different vein, Casado and Cerro[761] have focused on the relationship between the protection conferred by the Regulation and trade mark rights, claiming that this relationship gives rise to certain difficulties.

Yet not all the literature can be described as hostile by any stretch of the imagination: some authors[762] have broadly welcomed this Regulation.

---

[757] Para. 28 of the judgment.

[758] *op. cit.* n.731 above at 854–5.

[759] "La jurisprudence et la réglementation communautaires relatives à la protection des appellations d'origine, des dénominations géographiques et des indications de provenance" [1994] 4 R.M.U.E. 107.

[760] Such is the number and variety of the arguments deployed by Beier and Knaak in their onslaught on the Regulation that it is impossible to consider them all here.

[761] "Las diferentes modalidades de protección de los signos geograficos en el derecho comunitario: coexistencia y conflictos entre marcas y denominaciones de origen" [1993] G.J. Nos. 13 and Dec. 5.

[762] *e.g.* Brouwer, *op. cit.* n.751 above; Salignon, *op. cit.* n.759 above.

CHAPTER IX

Other Exception Clauses

9.01 The term "exception clause" is used in this Chapter as a convenient overall concept to cover provisions in the Treaty which permit measures to be taken which would otherwise fall foul of Articles 28 and 29. Such Treaty provisions are of various kinds: some vest the powers in question in the Member States as of right, while others require the adoption of a decision or other binding act by the Commission or, in some cases, the Council. This act will normally take the form of an authorisation to the Member State in question to take a particular measure. Again, some exception clauses such as Articles 30 (ex 36) and 296 (ex 223) may only be invoked on non-economic grounds, while the converse applies to others such as Articles 119 (ex 109H) and 120 (ex 109I), as they may be relied on only in cases of economic difficulty. However, all these provisions share one common trait: since they constitute an exception to a fundamental principle of the Treaty, namely the free movement of goods, measures taken pursuant to them may be no more restrictive than is necessary to realise the legitimate object in view.[1]

9.02 The Treaties of Maastricht and Amsterdam have repealed a number of the provisions considered in the previous editions of this book; and all the exception clauses which applied exclusively during the various transitional periods have lapsed. Only those provisions that are currently in force are analysed in this Chapter. Nevertheless, where previous provisions (or previous versions of existing provisions) may still be of practical importance today, the reader will be alerted as appropriate.

Article 30, which is by far the most important exception clause in relation to Articles 28 and 29, has already been discussed at length in the previous Chapter. It therefore requires no further examination here. Nor is it intended to consider here the exceptions (other than Article 134 (ex 115)) to the rule that on being put into free circulation, goods from third countries are assimilated to goods of Community origin; these exceptions have already been discussed at length in paragraphs 2.21 to 2.23 of this book. Article 38 (ex 46) will be considered at paragraph 10.05 below, since it relates only to agricultural produce. Moreover, in view of its limited geographical scope, Art. 299(2) has already been

---

[1] This rule of proportionality is expressly laid down in Art. 134(3) (ex 115(3)) but applies to all exception clauses; with respect to Art. 30 see Case 104/75 *de Peijper* [1976] E.C.R. 613; [1976] 2 C.M.L.R. 271 and paras 8.12 *et seq.* above; with respect to the former Art. 226 (deleted by the Treaty of Amsterdam), see Cases 73–74/63 *Handelsvereniging Rotterdam v Minister van Landbouw* [1964] E.C.R. 1; [1964] C.M.L.R. 198.

considered at para. 3.04 above.

This leaves the following Articles of the Treaty to be considered in turn in this Chapter: the new Article 16 and Articles 86 (ex 90), 100 (ex 103A), 119 (ex 109H) and 120 (ex 109I), 134 (ex 115), 295 (ex 222) to 298 (ex 225), 301 (ex 228A), 306 (ex 233) and 307 (ex 234). According to the Court's case law, Article 295 does not constitute an exception to Articles 28 and 29; the same probably applies to Article 16. Nevertheless, Articles 16 and 295 have been included for the purpose of examining their possible impact on this area of the law.

Article 16

9.03 The Treaty of Amsterdam inserted into the EC Treaty a new Article 16 drafted in the following terms:

> "Without prejudice to Articles 73, 86 and 87, and given the place occupied by services of general economic interest in the shared values of the Union as well as their role in promoting social and territorial cohesion, the Community and the Member States, each within their respective powers and within the scope of application of this Treaty, shall take care that such services operate on the basis of principles and conditions which enable them to fulfil their missions."

In addition, the following declaration was annexed to the final act of the Treaty of Amsterdam: "The provisions of Article 16 of the Treaty establishing the European Community on public services shall be implemented with full respect for the jurisprudence of the Court of Justice, *inter alia* as regards the principles of equality of treatment, quality and continuity of such services."

The legal impact of this ambiguously worded provision on the application of Articles 28 to 31 remains unclear.[2] However, one cannot ignore the "without prejudice" clause (which takes up nearly half the text of Article 16). Moreover, the requirement to "take care" is not far removed from a best endeavours clause. Last, an exception in favour of services of general economic interest was already enshrined in Article 86(2). For all these reasons, it seems unlikely that this new provision effects a substantive change to the law. Rather, it may be regarded as introducing a change of emphasis.

In any case, the insertion of this new provision into the Treaty has prompted the Commission to issue a Communication on services of general interest in Europe.[3]

---

[2] See Frenz, "Dienste von allgemeinem Wirtschaftlichem Interesse—Neuerungen durch Art. 16 EC" [2000] EuR 901; Königs, "Daseinsvorsorge durch Wettbewerb" [2001] EuzW 481; Rodrigues "Les services publics et le traité d'Amsterdam: genèse et portée juridique du projet de nouvel article 16 du traité CE" [1998] R.M.C. 37; Ross, "Art. 16 EC and Services of General Interest: From Derogation to Obligation" (2000) 25 E.L. Rev. 22; and Schwarze "Daseinsvorsorge im Lichte des europäischen Wettbewerbrechts" [2001] EuzW 334.

[3] [2001] O.J. C17/4.

Article 86 (ex 90)

9.04   Article 86 provides:

"1. In the case of public undertakings and undertakings to which Member States grant special or exclusive rights, Member States shall neither enact nor maintain in force any measure contrary to the rules contained in this Treaty, in particular to those rules provided for in Article 12 and Articles 81 to 89.
2. Undertakings entrusted with the operation of services of general economic interest or having the character of a revenue-producing monopoly shall be subject to the rules contained in this Treaty, in particular to the rules on competition, in so far as the application of such rules does not obstruct the performance, in law or in fact, of the particular tasks assigned to them. The development of trade must not be affected to such an extent as would be contrary to the interests of the Community.
3. The Commission shall ensure the application of the provisions of this Article and shall, where necessary, address appropriate directives or decisions to Member States".

9.05   These provisions are highly complex and give rise to considerable difficulties of interpretation. Moreover, there have been important developments in the interpretation and application of Article 86 together with Article 31 (ex 37).[4] In addition, as we have just noticed, the Treaty of Amsterdam inserted a new Article 16 into the EC Treaty, which relates to services of general economic interest.

In previous editions of this book, it was stated with some confidence that neither Article 86(1) nor (2) could constitute an exception to Articles 28 or 29. As will be seen, that view has recently been upheld as regards 86(1), but rejected with respect to Article 86(2).

9.06   As to Article 86(1), this provision does not constitute an exception clause at all. Thus in *Pigs Marketing Board v Redmond*[5] the Court noted that Article 86(1) expressly provides that as regards the undertakings in question the Member States "shall neither enact nor maintain in force any measure contrary to the rules contained in this Treaty". From this the Court concluded that Article 86(1) did not exempt such undertakings from the Treaty provisions on the free movement of goods.[6]

More recently, the Court confirmed that ruling in *Commission v Netherlands (electricity monopoly)*,[7] when it held:

"Article [86(1)] must be interpreted as being intended to ensure that the Member States do not take advantage of their relations with [the undertakings to which it

---

[4] See the judgments in Cases C-157/94 *Commission v Netherlands (electricity)* [1997] E.C.R. I-5699; C-158/94 *Commission v Italy (electricity)* [1997] E.C.R. I-5789; C-159/94 *Commission v France (electricity and gas)* [1997] E.C.R. I-5815; and C-189/95 *Franzén* [1997] E.C.R. I-5909, all noted by Slot (1998) C.M.L. Rev. 1183. For a discussion of developments with regard to Art. 31 (ex 37), see Ch. 11.
[5] Case 83/78 [1978] E.C.R. 2347 at 2369; [1979] 1 C.M.L.R. 177 at 201; see also generally Case 13/77 *GB Inno v ATAB* [1977] E.C.R. 2115; [1978] 1 C.M.L.R. 283.
[6] Art. 28, even read with Art. 86(1), is directly applicable: Case C-179/90 *Merci Convenzionali v Siderurgica Gabrielli* [1991] E.C.R. I-5889; see paras 5.10 and 6.10.
[7] See n.4 above.

refs] in order to evade the prohibitions laid down by other Treaty rules addressed directly to them, such as those in Articles [28, 29 and 31], by obliging or encouraging those undertakings to engage in conduct which, if engaged in by the Member States, would be contrary to those rules."[8]

9.07 As to Article 86(2), a detailed analysis of the voluminous case law interpreting that provision (other than in the context of the free movement of goods) is beyond the scope of this book.[9] This is because the Treaty rules from which the derogation in Article 86(2) is sought most frequently are Articles 81 and 82 (ex 85 and 86). However, the following principles may be briefly stated.

The services of "general economic interest" referred to in Article 86(2) include most commonly sectors such as transport,[10] energy[11] and communications.[12] The basic principle is that Article 86(2) "seeks to reconcile the Member States' interests in using certain undertakings, in particular in the public sector, as an instrument of economic or fiscal policy with the Community's interest in ensuring compliance with the rules on competition and the preservation of the unity of the common market".[13] Despite its vague wording, this provision has been held to be directly applicable.[14]

9.08 The first limb of Article 86(2) (whether the exclusive rights in question are necessary to enable the undertaking on which they are conferred to perform the particular tasks assigned to it) has been clarified by the Court in a number of recent cases.[15] In particular, the Court has held that:

> "for the Treaty rules not to be applicable to an undertaking entrusted with a service of general interest under Article [86(2)] of the Treaty, it is sufficient that the application of those rules obstruct the performance, in law or in fact, of the special obligations incumbent upon that undertaking. It is not necessary that the survival of the undertaking itself be threatened."[16]

---

[8] Para. 30; see also Case C-158/94, para. 41 and Case C-159/94, (see n.4 above) para. 41.

[9] See Bellamy & Child, *European Community Law of Competition*, (Sweet & Maxwell, 2001) Ch. 13; Buendia Sierra, *Exclusive rights and State monopolies under EC law: Article 86 (former Article 90) of the EC Treaty* (Oxford, 1999); Blum and Logue, *State Monopolies under EC Law* (Wiley, 1998); Bright, "Article 90, Economic Policy and the Duties of Member States" (1993) 6 E.C.L.R. 263; Edward and Hoskins, "Article 90: Deregulation and EC Law. Reflections arising from the XVI FIDE Conference" (1995) 32 C.M.L. Rev. 157; Ehlerman, "Managing Monopolies: the Role of the State in Controlling Market Dominance in the European Community" (1993) 2 E.C.L.R. 61; Hochbaum in Groeben, Thiesing and Ehlermann, *Kommentar Zum EWG—Vertrag* (5th ed., 1999), Vol. 2 at 1684.

[10] See, for example, Case 66/86 *Ahmed Saeed Flugreisen v Zentrale zur Bekämpfund unlauteren Wettbewerbs* [1989] E.C.R. 803; and C-266/96 *Corsica Ferries France v Gruppo Antichi Ormeggiatori del Porto di Genova* [1998] E.C.R. I-3949.

[11] See, for example, C-393/92 *Municipality of Almelo v NV Enegiebedrijf Ijsselmij* [1994] E.C.R. I-1477 and cases cited at n.4 above.

[12] See, for example, Cases 155/73 *Sacchi* [1974] E.C.R. 409; and C-320/91 *Corbeau* [1993] E.C.R. I-2533.

[13] C-67/96 *Albany* [1999] E.C.R. I-5751 at para. 103.

[14] Case C-393/92 (see n.11 above); reversing Case 10/71 *Muller—Hein* [1971] E.C.R. 723.

[15] See the electricity and gas cases cited at n.4 above. See also C-67/96 (see n.13 above); C-115–7/97 *Brentjens* [1999] E.C.R. I-6025; C-219/97 *Drijvende Bokken* [1999] E.C.R. I-6121.

[16] C-157/94 (See n.4 above), para. 43.

No threat to the financial balance or economic viability of the undertaking entrusted with the operation of a service of general economic interest need be shown. It is sufficient that, "in the absence of the rights at issue, it would not be possible for the undertaking to perform the particular tasks entrusted to it, defined by reference to the obligations and constraints to which it is subject".[17] Furthermore, "the conditions for application of [Article 86(2)] are fulfilled in particular if maintenance of those rights is necessary to enable the holder of them to perform the tasks of general economic interest assigned to it under economically acceptable conditions."[18]

9.09 The burden of proof of showing that Article 86(2) is fulfilled is on the Member State but:

"... that burden of proof cannot be so extensive as to require the Member State, when setting out in detail the reasons for which, in the event of elimination of the contested measures, the performance, under economically acceptable conditions, of the tasks of general economic interest which it has entrusted to an undertaking would, in its view, be jeopardized, to go even further and prove, positively, that no other conceivable measure, which by definition would be hypothetical, could enable those tasks to be performed under the same conditions."[19]

9.10 The second limb of Article 86(2) (whether the exclusive rights in question affect the development of trade to an extent contrary to the Community interest) entails an appraisal of the particular tasks entrusted to the undertaking concerned and the protection of the interests of the Community in relation to the development of trade. This must be weighed up against the consideration set out in the first limb.

9.11 As to the link between Article 86(2) and the Treaty provisions on the free movement of goods, the Greek Government argued in *Campus Oil v Ministry for Industry*[20] that Article 28 did not apply because the Irish oil refinery which the Irish Government sought to protect by means of the contested measures was caught by that provision. The Court rejected this suggestion in the following terms:

"Article [86(2)] is intended to define more precisely the limits within which, in particular, undertakings entrusted with the operation of services of general economic interest are to be subject to the rules contained in the Treaty. Article [86(2)] does not, however, exempt a Member State which has entrusted such an operation to an undertaking from the prohibition on adopting, in favour of that undertaking and with a view to protecting its activity, measures that restrict imports from other Member States contrary to Article [28] of the Treaty."

9.12 In the last edition of this book, the inference was drawn from this passage

---

[17] *ibid.* at para. 52.
[18] *ibid.* at para. 53.
[19] *ibid.* at para. 58.
[20] Case 72/83 [1984] E.C.R. 2727; [1984] 3 C.M.L.R. 5449.

that Article 86(2) can never constitute an exception to Article 28. That conclusion has now been overturned by a clutch of judgments handed down by the Court in infringement proceedings brought by the Commission which concerned alleged discrimination in the granting and exercise of exclusive rights to import and export natural gas and electricity.[21] In those cases, the Court maintained its view that Article 86(1) could not be relied on by Member States to evade Articles 28, 29 and 31 but that "it is against that background that Article [86(2)] lays down the conditions in which undertakings entrusted with the operation of services of general economic interest may exceptionally not be subject to the Treaty rules". The Court then concluded:

> "Having regard to the scope just attributed to paragraphs 1 and 2 of Article [86], and to their combined effect, paragraph 2 may be relied upon to justify the grant by a Member State, to an undertaking entrusted with the operation of services of general economic interest, of exclusive rights which are contrary to, in particular, Article [31] of the Treaty, to the extent to which performance of the particular tasks assigned to it can be achieved only through the grant of such rights and provided that the development of trade is not affected to such an extent as would be contrary to the interests of the Community."[22]

On the substance of those cases, the infringement proceedings were dismissed in each instance on the grounds that the Commission had failed to place before the Court sufficient economic, financial and social information to enable the Court to apply either limb of Article 86(2).

The Court's reasoning in these cases constitutes a fundamental reversal of *Campus Oil* in this regard. It should be noted that the burden of proof on the Member States under Article 86(2) is significantly lighter, and the burden on the opposing party correspondingly heavier, than under Article 30. At all events, there is every reason to suppose that this case law applies to the relationship of Article 86(2) with Articles 28 and 29 as well as with Article 31, although only the latter provision was expressly mentioned in the judgments.

9.13 Finally, as regards Article 86(3), it has been held that the Commission may take action under that paragraph to require Member States to put an end to infringements of Article 28 or Article 29 regarding undertakings covered by Article 86(1): *France v Commission*.[23] There the Court upheld a Commission Directive based on Article 86(3) requiring Member States to withdraw any exclusive rights granted to undertakings to import, bring into service or maintain telecommunications terminal equipment; such exclusive rights contravened Article 28, the Court held. It rejected the argument that the Commission had encroached on the powers conferred on the Council by Articles 95 (ex 100A) and 83 (ex 87), in the following terms:

---

[21] See n.4 above.
[22] See C-157/94 (see n.4 above), para. 32; C-158/94, (see n.4 above), para. 49; and C-159/94 (see n.4 above), para. 49.
[23] Case C-202/88 [1991] E.C.R. I-1223.

"Article [95] is concerned with the adoption of measures for the approximation of the provisions laid down by law, regulation or administrative action in Member States which have as their object the establishment and functioning of the internal market. Article [83] is concerned with the adoption of any appropriate regulations or directives to give effect to the principles set out in Articles [81] and [82], that is to say the competition rules applicable to all undertakings. As for Article [86], it is concerned with measures adopted by the Member States in relation to undertakings with which they have specific links referred to in the provisions of that article. It is only with regard to such measures that Article [86] imposes on the Commission a duty of supervision which may, where necessary, be exercised through the adoption of directives and decisions addressed to the Member States.

It must therefore be held that the subject-matter of the power conferred on the Commission by Article [86(3)] is different from, and more specific than, that of the powers conferred on the Council by either Article [95] or Article [83].

It should also be noted that, as the Court held in Joined Cases 188 to 190/80 (*France, Italy and United Kingdom v Commission* [1982] E.C.R. 2545, at paragraph 14), the possibility that rules containing provisions which impinge upon the specific sphere of Article [86] might be laid down by the Council by virtue of its general power under other articles of the Treaty does not preclude the exercise of the power which Article [86] confers on the Commission."

However, the Court did annul the Directive in so far as it required the Member States to withdraw "special" rights within the meaning of Article 86(1), but that was only because the Commission had failed to define "special" rights.[24][25]

Article 100 (ex 103A)

9.14   The first paragraph of Article 100 (ex Article 103A), which was inserted by the Treaty of Maastricht, provides:

"Without prejudice to any other procedures provided for in this Treaty, the Council may, acting unanimously on a proposal from the Commission, decide upon measures appropriate to the economic situation, in particular if severe difficulties arise in the supply of certain products".[26]

The second paragraph, which provides for financial assistance to be granted to Member States in certain circumstances, is not in point here. Article 100 has a number of features in common with the former Article 103,[27] although the latter provision related to "conjunctural policy" (*i.e.* short-term economic policy), whereas the new provision covers economic policy generally. The old Article 103 read as follows:

---

[24] The essence of this ruling was confirmed, in relation to a directive on services in the telecommunications sector, in Cases C-271/90, 281/90 and 289/90 *Spain, Belgium and Italy v Commission* [1992] E.C.R. I-5833.

[25] Acts adopted under Art. 86(3) must comply with the principle of the free movement of goods (see paras 4.10–4.25 above).

[26] The Treaty of Nice will replace the requirement for unanimity in the Council with a qualified majority.

[27] Smulders in Groeben, Boeckh, Thiesing and Ehlermann, *Kommentar Zum EWG—Vertrag* (5th ed., 1999), Vol. 3 at 55.

"1. Member States shall regard their conjunctural policies as a matter of common concern. They shall consult each other and the Commission on the measures to be taken in the light of the prevailing circumstances.

2. Without prejudice to any other procedures provided for in this Treaty, the Council may, acting unanimously on a proposal from the Commission, decide upon the measures appropriate to the situation.

3. Acting by a qualified majority on a proposal from the Commission, the Council shall, where required, issue any directives needed to give effect to the measures decided upon under paragraph 2.

4. The procedures provided for in this Article shall also apply if any difficulty should arise in the supply of certain products."

A brief examination of the case law relating to the old provision, and some of the legislation based on it, is therefore appropriate.[28]

9.15 In *SADAM v Comitato Interministeriale dei Prezzi*,[29] the Court held that a Member State could not rely on the old Article 103 to justify a measure falling under Article 28. Although that case concerned an agricultural product subject to a common organisation of the market, there is every reason to think that this ruling was of general application. It follows that the old Article 103 did not create an exception to Article 28 on which Member States could rely.

9.16 On the other hand, the old Article 103 granted the Council considerable freedom to adopt exceptional measures. The leading case was *Balkan v HZA Berlin-Packhof*[30] which concerned the validity of the system of monetary compensatory amounts. At the time of the events giving rise to the litigation, the relevant legislation was based on that provision. One of the questions referred by the German court hearing the case was whether the Regulation was invalid by virtue of its basis. The Court held that the agricultural provisions of the Treaty conferred power on the Community institutions to take short-term economic policy measures in the agricultural sector. On the other hand, Article 103 did not "relate to those areas already subject to common rules, as is the organisation of agricultural markets". In spite of this, the Court went on to rule that owing to the time needed to give effect to the procedures laid down in Articles 34 (ex 40) and 37 (ex 43), the Council was justified in making interim use of the powers conferred on it by the old Article 103 of the Treaty. In support of this conclusion the Court cited "the suddenness of the events with which the Council was faced, the urgency of the measures to be adopted, the seriousness of the situation and the fact that these measures were adopted in an area intimately connected with the monetary policies of Member States".

9.17 It is clear, then, that the powers conferred on the Community institutions by the old Article 103 were extensive. Thus:

---

[28] There is no case law on whether the old Art. 103(4) applied to cases of excess supply as well as to shortages.
[29] Cases 88–90/75 [1976] E.C.R. 323; [1977] 2 C.M.L.R. 183, see paras 7.77 *et seq.* above.
[30] Case 5/73 [1973] E.C.R. 1091.

(a) the *Balkan* ruling seemed to imply that Article 103 could be used as the basis for measures of a general nature which did not run counter to general principles of Community law such as the free movement of goods;

(b) by holding that Article 103 was inappropriate merely because it did not relate to "areas already subject to common rules", this judgment implied that a similar measure could be adopted under Article 103 if it fell within an area not yet subject to common rules;

(c) it is clear that even within those wide boundaries the Council enjoyed a considerable margin of discretion; this was stated by the Court in *Compagnie d'Approvisionnement v Commission*[31] and *Merkur v Commission*.[32]

9.18 The old Article 103 did not constitute an express exception to the general rules of the Treaty. Nevertheless, it was generally considered that in certain circumstances measures of conjunctural policy or supply policy based on the old Article 103 could be the basis for restrictions on inter-State trade.[33] This is clearly subject to the general rule that such measures may not be more restrictive than is necessary to attain the legitimate object in view. It was also suggested that exceptional measures based on the old Article 103 could only be of a temporary nature.[34] On the other hand, it would appear to follow from the broad wording of Article 103 ("measures appropriate to the situation") that the exceptional measures could be taken under it not only when a crisis actually occurred but also when there was an imminent threat of a crisis. At all events, the Commission and the Council appear to have arrived at an early stage at the conclusion that measures based on the old Article 103 could restrict inter-State trade in a way which would otherwise be contrary to Articles 28 and 29: by Decision 63/689,[35] the Council acting on the proposal of the Commission authorised Belgium to restrict exports of pork and live pigs for a fixed period, in view of the serious shortage of these products; such a restriction would normally have fallen foul of Article 29, if imposed by a Member State.

9.19 It is worth noting a dictum of the Court in *B.P. v Commission*,[36] an action for the annulment of a Commission Decision finding that the companies concerned had abused a dominant position contrary to Article 82 (ex 86) by various

---

[31] Cases 9 and 4/71 [1972] E.C.R. 391; [1973] C.M.L.R. 529.

[32] Case 43/72 [1973] E.C.R. 1055.

[33] Gori, *Les clauses de sauvegarde des traités CECA et CEE* (1967), 178–179; Müller-Heidelberg, *Schutzklauseln im Europäischen Gemeinschaftsrecht* (1970), 295.

[34] Lejeune, *Un droit des temps de crise: les clauses de sauvegarde de la CEE* (1975), 247. It might be noted, however, that a number of Decisions and Directives which were based on the old Art. 103 which were introduced in the wake of the oil crisis in the 1970s were only repealed in 1996: see Dir. 75/405 concerning the restriction of the use of petroleum products in power stations ([1975] O.J. L178/26) repealed by Decision 97/8 ([1997] O.J. L3/7); Dir. 75/339 obliging Member States to maintain minimum fossil fuel at thermal power stations ([1975] O.J. L153/6) repealed by Decision 97/7 ([1997] O.J. L3/6).

[35] [1963] J.O. 3108.

[36] Case 77/77 [1978] E.C.R. 1513; [1978] 3 C.M.L.R. 174.

practices during the acute oil shortage in the Netherlands of 1973–74. The Court in effect stated there that the old Article 103 was a legal basis for Community legislation imposing rationing in times of crisis. Indeed, it expressed its regret at the absence of any such rules at the relevant time; this in its view amounted to a serious failure to act which revealed "a neglect of the principle of Community solidarity which is one of the foundations of the Community".

9.20 It is clear, then, that various measures already adopted under the old Article 103 did create restrictions on intra-Community trade. Yet it should be pointed out that such measures only constituted a minority of the measures based on Article 103, some of which concerned such matters as the temporary suspension of customs duties on certain goods[37] or the co-ordination of the short term economic policies of Member States.[38]

At all events, there seems little room for doubt that the old Article 103 was the appropriate basis for Community measures restricting exports between Member States of goods in short supply, at least if they were of brief duration. In this respect it goes beyond the bounds within which the Community legislator must normally keep. It is not clear what other types of measure derogating from the free movement of goods were permitted by the old Article 103; but absolute import or export bans could probably be based on this provision in extreme cases only, if at all. Presumably, the same or similar principles now apply to Article 100.

Articles 119 (ex 109H) and 120 (ex 109I)

9.21 The Treaty of Maastricht replaced the former Articles 108 and 109 with Articles 109h and 109i. With the Treaty of Amsterdam those provisions in turn became Articles 119 and 120. Articles 119 and 120 ceased to apply from January 1, 1999 when the "third stage" of economic and monetary union began: Articles 119(4) and 120(4) respectively. However, that was only the case as regards the 11 Member States which were found to fulfil the economic convergence criteria laid down in the Treaty and participated in the single currency from the beginning of that stage.[39] Subsequently, Greece was admitted to the single currency with effect from January 1, 2001[40]; accordingly, Articles 119 and 120 have no longer been applicable to that Member State since that date. That leaves only 3 Member States outside the single currency: Denmark and the United Kingdom, both of which have so far declined, pursuant to their respective Protocols, to "opt in"; and Sweden, which is still not considered to fulfil the convergence criteria. By virtue of Article 122(6) read with paragraph 2 of the Protocol relating to Denmark and paragraph 6 of the Protocol relating to

---

[37] *e.g.* Decision 64/530 ([1964] J.O. 2389); Decision 65/266 ([1965] J.O. 1462); Reg. 2101/76 ([1976] O.J. L235/17).
[38] *e.g.* Decision of March 9, 1960 ([1960] J.O. 764); Decision 75/785 ([1975] O.J. L330/50).
[39] Council Decision 98/317 ([1998] O.J. L139/30).
[40] Council Decision 2000/427 ([2000] O.J. L167/19).

the United Kingdom, Articles 119 and 120 continue to apply to those three Member States. Consequently, a brief analysis of their effect is in order.

9.22 These provisions read as follows:

Article 119

"1. Where a Member State is in difficulties or is seriously threatened with difficulties as regards its balance of payments either as a result of an overall disequilibrium in its balance of payments, or as a result of the type of currency at its disposal, and where such difficulties are liable in particular to jeopardize the functioning of the common market or the progressive implementation of the common commercial policy, the Commission shall immediately investigate the position of the State in question and the action which, making use of all the means at its disposal, that State has taken or may take in accordance with the provisions of this Treaty. The Commission shall state what measures it recommends the State concerned to take.

If the action taken by a Member State and the measures suggested by the Commission do not prove sufficient to overcome the difficulties which have arisen or which threaten, the Commission shall, after consulting the Committee referred to in Article 114, recommend to the Council the granting of mutual assistance and appropriate methods therefor.

The Commission shall keep the Council regularly informed of the situation and of how it is developing.

2. The Council, acting by a qualified majority, shall grant such mutual assistance; it shall adopt directives or decisions laying down the conditions and details of such assistance, which may take such forms as:

(a) a concerted approach to or within any other international organizations to which Member States may have recourse;
(b) measures needed to avoid deflection of trade where the State which is in difficulties maintains or reintroduces quantitative restrictions against third countries;
(c) the granting of limited credits by other Member States, subject to their agreement.

3. If the mutual assistance recommended by the Commission is not granted by the Council or if the mutual assistance granted and the measures taken are insufficient, the Commission shall authorize the State which is in difficulties to take protective measures, the conditions and details of which the Commission shall determine.

Such authorisation may be revoked and such conditions and details may be changed by the Council acting by a qualified majority.

4. Subject to Article 122(6), this Article shall cease to apply from the beginning of the third stage."

Article 120

"1. Where a sudden crisis in the balance of payments occurs and a decision within the meaning of Article 119(2) is not immediately taken, the Member State concerned may, as a precaution, take the necessary protective measures. Such measures must cause the least possible disturbance in the functioning of the common market and must not be wider in scope than is strictly necessary to remedy the sudden difficulties which have arisen.

2. The Commission and the other Member States shall be informed of such protective measures not later than when they enter into force. The Commission may recommend to the Council the granting of mutual assistance under Article 119.

3. After the Commission has delivered an opinion and the Committee referred to in Article 114 has been consulted, the Council may, acting by a qualified majority, decide

that the State concerned shall amend, suspend or abolish the protective measures referred to above.

4. Subject to Article 122(6), this Article shall cease to apply from the beginning of the third stage."

Since these provisions are almost identical to the old Articles 108 and 109, we can draw heavily on sources relating to those two Articles.

9.23   The procedure under Article 119 is divided into three stages. At the first stage the Commission examines the monetary position of the Member State in question and makes recommendations as to the action which that State should take. Should this prove to be insufficient, the procedure moves on to the second stage, that of "mutual assistance" consisting of directives or decisions adopted by the Council by a qualified majority on a proposal put forward by the Commission. Only if "the mutual assistance recommended by the Commission is not granted by the Council or if the mutual assistance granted and the measures taken are insufficient" may the Commission authorise the Member State in difficulty to take exceptional measures. Such an authorisation, which, it would seem, must be granted by a decision within the meaning of Article 249 (ex 189),[41] may be revoked or altered by the Council acting by a qualified majority: Article 119(3), second paragraph.

9.24   The exceptional measures which the Commission may authorise under Article 119(3) include quantitative restrictions and measures of equivalent effect,[42] provided always that such draconian measures are necessary to counteract the balance of payments difficulties in question. Accordingly, by Decision 68/301[43] adopted under the old Article 108(3) the Commission authorised France to restrict imports of cars and certain other products, in order to overcome the economic difficulties encountered by France in the wake of the political unrest of May 1968. Another example was Decision 74/287,[44] by which the Commission authorised Italy to subject imports to the lodging with the Bank of Italy of a six-month interest-free loan amounting to not more than 50 per cent of the value of the goods. A particularly striking example of the use of the old Article 108(3) was Decision 85/594[45] which authorised Greece to require interest-free deposits to be lodged for the importation of certain goods; the list of goods concerned took up 28 pages of the Official Journal.

9.25   Where a Member State suffers a sudden crisis in its balance of payments and mutual assistance is not granted immediately by the Council under Article 119(2), then Article 120 empowers that State to take the necessary protective measures itself. As the two Articles are part of one and the same procedure, they

---

[41] Reischl A.G. in Case 27/74 *Demag v Finanzamt Duisburg* [1974] E.C.R. 1037 at 1057.
[42] Zuleeg and Amphoux in Groeben, Thiesing and Ehlermann, *"Kommentar zum EWG—Vertrag"* (4th ed., 1991), Vol. 2, p. 3104 (on the earlier provision).
[43] [1968] J.O. L178/15.
[44] [1974] O.J. L152/18.
[45] [1985] O.J. L375/9.

must be construed analogously. This means that protective measures adopted under Article 120 may include quantitative restrictions and measures of equivalent effect,[46] assuming that such measures may be authorised under Article 119(3). Article 120(1) states that "such measures must cause the least possible disturbance in the functioning of the common market and must not be wider in scope than is strictly necessary to remedy the sudden difficulties which have arisen". However, this is merely the expression of a general principle common to all exception clauses in the Treaty, which we noticed at the beginning of this Chapter.

9.26 It is clear, then, that Article 120 empowers Member States unilaterally to take exceptional measures striking at the very core of the Community on purely economic grounds. For this reason it is subject to important guarantees:

(a) Although the balance of payments difficulties must be of the same kind as those in Article 119, they must fulfil three additional conditions:

   (i) they must be in the nature of a crisis;
   (ii) this crisis must actually have occurred; and
   (iii) it must be sudden.

   Furthermore, Article 120 cannot be applied if mutual assistance under Article 119(2) is forthcoming.

(b) The unilateral measures are merely to act as a stop-gap until the crisis is dealt with by the Community. Hence the provision in Article 120(2) that "the Commission and the other Member States shall be informed of such protective measures not later than when they enter into force". The Court had occasion to interpret the same provision in the old Article 109(2) in *Commission v France*.[47] The background to this case was the economic crisis which arose in France in 1968. By Decision 68/301 based on the old Article 108(3),[48] the Commission authorised France to take various protective measures, including the fixing of a rediscount rate for exports more favourable than the general rate. However, that Decision stipulated that as from November 1, 1968 the difference between the two rates was not to exceed 1.5 points. When France exceeded that limit, the Commission brought infringement proceedings against it. In ruling that France had indeed committed an infringement, the Court rejected, *inter alia*, France's defence that the failure to respect the conditions attached to the Commission's decision was covered by the old Article 109 in view of a fresh monetary crisis which had arisen in the autumn of 1968.[49] The Court held that to rely on this provision a Member State must inform the

---

[46] Zuleeg and Amphoux, *op. cit.* n.42 above, 3116.
[47] Cases 6 and 11/69 [1969] E.C.R. 523; [1970] C.M.L.R. 43.
[48] See n.43 above.
[49] France had in fact relied on Art. 109 in June and July 1968 before Decision 68/301 was taken, but that was not in question before the Court.

Commission and the other Member States of its protective measures in accordance with Article 109(2) and in so doing must make express reference to Article 109. Since France had not done this, it could not rely on Article 109. Presumably this ruling would apply equally to the new Article 120.

9.27 At first sight it might appear from Article 120(2) and (3) that the Commission and the Council may stand back and refrain from all intervention, but it appears from the case law that it is incumbent on them to intervene at the earliest possible moment.[50] This is natural in view of the sweeping powers which Member States enjoy by virtue of these provisions.

Finally, it is not necessary in this context to explore all the procedural permutations which may occur.[51] Suffice it to point out the following possible trains of events:

— the Council may consider that there are no balance of payments difficulties such as to render Articles 119 and 120 applicable, in which case it must require the Member State concerned to abolish its unilateral measures or at least amend them so that they no longer constitute exceptional measures;

— the Commission may recommend mutual assistance under Article 119(2) to the Council; if the Council proceeds to adopt that recommendation, then Article 120 ceases to be applicable and Article 119 takes over;

— if the Commission recommends mutual assistance but the Council does not grant it or the mutual assistance granted proves insufficient, then the Commission may authorise exceptional measures under Article 119(3); once again, Article 120 ceases to have effect.

It would appear that Articles 119 and 120 have yet to be applied. Moreover, it would also seem that the old Articles 109h and 109I had not been applied either in the last few years.

Article 134 (ex 115)[52]

9.28 As amended by the Treaty of Maastricht, Article 134 provides as follows:

"In order to ensure that the execution of measures of commercial policy taken in accordance with this Treaty by any Member State is not obstructed by deflection of trade, or where differences between such measures lead to economic difficulties in

---

[50] Cases 6 and 11/69 (see n.47 above).
[51] For these, see in particular Lejeune, *op. cit.* n.34 above, 155; Zuleeg and Amphoux, *op. cit.* n. 42 above, 3117.
[52] Bourgeois, in Groeben, Thiesing and Ehlermann, *op. cit.* n.42 above, Vol. 3 at 883; Kretschmer, "Beschränkungen des innergemeinschaftlichen Warenverkehrs nach der Kommissionsentscheidung 80/47 EWG" (1981) EuR 63; Vogelzang, "Two Aspects of Article 115 EEC Treaty" [1981] C.M.L.R. 169.

one or more of the Member States, the Commission shall recommend the methods for the requisite co-operation between Member States. Failing this, the Commission shall authorise Member States to take the necessary protective measures, the conditions and details of which it shall determine.

In case of urgency, Member States shall request authorisation to take the necessary measures themselves from the Commission, which shall take a decision as soon as possible; the Member States concerned shall then notify the measures to the other Member States. The Commission may decide at any time that the Member States concerned shall amend or abolish the measures in question.

In the selection of such measures, priority shall be given to those which cause the least disturbance to the functioning of the common market."

It is somewhat anomalous that this provision did not expire at the end of the transitional period (*i.e.* on December 31, 1969) because Article 113 (now Article 133) required the common commercial policy in trade with third countries to be "based on uniform principles" from January 1, 1970. It was even more anomalous that the Single European Act failed to repeal this provision, although it provided for the completion of the internal market by January 1, 1993. To cap it all, as noted above, instead of repealing this provision, the Treaty of Maastricht actually amended it with the aim of reinforcing the exceptional powers of the Member States. Finally, the Treaty of Amsterdam has not altered or repealed this provision, and nor will the Treaty of Nice.

9.29 Despite the exceptional nature of this provision, recourse to it was originally widespread, particularly in relation to textiles. A bumper year for safeguard measures was 1979, when 260 requests from Member States were granted, but the numbers have steadily declined since then. Indeed, in view of Article 14 (ex 7A) of the Treaty,[53] recourse to this provision since January 1, 1993 has been hard to justify. It would appear that since then it has served as the legal basis only for a small number of unpublished Decisions relating to bananas; those decisions were adopted before the entry into force on July 1 of that year of Council Regulation 404/93 establishing a common market organisation for that product.[54] In addition, a Commission decision adopted on the basis of the old Article 115 before the entry into force of Regulation 404/93 was the subject of a challenge in *Lefebvre v Commission*.[55] In its judgment, the Court of First Instance held that since derogations allowed under the old Article 115 constitute an exception *inter alia* to Article 28, they "must be interpreted and applied strictly"[56] and that "where a Member State submits a request under Article 134, the Commission is under a duty to review the reasons put forward by the Member State concerned in order to justify the protective measures for which it seeks authorisation, and to verify whether those measures are consistent with the Treaty and necessary".[57]

In view of the limited and ever diminishing application of Article 134 in

---

[53] Para. 12.13.
[54] [1993] O.J. L47/1; see Ch. X below.
[55] T-571/93 [1995] E.C.R. I-2379.
[56] Para. 48 of the judgment.
[57] *ibid.*

practice, that provision must be regarded as moribund, if not actually dead. Accordingly, common sense would suggest that little purpose would now be served in setting out here a more detailed analysis of its history and the relevant case law. The reader is therefore referred to previous editions of this work.

Article 295 (ex 222)

9.30 Article 295 provides:

"This Treaty shall in no way prejudice the rules in Member States governing the system of property ownership."

Article 295 is not one of the most straightforward provisions in the Treaty. It appears to have been conceived primarily to show that nationalisation was compatible with the Treaty.[58] However, the position of nationalised industries under Community law cannot be explored here.[59] At all events, it is suggested that Article 295 does not permit discrimination by a nationalised industry against imported goods.[60]

This provision has been considered by the Court *inter alia* in *Consten and Grundig v Commission*,[61] *Parke, Davis v Centrafarm*[62] and *Italy v Commission*.[63] In each of these cases it held that Article 295 could not be relied on. In particular, in the first two cases the Court ruled that this provision did not preclude the general rules of the Treaty to affect the exercise of industrial property rights, so long as their existence was not affected.

Moreover, in *Commission v United Kingdom* (compulsory patent licences)[64] the Court ruled:

"Article [295] cannot be interpreted as reserving to the national legislature, in relation to industrial and commercial property, the power to adopt measures which would adversely affect the principle of free movement of goods within the common market as provided for and regulated by the Treaty."

Indeed, it is doubtful if Article 295 can ever constitute an exception to Articles 28 to 30.

Article 296 (ex 223)

9.31 Article 296 provides:

[58] Neri and Sperl, *Répertoire du Traité CEE* (1960) 410; see also Written Question 346/80 ([1980] O.J. C213/6.
[59] See paras 4.05 and 9.04 and Ch. XI of this book.
[60] Such a view is suggested by para. 7 of the judgment in Case 182/83 *Fearon v Irish Land Commission* [1984] E.C.R. 3677; [1985] 2 C.M.L.R. 228 which concerns establishment within the meaning of Art. 43 (ex 52) EEC. See also C-302/97 *Konle v Austria* [1999] E.C.R. I-3099 at para. 38.
[61] Cases 56 and 58/64 [1966] E.C.R. 299; [1966] C.M.L.R. 418.
[62] Case 24/67 [1968] E.C.R. 55; [1968] C.M.L.R. 47.
[63] Case 32/65 [1966] E.C.R. 389; [1969] C.M.L.R. 39.
[64] Case C-30/90 [1992] E.C.R. I-829 also discussed at para. 8.175 above.

"1. The provisions of this Treaty shall not preclude the application of the following rules:

(a) ...
(b) Any Member State may take such measures as it considers necessary for the protection of the essential interests of its security which are connected with the production of or trade in arms, munitions and war material; such measures shall not adversely affect the conditions of competition in the common market regarding products which are not intended for specifically military purposes.

2. The Council may, acting unanimously on a proposal from the Commission, make changes to the list, which it drew up on 15 April 1958, of the products to which the provisions of paragraph 1(b) apply."

This must be read in conjunction with Article 298 (ex 225), which provides:

"If measures taken in the circumstances referred to in Articles 296 and 297 have the effect of distorting the conditions of competition in the common market, the Commission shall, together with the State concerned, examine how these measures can be adjusted to the rules laid down in this Treaty.

By way of derogation from the procedure laid down in Articles 226 and 227, the Commission or any Member State may bring the matter directly before the Court of Justice if it considers that another Member State is making improper use of the powers provided for in Articles 296 and 297. The Court of Justice shall give its ruling in camera."

Regard must also be had to the European Union's common foreign and security policy enshrined in Articles 11 to 28 (ex J to J.11) of the Treaty on European Union—even though these provisions are not part of Community law, are not subject to the jurisdiction of the Court (Article 46 (ex L)) and do not amend the Treaty of Rome (Article 47 (ex M))[65]). Indeed, Gilsdorf has suggested[66] that Member States may not rely on Article 296 with respect to matters covered by joint action decided on by the Council in accordance with Article 14 (ex J.3) of the Treaty on European Union. In his view, it would only be otherwise where Article 14(6) TEU applies. Under that provision, a Member State may decline to carry out the joint action "in cases of imperative need arising from changes in the situation" and then may only take "the necessary measures as a matter of urgency"; the question must then be discussed in the Council pursuant to Article 14(7) (ex J.3(7)) TEU.

9.32 "Security" in Article 296(1)(b) refers both to internal and external threats to the State.[67] However, the use of the terms "war material" and "specifically military purposes" indicates that this provision does not cover security matters normally dealt with by the police, such as crime detection and

---

[65] The Court has been known to take cognisance of treaties which were not part of Community law: Cases 89/76 *Commission v Netherlands* [1977] E.C.R. 1355; [1978] 3 C.M.L.R. 630; and 44/84 *Hurd v Jones* [1986] E.C.R. 29. See generally Gilsdorf, "Les réserves de sécurité du traité CEE à la lumiére du Traité sur l'Union Européenne" [1994] R.M.C. 17.

[66] *op. cit.* n. 65 above, at p. 24.

[67] See *Sirdar v Secretary of State for Defence* [1999] E.C.R. I-7403, at para.17; and Case 83/94 *Leifer* [1995] E.C.R. I-3231 at para.26.

prevention and traffic regulation. These matters fall within the public security exception in Article 30.[68]

The term "arms, munitions and war material" is contrasted with "products which are not intended for specifically military purposes". Thus supplies such as petrol, which can be used for military purposes but are not specifically intended for them, are not arms, munitions or war material within the meaning of Article 296. Plainly, "war material" extends to items which are neither arms nor munitions, but the precise scope of this exception remains unclear.[69] As explained in paragraph 8.58 above, the Council has also adopted legislation relating to firearms and dual use goods.

Prior to its amendment by the Treaty of Amsterdam, paragraph 2 of this article provided that the list in question could only be adopted during the first year following the entry into force of the EC Treaty—with the result that the list drawn up on April 15, 1958 soon became wholly obsolete. Perhaps that is why, after steadfastly refusing to accede to requests to publish this list,[70] the Council has finally yielded.[71] At all events, this list can now be amended by the Council at any time, provided that it acts unanimously.[72]

9.33 It would seem clear that the measures which Member States may take under Article 296(1)(b) include quantitative restrictions and measures of equivalent effect with respect to goods figuring on the list[73] where such measures are necessary. Unlike the public security exception in Article 30, this provision applies only to goods appearing on the list.[74]

The Court delivered a land-mark judgment on this provision in *Commission v Spain*.[75] It was held there that the defendant was not entitled to exempt from VAT arms, ammunition and equipment used exclusively for military use. Spain's reliance on Article 296 was rejected, since it had failed to show that the exemption was "necessary for the essential interests of its security". Rather, the Court found that "the imposition of VAT on imports and acquisitions of armaments would not compromise that objective since the income from pay-

---

[68] Para. 8.52 above.

[69] See Gilsdorf and Kuijper, in Groeben, Thiesing and Ehlermann *op. cit.* n.42 above Vol. 5. p. 406.

[70] See, *e.g.* the Council's answer to Written Question 574/85 [1985] O.J. C287/9. A copy of the list was however published in Courades Allebeck, "The European Community: from the EC to the European Union" in Wulf (ed.), *Arms Industry Limited* (Oxford 1993) at 214. For criticism of the failure to publish the list officially, see Eikenberg, "Article 296 (ex 223) EC and external trade in strategic goods" (2000) 25 E.L. Rev. 117 at 128–130; and Vincentelli-Meria, "Vers une normalisation de l'application de l'article 296 du TCE dans le secteur des industries d'armement" [2001] R.M.C. 96 at 101.

[71] Answer to Written Question E-1324/01 ([2001] O.J. C364 E/85).

[72] The Council must act "on a proposal from the Commission" (Article 296(2)). Vincentelli-Meria, (see n. 70 above at 97) has pointed out that the Commission's right to propose amendments to the list has given the Commission a role in relation to the intergovernmental foreign and security policy.

[73] See generally the A.G. in Case 15/69 *Württembergische Milchverwerkung-Südmilch v Ugliola* [1969] E.C.R. 373; [1970] C.M.L.R. 194.

[74] Jacobs A.G. in Case C-367/89 *Aimé Richardt* [1991] E.C.R. I-4621 at 4643; Collet, "Le développement des actions communautaires dans le domaine des matériels de guerre, des armes et des munitions" [1990] R.T.D.E. 75.

[75] C-414/97 [1999] E.C.R. I-5585 at para.21.

ments of VAT on the transactions in question would flow into the State's coffers apart from a small percentage which would be diverted to the Community as own resources". This clearly illustrates that the Court is prepared to exercise effective judicial control of the application of this provision by Member States.[76]

9.34 Should the Commission or a Member State consider that another Member State is making improper use of these powers, then by virtue of Article 298 it can bring the matter to the Court without sending the reasoned opinion required by Articles 226 (ex 169) and 227 (ex 170) respectively. This exception was presumably created in view of the likely urgency of such an action. The stipulation in Article 298(2) that proceedings are to be held in camera is an exception to the rule in Article 28 of the Protocol on the Statute of the Court of Justice of the EC, which states that the hearings shall be in open court unless the Court "decides otherwise for serious reasons". As explained in paragraph 9.41 below, the first action ever brought by the Commission under Article 298 was subsequently discontinued and removed from the Court's register.

Article 297 (ex 224)

9.35 Article 297 provides:

> "Member States shall consult each other with a view to taking together the steps needed to prevent the functioning of the common market being affected by measures which a Member State may be called upon to take in the event of serious internal disturbances affecting the maintenance of law and order, in the event of war, serious international tension constituting a threat of war, or in order to carry out obligations it has accepted for the purpose of maintaining peace and international security."

At first sight this provision appears merely to impose an obligation on Member States to consult each other on the occurrence of one of the serious events enumerated there, but not to vest any powers in the Member States. However, that Article 297 does indeed give rise to powers on the part of the Member States is shown by the reference in Article 298 (ex 225) to "the powers provided for in Articles 296 and 297".[77]

Today Article 297 must be understood in the light of Articles 11 to 28 of the Treaty on European Union, which relate the Union's common foreign and security policy. This is despite the fact that these provisions are not technically part of Community law. Article 297 does not indicate whether the consultation required thereunder should take place solely within the Community legal framework or may take place within the European Union's foreign and security

---

[76] See also *Sirdar* (see n.67 above) at para.16 and C-285/98 *Kreil v Germany* [2000] E.C.R. I-69 at para.16. Also T-126–7/96 *BFM and EFIM v Commission* [1998] E.C.R. II-3437 at para. 89 where the Court of First Instance rejected an argument that the exception in Article 296 applied to State aid prohibited by Art. 87 (ex 92) on the grounds that "none of the aid called in question by the Commission was specifically linked with military projects forming part of the national defence policy". See also Gilsdorf, n. 65 above, at 18 and Eikenberg, n. 70 above, at 119.
[77] Jacobs A.G. in *Aimé Richardt* (see n.74 above) at 4643; for the text of Art. 298 see para. 9.31 above.

policy. However, the former view may be regarded as too formalistic.[78] It may be that Article 297 will cease to be applicable to matters covered by joint action agreed pursuant to Article 14 TEU, except where the derogation in point 6 of that article may be relied on.[79]

9.36 Unlike Article 296, the exceptional measures envisaged by this provision are not limited to arms, munitions and war material. It empowers Member States to impose quantitative restrictions and measures of equivalent effect with respect to any category of goods, including the sequestration of or import bans on goods of nationals of a particular third country or territory, which is a protagonist to international tension. This is possibly the only instance in the Treaty where goods can be discriminated against by reason of the nationality of their owner, rather than their origin.[80] Indeed, if the circumstances set out in Article 297 arise, virtually any provision of the Treaty may be disregarded.[81]

What are these circumstances? Broadly speaking, they are the existence or serious threat of war, civil war or sedition or the existence of obligations which a Member State has "accepted for the purpose of maintaining peace and international security" by which is meant primarily UN resolutions.[82] Thus a gamut of very different situations is covered. For instance, all the Member States may be affected in the same way, or only one may be affected. Again, the measures will normally be very urgent, but they may not be, as where measures are taken against a distant territory that constitutes no real security threat to the Member States.

9.37 It appears to follow from *Johnston v Chief Constable of the Royal Ulster Constabulary*[83] that Article 297 is a residual provision and will therefore not apply where another more specific provision is applicable. In view of the troubles in Northern Ireland, the United Kingdom claimed to be entitled under Article 297 to have a policy of discriminating against women in recruitment in the RUC full-time reserve. The Court described the unrest in Northern Ireland as "serious internal disturbances"; this could be taken to imply that in the Court's view it constituted "serious internal disturbances affecting the maintenance of law and order" within the meaning of Article 297. However, the Court found that the circumstances concerned were covered by one of the exceptions in Council Directive 76/207[84] on the implementation of the principle of equal treatment for men and women. From this it concluded that the national court's question on Article 297 did not arise. It is not clear whether the Court merely saw no need to decide the point; or whether, as a matter of substantive law, it considered Article 297 to be inapplicable. However, the latter view is consistent with

---

[78] See Koutrakos, "Is Article 297 EC a 'reserve of sovereignty'?" (2000) 37 C.M.L. Rev. 1339 at 1359–61.

[79] Gilsdorf, *op. cit.* n.65 above, at 24.

[80] See para. 2.24 above.

[81] See generally, *Ugliola*, n.73 above.

[82] Neri and Sperl, *op. cit.* n.58 above, at 412.

[83] Case 222/84 [1985] E.C.R. 1651; [1986] 3 C.M.L.R. 240.

[84] [1976] O.J. L39/40.

the maxim *lex specialis derogat generali* (the specific provision ousts the general one). It would follow that, as regards the free movement of goods, one must look notably to the public security exception in Article 30 before considering Article 297.

The latter view has been confirmed by recent case law. In *Leifer*,[85] which concerned German legislation requiring a special licence for the export of dual-use goods, the Court ruled on the compatibility of the German legislation with all other Treaty provisions (including Article 30), avoiding any analysis of Article 297 at all. Similarly, in *Sirdar*,[86] which concerned British legislation excluding women from certain special bodies of the British Army, the Court again ruled on all other grounds (including Article 30) but simply referred to the possible application of Article 297 as one "which concerns a wholly exceptional situation".[87] Finally, in *Albore*,[88] which concerned Italian legislation making the transfer of immovable property, situated in provinces adjoining frontiers or in areas of military importance, to non-Italian nationals subject to the approval by the local Prefect, the Court applied the "public security" derogation in Article 56 (ex 73b) and simply remarked that "the situation of the Member State concerned does not fall within the scope of Article [297] of the EC Treaty".[89]

In his Opinion in *Commission v Greece*,[90] Jacobs A.G. considered that:

> "the analogy between Articles [30] and [297] should not be taken too far ... Certainly it is correct to say that Articles [30] and [297] must both be construed strictly since they derogate from the ordinary rules of the Treaty. That much the two provisions have in common. There are, however, important differences. In the first place, whereas the situations covered by Article [30] (and by Articles [39(3) and 46(1)] respectively) may be described as exceptional, those covered by Article [297] are, as the Court recognised in paragraph 27 of the *Johnston* judgment, *wholly* exceptional. That is confirmed by the fact that Article [297] has so rarely been invoked, while recourse to Article [30] is relatively common. A second difference relates to the breadth of the possible derogations permitted by the two articles. Article [30] permits derogations from one aspect of the common market (admittedly a fundamental one); Article [297], on the other hand, permits derogations from the rules of the common market in general."[91]

9.38 It appears to follow from the above case law that the existence of a situation referred to in Article 297 does not in itself give the Member State concerned unlimited powers to derogate from Community law.[92] In *Johnston*, the United Kingdom had contended that in view of the troubles it was entitled to preclude recourse to the courts in this matter. The Court dismissed this argument on the grounds that "none of the facts before the Court and none of the observations submitted to it suggest that the serious internal disturbances in

---

[85] See n.67 above, noted by Govaere (1997) 34 C.M.L. Rev. 1019.
[86] See n.67 above.
[87] Para. 19 of the judgment.
[88] C-423/98 [2000] E.C.R. I-5965 noted by Hatzopoulos (2001) 38 C.M.L. Rev. 455.
[89] Para. 21 of the judgment.
[90] C-120/94 [1996] E.C.R. I-1513.
[91] Para. 46 of the Opinion.
[92] See Koutrakos, n.78 above at 1342–3.

Northern Ireland make judicial review impossible or that measures needed to protect public safety would be deprived of their effectiveness because of such review by the national courts". In *Albore* the Court did not explain why the situation in that case did not fall within the scope of Article 297. However, it is notable that Cosmas A.G. had embraced a remarkably extensive application of Article 297 (which he in the event found was not fulfilled).[93] The stark contrast between the Advocate General's approach and the Court's curt rejection of the application of Article 297 clearly confirms that the latter article is reserved for extreme conditions of disorder[94] or for what Jacobs A.G. has referred to as "massive breakdown of public order".[95]

The Court's restrictive interpretation of Article 297 is not surprising. Any other approach would give Member States the ability to bring all manner of general interests under the umbrella of Article 297, thereby undermining the application of Community law. The status accorded to measures that may fall within Article 297 as "wholly exceptional"[96] is thus fully justified.

9.39 Gilsdorf[97] takes the view that the consultation provided for in Article 297 must take place before the measures concerned are adopted, thereby rejecting the view suggested in the Commission's answer to Written Question 527/75,[98] according to which such consultations may be deferred until the functioning of the common market is in fact affected. Koutrakos[99] concurs with Gilsdorf, and points out that in practical terms it is not easy to imagine how it may be determined whether the "functioning of the common market is affected" without a consultation between the Member States and the State invoking Article 297. Moreover, the latter author notes that the procedural requirements laid down in Article 297 cannot be treated as a mere formality, given the "wholly exceptional" character of that provision. Thus, barring extreme urgency, the better view is indeed that the consultation provided for in Article 297 must take place before the measures concerned are adopted.[100] Gilsdorf also maintains[101] that the Commission must be involved in those consultations, since otherwise it would be unable to exercise its powers under Article 298.

9.40 Article 297 has been relied on frequently for the adoption of trade sanctions against third countries, often pursuant to resolutions of the United

---

[93] See, in particular, paras 31, 55 and 56 of the Opinion.
[94] Hatzopoulos, n.88 above, at 469.
[95] See n.90 above at para. 49 of the Opinion.
[96] See *Johnston*, n.83 above at para. 27 and *Sirdar*, n.67 above at para. 19.
[97] *op. cit.* n.42, 5607; see also Kuyper, "Sanctions against Rhodesia. The EEC and the Implementation of General International Rules" (1975) C.M.L. Rev. 231; *The Implementation of International Sanctions* (1978) at 195.
[98] [1976] O.J. C89/8.
[99] See n.78 above at 1356–59.
[100] In the case concerning the embargo that Greece imposed on the Former Yugoslav Republic of Macedonia, the Greek Government failed to consult the other Member States prior to imposing the embargo. Surprisingly, this point was not even mentioned by the Commission in its action before the Court.
[101] See n.97 above, 5607.

Nations Security Council. In the early days of the Community such sanctions were imposed by the Member States without any action being taken by the Community as such. This occurred with respect to Rhodesia[102] adopted after that country's Unilateral Declaration of Independence and Iran[103] after the taking of the American hostages in Teheran.

The sanctions imposed on Argentina at the time of the Falklands war were the first to be enshrined in a Community instrument, namely a Council Regulation[104] based on Article 133 (ex 113). The preamble to that Regulation refers to Article 297 but later Council Regulations imposing trade sanctions omit any reference to that provision.[105] The Treaty of Maastricht inserted a clear legal basis for Community trade sanctions into the Treaty of Rome, namely Article 301 (ex 228A). That provision will be considered below.

9.41 The first action ever brought under Article 298 (ex 225) related to the embargo imposed by Greece on the Republic of Macedonia on all trade passing through the port of Salonica, as a result of the dispute between the two countries relating in particular to the name by which the former Yugoslav republic wished to be known. The Commission claimed that this disagreement did not fall within any of the heads of Article 297 and that Greece was committing a serious infringement of Community law by blocking both intra-Community and external trade in all products other than goods which were absolutely essential for humanitarian purposes. The Commission also sought an interim order from the Court requiring Greece to suspend its blockade. Dealing with the latter application, the Court found that although the Commission had made out a *prima facie* case, the application for an interim order would be rejected on the grounds that the Commission had failed to show that any relevant damage was being suffered as a result of the embargo.[106]

In his Opinion on the main case, Jacobs A.G. also took the view that the Commission's action should be rejected. The following passage of his Opinion is of particular interest:

"When Article [297] speaks of 'serious internal disturbances affecting the main-

---

[102] See Kuyper, *op. cit.* n.97 above; Written questions 526/75 ([1976] O.J. C89/6) and 527/75, n.98 above.

[103] E.C. Bull. 5 [1980] 26.

[104] Reg. 877/82, [1982] O.J. L102/1, which was extended as regards most Member States by Regs 177/82, [1982] O.J. L136/1, and 1254/82, [1982] O.J. L146/1; and repealed by Reg. 1577/82 ([1982] O.J. L177/1). See Kuyper, "Community sanctions against Argentina: Lawfulness under Community and International law" in *Essays in European Law and Integration* (ed. O'Keefe and Schermers, Netherlands 1982); and Verhoeven, "Sanctions internationales et Communautés européennes" [1984] C.D.E. 259.

[105] See, *e.g.* the sanctions against Iran (Regs 2340/90, [1990] O.J. L213/1, 3155/90, [1990] O.J. L304/1); Libya (Reg. 945/92, [1992] O.J. L101/53); Serbia and Montenegro (Regs. 1432/92, [1992] O.J. L151/4 and 990/93, [1993] O.J. L102/14); and Haiti (Reg. 1608/93, [1993] O.J. L155/2); see Kuyper, "Trade Sanctions, Security and Human Rights and Commercial Policy" in *The European Community's Commercial Policy after 1992: the Legal Dimension* (ed. Maresceau, (1993)) pp. 387–422; and Vaucher, "L'évolution récente de la pratique des sanctions communautaires à l'encontre des Etats tiers" [1993] R.T.D.E. 39.

[106] Case 120/94 R [1994] E.C.R. I-3037.

tenance of law and order', it must in my view be read as envisaging a breakdown of public order on a scale much vaster than the type of civil unrest which might justify recourse to Article [30]. What seems to be envisaged is a situation verging on a total collapse of internal security, for otherwise it would be difficult to justify recourse to a sweeping derogation which is capable of authorising the suspension of all of the ordinary rules governing the common market."

The Advocate General found that this condition was not met in the present case. Next, he considered whether the situation amounted to a state of war or "serious international tension constituting a threat of war" within the meaning of Article 297. Stressing that it was extremely difficult to evaluate whether a threat of war existed and that this was primarily for the Member State concerned to assess, he concluded that Greece was not acting "wholly unreasonably". Thus it was in his view open to Greece to rely on this provision. Moreover, he found that Greece was not abusing its powers under Article 297, since such an abuse could scarcely be said to exist unless the real purpose of the Member State in imposing the embargo is to protect its economy rather than prosecute a political dispute with a third country.

Jacobs A.G. thus attributed a central role to the subjective view of the Member States and to the limited nature of the judicial review that may be carried out in the area covered by Article 297. Whilst the apparent latitude given to the Member States gives rise to initial concern, Jacobs A.G. is surely right to point out that there is a "paucity of judicially acceptable criteria that would permit this Court or any other court, to determine whether serious international tension exists and whether such tension constitutes a threat of war".[107] Moreover, as already mentioned, Article 297 only applies to situations that are "wholly exceptional". It is precisely because a situation is "wholly exceptional" that the scope and intensity of judicial review is limited.

After the Advocate General had delivered his Opinion and in view of subsequent developments, the Commission took the view that it no longer had an interest in pursuing the proceedings. The proceedings were accordingly discontinued and the case was removed from the Court's register.[108]

Article 301 (ex 228A)

9.42 Article 301, which was inserted into the EC Treaty by the Treaty of Maastricht, reads as follows:

"Where it is provided, in a common position or in a joint action adopted according to the provisions of the Treaty on European Union relating to the common foreign and security policy, for an action by the Community to interrupt or to reduce, in part or completely, economic relations with one or more third countries, the Council shall take the necessary urgent measures. The Council shall act by a qualified majority on a proposal from the Commission."[109]

---

[107] Para. 50 of the Opinion.
[108] C-120/94 (see n.90 above).
[109] See also Art. 60 (ex 73g) with regard to the free movement of capital.

Article 301 thus introduced for the first time a separate legal basis for Community sanctions against third countries.[110] It should be noted that the Council must act unanimously under the common foreign and security policy. Only then will it be able to adopt the sanctions by qualified majority in accordance with Article 301.

9.43 For present purposes, the important point is that isolated action by one or more Member States under Article 297 can still not be ruled out, as there is no guarantee that sanctions will always take the form of uniform Community measures. In the late 1980s Ireland and Denmark imposed certain sanctions of their own on South Africa.[111] Likewise, in 1994, Greece imposed an embargo on goods originating in, coming from and destined for the Former Yugoslav Republic of Macedonia. In the latter case, as was noted in the previous section of this Chapter, the Commission brought an action against Greece under Article 298, claiming *inter alia* that the unilateral measures taken by Greece amounted to an improper use of Article 297. As we noticed earlier, Jacobs A.G. confirmed in his Opinion that unilateral sanctions may still be imposed by individual Member States under Article 297.[112] In these circumstances the risk of national sanctions giving rise to restrictions on inter-State trade cannot be totally excluded.

Article 306 (ex 233)

9.44 Article 306 provides as follows:

"The provisions of this Treaty shall not preclude the existence or completion of regional unions between Belgium and Luxembourg, or between Belgium, Luxembourg and the Netherlands, to the extent that the objectives of these regional unions are not attained by the application of this Treaty."

The regional unions in question are, first, the Belgo-Luxembourg Economic Union created by a Convention of 1921 (which is now superseded by Economic

---

[110]For the position prior to the insertion of Article 301 see paras 9.40 above. Article 301 has been used as a legal basis for the imposition of sanctions against *inter alia*: the Taliban regime of Afghanistan (Reg. 467/2001 [2001] O.J. L67/1); the Al-Qaida network (Reg. 881/2002 [2002] O.J. L139/9); Angola (Reg. 1705/98 [1998] O.J. L215/1); Burma/Myanmar (Reg. 1081/2000 [2000] O.J. L122/29); Iraq (Reg. 2465/96 [1998] O.J. L337/1 amended by Reg. 1346/2002 [2002] O.J. L197/1); Libya (Reg. 836/1999 [1999] O.J. L106/1); Sierra Leone (Reg. 941/98 [1998] O.J. L136/1); and the Federal Republic of Yugoslavia (Reg. 1294/1999 [1999] O.J. L153/ 63); Zimbabwe (Reg. 310/2002 [2002] O.J. L50/4, amended by Reg. 1224/2002 [2002] O.J. L179/10) and certain persons and entities with a view to combating terrorism (Reg. 2580/2001 [2001] O.J. L344/70). The legislation relating to the Taliban is currently the subject of a challenge in Case T-306/01 *Abdirisak Aden v Commission*. See generally Paasivirta and Rosas "Sanctions, Countermeasures and Related Actions in the External Relations of the EU: a Search for Legal Frameworks" in Cannizzaro (ed.) *The European Union as an Actor in International Relations* (2002).
[111]Vaucher, *op. cit.* n.105 above. See generally Raux, "Les Sanctions de La Communauté européene et de ses Etats membres contre l'Afrique du Sud pour cause d'apartheid" [1989] R.M.C. 33; and Reg. 3302/86 [1986] O.J. L305/11.
[112]Para. 9.41 above.

and Monetary Union in which both countries participate); and the Benelux, set up in London during the Second World War by a Convention between the Governments in exile of Belgium, the Netherlands and Luxembourg.[113]

In *Pakvries v Minister for Agriculture and Fisheries*[114] the Court ruled that Article 306 "enables the three Member States concerned to apply, in derogation from the Community rules, the rules in force within their union in so far as it is further advanced than the common market".[115] It follows that by virtue of Article 306, the Member States concerned may integrate more rapidly than the Community as a whole. On the other hand, this provision does not apply where the objectives of these regional unions are attained by application of the Treaty of Rome.[116] Both Reuter[117] and Petersmann[118] agree that within these limits Article 306 constitutes an exception to the rule against non-discrimination—a fact which is obviously of some significance for the interpretation of Articles 28 to 30. It would appear to follow that the Member States concerned, acting within these limits, may grant preferential treatment to one another pursuant to the BLEU or Benelux Conventions; the resulting less favourable treatment of other Member States would not constitute arbitrary discrimination contrary to Article 30.

Article 307 (ex 234)

9.45 The first paragraph of Article 307 provides:

"The rights and obligations arising from agreements concluded before 1 January 1958 or, for acceding States, before the date of their accession, between one or more Member States on the one hand, and one or more third countries on the other, shall not be affected by the provisions of this Treaty."

This is qualified by the second paragraph, which reads:

"To the extent that such agreements are not compatible with this Treaty, the Member State or States concerned shall take all appropriate steps to eliminate the incompatibilities established. Member States shall, where necessary, assist each other to this end and shall, where appropriate, adopt a common attitude."

The third and final paragraph of this Article is not relevant for present purposes. As explained below, the Court appears to have held in *Conegate v H.M.*

---

[113] See Van Damme, "Benelux and its Relationship with the EEC" in *Legal Problems of an Enlarged European Community* (ed. Bathurst, 1972); Van der Woude, "La libre circulation des marchandises à l'intérieur du Bénélux dans une perspective communautaire" [1987] R.M.C. 83.

[114] Case 105/83 [1984] E.C.R. 2101 at 2115, [1985] 2 C.M.L.R. 602 at 613.

[115] See also to the same effect C-473/93 *Commission v Luxembourg* [1996] E.C.R. I-3207

[116] Thus, in Case C-367/93 *Roders v Inspecteur der Invoerrechten* [1995] E.C.R. I-2229 the Court held that Article 306 could not save an internal tax imposed pursuant to a Benelux treaty which infringed Article 90 (ex 95) EC: "such tax discrimination against imported products cannot be regarded as necessary for the functioning of the Benelux system and, therefore, as justified on the basis of Article [306] of the Treaty".

[117] In *Les Novelles, Droit des Communautés Européennes* (1969) para. 2.13.

[118] In Groeben, Boeckh, Thiesing and Ehlermann, *op. cit.* n.42 above, Vol. II, 1133.

Customs and Excise[119] that Article 307 can never constitute an exception to Articles 28 and 29. Nevertheless, for reasons which will be expounded below, it is appropriate to consider Article 307 in detail.

9.46 The exception clause contained in the first paragraph is limited in four ways. It is appropriate to consider the first two of these limitations together:

(a) It only applies to agreements concluded before the Treaty came into force or, for the new Member States, before accession.

(b) It only applies to agreements concluded between one or more Member States on the one hand and one or more third countries on the other. It therefore does not apply to agreements between Member States.

The foregoing principles were forcefully laid down by the Court in one of its earliest judgments concerning the EEC Treaty, in *Commission v Italy*.[120] The Commission claimed that Italy was infringing the Treaty by failing to reduce its customs duties on certain goods from other Member States in accordance with Article 25 (ex 12 and 14) of the Treaty which required the gradual abolition of customs duties between Member States. In its defence Italy claimed that it was obliged to charge the higher level of duty by virtue of the 1956 Geneva Agreements concluded under the auspices of GATT. To this end Italy invoked Article 307. However, this defence was rejected by the Court, which ruled that "in matters governed by the EEC Treaty, that Treaty takes precedence over agreements concluded between Member States before its entry into force, including agreements made within the framework of GATT".

9.47 Yet it is submitted that there are exceptions to this rule. If a Member State was required to carry out border controls under a prior treaty with a third State, that obligation would fall within Article 307—even as regards controls at frontiers with other Member States. Moreover, there is no reason why the result should be different where more than one Member State is bound by a prior treaty obligation.

This question was considered by Warner A.G. in *Henn and Darby*,[121] where the Court of Justice had been asked a series of questions by the House of Lords as to the compatibility with Community law of a prohibition on imports of indecent and obscene articles. In its seventh and final question the House of Lords asked, *inter alia*, whether this prohibition was lawful in view of the Geneva Convention of 1923 for the suppression of the traffic in obscene publications and of Article 307.

---

[119] Case 121/85, [1986] E.C.R. 1007; [1986] 1 C.M.L.R. 739.
[120] Case 10/61 [1962] E.C.R. 1; [1962] C.M.L.R. 187; see also Cases 235/87 *Matteucci v Communauté Francaise* [1988] E.C.R. 5589; 28 6/86 *Ministère Public v Deserbais* [1988] E.C.R. 4907; T-69/89 *R.T.E. v Commission* [1991] E.C.R. II-485 (the latter ruling of the CFI was upheld on appeal by the Court of Justice: C-241–2/91 P [1995] E.C.R. I-743); C-473/93 (see n. 115 above), para. 40; and C-364–5/95 *T. Port v Hauptzollamt Hamburg-Jonas* [1998] E.C.R. I-1023 at paras 56–64.
[121] Case 34/79 [1979] E.C.R. 3795; [1980] 1 C.M.L.R. 246; see paras 5.11, 8.17 and 8.41 above.

The Advocate General found that the 1923 Convention lent itself to two possible interpretations:

(i) either the Convention only created, at all events as regards imports and exports, a series of bilateral obligations between the parties; if so, the Convention had been superseded as between Member States by the EEC Treaty in line with the Court's ruling in *Commission v Italy*;

(ii) alternatively, the Convention created multilateral obligations between all the parties to it, so that States which are parties to the Convention but not Members of the Community have a right to the enforcement of the Convention even as respects imports and exports between Member States, on the basis that a "flourishing trade in obscene material" within the Community could prejudice other States' efforts to suppress the traffic in it.

Since the Court of Justice had no jurisdiction to interpret the 1923 Convention, the Advocate General concluded that it was for the national court to decide which of these two interpretations was correct.

The Court, however, saw no need to enter into these finer points: it merely replied that "in so far as a Member State avails itself of the reservation relating to the protection of public morality provided for in Article [30] of the Treaty, the provisions of Article [307] do not preclude that State from fulfilling the obligations arising from the Geneva Convention of 1923..."

9.48 This issue arose again in *Conegate*, which concerned imports into the United Kingdom of "inflatable dolls of a sexual nature" from Germany. The last question posed by the English High Court was whether an import ban imposed by a Member State in accordance with the Geneva Convention of 1923 and the Universal Postal Convention was consistent with Article 307. The Court held that "an agreement concluded prior to the entry into force of the Treaty may not be relied upon in order to justify restrictions on trade between Member States". This appears to mean that Article 307 can never constitute an exception to Articles 28 and 29. Yet the Court did not consider the view propounded by Warner A.G. in *Henn and Darby* and therefore gave no reason for rejecting it.

9.49 Happily, the precedent set by *Conegate* has not been followed. In *Deserbais*[122] the Court chose to use a different form of words, saying that a Member State could not rely on a pre-existing convention to maintain restrictions unless "the rights of non-member countries are ... involved...".

Moreover, in *R. v Secretary of State for the Home Department, Ex p. Evans Medical*[123]

---

[122] See n.121 above. See also Case C-158/91 *Levy* [1993] E.C.R. I-4287 (ILO convention banning night work by women inconsistent with Council Directive 76/207 on equal treatment between men and women).

[123] Case C-324/93 [1995] E.C.R. I-563; Lenz A.G. considered this issue at some length. See also to similar effect C-124/95 *R v HM Treasury Ex p. Centro-Com* [1997] E.C.R. I-81 at paras 56–59.

the Court was asked whether the United Kingdom could rely on Article 307 with respect to an import restriction on an opium derivative between Member States in view of the 1961 Single Convention on Narcotic Drugs. It ruled: "in order to determine whether a Community rule may be deprived of effect by an earlier international agreement, it is necessary to examine whether that agreement imposes on the Member State concerned obligations whose performance may still be required by non-Member States which are parties to it."[124] It was for the national court to decide this question, the Court held. In short, the Court has preferred the approach suggested by Warner A.G. This is to be welcomed.

9.50   (c) The exception clause in Article 307(1) is also subject to the limitation contained in Article 307(2): Member States are required to do everything in their power to eliminate any inconsistencies between the Treaty and prior agreements. At the very least, this means that, if an agreement with one or more third countries comes up for renewal after the Treaty entered into force (or, for new Member States, since accession), then no Member State may renew it unless elements incompatible with the Treaty are removed from that agreement. In *Commission v Portugal*,[125] the Court was called upon to consider the precise circumstances in which a Member State may maintain measures contrary to Community law in reliance upon a pre-Community convention concluded with a third country (*in casu*, the Republic of Angola). The Court confirmed that Member States are under an obligation to eliminate any incompatibilities existing between a pre-Community convention and the EC Treaty and moreover that "if a Member State encounters difficulties which make adjustment of an agreement impossible, an obligation to denounce that agreement cannot ... be excluded".[126]

9.51   (d) The exception laid down by Article 307(1) only applies to obligations of Member States and to rights of third States, and not the converse; thus a Member State cannot rely on Article 307 for the continued enjoyment of rights derived from a prior treaty with a third State, as the Court held in *Commission v Italy*.[127]

9.52   Further light on the meaning of this exception clause was shed by the ruling in *Attorney General v Burgoa*.[128] The defendant, the skipper of a Spanish vessel, was charged with various offences under Irish fisheries legislation alleged to have been committed within the exclusive fishery limits of the Irish State. Spain was not yet a Member State of the Community. During the hearing before the Irish Circuit Court the defendant relied on the London Fisheries Convention of 1964, to which both Spain and Ireland were party. Thereupon the Irish court referred to the Court of Justice a series of questions, the bulk of which

---

[124]See also T-2/99 *T. Port v Council* [2001] E.C.R. I-2093 at para. 77.
[125]C-62/98 [2000] E.C.R. I-5171, noted by Hillion (2001) C.M.L. Rev. 1269.
[126]See para. 49 of the judgment.
[127]See n.121 above.
[128]Case 812/79 [1980] E.C.R. 2787; [1981] 2 C.M.L.R. 193.

concerned Article 307. Only the first two questions are of relevance here:

First, the Irish court asked whether Article 307 created rights and obligations for the Community institutions as well as for the Member States. After confirming its ruling in *Commission v Italy* to the effect that the rights at issue were those of third countries only, the Court continued:

> "Although the first paragraph of Article [307] makes mention only of the obligations of Member States, it would not achieve its purpose if it did not impose a duty on the part of the institutions of the Community not to impede the performance of the obligations of Member States which stem from a prior agreement. However, that duty of the Community institutions is directed only to permitting the Member State concerned to perform its obligations under the prior agreement and does not bind the Community as regards the non-member country in question."

Second, the Irish court asked whether Article 307 or any other rule of Community law maintained or upheld rights of the beneficiaries of Treaties to which Article 307 applied, which national courts must apply. The Court replied:

> "since the purpose of the first paragraph of Article [307] is to remove any obstacle to the performance of agreements previously concluded with non-member countries which the accession of a Member State to the Community may present, it cannot have the effect of altering the nature of the rights which may flow from such agreements."

9.53 In conclusion, it is submitted that despite *Conegate* there will be exceptional cases in which a Member State should be able to rely on Article 307 as an exception to Article 28 or Article 29.

CHAPTER X

Agriculture

10.01 Central to the common agricultural policy is the concept of the common organisation of the market. Article 34(1) (ex 40(2)) of the Treaty provides:

> "This organisation shall take one of the following forms, depending on the product concerned:
>
> (a) common rules on competition;
> (b) compulsory co-ordination of the various national market organisations;
> (c) a European market organisation."

Option (c) has always been chosen. A common market organisation will normally include rules on price formation (under which supplies will usually be bought up when prices fall below a certain level), a system of direct income subsidies and measures relating to imports from outside the Community coupled with export refunds for goods exported to third countries.[1] In addition, all regulations establishing common market organisations during the transitional period—and some since—have included a provision prohibiting customs duties and taxes of equivalent effect and quantitative restrictions and measures of equivalent effect between Member States. However, for reasons explained in this Chapter it has become clear that such a clause is now superfluous.

The structure of this Chapter reflects the fundamental importance of common market organisations: the first section covers the application of the prohibition on quantitative restrictions and measures of equivalent effect in the absence of such an organisation, while the second deals with its application to products covered by such an organisation; in the third and final section we shall consider the completion of the internal market in agriculture.[2] It should be borne in mind that nearly all agricultural products[3] are now covered by common organisations; potatoes are now the only agricultural product of any significance which is still bereft of such an organisation. Until 1980, "sheepmeat"

---

[1] See generally Ackrill, *The Common Agricultural Policy* (2000); Barents, *The Agricultural Law of the E.C.* (1994); Blumann, *Politique agricole commune* (1996); Gencarelli, *La Politica agricola comune nella giurisprudenza comunitaria* (2000); Korte and van Rijn in Groeben, Thiesing, Ehlermann, *Kommentar zum EU-/EG-Vertrag* (5th ed., 1997), Vol. I, pp. 913 *et seq.*

[2] The scope of Article 37 (ex 43) EC, which constitutes the legal basis for agricultural legislation, is considered in para. 12.34 below.

[3] Agricultural products are those listed in Annex I (formerly Annex II) to the Treaty: Art. 32(3) (ex 38(3)). As to whether trees and forestry products are to be regarded as agricultural products, see Cases 164/97 and C-165/97 *Parliament v Council* [1999] E.C.R. I-1139 at p. 1164. See generally Barents; *op. cit.* at pp. 26 *et seq.*; Blumann, *op. cit.* at pp. 22 *et seq.*; Korte and van Rijn, *op. cit.* at pp. 918–9.

and "goatmeat" were not covered by a common organisation of the market,[4] while the common market organisation for bananas only came into force on July 1, 1993.[5]

I. WHERE NO COMMON MARKET ORGANISATION EXISTS

10.02 In the absence of a common market organisation for a product can a Member State maintain import or export quotas on that product, when those quotas form part of a national market organisation? Until the Court's judgment in *Charmasson v Minister of Economic Affairs*[6] it was widely thought that a Member State could maintain such quotas and indeed this was the view taken both by the Commission and by the Advocate General in that case. The Court was to reject that view in favour of a more integrationist approach. Its starting-point was Article 32(2) (ex 38(2)) EC which reads: "Save as otherwise provided in Articles 33 to 38 [ex 39 to 46], the rules laid down for the establishment of the common market shall apply to agricultural products." An examination of Articles 33 to 38 led the Court to conclude that, after the end of the transitional period laid down in Article 8 of the original Treaty of Rome (*i.e.* after 1969), the Treaty provisions on free movement of goods were fully applicable.

10.03 The Court subsequently applied this reasoning to measures of equivalent effect to quantitative restrictions on exports. During a potato shortage the French Government had published a notice to exporters in the French Journal Officiel requiring potato exporters to make an export declaration to be endorsed by the French authorities. In an action brought under Article 226 (ex 169), the Court confirmed the Commission's view that the measure infringed Article 29 (ex 34): *Commission v France.*[7]

10.04 In a series of cases, the Court then proceeded to apply the same reasoning to trade between the original Member States and various acceding States, although each of the Acts of Accession contained exception clauses which were arguably ambiguous on the point.[8] The last such exception clauses, Articles 76(2) and 244(2) of the Act of Accession of Spain and Portugal, lapsed

---

[4] Reg. 1837/80 ([1980] O. J. L183), now replaced.

[5] Reg. 404/93 ([1993] O.J. L47/1), described by Manservisi in "Die gemeinsame Marktorganisation für Bananen" [1994] EuZW 209. An attempt by Germany to obtain the interim suspension, and the annulment, of this Regulation failed: Case C-280/93R *Germany v Council* [1993] E.C.R. I 3667; and Case C-280/93 ([1994] E.C.R. I-4973). Also, the Community was held not liable in damages for the Commissions delay in proposing a Regulation on a common market organisation in bananas: Case T-571/93 *Lefebvre v Commission* [1995] E.C.R. II-2379.

[6] Case 48/74 [1974] E.C. R. 1383; [1975] 2 C.M.L.R. 208.

[7] Case 68/76 [1977] E.C.R. 515; [1977] 2 C.M.L.R. 161.

[8] Cases 118/78, *Meijer v Department of Trade* [1979] E.C.R. 1387; [1979] 2 C.M.L.R. 398, 31/78, *Commission v United Kingdom* (potatoes) [1979] E.C.R. 1447; [1979] 2 C.M.L.R. 427; 232/78 *Commission v France* (sheepmeat) [1979] E.C.R. 2729; [1980] 1 C.M.L.R. 418; 24/80R and 97/80R *Commission v France* (sheepmeat) [1980] E.C.R. 1319; [1981] 3 C.M.L.R. 25; 194/85 *Commission v Greece* (bananas) [1988] E.C.R. 1037. See generally paras 5.05 *et seq.* above.

at the end of 1995 and a detailed examination of this case law would therefore be out of place today. The reader who is sufficiently enthusiastic is referred to the previous edition of this book.

10.05 Finally, a discussion of this subject would not be complete without a brief mention of Article 38 (ex 46) of the Treaty, which reads:

> "Where in a Member State a product is subject to a national market organisation or to internal rules having equivalent effect which affect the competitive position of similar production in another Member State, a countervailing charge shall be applied by Member States to imports of this product coming from the Member State where such organisation or rules exist, unless that State applies a countervailing charge on export.
>
> The Commission shall fix the amount of these charges at the level required to redress the balance; it may also authorise other measures, the conditions and details of which it shall determine."

In *Ramel v Receveur des Douanes*[9] the Court held *obiter* that Article 38 lapsed at the end of the transitional period. However, that ruling was reversed in *St Nikolaus Brennerei v Hauptzollamt Krefeld*.[10] The Court therefore upheld the validity of Commission Regulation 851/76[11] requiring Germany and the Benelux countries to apply a countervailing charge on imports of subsidised French alcohol, which Regulation was based on Article 38. In reaching this conclusion, the Court relied on the fact that the Commission disposed of no other adequate basis for action with respect to State aids for agricultural products which were yet to be subject to a common market organisation.[12]

Although Article 38 is primarily concerned with countervailing charges, its final half-sentence would appear to contemplate the adoption of other forms of measure. Despite this, it scarcely seems conceivable that it would ever be appropriate to impose quantitative restrictions or measures of equivalent effect, since according to *St Nikolaus Brennerei* the purpose of countervailing measures adopted pursuant to Article 38 is to "re-establish equilibrium". It seems probable that only countervailing charges are proportionate to this aim. If that is so, then this provision cannot constitute an exception to Article 28. In any case, even though this article survived the cull of obsolete provisions effected by the Treaty of Amsterdam, it has not been applied for some years.[13]

---

[9] Cases 80–81/77 [1978] E.C.R. 927.
[10] Case 337/82 [1984] E.C.R. 1051; [1985] 3 C.M.L.R. 83; confirmed by Case C-201/90 *Gio Buton v Amministrazione delle Finanze dello Stato* [1991] E.C.R. I-2453; see also Cases 114/83 *Société d'Initiatives v Commission* [1984] E.C.R. 2589; [1985] 2 C.M.L.R. 767; and 289/83 *GAARM v Commission* [1984] E.C.R. 4295; [1986] 3 C.M.L.R. 15.
[11] [1976] O.J. L96/41.
[12] See Art. 36 (ex 42) EC and Reg. 22/62 ([1962] J.O. 993).
[13] In its Report on the Internal Market for 1993 (COM(94) 55) the Commission stated that the possibility of countervailing duties being applied to this product under Article 38 cannot be ruled out (at p. 58).

II. WHERE A COMMON MARKET ORGANISATION DOES EXIST

10.06 In view of the *Charmasson* judgment it has become clear that the provisions of Articles 28 to 30 apply to all agricultural products automatically, so that it is unnecessary to re-enact those provisions in regulations setting up a common market organisation.[14] Consequently, it has been the practice in recent years to forgo express provisions of this kind, since they are superfluous. This practice was endorsed by the Court in *Kramer*.[15] It held there that after the end of the transitional period (*i.e.* after 1969) the prohibition on measures of equivalent effect applied to products covered by a common market organisation, even where the regulation establishing that organisation did not expressly lay down the prohibition.[16]

10.07 When a national measure may be contrary to Article 28 or 29 and to a regulation setting up a common market organisation, should the Treaty provisions or the regulation be considered first? The Court has had occasion to rule on a considerable number of cases of this kind.[17] However, the practice of the persons bringing these matters before the Court has not been consistent: the Court has been asked to rule on the compatibility of national measures now with the Treaty provisions, now with the common market organisation, and sometimes with both. It is not surprising, then, that the Court has tended to mingle the two, with the consequence that it is often unclear whether a particular judgment is limited to the common market organisation in question, or whether it is an interpretation of Articles 28 and 29 applicable to all products. Nevertheless, in *Pigs and Bacon Commission v McCarren*[18] the Court stated:

> "In the event of proceedings relating to an agricultural sector governed by a common organisation of the market the problem raised must first be examined from that point of view having regard to the precedence necessitated by Article [32(2)] of the [EC] Treaty for the specific provisions adopted in the context of the common agricultural policy over the general provisions of the Treaty relating to the establishment of the Common Market."

Having decided that a national measure of the kind at issue contravened the regulation establishing the common market organisation, there was no need for the Court to consider its compatibility with the Treaty provisions.[19]

On this view a national measure, like a horse in a steeplechase, must clear the

---

[14] Indeed, the provisions of Community legislation governing the common market organisation must themselves be compatible with Articles 28 to 30: paras 4.10 *et seq.* above.

[15] Cases 3, 4 and 6/76 [1976] E.C.R. 1279; [1976] 2 C.M.L.R. 440.

[16] This was confirmed in Case 83/78 *Pigs Marketing Board v Redmond* [1978] E.C.R. 2347; [1979] 1 C.M.L.R. 177.

[17] *e.g.* Cases 190/73 *Van Haaster* [1974] E.C.R. 1123; [1974] 2 C.M.L.R. 521; 4/75 *Rewe-Zentralfinanz v Landwirtschaftskammer* [1975] E.C.R. 843; [1977] 1 C.M.L.R. 599; 89/74, 18–19/75 *Arnaud* [1975] E.C.R. 1023; [1975] 2 C.M.L.R. 490.

[18] Case 177/78 [1979] E.C.R. 2161; [1979] 3 C.M.L.R. 389.

[19] In *Krämer*, (see n.15 above), the Court adopted the same approach.

fence of the common market organisation before the fence of Articles 28 and 29. If it falls at the first fence, there is no need to consider these two articles. It is submitted that this is the most appropriate approach, because common market organisations will often contain specific provisions which have a bearing on the national measure in question, for example with respect to price formation.[20] In the absence of such provisions, one may fall back on Articles 28 and 30.

In other, quite unrelated, matters the Court has followed a similar approach to the relationship between Community legislation and Articles 28 to 30. One instance of this is the form of words used in the *"Cassis de Dijon"* case[21]: "in the absence of common rules relating to the production and marketing of alcohol ... it is for the Member States to regulate [these] matters." Another example is the Court's ruling to the effect that, once a Community Directive has harmonised measures necessary to protect public health, Member States can no longer adopt or maintain unilateral measures in reliance on Article 30 (ex 36).[22]

10.08   Consequently, judgments of the Court on measures of equivalent effect on imports and exports of products covered by common market organisations may be of limited significance as they may be applicable only to products covered by such an organisation. Those judgments, which appear to be of general application, have been discussed in Chapter VII. Others appear to be interpretations of the common market organisation in question, even if they expressly refer to Articles 28 and 29. It is by no means a simple matter to decide which judgments are of general application and which are not. The cases discussed below appear not to be of general application but deserve mention in this book precisely because this point is uncertain.

10.09   The *locus classicus* on this area of the law is *Pigs Marketing Board v Redmond.*[23] The facts of that case were that a police officer in Northern Ireland stopped a lorry containing 75 "bacon pigs", pigs weighing more than 77 kilograms. Under Northern Irish law it was an offence to transport bacon pigs otherwise than to one of the Pigs Marketing Board's purchasing centres with a document authorising transport, so that in effect the Board had a purchasing monopoly of all bacon pigs produced in Northern Ireland. Since the lorry driver was unable to produce the requisite certificate, the owner of the pigs was

---

[20] There is a large body of case law relating to national price controls on products covered by common market organisations: Cases 31/74 *Galli* [1975] E.C.R. 47; [1975] 1 C.M.L.R. 211; Case 154/77 *Dechmann* [1978] E.C.R. 1573; [1979] 2 C.M.L.R. 1; 223/78 *Grosoli* [1979] E.C.R. 2621; 10/79 *Toffoli* [1979] E.C.R. 3301; 95–96/79 *Kefer and Delmelle* [1980] E.C.R. 103; 216/86 *Antonini* [1987] E.C.R 2919; C-22/99 *Bertinetto* [2000] E.C.R. I-7629; see Berardis, "The common organisation of agricultural markets and national price regulations" [1980] C.M.L. Rev. 539; Colinet and Maresceau, "Interprétation et application du droit communautaire dans le domaine des réglementations des prix des produits agricoles de l'arrêt *Dechmann* à l'arrêt *Kefer-Delmelle*" [1980] C.D.E. 507. See also paras 7.75 *et seq.* above.
[21] Case 120/78 *Rewe-Zentral v Bundesmonopolverwaltung für Branntwein* [1979] E.C.R. 649; [1979] 3 C.M.L.R. 494; a similar form of words appears in Case 8/74 *Dassonville* [1974] E.C.R. 837; [1974] 2 C.M.L.R. 436.
[22] Paras 8.28 *et seq.* above.
[23] See n.16 above.

charged with an offence under the Regulations. The defendant having argued that the Regulations and certain provisions relating to the establishment of the Board were contrary to Community law, the Resident Magistrate referred a number of questions to the Court. These included the compatibility of the Northern Irish provisions with Articles 28 and 29 and Regulation 2759/75[24] setting up the common organisation of the market in pigmeat.

On these points the Court held:

"A marketing system on a national or regional scale set up by the legislation of a Member State and administered by a body which, by means of compulsory powers vested in it, is empowered to control the sector of the market in question or a part of it by measures such as subjecting the marketing of the goods to a requirement that the producer shall be registered with the body in question, the prohibition of any sale otherwise than to that body or through its agency on the conditions determined by it, and the prohibition of all transport of the goods in question otherwise than subject to the authorisation of the body in question are to be considered as incompatible with the requirements of Articles [28 and 29] of the EEC Treaty and of Regulation 2759/75...".

10.10 The principle of pre-emption has been described by the Court as follows:

"...once the Community has, pursuant to Article [34] of the Treaty, legislated for the establishment of a common organisation of the market in a given sector, Member States are under an obligation to refrain from taking any measure which might undermine or create exceptions to it."[25]

More specifically, in *Irish Creamery Milk Suppliers Association v Ireland*, the Court held that Member States must refrain from taking measures which "obstruct the working of the machinery established by the common organisations of the market".[26] This indicates that Member States will only fall foul of this principle if they interfere with the specific mechanisms of the common organisation. Thus national measures which merely run counter to the general aims of such an organisation without causing such harm are permissible.

The principle of pre-emption is neatly illustrated by some very clear cases at opposite ends of the spectrum: at one end, *Apple and Pear Development Council v Lewis*[27]; at the other, *Holdijk*[28] and *Annibaldi v Guidonia*.[29]

10.11 In the first of these cases, the Court was called upon to rule on whether a Member State was entitled to set up a body laying down quality standards for fruit. Under the common market organisation for fresh fruit and vegetables, highly detailed quality standards are laid down by the Community. It was little

---

[24] [1975] O.J. L282/1.
[25] *Pigs Marketing Board* (see n.16 above), para. 56.
[26] Cases 36 and 71/80 [1981] E.C.R. 735, para. 19.
[27] Case 222/82 [1983] E.C.R. 4083; [1984] 3 C.M.L.R. 733.
[28] Cases 141–143/81 [1982] E.C.R. 1299; [1983] 2 C.M.L.R. 635.
[29] Case C-309/96 [1997] E.C.R. I-7493.

wonder then that the Court held that this Community legislation was exhaustive and that "any attempt by such a body to impose compliance with [its recommendations as to quality] by applying any sort of penalties or by using the authority vested in it by its constitution to bring pressure to bear on growers or on traders would be unlawful." On the other hand, such a body could lawfully give advice on the quality and presentation of fruit, it was held.

10.12   At the other end of the spectrum is *Holdijk*. The defendants there were charged with keeping fatting calves in enclosures which fell below the minimum requirements stipulated in Dutch law. They contended *inter alia* that the relevant common organisation of the market precluded Member States from enacting such legislation. However, the Court found that "as it stands at present Community law contains no specific rules for the protection of animals kept for farming purposes." On this basis, it ruled:

> "the establishment of such an organisation pursuant to Article [34] of the Treaty does not have the effect of exempting agricultural producers from any national provisions intended to attain objectives other than those covered by the common organisation, even though such provisions may by affecting the conditions of production, have an impact on the volume or the cost of national production and therefore on the operation of the Common Market in the sector concerned...
>
> In those circumstances, the absence of any provision for the protection of animals kept for farming purposes in the regulations establishing common organisations of the agricultural markets cannot be interpreted as rendering the national rules in that field inapplicable pending the possible adoption of Community provisions at a later stage."[30]

Similarly, in *Annibaldi* the Court has in effect held that the establishment of a common market organisation does not preclude the Member States from adopting environmental or planning restrictions. The plaintiff in the main case, who was refused permission to plant an orchard in a regional park, claimed *inter alia* that this refusal fell foul of the prohibition in Article 34(2) on "discrimination between producers" imposed by, or pursuant to, a common market organisation. Quoting the passage from *Holdijk* cited here, the Court dismissed this argument—to the point where the question referred for a preliminary ruling was held to be inadmissible on the basis that it had no link with Community law!

10.13   Between these two extremes lies a grey area in which it is not nearly so easy to determine whether national legislation is pre-empted. This is illustrated by three cases delivered within a few months of one another.

A particularly generous approach towards the Member States was taken in *Jongeneel Kaas v Netherlands*.[31] That case concerned Dutch legislation relating to the quality of cheeses produced in the Netherlands. The Court held that

---

[30] See para. 8.114 above.
[31] Case 237/82 [1984] E.C.R. 483; [1985] 2 C.M.L.R. 53; noted by Waelbroeck (1985) C.M.L. Rev. 117.

national legislation of this kind was lawful, since there was no Community legislation on the matter. This in itself seems wholly uncontroversial. However, the Dutch legislation also set out an exhaustive list of cheeses which could be produced in the Netherlands (this naturally included traditionally Dutch cheeses such as Gouda and Edam, but it also covered Cheddar and Feta). Even though this in no way limited the varieties which could be sold in the Netherlands, the Court's ruling that such a measure was compatible with the common market organisation for milk and milk products seems questionable. Indeed, the Advocate General was of the opposite opinion, since he considered that "such a policy harms sales and thereby adversely affects the functioning of the common organisation of the market." It is submitted that, once a product is covered by a common market organisation, it should not be open to any Member State to prohibit its production, subject to considerations of public health, the protection of industrial and commercial property and the like.

Next, in *Prantl*[32] the Court was called upon to decide whether a German statutory provision to the effect that only wines from certain specified regions of Germany could be marketed in bottles of a particular shape known as "Bocksbeutel" was compatible with the Community legislation forming part of the common market organisation for wine. This case concerned imports from Italy which did not comply with the German measure; it therefore differed from *Jongeneel*, which related to the application of Dutch legislation to Dutch produce. The Council Regulation setting up that common market organisation stipulated that the Council "shall adopt, as necessary, the rules relating to the designation and presentation" of wine products, but the only implementing Regulation protecting the use of particular bottles concerned the bottle known as the *flûte d'Alsace*. Since the protection of bottles was only "of secondary importance in relation to a common organisation of the market" the Court ruled that, by adopting a Regulation protecting the *flûte d'Alsace*, the Community had not precluded Member States from protecting other types of bottle.[33]

Finally, the accused in *Pluimveeslachterij Midden-Nederland*[34] were Dutch companies which owned slaughterhouses and which were charged with infringing the Dutch legislation on the packaging and slaughtering of poultry. They claimed that the Dutch legislation was pre-empted by the common market organisation for poultry. However, although the Council Regulation establishing that organisation provided for legislation to be adopted on these matters, no relevant Community legislation had in fact been passed. The Commission had submitted a proposal to the Council several years before, but there had been a deadlock in the Council. Accordingly, the Court found that "there cannot in principle be any objection" to national legislation of the kind in question. However, it held that:

---

[32] Case 16/83 [1984] E.C.R. 1299; [1985] 2 C.M.L.R. 238.
[33] However, the Court went on to hold that such national legislation was contrary to Art. 28: see para. 8.154 above.
[34] Cases 47 and 48/83 [1984] E.C.R. 1721.

"such measures may not be regarded as involving the exercise of the Member State's own power, but as the fulfilment of the duty to cooperate in achieving the aims of the common organisation of the market which, in a situation characterised by the inaction of the Community legislature, Article [10 (ex 5)] of the Treaty imposes on them. Consequently, the measures adopted by the Member States may only be temporary and provisional in nature and they must cease to be applied as soon as Community measures are introduced."

While the national measures were held to be lawful in each of these cases, the fact remains that the Court's approach and reasoning have differed. Yet it seems safe to conclude with Waelbroeck[35] that "a presumption seems to exist that Member States retain the power to regulate a subject matter falling within the scope of a common organisation of the market, but not specifically regulated by that organisation, unless there is a clear indication that the Community intended the field to remain free."

10.14   One area of particular difficulty is the obligation to affiliate to a particular organisation before marketing goods.

The first case was *Vriend*.[36] There the defendant had been found guilty of selling several lots of chrysanthemum cuttings in the Netherlands without being affiliated to a body which bore the acronym NAKS. By virtue of a Dutch Royal Decree a person selling such products was required to be affiliated to this body. The Dutch court hearing the case referred two questions to the Court of Justice asking whether a requirement of this kind was compatible with Articles 28 to 38 of the Treaty and with Regulation 234/68[37] on the establishment of a common organisation of the market in trees and plants. The Court replied that:

"national rules of the kind referred to by the national court whereby a Member State, directly or through the intermediary of bodies established or approved by an official authority, reserves exclusively to persons affiliated to such bodies the right to market, resell, import, export and offer for export material for plant propagation such as chrysanthemum plants which are covered by the common organisation of the market in live trees and other plants ... established by Regulation 234/68 ... is incompatible with the said Regulation and also with Articles [28 and 29] of the [EC] Treaty."

The ruling in *Van Luipen*[38] was very much on the same lines. On the other hand, in *Apple and Pear Development Council*[39] it was held that the obligation to become a member of a body whose activities did not relate to intra- Community trade was lawful unless the activities of that body were themselves contrary to Community law.

Finally, in *Jongeneel Kaas*[40] it was held to be compatible with the Regulation setting up the common market organisation in milk products to require cheese

---

[35] *op. cit.*, n.31 above at p. 123.
[36] Case 94/79 [1980] E.C.R. 327; [1980] 3 C.M.L.R. 473.
[37] [1968] J.O. L55/1.
[38] Case 29/82 [1983] E.C.R. 151; [1983] 2 C.M.L.R. 681.
[39] See n.27 above.
[40] See n.31 above.

producers to be members of a national body whose function was to check that nationally produced cheese complied with national standards, provided that (i) the national standards were themselves compatible with Community law and (ii) the marketing, resale, importation, exportation and offer for exportation of cheese was not reserved to members of this body.

The state of the law thus seems somewhat unclear, but the present position may perhaps be summarised as follows:

— producers of an agricultural product subject to a common market organisation may be required to affiliate to a particular national body provided that the aims and activities of that body are themselves compatible
   with Community law;

— sales (other than by a producer to a wholesaler in the same Member
   State) may not be subject to the requirement to affiliate to a national
   body.

10.15 Another fraught question is to what extent Member States are entitled to impose production quotas. In two early cases, *Officier van Justitie v Van Haaster*[41] and *Officier van Justitie v Van den Hazel*,[42] such quotas were held to contravene the two common market organisations concerned. In *Van Haaster* the accused was charged with growing hyacinth bulbs without holding a licence required under Dutch law. This licensing system was tantamount to a production quota system. A reference for a preliminary ruling was made asking whether this scheme was compatible with Article 10 of Regulation 234/68[43] setting up a common market organisation in trees and plants, which Article prohibited quantitative restrictions and measures of equivalent effect. This is one of the simplest common market organisations, containing little more than rules relating to common quality standards. Nevertheless, "in the light of the objects and purposes of the Regulation within the framework of the principles laid down by the Treaty itself" the Court found that a national system of this kind was contrary to Article 10.

The decision in *Van den Hazel* was along similar lines. There a national scheme of slaughter quotas for poultry was held to be contrary to Regulation 123/67[44] setting up a common market organisation in poultry meat.

Yet in *Procureur de la République v Forest*[45] a French system of milling quotas was held to be compatible with Regulation 2727/75[46] on the common market organisation in cereals. The Court gave three reasons for this ruling: the quota system in issue did not concern the production of flour for export; the total sum of all the quotas allocated considerably exceeded demand within France; and Regulation 2727/75 provided for the setting of prices and other matters for

---

[41] See n.17 above.
[42] Case 111/76 [1977] E.C.R. 901.
[43] See n.37 above.
[44] [1967] J.O. 2301.
[45] Case 148/85 [1986] E.C.R. 3449; [1988] 2 C.M.L.R. 577.
[46] [1975] O.J. L281/1.

cereals, not flour. However, it is submitted as to the second point that the very fact that the defendants were prosecuted for exceeding their milling quotas showed that these quotas constituted a real restriction. As to the last point, one would have thought that any major interference by a Member State in the production of flour must inevitably undermine the Community market mechanisms for cereals.

10.16   In considering this area of the law, it should be remembered that in one respect common organisations of the market may go beyond Articles 28 and 29: the regulations setting up these common organisations often prohibit restrictions on trade even within each Member State.[47] On the other hand, in principle Articles 28 and 29 apply only to restrictions on trade between one Member State and another.[48]

10.17   On a different point, the Court has consistently held that national measures falling under Articles 28 or 29 cannot be justified on the grounds that they are designed to further the aims of the Common Agricultural Policy.[49]

III. THE COMPLETION OF THE INTERNAL MARKET

10.18   The impact of Article 14 (ex 7A) of the Treaty, which required the internal market to be completed by the end of 1992, is considered at length elsewhere in this book.[50] Among the myriad measures taken for the completion of the internal market in accordance with this provision are a certain number relating to agriculture. These include:

— the abolition of monetary compensation amounts[51];

— the adoption of a new common market organisation for "sheepmeat" and "goatmeat"[52]; and

— the adoption of a common market organisation for bananas[53].

---

[47] See, *e.g.* Art. 10 of Reg. 234/68, (see n.37 above).
[48] See paras 6.96 *et seq.* above.
[49] See para 8.37 above
[50] Paras 6.10, 7.04 and 12.12 *et seq.*
[51] Council Reg. 3813/92 ([1992] O.J. L387/1), para. 4.15 above.
[52] Council Reg. 3013/89 [1989] O.J. L289/1, replacing Council Reg. 1837/80 (see n.4 above); the later instrument has itself been superseded by Council Reg. 2467/98 [1998] O.J. L312/1.
[53] See n.5 above.

CHAPTER XI

State Monopolies of a Commercial Character

11.01 Article 31 (ex 37) of the Treaty provides as follows:

"1. Member States shall adjust any State monopolies of a commercial character so as to ensure that no discrimination regarding the conditions under which goods are procured and marketed exists between nationals of Member States.

The provisions of this Article shall apply to any body through which a Member State, in law or in fact, either directly or indirectly supervises, determines or appreciably influences imports or exports between Member States. These provisions shall likewise apply to monopolies delegated by the State to others.

2. Member States shall refrain from introducing any new measure which is contrary to the principles laid down in paragraph 1 or which restricts the scope of the Articles dealing with the abolition of customs duties and quantitative restrictions between Member States.

3. If a State monopoly of a commercial character has rules which are designed to make it easier to dispose of agricultural products or obtain for them the best return, steps should be taken in applying the rules contained in this Article to ensure equivalent safeguards for the employment and standard of living of the producers concerned."

This provision was amended by the Treaty of Amsterdam, essentially to remove the transitional provisions which lapsed at the end of 1969.[1]

It applies only to trading monopolies and not to monopolies on production or the provision of services. This is why it appears in the same chapter of the Treaty as the provisions relating to quantitative restrictions and measures of equivalent effect. However, it is also closely linked to the new Article 16 of the EC Treaty and to Articles 86 (ex 90) and 295 (ex 222), which have already been considered in Chapter IX.

11.02 This provision is no stranger to controversy, as evidenced in particular by the once renowned article by Collard which spoke of its "obscure clarity".[2]

---

[1] In addition, the former Art. 37(5), which exempted "existing international agreements", was also removed.

[2] "L'obscure clarté de l'article 37 du traité de la Communauté économique européenne" (1964) *Recueil Dalloz* 266. In this article the author criticises the *Conseil d'Etat* for refusing to refer a question on the interpretation of Art. 31 to the Court of Justice under Art. 234, because the *Conseil d'Etat* considered that the point was an *acte clair* and that a reference was therefore unnecessary (*Société des pétroles Shell Berre*—Act. Jur. 1964 II 438). Hence the ironic expression "obscure clarity".

Possibly as a result, it has undergone a number of vicissitudes, which are documented in earlier editions of this work.[3]

In recent years, it has enjoyed something of a renaissance. Until recently, the prevailing view was that this provision had become obsolete. Indeed, the Court's pre-1997 case law gave the distinct impression that Article 31 had little, if any, application independent of Article 28 (ex 30). Moreover, it appeared that the regulation of state monopolies fell to be considered under Article 86 (ex 90), to the virtual exclusion of Article 31. Hence the statement in the previous edition of this book that Article 31 was "ripe for repeal".[4]

However, predictions of the demise of Article 31 have proved to be premature. Not only has it survived the cull of redundant Treaty Articles following the entry into force of the Treaty of Amsterdam, but it has also been invested with renewed vigour by the Court of Justice in a series of cases decided in October 1997, namely: *Franzén*,[5] which related to the Swedish alcohol monopoly; and a raft of four infringement proceedings concerning gas and electricity monopolies.[6] What is more, the insertion of the new Article 16 into the Treaty could perhaps reinforce this trend, even if this provision is not regarded as an exception to the free movement of goods.

11.03   The tensions within this provision are laid bare in two apparently contradictory passages of the judgment in *Franzén*. First, repeating a statement made in a number of earlier rulings,[7] the Court summarised the essence of Article 31 as follows:

> "It is clear not only from the wording of Article [31] but also from the position which it occupies in the general scheme of the Treaty that the article is designed to ensure compliance with the fundamental principle that goods should be able to move freely throughout the common market, in particular by requiring quantitative restrictions and measures having equivalent effect in trade between Member States to be abolished, and thereby to ensure maintenance of normal conditions of competition between the economies of Member States in the event that a given product is subject, in one or other of those States, to a national monopoly of a commercial character...".[8]

Two paragraphs later, it added:

---

[3] See generally Buendia Sierra, *Exclusive Rights and State Monopolies under EC law* (OUP, 1999) at pp. 75–128; Hochbaum in Groeben, Thiesing, Ehlermann *Kommentar, zum EU-/EG-Vertrag* (5th ed. 1997) Vol. I, 846; de Cockborne in Mégret, *Le droit de la CEE* (2nd ed., 1992) Vol. I, 307; Wyatt and Dashwood, *European Union Law* (4th ed., 2001) 357.

[4] At p. 352; see also Tesauro, "The Community's Internal Market in the light of the Recent Case-law of the Court of Justice" (1995) 15 Y.E.L. 1 at 16 where Article 31 was described as "obsolete".

[5] C-189/95 [1997] E.C.R. I-5909.

[6] Cases C-157/94 *Commission v Netherlands* [1997] E.C.R. I-5699; C-158/94 *Commission v Italy* [1997] E.C.R. I-5789; C-159/94 *Commission v France* [1997] E.C.R. I-5815; and C-160/94 *Commission v Spain* [1997] ECR I-5851. See note by Slot (1998) 35 C.M.L. Rev. 1183.

[7] Case 59/75 *Pubblico Ministero v Manghera* [1976] E.C.R. 91; [1976] I C.M.L.R. 557, para. 9; Case 91/78 *Hansen v Hauptzollamt Flensburg* [1979] E.C.R. 935, para. 8; Case 78/82 *Commission v Italy* [1983] E.C.R. 1955, para. 11; Case C-347/88 *Commission v Greece* [1990] E.C.R. I-4747, para. 42; and Case C-387/93 *Banchero* [1995] E.C.R. I-4663, para. 27.

[8] Para. 37.

"The purpose of Article [31] is to reconcile the possibility for Member States to maintain certain monopolies of a commercial character as instruments for the pursuit of public interest aims with the requirements of the establishment and functioning of the common market. It aims at the elimination of obstacles to the free movement of goods, save, however, for restrictions on trade which are inherent in the existence of the monopolies in question."[9]

As explained in paragraph 11.14 below, the question as to what restrictions might be regarded as "inherent in the existence of the monopolies in question" is fraught with difficulty.

Some Established Principles

11.04   Whilst it is true that Article 31 has taken on a new lease of life in recent years, that in no way precludes various long-established principles from continuing to apply. First among these is that Article 31(1) and (2) are both directly applicable: in *Pubblico Ministero v Manghera*[10] and *Rewe-Zentral v HZA Landau*[11] the Court ruled that Article 31(1) was directly applicable since the end of the transitional period, while in *Costa v ENEL*[12] Article 31(2) was held to have possessed this quality since the entry into force of the Treaty.

11.05   Second, the Court has always made it clear that Article 31 does not require national monopolies having a commercial character to be abolished, but merely their adjustment in such a way as to ensure that no discrimination regarding the conditions under which goods are procured and marketed exists between nationals of Member States.[13]

11.06   Third, it is also well established that Article 31 only applies to "goods", which concept has the same meaning as in Articles 28 and 29. The Court of Justice reached this conclusion in *Sacchi*[14] on the basis of the position of Article 31 in the Treaty (in the Chapter on quantitative restrictions) and of its use of the terms "imports", "exports" and "products". It followed that a monopoly of television advertising, being a service within the meaning of Article 49 (ex 59), did not fall within Article 31.

In *Société Coopérative du Béarn v Mialocq*,[15] the Court confirmed this ruling, adding however that:

"the possibility cannot be ruled out that a monopoly over the provision of services may

---

[9] Para. 39.
[10] See n.7 above.
[11] Case 45/75 [1976] E.C.R. 181; [1976] 2 C.M.L.R. 1.
[12] Case 6/64 [1964] E.C.R. 585; [1964] C.M.L.R. 425.
[13] Case 59/75 (see n.7 above) para. 5; Case 91/78 (see n.7 above), para. 8; Case 78/82 (see n.7 above), para. 11; C-387/93 (see n.7 above) para. 27; C-157/94 (see n.6 above), para 14; and *Franzén*, (see n.5 above) para. 38.
[14] Case 155/73 [1974] E.C.R. 409; [1974] 2 C.M.L.R. 177.
[15] Case 271/81 [1983] E.C.R. 2057; confirmed in Cases 30/87 *Bodson v Pompes Funèbres* [1988] E.C.R. 2479; and C-17/94 *Denis Gervais* [1995] E.C.R. I-4353.

have an indirect influence on trade in goods between Member States. Thus an undertaking or group of undertakings which exercises a monopoly over the provision of certain services may contravene the principle of the free movement of goods, if, for example, such a monopoly leads to discrimination against imported products as opposed to products of domestic origin."

11.07 Fourth, Article 31 applies to goods originating in third countries but put into free circulation in the Community, as is clear from Article 23 (2) (ex 9(2))[16]; but it does not apply to direct trade with third countries. In *Hansen v HZA Flensburg*[17] (Hansen II) the Court deduced this also from the position and the wording of Article 31. It concluded that "the provisions of that Article cannot be applied to products imported from third countries since the arrangements for the importation of such products are subject not to the provisions governing the internal market but to those relating to commercial policy".

11.08 Fifth, although the Court has not yet ruled on the point, a production monopoly is generally considered not to constitute a State monopoly "of a commercial character" (*Handelsmonopol* in the German version), within the meaning of Article 31.[18] However, difficulties will arise in so far as a body enjoying a monopoly of production is also granted exclusive rights to sell its produce, at least at the retail stage.[19]

It should also be noted that a State monopoly "of a commercial character" was found to exist in *Commission v Netherlands (electricity)*[20] despite the Dutch Government's argument that the monopoly in question (SEP) did not have a "commercial character" because its principal task was the planning and commissioning of production units and the pooling of production and transmission costs at national level. The Court rejected that argument simply by recalling that Article 31 applied to situations in which the national authorities were in a position to control, direct or appreciably influence trade between Member States through a body established for that purpose.[21] The fact that SEP did not carry on any commercial activity in the strict sense was thus irrelevant.

11.09 Sixth, Article 31 covers retail monopolies as well as wholesale monopolies. This emerges clearly from *Commission v France* where retail price controls on tobacco were held to be contrary, *inter alia*, to Article 31, since a State monopoly enjoyed exclusive rights of manufacture and retail sale.[22]

---

[16] Case 119/78 *Peureux v Directeur des Services Fiscaux* [1979] E.C.R. 975; [1980] 3 C.M.L.R. 337.
[17] See n.7 above.
[18] De Cockborne, *op. cit.*, see n.3 above, at 331.2.
[19] Case 90/82 *Commission* v *France* (manufactured tobacco) [1983] E.C.R. 2011; [1984] 2 C.M.L.R. 516. Hochbaum, *op. cit.* at 867, suggests that this will apply where the production monopoly enjoys the exclusive right to sell at the wholesale stage.
[20] See n.6 above.
[21] Para. 20 of the judgment.
[22] See n.19 above.

The Definition of a "State Monopoly"

11.10 The second sub-paragraph of Article 31(1) lays down a wide definition of the term "State monopoly", which is not limited to public bodies but extends also to monopolies delegated by the State to a private enterprise. However, the expression "in law or in fact" is not to be taken as extending Article 31 to private enterprises enjoying a monopoly without any intervention from the State; rather, this limb of the second sub-paragraph is to be construed as covering only those private bodies on which the State has conferred certain powers amounting in fact to a monopoly.[23] Otherwise Article 31 would encroach on Article 82 (ex 86); and, as we noticed in Chapter IV, Title I in general relates only to acts attributable to the Member States.

Furthermore, it is not entirely free from doubt whether the monopoly must have some institutional structure, as the term "body" in the English text and similar terms in most of the other language texts would suggest. Today, the prevailing view would seem to be that some such structure is required,[24] despite the use of the word "*Einrichtung*" (which can mean "arrangement") in the German text. Certainly, the Court's ruling in Case *Commission v France* (artificial insemination)[25] established that an import licensing system does not in itself constitute a State monopoly, a point which the Commission in any event conceded. Moreover, in *Bodson v Pompes Funèbres*[26] the Court held that "Article [31] applies in particular to situations in which the national authorities are in a position to supervise, determine or even appreciably influence trade between Member States through *a body* established for that purpose or a monopoly delegated to others" (emphasis added).[27]

What if the territory of a Member State is divided up into different areas and each local authority is entitled or obliged to exercise or grant a monopoly in its area? This situation arose in *Bodson*. The Court held that Article 31 does indeed apply to monopolies "operated by an undertaking or group of undertakings, or by the territorial units of a State such as communes". It has thus given a liberal construction to the term "State monopolies" ("*monopoles nationaux*" in the French text). This ruling is to be welcomed since, as the Advocate General pointed out, Member States could otherwise circumvent the prohibition in Article 31 by the simple expedient of creating a large number of local monopolies. Quite what proportion of the national territory (or trade) must be covered before such a series of local monopolies can be said to exercise

---

[23] De Cockborne, *op. cit.* n.3 above at 313.

[24] De Cockborne *op. cit.*, at 313; Hochbaum, *op. cit.* at 869. In the early years the contrary view prevailed: see the Commission's Recommendation to France on the allocation of import licences to private undertakings ([1963] J. O. 2271) and Gand A.G. in Case 20/64 *Albatros v Sopéco* [1965] E.C.R. 29 at 44; [1965] C.M.L.R. 159.

[25] Case 161/82 [1983] E.C.R. 2079.

[26] See n.15 above, para. 13 of the judgment. See also Case C-393/92 *Amelo v Energiebedrijf Ijsseelmij* [1994] E.C.R. I-1477, para. 29, and *Banchero*, (see n.7 above) para. 26.

[27] See also, to identical effect Case C-157/94 *Commission v Netherlands* (see n.6 above), at para. 20.

"appreciable influence" on inter-State trade and thus to fall under Article 31 remains obscure.[28]

However, in *Commission v Greece* (oil and petroleum products)[29] a State monopoly of a commercial character was held to exist where the body in question enjoyed the exclusive right to import and market 65 per cent of the requirements of the domestic market. This right, held the Court, gave Greece "an appreciable influence" over imports from other Member States. The Court did not state what percentage was necessary to constitute an "appreciable influence".

In *Commission v Netherlands* (electricity), citing that earlier judgment, the Court held in effect that the Dutch body in question (SEP) constituted a State monopoly for the purposes of Article 31 although final consumers were free to import electricity for their own needs: it was not disputed that SEP alone was authorised to import electricity for public distribution.[30]

11.11   As already mentioned, the Court held in *Commission v France* (artificial insemination) that an import licensing system does not constitute a "State monopoly". It seems hard to quibble with this conclusion: the term "State monopoly" scarcely seems apt to describe a scheme established by the State under which any applicant is entitled to an import, export or retail sales licence (as the case may be), subject only to objective conditions that are easily met. There are two reasons for this: a scheme in which any comers are able to participate, both as a matter of law and as a matter of fact, is not a "monopoly" at all; and such an arrangement does not enable the State to "supervise, determine or appreciably influence" imports or exports, as required by the second sub-paragraph of Article 31(1).

The scheme in issue in *Banchero*[31] was not far removed from this. That case concerned Italian legislation creating a "State monopoly" over the importation of and trade in manufactured tobacco. These activities were limited to holders of licences granted by the Autonomous Administration of State Monopolies (AAMS); that body also owned the warehouses in which imports were required to be kept, unless it specifically authorised storage in private warehouses. Imports were subject to a special tax of the same amount as the consumption tax, and a stamp was then affixed. Over 70,000 retail sales outlets were duly licensed within Italy. The AAMS laid down various conditions as to locations and times of sales and other matters, but did not influence the retailer's choice of product. It must be said, however, that the report of the judgment does not give an exhaustive account of the requirements imposed by the AAMS. At all events,

---

[28] Note that the Court went on to hold that, where a certain number of communes constituting a significant proportion of the national territory had granted an exclusive concession to members of the same group of undertakings and that group was therefore able to influence patterns of trade, no State monopoly existed. The reason given by the Court for the latter conclusion was— rather surprisingly—that the position of the group was not then attributable to any act of the public authorities, but to the conduct of the group itself.

[29] Case C-347/88 (see n.7 above).

[30] Paras 16 to 18 of the judgment.

[31] See n.7 above.

unlawful possession of tobacco within Italy was punishable as smuggling, and the accused in the main case was charged with that offence. Given the unintrusive nature of this scheme and the very large number of authorised retailers, one might have expected the Court to rule that no State monopoly within the meaning of Article 31 existed at all, whatever its denomination in national law. However, the Court avoided the issue by finding that the measures at issue "do not concern the exercise by a public monopoly of its exclusive right but apply in a general manner to the production and marketing of goods, whether or not they are covered by the monopoly in question".[32] As explained further below, the Court therefore concluded that those measures fell to be examined under Article 28, not Article 31. Yet, it would surely have been more logical for the Court to decide first whether a State monopoly within the meaning of the latter provision existed at all.

The situation in *Franzén* was clearly at the other end of the scale. The Swedish State had created a body, *Systembolaget*, which undoubtedly constituted a State monopoly for the sale and importation of alcohol. While import licences could be granted to other parties, the conditions for the award of such licences were very stringent, both in financial and in other respects. Accordingly, there could be no doubt that Systembolaget was indeed a State monopoly—although it is striking that the Court examined the import licensing system under Article 28, not Article 31.

Clearly, then, in determining this question one must have regard to the economic realities, and in particular the stringency of the conditions imposed for the grant of licences.

11.12 The concept of "collective dominance" under Article 82 (ex 86) is well known.[33] It arises because that provision speaks of an abuse of a dominant position held by "one or more undertakings". In contrast, there would appear to be little room for the concept of a "collective State monopoly" under Article 31 where the right to trade is limited to a small number of enterprises in a particular territory—except where they are truly acting as a single entity. The idea that a number of discrete entities acting separately could constitute a "collective monopoly" must be regarded as something of a contradiction in terms. If it is right that only bodies having some institutional structure can constitute State monopolies within the meaning of this provision, then such a concept is excluded in any event.

The Prohibitions in Article 31(1) and (2)

11.13 Article 31(1) provides that Member States shall "adjust" their State monopolies so as to ensure that no discrimination in the procurement or

---

[32] Para. 29 of the judgment.
[33] See, *e.g.* Cases C-395–6/95P *Compagnie Maritime Belge v Commission* [2000] 4 C.M.L.R. 1076; Monti, "The Scope of Collective Dominance under Article 82 EC" [2001] C.M.L. Rev. 131; Whish, "Collective Dominance" in O'Keeffe and Bavasso (eds.) *Liber Amicorum in Honour of Lord Slynn of Hadley*, Vol. I: Judicial Review in European Law p. 581.

marketing of goods occurs. Read literally, this would appear to suggest that non-discriminatory restrictions on the free movement may be tolerated. In contrast, the scope of Article 31(2), which prohibits the introduction of new restrictions, is worded more broadly: "Member States shall refrain from introducing any new measure which is contrary to the principles laid down in paragraph 1 or which restricts the scope of the Articles dealing with the abolition of customs duties and quantitative restrictions between Member States". No mention is made here of discrimination, but then measures of equivalent effect are not mentioned either.

In *Rewe v Bundesmonopolverwaltung für Branntwein* ("Cassis de Dijon"),[34] the Advocate General took the view that non-discriminatory measures of equivalent effect fall outside Article 31(1); indeed, that was the case with the minimum alcohol requirement at issue in those proceedings. Yet, as we noticed in paragraph 11.03 above, the Court has repeatedly held that Article 31 "is designed to ensure compliance with the fundamental principle that goods should be able to move freely throughout the common market, in particular by requiring quantitative restrictions and measures having equivalent effect in trade between Member States to be abolished". This very broad formulation covers all types of quantitative restriction and measures of equivalent effect.

In the same passage quoted in paragraph 11.03, the Court also held that Article 31 is equally designed to "ensure maintenance of normal conditions of competition between the economies of Member States in the event that a given product is subject, in one or other of those States, to a national monopoly of a commercial character".[35] Whether this statement incorporates by reference concepts derived from Articles 81 and 82 (ex 85 and 86) and the Treaty provisions on State aids is a moot point.[36]

11.14 As we also noticed in paragraph 11.03, the Court in *Franzén* created a bold new exception covering "restrictions on trade which are inherent in the existence of the monopolies in question". The precise scope of this exception can only be a matter of speculation, as the Court has never applied it. Some commentators have suggested that it is possible that the Court intended by that passage in *Franzén* to introduce a "rule of reason" as a justification for national measures that would otherwise infringe Article 31.[37] That would, to some extent at least, be consistent with the Court's finding that Article 30 cannot serve as a justification for restrictions prohibited by Article 31.[38] However, the mystery surrounding the apparent exception mentioned in *Franzén* is compounded by

---

[34] Case 120/78 [1979] E.C.R. 649 at 667; [1979] 3 C.M.L.R. 494 (paras 6.43 *et seq.* above).
[35] See also C-347/88 (see n.7 above), para. 42; and C-387/93 (see n.7 above), para. 27.
[36] In Case 78/82 (see n.7 above), the Court set out the same statement (at para. 11 of the judgment) which it then applied at paras 16 to 19 of the judgment. However, the requirement that the "maintenance of normal conditions of competition" be ensured was applied in accordance with the Court's case law on price fixing and the free movement of goods (see discussion at paras 7.75 *et seq.* of this work) and did not, in that case at least, import concepts derived from the Treaty's competition rules.
[37] See Mortelmans, [1998] S.E.W. 30 at 33; and Slot, (1998) 35 C.M.L. Rev. 1183 at 1195–6.
[38] But see discussion at para. 11.21 below.

the fact that it applies cumulatively with that in Article 86(2).[39] It is also notable that in *Franzén* itself, the Court did not apply the exception (since it concluded that the Swedish measures in question were not discriminatory or apt to put imported products at a disadvantage). There is thus considerable uncertainty as to the existence, nature and scope of the apparent exception in *Franzén* for "restrictions on trade which are inherent in the existence of the monopolies in question".[40]

11.15 At all events, it is axiomatic that, in principle, Article 31 requires exclusive import rights enjoyed by State monopolies to be abolished,[41] as must exclusive export rights.[42] In some of the earlier cases, the Commission argued that the same must apply to the exclusive right to market imported goods, since otherwise the abolition of the exclusive import right would be a hollow gesture. However, in *Franzén* the Court held the monopoly over retail alcohol sales in Sweden to be lawful.

11.16 A consideration of the Court's more detailed examination of the Swedish alchohol monopoly in *Franzén* is especially instructive. After examining the various aspects of the Swedish scheme, the Court held them all to fall outside Article 31. First, the Court found that the product selection system operated by the monopoly (*Systembolaget*) did not appear to be either discriminatory or apt to put imported products at a disadvantage.[43] Second, the Court acknowledged that the sales network maintained by *Systembolaget* was restricted, but held that such imperfections did not adversely affect the sale of alcoholic beverages from other Member States more than the sale of alcoholic beverages produced in Sweden.[44] Finally, the Court held that the restrictions that operated on the promotion of alcoholic beverages, namely those that confined such "promotion" to the provision of information by the monopoly alone without the control and direction of suppliers, was compatible with Article 31 insofar as it applied independently of the products' origin and was

---

[39] Para. 9.12 above. Mortelmans has pointed out (*op. cit.* at 33) that para. 39 of the judgment in *Franzen* dealing with the apparent new rule of reason exception to Article 31 ("The purpose of Article [31] of the Treaty is to reconcile the possibility for Member States to maintain certain monopolies of a commercial character as instruments for the pursuit of public interest aims with the requirements of the establishment and functioning of the common market") is strikingly similar to paragraph 39 of *Commission v Netherlands (electricity)* dealing with the exception in Article 86(2) ("Article [86(2)] seeks to reconcile the Member States' interest in using certain undertakings, in particular in the public sector, as an instrument of economic or fiscal policy with the Community's interest in ensuring compliance with the rules on competition and the preservation of the unity of the common market"). Given this, the fact that the apparent new rule of reason applies cumulatively with the exception in Art. 86(2) may thus be less troublesome than at first appears.

[40] See Blum, "De Sacchi à Franzén en passant par La Crespelle" [1999] *Gazette du Palais* III Doct.p. 1031 at 1036–7; and Mortelmans, [1998] S.E.W. 30 at 33.

[41] Case 59/75 (see n.7 above) para. 33; Case C-347/88 (see n.7 above) para. 44; Case C-159/94 (see n.6 above), para. 33.

[42] Case C-159/94 (see n.6 above), para. 34.

[43] Paras. 43 to 52 of the judgment.

[44] Paras. 53 to 57 of the judgment.

not in itself apt to put at a disadvantage beverages imported from other Member States in relation to those produced on national territory.[45] The indulgent approach may be explained in part by the fact that Mr Franzén had not challenged the ban on advertising virtually all alcoholic products outside the point of retail sale.[46]

Significantly, in *Konsumentombudsmannen v Gourmet International*[47] where the latter ban was directly challenged, it was found to be discriminatory and thus caught by Article 28. One of the factors taken into account by the Court was that all points of retail sale were in the hands of the monopoly, which only distributed its own literature. At the least, that judgment must be regarded as reflecting a hardening of the Court's position in *Franzén* on this point.

11.17   Further light has been shed on the requirements of Article 31(1) and (2) by the decisions in the gas and electricity cases mentioned earlier. In each case, the Court held that there was a *prima facie* breach of Article 31[48]— although, as explained in paragraph 9.12 above, it went on to rule that such measures might be cured by Article 86(2).[49]

In *Commission v Italy* (electricity), the Court rejected the Italian Government's argument that it was necessary for the purposes of Article 31 for there to be evidence of the existence of an actual obstacle and therefore of real discrimination suffered by the imported product as compared to the domestic product. Thus, evidence adduced by the Italian Government to the effect that the level of imports of electricity into Italy had constantly increased in recent years was held to be irrelevant.[50] The Italian Government's reliance on the judgment in *Keck and Mithouard*[51] with respect to the exclusive import rights in question was also roundly rejected on the basis that that judgment was concerned only with national provisions which limited or prohibited certain selling arrangements and not national legislation designed to regulate trade in goods between Member States.[52]

As to export restrictions, the Court incorporated its case law interpreting Article 29 (ex 34) into Article 31.[53] Thus in *Commission v France* (electricity and gas),[54] once the French Government had conceded that available national production both of electricity and of gas was reserved as a matter of priority to users within French territory, the Court held that the relevant monopoly's exclusive export rights had, if not the object, at least the effect of "specifically restricting patterns of exports and thereby establishing a difference in treat-

---

[45] Paras. 58 to 65 of the judgment.
[46] Para. 61 of the judgment.
[47] Case C-405/98 [2001] E.C.R. I-1795; see para. 7.45 above.
[48] See n.6 above.
[49] See C-158/94 (see n.6 above), para. 43; C-157/94 (see n.6 above), para. 32; and C-159/94 (see n.6 above), para. 49.
[50] Para. 32 of the judgment.
[51] C-268/91 [1993] E.C.R. I-6097. See paras 6.54 *et seq.*
[52] Para. 31 of the judgment.
[53] See paras 6.79 *et seq.*
[54] See n.6 above.

ment between domestic trade and export trade, in such a way as to provide a special advantage for the French domestic market".[55]

The Court's finding of breaches of Article 31 in each of the above cases was somewhat softened by its further finding that Article 86(2) was capable of justifying the grant by a Member State to an undertaking entrusted with the operation of services of general economic interest of exclusive rights which are contrary to Article 31. This aspect of the judgments was discussed at paragraph 9.12 above.

Article 31 and other Treaty Articles

11.18 Until recently, the Court has given the appearance of preferring to decide cases on the basis of other Treaty provisions instead of Article 31. It has regularly held:

> "the rules contained in Article [31] concern only activities intrinsically connected with the specific business of the monopoly and are irrelevant to national provisions which have no connection with such specific business".[56]

In *"Cassis de Dijon"*[57] it ruled:

> "Article [31] relates specifically to State monopolies of a commercial character. That provision is therefore irrelevant with regard to national provisions which do not concern the exercise by a public monopoly of its specific function—namely, its exclusive right—but apply in a general manner to the production and marketing of alcoholic beverages, whether or not the latter are covered by the monopoly in question. That being the case, the effect on intra-Community trade of the measure referred to by the national court must be examined solely in relation to the requirements under Article [28]."

The Court went further in *Commission v Greece* (oil and petroleum monopoly),[58] holding that an exclusive importing right conferred by the State on its monopoly infringed Article 28 as well as Article 31. It was to confirm this view in *France v Commission*[59] (telecommunications). Hence the conclusion in the last edition of this book that Article 31 had become largely or wholly redundant.

11.19 As mentioned at the outset, this state of affairs has changed in recent years and Article 31 has enjoyed something of a renaissance as a provision with independent force. In *Franzén*,[60] the Court reverted to a demarcation between Articles 28 to 30 (ex 30 to 36) and Article 31, which it had developed in an

---

[55] Para. 35 of the judgment. See also C-158/94 (see n.6 above), para. 25.

[56] *e.g.* Cases 86/78 *Peureux v Directeur des Services Fiscaux v Directeur des Services Fiscaut* [1979] E.C.R. 897; [1980] 3 C.M.L.R. 337, 119/78 (see n.16 above); and C-78/90 *Compagnie Commerciale de L'Ouest v Receveur principal des Douanes* [1992] E.C.R. I-1847.

[57] See n.34 above.

[58] See n.7 above.

[59] Case C-202/88 [1991] E.C.R. I-1223.

[60] See n.5 above.

earlier phase.[61] On the one hand, Article 31 is applicable to the exercise by a domestic commercial monopoly of its exclusive rights.[62] On the other hand, the effect on intra-Community trade of the other provisions of national legislation "which are separable from the operation of the monopoly although they have a bearing upon it" is governed by Article 28.[63]

Nevertheless, it is not easy to see the precise location of the distinction between provisions as to the exercise of exclusive rights and those which merely bear upon, but are separable from, the monopoly. In *Franzén* itself, the Court treated Swedish requirements that the monopoly obtain supplies of alcoholic beverages only from holders of production licences or wholesale licences (whose grant is subject to restrictive conditions) as separable from the monopoly, and thus subject to the scrutiny of Article 28 rather than 31.[64]

What is more, the electricity and gas cases are of no assistance on this point. In those cases the Court simply held that "[t]he arguments concerning Article 31 should be examined first"[65] without giving reasons as to why that was the case. Then, having found breaches of Article 31, the Court simply observed that it was unnecessary to consider the application of Articles 28 to 30.[66] It is not clear how the latter finding can be consistent with the distinction drawn in *Franzén*. On the one hand, if all the measures at issue in those cases fell within the exercise of exclusive rights, one would expect, on the basis of *Franzén*, that that would have itself provided a reason for excluding the application of Articles 28 to 30. On the other hand, if some of the measures at issue were separable from the monopoly (though bearing on it), then Articles 28 to 30 should have been applied to those issues.

Regrettably, therefore, the demarcation (if any) between Articles 28 to 30 on the one hand and Article 31 on the other, remains unclear.

Article 31(3)

11.20   Can Article 31(3) constitute an exception to the prohibitions contained in Article 31? This paragraph reproduces the former Article 37(4) without the last limb, which lapsed at the end of 1969. In *Charmasson v Minister of Economic Affairs*[67] the Court held that this paragraph had never allowed any derogation from Article 31 and that "equivalent safeguards" referred to in Article 31(3) must themselves be compatible with Article 31(1) and (2). Furthermore, in *Miritz*[68] the Court expressly held that this provision does not derogate from the

---

[61] Case 91/75 *Hauptzollamt Göttingen v Miritz* [1976] E.C.R. 217, para. 5; "Cassis de Dijon" (n.34 above), para 7; *Hansen* (n.7 above), paras 9 and 10.
[62] Para. 35 of the judgment.
[63] Para. 36 of the judgment.
[64] See paras 67–73 of the judgment.
[65] See C-159/94 (See n.6 above), para 30.
[66] See para. 41 of the judgment. The lack of reasoning in the Court's judgment on this point is open to serious criticism: see Mortelmans *op. cit.* at 31–2.
[67] Case 48/74 [1974] E.C.R. 1383; [1975] 2 C.M.L.R. 208, discussed at para. 10.02 above.
[68] See n.61 above.

other provisions of Article 31: on the contrary it was expressed to have effect "in applying the rules" contained in that Article.

The Link with Article 30 (ex 36)

11.21   There is some doubt as to whether Article 30 (ex 36) can be applied to exempt measures falling under Article 31. Article 30 is expressed only to apply to restrictions covered by Articles 28 to 29, and, as already pointed out,[69] Article 30 must be restrictively interpreted.[70]

Yet in *SAIL*[71] the Commission claimed that Article 30 could constitute an exemption from the prohibitions contained in Article 31, in view of the parallelism between that provision and Articles 28 to 29. The Advocate General considered this argument to be at least plausible, although he found the measure in question unnecessarily restrictive and thus incapable of being justified by Article 30 in any case. Again, in *Commission v Greece* (oil and petroleum products) the Court dismissed the defendant's contention based on the public security exception in Article 30 on the grounds of lack of justification, without ruling on whether Article 30 could ever be relied on in relation to Article 31. This judgment appears to imply that Article 30 can be relied on in this way.

More recently however, and as noted above, the Court has held in the electricity and gas cases[72] that since it had found that Article 31 had been breached, it was unnecessary for it to consider the application of Articles 28 to 30.[73] Yet, if Article 30 was indeed capable of forming a justification for restrictions prohibited by Article 31, one would expect consideration of Article 30 to have been necessary. Some authors have deduced from this more recent authority that Article 30 *cannot* be applied to exempt measures falling under Article 31.[74]

On a cynical assessment, given the Court's haphazard approach to the demarcation of this provision from Articles 28 and 29, this question is purely academic: when the Court wishes to find a restriction linked to a State monopoly justified under Article 30, it will contrive to examine the restriction under Articles 28 and 29, thereby conveniently side-stepping the difficulty. For instance, in *Franzén* the import licensing system for alcoholic products was held to fall under Article 28 rather than Article 31, thereby conveniently enabling the Court to consider whether this system was covered by the public health exception in Article 30.[75]

---

[69]   Para. 8.01 above. See also Case 7/68 *Commission v Italy* (art treasures) [1968] E.C.R. 423; [1969] C.M.L.R. 181.
[70]   Thus Mattera, *Le marché unique européen* (1990) at 56 claims that Art. 30 cannot apply to measures falling under Art. 31.
[71]   Case 82/71 [1972] E.C.R. 119; [1972] C.M.L.R. 723.
[72]   See n.6 above.
[73]   See C-159/94 (See n.6 above), para. 41.
[74]   See Slot, (1998) 35 C.M.L. Rev. 1183 at 1194–5; and Blum, *op. cit.* n.40 at 1035. However, the Court went on to dismiss those actions on other grounds; see para. 9.12 above.
[75]   See para. 8.95 above.

Assessment

11.22   While the Court has recently revived Article 31, it has done nothing to dispel the "obscure clarity" of this provision, which has bedevilled it since its inception. None of the fundamental questions surrounding it—such as the precise nature of the obligation imposed on Member States by Article 31(1), or the demarcation between this provision and Articles 28 and 29—has been solved. Moreover, in *Franzén* the Court has now added a further element of potential confusion in the shape of its new-found and open-ended exception for restrictions "inherent in the existence of the monopolies in question".

CHAPTER XII

Community Legislation Relating to the Free Movement of Goods

12.01 A fully fledged discussion of harmonisation in the Community in all its aspects falls outside the scope of this book. Rather, the intention of this Chapter is more limited: to show the reader how Community legislation can set aside the obstacles to the free movement of goods discussed in the previous Chapter, and the relationship between such legislation and Articles 28 to 30 (ex 30 to 36).

After a general section summarising the applicable general principles, we shall go on to consider the legal bases of harmonisation and then the techniques of harmonisation. Next, we shall examine certain Community legislative enactments which are of particular importance in the context of this book, and finally look at the relationship between harmonisation and Articles 28 to 30.

It cannot be sufficiently stressed that this area of law was fundamentally altered by the Single European Act which came into force on July 1, 1987. Some additional amendments were also effected by the Treaty of Maastricht, which entered into force on November 1, 1993 and by the Treaty of Amsterdam, which entered into force on May 1, 1999. The Treaty of Nice, which was signed on February 26, 2001,[1] will make further amendments, which will also be discussed.

The geographical scope of the Treaty provisions on harmonisation has already been considered in Chapter III.

I. GENERAL PRINCIPLES

12.02 Community legislation is governed by a wide range of principles. While not attempting an exhaustive summary, the following paragraphs outline some of the principles which are most important in the context of the free movement of goods.

A. Fundamental Rights

12.03 The role of fundamental rights in the interpretation and application of Article 30 has already been considered in paragraphs 8.38 to 8.40 above. It is

---

[1] [2001] O.J. C80/1.

also clear that, when asked to determine the validity of harmonising measures, the Court will assess the compatibility of the measures with fundamental rights.[2] However, as described previously, the Court has only had clear jurisdiction to do so since the Treaty of Amsterdam, under Article 6(2) of the Treaty on European Union. Accordingly, it is anticipated that there will be a growing number of challenges to harmonisation brought on this basis in the future. It is also possible that the Court will increasingly refer to the Charter of Fundamental Rights which was signed at Nice.[3]

B. Subsidiarity

12.04   The second paragraph of Article 5 (ex 3B), which was inserted into the EC Treaty by the Treaty of Maastricht, reads as follows:

"In areas which do not fall within its exclusive competence, the Community shall take action, in accordance with the principle of subsidiarity, only if and in so far as the objectives of the proposed action cannot be sufficiently achieved by the Member States and can therefore, by reason of the scale or effects of the proposed action, be better achieved by the Community."

Much ink has flowed over the principle of subsidiarity,[4] which is also referred to in Article 2 (ex B) of the Treaty on European Union. It should be noted that this principle applies only "in areas which do not fall within [the Community's] exclusive competence".

---

[2] Case C-377/98 *Netherlands v Parliament and Council* ("biotechnology Directive") [2001] E.C.R. I-7079, paras 69-81 (right to human dignity and integrity). The issue was also raised in Case C-376/98 *Germany v Parliament and Council* ("tobacco advertising") [2000] E.C.R. I-8419, notably as regards freedom of expression and the right to property; the Court did not consider the point, as it annulled the Directive on other grounds, but Fennelly A.G. advised that the Directive should also be partly or wholly annulled on the basis of infringements of these fundamental rights (paras 146-176); see para. 8.102 above. See also the Opinion dated September 10, 2002 of Geelhoed A.G. in Case C-491/01 *The Queen on the application of British American Tobacco and Imperial Tobacco against Secretary of State for Health* (pending).

[3] [2000] O.J. C 364/1; see generally Oliver, "EU and National Constitutions", Community report for FIDE 2002 (www.fide2002.org).

[4] The literature is vast. See for example, the proceedings of the colloquium entitled "Subsidiarité, défi du changement" held at the European Institute of Public Administration in Maastricht in 1991 (contributions of President Delors and others); the 1994 FIDE reports on subsidiarity; Bernard, "The Future of European Economic Law in the light of the Principle of Subsidiarity" (1996) 33 C.M.L.Rev. 633; von Borries, "Das Subsidiaritätsprinzip im Recht der Europäischen Union" [1994] EuR 263; Calliess, *Subsidiaritäts- und Solidaritätsprinzip in der Europäischen Union* (1999); Lambers, "Subsidiarität in Europa–Allheilmittel oder juristische Leerformel?" [1993] EuR 229; Lenaerts and van Ypersele, "Le principe de la subsidiarité et son contexte: étude de l'article 3B du Traité" [1994] C.D.E. 3; Pipkorn "Das Subsidiaritätsprinzip im Vertrag über die Europäische Union–rechtliche Bedeutung und gerichtliche Überprüfbarkeit" [1992] EuZW 697; Rohe, "Binnenmarkt oder Interessenverband ? Zum Verhältnis von Binnenmarktziel und Subsidiaritätsprinzip nach dem Maastricht-Vertrag" [1997] RabelsZ. 1; Soares, "Pre-Emption, Conflicts of Powers and Subsidiarity" (1998) 23 E.L.Rev. 132; Stewing, *Subsidiarität und Föderalismus in der Europäischen Union* (1992); Toth, "The Principle of Subsidiarity in the Maastricht Treaty" [1992] C.M.L.Rev. 1079; Wyatt, "Subsidiarity and Judicial Review" in Liber Amicorum in Honour of Lord Slynn of Hadley (2000), Vol. 1 "Judicial Review in European Union Law" at 505. For a comparison with the United States see Bermann, "Taking Subsidiarity Seriously: Federalism in the European Community and the United States" [1994] Columbia L.Rev. 331.

12.05 The principle has been the subject of several "soft law" instruments, including: a statement of the European Council held at Edinburgh in December 1992[5]; an inter-institutional agreement initialled by the Parliament, the Council and the Commission on October 29, 1993[6]; and annual Commission communications since 1992.[7] The Treaty of Amsterdam added to these instruments the Protocol on the application of the principles of subsidiarity and proportionality, which it annexed to the EC Treaty.[8] The Protocol lays down the rules for the application of these principles.

12.06 Point 5 of the Protocol sets out in detail the requirements of the principle of subsidiarity which must be met to justify Community action: "the objectives of the proposed action cannot be sufficiently achieved by the Member States' action in the framework of their national constitutional system and can therefore be better achieved by action on the part of the Community." It then sets out three matters which are to be addressed in assessing this, namely whether:

"— the issue under consideration has transnational aspects which cannot be satisfactorily regulated by action by Member States;
— actions by Member States alone or lack of Community action would conflict with the requirements of the Treaty (such as the need to correct distortion of competition or avoid disguised restrictions on trade or strengthen economic or social cohesion) or would otherwise significantly damage Member States' interests;
— action at Community level would produce clear benefits by reason of its scale or effects compared with action at the level of the Member States."

Even where a Community measure meets these requirements, Point 7 of the Protocol requires that "Community measures should leave as much scope for national decision as possible, consistent with securing the aim of the measure and observing the requirements of the Treaty." So far as possible, this means respecting "well established national arrangements and the organisation and working of Member States' legal systems" and allowing Member States the choice of "alternative ways to achieve the objectives of the measures".

However, Point 8 declares that, where the application of the principle of subsidiarity leads to no action being taken by the Community, Member States remain bound by Article 10 of the Treaty to take "all appropriate measures to ensure fulfilment of their obligations under the Treaty" and to abstain from "any measure which could jeopardise the attainment of the objectives of the Treaty". It should also be noted that, according to Point 6, "other things being

---

[5] Bull.E.C. 12-1992 p. 13
[6] [1993] O.J. C 329/132.
[7] SEC(92) 1990, COM(93) 545, COM(94) 553, CSE(95) 580, CSE(96) 7, COM(97) 626, COM(98) 715, COM(99) 562, COM(2000) 772 and COM(2001)728. Since 1995 these have gone under the title "Better Lawmaking", and since 1998 the Commission has been required to submit them under Point 9 of the Protocol on the application of the principles of subsidiarity and proportionality, annexed to the EC Treaty by the Treaty of Amsterdam ([1997] O.J. C340/105).
[8] See n.7; also Constantinesco, "Le protocole sur l'application des principes de subsidiarité et de proportionalité" (1997) 33 R.T.D.E. 765.

equal, Directives should be preferred to Regulations and framework Directives to detailed measures".

12.07   The Protocol also answers one of the most hotly disputed questions of the past: whether the principle of subsidiarity is justiciable. Point 13 of the Protocol states that "compliance with the principle of subsidiarity shall be reviewed in accordance with the rules laid down by the Treaty." However, the Court had already reached the same conclusion in *United Kingdom v Council* ("working time Directive"). [9]

12.08   Nevertheless, the Court has not to date treated the principle of subsidiarity as a significant fetter on the discretion of the Community institutions. The principle only applies "in areas which do not fall within [the] exclusive competence" of the Community. In *United Kingdom v Council*,[10] the Court held that, once the need to harmonise was demonstrated, this "necessarily presupposes Community-wide action" and any questions about scope or extent of the measures must be considered under the heading of proportionality. If there is no need to harmonise, the measure is likely to be held invalid for want of a proper legal basis in any event and so it is unnecessary to look to the principle of subsidiarity.

In *Netherlands v Parliament and Council* ("biotechnology Directive"), the Court held:

> "The objective pursued by the Directive, to ensure the smooth operation of the internal market by preventing or eliminating differences between the legislation and practice of the various Member States in the area of the protection of biotechnological inventions, could not be achieved by action taken by the Member States alone. As the scope of that protection has immediate effects on trade, and accordingly, on intra-Community trade, it is clear that, given the scale and effects of the proposed action, the objective in question could be better achieved by the Community".[11]

In addition, the Court has considered whether a Directive was adequately reasoned with regard to the respect of the principle of subsidiarity, although it has held that "an express reference to that principle cannot be required".[12]

These cases all related to legislation adopted prior to the entry into force of the Protocol. Consequently, it remains to be seen to what extent the Protocol will be of practical assistance to the Court in carrying out the delicate and elusive task of assessing compliance with the principle of subsidiarity. At least, it seems clear that its provisions have placed additional requirements on the Community institutions to provide reasons for their acts as regards subsidiarity.

12.09   In any event, it is questionable whether the principle of subsidiarity

---

[9] Case C-84/94 [1996] E.C.R. I-5755, paras 46-47.
[10] *ibid.*
[11] See n.2 above, para. 32.
[12] Case C-233/94 *Germany v Parliament and Council* ("Directive on deposit-guarantee schemes") [1997] E.C.R. I-2405, paras 22-29 (especially para. 28).

applies at all to legislation adopted prior to the Maastricht Treaty, given that the *acquis communautaire* must be respected under Articles 2 and 3 (ex B and C) of the Treaty on European Union, as supplemented by Article 2 of the Protocol on subsidiarity and proportionality.[13]

C. Proportionality

12.10   In stark contrast to subsidiarity, the principle of proportionality was well established in the Court's case law long before the Treaty of Maastricht.[14] However, that Treaty inserted into the EC Treaty a provision (now the third paragraph of Article 5), which makes it explicit that:

> "Any action by the Community shall not go beyond what is necessary to achieve the objectives of the Treaty."

This provision is supplemented by the Protocol on the application of the principles of subsidiarity and proportionality.[15] Proportionality is, like subsidiarity, declared to be justiciable under Point 13 of the Protocol—but, as already mentioned, this was scarcely novel with respect to proportionality.

A further difference between the two principles is that proportionality comes into play at a later stage: subsidiarity determines whether Community action may be taken at all, whereas proportionality determines the nature of measures which may be enacted.[16]

12.11   The Court has held that "in order to establish whether a provision of Community law complies with the principle of proportionality, it must be ascertained whether the means which it employs are suitable for the purpose of achieving the desired objective and whether they do not go beyond what is necessary to achieve it ...".[17]

In practice, the Court only exercises marginal review, since it considers that it

> "... cannot, without risk of overriding the wide discretion of the Council, substitute its assessment for that of the Council as to the choice of the most appropriate measure to

---

[13] Broadly speaking, the "*acquis communautaire*" means the body of law established by the European Union and/or the Community at the material time. See Delcourt, "The *Acquis Communautaire*: Has the Concept had its Day?" [2001] C.M.L.Rev. 829.

[14] See paras 8.10 and 9.01 above; see also Lenaerts and van Ypersele, *op. cit.* n.4 above at 52-70. On proportionality generally see De Búrca, "The Principle of Proportionality and its Application in EC Law" [1994] Y.E.L. 105; Emiliou, *The Principle of Proportionality in European Law—A Comparative Study* (1996); Jacobs, "Recent Developments in the Principle of Proportionality in European Community Law" in Ellis "The Principle of Proportionality in the Laws of Europe" (1999) pp. 1-21; Jans, "Evenredigheid Revisited" [2000] S.E.W. 270; and Tridimas, *The General Principles of EC Law* (1999), Ch. 3.

[15] See n.7 above.

[16] Léger A.G. in Case 84/94, see n. 9 above at p. 5783, endorsing Lenaerts and van Ypersele, *op. cit.*

[17] Case C-110/97 *Netherlands v Council* (judgment of November 22, 2001), para. 122, where the Court also referred to Case C-233/94, see n.12 above, para. 54; Case C-284/95 *Safety Hi-Tech v S & T* [1998] E.C.R. I-4301, para. 57; and Case C-390/95 P *Antillean Rice Mills v Commission* [1999] E.C.R. I-769, para. 52.

prevent disturbances to the Community market in rice if those measures have not been proved to be manifestly inappropriate for achieving the objective pursued ... ".[18]

One can only agree with Jacobs A.G.'s extra-judicial statement that "proportionality is a flexible tool of judicial review, which is applied differently in different contexts".[19] This idea is echoed by Tridimas, when he says that "far from dictating a uniform test, proportionality is a flexible principle which is used in different contexts to protect different interests and entails varying degrees of judicial scrutiny."[20] The Court has tended to be most exacting in the agricultural sector, especially when considering penalties and similar measures.[21] On the other hand, when it considers measures such as harmonisation, where the institutions have a wide discretion in making social policy choices and carrying out complex assessments, the Court applies a relatively light degree of scrutiny.[22]

D. Removal of Border Restrictions between Member States

12.12 In 1984, the European Parliament drew up a draft Treaty establishing the European Union[23] which, despite being regarded as too ambitious for its time, created a momentum for the conclusion of a new Community Treaty.

In the following year, the Commission published its White Paper on Completing the Internal Market.[24] This imaginative document set as its goal the creation of a fully unified internal market by 1992. Important sections related to the free movement of goods and the elimination of technical barriers to trade, while other sections were devoted to persons, services, capital and tax barriers to trade. The White Paper contained a specific legislative programme, setting out for each measure the year in which the Commission's draft legislation was to reach the Council and the date of its expected adoption by the Council.

These two events provided the impetus for the adoption of the Single European Act, which was signed in February 1986 and which came into force on July 1, 1987.

12.13 The provisions which are now to be found in Article 14(1) and (2) were inserted into the EC Treaty by the Single European Act, and indeed they con-

---

[18] Case C-110/97, see n.17 above, para. 126, where the Court also referred to Cases C-280/93 *Germany v Commission* [1994] E.C.R. I-4973, para. 94; and C-189/01 *Jippes v Minister of Agriculture* [2001] E.C.R. I-5689, para. 83).

[19] *op. cit.*, p. 20.

[20] *op. cit.*, p. 76; also Jans, *op. cit.*, p. 281.

[21] *e.g.* Case 114/76 *Bela-Mühle v Grows-Farm* [1977] E.C.R. 1211.

[22] Case 138/78 *Stölting v Hauptzollamt Hamburg-Jonas* [1979] E.C.R. 713, para. 7; Case 59/83 *Biovilac v EEC* [1984] E.C.R. 4057, para.17; Joined Cases 279/84, 280/84, 285/84 and 286/84 *Walter Rau Lebensmittelwerke v Commission* [1987] E.C.R. 1069, paras 34-37; Case C-331/88 *R v Minister for Agriculture, Fisheries and Food, Ex p. Fedesa and others* [1990] E.C.R. I-4023, paras 13-17; Case C-426/93 *Germany v Commission* [1995] E.C.R. I-3723, para. 42; Case C-84/94, see n.9 above, paras 57-67.

[23] [1984] O.J. C77/23. See Bieber, Jacqué and Weiler, *An Ever Closer Union* (1985), 110; Capotorti, Hilf, Jacobs and Jacqué, *Le Traité d'union européenne* (1985), *Der Vertrag zur Gründung der Europäischen Union* (1984).

[24] COM (85) 310 final.

stituted the very cornerstone of that instrument. Article 14 reads as follows:

"1.   The Community shall adopt measures with the aim of progressively establishing the internal market over a period expiring on December 31, 1992, in accordance with the provisions of this Article and of Articles 15, 26, 47(2), 49, 80, 93 and 95 and without prejudice to the other provisions of this Treaty.

2.   The internal market shall comprise an area without internal frontiers in which the free movement of goods, persons, services and capital is ensured in accordance with the provisions of this Treaty.

3.   The Council, acting by a qualified majority on a proposal from the Commission, shall determine the guidelines and conditions necessary to ensure balanced progress in all the sectors concerned."[25]

As we observed in paragraph 1.07 above, the better view today is that the concept of the "internal market" is indistinguishable from that of the "common market", an approach which also has the merit of great simplicity.

12.14   The question as to whether Article 14(1) has automatic direct effect, thereby removing barriers to the internal market even in the absence of the envisaged legislation, was hotly debated at the time of the Single European Act. A declaration by the Conference of the Representatives of the Governments of the Member States annexed to that Act stated: "Setting the deadline of 31 December 1992 does not create an automatic legal effect." The stronger view always appeared to be that Article 14(1) did not have such an effect, as it was not intended as a substitute for legislation.[26] Indeed, the Parliament, by bringing an action under Article 232 (ex 175) EC against the Commission for failure to propose the measures necessary to realise the objective of Article 14 in relation to the free movement of persons,[27] tacitly conceded that the latter provision has no automatic effect.

In *INCS v Baglieri*,[28] Jacobs A.G. firmly endorsed the view that Article 14(1) does not have an automatic effect; and the Court confirmed this approach, albeit without considering the matter in any detail. In *Wijsenbeek*, which concerned the abolition of border controls on persons, the Court reached the same

---

[25] Paras 1 and 2 were originally located in Art. 8A, before being moved by the Treaty of Maastricht to Art. 7A. Meanwhile, what is now para. 3 has led an equally unsettled existence, having started life as the second para. of Art. 8B, before being shifted to the second para. of Art. 7B.
    It should be noted that the Single European Act provided for a deadline of the end of 1992, rather than the beginning of that year as envisaged in the White Paper.

[26] Schermers, "The Effect of the Date of 31 December, 1992" [1991] C.M.L.Rev. 275; *contra* Mattera editorial [1992] R.M.U.E. 5. See generally Ayral, "La suppression des contrôles aux frontières intracommunautaires" [1993] R.M.U.E. 13; Ehlermann, "The Internal Market Following the Single European Act" [1987] C.M.L.Rev. 361 at 372; Glaesner, "Die Einheitliche Europäische Akte" (1986) EuR 119 at 133; Schockweiler, "Les conséquences de l'expiration du délai imparti pour l'établissement du marché intérieur" [1991] R.M.C. 882.

[27] C-445/93 (now withdrawn).

[28] Case C-272/92 [1993] E.C.R. I-5211, paras 11-13 of the Opinion.

conclusion on the basis of the following reasoning:

"[Article 14] cannot be interpreted as meaning that, in the absence of measures adopted by the Council before 31 December 1992 requiring the Member States to abolish controls of persons at the internal frontiers of the Community, that obligation automatically arises from expiry of that period. As the Advocate General points out in point 77 of his Opinion, such an obligation presupposes harmonisation of the laws of the Member States governing the crossing of the external borders of the Community, immigration, the grant of visas, asylum and the exchange of information on those questions (see, to this effect, as regards social security, *Baglieri*, cited above, paragraphs 16 and 17)."[29]

Although this judgment was delivered in the context of free movement of persons, namely the requirement to present a passport when travelling between Member States, there is no basis for believing that the approach would be any different as regards the free movement of goods. Consequently, it is clear that Article 14 on its own cannot be relied upon to strike down border controls imposed on goods.[30]

12.15   In any case, with respect to goods virtually all the requisite measures were in place by the deadline of December 31, 1992—in glaring contrast to the free movement of persons. Accordingly, as regards the free movement of goods, the question as to whether Article 14 had automatic legal effect was of no practical interest in any event. Moreover, the Court has held that Article 14 merely defines "general objectives" and must be read in conjunction with Treaty provisions designed to implement those objectives, notably Articles 28 to 30.[31]

It cannot be sufficiently emphasised that prior to 1993 systematic border controls on goods passing between Member State were actually **required** by Community legislation. Thus compliance with Article 14 entailed a vast legislative programme to abolish the provisions concerned and to remove the need for border controls altogether. Some 265 legislative instruments were enacted to this end in the period leading up to the end of 1992.[32]

---

[29] Case C-378/97 [1999] E.C.R. I-6207, para. 40.

[30] In Case T-113/96 *Edouard Dubois v Council and Commission* [1998] E.C.R. II-125, para. 46, the CFI held that the Community could not be held liable to compensate customs agents for the loss caused by the abolition of internal customs controls because this was a "direct result" of the Single European Act. It is submitted that there is no contradiction between the rulings in *Wijsenbeek* and *Edouard Dubois*: in the latter case, the CFI merely recognised the fact that the Community institutions were bound to fulfil their obligations under Art. 14.

[31] Case C-9/99 *Échirolles Distribution v Association du Dauphiné* [2000] E.C.R. I-8207 at para. 24.

[32] *e.g.* Council Dir. 91/477 on control of the acquisition and possession of weapons [1991] O.J. L256/51; Council Dir. 93/7 on the return of cultural objects unlawfully removed from a Member State [1993] O.J. L74/74; Council Dirs 93/36, 93/37 and 93/38 on public procurement [1993] O.J. L199/1 54 and 84; Council Dir. 92/12 on excise duties [1992] O.J. L76/1; Council Dirs 91/680, 92/77 and 92/111 on temporary new rules on VAT [1991] O.J. L376/1, [1992] O.J. L316/1 and [1992] O.J. L384/47; Council Reg. 259/93 on the transport of waste [1993] O.J. L30/1; Council Dir. 92/59 on general product safety [1992] O.J. L228/24. The last-mentioned Act is one of many requiring Member States to carry out the necessary controls within their territory rather than at the internal borders. As to the measures adopted in agriculture, see para 10.18 above.

12.16 However, the Commission has in general avoided proposing any legislation expressly requiring the abolition of internal border controls. An important exception was Article 1 of Council Regulation 3925/91 concerning the elimination of controls and formalities applicable to the cabin and hold baggage of persons taking an internal Community flight and the baggage of persons making an inter-Community sea crossing[33] (the "baggage Regulation"), which came into force on January 1, 1993.

That Regulation was adopted to take account of the problems posed by international air and sea ports, since passengers arrive there both from within the Community and from third countries; to use the language of the preamble to that Regulation, "ports and airports stand apart as either may constitute, at the same time, an external frontier and an internal border". It was therefore necessary to specify at what point their luggage might be checked. This amounts indirectly to defining what is meant for the purposes of Article 14 by the external frontiers of the Community—and therefore by necessary implication the internal frontiers of the Member States; (but, as will be seen, these provisions are quite distinct from Article 3 of Council Regulation 2913/92[34] establishing the Community Customs Code, which sets out the customs territory of the Community). It was thought necessary to prohibit internal border controls expressly in the same Regulation.

None of the provisions of this Regulation has been repealed. However, Articles 2, 3, 4 and 5 are in effect reproduced in Articles 189 to 197 of the Commission Regulation 2454/93[35] implementing the Community Customs Code, as were the provisions of the Commission Regulation[36] which implements the baggage Regulation. Regulation 2454/93 came into force on January 1, 1994.

Article 1(1) of the Regulation prohibits the application of all controls or formalities on the baggage of those making intra-Community flights or sea crossing, except as permitted by the Regulation. Article 1(2) makes it clear that the Regulation does not affect security checks nor any prohibitions or restrictions laid down by the Member States which are compatible with the Treaties. Article 2 (Articles 190 and 191 of the Community Customs Code) sets out of the relevant definitions, while Articles 3 to 5 (Articles 192 to 194 of the Community Customs Code) lay down rules for flights and sea crossings which involve (or may involve) a stop outside the Community. The rules essentially provide that baggage entering or leaving the Community should be checked at the port or airport where it is first loaded or finally unloaded, except for baggage on private aeroplanes and for cabin baggage on flights involving a change of aeroplane, which should be checked at the airport where the aeroplane enters or leaves the

---

[33] [1991] O.J. L374/4; see Ayral, *op. cit.*, n.26 above; Buekenhoudt and Goosens, "1er janvier 1993: abolition des douanes?" [1993] Revue des Affaires Européennes part 1 p. 31 and part 2 p. 17; and Vaulont, "La suppression des frontières intérieures et la réglementation douanière communautaire" [1993] R.M.U.E. 51.

[34] [1992] O.J. L302/1; on Art. 3 see para. 3.08 above.

[35] [1993] O.J. L253/1.

[36] Reg. 1823/92: [1992] O.J. L185/8. That Regulation was repealed by Art. 913 of Reg. 2454/93.

Community. Checks on baggage on private boats, which do not have fixed itineraries, are not prohibited.

12.17   Furthermore, a series of customs Regulations, culminating with the Community Customs Code and the implementing Regulation (Regulation 2454/93), have introduced a number of major reforms rendering border controls unnecessary and, in most cases, even impossible.

Thus the internal transit regime, which related to goods falling under Article 23(2) of the Treaty, has now been abolished save in two cases: where goods transit through a third country (*e.g.* goods exported from Germany to Italy via Switzerland)[37]; and where "a Community provision makes express provision for its application".[38] Despite the broad language of the latter provision, it would seem that recourse to it is likely to be rare.[39]

It follows from all these provisions that in the overwhelming majority of cases, goods falling within Article 23(2) EC are no longer accompanied by customs documents at all, so that customs controls are not possible.

12.18   In short, the measures adopted for the completion of the internal market in respect of goods have created the conditions making internal border controls superfluous. This has been achieved in particular by requiring the relevant controls to be carried out within the territory of the Member States and, where necessary, at their external borders.

Moreover, to all intents and purposes the infrastructure for carrying out internal border controls has been removed, thus making such controls impossible. For instance, goods originating in the Community or put into free circulation are in general not covered by customs documents. What is more, customs officers have been moved from border posts and assigned to other tasks.

12.19   Now that the measures for the implementation of Article 14 are in place with respect to goods, the obvious question is: what does that provision actually require? Since the Court has not yet had occasion to rule on this issue, one can scarcely do better than turn to the Commission's Communication of May 8, 1992 on the abolition of border controls. According to that Communication, Article 14:

> "establishes a clear and simple objective that allows no margin of discretion. But the abolition of border controls does not deprive the competent authorities of their power to act throughout their territory and up to the frontier of that territory. However as the crossing of the frontier may no longer give rise to controls, such intervention must form part of internal monitoring arrangements covering the whole of the territory. Powers to impose controls or penalties which were exercised only on the occasion of,

---

[37] Art. 163 of the Community Customs Code.
[38] Art. 165 of the Code.
[39] Vaulont, *op. cit.* n.33 above at 58. Moreover, the use of the Single Administrative Document is also restricted to these two cases: Council Regulation 717/91 [1991] O.J. L78/1, now replaced by Articles 205 to 215 of Regulation 2454/93.

or in connection with, the crossing of an internal frontier would, therefore, be contrary to Article [14]".[40-41]

Accordingly, Member States may carry out controls at their internal borders, but only to the same extent as within their territory. Internal border controls exceeding that level will fall foul of Article 28 or Article 29, as the case may be.[42] However, that is subject to Article 30. Thus, for instance, where the authorities of a Member State are warned by a reliable source of the impending arrival of a dangerous criminal in a car of a given description, they are entitled to stop and search that vehicle and its occupants. Such controls would be covered by the public policy and/or public security exceptions in Article 30.

12.20 As to Article 14(3), it would seem that no legislation has ever been enacted on the basis of that provision.

E. Regional Disparities in the Internal Market

12.21 Article 15 EC reads:

"When drawing up its proposals with a view to achieving the objectives set out in Article 14, the Commission shall take into account the extent of the effort that certain economies showing differences in development will have to sustain during the period of establishment of the internal market and it may propose appropriate provisions.

If these provisions take the form of derogations, they must be of a temporary nature and must cause the least possible disturbance to the functioning of the common market."[43]

In the previous edition of this book, it was argued that this provision had lapsed at the end of 1992.[44] On this view, clear wording would have been required to make such an exemption clause permanent, constituting as it does a departure from the fundamental principle of the uniformity of Community law. However, the fact that this provision was not repealed by the Treaties of Maastricht, Amsterdam or Nice gives some indication that the Member States reject this view, as does the Commission's subsequent use of the Article. The survival of this provision is no doubt due in part to its express requirement that derogations be temporary in nature and cause the least possible disruption to the common market.

12.22 As Glaesner pointed out,[45] the reference to "economies" might be regarded as allowing for different regions of the same Member State to be

---

[40-41] COM(92) 877 final.
[42] See paras 6.10 and 7.04 above.
[43] This provision, which was first introduced by the Single European Act as Art. 8C, became Art. 7C by virtue of the Treaty of Maastricht, before bearing its current number.
[44] On this issue, see generally Ehlermann, *op.cit.* (see n. 26 above) at 373; also Forwood and Clough, "The Single European Act and Free Movement–Legal Implications of the Provisions for the Completion of the Internal Market" [1986] E.L.Rev. 383 at 399.
[45] *op. cit.* n.26 above at 134.

accorded different treatment. This view is borne out by Articles 158 (ex 130A) and 162 (ex 130E) which are discussed below.

Also, it has been suggested[46] that Article 15 might perhaps relate only to legislation based on the Articles referred to in Article 14. Yet, this seems unlikely since the objectives set out in Article 14 can also be achieved on the basis of other Articles of the Treaty. Indeed, this is expressly recognised by the words "without prejudice to the other provisions of this Treaty" in Article 14.

Article 15 is to be read in the light of Articles 158 to 162 relating to "economic and social cohesion", which were inserted into the Treaty by the Single European Act[47]; (these provisions have undergone significant amendments as a result of the Treaty of Maastricht, but those amendments are not directly in point here). The first of these provisions states that the Community shall strengthen its "economic and social cohesion", in particular by "reducing disparities between the levels of development of the various regions and the backwardness of the least favoured regions, including rural areas". Article 159 begins:

> "Member States shall conduct their economic policies and shall coordinate them in such a way as, in addition, to attain the objectives set out in Article 158. The formulation and implementation of the Community's policies and actions and the implementation of the internal market shall take into account the objectives set out in Article 158 and shall contribute to their achievement."

12.23 As to the practice relating to Article 15, that provision is referred to in the preambles to Directive 88/361[48] and Directive 90/650[49] and in Article 7 of Directive 90/387.[50] The Commission considered and rejected the need to rely on Article 15 when it made the proposal which became Directive 98/44 on the legal protection of biotechnological inventions,[51] and when it proposed amendments to Directive 85/374 on product liability.[52] However, the Article was referred to in Directive 98/30 on common rules for the internal market for natural gas.[53]

F. "All Pervasive" Policies

12.24 The Treaty of Amsterdam amended Article 2 EC so that, for the first time, "sustainable" economic development is declared to be one of the tasks of

---

[46] Forwood and Clough, *op. cit.* at 399.
[47] Mortelmans, "De 'Economische en Sociale Samenhang' en de 'Interne Market': Enkele juridische aspecten van een LAT—relatie" [1989] S.E.W. 766.
[48] [1988] O.J. L178/5 (abolition of restrictions on movement of capital - transitory measures for Greece, Ireland, Portugal and Spain until December 31, 1992).
[49] [1990] O.J. L353/39 (transitory measures for the application of Directives on the harmonisation of technical rules to products from the former German Democratic Republic until December 31, 1992).
[50] [1990] O.J. L192/1 (framework for harmonisation of access to public telecommunications networks - provision for further Council action under Article 95 taking into account Article 15).
[51] COM (96) 661 final, para.34.
[52] COM (97) 478 final, para.11.
[53] [1998] O.J. L204/1.

the Community. Moreover, Article 6 EC which was inserted at Amsterdam provides:

"Environmental protection requirements must be integrated into the definition and implementation of the Community policies and activities referred to in Article 3, in particular with a view to promoting sustainable development."

Article 174 (ex 130r) then states:

"1. Community policy on the environment shall contribute to pursuit of the following objectives:
  — preserving, protecting and improving the quality of the environment;
  — protecting human health;
  — prudent and rational utilisation of natural resources;
  — promoting measures at international level to deal with regional or worldwide environmental problems.
2. Community policy on the environment shall aim at a high level of protection taking into account the diversity of situations in the various regions of the Community. It shall be based on the precautionary principle and on the principle that preventive action should be taken, that environmental damage should as a priority be rectified at source and that the polluter should pay.
    In this context, harmonisation measures answering environmental protection requirements shall include, where appropriate, a safeguard clause allowing Member States to take provisional measures, for non-economic environmental reasons, subject to a Community inspection procedure."

12.25   Article 151(4) (ex 128(4)) is drafted in the following terms:

"The Community shall take cultural aspects into account in its action under other provisions of this Treaty, in particular in order to respect and to promote the diversity of its cultures."

12.26   Article 152 (ex 129) reads as follows:

"1. A high level of human health protection shall be ensured in the definition and implementation of all Community policies and activities.
    Community action, which shall complement national policies, shall be directed towards improving public health, preventing human illness and diseases, and obviating sources of danger to human health. Such action shall cover the fight against the major health scourges, by promoting research into their causes, their transmission and their prevention, as well as health information and education.
    The Community shall complement the Member States' action in reducing drugs-related health damage, including information and prevention."

12.27   Article 153 (ex 129a) provides:

"1. In order to promote the interests of consumers and to ensure a high level of consumer protection, the Community shall contribute to protecting the health, safety and economic interests of consumers, as well as to promoting their right to information, education and to organise themselves in order to safeguard their interests.
2. Consumer protection requirements shall be taken into account in defining and implementing other Community policies and activities."

3.   The Community shall contribute to the attainment of the objectives referred to in paragraph 1 through:

   (a)   measures adopted pursuant to Article 95 in the context of the completion of the internal market;

   . . . "

12.28   As a result of these provisions, the Community must take account of all three principles. For the environment and for human health, the Community is required to ensure a high level of protection; by way of contrast, the provisions relating to culture and consumer protection merely state that such requirements shall be taken into account. This is in addition to the specific legal bases which allow harmonisation in order to protect the environment, public health and consumers, and to promote culture and cultural diversity.[54]

It should be noted that, although these provisions do not act as grounds for harmonising legislation themselves, they do operate to protect legislation from challenge on proportionality grounds. They may also act as grounds for challenging legislation which fail to take the policies into account and, in the case of the environment and public health, which fail to ensure a high level of protection.[55]

G. Legal Certainty and Legitimate Expectation

12.29   Neither the principle of legal certainty nor the principle of legitimate expectation is enunciated in the Treaty and both are thus creatures of case law.[56] In *Amministrazione delle Finanze dello Stato v Salumi*,[57] the Court summarised the two principles as follows:

" . . . [according to] the principles of legal certainty and the protection of legitimate expectations . . . Community legislation must be clear and predictable for those who are subject to it."

The principle of legal certainty is highly diffuse in nature and cannot be examined exhaustively here. However, to give one illustrative example, the Court held that this principle "requires that rules imposing charges on the taxpayer must be clear and precise so that he may know without ambiguity what are his rights and obligations and may take steps accordingly".[58]

The principle of legitimate expectation is more specific. Indeed, it has been described as a "specific expression of legal certainty".[59] Legislation which imposes a burden retroactively will be contrary to this principle in the absence of overriding justification, as will legislation which imposes new rules with

---

[54] See paras 12.62 *et seq.* below.

[55] In *Safety Hi-Tech* (n.17 above), the Court appeared to treat as justiciable the obligation in Article 174(2) to ensure a high level of environmental protection.

[56] See generally Tridimas, *op. cit.* n.14 above, Ch. 5.

[57] Cases 212-217/80 [1981] E.C.R. 2735, para. 20. Schermers and Waelbroeck, "Judicial Protection in the European Union" (6th ed., 2001) paras 117 *et seq.*

[58] Case 169/80 *Administration des Douanes v Gondrand* [1981] E.C.R. 1931, paras 17-18.

[59] Tridimas, *op. cit.* p. 163.

immediate effect on persons who have entered into an irrevocable arrangement on the basis of the previous legislation.[60] However, no legitimate expectation will arise where the introduction of the new measure was reasonably foreseeable.[61] Thus "the principle of the protection of legitimate expectations may be invoked as against Community rules only to the extent that the Community itself has previously created a situation which can give rise to a legitimate expectation".[62]

H. Equality

12.30 A number of provisions of the EC Treaty prohibit discrimination of certain kinds, such as: Articles 12 (ex 6) (nationality), 34(2) (ex 40(3)) (discrimination between agricultural producers or between agricultural consumers) and 141 (ex 119) (sex). However the Court has held that such provisions are a "specific enunciation of the general principle of equality which is one of the fundamental principles of Community law".[63] According to the time-honoured formula, discrimination in substance (*i.e.* a breach of the principle of equality) may consist either in treating similar situations differently or in treating different situations similarly.[64] Thus measures which appear to constitute discrimination do not do so in fact, where the difference in treatment is justified.[65]

The distinct function of the principle of equality has been described by Tesauro A.G. in the following terms:

" ... the principle of equal treatment is fundamental not only because it is a cornerstone of contemporary legal systems but also for a more specific reason: Community legislation chiefly concerns economic situations and activities. If, in this field, different rules are laid down for similar situations, the result is not merely inequality before the law, but also, and inevitably, distortions of competition which are absolutely irreconcilable with the fundamental philosophy of the common market."[66]

Tridimas has aptly summarised this passage as follows: "Equality, therefore, is not only a constitutional necessity but also a keystone of integration".[67]

---

[60] Cases 74/74 *CNTA v Commission* [1975] E.C.R. 533; 120/86 *Mulder v Minister van Landbouw* [1988] E.C.R. 2321; C-152/88 *Sofrimport v Commission* [1990] E.C.R. I-2477; C-368/89 *Crispoltoni v Fattoria Autonoma Tabacchi* [1991] E.C.R. I-3695.

[61] Case 108/81 *Amylum v Council* [1982] E.C.R. 3107, para. 11.

[62] Case C-177/90 *Kühn v Landwirtschaftskammer Weser-Ems* [1992] E.C.R. I-35, para. 14; Case C-63/93 *Duff v Minister for Agriculture* [1996] E.C.R. I-569, para. 20.

[63] Case 117/76 *Ruckdeschel v HZA Hamburg St.-Annen* [1977] E.C.R. 1753, para 7; Case C-56/94 *SCAC v Associazione dei Produttori Ortofrutticoli* [1995] E.C.R. I-1769, para. 27. See Dashwood and O'Leary (eds.), *The Principle of Equal Treatment in EC Law* (1997); Lenaerts, "L'égalité de traitement en droit communautaire" [1991] C.D.E. 3; Schermers and Waelbroeck, *op. cit.* paras 160 *et seq.* Tridimas, *op. cit.* Ch. 2.

[64] Cases 13/63 *Italy v Commission* [1963] E.C.R. 165 at 183; C-309/89 *Codorniu v Council* [1994] E.C.R. I-1853, para. 26; *SCAC*, para. 27.

[65] *Ruckdeschel*, para. 7; *Codorniu*, para. 26; *SCAC*, para. 27.

[66] Case C-63/89 *Assurances du Crédit v Council and Commission* [1991] E.C.R. I-1799 at 1829.

[67] *op. cit.* at 45.

II. THE LEGAL BASES FOR HARMONISATION

A. Introduction

12.31   The first paragraph of Article 5 (ex 3B), which was inserted into the EC Treaty by the Treaty of Maastricht, reads as follows:

> "The Community shall act within the limits of the powers conferred upon it by the Treaty and of the objectives assigned to it therein."

This confirms that the Community is restricted to legislating where it has been given the power to do so by the Treaties and is not endowed with general law-making competence.[68] However, such powers need not be expressly set out in the Treaties; they may be implied, where this is necessary to supplement express powers.[69]

12.32   Certain fundamental principles governing the choice of a legal basis must also be examined.[70] First, this choice may not depend on an institution's conviction as to the objective pursued but must be based on objective factors which are amenable to judicial review.[71] Second, where an institution's power is based on two provisions of the Treaty, it is bound to adopt the relevant measures on the basis of both.[72] However, that rule only applies where the two provisions concerned provide for adoption of legislation according to the same procedure. In other cases—or at least where one article provides for unanimous voting in the Council, while the other requires the co-operation procedure to be followed—the legislation must be based on one provision alone.[73] The reason is that otherwise "the very purpose of the co-operation procedure, which is to increase the involvement of the European Parliament in the legislative process of the Community, would be jeopardised".[74] The same reasoning applies *a fortiori* to the co-decision procedure in Article 251 (ex 189B). Accordingly, in

---

[68] Bogdandy and Bast, "The European Union's Vertical Order of Competences: the Current Law and Proposals for its Reform" [2002] C.M.L.Rev. 227; Dashwood, "The Limits of European Community Powers" (1996) 21 E.L. Rev. 113; Piris, "L'Union européenne a-t-elle une constitution? Lui en faut-il une?" [1999] R.T.D.E. 599 (also published in English "Does the European Union have a Constitution ? Does it Need One ?" Jean Monnet Working Papers 5/00 *www.jeanmonnetprogram.org/papers/00/000501.html*).

[69] Cases 281/85 *Germany and others v Commission* [1987] E.C.R. 3203; C-295/90 *Parliament v Council* (Directive on residence of students) [1992] E.C.R. I-4193; Opinion 1/94 [1994] E.C.R. I-5267, paras 72 *et seq.* See Dashwood, *op. cit.* at p. 124; Lenaerts and Desomer, "Bricks for a Constitutional Treaty of the European Union: values, objectives and means" [2002] E.L.Rev. 377 at 385.

[70] See Barents, "The Internal Market Unlimited: Some Observations on the Legal Basis of Community Legislation" [1993] C.M.L.Rev. 85.

[71] Case 45/86 *Commission v Council* ("generalised tariff preferences") [1987] E.C.R. 1493, para. 11; Case C-300/89 *Commission v Council* ("titanium dioxide") [1991] E.C.R. I-2867, para. 10; C-209/97 *Commission v Council* (mutual assistance) [1999] E.C.R. I-8067, para. 13.

[72] Case 165/87 *Commission v Council* ("Convention on the Harmonised System") [1988] E.C.R. 5543.

[73] Case C-300/89, see n.71 above.

[74] *ibid.*, para. 20 of the judgment. The co-operation procedure, which was initially established by the Single European Act, is now enshrined in Art. 252 (ex 189C) EC.

determining whether two given legal bases may be combined, it is essential to consider which legislative procedures they require to be followed. As will be seen shortly, the Single European Act and the Treaties of Maastricht, Amsterdam and Nice altered the legislative procedures under a number of the provisions considered here.

12.33   Prior to the entry into force of the Single European Act, the most important legal basis for harmonising provisions relating to goods was Article 94 (ex 100). Since then it has been Article 95 (ex 100A). Rather than begin with these provisions at once, it is appropriate to examine the various relevant articles in numerical order. Having said that, what follows does not purport to be an exhaustive list of all the Treaty provisions which may be used for the harmonisation of provisions relating to goods.

B. Agriculture

12.34   Article 37 (ex 43) is the appropriate basis for harmonising legislation relating to agricultural products.[75]

In a number of cases relating to legislation adopted before Article 95 was in force, the Court construed Article 37 broadly in relation to Article 94. Article 37 provides for majority voting in the Council and may be used as the legal basis for regulations, directives and decisions. In contrast, Article 94 requires unanimous voting in the Council and provides for the adoption of directives only.

In two separate cases,[76] the United Kingdom contested the validity of Directive 85/649[77] prohibiting the use in livestock of certain substances having a hormonal action and of Directive 86/113[78] laying down minimum standards for the protection of laying hens kept in battery cages, on the grounds that they were based on Article 37 alone instead of Articles 37 and 94 together. The Court rejected the United Kingdom's arguments on this point. It interpreted Article 37 widely, stating that it "is the appropriate legal basis for any legislation concerning the production and marketing of agricultural products ... which contributes to the achievement of one or more of the objectives of the common agricultural policy set out in Article [33] of the Treaty". It went on to hold that "even where the legislation in question is directed both to objectives of agricultural policy and to other objectives which, in the absence of specific provisions, are pursued on the basis of Article [94] of the Treaty, that Article, a general one under which Directives may be adopted for the approximation of the laws of the Member States, cannot be relied on as a ground for restricting the field of application of Article [37] of the Treaty." Moreover, the applicant

---

[75] Agricultural products for this purpose are those listed in Annex I to the Treaty: Art. 32(3). See Cases 164/97 and C-165/97 *Parliament v Council* (protection of forests) [1999] ECR I-1139 (para. 10.01 below).

[76] Cases 68/86 *United Kingdom v Council* [1988] E.C.R. 855; [1988] 2 C.M.L.R. 543; and 131/86 *United Kingdom v Council* [1988] E.C.R. 905; [1988] 2 C.M.L.R. 364; see also C-331/88, see n.22 above.

[77] [1985] O.J. L382/228.

[78] [1986] O.J. L95/45.

contended that the Council had departed from its consistent practice of basing measures in these fields on Articles 37 and 94 together. The Court dismissed this argument on the grounds that the practice of the Council could not alter the rules laid down in the Treaty.

The Court was to confirm this approach in *Commission v Council*,[79] where it annulled Council Directive 87/64[80] laying down certain health measures for meat products on the grounds that it had wrongfully been adopted on the basis of Articles 94 and 133 (ex 113) of the Treaty rather than Article 37.

12.35   In so far as this case law relates to "measures in the veterinary and phytosanitary fields which have as their direct objective the protection of public health", it is no longer good law. The Treaty of Amsterdam has narrowed the scope of Article 37, by inserting into Article 152 on public health an express provision that such measures are to be based on the latter provision to the exclusion of Article 37 (Article 152(4(b)).[81] Nevertheless, Article 37 continues to constitute the correct legal basis for other veterinary and phytosanitary legislation.

C. Internal Market

(i) General

12.36   Since the Treaty of Amsterdam, Article 94 has read as follows:

> "The Council shall, acting unanimously on a proposal from the Commission and after consulting the European Parliament and the Economic and Social Committee, issue Directives for the approximation of such laws, regulations or administrative provisions of the Member States as directly affect the establishment or functioning of the common market."

Until the Single European Act came into force, this provision was by far the most important Treaty provision relating to harmonisation, although its wording was very different. However, that Act rendered that provision largely redundant: it inserted Article 95 into the Treaty, which must be used as a legal basis in all cases hitherto covered by Article 94 "save where otherwise provided in this Treaty" and subject to the exceptions set out in Article 95(2). Thus Article 94 now only covers the categories of legislation listed in Article 95(2).

For the present purposes the salient features of Article 94 may be summarised as follows:

— the only category of instrument which may be based on Article 94 is the Directive;

---

[79] Case C-131/87 [1989] E.C.R. 3743.
[80] [1987] O.J. L34/52.
[81] See Gencarelli, "La politique agricole commune et les autres politiques communautaires : la nouvelle frontière" [2001] R.D.U.E. 173.

— while the concept of provisions which "directly affect the establishment or functioning of the common market" is vague, there can be no doubt that it covers national provisions creating barriers to trade which are justified under Article 30.[82] Article 94 has also been used frequently as a basis for customs legislation;

— it is not necessary that all Member States possess measures covering the field to be harmonised. It is enough that one Member State has such a measure or perhaps even that is not necessary.[83]

12.37 Article 95 was inserted into the Treaty of Rome by the Single European Act. Following its amendment by the Treaties of Maastricht and Amsterdam, this provision now reads as follows:

"1. By way of derogation from Article 94 and save where otherwise provided in this Treaty, the following provisions shall apply for the achievement of the objectives set out in Article 14.

   The Council shall, acting in accordance with the procedure referred to in Article 251 and after consulting the Economic and Social Committee, adopt the measures for the approximation of the provisions laid down by law, regulation or administrative action in Member States which have as their object the establishment and functioning of the internal market.

2. Paragraph 1 shall not apply to fiscal provisions, to those relating to the free movement of persons nor to those relating to the rights and interests of employed persons.

3. The Commission, in its proposals envisaged in paragraph 1 concerning health, safety, environmental protection and consumer protection, will take as a base a high level of protection, taking account in particular of any new development based on scientific facts.

   Within their respective powers, the European Parliament and the Council will also seek to achieve this objective.

4. If, after the adoption by the Council or by the Commission of a harmonisation measure, a Member State deems it necessary to maintain national provisions on grounds of major needs referred to in Article 30, or relating to the protection of the environment or the working environment, it shall notify the Commission of these provisions as well as the grounds for maintaining them.

5. Moreover, without prejudice to paragraph 4, if, after the adoption by the Council or by the Commission of a harmonisation measure, a Member State deems it necessary to introduce national provisions based on new scientific evidence relating to the protection of the environment or the working environment on grounds of a problem specific to that Member State arising after the adoption of the harmonisation measure, it shall notify the Commission of the envisaged provisions as well as the grounds for introducing them.

6. The Commission shall, within six months of the notifications as referred to in paragraphs 4 and 5, approve or reject the national provisions involved after having verified whether or not they are a means of arbitrary discrimination or a disguised restriction on trade between Member States and whether or not they shall constitute an obstacle to the functioning of the internal market.

   In the absence of a decision by the Commission within this period the national

---

[82] Paras 12.103 *et seq.* below.
[83] Taschner, "Commentary on Article 100 (old numbering)" in Groeben, Thiesing, Ehlermann, *Kommentar zum EU-/-EG-Vertrag* (5th ed., 1997) Vol. II at 2217.

provisions referred to in paragraphs 4 and 5 shall be deemed to have been approved.

When justified by the complexity of the matter and in the absence of danger for human health, the Commission may notify the Member State concerned that the period referred to in this paragraph may be extended for a further period of up to six months.

7. When, pursuant to paragraph 6, a Member State is authorised to maintain or introduce national provisions derogating from a harmonisation measure, the Commission shall immediately examine whether to propose an adaptation to that measure.

8. When a Member State raises a specific problem on public health in a field which has been the subject of prior harmonisation measures, it shall bring it to the attention of the Commission which shall immediately examine whether to propose appropriate measures to the Council.

9. By way of derogation from the procedure laid down in Articles 226 and 227, the Commission and any Member State may bring the matter directly before the Court of Justice if it considers that another Member State is making improper use of the powers provided for in this Article.

10. The harmonisation measures referred to above shall, in appropriate cases, include a safeguard clause authorising the Member States to take, for one or more of the non-economic reasons referred to in Article 30, provisional measures subject to a Community control procedure."

This wording differs in several ways from that applicable before the Treaty of Amsterdam came into force. In particular, paragraphs 5 to 8 are entirely new.

12.38   Article 95 is more flexible than Article 94 in two significant respects: it enables the Council to act by a qualified majority; and it provides for the adoption of regulations as well as directives.[84] However, the price for this was the procedure now enshrined in paragraphs 4 to 9 of Article 95.

At all events, the words "shall apply" in the opening sentence of paragraph 1 make it clear that, where this Article is applicable, the Council may not opt to base legislation on Article 94 instead.[85] This is quite understandable since Article 94 merely requires the Parliament to be consulted, whereas Parliament is more actively involved in the adoption of proposals based on Article 95.

The phrase "save where otherwise provided in this Treaty" in the initial sentence of Article 95(1) is important. It follows from it that a particular Regulation or Directive, which could have been based on, say, Article 37 alone before the Act came into force, may still have precisely the same legal basis.

12.39   Paragraph 2 excludes three areas from the scope of Article 95, presumably because the Member States regarded them as too sensitive to be subject to majority voting. None of those areas is relevant to this book.

---

[84] It should also be noted that, unlike Article 94, Article 95 is not restricted to the harmonisation of measures directly affecting the common market. However, this is of little practical importance, since the concept of directness in Article 94 is somewhat vague in any event: Taschner, *op. cit.* at 2811-12.

Moreover, Art. 94 refers to the "common market", whereas Art. 95 speaks of attaining the objectives of Art. 14, where the term "internal market" is used. Yet, as explained in para. 13.04 below, the better view is that the two concepts are identical.

[85] Ehlermann, *op.cit.* (see n.26 above) at 382.

12.40   In view of its imprecise nature, the requirement in paragraph 3 to "take as a base a high level of protection" in certain matters was described by Ehlermann[86] as "hardly justiciable". However, the case law regarding the analogous provision in Article 174(2) suggests otherwise.[87]

(ii) The scope of Article 95

12.41   As is plainly indicated by its opening words, Article 95 is closely linked to Article 14 of the Treaty, which has already been discussed at paragraphs 12.12 to 12.20 above.

The scope of Article 95 has been interpreted broadly by the Court. Thus in *Spain v Council*,[88] the Court held:

> " ... harmonising measures are necessary to deal with disparities between the laws of the Member States in so far as such disparities are liable to hinder the free movement of goods within the Community."[89]

However, in *Commission v Council* ("Titanium Dioxide"), the Court also recognised the following alternative circumstance in which the Community legislator may have recourse to this provision:

> "In order to give effect to the fundamental freedoms mentioned in Article [14], harmonising measures are necessary to deal with disparities between the laws of the Member States in areas where such disparities are liable to create or maintain distorted conditions of competition. ... ".[90]

What is more, Article 95 has been held to empower the Community institutions to adopt legislation designed to prevent the emergence of future obstacles to trade resulting from multifarious development of national laws provided that the emergence of such obstacles is likely.[91]

Prior to the momentous ruling in *Germany v Parliament and Council* ("Tobacco Advertising"),[92] the Court had consistently upheld Article 95 as the appropriate legal basis for legislation. The only exception concerned legislation primarily related to some other purpose covered by some other Treaty provision (e.g. Article 175 (ex 130S) in relation to the environment) so that the elimination of such disparities was only of secondary importance.[93]

Thus, for instance, Article 95 has been held to constitute the proper basis for

---

[86] *op.cit.* (see n.26 above) at 389.
[87] *Safety Hi-Tech*, see n.17 above.
[88] Case C-350/92 [1995] E.C.R. I-1985.
[89] para. 33. Moreover, this was confirmed in Case C-350/92, see n.88 above, para. 32.
[90] Case C-300/89 (see n. 71 above), para. 15 of the judgment.
[91] Case C-350/92, see n.88 above, para. 35; see Case C-377/98, see n.2 above.
[92] See n.2 above.
[93] Cases C-70/88 *Parliament v Council* [1991] E.C.R. I 4529 (contested regulation properly based on Art. 31 Euratom), para. 17; C-209/97 *Commission v Council* (mutual assistance) (see n.71 above), para 35. However, in *Titanium Dioxide* the Court construed Art.95 very widely at the expense of Art. 175; see para. 12.66 below.

legislation harmonising national laws on intellectual property.[94] In addition, legislation empowering the Commission to take individual temporary measures with respect to unsafe products may also be based on Article 95, provided that that legislation is aimed at "the establishment and functioning of the internal market"—even though this does not entail the harmonisation of national measures.[95]

12.42   Then came the momentous judgment in the *Tobacco Advertising* case. In that case, Germany successfully challenged the legal basis of Directive 98/43 on the approximation of the laws, regulations and administrative provisions of the Member States relating to the advertising and sponsorship of tobacco products.[96] This Directive was based not only on Article 95, but also on the Treaty provisions relating to establishment and services (respectively Articles 47(2) (then 57(2) and 55 (then 66)); it could not be based on Article 152 (then 129) relating to public health, because that provision expressly excluded harmonising measures in this area.[97] Subject to certain exceptions, it prohibited all forms of advertising and sponsorship of tobacco products within the Community.

The following statements of the Court deserve particular note:

"Those provisions, read together, make it clear that the measures referred to in Article [Article 95(1)] of the Treaty are intended to improve the conditions for the establishment and functioning of the internal market. To construe [Article 95] as meaning that it vests in the Community legislature a general power to regulate the internal market would not ... be incompatible with the principle embodied in Article [5] EC that the powers of the Community are limited to those specifically conferred on it.

Moreover, a measure adopted on the basis of Article [95] of the Treaty must genuinely have as its object the improvement of the conditions for the establishment and functioning of the internal market. If a mere finding of disparities between national rules and of the abstract risk of obstacles to the exercise of fundamental freedoms or of distortions of competition liable to result therefrom were sufficient to justify the choice of Article [95] as a legal basis, judicial review of compliance with the proper legal basis might be rendered nugatory. The Court would then be prevented from discharging the function entrusted to it by Article 164 of the EC Treaty (now Article 220 EC) of ensuring that the law is observed in the interpretation and application of the Treaty."[98]

The Court then proceeded to scrutinise the Directive under the two separate heads which we noticed in para. 12.41, namely: the elimination of obstacles to the free movement of goods (and, in this instance, services as well, given that

---

[94] Opinion 1/94 (n.69 above), para. 59. In *Spain v Council* the Court rejected the contention that Article 95 does not constitute the proper legal basis for Council Reg. 1768/92 concerning the supplementary protection certificate for medicinal products ([1992] O.J. L182/1). See para. 8.177 above.

[95] Case C-359/92 *Germany v Council* [1994] E.C.R. I-3681, upholding Art. 9 of Council Dir. 92/59 on general product safety (n.32 above). Similarly, Art. 95 has been used as the basis for Reg. 141/2000 on orphan medical products, which lays down a *Community* procedure for designating such products and provides incentives for research and development in relation to them.

[96] [1998] O.J. L213/9.

[97] See para. 12.63 below.

[98] Paras 83 and 84 of the judgment.

the Directive was also based on Article 55); and the elimination of distortions of competition.

As to the first of these two heads, it sufficed to show that obstacles to free movement "may well arise".[99] This condition was fulfilled with respect to tobacco advertising in periodicals, magazines and newspapers. However, the same could not be said of the prohibition of such advertising on "posters, parasols, ashtrays and other articles used in hotels, restaurants and cafés" and in cinemas, since these prohibitions "in no way help facilitate trade in the products concerned".[100] Moreover, as regards diversification products, the Directive did not ensure free movement: not only did one article of the Directive expressly authorise Member States to impose stricter rules, but the Directive did not even contain a clause ensuring free movement.

As to the elimination of distortions of competition, the Court laid down a more rigid test: the use of this Article could be upheld only where the distortion was "appreciable".[101] It added:

> "In the absence of such a requirement, the powers of the Community legislature would be practically unlimited. National laws often differ regarding the conditions under which the activities they regulate may be carried on, and this impacts directly or indirectly on the conditions of competition for the undertakings concerned. It follows that to interpret Articles [95, 47(2) and 55] of the Treaty as meaning that the Community legislature may rely on those articles with a view to eliminating the smallest distortions of competition would be incompatible with the principle, ... that the powers of the Community are those specifically conferred on it."[102]

Again, the Court found that this requirement was not fulfilled in the present case, since no "appreciable" distortion of competition was involved—except as regards sponsorship of "certain sports events", which were in danger of being relocated "with considerable repercussions on the conditions of competition for undertakings associated with such undertakings".[103]

Finally, the Court ruled that, although the Directive was lawful as regards periodicals, magazines and newspapers and with respect to "certain sports events", that did not suffice to save the Directive, as severance was impossible. Accordingly, the Court quashed the Directive in its entirety.

The Court appears to have been influenced by the suggestion that the Parliament and the Council had circumvented the express exclusion of harmonisation in relation to public health laid down in Article 152(5) (then 129(4)).[104] Nevertheless, the Court took care to acknowledge that the Community legislature cannot be prevented from harmonising public health measures on the basis of other provisions of the Treaty.[105] [106]

---

[99] Para. 96.
[100] Para. 99.
[101] Para. 106.
[102] Para. 107.
[103] Para. 110.
[104] Para. 79.
[105] Para. 88.
[106] Following that ruling the Commission submitted a new proposal for a Directive on the advertising and sponsorship of tobacco products ([2001] O.J. C270E/12).

12.43   For completeness, it should be recorded that in *British American Tobacco*[107] Geelhoed A.G. has distilled the following propositions from the complex ruling in *Tobacco Advertising*:

"— The measures must improve the conditions for the establishment and functioning of the internal market. Article 95 EC does not confer any general power to regulate the internal market.
— The measures must have as their object the removal of obstacles to the exercise of fundamental freedoms or the removal of distortions of competition.
— There must be a serious risk. Article 95 EC may be used to prevent the emergence of future obstacles to trade resulting from multifarious development of national laws. However, the emergence of such obstacles must be probable and the measure in question must be designed to prevent them.
— A directive may incorporate provisions which contribute only indirectly to the removal of obstacles. These are provisions which are necessary to prevent the circumvention of prohibitions directly involving the removal of obstacles.
— Distortions of competition are, according to established case law, relevant only if they are appreciable.
— The Court regards as a distortion of competition any restriction of forms of competition applicable to all market participants in a Member State, for instance through the fact that a particular course of action is prohibited. Such a distortion does not by itself justify Article 95 EC as a legal basis for the general application to the entire European Union of a stringent prohibition existing in one Member State."

The *British American Tobacco* case relates to Directive 2001/37 concerning the manufacture, presentation and sale of tobacco products, which is based on Articles 95 and 133 (ex 113) EC.[108] That Directive contains very detailed provisions on labelling and also prohibits any words or symbols on the packaging of tobacco products suggesting that "a particular tobacco product is less harmful than others"; but it does not contain any measures on advertising. Geelhoed A.G. recommended that the challenge to the validity of this Directive be dismissed. The case is still pending.

12.44   The *Tobacco Advertising* judgment has given rise to a substantial body of literature.[109] While that literature can obviously not be considered exhaustively here, a few salient points should be drawn to the reader's attention.

First, Mortelmans and van Ooik note that the Court has not departed from its earlier alternative test whereby legislation must aim to eliminate either obstacles to free movement or distortions of competition.[110] They acknowledge that in

---

[107] See n.2 above, para. 18 of the Opinion.
[108] [2001] O.J. L194/26; (see Schroeder, "Vom Brüsseler Kampf gegen den Tabakrauch—2. Teil" [2001] EuZW 489).
[109] Drijber, Casenote [2001] S.E.W. 314 and "Les communications commerciales au carrefour de la dérégulation et de la régulation" [2002] C.D.E (forthcoming); Hervey, "Up in Smoke? Community Anti-Tobacco Law and Policy" [2001] E.L.Rev. 101 and "Community and National Competence in Health after *Tobacco Advertising*" [2001] C.M.L.Rev. 1421; Mortelmans and van Ooik, "Het Europese verbod op tabaksreclam: verbetering van de interne markt of bescherming van de volksgezondheid?" [2001] Ars Aequi 114; Möstl, "Grenzen der Rechtsangleichung im europäischen Binnenmarkt" [2002] EuR 318; Usher, Casenote [2001] C.M.L.Rev. 1519.
[110] *op. cit.* at 121. Likewise Drijber, Casenote in [2001] S.E.W. at 317.

paragraph 95 the Court appears to speak of the two conditions as cumulative. Yet in their view this was not the Court's intention, since otherwise it would not have troubled at all to consider whether the second condition was fulfilled. This interpretation appears to be shared by Geelhoed A.G., to judge by the second of his six propositions in *British American Tobacco* cited above.

Second, shortly after the Court significantly cut down the scope of Article 28 in *Keck*,[111] Mortelmans[112] and Defalque[113] suggested that the scope of Article 95 was similarly reduced. Not surprisingly, Mortelmans (writing with van Ooik) regards the *Tobacco Advertising* judgment as bearing out that prediction[114]; and Usher is of the same view.[115]

Third, there can be no easy answer to the question as to where this ruling leaves the relationship between Article 95 on the one hand and Articles 28 to 30 on the other. As Usher points out, shortly after this judgment the Court ruled in *KO v Gourmet International*[116] that a similar advertising ban at national level might be caught by Article 28 but be justified under Article 30. If so, Usher asks, can Article 95 not be used to replace that national ban with a Community-wide ban ?[117]

Perhaps some of these concerns will be addressed by the Court in its forthcoming judgment in *British American Tobacco*.

(iii) The exception clauses in Article 95(4) to (9)

12.45 The exception clause first inserted into the Treaty by the Single European Act as Article 100A(4)—now Article 95(4) to (9) - was initially the subject of tremendous controversy.[118] The reason is that in certain circumstances it entitles a Member State to continue to impose a particular standard even after Community harmonising legislation has come into force. Indeed, some Members of the European Parliament posed a written question asking the Council whether it agreed that this paragraph "constitutes a threat to the achievement of a genuine single Community market" and "could make the common market more compartmentalised than it is now"; in its answer[119] the Council did not wholly reject this suggestion.

Despite this controversy, recourse to this provision has so far been rare.[120] At

---

[111] Cases C-267-8/91 [1993] E.C.R. I 6097; see para. 6.55 above.
[112] Casenote [1994] S.E.W. at 127.
[113] "L'harmonisation des législations: une alternative à la jurisprudence" [1994] J.T.D.E. 166.
[114] *op.cit.* at pp. 125 *et seq.*
[115] *op.cit.* at p. 1535.
[116] Case C-405/98 [2001] E.C.R. I-1795, see paras 6.00 and 7.45 above.
[117] *op.cit.* at p. 1538.
[118] See, *e.g.* Ehlermann, *op.cit.* (see n.26 above) at 389; Jacqué, "L'acte unique européen" [1986] R.T.D.E. 575 at 599; also see generally Edward, "The Impact of the Single Act on the Institutions" [1987] C.M.L.Rev. 19.
[119] Written question 1893/86 ([1987] O.J. C112/39).
[120] According to De Sadeleer ("Les clauses de sauvegarde prévues à l'article 95 du Traité CE" [2002] R.T.D.E. 53 at 54), the Commission has only applied this exception clause about ten times.

all events, as already mentioned, the Treaty of Amsterdam substantially modified paragraph 4 and added paragraphs 5 to 8, thereby clarifying a number of hotly debated issues.

12.46   Thus, for the first time, paragraph 5 makes it clear that a Member State may introduce a new national provision after the adoption of the relevant Community legislation. This is in contrast to paragraph 4, under which Member States may be authorised to retain certain legislation that pre-dated the Community legislation.[121]

The conditions for applying paragraph 5 are more restrictive than those relating to paragraph 4. At first sight, there would appear to be three differences. First, paragraph 5 may only be invoked in relation to the protection of the environment or the working environment, and not on grounds expressly set out in Article 30—including public health. Second, under paragraph 5 the Member State must be able to rely on "new scientific evidence". Finally, under paragraph 5 the problem must be "specific to that Member State".

However, the last point is perhaps common to both paragraphs: in *Denmark v Commission*[122] Tizzano A.G. has explained at length why in his view paragraph 4 is also confined to circumstances specific to the requesting Member State, even though this condition is not spelt out there.[123] He reached this conclusion on the basis of the analysis of the whole scheme of Article 95. In particular, he found that, when enacting legislation under Article 95, the Parliament and the Council are required to have regard to considerations which are common to all or several Member States—notably because under Article 95(3) they must "take as a base a high level of protection". Accordingly, he reasoned, paragraph 4 can only apply to difficulties specific to the requesting State. This case is still pending and it therefore remains to be seen whether the Court will follow this bold approach.

At all events, in most other respects paragraphs 4 and 5 are similar, as is shown by paragraphs 6 to 9. In particular, as exception clauses, both paragraph 4 and paragraph 5 are to be construed narrowly.[124]

12.47   Whereas Article 100A(4) was expressed to apply only to legislation adopted by qualified majority, that condition was removed by the Treaty of Amsterdam. Accordingly, Article 95(4) and (5) may both be applied to legislation adopted by unanimous vote.

What is more, it is conceivable that a Member State may rely on paragraph 4 even if it has voted in favour of the proposal concerned - although the point is

---

[121] For the distinction between the two paragraphs, see Tizzano A.G. in Case C-512/99 *Germany v Commission* (pending).

[122] Case C-3/00 (pending).

[123] *contra* de Sadeleer, *op. cit.* at p. 63.

[124] See Tesauro A.G. in Case C-41/93 *France v Commission* ("PCP") [1994] E.C.R. I-1829; also Tizzano A.G. in Cases C-512/99 and C-3/00 (nn.121 and 122 above). Paras. 8.01 and 9.01 above.

not free from doubt.[125] An analogy can be drawn here with *Italy v Council*[126]; it was held there that a Member State can bring an action under Article 230 (ex 173) despite having voted in favour of the contested act. Having said that, it should be recalled that, according to Article 205(3) of the Treaty, a vote is considered unanimous despite one or more abstentions.

In any event, it seems clear that a Member State is not debarred from relying on paragraph 5 merely because it has voted in favour of the Community legislation in question: this provision clearly stipulates that it only applies where "new scientific evidence" comes to light after the adoption of the Community legislation; and by definition no Member State can be taken to task for voting in favour of legislation which subsequent scientific discoveries prove to be harmful.

12.48   A further point of controversy was whether Article 95(4) extends to Commission acts implementing Council legislation based on Article 95. Again, the Treaty of Amsterdam has laid this controversy to rest by stating explicitly that paragraph 4 applies to acts of the Commission as well as to those adopted by the Council. Moreover, the new paragraph 5 contains a statement to the same effect.

12.49   The first subparagraph of Article 95(4) states that the Member State must notify its request after the legislation has been adopted, without specifying when. It is clear from *France v Commission* ("PCP")[127] that the Member State may lodge its request at any time after the adoption of the legislation; in the case of Directives this may occur either before or after the expiry of the deadline for implementation. However, it is equally plain from the judgment that in no case may the Member State act unilaterally: on no account may it apply the notified national provisions before they have been approved by the Commission. This was subsequently confirmed in *Kortas*,[128] where the Court also ruled that a Directive continues to be fully effective in the Member State concerned, unless and until the Commission grants that State's application.[129]

Thus the Member State has an incentive to effect the notification as speedily as possible. What is more, the Court has held that it is incumbent on the Member State to do so.[130] No doubt, the same principles apply to paragraph 5.

---

[125] Ehlermann, *op.cit.* (see n.26 above) at 394, expresses uncertainty on this point. Michel Waelbroeck, "Le role de la Cour de justice dans la mise en oeuvre de l'Acte unique européen" [1989] C.D.E. 42 at 57, maintains that the Member State must have voted against the measure if it is to rely on Art. 95(4).

[126] Case 166/78 (potato starch) [1979] E.C.R. 2575; [1981] 3 C.M.L.R. 770.

[127] See n.124 above.

[128] Case C-319/97 [1999] E.C.R. I-3143, para. 35.

[129] This must be read with the ruling in Case C-129/96 *Inter-Environnement Wallonie v Région Wallonne* [1997] E.C.R. I-7411. It was held there that a Member State need not implement a Directive before the date set for its implementation and thus need not repeal any incompatible pre-existing measures; but that, prior to that date, the Member State must "refrain from taking any measures liable seriously to compromise the result prescribed" (para. 45).

[130] *Kortas*, para. 35.

12.50   Prior to the Treaty of Amsterdam, the then Article 100A(4) imposed no time-limit on the Commission for deciding on the application by a Member State. In the *PCP* case, the Advocate General criticised the Commission for its delay, and in *Kortas* the Court itself was equally disapproving. This problem has now been solved by Article 95(6).

12.51   The prevailing view[131] has always been that the act whereby the Commission confirms or rejects a national measure is in the nature of a decision and is not therefore analogous to a reasoned opinion under Article 226 (ex 169). This approach was not contested by any of the parties in the *PCP* case. Moreover, it was expressly endorsed by the Advocate General and tacitly accepted by the Court. Accordingly, a Commission decision rejecting a Member State's application may well be capable of being relied on before national courts, at least against the authorities of that State.[132]

12.52   In the previous two editions of this book, it was suggested that, despite the rule that exceptions to fundamental Treaty rules are to be construed restrictively, Member States could perhaps rely on paragraph 4 with respect to any of the mandatory requirements, not merely the protection of the environment and protection of the working environment.[133] It was claimed that there was no logical reason why the other mandatory requirements should not apply in this context; this was particularly the case with consumer protection which is expressly mentioned in paragraph 3. However, in *France v Commission* ("PCP")[134] Tesauro A.G. expressed the contrary view, seeing no need to depart from the rule that exceptions to fundamental Treaty rules are to be read narrowly. Indeed, he found this approach to be:

> "further justified by the fact that the derogations from the principle of free movement of goods upheld by those decisions relate to pre-existing national measures or sectors in which harmonisation has not taken place, whereas those which may be based on the provision at issue here actually presuppose the existence of a Community harmonisation measure, for the adoption of which account was taken of the 'major needs' invoked by the various Member States."

12.53   By the same token, it was also suggested in the last two editions that the words "major needs referred to in Article [30]" should merely be taken as a

---

[131]Ehlermann *op.cit.* (see n.26 above) at 397-398; Flynn, "How Will Article 100A(4) Work ? A Comparison with Article 92" [1987] C.M.L.Rev. 689 at 702; Forwood and Clough *op. cit.* n.44 above at 403; Glaesner *op. cit.* n.26 above at 135; Jacqué, *op. cit.* n. 118 above, at 600; and Langeheine, "Rechtsangleichung unter Artikel 100A EWGV–Harmonisierung v nationale Schutzinteressen" [1988] EuR 235 at 253.

[132]Forwood and Clough, *op. cit.* n.44 above at 403. The *PCP* decision was not published as such in the Official Journal but its salient features were summarised in a Commission Communication ([1992] O.J. C334/8). It was held in Case C-192/89 *Sevince v Staatssecretaris van Justitie* [1990] E.C.R. I-3461 that an unpublished decision may have direct effect, although it may obviously not be invoked against private parties.

[133]It appears from Art. 137 that by "the working environment" is meant the health and safety of workers, Ehlermann *op.cit.* (see n.26 above) at 393.

[134]See n.124 above, para. 5 of the Opinion.

reminder that that provision is not to be invoked lightly, and should not be regarded as precluding reliance on Article 30 with regard to other types of "need". On this view, this language is not to be read as creating two classes of "need" under Article 30. This appears to be the prevailing view.[135]

12.54 Where a Member State's standard is higher than that enshrined in Community legislation based on Article 95, it does not automatically follow that the Commission may confirm the national measure. In the *PCP* case, the Commission's decision authorising the German measure was annulled for want of proper reasoning. Having established that the German standard was more stringent, the Commission simply stated in the crucial passage of its decision that:

> "the national provisions apply without distinction to both national and imported products. They are designed to protect public health and the environment and do not seem to be a manifestly disproportionate way of attaining these objectives. Furthermore, they do not appear to be a means of arbitrary discrimination or a disguised restriction on trade between Member States."

Following the Advocate General, the Court found that the Commission had failed to set out the reasons of fact and law which had led it to the conclusion that the conditions set out in Article 95(4) were fulfilled; and that the Commission's decision thus failed to fulfil the requirements of Article 253 (ex 190). Consequently, the Court found it unnecessary to consider France's primary argument, which was that as a matter of substance the conditions laid down by Article 95(4) had not been fulfilled.[136] The ruling in this case indicates most plainly that, in view of its exceptional nature, recourse to that provision cannot be authorised lightly.

12.55 Moreover, in the last edition it was also claimed that the normal rule as to burden of proof applies, namely that there is a presumption that a restriction on imports or exports is not justified.[137] That view was implicitly confirmed by the Court in the following passage of its *PCP* judgment, when it said:

> "The Commission must ... satisfy itself that all the conditions for a Member State to be able to rely on the exception provided for by Article 95(4) are fulfilled. In particular, it must establish whether the provisions in question are justified on grounds of the major needs mentioned in the first subparagraph of Article 95(4) and are not a means of arbitrary discrimination or a disguised restriction on trade between Member States."[138]

---

[135] De Sadeleer, *op.cit.* at p. 62 and other sources cited there.
[136] Subsequently, the Commission adopted a fresh Decision authorising Germany to maintain the measure: Decision 94/783 ([1994] O.J. L316/43).
[137] Para. 8.11 above.
[138] See n.124 above, para. 27 of the judgment.

More recently, this point was stated in express terms by Tizzano A.G. in *Germany v Commission.*[139]

12.56 According to Article 95(6), the Commission is required to check whether the notified national measure is a "means of arbitrary discrimination or a disguised restriction on trade" and whether it constitutes an "obstacle to the functioning of the internal market". It seems clear that in reality the Commission is obliged to proceed to a general scrutiny of the compatibility of the national measure with Community law; and this particularly includes the principle of proportionality.[140] Indeed, in *Denmark v Commission*[141] the Advocate General has considered the question of proportionality at some length.

12.57 The wording of the paragraph 9 also raises a number of questions. This provision does not state at what stage the action must be lodged with the Court. Although this is not expressly stipulated, common sense would suggest that the Commission must first formally decide to reject the national measure and inform the Member State of its decision. Moreover, if the Member State complies with the decision at that stage, the Commission need not bring the matter before the Court at all.

In contrast, it would appear to be open to another Member State to commence proceedings before the Court without waiting for the Commission to decide whether to confirm the national measure. There seems to be no reason to make the rights of action of Member States dependent on the course of events within the Commission.

If the Commission confirms the measure of one Member State but another Member State objects, the latter State would appear to be faced with a choice: it can seek the annulment of the Commission decision under Article 230 (ex 173); it can bring an action under the Article 95(9) against the Member State whose measure it contests; or it can do both. It is probably open to the dissatisfied State to bring an action under paragraph 9 even after the date for bringing annulment proceedings under Article 230 has expired.

(iv) Article 95(10)

12.58 Paragraph 10 (ex Article 100A(5)) provides that harmonisation measures shall, where appropriate, contain safeguard clauses of a type which was already common prior to its insertion into the EC Treaty by the Single European Act. It does not entail any change in practice. Glaesner[142] expressed the view that, where a regulation or directive contains such a safeguard clause, Member States may not have recourse to paragraph 4; Gulmann[143] took the opposite view.

---

[139] Case C-512/99 (see n.121 above), point 71 of the Opinion.
[140] De Sadeleer, *op. cit.* at p. 68.
[141] See n.122 above.
[142] *op. cit.* n.26 above at 134.
[143] "The Single European Act: Some Remarks from a Danish Perspective" [1987] C.M.L.Rev. 31 at 38; similarly Ehlermann, *op.cit.* (see n.26 above), at 399. Jacqué (*op. cit.* n.42 above at 599-600) leaves the point open.

What is striking, however, is that the scope of this paragraph is limited to the "non-economic reasons referred to in Article 30"—whereas that of paragraph 4 covers "major needs referred to in Article 30" and to the environment and the working environment, and paragraph 5 refers exclusively to the environment and the working environment. These inconsistencies appear difficult to justify. In any case, it seems clear that there is nothing to preclude the Community legislator from laying down safeguard clauses in relation to grounds of justification not expressly set out in Article 30.

D. Competitive Distortions

12.59 In addition to these legislative provisions, Article 96 (ex 101) provides for a special procedure for ironing out distortions caused by differences between national measures. If it finds the existence of such a distortion, the Commission must consult the Member States concerned and, if necessary, it may propose to the Council a separate Directive which the Council may adopt by qualified majority after the end of the first stage of the transitional period. Article 97 (ex 102) further requires a Member State wishing to adopt a measure likely to cause such a distortion to consult the Commission, which is then required to recommend the appropriate measures to the Member States concerned. If the Member State in question adopts the measure contrary to the recommendation of the Commission, Article 97 states that other Member States cannot be required to amend their provisions under Article 96. In fact, Articles 96 and 97 have had very little impact: a handful of Commission recommendations have ensued, but no Directives.

E. Customs Co-operation

12.60 Article 135 reads as follows:

> "Within the scope of application of this Treaty, the Council, acting in accordance with the procedure referred to in Article 251, shall take measures in order to strengthen customs co-operation between Member States and between the latter and the Commission. These measures shall not concern the application of national criminal law or the national administration of justice."

This provision, which was inserted into the EC Treaty at Amsterdam, is drawn from the former Article K.1(8) TEU. Neither provision has been the basis for any legislation to date, perhaps because of their narrow scope: only co-operation "between Member States and between the latter and the Commission" is covered, which thus excludes most customs legislation. Accordingly, Regulation 2700/2000,[144] the only Regulation to amend the Common Customs Code since the entry into force of the Treaty of Amsterdam, is based not on Article 135, but on Articles 26 (ex 28), 95 and 133 (ex 113).

---

[144] [2000] O.J. L311/17.

F. Worker Protection

12.61   Before the Treaty of Amsterdam, according to the then Article 118A(1), "Member States shall pay particular attention to encouraging improvements, especially in the working environment, as regards the health and safety of workers ... ". The meaning of the words "especially in the working environment" was not wholly clear, but the provision was obviously concerned with health and safety at work.[145]

Now, according to Article 137(a), "the Community shall support and complement the activities of the Member States in the following fields:

— improvement in particular of the working environment to protect workers' health and safety;
— working conditions;
— the information and consultation of workers;
— the integration of persons excluded from the labour market, without prejudice to Article 150;
— equality between men and women with regard to labour market opportunities and treatment at work."

Article 137(2) provides for directives—though not regulations—to be adopted by the Council "to this end". Since this paragraph was amended by the Treaty of Amsterdam, legislation is to be adopted according to the co-decision procedure set out in Article 251, after the Economic and Social Committee has been consulted. A major difference from Article 95 is that the Directives based on Article 137 are merely to lay down "minimal requirements for gradual implementation".

Article 137(5) states: "The provisions adopted pursuant to this Article shall not prevent any Member State from maintaining or introducing more stringent measures for the protection of working conditions compatible with the Treaty."

It is unlikely that legislation on goods could be based on this provision. One could conceivably argue that Article 137(2) is the proper legal basis for health and safety standards for goods used exclusively or almost exclusively in the workplace, such as tools and industrial machines. Yet this would lead to the inconvenient result that Article 95 could not be used as a legal basis for such legislation, since the latter provision is expressed to apply "save where otherwise provided in this Treaty" (see Article 95(1)). That would scarcely appear a reasonable result.

The Treaty of Nice is set to replace this Article with a wholly new provision, which will be considerably wider in scope as it will extend to such matters as social security. However, Article 137(4) will provide: "The provisions adopted pursuant to this Article shall not affect the right of Member States to define the fundamental principles of their social security systems and must not significantly affect the financial equilibrium thereof ... ".

---

[145] See generally Case C-84/94 (see n.9 above).

G. Culture

12.62 For good measure, it should be mentioned that, while Article 151 (ex 128) EC empowers the Community to take certain measures in relation to culture, paragraph 5 provides that this article may not be used for harmonisation.[146] Nevertheless, it seems clear that there is nothing to preclude the adoption of harmonising legislation based on other provisions of the Treaty, which have an impact on cultural policy.[147]

H. Public Health Protection

12.63 Article 152(1) has already been cited at paragraph 12.26 above. Article 152(4) and (5) read as follows:

> "4. The Council, acting in accordance with the procedure referred to in Article 251 and after consulting the Economic and Social Committee and the Committee of the Regions, shall contribute to the achievement of the objectives referred to in this Article through adopting:
>
> (a) measures setting high standards of quality and safety of organs and substances of human origin, blood and blood derivatives; these measures shall not prevent any Member State from maintaining or introducing more stringent protective measures;
> (b) by way of derogation from Article 37, measures in the veterinary and phytosanitary fields which have as their direct objective the protection of public health;
> (c) incentive measures designed to protect and improve human health, excluding any harmonisation of the laws and regulations of the Member States.
>
> The Council, acting by a qualified majority on a proposal from the Commission, may also adopt recommendations for the purposes set out in this Article.
> 5. Community action in the field of public health shall fully respect the responsibilities of the Member States for the organisation and delivery of health services and medical care. In particular, measures referred to in paragraph 4(a) shall not affect national provisions on the donation or medical use of organs and blood."

This provision falls well short of creating a common public health policy. On the contrary, the powers which it confers on the Community are relatively limited. Indeed, paragraph 4(c) expressly excludes harmonisation except in the fields covered by paragraph 4(a) and (b). Having said that, there is nothing to preclude the adoption of harmonising legislation based on other provisions of the EC Treaty, which have an impact on public health.[148] Finally, as we noticed earlier, Article 152(4)(b) restricts the scope of Article 37.

---

[146] See generally Case C-85/94 *Piageme v Peeters* [1995] E.C.R. I-2955 at para. 19, relating to the earlier provision.
[147] See footnote for the case law on the equivalent provision in Art. 152.
[148] Case C-376/98, see n.2 above, paras 78, 79 and 88; Opinion of Geelhoed A.G. dated September 10, 2002 in Case C-491/01, see n.2 above, para. 114.

I. Consumer Protection

12.64   Article 153 (ex 129a), which was introduced by the Treaty of Maastricht and amended by the Treaty of Amsterdam, is entitled "Consumer Protection". Paragraphs 1 and 2 are set out at paragraph 12.27 above. Article 153(3) to (5) read as follows:

> "3. The Community shall contribute to the attainment of a high level of consumer protection through:
>
> (a) measures adopted pursuant to Article 95 in the context of the completion of the internal market;
> (b) measures which support, supplement and monitor the policy pursued by the Member States.
>
>   4. The Council, acting in accordance with the procedure referred to in Article 251 and after consulting the Economic and Social Committee, shall adopt the measures referred to in paragraph 3(b).
>   5. Measures adopted pursuant to paragraph 4 shall not prevent any Member State from maintaining or introducing more stringent protective measures. Such measures must be compatible with this Treaty. The Commission shall be notified of them."

The restrictive language of paragraph 3(b) should be noted.[149] As to paragraph 5, it is broadly analogous to Article 95(4), but confers no powers of decision on the Commission.[150]

J. Environmental Protection

12.65   Articles 174 to 176 (ex 130r to 130t), which relate to the environment, were first introduced by the Single European Act, but were substantially amended by the Treaties of Maastricht and Amsterdam. Article 174(1) and (2) have already been cited *in extenso* at paragraph 12.24 above. Article 175(1) provides for legislation to be enacted according to the co-decision procedure; by virtue of Article 175(3), general action programmes are to be adopted following the same procedure. Article 175(2) is drafted in the following terms:

> "By way of derogation from the decision-making procedure provided for in paragraph 1 and without prejudice to Article 95, the Council, acting unanimously on a proposal from the Commission and after consulting the European Parliament, the Economic and Social Committee and the Committee of the Regions, shall adopt ... measures significantly affecting a Member State's choice between different energy sources and the general structure of its energy supply. ... ".

Article 175(2)—and only that paragraph—is expressed to be without prejudice to Article 95. However, the procedure in paragraphs 1 and 3 is identical to that in Article 95. Accordingly, conflicts between the two Articles may only arise where measures under paragraph 2 are involved.

---

[149] The ruling in *Piageme v Peeters* (see n.146 above) applies equally to this provision.
[150] See para. 12.72 below.

Article 176 states that the adoption of such legislation shall not preclude the Member States from maintaining or introducing more stringent protective measures, provided that they are otherwise compatible with the Treaty.[151]

12.66   The Court has decided three cases on the relationship between Article 95 and Article 175. Although those cases relate to Article 175 as it stood prior to the entry into force of the Treaty of Maastricht, they are still in point today.[152]

The first case, *Commission v Council* ("Titanium Dioxide")[153] concerned Directive 89/428 on the progressive elimination of pollution caused by titanium dioxide.[154] The Commission claimed that the proper legal basis for this Directive was Article 95, whereas the Council had chosen to base it on Article 175 instead. On an analysis of the text of the Directive, the Court found that it was concerned "indissociably with both the protection of the environment and the elimination of disparities in conditions of competition". Accordingly, it "displayed features" linking it both to Article 95 and to Article 175. However, it was not possible to combine the two legal bases, since at the material time Article 95 required legislation to be adopted according to the co-operation procedure, whereas under Article 175 a unanimous vote was required in the Council. The Court found that sufficient account could be taken of environmental needs under Article 95, particularly as Article 95(3) enjoined the Commission to take as a base a high level of environmental protection when drafting proposals under paragraph 1. Thus Article 95 was held to be the appropriate legal basis. The Court therefore annulled the Directive.

The Court then proceeded to qualify that ruling in the next case, *Commission v Council* ("Directive on waste").[155] It was held there that Directive 91/156 on waste[156] had been correctly based on Article 175, since it was primarily concerned with the protection of the environment.[157] That Directive therefore differed from the Directive on titanium dioxide which concerned the protection of the environment and harmonising conditions of competition in equal measure. In this case the Court plainly heeded the warning of Tesauro A.G. that, if it went any further down the path followed in the earlier case, it would render Article 175 virtually otiose.[158]

---

[151] See para. 12.72 below.
[152] See also generally Case 62/88 *Greece v Council* [1990] E.C.R. 1527 on the relationship between Arts 133 and 175.
[153] Case C-300/89, see n.71 above; see Barents, *op. cit.* n.70 above and "Milieu en interne markt" [1993] S.E.W. 5; Everling, "Abgrenzung der Rechtsangleichung zur Verwirklichung des Binnenmarktes nach Art. 100A EWGV durch den Gerichtshof" [1991] EuR 179; Krämer, "L'Environnement et le Marché unique européen" [1993] R.M.U.E. 45.
[154] [1989] O.J. L201/56.
[155] Case C-155/91 [1993] E.C.R. I 939, noted by Wachsmann [1993] C.M.L.Rev. 105.
[156] [1991] O.J. L78/32.
[157] In this regard the Court relied on its earlier judgment in Case C-70/88, see n.93 above; it had held there that legislation need not be based on Art. 95 where it only had the "incidental effect of harmonising the conditions for the free movement of goods within the Community"; the Court in Case C-70/88 had therefore found that the contested Regulation was lawfully based on the now deleted Art. 31 of the Euratom Treaty.
[158] See also Everling, *op. cit.* n.153 above.

Next, in *Parliament v Council*[159] the applicant institution sought the annulment of Council Regulation 259/93 on the supervision and control of shipments of waste within, into and out of the European Community.[160] That Regulation was adopted under Article 175 but Parliament maintained that it should have been based on Articles 95 and 133. The action failed, since once again the primary object of the contested measure was held to be the protection of the environment. The Court referred with approval to Jacobs A.G.'s statement that: "The aim of the Regulation is not to define those characteristics of waste which will enable waste to circulate freely within the internal market; rather it is to provide a harmonised set of procedures whereby movements of waste can be prevented and controlled in accordance with national law and with the requirements imposed by the Directive on waste."[161]

12.67 Article 175(2) is set to be substantially reworded by the Treaty of Nice.

K. General Objectives

12.68 Article 308 (ex 235) provides:

"If action by the Community should prove necessary to attain, in the course of the operation of the common market, one of the objectives of the Community and this Treaty has not provided the necessary powers, the Council shall, acting unanimously on a proposal from the Commission and after consulting the Assembly, take the appropriate measures."

This provision only applies if "this Treaty has not provided the necessary powers". Thus the Court has repeatedly held[162] that it may only be relied on as a legal basis of last resort, when no other legal basis in the Treaty is available. Accordingly, after the Single European Act added a number of new legal bases for harmonisation (*e.g.* for the environment), recourse to Article 308 became less frequent than it had been. With the addition of further provisions by the Treaties of Maastricht and Amsterdam, this provision is used sparingly today.[163]

This provision does not confer *Kompetenz-Kompetenz* (*i.e.* the power to extend one's own competences) on the Community. That was clearly stated by the Court in Opinion 2/94 where it held:

---

[159] Case C-187/93 [1994] E.C.R. I 2857.

[160] [1993] O.J. L30/1.

[161] On the scope of Articles 174-176, see also Cases C-164 and C-165/97 *Parliament v Council* (see n.75 above); Opinion 2/00 on the Cartagena Protocol on the prevention of biotechnological risks [2001] E.C.R. I-9713; and Case C-36/98 *Spain v Council* (Danube Convention) [2001] E.C.R. I-779.

[162] See generally Cases 8/73 *Hauptzollamt Bremerhaven v Massey-Ferguson* [1973] E.C.R. 897; 45/86, see n.71 above; [1988] 2 C.M.L.R. 131; and C-295/90, see n.69 above.

[163] The Court has held that it constitutes the correct legal basis for legislation creating new Community intellectual property rights, but by definition that does not entail the harmonisation of national laws: Opinion 1/94 (see n.69 above), para. 59. Thus Council Regulation 40/94 on the Community trade mark ([1994] O.J. L11/1) is based on Article 308, as is the proposed Regulation on the Community patent ([2000] O.J. C337E/278).

"Article [308] is designed to fill the gap where no specific provisions of the Treaty confer on the Community institutions express or implied powers to act, if such powers appear none the less to be necessary to enable the Community to carry out its functions with a view to attaining one of the objectives laid down by the Treaty.

That provision, being an integral part of an institutional system based on the principle of conferred powers, cannot serve as a basis for widening the scope of Community powers beyond the general framework created by the provisions of the Treaty as a whole and, in particular, by those that define the tasks and the activities of the Community. On any view, Article [308] cannot be used as a basis for the adoption of provisions whose effect would, in substance, be to amend the Treaty without following the procedure which it provides for that purpose."[164]

L. Police and Judicial Co-operation

12.69   For completeness a brief mention should be made of Title VI of the TEU ("Provisions on police and judicial co-operation in criminal matters"), which covers Articles 29 to 42 (ex K to K14) of that Treaty. These Articles provide for certain matters to be the subject of consultation between the Member States and, where appropriate, of inter-governmental conventions. The Community as such is not involved, although its institutions do have a role to play.

Among the items covered by this title is "closer co-operation between police forces, customs authorities and other competent authorities of the Member States" (Article 29). However, the opening words of that provision stipulate that these provisions are to apply "without prejudice to the powers of the European Community". Article 95 EC is the appropriate basis for customs legislation in the internal market, while Articles 26 and 133 (ex 28 and 113) EC are the appropriate bases for customs legislation relating to trade with third countries. Accordingly, it is not easy to see what room there is left for customs measures adopted under Title VI —save perhaps in relation to criminal law.

M. Closer Co-operation

12.70   Since the Treaty of Maastricht, the Treaty on European Union has provided for the possibility for some Member States to engage in "closer co-operation" with one another without the participation of others. Precisely for this reason, such measures do not constitute harmonisation in the traditional sense at all.[165]

The important point to notice in the present context is that such co-operation may not involve restrictions on trade between Member States: Article 43(1)(e) TEU makes it clear that such measures may not "affect the '*acquis communautaire*'". Moreover, under Article 43(1)(f) such action may not "affect

---

[164] [1996] E.C.R. I-1759, paras 29 and 30; confirmed in C-249/96 *Grant v South West Trains* [1998] E.C.R. I-621, para.45.

[165] See generally Bribosia, "Différenciation et avant-gardes au sein de l'Union européenne" [2000] C.D.E. 57; Ehlermann, "Différenciation, flexibilité, coopération renforcée : les nouvelles dispositions du traité d'Amsterdam" [1997] R.M.U.E. 53; Gaja, "How flexible is flexibility under the Amsterdam treaty ?" [1998] C.M.L.Rev. 855; Tuytschaever, *Differentiation in European Law* (1999).

the ... rights, obligations and interests of those Member States which do not participate therein". Indeed, the new Article 11(1)(e) EC expressly provides that, if such co-operation is carried out under the auspices of the EC institutions and according to EC procedures, then it must not "constitute a discrimination or a restriction of trade between Member States" and must not "distort the conditions of competition between the latter".

Both provisions will be substantially amended by the Treaty of Nice. Thus "closer co-operation" will become known as "enhanced co-operation". Nevertheless, measures involving restrictions on trade between Member States will still be prohibited. Article 43 TEU will continue to provide that the "*acquis communautaire*" must be respected (paragraph(c)), and will also expressly stipulate that closer co-operation must not "constitute a barrier to or discrimination in trade between the Member States" and must not "distort competition between them" (paragraph (f)).

III. TECHNIQUES OF HARMONISATION

A. Total and Optional Harmonisation

12.71   Having considered the various bases in the Treaty for harmonisation, it is now necessary to discuss the two basic types of harmonisation: total and optional. Total harmonisation imposes a two-fold obligation on the Member States:

— to permit goods complying with the Directive to be freely imported and marketed (the free movement clause); and

— to prohibit the sale of goods not complying with the Directive (the exclusivity clause).

On the other hand, optional harmonisation involves the first obligation only: the Member States are then free to allow the sale of goods not meeting the standards laid down in the Directive. This means that, should a Member State so wish, it can allow national norms to co-exist with the Community ones. It is then open to small producers to produce only according to national norms, although this reduces the possibility of exporting their goods. This can best be illustrated by reference to examples. Directive 76/768[166] on the approximation of laws relating to cosmetic products provides for total harmonisation. Article 7(1) of that Directive provides:

"Member States may not, for reasons related to the requirements laid down in this Directive and the annexes thereto, refuse, prohibit or restrict the marketing of any cosmetic products which comply with the requirements of this Directive and the Annexes thereto" (the free movement clause).

---

[166] [1976] O.J. L262/169. This Directive has been amended on numerous occasions, but those amendments are not in point here, since the Directive is only being taken as an example.

In addition, Article 3 provides:

> "Member States shall take all necessary measures to ensure that only cosmetic products which confirm to the provisions of this Directive and its Annexes may be put on the market" (the exclusivity clause).

On the other hand, Directive 71/316[167] on the approximation of laws relating to common provisions for both measuring instruments and methods of methodological control provides for optional harmonisation. It contains a free movement clause (broadly similar to Article 7(1) of Directive 76/768) but no exclusivity clause.

Optional harmonisation is more flexible and less likely to stifle innovation than total harmonisation. It is also more attractive to small companies producing only for the market of their own Member State: for such companies total harmonisation entails the expense of changing over to new standards without any compensating advantage. Consequently optional harmonisation has come to be more frequently used. On the other hand, optional harmonisation does not necessarily remove differences between national standards and these differences can sometimes be successfully exploited by multinationals so as to restrict parallel imports. Other weaknesses in optional harmonisation are discussed in paragraphs 12.109 and 12.110.

B. Minimum Standards

12.72 We have already noticed that provisions such as Articles 137, 153 and 175 (read with Article 176) only empower the Council to adopt minimum standards, leaving the Member States free to maintain or introduce more stringent measures if they wish.[168] None of these provisions appeared in the original Treaty of Rome.

Yet the practice is not new.[169] Thus Council Directive 85/577 to protect the consumer in respect of contracts negotiated away from business premises[170] (frequently referred to as the "doorstep selling" Directive) contains a minimum standards clause.

. This was the Directive in issue in *Buet*[171] which concerned a total ban imposed by France on doorstep selling. The Court held this ban to be compatible with the Directive (in view of the minimum standards clause) and with Article 28. As this case illustrates, where a Member State takes advantage of a minimum standards clause in a Directive to impose a more stringent standard and that

---

[167] [1971] O.J. L202/1, subsequently amended. Again, this Directive is mentioned here purely by way of illustration so that it is unnecessary to have regard to any amendments.

[168] For a case on Art. 175 EC, see C-203/96 *Chemische Afvalstoffen Dusseldorp v Minister van Milieubeheer* [1998] E.C.R. I-4075. See generally Van Calster, "Export restrictions—a Watershed for Article 30" [2000] E.L.Rev. 335.

[169] See Dougan, "Minimum Harmonisation and the Internal Market" [2000] C.M.L.Rev. 853; Slot, "Harmonisation" [1996] 21 E.L.Rev. 378; Temmink, "Minimumnormen in EG-Richtlijnen" [1995] S.E.W. 79.

[170] [1985] O.J. L372/31.

[171] Case 382/87 [1989] E.C.R. 1233.

standard is also applied to imports, the measure concerned will only be compatible with Community law if it satisfies the conditions of Article 30, including the mandatory requirements.[172]

12.73 When can a minimum standards clause be implied?[173] Traditionally, the judgment in *Ratti*[174] is seen as the *locus classicus* on this question. The Court's position on this issue in that ruling is simple: such a clause cannot be implied. It was held that the Directive in question, which related to solvents, precluded Member States from laying down more stringent rules, since it stipulated that only solvents which complied with its provisions could be placed on the market.

However, doubt has been cast on that judgment by the decision in *R. v Secretary of State for Health, Ex p. Gallaher*.[175] That case related to Council Directive 89/622 on the labelling of tobacco products,[176] which was based on Article 95. Articles 3(3) and 4(4) of that Directive required certain information to be indicated on cigarette packets in print covering "at least 4%" of the surface concerned. Article 8(1) provided that "Member States may not, for reasons of labelling, prohibit or restrict the sale of products which comply with this Directive." Nevertheless, the United Kingdom required the print to cover at least 6 per cent of the surface in question, but exempted imports from other Member States from this more stringent requirement.

The Court read Article 8(1) as relating only to imports from other Member States. It took the words "at least" in Article 3(3) and 4(4) as constituting an implied authorisation to Member States to go beyond the requirements of those two provisions. Thus it found the British measure to be compatible with the Directive.

Since the 6 per cent requirement related only to the sale within the United Kingdom of goods produced there, neither Article 28 nor Article 29 was in point.[177] Yet the outcome may be regarded by some as being less than wholly conducive to the elimination of disparities in conditions of competition, which is said to be the purpose of Article 95.[178]

---

[172] See also Cases C-1/96 *R. v Minister of Agriculture Ex p. Compassion in World Farming* [1998] E.C.R. I-1251; C-203/96, see n.168 above; and C-389/96 *Aher-Waggon v Germany* [1998] E.C.R. I-4473. See van Calster, *op. cit.*

[173] This question is to be distinguished from the question as to whether a Community legislative act is to be regarded as exhaustive (*i.e.* whether it leaves room for Member States to take action against the products concerned on grounds not covered by that act); on that issue, see paras 8.28 *et seq.* above.

[174] Case 148/78 [1979] E.C.R. 1629; [1980] 1 C.M.L.R. 96.

[175] Case C-11/92 [1993] E.C.R. I 3545; noted by Robert [1994] C.M.L.Rev. 165; and Weatherill [1994] E.L.Rev. 56. See also Case C-222/91 *Ministero delle Finanze v Philip Morris Belgium* [1993] E.C.R. I-3469.

[176] [1989] O.J. L359/1, since replaced by Dir. 2001/37 (see n.108 above).

[177] Paras 6.96 *et seq.* above.

[178] See also Case C-389/96 *Aher-Waggon* (see n.172 above), para 15. That judgment is also discussed at para. 8.161 above.

C. Safeguard Clauses

12.74 It is also quite common for a Directive to contain a safeguard clause. An example is Article 12(1) of Directive 76/768 already referred to, which reads as follows:

> "If a Member State notes, on the basis of a substantiated justification, that a cosmetic product, although complying with the requirements of the Directive, represents a hazard to health, it may provisionally prohibit the marketing of that product in its territory or subject it to special conditions. It shall immediately inform the other Member States and the Commission thereof, stating the grounds for its decision."

Subsequent provisions of the Directive require the Commission to deliver an opinion on whether the product constitutes a health hazard and, if necessary, to propose the technical adaptation of the Directive.[179] As will be clear from paragraphs 12.58 and 12.24 respectively, Articles 95(10) and 174(2) make specific provision for such safeguard clauses to be inserted into legislative acts in "appropriate cases".

D. Technical Adaptation

12.75 In order to bring legislation into line with technical developments, it is obviously necessary to amend it from time to time. Clearly, it would be too cumbersome to follow the same procedure as for the basic directive on each occasion, culminating in the adoption of an amending directive by the Council. To avoid this, it is the practice for the Council to delegate to the Commission power to elaborate technical adaptations with the assistance of one of the committees provided for in Council Decision 1999/468 laying down the procedures for the exercise of implementing powers conferred on the Commission.[180] Such a procedure is provided for, for instance, by Articles 9 and 10 of Directive 76/768.[181]

E. The "New" Approach

12.76 It was anticipated that the entry into force of Directive 83/189[182] (now repealed and consolidated by Directive 98/34)[183] would bring to light new areas in which harmonisation was needed. This, it was felt, would aggravate the pre-existing difficulties encountered in harmonising national measures according to the practice of incorporating detailed technical specifications into Directives.

---

[179] See para. 12.75 below.
[180] [1999] O.J. L184/23.
[181] In Case C-314/99 *Netherlands v Commission* (judgment of June 18, 2002), the Court quashed a Commission Directive of this kind, on the grounds that it did not constitute technical adaptation at all and that the Commission had therefore exceeded its powers: the contested Directive merely extended in time a derogation granted to Austria and Sweden in the 1994 Act of Accession.
[182] [1983] O.J. L109/8.
[183] [1998] O.J. L204/37.

Thus the Directive, together with the perceived need to quicken the pace of harmonisation, led to the adoption of the "new approach to technical harmonisation and standards" set out in detail in the Resolution of the Council of May 7, 1985.[184] The "new" approach is based on various principles set out at length in the Annexes to the Resolution. According to these principles, total harmonisation is to be used whenever possible and the task of drawing up standards is to be delegated to standards organisations; and only the essential elements of standards are to be harmonised. An example of Community legislation based on this approach is Council Directive 87/404 on pressure vessels.[185]

The Resolution of 1985 was followed up by: Council Decision 90/683 on conformity assessment procedures[186]; the Commission's Green Paper on the development of European standardisation[187]; a Council Resolution of June 18, 1992 on the role of European standardisation in the European economy[188]; a Commission report of May 13, 1998[189]; and a further Council Resolution dated May 19, 2000.[190]

IV. NOTIFICATION OF NATIONAL MEASURES

A. Directive 98/34

12.77 Directive 98/34[191] lays down a procedure for the provision of information in the field of technical standards and regulations. This Directive repealed and consolidated Directive 83/189[192] which had been materially amended by Directives 88/182[193] and 94/10.[194] This consolidation, which was carried out "for reasons of clarity and rationality",[195] left the substance of the amended provisions of Directive 83/189 untouched.[196] However, less than one

---

[184] [1985] O.J. C136/1. See Written question 119/86 ([1987] O.J. C19/4); and Lopez Escudero, *Los obstáculos técnicos al comercio en la Comunidad Económica Europea* (1991) at 420; McMillan, "La 'certification', la reconnaissance mutuelle et le marché unique" [1991] R.M.U.E. 181.
[185] [1987] O.J. L 220/48.
[186] [1990] O.J. L380/3.
[187] [1991] O.J. C20/1.
[188] [1992] O.J. C173/1.
[189] COM(98)291 final.
[190] [2000] O.J. C141/1.
[191] See n.183 above.
[192] See n.182 above.
[193] [1988] O.J. L81/75.
[194] [1994] O.J. L100/30.
[195] Recital (1) of the Preamble to Dir. 98/34. On the emphasis towards simplifying and consolidating Community legislation in order to make it more transparent, see Council Resolution on the quality of drafting of Community legislation [1993] O.J. C166/1; and Council Resolution on legislative and administrative simplification in the field of the internal market [1996] O.J. C224/5. See also the establishment of the high level Molitor Group in 1994 to recommend areas of Community law that could be abolished in order to enhance the competitiveness of industry within the Community (COM (95) 288), and the launching in May 1996 of the SLIM pilot project (Simpler Legislation for the Single Market).
[196] For commentary on the provisions of Dir. 83/198, see Fronia and Casella "La procédure de contrôle des réglementations techniques prévue par la nouvelle Directive 83/189 CEE" [1995] 2 R.M.U.E. 37; Fronia, 'Transparenz und Vermeidung von Handelshemnissen bei Producktspezi-

month after the provisions were consolidated in Directive 98/34, the latter was subject to yet further amendment extending its scope to "Information Society" services,[197] but these are not relevant to the free movement of goods.

12.78 Directive 98/34 as amended covers products which are defined as "any industrially manufactured product and any agricultural product, including fish products" (Article 1(1)).

The most important subparagraphs of Article 8(1) read as follows:

"Subject to Article 10, Member States shall immediately communicate to the Commission any draft technical regulation, except where it merely transposes the full text of an international or European standard, in which case information regarding the relevant standard shall suffice; they shall also let the Commission have a statement of the grounds which make the enactment of such a technical regulation necessary, where these have not already been made clear in the draft.
. . .

The Commission shall immediately notify the other Member States of the draft and all documents which have been forwarded to it; it may also refer this draft, for an opinion, to the Committee referred to in Article 5 and, where appropriate, to the committee responsible for the field in question.

With respect to the technical specifications or other requirements or rules on services referred to in the third indent of the second subparagraph of point 11 of Article 1, the comments or detailed opinions of the Commission or the Member States may concern only aspects which may hinder trade or, in respect of rules on services, the free movement of services or the freedom of establishment of service operators and not the fiscal or financial aspect of the measure."

Article 1(11) defines "technical regulation" as follows:

"technical specifications and other requirements or rules on services, including the relevant administrative provisions, the observance of which is compulsory, *de jure* or *de facto*, in the case of marketing, provision of services, establishment of a service operator or use in a Member State or a major part thereof, as well as laws, regulations or administrative provisions of Member States, except those provided for in Article 10, prohibiting the manufacture, importation, marketing or use of a product or prohibiting the provision or use of a service or establishment as a service provider."

This comprises "technical regulations imposed by the authorities designated by the Member States and appearing on a list to be drawn up by the Commission before August 5, 1999, in the framework of the Committee referred to in Article 5". The same procedure shall be used for amending this list.

De facto technical regulations include:

— "laws, regulations or administrative provisions of a Member State which refer

fikationen im Binnenmarkt' (1996) Eu.Z.W. 101; Lecrenier, "Vers l'achèvement du marché intérieur: l'évolution des procédures de contrôle prévues par la Directive 83/189 CEE depuis quatre ans" [1988] R.M.C. 121; Mattera, *Le marché unique Européen: ses règles, son fonctionnement* (2nd ed., 1990) at 147; and Weatherill, "Compulsory Notification of Draft Technical Regulations: the Contribution of Directive 83/189 to the Management of the Internal Market" (1996) 16 Y.E.L. 129.
[197] Dir. 98/48 [1998] O.J. L217/18.

either to technical specifications or other requirements or to rules on services or to professional codes or codes of practice which in turn refer to technical specifications or other requirements or to rules on services compliance with which confers a presumption of conformity with the obligations imposed by the aforementioned laws, regulations or administrative provisions;

— voluntary agreements to which a public authority is a contracting party and which provide, in the public interest, for compliance with technical specifications or other requirements or rules on services, excluding public procurement tender specifications;

— technical specifications or other requirements or rules on services which are linked to fiscal or financial measures affecting the consumption of products or services by encouraging compliance with such technical specifications or other requirements or rules on services; technical specifications or other requirements or rules on services linked to national social-security systems are not included.''

Article 9 provides:

''1. Member States shall postpone the adoption of a draft technical regulation for three months from the date of receipt by the Commission of the communication referred to in Article 8(1).

    2. Member States shall postpone:

— for four months the adoption of a draft technical regulation in the form of a voluntary agreement within the meaning of the second indent of the second subparagraph of point 11 of Article 1,

— without prejudice to paragraphs 3, 4 and 5, for six months the adoption of any other draft technical regulation (except for draft rules on services),

from the date of receipt by the Commission of the communication referred to in Article 8(1) if the Commission or another Member State delivers a detailed opinion, within three months of that date, to the effect that the measure envisaged may create obstacles to the free movement of goods within the internal market.
    ...
    The Member State concerned shall report to the Commission on the action it proposes to take on such detailed opinions. The Commission shall comment on this reaction.
    ...
    3. ... Member States shall postpone the adoption of a draft technical regulation for 12 months from the date of receipt by the Commission of the communication referred to in Article 8(1) if, within the three months of that date, the Commission announces its intention of proposing or adopting a directive, regulation or decision on the matter in accordance with Article [249] of the Treaty.

    4. Member States shall postpone the adoption of a draft technical regulation for 12 months from the date of receipt by the Commission of the communication referred to in Article 8(1) if, within the three months following that date, the Commission announces its finding that the draft technical regulation concerns a matter which is covered by a proposal for a directive, regulation or decision presented to the Council in accordance with Article [249] of the Treaty.

    5. If the Council adopts a common position during the standstill period referred to in paragraphs 3 and 4, that period shall, subject to paragraph 6, be extended to 18 months.

    6. The obligations referred to in paragraphs 3, 4 and 5 shall lapse:

— when the Commission informs the Member States that it no longer intends to propose or adopt a binding Community act,

— when the Commission informs the Member States of the withdrawal of its draft or proposal,

when the Commission or the Council has adopted a binding Community act.
    7. Paragraphs 1 to 5 shall not apply in cases where:

— for urgent reasons, occasioned by serious and unforeseeable circumstances relating to the protection of public health or safety, the protection of animals or the preservation of plants, and for rules on services, also for public policy, notably the protection of minors, a Member State is obliged to prepare technical regulations in a very short space of time in order to enact and introduce them immediately without any consultations being possible or
— for urgent reasons occasioned by serious circumstances relating to the protection of the security and the integrity of the financial system, notably the protection of depositors, investors and insured persons, a Member State is obliged to enact and implement rules on financial services immediately.

In the communication referred to in Article 8, the Member State shall give reasons for the urgency of the measures taken. The Commission shall give its views on the communication as soon as possible. It shall take appropriate action in cases where improper use is made of this procedure. The European Parliament shall be kept informed by the Commission.''

Article 10 is in the following terms:

''1. Articles 8 and 9 shall not apply to those laws, regulations and administrative provisions of the Member States or voluntary agreements by means of which Member States:

— comply with binding Community acts which result in the adoption of technical specifications or rules on services,
— fulfil the obligations arising out of international agreements which result in the adoption of common technical specifications or rules on services in the Community,
— make use of safeguard clauses provided for in binding Community acts,
— apply Article 8(1) of Directive 92/59/EEC,
— restrict themselves to implementing a judgment of the Court of Justice of the European Communities,
— restrict themselves to amending a technical regulation within the meaning of point 11 of Article 1 in accordance with a Commission request, with a view to removing an obstacle to trade .... .

    2. Article 9 shall not apply to the laws, regulations and administrative provisions of the Member States prohibiting manufacture insofar as they do not impede the free movement of products.
    3. Paragraphs 3 to 6 of Article 9 shall not apply to the voluntary agreements referred to in the second indent of the second subparagraph of point 11 of Article 1.
    4. Article 9 shall not apply to the technical specifications or other requirements or the rules on services referred to in the third indent of the second subparagraph of point 11 of Article 1.''[198]

12.79   The notification procedure in Directive 98/34 is thus designed to secure the communication of information on national technical standards before they

---

[198] As to Dir. 92/59, see n.32 above.

are adopted by Member States and it empowers the Commission and other Member States to delay, and object to, the adoption or drafting of those standards.[199] Clearly, this notification procedure is an essential aspect of the strategy for consolidating the internal market through increased communication, access to justice and administrative co-operation.[200] Thus the preamble to the Directive states that "in order to promote the smooth functioning of the internal market, as much transparency as possible should be ensured" and that "the aim of the internal market is to create an environment that is conducive to the competitiveness of undertakings".

12.80 The consequences which flow from a Member State's failure to notify a draft technical regulation in accordance with the Directive have been clarified by the Court in *CIA Security International v Signalson and Securitel*.[201] That case concerned a Belgian decree of 1991 which required alarm systems supplied by security firms in Belgium to be tested and approved by a special committee. CIA Security, a security firm, had sought an order from the Belgian court to require Signalson and Securitel, two competitors, to cease unfair trading practices involving claims by the defendants that an alarm system marketed by CIA did not comply with Belgian legislation. Signalson and Securitel counter-claimed for an order to restrain CIA from marketing an alarm system that had not been approved under the Belgian legislation. The Belgian decree of 1991 had not been notified to the Commission under Directive 83/189. The Commercial Court in Liège referred questions to the Court seeking in essence to ascertain the consequences that follow from a failure to notify.

Upholding the view expounded by the Commission in a communication devoted to this matter,[202] the Court of Justice ruled that Articles 8 and 9 of Directive 83/189 were unconditional and sufficiently precise and could thus be relied on by individuals before national courts against national technical regulations which had not been notified in accordance with the Directive. The Court reasoned that, since the aim of the Directive was to protect freedom of movement for goods by means of preventive control and the obligation to notify was essential for achieving such Community control, "the effectiveness of Community control will be that much greater if the Directive is interpreted as meaning that breach of the obligation to notify constitutes a substantial pro-

---

[199] In 2000 and 2001 there were respectively 751 and 530 notifications: see full statistics published at [2001] O.J. C207/5 and [2002] O.J. C119/17 respectively. See also detailed analysis of notification under the Directive by Weatherill, n.196 above at 153-168.

[200] See generally "The Internal Market After 1992—Meeting the Challenge" SEC (92) 2277 final; also the follow-up to the foregoing in the Commission's Communication, "Making the Most of the Internal Market: Strategic Programme" COM (93) 632 final; "Follow-up to the Sutherland Report: Legislative consolidation to enhance the transparency of Community law in the area of the internal market" COM (93) 361 final and Council Resolution on the development of administrative co-operation in the implementation and enforcement of Community legislation in the internal market [1994] O.J. C179/1.

[201] Case C-194/94 [1996] E.C.R. I-2201. See annotation by Slot, (1996) 33 C.M.L.Rev. 1035; also Candela Castillo, "La confirmation par la Cour du principe de non-opposabilité aux tiers des règles techniques non notifiées dans le cadre de la Directive 83/189/CEE" [1997] R.M.U.E. 51.

[202] [1986] O.J. C245/4.

cedural defect such as to render the technical regulations in question inapplicable to individuals".[203] Needless to say, this ruling has had far-reaching repercussions.

12.81 This expansive judgment in *CIA Security* were somewhat refined in *Lemmens*.[204] In that case, questions were referred to the Court in the context of criminal proceedings which concerned the driving of a vehicle while under the influence of alcohol. The prosecutor relied on the results of a breath analysis carried out by the Dutch police using breath-analysis apparatus, the technical requirements for which, had not been notified to the Commission under Directive 83/189. The Court held that the failure to notify the technical regulation applicable to the breath-analysis apparatus did not preclude the use by the police of the results of a test taken with that apparatus as evidence in criminal proceedings. The following passage is of particular note:

> "While failure to notify technical regulations, which constitutes a procedural defect in their adoption, renders such regulations inapplicable inasmuch as they hinder the use or marketing of a product which is not in conformity therewith, it does not have the effect of rendering unlawful any use of a product which is in conformity with regulations which have not been notified.
>
> The use of the product by the public authorities, in a case such as this, is not liable to create an obstacle to trade which could have been avoided if the notification procedure had been followed."[205]

12.82 The Court's ruling in *CIA Security* was confirmed and extended by its judgment in *Unilever Italia*.[206] It will be recalled that *CIA Security* concerned a dispute between individuals relating to unfair competition. In *Unilever Italia*, the Court held that its ruling in *CIA Security* applied with equal force to a dispute between individuals concerning contractual rights and obligations.[207] In other words, a national court is required, in civil proceedings between individuals concerning contractual rights and obligations, to refuse to apply a national technical regulation which was adopted in breach of the notification and postponement requirements in Articles 8 and 9 of Directive 98/34.[208]

12.83 The Court's judgment in *CIA Security* has brought the definition of a

---

[203] Para. 48 of the judgment.
[204] Case C-226/97 [1998] E.C.R. I-3711.
[205] Paras 35 and 36 of the judgment.
[206] Case C-443/98 [2000] E.C.R. I-7535; noted by Dougan, [2001] C.M.L.Rev. 1503; and Weatherill, [2001] E.L.Rev. 177.
[207] Para. 49 of the judgment. See also C-159/00 *Sapod Audic v Eco-Emballages* (judgment of June 6, 2002).
[208] The result in *Unilever Italia* comes close to according "horizontal" direct effect to directives; that is to say, a finding that a directive imposes obligations on individuals that can be relied on as such against an individual. The Court has always refused to countenance horizontal direct effect for directives: see, for example C-91/92 *Faccini Dori* [1994] E.C.R. I-3325 at para. 20. The Court's distinguishing of that case law in *Unilever Italia* (see paras 50 to 51 of the judgment) is regarded in some quarters as unconvincing: see note by Weatherill, *op cit* n.206.

"technical regulation" in Article 1(11) of the Directive into sharp focus.[209] Each case turns on its facts, while the following judgments give a good indication of the approach adopted by the Court:

(a) In *Bic Benelux v Belgium*[210] the Court held that, where a national measure was adopted in order to protect the environment or does not implement a technical standard which may itself constitute a barrier to free movement, that circumstance does not preclude the measure in question from constituting a technical regulation within the meaning of the Directive. Moreover, the Court held that "there is no basis in Directive [98/34] for an interpretation limiting its application to national measures capable of harmonisation only on the basis of Article [95] of the Treaty".[211]

(b) In *Semeraro Casa Uno v Erbusco*[212] the Court held that "the obligation to notify laid down by [Directive 98/34] does not ... apply to national rules which do not lay down the characteristics required of a product but are confined to regulating the closing times of shops".

(c) In *Colim v Bigg's Continent Noord*[213] the obligation to express labelling information in a specified language was held not to amount to a technical regulation but merely "an ancillary rule necessary in order for the information to be effectively communicated".[214]

(d) In *Snellers Auto's v Algemeen Directeur van de Dienst Wegverkeer*[215] a national regulation laying down a number of criteria for establishing the date on which a vehicle is deemed to have been first registered was held not to define any characteristic required of a product and, as such, to be outside the scope of the Directive.

(e) In *Donkersteeg*[216] the Court found that Dutch provisions required disinfectant containers or appropriate cleaning facilities for disinfecting footwear to be present on pig farms did not concern the production of a product in the strict sense and thus did not constitute a technical requirement. The Court also held that a provision which imposed no restrictions on either the marketing or the use of the products concerned did not constitute a technical regulation.

(f) Finally, in *Van der Burg*[217] the Court held that Dutch legislation prohi-

---

[209] It should be noted that the concept of a "technical regulation" which must be notified under Dir. 98/34 is narrower than the concept of a measure having equivalent effect to a quantitative restriction under Art. 28 of the Treaty.
[210] Case C-13/96 [1997] E.C.R. I-1753. See also Case C-289/94 *Commission v Italy* [1996] E.C.R. I-4405.
[211] Para. 19 of the judgment.
[212] Cases C-418-421/93 [1996] E.C.R. I-2975 at para. 38.
[213] C-33/97 [1999] ECR I-3175 at para. 22.
[214] Para. 29 of the judgment.
[215] C-314/98 [2000] E.C.R. I-8633.
[216] C-37/99 [2000] E.C.R. I-10223.
[217] C-278/99 [2001] E.C.R. I-2015.

biting commercial advertising of transmitting equipment of a non-approved type did not constitute a technical regulation, because it merely prohibited a marketing method without laying down the characteristics required of a product.

Manifestly, having laid down in *CIA Security* the severe consequences of a failure by a Member State to observe its obligation to notify, the Court has been at pains not to define too broadly the concept of "technical regulation".

12.84 Technical regulations introduced in order to honour obligations under Community legislation are exempt from notification.[218] The latter will not, however, be the case where the Community legislation in question is drafted in general terms, leaving Member States sufficient room for manoeuvre[219] or where it does not lay down a binding Community requirement.[220]

12.85 In *Commission v Italy*[221] the Court had the opportunity to stress that the duty of notification under Article 8(1) of the Directive required the communication of the *full* text of the proposed measure, even where many of the provisions of the measure did not constitute technical regulations.[222] However, the Court also made it clear that this does not preclude the Member State from bringing into force immediately those provisions of the enactment which do not constitute technical measures - without waiting for the outcome of the examination procedure provided for by the Directive.[223]

12.86 In *Commission v Germany* (medical instruments)[224] the defendant State denied that it had infringed Article 8 of the Directive by failing to notify a new measure: since it had merely extended an existing measure to new products, it maintained that the obligation to notify did not apply. The Court dismissed this argument, on the grounds that as regards the new products concerned the measure constituted a new instrument and must be notified as such. Moreover, the Court saw no merit in Germany's argument that it had in fact complied with Article 8, since the contested instrument was based on an enabling provision which had been notified at the appropriate time: a measure implementing an enabling provision was a distinct measure in its own right and must therefore be notified separately. Although this ruling relates to the Directive as worded in March 1988, there can be little doubt that these principles are equally applicable to its present version.

---

[218] See Article 10 of Directive 98/34; and C-425 to 427/97 *Albers* [1999] E.C.R. I-2947; and C-246/98 *Berendse-Koenen and others* [2000] E.C.R. I-1777.
[219] See *Unilever Italia*, at para. 29; also *Sapod Audic*, at para. 44.
[220] See C-390/99 *Canal Satélite Digital v Administración General del Estato* (judgment of January 22, 2002) at paras 48 to 49.
[221] Case C-279/94 [1997] E.C.R. I-4743.
[222] Para. 41 of the judgment.
[223] Para. 42 of the judgment.
[224] Case C-317/92 [1994] E.C.R. I-2039. See also Case C-273/94 *Commission v Netherlands* [1996] E.C.R. I-31; and *Colim v Bigg's*, see n.213 above at para. 22.

12.87   Next, what is the nature of the "detailed opinion" referred to in Article 9(2) of Directive 98/34? It seems clear that, despite being called an "opinion", this instrument constitutes a decision which can be annulled under Article 230 (ex 173) of the Treaty. This is because it produces legal effects, as the Member State to which it is addressed is bound to defer the adoption of the measure in that State for a further period.[225] Having said that, a Member State has little to gain in practice by attacking a "detailed opinion" under Article 230 in view of the short period of time during which its legal effects are felt. This is all the more so as it is open to Member States to rely on Article 9(7) of Directive 98/34 in urgent cases. Equally, it is difficult to envisage circumstances in which private parties would have the standing or the incentive to initiate a judicial challenge under Article 230 of a "detailed opinion" of the Commission under Article 9 of Directive 98/34.

12.88   For many years, the Commission took the view that, when issued by the Commission, a detailed opinion constitutes, or could be combined with, a letter of formal notice initiating the procedure under Article 226 (ex 169) of the Treaty.[226] The Commission's practice was to incorporate into each detailed opinion a statement that that document was also to be viewed as a letter of formal notice, if the draft of the technical regulation concerned were to be adopted without account being taken of the Commission's objections; and that the Commission reserved the right to issue a reasoned opinion under Article 226 of the Treaty, if need be. This practice was based on the premise that Article 226 does not prevent a letter of formal notice being sent before the measure complained of is adopted.

However, this practice has now been rejected by the Court in *Commission v Netherlands*.[227] There the Court dismissed as inadmissible an action brought pursuant to Article 226 and based on such a letter of formal notice. To issue such a letter even before an alleged infringement commenced was contrary to the principle of legal certainty, it held.

12.89   Arguably, the announcement referred to in Article 9(3) is also a decision which can be annulment under Article 230, even though at first sight it is no more than a mere statement of intention: again, such an announcement produces legal effects for the Member State.

As to the announcement provided for in Article 9(4), it may also be subject to proceedings under Article 230 because of its legal effects, although it contains nothing more than a finding that a particular state of affairs exists.

B. Decision 3052/95

12.90   The provisions of Directive 98/34 have been supplemented by Decision

---

[225] See generally Cases 8 and 11/66 *Cimenteries v Commission* [1967] E.C.R. 75; [1967] C.M.L.R. 77.
[226] COM (88) 722 final at 42 and 64-5.
[227] Case C-341/97 [2000] E.C.R. I-6611.

3052/95 which establishes a procedure for the exchange of information on national measures derogating from the principle of the free movement of goods within the Community.[228] The preamble to this Decision, which became applicable on January 1, 1997, states that its aim is to facilitate transparency by means of "a simple and pragmatic procedure ... so that any problems that may arise in connection with the operation of the internal market can be settled satisfactorily for both businesses and consumers".

12.91 Article 1 of the Decision provides that:

"Where a Member State takes steps to prevent the free movement or placing on the market of a particular model or type of product lawfully produced or marketed in another Member State, it shall notify the Commission accordingly where the direct or indirect effect of the measure is:

— a general ban on the goods,
— a refusal to allow the goods to be placed on the market,
— the modification of the model or type of product concerned before it can be placed or kept on the market, or
— withdrawal of the goods from the market."

Article 2 specifies *inter alia* that judicial decisions are not covered by Article 1.

12.92 Not surprisingly, in *Commission v France* (transit of spare parts)[229] the Court dismissed the defendant's claim that the Member States must necessarily be entitled to adopt measures of the kind referred to in Article 1. As the Court pointed out, the main purpose of Decision 3052/95 was to "make it possible to enhance knowledge concerning the implementation of the free movement of goods in non-harmonised sectors and to identify the problems encountered with a view to finding appropriate solutions to them"; and its purpose was not to "define the type of measures which are compatible with the rules of the Treaty relating to the free movement of goods".[230]

12.93 Article 3 provides:

"1. The notification requirement laid down in Article 1 shall apply to measures taken by the competent authorities of the Member States so authorised, with the exception of judicial decisions.
     Where a particular model or type of product is the subject of several measures, adopted under identical substantive conditions and procedures, only the first of those measures shall be subject to the notification requirement.
     2. Article 1 shall not apply to:

— measures taken solely in pursuance of Community harmonisation measures,
— measures notified to the Commission under specific provisions,
— draft measures notified to the Commission under specific Community provisions,
— measures preparing or leading up to the main measure referred to in Article 1,

---

[228] [1995] O.J. L321/1.
[229] Case C-23/99 [2000] E.C.R. I-7653.
[230] Both quotations are taken from para. 27 of the judgment.

such as preventive measures or investigations,
— measures relating solely to the protection of public morality or public order,
— measures relating to second-hand goods which, with time or use, have become
  unsuitable for being placed or kept on the market.

   3. The initiation of proceedings for judicial review of such a main measure shall
under no circumstances result in suspension of the application of Article 1.''

It follows from the second and third indents of Article 3(2) that this Decision is
residuary in nature, since it yields to other legislation requiring national measures to be notified, including Directive 98/34. This is in line with the tenth
recital to the Decision, according to which the procedure set out therein "shall
not duplicate notification or information procedures provided for by other
Community measures". Despite the wording of these two indents, it seems clear
that national measures covered by Community legislation such as Directive
98/34 fall outside the scope of Decision 3052/95, whether or not they have
been notified in fact.[231]
   The fourth indent of Article 3(2) ("measures preparing or leading up to the
main measure") has been held to include a "seizure measure the duration of
which is limited to the time necessary to check the conformity of the good in
question" which is accordingly exempted from the Article 1 notification
requirement.[232] However, where the seizure extends beyond that time, it does
not fall within the exception in the fourth indent and must therefore be notified pursuant to Article 1.[233]

12.94   Article 4 contains details of information to be notified and provides that
this should be done "in sufficient detail and in clear and comprehensible
form" and should consist in the dispatch of an information sheet containing
the particulars listed in an annex to the Decision together with a copy of the
measure taken by the authorities. Article 4(2) stipulates that this information is
to be communicated within 45 days of the date on which the measure is taken.
Article 4(3) requires the Commission to send a copy to the other Member
States. It is clear that the intention is that Decision 3052/95 will complement
Directive 98/34 and will not apply to measures which must be notified under
that Directive (Article 3(2) of the Decision). The complementary nature of
Decision 3052/95 is reinforced by Article 10 of the Decision which requires the
Commission to keep the Standing Committee set up by Directive 83/189 (and
therefore Directive 98/34) regularly informed of the functioning of the pro-
cedure provided for in the Decision and of measures notified by Member States.

12.95   Given that Decision 3052/95 does not impose a standstill on Member
States and that it only provides for notification of action taken (rather than

---

[231] Gippini Fournier and La Pergola, "La nouvelle procédure d'information mutuelle sur les
mesures nationales dérogeant au principe de libre circulation des marchandises à intérieur de la
Communauté" [1996] R.M.U.E. 145 at 161.
[232] C-388 and 429/00 *Radiosistemi v Prefetto di Genova* (judgment of June 20, 2002).
[233] *ibid.*

proposed), it seems that disregard of the notification obligations could not fall within the reasoning of the Court in *CIA Security*,[234] and therefore could not render any national action unenforceable at national level.

V. EARLY WARNING SYSTEM

12.96 Following the judgement in *Commission v France* (violent action by farmers),[235] the Council enacted Regulation 2679/98 on the functioning of the internal market in relation to the free movement of goods among the Member States.[236] This instrument establishes a mechanism for the exchange of information and for pressurising a Member State to which an obstacle to the free movement of goods contrary to Articles 28 to 30 is attributable as a result of its or inaction. The Regulation comes into play where the obstacle:

"(a) leads to serious disruption of the free movement of goods by physically or otherwise preventing, delaying or diverting their import into, export from or transport across a Member State,
(b) causes serious loss to the individuals affected, and
(c) requires immediate action in order to prevent any continuation, increase or intensification of the disruption or loss in question." (Article 1(1))

Either on its own initiative or at the instigation of another Member State, the Commission must bring the existence of such an obstacle to the notice of the Member State concerned, whereupon that State is required to take "all necessary and proportionate measures" to remove that obstacle (Article 4(1)). Article 5(1)) provides: "Where the Commission considers that an obstacle is occurring in a Member State, it shall notify the Member State concerned of the reasons that have led the Commission to such a conclusion and shall request the Member State to take all the necessary and proportionate measures to remove the said obstacle within a period which it shall determine with reference to the urgency of the case". Regrettably, the Regulation does not specify the consequences of a failure by the Member State to comply with such a "request" from the Commission. At all events, the latter institution may publish in the Official Journal the text of its summons to act (Article 5(3)). Within five working days of the receipt of that summons, the Member State must either "inform the Commission of the steps which it has taken or intends to take" or "communicate a reasoned submission as to why there is no obstacle constituting a breach of Articles [28 to 30]".

Whether the notification sent pursuant to Article 5(1) may be combined with

---

[234] See n.201 above.
[235] Case C-265/95 [1997] E.C.R. I-6959; noted by Jarvis, [1998] C.M.L.Rev. 1371; Muylle, [1998] E.L.Rev. 467. See paras 4.09 and 6.109 above.
[236] [1998] O.J. L337/8. See Mattera, "Un instrument d'intervention rapide pour sauvegarder l'unicité du marché intérieur : le règlement 2679/98" [1999] R.M.U.E. 29; Romero Melchor, "El Reglamento n° 2679/98 para situaciones de emergencia : ¿un instrumento útil a fin de asegurar la libre circulación de mercancías ?" [2000] Comunidad Europea Aranzadi 38.

a letter of formal notice initiating proceedings under Article 226 EC is a moot point. It seems clear that the ruling in *Commission v Netherlands*[237] may be distinguished: as explained earlier, it was held there that a detailed opinion sent in accordance with Article 9 of Directive 98/34 could not be treated as a letter of formal notice, because the infringement had not yet commenced when the opinion was sent; that would not be the case with a notification under Article 5(1) of Regulation 2679/98.

At all events, the powers conferred on the Commission by this Regulation fall well short of those envisaged by the Commission's proposal, which would have established a fully-fledged expedited infringement procedure.[238] That proposal provided for the Commission to lodge an Application with the Court directly after exhausting the procedures laid down there. The Council objected to this radical approach, *inter alia* on the grounds that this would amount to tampering with the mechanism set out in Article 226 and could thus be effected only by amending the Treaty itself.

12.97   Moreover, a potentially significant exception is enshrined in Article 2, which provides:

"This Regulation may not be interpreted as affecting in any way the exercise of fundamental rights as recognised in Member States, including the right or freedom to strike. These rights may also include the right or freedom to take other actions covered by the specific industrial relations systems in Member States."

This exception would not appear to cover farmers' protests, and it would only extend to violent action in the unlikely event of this being protected as a right or freedom in the laws of the Member States.

12.98   In its report to the Council and the Parliament on the application of this Regulation,[239] the Commission stated that it had had recourse to this Regulation on four occasions during the course of 1999 and eighteen times in 2000.[240] This included: the case of action taken by Belgian lorry drivers and farmers in June 1999 in protest at measures adopted following discovery that a significant quantity of dioxine had entered the food chain in Belgium; and that of action by French lorry drivers in January 2000. It would appear that in each case the crisis ended at a relatively early stage, so that the mechanism enshrined in the Regulation was not tested to the full.

In its report, the Commission concluded:

"The experience gained in applying the Regulation has shown its limits. Although it is an instrument born of political will, the Member States have not given it any teeth by

---

[237] See n.227 above.
[238] [1998] O.J. C10/14. For a detailed discussion of this proposal and the reasons for the Council's opposition to it, see Mattera *op. cit.*
[239] COM(2001) 160 final.
[240] See also Gonzalez Vaqué, "A propos des transporteurs : les entraves graves à la circulation des marchandises" [2000] J.T.D.E. 177.

including effective means of intervention in the text."[241]

Accordingly, the Commission suggested that various amendments to the Regulation would be welcome. At the same time, the Commission recognised that this would require a broad political consensus, given that the Regulation is based on Article 308 of the Treaty and can therefore only be amended by a unanimous vote in the Council.

VI. PUBLIC PROCUREMENT

12.99 We saw in Chapter VII[242] how discrimination in the award of public supply contracts is contrary to Article 28. Council Directive 77/62,[243] based on Article 94, was designed to supplement the prohibition in Article 28 "by the co-ordination of the procedures relating to public supply contracts in order, by introducing conditions of competition for such contracts in all the Member States, to ensure a degree of transparency allowing the observance of this prohibition to be better supervised".[244]

That Directive was amended on a number of occasions, notably by Directive 88/295,[245] before being replaced by Directive 93/36[246] co-ordinating procedures for the award of public supply contracts. The 1988 Directive was enacted in pursuance of the White Paper on Completing the Internal Market,[247] in which the Commission admitted that the Directives on public contracts had not been a success: "less than 1 ECU in 4 of public expenditure in the areas covered by the co-ordination Directives is the subject of publication in the Official Journal and thus, even theoretically, of Community-wide competition."

The 1993 Directive was essentially a consolidating measure. What follows is a brief summary of the latter Directive, which makes no claim to being exhaustive.[248]

12.100 In essence this Directive defines public supply contracts as contracts for the delivery of products, whether or not such delivery includes siting and

---

[241] p.12 of the report.
[242] Paras 7.14 *et seq.*
[243] [1977] O.J. L13/1. This was only the second Directive on public contracts, the first being Dir. 71/305 ([1971] O.J. L185/5), which has now been replaced by Dir. 93/37 ([1993] O.J. 199/54). The latter Directive only concerns contracts to carry out work; it therefore relates to the provision of services rather than the movement of goods and thus falls outside the scope of this book.
[244] Second recital to the Directive; clearly this Directive does not, and could not, alter the scope of Art. 28; see also generally para. 33 of the judgment in Case 243/89 *Commission v Denmark* (Great Belt Bridge) [1993] E.C.R. I 3353 (see para. 7.17 above).
[245] [1988] O.J. L127/1.
[246] [1993] O.J. L199/1.
[247] COM(85) 310.
[248] Commentaries include: Arrowsmith, *The Law of Public and Utilities Procurement* (1996); Cox, *Public Procurement in the European Community* (1993); Diggings and Bennett, *EC Public Procurement Law and Practice* (1993); Trepte, *Public Procurement in the EC* (1993); and Weiss, *Public Procurement in European Community Law* (1993).

installation operations (Article 1(a)). It applies to the contract entered into by the State, regional or local authorities and certain other public authorities (Article 1(b)). By virtue of Article 2(1)(a), certain contracts for utilities are excluded, since they are covered by other legislation discussed below. In addition, the Directive does not apply to "contracts which are declared secret or the execution of which must be accompanied by special security measures in accordance with the laws, regulations or administrative provisions in force in the Member States concerned or when the protection of the basic interests of the Member State's security so requires" (Article 2(1)(b)). On the other hand, it does cover contracts "awarded by contracting authorities in the field of defence, except for the products to which Article [296(1)(b)] of the Treaty applies" (Article 3). The Directive relates only to public supply contracts whose estimated value net of VAT is not less than €200,000 or, in the case the central government authorities listed in Annex 1 to the Directive, €130,000 (Article 5(1)(a)).

The Directive does not aim to create a single Community procedure for the award of public supply contracts, but requires the Member States to adapt their national procedures in accordance with its provisions. The first substantive part of the Directive is Title II, entitled "Common rules in the technical field". Article 8(1) provides that the technical specifications defined in Annexe III shall figure in the general or the contractual documents relating to each contract. Article 8(6) provides in particular:

"Unless such specifications are justified by the subject of the contract, Member States shall prohibit the introduction into the contractual clauses relating to a given contract of technical specifications which mention goods of a specific make or source or of a particular process and which therefore favour or eliminate certain suppliers or products. In particular, the indication of trade marks, patents, types or of a specific origin or production shall be prohibited. However, if such indication is accompanied by the words 'or equivalent' it shall be authorised in cases where the contracting authorities are unable to give a description of the subject of the contract using specifications which are sufficiently precise and fully intelligible to all parties concerned."[249]

Title III relates to common advertising rules. It provides that where a public authority intends to award a contract covered by the Directive, it must advertise its intention by a notice in the Official Journal of the European Communities.

Title IV relates to participation in the bidding procedure and the actual award of contracts. Article 20 states that a supplier may be excluded on a number of grounds, such as that he is bankrupt or that he has failed to pay social security contributions or tax due in the country where he is established or the country of the contracting authority. The following Articles relate to similar matters such as proof of the supplier's financial standing (Article 22) and of his technical ability (Article 23). Article 26(1) concerns the criteria for the award of public contracts, which shall be:

---

[249] In Case C-359/93 *Commission v Netherlands* [1995] E.C.R. I-157, a national measure infringing the equivalent provision in the earlier Directives was held to constitute a breach of Art. 28 as well; see para. 7.18 above.

"(a) either the lowest price only;
(b) or, when the award is made to the most economically advantageous tender, various criteria according to the contract in question: *e.g.* price, delivery date, running costs, cost-effectiveness, quality, aesthetic and functional characteristics, technical merit, after-sales service and technical assistance."

Article 26(2) provides:

"In the case referred to in point (b) of paragraph 1, the contracting authority shall state in the contract documents or in the contract notice all the criteria they intend to apply to the award, where possible in descending order of importance."

12.101 The water, energy, transport and telecommunications sectors fell outside the public procurement legislation until the enactment of Council Directive 90/531.[250] In the meantime, that Directive has been replaced by Council Directive 93/38.[251] That instrument lays down procedures and requirements for those sectors which broadly correspond to those of Directive 93/36.[252]

12.102 In 1996 the Commission published a Green Paper reviewing the application of the procurement rules in the European Community.[253] A Communication of March 1998[254] set out the responses received to the Green Paper, many of which were critical of the current legislation, deeming it to be unsuited in many respects to the prevailing economic environment. In response, the Commission has proposed the adoption of two new Directives to replace all existing Directives on the procurement of works, supplies and services[255] and procurement by the utilities.[256] These proposals are expected to be adopted in early 2003.

VII. RELATIONSHIP BETWEEN HARMONISATION AND ARTICLES 28 TO 30

12.103 A dynamic relationship exists between the Court's case law interpreting Articles 28 to 30 on the one hand and Community harmonisation legislation on the other. This dynamic relationship is characterised by the fact that these two tools of integration complement one another. On the one hand, the Court's case law constitutes "negative" integration in the sense that it involves national provisions being held to be contrary to Articles 28 to 30 in individual cases. On the other hand, Community harmonisation legislation contributes towards

---

[250] [1990] O.J. L297/1.
[251] [1993] O.J. L199/34.
[252] Both Directives have been amended by Commission Dir. 2001/78 [2001] O.J. L285/1 prescribing new standard forms.
[253] Public Procurement in the European Union: Exploring the Way Forward. COM (96) 583 final.
[254] COM(98) 143 final.
[255] [2001] O.J. C29E/11, amended [2002] O.J. C203E/210.
[256] [2001] O.J. C29E/112, amended [2002] O.J. C203E/183.

"positive" integration by introducing new standards at Community level which apply horizontally to promote free movement.[257]

12.104 Any attempt to define the scope of Articles 28 to 30 by reference to Article 94 (or other Articles providing for Community legislation) has always signally failed. The Court has always refused to find that the restriction on imports resulting from a particular measure could be set aside under Article 94 and that such a measure therefore fell outside Article 28. In *Commission v Italy*[258] the Court rejected this line of argument which the defendant Government had put forward, in the following terms:

> "It is apparent that the purposes of Articles [28] and [94] are different. The purpose of Article [28] is, save for certain specific exceptions, to abolish in the immediate future all quantitative restrictions on the imports of goods and all measures having an equivalent effect, whereas the general purpose of Article [94] is, by approximating the laws, regulations and administrative provisions of the Member States, to enable obstacles of whatever kind arising from disparities between them to be reduced. The elimination of quantitative restrictions and measures having an equivalent effect, which is unreservedly affirmed in Article 3(a) of the Treaty and carried into effect by Article [28], may not therefore be made dependent on measures which, although capable of promoting the free movement of goods, cannot be considered to be a necessary condition for the application of that fundamental principle."

12.105 Frequently, Community legislation is designed to harmonise measures justified under Article 30. It will be recalled that where Community legislation provides exhaustive health or other guarantees, Member States may no longer rely on Article 30.[259] As we noticed in paragraph 12.44 above, the *Tobacco Advertising* judgment gives rise to a concern that some national restrictions justified under Article 30 may now be beyond the reach of Article 95 and thus cannot be harmonised on the basis of that provision. No doubt, this will be clarified by future case law.

Exceptionally, such Community legislation has the effect of supplementing Articles 28 and 29 and ensuring their observance. An example of such legislation is to be found in the public supply Directives discussed above.

12.106 At the same time that Community legislation may not create or permit unnecessary restrictions to interstate trade.[260] Having said that, it seems clear that, in the performance of the tasks with which they are entrusted, the Community institutions have greater freedom of action than do the Member States. Furthermore, while a norm enacted by some Member States only will restrict inter-State trade, it will cease to do so once it is introduced throughout the Community.[261]

---

[257] See discussion by Slot, *op.cit.* n.169 above, at 379-82.

[258] Case 193/80 [1981] E.C.R. 3019.

[259] See detailed discussion of this at paras 8.28 *et seq.* above. See, for example, Case C-350/97 *Monsees* [1999] E.C.R. I-2921 at para. 24.

[260] See paras 4.10 *et seq.* above. See, most recently, C-169/99 *Schwarzkopf v Zentrale zur Bekämpfung unlauteren Wettbewerbs* [2001] E.C.R. I-5901 at para 37.

12.107 In these circumstances, it is suggested that the Court's broad construction of Article 28 has actually acted as a catalyst to harmonisation. Evidence of this is provided by the adoption of Council Directive 83/189 (now repealed and consolidated by Directive 98/34) laying down a procedure for the provision of information in the field of technical standards and regulations.[262]

It is suggested that the reasons for this are twofold:

— even where national measures are not justified, an analogous measure may in some cases be adopted by the Community[263];

— in so far as national measures are so justified, Member States still have to allow imports conforming to norms providing equivalent guarantees.[264] This means that a Member State may have to check the equivalence of other norms and, if need be, apply those other norms alongside its own. This could result in one and the same Member State applying a plethora of different norms. It is simpler to resort to harmonisation by a Community Directive.

12.108 Supposing, then, that certain barriers to interstate trade have been removed by a harmonising directive, it is submitted that the compatibility of a national measure with Community law should first be examined by reference to that directive.[265] Only if the national measure is compatible with the directive should it be examined in the light of Articles 28 to 30. This is because the directive will contain more specific rules than those provisions, which are of a general nature. Again, as we have just noticed, a directive harmonising health or other guarantees covered by Article 30 may have exhausted the Member State's right to rely on that provision.[266] This approach is also suggested by the form of words used in the *"Cassis de Dijon"* case: "in the absence of common rules relating to the production and marketing of alcohol ... it is for the Member States to regulate [these] matters."[267] At all events, it is plain that the adoption of Community legislation does not remove a matter from the scope of Article 28.

12.109 On another point, when optional harmonisation is adopted, importers of goods not conforming to the standard laid down in the Directive (standard A) may still rely on Article 28. Thus goods produced in one Member State according to the standard of that State (standard B) may be imported into another Member State which has a different standard (standard C). If standards

---

[261] See paras 6.93 *et seq.* above.
[262] See paras 12.77 *et seq.* above.
[263] See paras 4.10 *et seq.* above.
[264] Paras 6.70 *et seq.* above.
[265] Case C-37/92 *Vanacker* [1993] E.C.R. I-4947. A particularly striking example is to be found in Case C-1/00 *Commission v France* (BSE) (judgment of December 13, 2001). See also para. 10.07 above.
[266] Paras 8.28 *et seq.* above.
[267] A similar form of words was used in Case 8/74 *Dassonville* [1974] E.C.R. 837; [1974] 2 C.M.L.R. 436.

B and C are equivalent to one another, then Article 28 precludes the latter State from restricting the importation and sale of those goods.[268]

12.110 What then if the importing Member State has rendered the Community standard (standard A) compulsory and abolished its own national standard? This delicate issue was raised in Written Question 1176/81. The question referred to Directive 80/232[269] on the ranges of nominal quantities and capacities permitted for certain pre-packaged products, which provides for optional harmonisation. Belgium was apparently considering making the implementation of the provisions of the Directive mandatory, so that only the ranges listed in the Directive could be marketed in Belgium. If another Member State, say France, were to proceed with optional harmonisation and allow other standards not set out in the Directive, the French goods conforming to those other standards could not then be sold in Belgium. In view of "*Cassis de Dijon*" the questioner asked whether Belgium would then be infringing Article 28. If so, why did the Directive provide for optional rather than total harmonisation? The very principle of optional harmonisation was thus fundamentally put in question. In its reply,[270] the Commission stated:

"arguments based on the Cassis de Dijon judgment cannot be used in this instance to force a Member State which has made the provisions of the Directive mandatory to accept products which do not conform to it."

12.111 A related question was raised in *Denkavit Futtermittel v Land Baden-Württemberg*.[271] The Directive in issue there empowered Member States to require the ingredients of compound foodstuffs to be indicated, but did not render this compulsory for Member States. Denkavit imported such goods into Germany, which required this information to be indicated, from the Netherlands, which did not; and the packaging did not in fact bear the information concerned. Denkavit contended that in these circumstances it was contrary to Article 28 for the German authorities to impose this requirement. The Court rejected this argument, finding instead that the requirement was justified on human and animal health grounds as well as on the grounds of consumer protection and the prevention of unfair competition. It deduced this in part from the preamble to the Directive, but it was also influenced by the fact that, after the material date, the Council had rendered such labelling compulsory. That ruling was confirmed in *Van der Veldt*,[272] which related to the labelling of bread.

Plainly, there is a major difference between these two cases and the situation described in Written Question 1176/81: in neither *Denkavit* nor *Van der Veldt* was it suggested that the goods complied with standards equivalent to those laid down in the importing State.

---

[268]For the principle of equivalence, see paras 6.79 *et seq.* above.
[269][1980] O.J. L51/1.
[270][1982] O.J. C92/2.
[271]Case C-39/90 [1991] E.C.R. I 3069, para. 4.17 above.
[272]Case C-17/93 [1994] E.C.R. I 3537.

12.112   Finally, national rules adopted in order to comply with a Directive in the general interest of the Community cannot be characterised as a measure having equivalent effect to a quantitative restriction on imports or exports prohibited by Articles 28 or 29.[273]

---

[273] C-246/98, see n.218 above at paras 24–5. See also in relation to charges having an effect equivalent to a customs duty; Case 46/76 *Bauhuis v Netherlands* [1977] E.C.R. 5 at paras 28–9.

CHAPTER XIII

The European Economic Area

I. INTRODUCTION

13.01 Relations between the Community and its trading partners in Western Europe have always been the source of the utmost interest to both sides. The reason is simple: the two groups conduct a major part of their external trade with one another. The figure is particularly striking as regards EFTA trade: in 1988 for instance, 55.9 per cent of the exports of EFTA countries went to the Community; that figure rose to 65.2 per cent when intra-EFTA trade was excluded.

In 1960 the Convention establishing the European Free Trade Association was signed by seven countries which at that time could not, or did not wish to, join the Community, namely: Austria, Denmark, Norway, Portugal, Sweden, Switzerland and the United Kingdom. The Convention came into force in the same year. Initially, Finland was prevented by its delicate relationship with the Soviet Union from seeking full membership, so that it was only as from January 1, 1986 that Finland became a full member of EFTA. However, by virtue of the 1961 Finland-EFTA Agreement it did for all practical purposes acquire this status much earlier. Iceland joined in 1970.

In 1973 Denmark and the United Kingdom left EFTA to join the Community. This prompted the EEC to conclude a series of almost identical Free Trade Agreements (the first of their kind) with each of the remaining EFTA countries, namely: Austria, Finland, Iceland, Norway (which had just rejected accession to the Community in a referendum), Portugal, Sweden, and Switzerland.[1] No treaty could be concluded with the EFTA as such, since that organisation is a treaty making power with no legal personality. These agreements, which came into force on various dates in 1973 and 1974, were supplemented by a tripartite Agreement between the EEC, Switzerland and Liechtenstein,[2] which extended the provisions of the EEC-Switzerland Agreement to the Principality. Liechtenstein was not then a member of EFTA but the EFTA Convention was applicable to it due to its customs union of 1923 with Switzerland, which

---

[1] Respectively [1972] O.J. L300, [1973] O.J. L171, [1972] O.J. L301/1, [1973] O.J. L171, [1972] O.J. L301/66, [1972] O.J. L300 and [1972] O.J. L300.
[2] [1972] O.J. L300/281.

represented its interests in EFTA. Liechtenstein became a member of EFTA only in 1991. The Agreement with Portugal lapsed in 1986 when that country joined the Community.

The Community concluded these Free Trade Agreements on the basis of Article 133 (ex 113) EC, which relates to the common commercial policy. As their name implies, taken together they established a free trade area—not a customs union—between the Community and the EFTA countries. Quantitative restrictions and measures of equivalent effect between the parties were abolished (subject to an exception clause almost identical to Article 30 (ex 36) EC), as were customs duties and charges of equivalent effect. However, these Agreements did not relate to agricultural or fisheries products.[3]

In addition, the Community has at various times concluded a plethora of more specific treaties with the individual EFTA countries on such diverse matters as cheese, fisheries and transport. As will be seen, many of these treaties are still in force, as they have not all been superseded by the Agreement on the European Economic Area.

13.02 The Court has held that provisions of treaties concluded between the Community and third countries are subject to its jurisdiction since they are instruments of Community law[4]; and that they may be directly applicable.[5] However, the judgment in *Polydor v Harlequin Record Shops*[6] showed in the clearest possible terms that the Free Trade Agreements fell well short of integrating the EFTA countries into the common market. The case turned on two provisions of the Agreement between the Community and Portugal which reproduced, *mutatis mutandis*, the terms of Articles 28 and 30 (ex 30 and 36) of the Treaty of Rome. Records had been produced under copyright licence in Portugal and had been imported into the United Kingdom. The copyright in the two countries belonged to one company. Had Portugal then been a part of the Community, the doctrine of exhaustion of intellectual property rights would undoubtedly have applied.[7] The question which therefore arose was whether this doctrine was applicable under the Free Trade Agreement.

The Court held that it was not. It did so on the following grounds:

"The considerations which led to that interpretation of Articles [28 and 30] of the Treaty [on the exhaustion of rights] do not apply in the context of the relations between the Community and Portugal as defined in the Agreement. It is apparent from the examination of the Agreement that although it makes provision for the unconditional abolition of certain restrictions on trade between the Community and Portugal, such as quantitative restrictions and measures having equivalent effect, it

---

[3] For an assessment of these Agreements, see Steenbergen, "EG/EFTA en de Europe economische ruimte" [1991] S.E.W. 15.

[4] Cases 181/73 *Haegeman v Belgium* [1974] E.C.R. 449; and C-192/89 *Sevince v Staatssecretaris Van Justitie* [1990] E.C.R. I-3461.

[5] Case 104/81 *Hauptzollamt Mainz v Kupferberg* [1982] E.C.R. 3641 (provision in Free Trade Agreement with Portugal equivalent to Art. 90 (ex 95) EC was directly applicable).

[6] Case 270/80, [1982] E.C.R. 329. See, however, Case C-207/91 *Eurim-Pharm v Bundesgesundheitsamt* [1993] E.C.R. I-3723.

[7] Paras 8.197 *et seq.* above.

does not have the same purpose as the EEC Treaty, in as much as the latter, as has been stated above, seeks to create a single market reproducing as closely as possible the conditions of a domestic market.

It follows that in the context of the Agreement restrictions on trade in goods may be considered to be judged on the grounds of the protection of industrial and commercial property in a situation in which their justification would not be possible within the Community.''

13.03 At the first joint Ministerial Meeting between EEC and EFTA Members and the EC Commission held in Luxembourg in April 1984, it was agreed to follow up the creation of the world's biggest Free Trade Area by embarking upon co-operation in other areas, thereby creating a dynamic European Economic Space (EES).

One reason for pursuing further integration was the fact that the EFTA countries and the Community were not involved in drafting each other's legislation. This was a source of difficulty, particularly in relation to technical standards. This problem became more acute with the publication and implementation of the Commission's White Paper of 1985, and the conclusion of the Single European Act.[8] In short, although the Free Trade Agreements provided the framework for close trading relations between the Community and the EFTA countries, they still constituted commercial treaties of the classic type.

13.04 During the work on the creation of the EES, it became increasingly clear that a more ambitious approach was required. In a speech to the European Parliament in January 1989 the President of the Commission, M. Jacques Delors, proposed that in order to create a dynamic and homogeneous European Economic Area (EEA) a new form of association with joint decision-making and institutions be found with the EFTA countries. Those countries gave a favourable response to this initiative, and intensive preparatory negotiations were formally commenced in June 1990. These negotiations were to reach a successful conclusion nearly two years later.

13.05 The Agreement on the European Economic Area[9] was signed in Oporto on May 2, 1992 between the EEC, the ECSC and their Member States, on the one hand, and the seven EFTA countries (Austria, Finland, Iceland, Liechtenstein, Norway, Sweden and Switzerland) on the other. Article 129(3) of that Agreement stipulated that it was to come into force on January 1, 1993, provided that all the Contracting Parties deposited their instruments of ratification or approval before that date.

In the event that deadline was not met, since the Swiss people rejected the

---

[8] See paras 12.12 *et seq.*
[9] [1994] O.J. L1/3. See Blanchet et al, *The Agreement on the European Economic Area (EEA): A Guide to the Free Movement of Goods and Competition Rules* (1994); Bourgeois, "L'espace économique européen" (1992) 2 R.M.U.E. 11; Jacot-Guillarmod (ed.), *The EEA Agreement* (1992); Norberg *et al.*, *EEA law* (1993); Steenbergen, "Het EER-Verdrag, een beknopte samenvatting" [1993] S.E.W. 140.

Agreement in a referendum held on December 6, 1992.[10] As a result, on March 17, 1993 a Protocol adjusting the Agreement on the European Economic Area[11] was signed by all the signatories to the Oporto Agreement other than Switzerland. The Protocol made provision for the Agreement to enter into force without that country. As to Liechtenstein, the Protocol provided that that Principality could accede to the EEA after its entry into force, on condition that its relationship with Switzerland was regarded by the EEA Council as not impairing the good functioning of the Agreement.

The Oporto Agreement as amended by the Protocol was duly ratified before the end of December 1993 by all the original signatories other than Switzerland. The instruments therefore came into force on January 1, 1994 with respect to all the original signatories apart from that country and Liechtenstein.

Following the amendment of its treaty relations with Switzerland, the Principality acceded to the EEA with effect from May 1, 1995.[12] By then Austria, Finland and Sweden had become Member States of the Community on January 1, 1995. Thus Iceland, Liechtenstein and Norway are currently the only EFTA States within the EEA.

13.06 The EEA does not entirely replace the Free Trade Agreements and other bilateral and multilateral agreements between the Community and the participating EFTA countries. Nevertheless, Article 120 EEA provides that it replaces those earlier agreements to the extent of any inconsistency, unless the contrary is specified in the EEA itself or the Protocols thereto.[13] With regard to the trade in certain agricultural and fisheries products a number of bilateral agreements between the EC and individual EFTA countries remain.

II. ANALYSIS OF THE AGREEMENT

A. General

13.07 According to the fourth recital in the preamble to the EEA, its objective was to establish "a dynamic and homogeneous European Economic Area, based on common rules and equal conditions of competition and providing for the adequate means of enforcement including at the judicial level, and achieved on the basis of equality and reciprocity and of an overall balance of benefits, rights and obligations for the Contracting Parties". This concept of "homogeneity",

---

[10] Switzerland has now concluded a series of seven agreements with the EC and Euratom and their Member States (Decision 2002/309 EC, Euratom [2002] O.J. L114/1). Those agreements entered into force on June 1, 2002. In so far as these new agreements relate to goods, they supplement the Free Trade Agreement of 1972 between the Community and Switzerland (see n.1 above).

[11] [1994] O.J. L1/572.

[12] Decision 1/95 of the EEA Council ([1995] O.J. L86/58).

[13] See Case T-115/94 *Opel Austria v Council* [1997] E.C.R. II-39, para. 97. Certain earlier treaties are expressly saved by Protocols 41, 43 and 44 to the EEA, but none of them concern the free movement of goods.

which is also spelt out in Article 1(1) of the Agreement, permeates the whole operation of the EEA. Both the EFTA Court and the Court of First Instance have attached considerable importance to this passage of the preamble in their landmark cases on the EEA.[14]

13.08 As already indicated, the EEA Agreement is a mixed agreement (*i.e.* it was concluded both by the Community and its Member States). Article 2 provides, in so far as is relevant:

> "For the purposes of the Agreement: ...
> (c) the term 'Contracting Parties' means, concerning the Community and the EC Member States, the Community and the EC Member States, or the EC Member States. The meaning attributed to this expression in each case is to be deduced from the relevant provisions of this Agreement and from the relevant provisions of this Agreement and from the respective competences of the Community and the EC Member States as they follow from the Treaty establishing the European Economic Community and the Treaty establishing the European Coal and Steel Community."

In fact, the Community's competence extends to almost every matter subject to the EEA. The EC has concluded this Agreement on the basis of Article 310 (ex 238) of the Treaty, which empowers the Community to enter into association agreements. In *Demirel v Stadt Schwäbisch Gmund* which concerned the Association Agreement with Turkey, the Court held:

> "since the agreement in question is an association agreement creating special, privileged links with a non-member country which must, at least to a certain extent, take part in the Community system, Article [310] must necessarily empower the Community to guarantee commitments to non-member countries in all fields covered by the Treaty...".[15]

However, in the same case, the Court stressed that Member States might bear some responsibility for the fulfilment of commitments entered into by the Community on the basis of Article 310.

At all events, the free movement of goods surely forms part of the hard core of the Community's competence. The provisions of Articles 25 (ex 12 to 17) and 28 to 31 (ex 30 to 37) EC are matched by Article 113 (ex 133) EC, which creates a common commercial policy governing relations between the Community and third countries. Similarly, all or virtually all EEA legislation relating to goods is a matter of Community competence by virtue of the doctrine in the "ERTA" case,[16] according to which treaty-making powers are vested in the Community with respect to matters covered by internal Community legislation. In short, such powers as the Member States may retain in relation to the EEA are unlikely to have any bearing on the subject matter of this book.

---

[14] Respectively Case E-1/94 *Restamark* (1994 Efta Court Reports, p. 15), para. 32; E-9/97 *Sveinbjörndóttir v Iceland* (judgment of December 10, 1998[1998] EFTA Court Reports 95), paras 49–56; and Case T-115/94 (see n.13 above), para. 108.
[15] Case 12/86 [1987] E.C.R. 3719 at 3751.
[16] Case 22/70 *Commission v Council* [1971] E.C.R. 263.

507

13.09 The most casual glance at the Oporto Agreement will give an idea of its importance and complexity. Although the body of the agreement comprises a mere 129 articles, it is accompanied by 41 protocols (many of which themselves have appendices), a total of 71 declarations, two "arrangements" and a set of agreed minutes.

The length of this document is largely explained by one important innovation: this is the first treaty to "extend" to any third country considerable portions of Community legislation, which after a few adjustments has become EEA legislation. The various appendices to the EEA Agreement are taken up in large part with lists of EC legislation together with the amendments required to transform it into EEA legislation.

So many Community policies and measures are carried over into the EEA that it is easier to list those which are not covered by the Agreement. The most important Community policies to fall outside the EEA are:

(a) the common agricultural policy;

(b) the common fisheries policy;

(c) the common transport policy;

(d) the common policy on indirect taxation;

(e) the common economic and monetary policy; and

(f) the common commercial policy.

Furthermore, while the scope of the EEA broadly reflects that of the EEC in 1992, new EU policies have not been added. In addition, as one would expect, the institutional structure of the EEA is wholly different from that of the Community.

13.10 The nature of the EEA legal order is perhaps best encapsulated in the judgment of the EFTA Court in *Sveinbjörndóttir v Iceland*,[17] where it held: "the EEA is an international treaty *sui generis* which contains a distinct legal order of its own. ... The depth of integration of the EEA Agreement is less far-reaching than under the EC Treaty, but the scope and objective of the EEA Agreement goes beyond what is usual for an agreement under public international law."

13.11 By definition, a comprehensive examination of the EEA would be out of place in this book. Only the following aspects are of interest here: the free movement of goods, "old" legislation, the decision-making procedure, enforcement and dispute settlement. These will now be examined in turn.

First, a note of caution should be sounded: while the three Articles which correspond to Articles 28 to 30 EC will be analysed in some depth, the following sections make no claim to constituting an exhaustive account of the relevant

---

[17] See n.14 above, para. 59.

provisions, in view of their extreme complexity. Rather, they aim to assist the reader by highlighting the basic principles.

B. The Free Movement of Goods

13.12 Article 10 EEA prohibits customs duties and charges of equivalent effect between the Contracting Parties, Article 11 EEA prohibits quantitative restrictions on imports and all measures of equivalent effect between Contracting Parties, while Article 12 bars quantitative restrictions on exports and measures of equivalent effect. Article 13 EEA reproduces *mutatis mutandis* the terms of Article 30 of the Treaty of Rome. Article 16 requires the Contracting Parties to "ensure that any State monopoly of a commercial character be adjusted so that no discrimination regarding the conditions under which goods are procured and marketed will exist between nationals of EC Member States and EFTA States". It thus broadly corresponds to Article 31 (ex 37) EC.

As explained below, the EFTA Court has already decided a number of cases relating to the free movement of goods in the EEA Treaty.

13.13 Article 6 EEA reads as follows:

> "Without prejudice to future developments of case law, the provisions of this Agreement, in so far as they are identical in substance to corresponding rules of the Treaty establishing the European Economic Community and the Treaty establishing the European Coal and Steel Community and to acts adopted in application of these two Treaties, shall, in their implementation and application, be interpreted in conformity with the relevant rulings of the Court of Justice of the European Communities given prior to the date of signature of this Agreement."

The importance of this provision cannot be over-emphasised, since it precluded the application of the ruling in *Polydor* to the EEA. Thus, the case law of the Court on Articles 28 to 30 EC applies to Articles 11, 12 and 13 EEA respectively.

However, this rule is expressly limited to judgments delivered by the Court on or prior to May 2, 1992, the date of signature of the Agreement. The position as regards subsequent case law will be discussed below. It is also true that despite Article 6 the Court held in Opinion 1/91[18] that the EEA provisions were to be construed in the light of the aims of that EEA Agreement which were to be more limited than those of the Treaty of Rome. The Agreement was merely concerned with the application of rules on free trade and competition in economic and commercial relations between the Contracting Parties, whereas the Treaty of Rome sought to "make concrete progress towards European Unity" and to establish an internal market and economic and monetary union; and "the provisions of the EEC Treaty on free movement and competition, far from being an end in themselves, are only a means for attaining those objectives".

---

[18] [1991] E.C.R. I-6079, paras 13–18, see case notes by Auvret-Finck (1993) C.D.E. 38; and Schermers [1992] C.M.L. Rev. 1991.

13.14 The EEA is a free trade area and not a customs union, as the EFTA Court recognised in *Mag Instruments v California Trading Company Norway.*[19] Article 8(2) provides that "unless otherwise specified, Articles 10 to 15, 19, 20 and 25 to 27 shall apply only to products originating in the Contracting Parties". The rules of origin are set out in Protocol 4 to which Article 9 refers. Title V of that Protocol requires goods to be accompanied by certain documents which constitute proof of their origin. Consequently, notwithstanding Article 6 EEA, the Court's case law holding the requirement of certificates of origin to be contrary to Article 28[20] cannot apply to the EEA in so far as documentation is required by these provisions.[21]

The opening words of Article 8(2) would appear to indicate that there are, or may be, instances in which Articles 11 to 13 do exceptionally apply to goods originating in third countries. Yet it seems hard to imagine how this could be so, given that the EEA is not a customs union. Articles 22 and 23, which are not among the provisions mentioned in Article 8(2), do appear to apply to goods originating in third countries, but it is not clear that Articles 11 to 13 are in point.

Article 22 establishes a notification procedure with respect to any proposed reduction by a Contracting Party of the effective level of its duties or charges of equivalent effect applicable to third countries benefiting from most favoured nation treatment, or which is considering the suspension of their application. However, Article 22 is not one of the provisions referred to in Article 8(2). More importantly, Article 23(a) provides that the specific provisions and arrangements laid down in Protocol 12 and Annex II in relation to technical regulations, standards, testing and certification "shall apply to all products unless otherwise specified". Yet once again Article 23 is not one of the provisions to which Article 8(2) refers.

13.15 Article 8(3) excludes agricultural and fisheries products from the scope of the Agreement; it will be recalled that the Free Trade Agreements did not apply to these products either. Moreover, the same applies to certain industrial products processed from agricultural products, by virtue of the same provision read with Protocol 2.

However, "exceptional" cases of EEA provisions applicable to agricultural and fisheries products abound. In the first place, by the combined effect of Article 8 (3) and Protocol 3, the agricultural products specified in that Protocol are subject to the special arrangements set out there.

Moreover, these products are only excluded "unless otherwise specified". Indeed, Articles 17 to 20 are specifically devoted to trade in agricultural and fisheries products. Also, Article 21 which provides for the simplification of border controls and formalities is expressed to apply to such products, notwithstanding Article 8(3). Again, Article 23 is expressed to apply to all products

---

[19] Case E-2/97 (1997 EFTA Court Reports, p. 127), para. 25. As to the difference between a customs union and a free trade area, see para. 1.05 above.
[20] Para. 7.05.
[21] Norberg *et al., op. cit.* n.9 above, at p. 341.

unless otherwise specified; (Article 23(a) has already been discussed and Article 23(b) refers to Protocol 47 on the abolition of technical barriers to trade in wine). The same holds good for the provisions on intellectual property by virtue of Article 65(2).[22]

To return to Articles 17 to 20, the first of these provisions refers to Annex I which incorporates the bulk of Community veterinary and phytosanitary legislation subject to certain adaptations. Article 18 provides:

> "Without prejudice to the specific arrangements governing trade in agricultural products, the Contracting Parties shall ensure that the arrangements provided for in Articles 17 and 23(a) and (b), as they apply to products other than those covered by Article 8(3), are not compromised by other technical barriers to trade. Article 13 shall apply."

The nature of the "specific arrangements" referred to here will be discussed shortly. The wording of the last sentence of Article 18 leaves a good deal to be desired: how can Article 13 (which corresponds to Article 30 EC) apply if Articles 11 and 12 (the equivalent of Articles 28 and 29 EC) do not? One plausible view is that "other technical barriers to trade" may not constitute "a means of arbitrary discrimination or a disguised restriction on trade between the Contracting Parties" within the meaning of Article 13.

Alternatively, Norberg et al.[23] suggest, albeit somewhat tentatively, that Articles 11 and 12 do in fact apply to goods covered by the legislation referred to in Articles 17, 23(a) and 23(b) in so far as restrictions take the form of technical barriers to trade. Yet this interpretation would appear to render Articles 11 and 12 applicable "by the back door" so as to prohibit most restrictions on trade in agricultural products. One might wonder whether this result would reflect the intentions of the signatories to the Agreement.

Article 19(3) requires the Contracting Parties to undertake regular reviews of the conditions of their trade in agricultural products with a view to achieving progressive liberalisation. Article 19(4) provides:

> "In the light of the results of these reviews, within the framework of their respective agricultural policies, and taking into account the results of the Uruguay Round, the Contracting Parties will decide, within the framework of this Agreement, on a preferential bilateral or multilateral, reciprocal and mutually beneficial basis, on further reductions of any type of barriers to trade in the agricultural sector, including those resulting from State monopolies of a commercial character in the agricultural field."

Moreover, a number of bilateral agreements were concluded with EFTA countries in relation to specific agricultural products. These are quite separate from the EEA, although they are mentioned in Protocol 42. Finally, trade in fish and other marine products is governed by Protocol 9, to which Article 20 refers.

---

[22] Art. 65(2) refers to Annex XVII and Protocol 28. On the latter, see Case C-13/00 *Commission v Ireland* (judgment of March 19, 2002), discussed in para. 8.178 above.
[23] *op. cit.*, n.9 above, at pp. 358–359.

C. "Old" Legislation

13.16   The reader will by now be aware that substantial portions of Community legislation have been incorporated, subject to certain amendments, into the EEA. It was obviously not possible to take account of developments in Community legislation up to the very date of signature of the Agreement. Consequently, it was decided to take July 31, 1991 as the "cut-off" date; Community legislation adopted thereafter could only be incorporated into the EEA after the entry into force of the. For ease of reference, relevant legislation adopted on or before July 31, 1991 will be referred to here as "old" legislation, while subsequent acts will be referred to as "new" legislation. It should be stressed, however that these are neither terms of art nor even EEA jargon.

13.17   The various Protocols and Annexes to the Agreement do not set out *in extenso* old legislation as adjusted to the EEA. Instead, the various acts are listed in these Protocols and Annexes, and the reader is in effect given instructions as to how to "adapt" them himself.

Each Act concerned must be read subject to the following two sets of adjustments:

(a) those provided for in the particular Protocol or Annex where the act is listed;

(b) those provided for in Protocol 1 on horizontal adaptations which apply to all Acts.

The opening words of Protocol 1 state: "The preambles of the acts referred to are not adapted for the purposes of the Agreement. They are relevant to the extent necessary for the proper interpretation and application, within the framework of the Agreements, of the provisions contained in such acts." Point 2 stipulates that "procedures, institutional arrangements or other provisions concerning EC committees contained in the acts referred to are to be replaced by the provisions of the Agreement." According to point 8, references in relevant Community acts to the "Community" or "the Common Market" shall be taken to cover the EEA. Similarly, point 9 reads as follows: "whenever the acts referred to contain references to nationals of EC Member States, the references shall for the purposes of the Agreement be understood to be references also to the nationals of EFTA States."[24] Point 11 provides that, regardless of the date specified in the Community act for its entry into force, all old EEA legislation is to come into force on the same date as the Agreement itself.

13.18   To illustrate how these rules operate, it is helpful to take as an example

---

[24] According to Art. 2(b) of the Agreement, "the term 'EFTA States' means the Contracting Parties, which are members of the European Free Trade Association". Since Switzerland is not a Contracting Party, it is not an "EFTA State" for these purposes.

Council Directive 83/189 laying down a procedure for the provision of information in the field of technical standards and regulations.[25] This Directive was listed in Part XIX of Annex II to the Agreement, which sets out a number of adjustments. It follows from this Annex read with Protocol 1 that, whereas EC Member States were to continue to notify their draft technical regulations to the Commission, EFTA countries were required to notify their drafts to the EFTA Surveillance Authority; and that these two bodies were to communicate such drafts to one another. A number of other adjustments to the Directive were effected by Annex II and Protocol 1.

13.19 The EEA version of Directive 83/189 has a life of its own, quite separate from the EC version. Thus, if the EEA version is "provisionally suspended" pursuant to Article 102(5) EEA (discussed below), this in no way affects the application of the EC version within the Community. Indeed, the two must be regarded as two separate acts: an EC Directive, and an "EEA Directive". The same applies to all other items of EC legislation incorporated into the EEA. In this context mention must be made of Article 7 of the Agreement which provides in terms reminiscent of Article 249 (ex 189) EC:

"Acts referred to or contained in the Annexes to the Agreement or in decisions of the EEA Joint Committee shall be binding upon the Contracting Parties, and be, or be made, part of their internal legal order as follows:

(a) an act corresponding to an EC regulation shall as such be made part of the internal legal order of the Contracting Parties;

(b) an act corresponding to an EC directive shall leave to the authorities of the Contracting Parties the choice of form and method of implementation".

D. "New" Legislation

13.20 It follows from Article 98 EEA that any amendment to EC acts listed in the Annexes to the Agreement, or in certain Protocols, must be submitted to the EEA Joint Committee so as to be carried over into the EEA. As already mentioned, this applies to all EC amendments enacted after the "cut-off" date of July 31, 1991.

The EFTA States do not vote on proposed new EC legislation; thus there is no interference with the institutions and mechanisms laid down in the Treaty of Rome. However, when drawing up such legislation the EC Commission shall "informally seek advice from experts of the EFTA States in the same way as it seeks advice from experts of the EC Member States for the elaboration of its proposals" (Article 99). What is more, in certain cases experts from EFTA States

---

[25] [1983] O.J. L109/8. That instrument has now been replaced by Directive 98/34 ([1998] O.J. L204/37) (see paras 12.77 *et seq.* above), but this example nevertheless remains valid.

participate in committees which assist the Commission (Articles 81, 100 and 101).

When the Commission transmits its proposal to the Council, it must send copies to the EFTA States (Article 99(2)). Then, during the phase preceding the decision of the Council of the European Communities, a "continuous information and consultation process" occurs within the EEA Joint Committee, which consists of "representatives of the Contracting Parties " (Article 93(2)).

13.21 Only after the EC act is adopted do the EFTA States play a role which is more than purely consultative. As soon as possible after the adoption of the EC act, the Joint Committee must decide whether to carry it over into the EEA (Article 102(1)). Although this is nowhere specified, the Joint Committee must logically have the power to adjust the EC act when incorporating it into the EEA. The Joint Committee takes decisions by agreement between the Community, on the one hand, and the EFTA States speaking with one voice, on the other (Article 93(2)). In other words, decisions are taken by bilateral consensus. The Agreement is silent on the procedure by which the Community decides on the position which it will adopt within the Joint Committee. That is a matter for the Community alone.

Those procedures were laid down in Council Regulation 2894/94[26] concerning arrangements for implementing the Agreement on the EEA. Article 1(2) of that Regulation provides: "The Community's position regarding EEA Joint Committee decisions which simply extend acts of Community legislation to the EEA, subject to any technical amendments needed, shall be adopted by the Commission." By virtue of Article 1(3)(a), where more than mere technical amendments are involved, it shall be for the Council to decide on the Community's position, acting by the majority laid down in the Treaty of Rome for the Community act which is to be extended to the EEA. The EFTA States have decided to act by unanimous vote, save in certain specified circumstances, which means that one single EFTA State can block a measure.[27]

The Joint Committee is to take its decision as soon as possible after the adoption of the corresponding EC legislation "with a view to permitting a simultaneous application of the latter as well as of the amendments of the Annexes to the Agreement" (Article 102(1)). According to Article 102(3), "the Contracting Parties shall make all efforts to arrive at an agreement on matters relevant to this Agreement". If, despite all their efforts, the Contracting Parties still cannot reach an agreement, then "the EEA Joint Committee shall examine all further possibilities to maintain the good functioning of this Agreement and take any decisions necessary to this effect, including the possibility to take notice of the equivalence of legislation" (Article 102(4)).

Should all else fail, then at the end of the period specified in Article 102(4) the "affected part" of the Annex concerned shall be regarded as being "pro-

---

[26] [1994] O.J. L305/6.
[27] Art. 6 of the Agreement on a Standing Committee of the EFTA States (Annex III to Norberg *et al. op. cit.* n.9).

visionally suspended" within the EEA (Article 102(5)). The same provision specifies that "such a suspension shall take effect six months after the end of the period referred to in paragraph 4, but in no event earlier than the date on which the corresponding EC Act is implemented in the Community". An agreed minute annexed to the Final Act states that such a suspension shall be "adequately published". The practical consequences of the suspension are to be discussed in the Joint Committee (Article 102(6)). At all events, "the rights and obligations which individuals and economic operators have already acquired under this Agreement shall remain" (Article 102(6)).

An agreed minute on the latter paragraph declares that this provision applies only to "actually acquired rights but not expectations only" and it goes on to give certain examples. Finally, Article 102(6) also stipulates that "the Contracting Parties shall, as appropriate, decide on the adjustments necessary due to the suspension". Plainly, the practical difficulties involved in provisionally suspending an EEA act are likely to be considerable, particularly where it is a directive: the idea of all Member States and EFTA States acting in unison to suspend the directive and subsequently ending the suspension may seem workable in theory, but the practice might well turn out to be somewhat different. Fortunately, to date there has not yet been any need to suspend any EEA act.

Article 103(1) states that, where a Decision of the Joint Committee can only become binding on a Contracting Party after it has followed certain procedures provided for by its Constitution, then that measure shall only come into force after the Party has notified its completion of those procedures. According to Article 103(2), where the Party fails to complete the procedures concerned, the Decision may be applied provisionally unless any Party objects.

Article 104 provides:

"Decisions taken by the EEA Joint Committee in the cases provided for in this Agreement shall, unless otherwise provided for therein, upon their entry into force be binding on the Contracting Parties which shall take the necessary steps to ensure their implementation and application."

13.22 Suppose that the Community were now to enact legislation on a matter covered by the Agreement but that this legislation does not amend any regulation or directive listed in the Protocols or Annexes. Could the Joint Committee then incorporate the new Community legislation into the EEA?

The better view is that the procedure referred to above must be followed if the new Community legislation affects the functioning of the EEA. This view appears to be borne out by Article 97 which provides:

"This Agreement does not prejudice the right for each Contracting Party to amend, without prejudice to the principle of non-discrimination and after having informed the other Contracting Parties, its internal legislation in the areas covered by this Agreement:

— if the EEA Joint Committee concluded that the legislation as amended does not affect the good functioning of this Agreement; or
— if the procedures referred to in Article 98 have been completed."

Moreover, Article 99 (which lays down the procedure to be followed prior to the adoption of Community legislation by the Council) applies whenever new legislation is being drawn up "in a field which is governed by this Agreement". This language is not confined to the amendment of legislation listed in the Annexes and Protocols to the EEA. Having said that, the wording of Article 102 (which governs the actual adoption of EEA legislation) is narrower, since it is expressed to apply to legislative acts constituting "an amendment to an Annex to this Agreement". Nevertheless, having regard to Articles 97 and 99 and to the general purposes of the Agreement, it would be surprising if the narrow view were to prevail.

13.23   The complexity of the decision-making procedure is illustrated by the following anomaly. Let us imagine that EC Directive A/90 is listed in one of the Annexes to the EEA and is thus incorporated into the EEA, and that the EC Council of Ministers subsequently enacts Directive B/94 which primarily relates to another matter but amends one provision of Directive A/90. Let us imagine further that one EFTA State (for example, Norway) is opposed to the amendment. Since the EFTA States have decided to act by consensus, Norway could prevent the Joint Committee carrying over the amendment. If the deadlock is not broken, EEA Directive A/90 will ultimately be provisionally suspended throughout the EEA, in accordance with Article 102(5). However, EC Directive A/90 will be unaffected within the Community.

E. Enforcement

13.24   It follows clearly from Article 7 EEA (cited above) that an EEA regulation is directly applicable in the same manner as an EC Regulation; and that an EEA directive may have direct effect in the same way as an EC directive. As is plain from its wording, Article 7 governs both "old" legislation set out in the Annexes to the Agreement and "new" legislation.

As to the provisions of the Agreement itself and the Protocols thereto, the principle of direct applicability is not spelt out. Nevertheless, it follows from the principles discussed in paragraph 13.02 above that such provisions may be directly applicable in *Community law* in any event; and this has now been confirmed by the Court of First Instance in *Opel Austria v Council* discussed at paragraph 13.29 below.

Hence it is by no means surprising to find the EFTA Court ruling that:

> "...the provisions of the EEA Agreement are, to a great extent, intended for the benefit of individuals and economic operators throughout the European Economic Area. Therefore, the proper functioning of the EEA Agreement is dependent on those individuals and economic operators being able to rely on the rights thus intended for their benefit."[28]

---

[28] *Sveinsbjörnsdóttir* (see n.14 above), para. 58. This view is also strongly supported by such highly authoritative experts on the EEA as Sevón and Johansson "The Protection of Individual Rights under the EEA Agreement" [1999] E.L. Rev. 373; Norberg "Perspectives on the Future Devel-

Regrettably, however, Norway and Iceland still do not accept that they are required to treat EEA provisions as capable of being directly applicable. Two former judges[29] of the EFTA Court have urged those countries to reconsider their position; they point to the danger that otherwise the Court of Justice might regard the aims of the EEA Agreement as being little more than the former Free Trade Agreements, thereby in effect downgrading the EEA.[30] Equally, the other "Community institutions and the EC Member States might lose interest in the EEA Agreement, ... and ... worry less about the input of the EFTA States in the decision-making process."[31]

13.25   At all events, the Commission may bring proceedings under Article 226 (ex 169) EC against any Member State of the Community for infringing any EEA provisions. Indeed, Article 109(1) EEA specifically requires the Commission to monitor "the fulfilment of the obligations under this Agreement ... acting in conformity with [the EC Treaty, the ECSC Treaty] and this Agreement". Thus the Commission has successfully brought proceedings against Ireland for failure to accede to various international conventions on intellectual property as required by Protocol 28 to the EEA Agreement.[32]

At the same time, the EFTA States have established an independent EFTA Surveillance Authority, as required by Article 108 EEA.[33] One of the primary functions of the Authority is to monitor the application of the Agreement by the EFTA States (Article 109) and it may bring infringement proceedings before the EFTA Court (Article 108). These provisions are supplemented by an Agreement between the EFTA States on the establishment of a Surveillance Authority and a Court of Justice.[34] The Commission and the EFTA Surveillance Authority are required to "cooperate, exchange information and consult each other on surveillance policy issues and individual cases" (Article 109(2)).

F. Dispute Settlement

13.26   During the negotiation of the EEA Agreement, judicial control of "EEA law" proved to be one of the most thorny issues. This was in part because the initial regime was rejected by the Court of Justice in Opinion 1/91, whereupon a wholly different scheme had to be devised. In a second Opinion the Court upheld the new scheme.[35]

The central feature of the initial regime was an EEA Court composed of five

---

opment of the EEA" in Festschrift for Thor Vilhjámsson and van Gerven "The Genesis of 'EEA law' and the Principles of Primacy and Direct Effect" (1993) 16 Fordham International Law Journal 955.

[29] Sevón (writing with Johansson) and Norberg (see previous footnote).

[30] See para. 13.02 above.

[31] Sevón and Johansson, *op. cit.* p. 385.

[32] Case C-13/00 (see n.22 above).

[33] Agreement between the EFTA States on the establishment of a surveillance authority and a Court of Justice ([1994] O.J. L344/1).

[34] See Annex II to Norberg *et al.* "EEA Law".

[35] Opinion 1/92 [1992] E.C.R. I-2821, noted by Auvret-Finck (*op. cit.* n.18 above) and Schermers (*op. cit.* n.18 above).

judges of the Court of Justice and three EFTA judges (each of the EFTA States would have nominated one judge but only three of those judges would have heard any given case). The Commission sought an Opinion from the Court under Article 300 (ex 228) EC as to whether this system was compatible with Community law. In Opinion 1/91 the Court held most emphatically that it was not, since the jurisdiction to be conferred on the EEA Court by the Agreement was:

> "...likely adversely to affect the allocation of responsibilities defined in the Treaties and, hence, the autonomy of the Community legal order, respect for which must be assured by the Court of Justice pursuant to Article 164 of the EEC Treaty [now Article 220 EC]. This exclusive jurisdiction of the Court of Justice is confirmed by Article 219 of the EEC Treaty [now Article 292 EC], under which Member States undertake not to submit a dispute concerning the interpretation or application of that Treaty to any method of settlement other than those provided for in the Treaty. Article 87 of the ECSC Treaty embodies a provision to the same effect.
> Consequently, to confer that jurisdiction on the EEA Court is incompatible with Community law."[36]

13.27 There followed a period of renegotiation of the relevant provisions of the Agreement. The EEA Court was consigned to history, as required by Opinion 1/91. In its place, the Contracting Parties established an EFTA Court with jurisdiction, *inter alia*, to hear infringement proceedings brought against EFTA States by the EFTA surveillance authority, as well as disputes between EFTA States (Article 108).[37] This court originally sat in Geneva, but now sits in Luxembourg.

Article 105 requires the EEA Joint Committee to preserve the homogeneous interpretation of the Agreement and to "keep under constant review the development of the case law of the Court of Justice of the European Communities and the EFTA Court". Article 105(3) provides that, if the Joint Committee has not been able to settle a difference between the case law of the two courts, the procedures in Article 111 may be applied.

The latter provision governs any dispute as to the interpretation or application of the Agreement, whether or not there is divergent case law. The procedures which it lays down are highly complex, but their essence is this: in no case may the Contracting Parties depart from the case law of the Court of Justice and, if at the end of the day they fail to resolve their dispute, the aggrieved party may resort to safeguard measures under Article 111 itself read with Articles 112 to 113. In such a case, any other Contracting Party is entitled to take "such appropriate rebalancing measures as are strictly necessary to remedy the imbalance", pursuant to Article 114.

Under Article 111(3), if the dispute relates to the interpretation of the EEA provisions which are identical in substance to provisions of Community law and the dispute has not been settled within three months of being brought before

---

[36] Paras 35 and 36 of the Opinion.
[37] See the Agreement referred to in n.33 above; also Protocol 5 thereto on the Statute of the EFTA Court.

the Joint Committee, the Contracting Party may agree to request a binding ruling from the Court of Justice. At the time of writing, no such ruling has been sought.

Under Article 111(4), where a dispute relates to safeguard measures, any Contracting Parties may seek binding arbitration under the procedures laid down in Protocol 33. Article 111(4) specifically provides that no question of interpretation of the provisions of the Agreement which are identical in substance to provisions of Community law may be dealt with in such procedures. Last, Protocol 34, to which Article 107 of the agreement refers, contains provisions under which the EFTA States may authorise their courts to request the Court of Justice to give a binding ruling on the interpretation of a provision of the agreement which is identical in substance to a provision of Community law. However, none of the EFTA States has taken advantage of this possibility.

In Opinion 1/92,[38] also delivered pursuant to Article 228 EEC, the Court gave its blessing to these new provisions, since it found that they did not "call in question the binding nature of the Court's case law or, the autonomy of the Community legal order". Two closely related features of the new system commended themselves to the Court: in no circumstances was it open to the Contracting Parties to depart from the case law of the Court; and any ruling requested from the Court pursuant to the Agreement would be binding.[39]

III. SUBSEQUENT DEVELOPMENTS

A. General

13.28 This section describes the major developments which have occurred since January 1, 1994, when the EEA Agreement came into force.[40]

Without question the most important development has been the accession of Austria, Finland and Sweden to the Community on January 1, 1995.[41] They thus moved from the EFTA to the EC side of the EEA. This required no amendment to the EEA Treaty. Transitional provisions relating to matters pending before the EFTA institutions are contained in Article 172 of the Act of Accession.

One must also mention the adoption of Council Regulation 2894/94 concerning arrangements for implementing the Agreement on the EEA,[42] which lays down the various Community procedures to be followed in relation to EEA matters. Unfortunately, that Regulation was not enacted until late November 1994, 11 months after the EEA Treaty came into force.

---

[38] See n.35 above.

[39] In Opinion 1/91 (paras 54 to 65) the Court had struck down provisions of the earlier scheme under which the courts of EFTA States could seek non-binding preliminary rulings from the Court, but only on the grounds that preliminary rulings must be binding.

[40] See Forman "The EEA Agreement Five Years On: Dynamic Homogeneity in Practice and its Implementation by the Two EEA Courts" [1999] C.M.L. Rev. 751.

[41] [1994] O.J. C241, as amended by the adjusting Decision for Norway ([1995] O.J. L1).

[42] See n.26 above.

B. ECJ and CFI Judgments

13.29   The *locus classicus* on the EEA in the case law of the Community courts is *Opel Austria v Council*.[43] In that case, the CFI found that Article 10 EEA prohibiting customs duties and charges of equivalent effect between the Contracting Parties has direct effect. It would seem to follow that the same applies to the other EEA provisions on the free movement of goods.

Moreover, on the basis of Article 6 EEA, the Court held that the Article 10 was to be interpreted in precisely the same way as the corresponding provisions of the EC Treaty. The Court based this finding on the following considerations: the purpose of the EEA was to "eliminate virtually all trade barriers, in conformity with the provisions of the GATT on the establishment of free-trade areas"; in that context, "the EEA Agreement involves a high degree of integration, with objectives which exceed those of a mere free-trade agreement"; in addition, "the rules applicable to relations between the Contracting Parties essentially correspond to the parallel provisions of the EC and ECSC Treaties and the measures adopted in pursuance of those treaties."; and the fourth recital in the preamble to the Agreement (cited above) speaks of the purpose of the Agreement being to establish "a dynamic and homogeneous European Economic Area".[44]

Accordingly, the contested Council Regulation, which imposed a countervailing charge on the applicant's gear boxes manufactured in Austria by reason of a State aid granted by that country, was held to contravene Article 10 EEA.

13.30   Another judgment concerning the EEA was *Andersson v Sweden*.[45] The Court held there that it had no jurisdiction to hear a reference for a preliminary ruling from a Swedish court as to the rights and liabilities arising under EEA provisions in Sweden in 1994, when that country was on the EFTA side of the EEA. This was because the material facts arose at a time when Sweden was not in the Community and the Court had no power to rule on the application of the EEA in the EFTA States. What is more, it was found to be of no consequence that Sweden had acceded to the Community in the meantime. Clearly, the Swedish court was no longer entitled to seek the assistance of the EFTA Court either.

C. EFTA Court Judgments

13.31   The EFTA Court has delivered a large number of judgments relating to the free movement of goods.

Indeed, as it happened, its very first judgment concerned this part of the EEA Treaty: *Restamark*.[46] The plaintiffs in that case, who had imported into Finland

---

[43] See n.13 above.
[44] Paras 106–108 of the judgment.
[45] Case C-321/97 [1999] E.C.R. I-3551. See Oliver "La recevabilité des questions préjudicielles: la jurisprudence des années 1990" [2001] C.D.E. 15.
[46] See n.14 above.

wine from Italy and whisky from Germany, contested the Finnish legislation whereby such goods could not be imported without an authorisation from the State alcohol monopoly. The Finnish tribunal made a reference to the EFTA Court for a preliminary ruling pursuant to Protocol 34. That Court began the substantive part of its ruling with a few general remarks about the interpretation of the EEA, noting in particular that "the objective of the Contracting Parties was to create a dynamic and homogeneous European Economic Area". The Court held that such a restriction infringed Article 11 EEA (which corresponds to Article 28 EC); that it was not justified on health grounds under Article 13 EEA (which corresponds to Article 30 EC), since other less restrictive means could be found of preventing alcohol abuse; and that the same restrictions also fell foul of Article 16 (which corresponds to Article 37 EC).

Another important ruling of the EFTA Court was that in *Mag Instruments*,[47] where it held that the EEA version of the First Trade Mark Directive leaves it open to the EFTA States to decide whether or not to apply the principle of the international exhaustion of trade mark rights with regard to goods originating in countries outside the EEA. This conclusion does not in itself impinge directly on the movement of goods within the EEA: the Court's permissive interpretation of the EEA version of the Directive was based precisely on the fact that the EEA is a free trade area, not a customs union.[48] Hence it is not surprising that the European Court of Justice subsequently reached the opposite conclusion on the EC version of the same Directive in *Silhouette International Schmied v Hartlauer*.[49]

Another case worthy of note is *EFTA Surveillance Authority v Norway*,[50] where the EFTA Court held that, by prohibiting the importation and marketing of cornflakes fortified with vitamins, the defendant State was in breach of Article 11 EEA. The Court dismissed the suggestion that the ban was justified on public health grounds.[51]

IV. CONCLUSION

13.32 The EEA has created a greatly enhanced free trade area between the Community and certain EFTA countries. However, trade in agricultural and fisheries products has been liberalised only in part. On the other hand, the unique feature of this Agreement is that large portions of EC legislation are rendered applicable, subject to specified adjustments, to the other Contracting

---

[47] See n.19 above.
[48] See generally Baudenbacher, "Erschöpfung der Immaterialengüterrechte in der EFTA und die Rechtslage in der EU" [2000] G.R.U.R. Int. 584.
[49] Case C-355/96 [1998] E.C.R. I-4799, see paras 8.217 *et seq.* above.
[50] Case E-3/00 (judgment of April 5, 2001).
[51] Other relevant judgments of the EFTA Court include those delivered in Cases E-5/96 *Ullensarker commune v Nille* ([1997] EFTA Court Reports 30) (sales of video cassettes); E-1/98 *Norway v Astra Norge* ([1998] EFTA Court Reports 140) (parallel imports of pharmaceuticals); and E-5/98 *Fagtún v Iceland* ([1999] EFTA Court Reports 51) (public works contracts).

Parties. No treaty concluded with a third country has ever incorporated Community legislation in this way.

The cumbersome nature of the procedures for adopting new EEA Acts and for settling disputes must be a cause for concern. In attempting to preserve the autonomy of the Community while respecting in so far as possible the wish of the EFTA countries to avoid sacrificing their sovereignty, the Contracting Parties have devised a structure of startling complexity. Thus Schermers has written:

"it is unlikely that the compromises found will lead to a system which remains workable in the long-term. They are too much of an effort to combine the uncombinable. Most probably the Agreement will only apply during an interim period."[52]

A very different view has recently been expressed by Norberg, when he wrote:

"... the EEA functions well and can continue to do so as long as all the parties and the institutions in the EFTA pillar do their best to play by the rules. On the other hand, one should not forget that the delicate institutional balance is vulnerable to obstructions."[53]

By this is meant that, unless Norway and Iceland recognise the principle of direct applicability, the Community may in practice downgrade the EEA.[54]

---

[52] *op. cit.* n.18 above at 1005.
[53] *op. cit.* n.28 above at p. 379.
[54] See para. 13.24 above.

ANNEX I

Treaty of Amsterdam: Table of Equivalences*

Old Number	New Number	Old Number	New Number
B: Treaty establishing the European Community		Article 36	Article 30
		Article 37	Article 31
Article 2	Article 2	Article 38	Article 32
Article 3	Article 3	Article 39	Article 33
Article 3b	Article 5	Article 40	Article 34
Article 3c	Article 6	Article 41	Article 35
Article 4b	Article 9	Article 43	Article 37
Article 5	Article 10	Article 46	Article 38
Article 5a	Article 11	Article 48	Article 39
Article 6	Article 12	Article 49	Article 40
Article 6a	Article 13	Article 50	Article 41
Article 7a	Article 14	Article 51	Article 42
Article 7c	Article 15	Article 52	Article 43
Article 7d	Article 16	Article 54	Article 44
Article 8	Article 17	Article 55	Article 45
Article 8a	Article 18	Article 56	Article 46
Article 8b	Article 19	Article 57	Article 47
Article 8c	Article 20	Article 58	Article 48
Article 8d	Article 21	Article 59	Article 49
Article 8e	Article 22	Article 60	Article 50
Article 9	Article 23	Article 61	Article 51
Article 10	Article 24	Article 62 (repealed)	—
Article 12	Article 25	Article 63	Article 52
Articles 18–27 (repealed)		Article 64	Article 53
Article 28	Article 26	Article 65	Article 54
Article 29	Article 27	Article 66	Article 55
Article 30	Article 28	Article 73b	Article 56
Articles 31–33 (repealed)		Article 73c	Article 57
Article 34	Article 29	Article 73d	Article 58
Article 35 (repealed)		Article 73f	Article 59

* This is a table of equivalences for Articles mentioned in the text of this book, not a complete guide.

Old Number	New Number	Old Number	New Number
Article 73g	Article 60	Article 129a	Article 153
Article 74	Article 70	Article 130a	Article 158
Article 75	Article 71	Article 130b	Article 159
Article 76	Article 72	Article 130c	Article 160
Article 77	Article 73	Article 130d	Article 161
Article 78	Article 74	Article 130e	Article 162
Article 79	Article 75	Article 130r	Article 174
Article 80	Article 76	Article 130s	Article 175
Article 81	Article 77	Article 130t	Article 176
Article 82	Article 78	Article 131	Article 182
Article 83	Article 79	Article 132	Article 183
Article 84	Article 80	Article 133	Article 184
Article 85	Article 81	Article 134	Article 185
Article 86	Article 82	Article 135	Article 186
Article 87	Article 83	Article 136	Article 187
Article 90	Article 86	Article 136a	Article 188
Article 92	Article 87	Article 148	Article 205
Article 93	Article 88	Article 164	Article 220
Article 94	Article 89	Article 169	Article 226
Article 95	Article 90	Article 170	Article 227
Article 99	Article 93	Article 173	Article 230
Article 100	Article 94	Article 175	Article 232
Article 100a	Article 95	Article 176	Article 233
Article 101	Article 96	Article 177	Article 234
Article 102	Article 97	Article 189	Article 249
Article 102a	Article 98	Article 189b	Article 251
Article 103	Article 99	Article 189c	Article 252
Article 103a	Article 100	Article 190	Article 253
Article 104	Article 101	Article 209a	Article 280
Article 105a	Article 106	Article 215	Article 288
Article 109b	Article 113	Article 219	Article 292
Article 109c	Article 114	Article 222	Article 295
Article 109g	Article 118	Article 223	Article 296
Article 109h	Article 119	Article 224	Article 297
Article 109i	Article 120	Article 225	Article 298
Article 109k	Article 122	Article 226 (repealed)	—
Article 113	Article 133	Article 227	Article 299
Article 115	Article 134	Article 228	Article 300
Article 116	Article 135	Article 228a	Article 301
Article 117	Article 136	Article 232	Article 305
Article 118	Article 137	Article 233	Article 306
Article 118a	Article 138	Article 234	Article 307
Article 119	Article 141	Article 235	Article 308
Article 122	Article 145	Article 238	Article 310
Article 127	Article 150	Article 240	Article 312

Cases and Materials

COMMISSION DIRECTIVE OF 22 DECEMBER 1969

based on the provisions of Article 33(7), on the abolition of measures which have an effect equivalent to quantitative restrictions on imports and are not covered by other provisions adopted in pursuance of the EEC Treaty (70/50/EEC).

The Commission of the European Communities,

Having regard to the provisions of the Treaty establishing the European Economic Community, and in particular Article 33(7) thereof,

Whereas for the purpose of Article 30 *et seq.* "measures" means laws, regulations, administrative provisions, administrative practices, and all instruments issuing from a public authority, including recommendations;

Whereas for the purposes of this directive "administrative practices" means any standard and regularly followed procedure of a public authority; whereas "recommendations" means any instruments issuing from a public authority which, while not legally binding on the addressees thereof, cause them to pursue a certain conduct;

Whereas the formalities to which imports are subject do not as a general rule have an effect equivalent to that of quantitative restrictions and, consequently, are not covered by this directive;

Whereas certain measures adopted by Member States, other than those applicable equally to domestic and imported products, which were operative at the date of entry into force of the Treaty and are not covered by other provisions adopted in pursuance of the Treaty, either preclude importation or make it more difficult or costly than the disposal of domestic production;

Whereas such measures must be considered to include those which make access of imported products to the domestic market; at any marketing stage, subject to a condition which is not laid down for domestic products or to a condition differing from that laid down for domestic products, and more difficult to satisfy, so that a burden is thus placed on imported products only;

Whereas such measures must also be considered to include those which, at any marketing stage, grant to domestic products a preference, other than an aid, to which conditions may or may not be attached, and where such measures totally or partially preclude the disposal of imported products;

Whereas such measures hinder imports which could otherwise take place, and thus have an effect equivalent to quantitative restrictions on imports;

Whereas effects on the free movement of goods of measures which relate to the marketing of products and which apply equally to domestic and imported products are not as a general rule equivalent to those of quantitative restrictions, since such effects are normally inherent in the disparities between rules applied by Member States in this respect;

Whereas, however, such measures may have a restrictive effect on the free movement of goods over and above that which is intrinsic to such rules; Whereas such is the case where imports are either precluded or made more difficult or costly than the disposal of domestic production and where such effect is not necessary for the attainment of an objective within the scope of the powers for the regulation of trade left to Member States by the Treaty; whereas such is in particular the case where the said objective can be attained just as effectively by other means which are less of a hindrance to trade; whereas such is also the case where the restrictive effect of these provisions on the free movement of goods is out of proportion to their purpose;

Whereas these measures accordingly have an effect equivalent to that of quantitative restrictions on imports;

Whereas the customs union cannot be achieved without the abolition of such measures having an equivalent effect to quantitative restrictions on imports;

Whereas Member States must abolish all measures having equivalent effect by the end of the transitional period at the latest, even if no Commission Directive expressly requires them to do so;

Whereas the provisions concerning the abolition of quantitative restrictions and measures having equivalent effect between Member States apply both to products originating in and exported by Member States and to products originating in third countries and put into free circulation in the other Member States;

Whereas Article 33(7) does not apply to measures of the kind referred to which fall under other provisions of the Treaty, and in particular those which fall under Articles 37(1) and 44 of the Treaty or form an integral part of a national organisation of an agricultural market;

Whereas Article 33 (7) does not apply to the charges and taxation referred to in Article 12 *et seq.* and Article 95 *et seq.* or to the aids mentioned in Article 92.

Whereas the provisions of Article 33 (7) do not prevent the application, in particular, of Articles 36 and 223;

Has adopted this Directive:

Article 1

The purpose of this directive is to abolish the measures referred to in Articles 2 and 3, which were operative at the date of entry into force of the EEC Treaty.

Article 2

1. This directive covers measures, other than those applicable equally to domestic or imported products which hinder imports which could

otherwise take place, including measures which make importation more difficult or costly than the disposal of domestic production.

2. In particular, it covers measures which make imports or the disposal, at any marketing stage, of imported products subject to a condition—other than a formality—which is required in respect of imported products only, or a condition differing from that required for domestic products and more difficult to satisfy. Equally, it covers, in particular, measures which favour domestic products or grant them a preference, other than an aid, to which conditions may or may not be attached.

3. The measures referred to must be taken to include those measures which:

    (a) lay down, for imported products only, minimum or maximum prices below or above which imports are prohibited, reduced or made subject to conditions liable to hinder importation;

    (b) lay down less favourable prices for imported products than for domestic products;

    (c) fix profit margins or any other price components for imported products only or fix these differently for domestic products and for imported products, to the detriment of the latter;

    (d) preclude any increase in the price of the imported product corresponding to the supplementary costs and charges inherent in importation;

    (e) fix the prices of products solely on the basis of the cost price or the quality of domestic products at such a level as to create a hindrance to importation;

    (f) lower the value of an imported product, in particular by causing a reduction in its intrinsic value, or increase its costs;

    (g) make access of imported products to the domestic market conditional upon having an agent or representative in the territory of the importing Member State;

    (h) lay down conditions of payment in respect of imported products only, or subject imported products to conditions which are different from those laid down for domestic products and more difficult to satisfy;

    (i) require, for imports only, the giving of guarantees or making of payments on account;

    (j) subject imported products only to conditions, in respect, in particular of shape size weight composition presentation identification or putting up, or subject imported products to conditions which are different from those for domestic products and more difficult to satisfy;

    (k) hinder the purchase by private individuals of imported products only, or encourage, require or give preference to the purchase of domestic products only;

    (l) totally or partially preclude the use of national facilities or equipment in respect of imported products only, or totally or partially confine the use of such facilities or equipment to domestic products only;

(m) prohibit or limit publicity in respect of imported products only, or totally or partially confine publicity to domestic products only;

(n) prohibit, limit or require stocking in respect of imported products only; totally or partially confine the use of stocking facilities to domestic products only, or make the stocking of imported products subject to conditions which are different from those required for domestic products and more difficult to satisfy;

(o make importation subject to the granting of reciprocity by one or more Member States;

(p) prescribe that imported products are to conform, totally or partially, to rules other than those of the importing country;

(q) specify time limits for imported products which are insufficient or excessive in relation to the normal course of the various transactions to which these time limits apply;

(r) subject imported products to controls [or], other than those inherent in the customs clearance procedure, to which domestic products are not subject or which are stricter in respect of imported products than they are in respect of domestic products, without this being necessary in order to ensure equivalent protection;

(s) confine names which are not indicative of origin or source to domestic products only.

Article 3

This directive also covers measures governing the marketing of products which deal, in particular, with shape, size, weight, composition, presentation, identification or putting up and which are equally applicable to domestic and imported products, where the restrictive effect of such measures on the fee movement of goods exceeds the effects intrinsic to trade rules.

This is the case, in particular, where:

— the restrictive effects on the free movement of goods are out of proportion to their purpose;

— the same objective can be attained by other means which are less of a hindrance to trade.

Article 4

1. Member States shall take all necessary steps in respect of products which must be allowed to enjoy free movement pursuant to Articles 9 and 10 of the Treaty to abolish measures having an effect equivalent to quantitative restrictions on imports and covered by this directive.

2. Member States shall inform the Commission of measures taken pursuant to this directive.

Article 5

1. This directive does not apply to measures:

    (a) which fall under Article 37 1
        of the EEC Treaty;
    (b) which are referred to in Article 44 of the EEC Treaty or integral
        part of a national organisation of an agricultural market not yet
        replaced by a common organisation.

2. This directive shall apply without prejudice to the application, in particular, of Articles 36 and 223 of the EEC Treaty.

Article 6

This directive is addressed to the Member States.

Done at Brussels, 22 December 1969.

For the Commission
The President
Jean Rey

Table of Cases

Case 8/74 *Procureur du Roi v. Dassonville*
[1974 E.C.R. 837 at 852, [1974] 2 C.M.L.R. 436 at 453

5. All trading rules enacted by Member States which are capable of hindering, directly or indirectly, actually or potentially, intra-Community trade are to be considered as measures having an effect equivalent to quantitative restrictions.

Case 104/75 *Officier van Justitie v. De Peijper*
[1976] E.C.R. 613 at 635–636, [1976] 2 C.M.L.R. 271 at 304

4. National measures of the kind in question have an effect equivalent to a quantitative restriction and are prohibited under Article 30 of the Treaty if they are likely to constitute an obstacle, directly or indirectly, actually or potentially, to imports between Member States.
    Rules or practices which result in imports being channelled in such a way that only certain traders can effect these imports, whereas others are prevented from doing so, constitute such an obstacle to imports ...

16. Nevertheless, it emerges from Article 36 that national rules or practices which do restrict imports of pharmaceutical products or are capable of doing so are only compatible with the Treaty to the extent to which they are necessary for the effective protection of health and life of humans.

17. National rules or practices do not fall within the exception specified in '1 Article 36 if the health and life of humans can be as effectively protected by measures which do not restrict intra-Community trade so much.

Case 120/78 *Rewe-Zentral A.G. v. Bundesmonopolverwaltung für Branntwein*
("Cassis de Dijon")
[1979] E.C.R. 649 at 662–664, [1979] 3 C.M.L.R. 494 at 508

8. In the absence of common rules relating to the production and marketing of alcohol—a proposal for a regulation submitted to the Council by the Commission on 7 December 1976 (*Official Journal* C309, p. 2) not yet having received the Council's approval—it is or the Member States to regulate all matters relating to the production and marketing of alcohol and alcoholic beverages on their own territory.
    Obstacles to movement within the Community resulting from dis-

parities between the national laws relating to the marketing of the products in question must be accepted in so far as those provisions may be recognised as being necessary in order to satisfy mandatory requirements relating in particular to the effectiveness of fiscal supervision, the protection of public health, the fairness of commercial transactions and the defence of the consumer.

It is clear from the foregoing that the requirements relating to the minimum alcohol content of alcoholic beverages do not serve a purpose which is in the general interest and such as to take precedence over the requirements of the free movement of goods, which constitutes one of the fundamental rules of the Community.

In practice, the principal effect of requirements of this nature is to promote alcoholic beverages having a high alcohol content by excluding from the national market products of other Member States which do not answer that description.

It therefore appears that the unilateral requirement imposed by the rules of a Member State of a minimum alcohol content for the purposes of the sale of alcoholic beverages constitutes an obstacle to trade which is incompatible with the provisions of Article 30 of the Treaty.

There is therefore no valid reason why, provided that they have been lawfully produced and marketed in one of the Member States, alcoholic beverages should not be introduced into any other Member State; the sale of such products may not be subject to a legal prohibition on the marketing of beverages with an alcohol content lower than the limit set by the national rules.

Consequently, the first question should be answered to the effect that the concept of "measures having an effect equivalent to quantitative restrictions on imports" contained in Article 30 of the Treaty is to be understood to mean that the fixing of a minimum alcohol content for alcoholic beverages intended for human consumption by the legislation of a Member State also falls within the prohibition laid down in that provision where the importation of alcoholic beverages lawfully produced and marketed in another Member State is concerned.

Case C-267 and 268/91 *Bernard Keck and Daniel Mithouard*
[1993] E.C.R. I 6097, [1995] 1 C.M.L.R. 101.

12. It is not the purpose of national legislation imposing a general prohibition on resale at a loss to regulate trade in goods between Member States.

13. Such legislation may, admittedly, restrict the volume of sales, and hence the Volume of sales of products from other Member States, in so far as it deprives traders of a method of sales promotion. But the question remains whether such a possibility is sufficient to characterise the legislation in question as a measure having equivalent effect to a quantitative restriction on imports.

14. In view of the increasing tendency of traders to invoke Article 30 of the

Treaty as a means of challenging any rules whose effect is to limit their commercial freedom even where such rules are not aimed at products from other Member States, the Court considers it necessary to re-examine and clarify its case law on this matter.

15. In "Cassis de Dijon" (Case 120/78 *Rewe-Zentral v. Bundesmono-polverwaltung für Branntwein* [978] E.C.R. 649) it was held that, in the absence of harmonisation of legislation, measures of equivalent effect prohibited by Article 30 include obstacles to the free movement of goods where they are the consequence of applying rules that lay down requirements to be met by goods (such as requirements as to designation, form, size, weight, composition, presentation, labelling, packaging) to goods from other Member States where they are lawfully manufactured and marketed, even if those rules apply without distinction to all products unless their application can be justified by a public interest objective taking precedence over the free movement of goods.

16. However, contrary to what has previously been decided, the application to products from other Member States of national provisions restricting or prohibiting certain selling arrangements is not such as to hinder directly or indirectly, actually or potentially, trade between Member States within the meaning of the *Dassonville* judgment (Case 8/74 [1974] E.C.R. 837), provided that those provisions apply to all affected traders operating within the national territory and provided that they affect in the same manner, in law and in fact, the marketing of domestic products and of those from other Member States.

17. Where those conditions are fulfilled, the application of such rules to the sale of products from another Member State meeting the requirements laid down by that State is not by nature such as to prevent their access to the market or to impede access any more than it impedes the access of domestic products. Such rules therefore fall outside the scope of Article 30 of the Treaty.

Selected Bibliography on Articles 28 to 30

Baquero Cruz	"Free movement and private autonomy" (1999) 24 E.L.Rev. 603.
Barents	"New Developments in Measures having Equivalent Effect" [1981] C.M.L.Rev. 271.
Barnard	"Fitting the remaining pieces into the goods and persons jigsaw?" (2001) 26 E.L.Rev. 35.
Becker	"Von *Dassonville* über *Cassis* zu *Keck*: Der Begriff der Maßnahmen gleicher Wirkung in Art. 30 EGV" [1994] EuR 162.
Béraud	"Les mesures d'effet équivalent au sens des articles 30 et suivants du Traité de Rome" [1968] R.T.D.E. 265.
Bermann, Goebel, Davey and Fox	*Cases and Materials on European Union Law* (2nd ed., 2002) Ch. 13.
Capelli	"Les malentendus provoqués par l'arrêt 'Cassis de Dijon'" [1981] R.M.C. 421.
Chalmers	"Free Movement of Goods within the European Community: an Unhealthy Addiction to Scotch Whisky?" [1993] I.C.L.Q. 269.
Daniele	"Réflexions d'ensemble sur la notion de mesures ayant un effet équivalent à des restrictions quantitatives" [1984] R.M.C. 477.
Dashwood	"The Cassis de Dijon Line of Authority" from *In Memoriam D.D.B. Mitchell* (1983).
Dauses	"La jurisprudence de la Cour de justice en matière de libre circulation des marchandises' dans la Communauté européene" [1985] R.T.D.E. 1.
Davey	*See* Bermann.

Defalque	(1) "Le concept de discrimination en matière de libre circulation des marchandises" [1987] C.D.E. 471. (2) Commentary on Articles 30 to 36 in *Commentaire Mégret – Le droit de la CEE* (2nd. ed., Brussels, 1992) Vol.1.
Dona	"Les mesures d'effet équivalent à des restrictions quantitatives" [1973] R.M.C. 224.
Ehlermann	(1) "Die Bedeutung des Artikels 36 EWG für die Freiheit des Warenverkehrs" [1973] EuR 1. (2) Commentary on Articles 30 to 36 in Groeben, Boeckh, Thiesing, *Kommentar zum EWG-Vertrag* (2nd ed., Baden- Baden, 1974) Vol 1. (3) "Das Verbot der Massnahmen gleicher Wirkung in der Rechtsprechung des Gerichtshofes" in *Festschrift für Ipsen* (Hamburg, 1977).
Evans	"Economic Policy and the Free Movement of Goods in EEC Law" [1983] I.C.L.Q. 577.
FIDE	"The Elimination of Non-Tariff Barriers with Particular Reference to Industrial Property Rights including Copyright" (1982).
Fox	*See* Bermann.
Goebel	*See* Bermann.
González Vaqué	"La jurisprudence relative à l'article 28 CE (ex article 30) après l'arrêt 'Keck et Mithouard'" [2000] R.D.U.E. 395.
Gormley	(1) *Prohibiting Restrictions on Trade within the EEC* (The Hague, 1985). (2) "Actually or Potentially, Directly or Indirectly? Obstacles to the Free Movement of Goods" [1990] Y.E.L. 197. (3) "Recent Case Law on the Free Movement of Goods: Some Hot Potatoes" [1990] C.M.L.Rev. 825. (4) "Reasoning Renounced? The Remarkable Judgment in *Keck and Mithouard*" [1994] E.B.L.R. 63.
Grabitz	"Das Recht auf Zugang zum Markt nach dem EWG-Vertrag" in *Festschrift für Ipsen* (Hamburg, 1977).

Graf — *Der Begriff "Massnahmen gleicher Wirkung wie mengenmässige Einfuhrbeschränkungen" im EWG-Vertrag* (Munich, 1972).

Gulmann — Handelshindringer i EF-Retten (Denmark, 1980).

Hatzopoulos — "Exigences essentielles, imperatives ou impérieuses: une théorie, des theories ou pas de théorie du tout?" (1998) 34 R.T.D.E. 191.

Joliet — "La libre circulation des marchandises: l'arrêt Keck et Mithouard dans les nouvelles orientations de la jurisprudence" [1994] J.T.D.E. 145.

Leitao — "Quelques réflexions politico-juridiques autour de l'élimination des mesures d'effet équivalent: unité du marché commun, principe logique ou principe organique?" [1986] R.M.C. 21.

Lopez Escudero — "La jurisprudencia Keck y Mithouard: una revision del concepto de medida de efecto equivalente" [1994] Revista de Instituciones Europeas 379.

Mackenzie Stuart — "The Free Movement of Goods" (1979) 12 Bracton L.J. European Supplement 17.

Marenco —
(1) "Pour une interprétation traditionnelle de la notion de mesures d'effet équivalant à une restriction quantitative" [1984] C.D.E. 291.
(2) "La giurisprudenza comunitaria sulle misure di effetto equivalente a una restrizione quantitativa" (1984-1986) [1988] Il Foro Italiano IV 166.

Masclet —
(1) "Les articles 30, 36 et 100 du traité CEE à la lumière de l'arrêt 'Cassis de Dijon'" [1980] R.T.D.E. 611.
(2) "La libre circulation des marchandises dans les Communautés européennes" [1986] R.T.D.E. 243.

Mattera —
(1) "Libre circulation des marchandises et articles 30 à 36 du Traité CEE" [1976] R.M.C. 500.
(2) "L'arrêt "Cassis de Dijon": une nouvelle approche pour la réalisation et le bon fonctionnement du marché intérieur" [1980] R.M.C. 505.
(3) "Les nouvelles formes du protectionnisme

économique et les articles 30 et suivants du Traité CEE" [1983] R.M.C. 252.

(4) *Le marché unique européen—ses règles, son fonctionnement* (2nd ed., Paris, 1990).

(5) "L'article 30 du Traité CEE, la jurisprudence *Cassis de Dijon* et le principe de la reconnaissance mutuelle" [1992] R.M.U.E. 13.

(6) "De l'arrêt *Dassonville* à l'arrêt *Keck*: l'obscure clarté d'une jurisprudence riche en principes novateurs et en contradictions" [1994] R.M.U.E. 117.

(7) "L'arrêt 'foie gras' du 22 octobre 1998 : porteur d'une nouvelle impulsion pour le perfectionnement du Marché unique européen" [1998] R.M.U.E. 113.

Matthies

(1) "Herkunftsangaben und Europäisches Gemeinschaftsrecht" in *Festschrift für Schiedermair* (Munich, 1976) at 395.

(2) "Die Verantswortung der Mitgliedstaan für den freien Warenverkehr im Gemeinsamen Markt" in *Festschrift für Ipsen* (Tübingen, 1977) at 669.

(3) "Die Verfassung des Gemeinsamen Marktes" in 'Das Europa der zweiten Generation', *Gedächtnisschrift für Sasse* (Baden-Baden, 1981), Vol. I at 115.

(4) Commentary on Arricles 30 to 37 in *Kommentar zum EWG-Vertrag* (ed. Grabitz) (Munich, looseleaf with updates).

Meier

(1) Commentary in Ehle and Meier, *EWG-Warenverkehr* (Cologne, 1971), 158 et seq.

(2) "Zur Kombination von nationalen Lebesmittel- Begriffsbestimmungen und Vorschriften zum Schutz des Verbrauchers gegen Irreführungen als Rechtsfertigungsgründe nach Art 36 EWGV" [1980] W.R.P.59.

(3) "Kennzeichnung statt Verkehrsverbote-Die Rechtsprechung als Schrittmacher des Lebensmittelrechts" in *Schriftenreihe des Bundes für Lebensmittelrecht und Lebensmittelkunde*, Heft 94, 47.

Meij and Winter

"Measures having an equivalent effect to quantitative restrictions" [1976] C.M.L.Rev. 79.

Melgar   See Wainwright.

Mestmäcker   Die Vereinbarkeit von Preisregelungen und dem
                           Arzneimittelmarkt mit dem Recht der
                           Europäischen Wirtschaftsgemeinschaft (Baden-
                           Baden, 1980).

Mortelmans   (1) "Article 30 of the EEC Treaty and Legislation
                               Relating to Market Circumstances: Time to
                               Consider a New Definition?" [1991]
                               C.M.L.Rev. 115.
                           (2) Casenote on *Keck* in [1994] S.E.W. 120.
                           (3) "Excepties bij non-tarifaire
                               intracommunautaire belemmeringen:
                               assimilaties in het nieuwe EG-Verdrag"
                               [1997] S.E.W. 182.
                           (4) "The Common Market, the Internal Market
                               and the Single Market, What's in a Market"
                               (1998) 35 C.M.L.Rev. 101.
                           (5) "Towards convergence in the application of
                               the rules on free movement and on
                               competition" (2001) 38 C.M.L.Rev. 613.

Müller-Graff   Commentary on Articles 30 to 36 EC in Groeben,
                           Thiesing, Ehlermann *Kommentar zum EWG- Vertrag*
                           (5th ed., Baden-Baden, 1997) Vol.I at 631 *et seq.*

Nic Shuibne   "The Free Movement of Goods and Article 28
                           EC: An Evolving Framework" [2002] E.L.Rev.
                           408.

Oliver   (1) "A Review of the Case Law of the Court of
                               Justice on Articles 30 to 36 EEC in 1983"
                               [1984] C.M.L.Rev. 221.
                           (2) "A Review of the Case Law of the Court of
                               Justice on Articles 30 to 36 EEC in 1984"
                               [1985] C.M.L.Rev. 301.
                           (3) "A Review of the Case Law of the Court of
                               Justice on Articles 30 to 36 EEC in 1985"
                               [1986] C.M.L.Rev. 325.
                           (4) "Some further reflections on the scope of
                               Articles 28-30 (ex 30-36) EC" (1999) 36
                               C.M.L.Rev. 783.
                           (5) "Goods and Services: Two Freedoms
                               Compared" in *Mélanges en homage à Michel
                               Waelbroeck* (1999, Bruylant).

Page   "The Concept of Measures having an Effect
                           Equivalent to Quantitative Restrictions" [1977]
                           E.L.Rev. 105.

Picod	"La nouvelle approche de la Cour de justice en matière d'entraves aux échanges" (1998) 34 R.T.D.E. 169.
Poiares Maduro	*We, the Court – A Critical Reading of Article 30 of the EC Treaty* (1998).
Reich	"The 'November Revolution' of the European Court of Justice: *Keck, Meng* and *Audi* Revisited" [1994] C.M.L.Rev. 459.
Schiller	"Gewährt Art. 30 des EWG-Vertrages dem Gemeinschaftsbürger neben einem subjektiven Abwehrrecht auch ein subjektives Leistungsrecht?" [1980] R.I.W./A.W.D. 569.
Schilling	"Rechtsfragen zu Art. 30 EGV" [1994] EuR 50.
Schwintowski	"Freier Warenverkehr im europäischen Binnenmarkt – eine Fundamentalkritik an der Rechtsprechung des EuGH au Art. 28 EGV" [2000] RabelZ 38.
Seidel	"Der EWG-rechtliche Begriff der 'Massnahmen gleicher Wirkung wie eine mengemässige Beschränkung'" [1967] N.J.W. 2081.
Steindorff	"Unvollkommener Binnenmarkt" [1994] Z.H.R. 149.
Steiner	"Drawing the Line: Uses and Abuses of Article 30 EEC" [1992] C.M.L.Rev. 749.
Stoffel Vallotton	La prohibicíon de restricciones a la libre circulacion de mercancias en la Comunidad Europea (Madrid, 2000).
Touffait	"Les entraves techniques à la libre circulation des marchandises" [1982] *Recueil Dalloz-Sirey*, Chronique 37.
Ulmer (Peter)	"Zum Verbot mittelbarer Einfuhrbeschränkungen im EWG-Vertrag" [1973] G.R.U.R.Int. 502.
Van Calster	"Export Restrictions – a Watershed for Article 30" [2000] E.L.Rev. 335.
Van Gerven	'The Recent Case Law of the Court of Justice concerning Articles 30 and 36 of the EEC Treaty" [1977] C.M.L.Rev. 5.

Van Rijn
"A Review of the Case Law of the Court of Justice on Articles 30 to 36 in 1986 and 1987" [1988] C.M.L.Rev. 593.

Veelken
"Massnahmen gleicher Wirkung wie mengenmässige Beschränkungen" [1977] EuR 311.

Verloren van Thermaat
(1) "Bevat art. 30 van het EEG-Verdrag slechts een non-discriminatie-beginsel ten anzien van invoerbeperkingen?" 15 S.E.W. 632.
(2) "Zum Verhältnis zwischen Artikel 30 und Artikel 85 EWG-Vertrag" in *Festschrift für Gunther* (Baden-Baden, 1976) at 373.
(3) "De artikelen 30-36 van het EEG–Verdrag" [1980] R.M. Themis 4/5 at 378.
(4) "La libre circulation des marchandises après 'Cassis de Dijon'" [1982] C.D.E. 123.

Waegenbaur
Commentary on Articles 30 to 36 in Groeben, Boeckh, Thiesing, Ehlermann, *Kommentar zum EWG-Vertrag* (3rd ed., Baden-Baden, 1983) Vol. I.

Waelbroeck (Denis)
"L'arrêt *Keck et Mithouard*: les conséquences pratiques" [1994] J.T.D.E. 160

Waelbroeck (Michel)
(1) Commentary on Articles 30 to 36 in *Le droit de la Communauté économique européenne* (Brussels, 1970) Vol. I.
(2) *Les réglementations nationales de prix et le droit communautaire* (Brussels, 1975).
(3) "Mesures d'effet équivalent, discrimination formelle et matérielle dans la jurisprudence de la Cour de Justice" in *Liber Amicorum Frédéric Dumon* (Antwerp).

Wainwright (with Melgar)
"Bilan de l'article 30 après vingt ans de jurisprudence: de Dassonville à Keck et Mithouard" [1994] R.M.C. 533.

Weatherill
(1) "Article 30 EEC: Caution in the European Court" [1990] M.L.R. 699.
(2) "After *Keck*: Some Thoughts on How to Clarify the Clarification" (1996) 33 C.M.L.Rev. 783.
(3) "Recent case law concerning the free movement of goods: mapping the frontiers of market deregulation" (1999) 36 C.M.L.Rev. 51.

White   "In Search of Limits to Article 30 of the EEC
                               Treaty" [1989] C.M.L.Rev. 235.

Wils   "The Search for the Rule in Article 30 EEC:
                               Much Ado about Nothing?" [1993] E.L.Rev. 475.

Winkel   "Die Vereinbarkeit staatlicher
                               Preislenkungsmassnahmen mit dem EWG-
                               Vertrag" [1976] N.J.W. 2048.

Winter   *See* Meij.

INDEX